THE PENGUIN DICTIONARY OF CLASSICAL MYTHOLOGY

Pierre Grimal was born in Paris in 1912. He was a teacher at the Lycée de Rennes and Senior Lecturer in Literature at Caen University from 1941 to 1952. He was Professor of Literature at Bordeaux from 1945 to 1952 and Professor at the Sorbonne University from 1952 to 1982. He was a member of the Institut de France (Académie des Inscriptions et Belles-Lettres). He edited and translated many books on Greek and Latin literature, and his own books include *Horace* (1958), *Mythologies* (1964), *Le Siècle d'Auguste* (1965), *Etudes de chronologie cicéronienne* (1977), *La Mythologie grecque* (1978), *Le Lyrisme à Rome* (1978), *Le Théâtre antique* (1978) and *L'Amour à Rome* (1979). He died in 1996.

THE PENGUIN DICTIONARY OF CLASSICAL MYTHOLOGY

PIERRE GRIMAL

EDITED BY
STEPHEN KERSHAW
FROM THE TRANSLATION BY
A. R. MAXWELL-HYSLOP

PENGUIN BOOKS

PENGUIN BOOKS

Published by the Penguin Group
Penguin Books Ltd, 80 Strand, London WC2R 0RL, England
Penguin Putnam Inc., 375 Hudson Street, New York, New York 10014, USA
Penguin Books Australia Ltd, 250 Camberwell Road, Camberwell, Victoria 3124, Australia
Penguin Books Canada Ltd, 10 Alcorn Avenue, Toronto, Ontario, Canada M4V 3B2
Penguin Books India (P) Ltd, 11 Community Centre, Panchsheel Park, New Delhi – 110 017, India
Penguin Books (NZ) Ltd, Cnr Rosedale and Airborne Roads, Albany, Auckland, New Zealand
Penguin Books (South Africa) (Pty) Ltd, 24 Sturdee Avenue, Rosebank 2196, South Africa

Penguin Books Ltd, Registered Offices: 80 Strand, London WC2R 0RL, England

www.penguin.com

First published in France, under the title *Dictionnaire de la mythologie grecque et romaine*, by Presses Universitaires de France, Paris 1951
This translation, under the title *The Dictionary of Classical Mythology*, first published in Great Britain by Basil Blackwell 1986
A concise edition entitled *A Concise Dictionary of Classical Mythology* first published by Basil Blackwell 1990
Published under the present title in Penguin Books 1991
15

Printed in England by Clays Ltd, St Ives plc

CONTENTS

PUBLISHER'S NOTE

THE *Dictionary of Classical Mythology* originally published in French by Pierre Grimal in 1951 as the *Dictionnaire de la Mythologie Grecque et Romaine* established itself quickly as one of the standard single-volume dictionaries on the subject of the mythology of the classical period. In particular, Grimal's impressive list of classical sources which he had used in compiling the variant versions of several myths gave the book a validity which has established it as a lexical work of considerable scholarly value.

This dictionary was translated into English under the supervision of A. R. Maxwell-Hyslop and published by Basil Blackwell in 1985. For the Blackwell edition, the full scholarly apparatus of the original French version was collected together in a series of appendices, and the forty-odd genealogical tables were grouped together at the end of the volume.

The size and price of the dictionary tended to put it beyond the reach of the lay-reader interested in the principal myths from classical literature. As a consequence of the demand for such a book, but one which nevertheless contains the authoritative treatment of sources of Grimal's original dictionary, we have prepared this concise version of Grimal's text under the editorial supervision of Stephen Kershaw. Some of the minor supplementary variant myths have been deleted and a number of small extra entries have been added, giving brief descriptions of characters and events important to understanding the canon of this literature. A more comprehensive cross-reference system has been introduced, so that readers can follow information through a lattice of references throughout the volume. It is hoped that this volume will make the caucus of classical mythology available to the lay reader, and explain the most important myths and legends in a clear and accessible way.

A

Abas (*Ἄβας*)

1. The eponym of the Abantides, a tribe in Euboea mentioned in the *Iliad*. He is said to have been the son of Poseidon and the Nymph Arethusa (1), but a late Athenian myth makes him a descendant of Metion. Abas had two sons, Chalcodon (1) and Canethus.

2. The best known Abas was the king of Argos, son of Lynceus (1) and Hypermestra (1). He was descended from the two feuding brothers, Danaus and Egyptus, and was the ancestor of Perseus and his family (Table 7). He was considered to be the founder of the Phocian town of Abae. With his wife, Aglaea, Abas had twin sons, Acrisius and Proetus. He is also said to have had an illegitimate son Lyrcus (2).

3. The great-grandson of Abas (2). He is said to have been the father of Lysimache (Table 1), Idmon and of Coeranus (see POLYIDUS (2)).

4. The son of Eurydamas. He was slain by Diomedes (2) (cf. Polyidus (2)).

Aborigines The earliest inhabitants of central Italy, according to Roman legends, and supposedly sons of the trees. They lived as nomads, without laws, and their food was wild fruit. Their name is generally taken to mean 'the original population'. When Aeneas arrived in Latium the Aborigines were ruled by LATINUS. When they were united with the Trojans they formed the Latin race.

Acacallis (*Ἀκακαλλίς*) One of the daughters of Minos, loved first by Hermes, by whom she had Cydon, and then by Apollo, by whom she had three sons; Naxos, Miletus and Amphitemis who was also known as Garamas. While Acacallis was expecting Amphitemis, Minos, in a fit of anger, banished her to Libya, where her son became the progenitor of the nomadic people, the Garamantes. Acacallis had also fled from her father's anger before the birth of Miletus. She sought refuge in the woods, where she gave birth to Miletus and, unable to rear him herself, she left him at the foot of a tree. In obedience to Apollo, the she-wolves in the forest suckled him until some shepherds found him and brought him up.

Acacallis is sometimes called Acacalle, which in Greek means 'the Egyptian tamarisk' (see PHILANDRUS).

Acacus (*Ἄκακος*) The son of Lycaon (2) and founder of the town of Acacesion in Arcadia. According to some traditions he was the foster-father of Hermes.

Academus (*Ἀκάδημος*) An Attic hero who told the Dioscuri where Theseus was holding their sister Helen prisoner when they were searching for her. His tomb on the outskirts of Athens was surrounded by a sacred wood in which Plato set up his Academy.

Acalanthis (*Ἀκαλανθίς*) One of the PIERIDES. With her sisters she challenged the Muses to match her at singing, and in indignation the goddesses changed all nine girls into birds. Acalanthis became a goldfinch.

Acamas (*Ἀκάμας*)

1. A Trojan, the son of Antenor and Theano, who played a brilliant part in the attack on the Greek camp. He was killed by Meriones.
2. The uncle of Cyzicus. He fought for the Trojans and was leader of a Thracian contingent. He was killed by Ajax (2).
3. The son of Theseus and Phaedra. He gave his name to the Attic clan of the Acamantides. He does not feature in Homer, though later myths give him and his brother Demophon (2) a part in the capture of Troy. Acamas is said to have accompanied Diomedes (2) to Troy, before the war broke out, to demand the return of Helen. While he was there Laodice (4) fell in love with him. She confided her feelings to Philobia, the wife of the ruler of the town of Dardanus in the Troad, who decided to help. Philobia persuaded her husband to invite the two young people to a feast separately and seat them side by side, Laodice pretending to be a member of Priam's harem. By the end of the feast Laodice had become Acamas' wife. Their marriage resulted in a son, MUNITUS. After the fall of Troy Munitus returned to Acamas and they set out for Attica, but Munitus died on the way after being bitten by a snake while hunting at Olynthus.

There is a story that Acamas was one of those inside the Wooden Horse at the capture of Troy. On his way home from Troy he spent a long time in Thrace on account of his love for PHYLLIS. Later he founded a colony in Cyprus where he is said to have died when he was impaled on his own sword. This legend is more generally thought, though, to refer to Acamas' brother DEMOPHON (2).

According to other legends, Acamas took part in the capture of Troy with Demophon and returned to Attica, where he resumed power and reigned peacefully.

Acanthis (*Ἄκανθίς*) The daughter of Autonous who had four sons, Anthus, Erodius, Schoeneus (2) and Acanthus. Acanthis was also known as Acanthyllis. The family farmed a large area of land but, since they did not work hard, it was not very productive, and their fields were always full of thistles and rushes. This was appropriate to the name of Schoeneus and Acanthus, whose names in Greek mean respectively 'rush' and 'thistle'. Their main occupation was horse breeding, and they were in the habit of leaving mares to graze on the marshes. One day Anthus went to fetch the mares and they, reluctant to leave their grazing, reared up in anger and fell on him, crushing him to death. The whole family was cast into such despair by this that Zeus and Apollo, out of pity for their grief, turned them all into birds. Acanthis probably became a goldfinch (see ACALANTHIS).

Acarnan (*Ἀκαρνάν*) Son of Alcmaeon (1) of Argos and of Callirhoe (2). Callirhoe coveted the necklace and dress of HARMONIA (1), and Alcmaeon had stolen these from King Phegeus of Psophis, but had been killed by Phegeus' children for doing so. When Callirhoe heard of this she asked Zeus, her lover, to make her sons Acarnan and Amphoterus grow up immediately; he granted her request, and they took revenge on Phegeus and his sons, subsequently fleeing to Tegea. After dedicating the necklace and dress at Delphi, they went to the land of the Curetes and founded Acarnania, whose inhabitants took their name from Acarnan. According to one tradition, Acarnan was killed while trying to marry Hippodamia (1), whose father put her suitors to death.

Acastus (Ἄκαστος) The son of PELIAS and Anaxibia (Table 6). Acastus took part in the voyage of the ARGONAUTS against his father's wishes, Pelias having conceived the expedition as a means of getting rid of JASON whom he regarded as a threat to his throne. Acastus also took part in the hunt for the wild boar of Calydon. After the murder of his father by MEDEA Acastus reigned in Iolcos.

Acastus played an indirect part in the legend of PELEUS. During the hunt of the Calydonian boar Peleus accidentally killed EURYTION, and to purify himself he went to Iolcos. While he was there Astydamia, the wife of Acastus, fell in love with him. When Peleus rejected her advances she sent a message to his wife saying that her husband was about to leave her in order to marry STEROPE (5), the daughter of Acastus. Peleus' wife hanged herself in despair. Astydamia did not think that she had yet exacted sufficient revenge, and accused Peleus of trying to rape her. Acastus believed the story and, not daring to kill his guest, lured Peleus to a hunt on Pelion. During the hunt Peleus merely cut out the tongues of the animals he killed, while the other hunters bagged their game. When his companions mocked him, he proved his courage by showing them the tongues. In the evening Peleus fell asleep. Acastus abandoned him, having first hidden his sword in a dung heap. The unarmed Peleus was almost put to death by the Centaurs who lived on the mountain, but one of them, CHIRON woke him in time and gave him back his sword. (Another version said that the sword was sent by Hephaestus.)

When Peleus returned to his kingdom he thought about revenge. In some accounts he captured Iolcos, perhaps with the help of Jason, CASTOR and POLLUX, killing Astydamia, and scattering her limbs so that his army could march between the various pieces of the dismembered body. He also killed Acastus.

Other writers claim that Peleus was attacked by Acastus during the Trojan War and forced to flee. There is also a tradition that besides Astydamia, Acastus had another wife, Hippolyta Cretheis, the daughter of CRETHEUS.

Acca Larentia

1. During the reign of either Romulus or Ancus Martius, the keeper of the temple of Hercules in Rome invited the god to a game of dice. The prize was to be a feast and a beautiful girl. Hercules accepted and won both the feast and the favours of Acca Larentia. When Hercules gave Acca up he advised her, by way of

compensation, to put herself at the disposal of the first man she should meet. This was Tarutius, a wealthy Etruscan, who married her but died shortly afterwards; Acca Larentia inherited his large estates, later bequeathing them to the Roman people. This legend may have been devised to justify the ownership of land claimed by Rome.

2. The wife of a shepherd named FAUSTULUS. She had twelve children, as well as Romulus and Remus whom she adopted. The college of the twelve Arval Brothers was said to have been constituted in memory of her twelve children.

Acestes See AEGESTES.

Achaemenides (Ἀχαιμενίδης) A companion of Odysseus, who accidentally abandoned him on the island of the Cyclopes. However, Achaemenides saved himself by going into hiding and he was subsequently rescued by Aeneas.

Achates (Ἀχάτης) A Trojan, the faithful friend of AENEAS and companion on his travels until he reached Italy. There is a tradition that Achates killed PROTESILAUS, the first Greek to land on Trojan soil.

Achelous (Ἀχελῷος) The name of the largest river in Greece (in Boeotia) and of the river-god. Achelous was said to be the son of Oceanus and Tethys, and was the oldest of the three thousand river-gods who were his brothers.

Other legends say that Achelous was the son either of Helios and Gaia, or one of the sons of Poseidon. One day Achelous was killed by an arrow while crossing a river. He fell in and the river was later named after him.

Achelous is said to have had various affairs, first with Melpomene, by whom he fathered the SIRENS, and then with some of the other MUSES. He was also the father of several streams: of Pirene, Castalia, Dirce and Callirhoe (2) (see ALCMAEON (1) and ACARNAN).

Achelous and Heracles were rivals for the hand of Deianeira. Achelous had the power of assuming whatever form he liked, but this proved unattractive to Deianeira, so when Heracles asked for her hand she accepted immediately. Even so, Heracles had to win her by force in a fight in which Achelous used all his resources and Heracles all his strength. During the struggle Achelous changed himself into a bull and Heracles tore off one of his horns, whereupon Achelous surrendered and conceded Deianeira to Heracles on condition that his horn was returned. Heracles gave him the horn of the she-goat AMALTHEA which was miraculously filled with fruit and flowers (although some authors claim that this horn belonged to Achelous himself).

Achelous also created the Echinades Islands, which lie at the river's mouth. Four local nymphs failed to include the river-god in a sacrifice, which so angered him that he made his waters rise and swept them out to sea, where they became islands. The fifth island in the group, Perimele, was originally a virgin raped by Achelous. Her outraged father Hippodamus threw her into the sea, but Achelous persuaded Poseidon to change her into an island, and thus she became immortal.

The modern name of the Achelous, which flows into the Ionian Sea at the entrance to the gulf of Patras, is the Aspropotamo.

Acheron (*Ἀχέρων*) The first mention of the River Acheron occurs in the *Odyssey*, where it is described as being in the Underworld, together with Pyriphlegethon and COCYTUS. The Acheron is the river which souls have to cross to reach the empire of the Dead. A ferryman, CHARON, carries them across. The river is almost stagnant and its banks are thick with reeds and mud. According to tradition Acheron was a son of GAIA, condemned to stay underground for having allowed the GIANTS to drink his waters after their struggle with the Olympians.

There was a River Acheron in Epirus which disappeared into a deep cleft. When it surfaced again, it formed an unhealthy marsh set in a barren landscape. An etymological mistake (according to which its name was thought to be derived from the Greek word for sorrow) as well as the characteristics of the river in Epirus undoubtedly contributed to the idea that it was associated with the Underworld, and its earthly features were transferred to the subterranean world.

In the mystical beliefs of the Roman Empire, the Acheron was regarded as lying near the South Pole, among the constellations of the Antipodes.

Achilles (*Ἀχιλλεύς*) The legend of Achilles owes its fame largely to the *Iliad*, which has as its main theme not the capture of Troy but the 'wrath of Achilles'. Other poets and popular legends filled gaps left by the Homeric accounts, and so an 'Achilles cycle' gradually came into being, overlaid with incidents and legends which, though frequently inconsistent with each other, continued to be an inspiration to poets throughout antiquity.

Childhood Achilles was the son of PELEUS. On his father's side he was a direct descendant of Zeus, while his mother was the goddess THETIS. There are varying accounts of his upbringing. One version depicts him as being brought up by his mother in his father's house, under the guidance of his teacher PHOENIX (3) or the Centaur CHIRON. Another says that he was the involuntary cause of a quarrel between his father and mother and tells how, after Thetis had left her husband, Achilles was put in the care of Chiron, who lived on the mountain of Pelion. Achilles was said to have been the seventh child of the marriage and Thetis had tried to purge each of her offspring of the mortal elements which indicated that Peleus was their father. She did this by thrusting them into a fire and so killing them, but when she was about to incinerate the seventh child, Peleus awoke. He snatched the child from her and Achilles was found to have suffered nothing worse than the scorching of his lips and of a small bone in his right foot. Thetis, in her anger, went back to the depths of the sea. Peleus asked Chiron, who was skilled in the art of medicine, to replace the scorched bone. So Chiron exhumed the body of a giant called DAMYSUS, who had been a notably swift runner, and replaced the missing bone with the corresponding one from the giant. This explains the extraordinary runner's gifts which Achilles possessed. Another legend asserts that in his infancy Achilles was bathed in the River STYX, whose waters had the power of making invulnerable all who were steeped in them, but the heel by which Thetis was holding him was untouched by the waters and remained vulnerable.

On Mount Pelion Achilles was looked after by Chiron's mother PHILYRA and his wife, Chariclo (1). When he was older he began to practise hunting, breaking horses, and medicine. In addition he learned to sing and play the lyre and talked with Chiron about the ancient virtues. He was fed on nothing but the entrails of lions and wild boars (to instil in him the strength of these animals), honey (to give him gentleness and persuasiveness) and bear's marrow. Chiron named him Achilles: previously he had been called Ligyron.

Departure for Troy According to the *Iliad* Achilles took part in the Trojan expedition on the invitation of NESTOR, ODYSSEUS and PATROCLUS. He led a fleet of fifty warships sailed by a body of Myrmidons and was accompanied by Patroclus and PHOENIX (3). As he left, Peleus made a vow to dedicate the hair of his son to the River SPERCHEIUS if he returned safely. Thetis, for her part, warned Achilles of the fate which awaited him: if he went to Troy he would win a dazzling reputation but his life would be short; if he stayed at home his life would be long but inglorious. Achilles chose the former alternative. This is the Homeric version, but later poets, and especially the tragedians, give a very different account. According to them an oracle had disclosed to Peleus (or, in some versions, Thetis) that Achilles was fated to die at the gates of Troy. When the Greeks were discussing whether to go to Troy, Peleus (or Thetis) had the idea of hiding Achilles by dressing him in women's clothes and making him live at the court of LYCOMEDES, King of Scyros, where he shared the life of the king's daughters. He stayed there for nine years. He was known as Pyrrha (the red-haired girl) because of his fiery auburn locks and while in this disguise he married Deidamia, one of Lycomedes' daughters, by whom he had a son, NEOPTOLEMUS. This disguise failed to cheat Fate, however, as Odysseus had learned from the soothsayer CALCHAS (1) that Troy could not be taken without the help of Achilles. He immediately sought Achilles and eventually learned where he had taken shelter. Odysseus then presented himself at the court of Lycomedes and, offering a pedlar's pack, made his way into the women's quarters. The women chose embroidery materials but Odysseus had mixed up some weapons with them and these were the choice of 'Pyrrha'. Odysseus had no difficulty in persuading the young man to reveal his identity. In another version Odysseus arranged for the sound of the trumpet to be heard in the middle of the harem of Lycomedes. While the women fled, Achilles stood his ground and called for weapons. Peleus and Thetis had therefore to accept that Achilles' warlike vocation could not be thwarted. On his departure from Aulis, where the Greek fleet had assembled, Thetis gave the hero a suit of armour, given by HEPHAESTUS to Peleus as a wedding gift, and she added the horses which POSEIDON had given on the same occasion. She also placed near her son a slave whose only duty was to prevent Achilles from killing a son of Apollo; for an oracle had affirmed that Achilles was bound to die a violent death if he did this.

The First Expedition According to the *Iliad*, the Greek army made its way directly from Aulis to Troy, but later legends speak of a first attempt at landing which failed. The first time the fleet left Aulis there was a mistake in the navigation and the army came ashore in Mysia. Thinking that they were in the Troad, the Greeks ravaged the country, but its king, TELEPHUS, advanced to meet them and a battle ensued in which Achilles wounded Telephus. The Greeks then realized their mistake and re-embarked to head for Troy, but a storm scattered the fleet and each contingent found itself back where it had started. Achilles was driven ashore on Scyros. The Greeks reassembled at Argos, and there Telephus came to ask Achilles to heal the wound he had inflicted, for, according to the Delphic oracle, only filings from Achilles' spear could heal the wounds it had made.

The Second Expedition The Greek fleet made its way to Aulis where it lay becalmed, an event said by Calchas to have been caused by ARTEMIS who demanded the sacrifice of AGAMEMNON's daughter IPHIGENIA. Agamemnon agreed to this demand and pretended that he wanted to betroth her to Achilles. By the time Achilles discovered what the king had planned Iphigenia had arrived at Aulis. He tried to resist the sacrifice, but the soldiers, roused in opposition to him, would have stoned him to death, and he was forced to acquiesce. Favourable winds sprang up and the army, guided by Telephus, arrived at Tenedos where Achilles and Agamemnon quarrelled for the first time. It was also in Tenedos that Achilles killed Tenes, a son of Apollo, whose sister he tried to abduct. Realizing too late that he had fulfilled the oracle, he arranged a magnificent funeral for Tenes and killed the slave whose duty it had been to prevent the murder.

The Greeks besieged Troy for nine years before the events which form the story of the *Iliad* began. The *Iliad* speaks of a whole range of exploits in Asia Minor, especially against Thebes in Mysia, which was captured by Achilles who killed King EËTION, together with his seven sons, and abducted the queen. To the same group of stories belongs the campaign against Lyrnessos during which Achilles captured BRISEIS, while Agamemnon captured CHRYSEIS in the Theban operation. With Patroclus, Achilles raided the herds of oxen which AENEAS grazed on Mount Ida. Other episodes of the first nine years include those which took place during the Greek disembarkation when the Trojans, initially victorious, were routed by Achilles who killed CYCNUS (2). It was also said that Achilles, who was not among the suitors of Helen, was curious to see her and that Aphrodite and Thetis arranged for them to meet. No one, though, seems to have portrayed Achilles as Helen's lover.

The real Homeric stories and the quarrel over Briseis begin with the tenth year of the war. When a plague afflicted the Greek ranks, Calchas revealed that the calamity was due to the wrath of APOLLO, sent at the request of his priest CHRYSES (I) whose daughter Chryseis had been abducted by Agamemnon. Achilles summoned the chiefs and compelled Agamemnon to surrender the girl. In retaliation Agamemnon demanded that Achilles should give back his own prize, Briseis, whereupon Achilles retired to his tent and refused to take any part in the struggle. When the heralds came to reclaim her he returned her, but protested against this injustice. Then he appealed to Thetis, who advised him to let the Trojan attack get as far as the ships, in order to prove his indispensability, for, as she well knew, he was the only man who could prevent the enemy from attacking the Greeks effectively. Thetis went to ZEUS and asked him to grant the Trojans victory as long as Achilles kept away from the fighting. Zeus agreed and the Greeks suffered a series of defeats. Agamemnon sent a mission to appease Achilles, promising him Briseis and a magnificent ransom, but Achilles remained unmoved. The battle came close to the camp but Achilles watched from the deck of his ship. Patroclus eventually asked Achilles to let him help the Greeks, whose ships were in danger of being burnt. Achilles agreed to lend his armour, but Patroclus (after a certain degree of success, which lasted as long as the Trojans believed him to be Achilles) was killed by Hector. Achilles was overcome by indescribable grief. His cries were heard by Thetis, who promised him a fresh suit of armour in place of that which Hector had just stripped from Patroclus' body. Though unarmed, Achilles joined the battle and his voice put to flight the Trojans who were struggling against the Greeks for possession of the corpse of Patroclus.

The next morning Achilles made his peace with Agamemnon, who in his turn asked Achilles' forgiveness and returned Briseis; Achilles rejoined the fighting, whereupon his horse, Xanthus, which had been momentarily endowed with the gifts of prophecy and speech, foretold the imminent death of his master. Despite this, Achilles advanced and the Trojans fled; Aeneas alone, under the inspiration of Apollo, stood up to him. Achilles' spear pierced Aeneas' buckler; Aeneas brandished a huge stone and Poseidon rescued both of them by enveloping them in a cloud. Hector also wanted to attack Achilles, but in vain: fate for the moment did not allow the two heroes to meet face to face. Achilles continued his advance. After fording the River SCAMANDER, he took twenty young Trojans prisoner, intending to sacrifice them at Patroclus' tomb. The river-god wanted to stop the bloodshed and kill Achilles, whose victims were blocking his course. The river became swollen, overflowed its banks and pursued the hero, but Hephaestus made it return to its course. Achilles continued his attack in order to cut off the Trojan retreat, but he was diverted into a fruitless pursuit of Apollo, and so lost his opportunity. Hector was alone in front of the Scaean Gate, but, just as Achilles was drawing close and they were on the point of fighting, he took fright and Achilles chased him round the walls until at last Zeus, raising the scales of fate, weighed Achilles' lot against Hector's, whose scale tipped towards Hades. Apollo then abandoned Hector. ATHENA appeared and, assuming the likeness of his brother DEIPHOBUS, inspired Hector with the wish to confront his opponent; he was soon killed, uttering a warning to Achilles that he himself had not long to live. On the point of death he asked Achilles to return his body to PRIAM, but Achilles refused and dragged the corpse behind his chariot into the Greek camp.

Each day for twelve days Achilles did the same, but then Thetis was bidden by Zeus to tell him that the gods were angry at his lack of respect for the dead, and when Priam came to ask for Hector's body, he was kindly received by Achilles, who gave him back the corpse. That moment is the climax of the *Iliad*.

In the *Odyssey* we find Achilles in Hades. He is surrounded by heroes who were his friends during the war, amongst them was Agamemnon who told Odysseus of the death of Achilles, although he did not give the name of his killer. The *Odyssey* gives an account of Achilles' funeral games, and the subsequent quarrel caused by the way in which the hero's arms were awarded (see AJAX (2) and ODYSSEUS).

Other stories in the Homeric poems bring the cycle to its close. First there is the tale of the struggle against the Amazon queen, PENTHESILEA. Initially she forced the Greeks to retreat, but Achilles wounded her and, just as she was on the point of death, he exposed her face. Confronted by such beauty he was stricken with a sorrow so obvious (for he was incapable of concealing his emotions) that THERSITES derided his love for a corpse. Achilles killed him with one blow of his fist.

A further story records Achilles' struggle against MEMNON, which took place in the presence of their respective mothers, Thetis and EOS.

Finally comes the tale of Achilles' love for POLYXENA. Achilles fell so deeply in love with her that he promised her father, Priam, that he would come over to the side of the Trojans if he would agree to their marriage. Priam accepted, and the betrothal was to be ratified in the temple of Apollo Thymbrius. Achilles appeared unarmed and PARIS, hidden behind the statue of Apollo, shot him. The Trojans seized his corpse and demanded the same ransom as they had had to pay for Hector's body.

This version of the hero's end seems to be a late one: other authors say that Achilles met his end in battle at a moment when he had driven the Trojans back to the walls of their city. Apollo confronted him and ordered him to withdraw and, when he refused, shot him with an arrow. In some versions the archer is said to be Paris, although Apollo guided the arrow to strike Achilles at his only vulnerable place, his heel. (See also DAMYSUS.) A struggle took place round Achilles' body, from which AJAX (2) and ODYSSEUS eventually carried the body back to the camp. The funeral was celebrated by Thetis and the MUSES, or the NYMPHS. Athena anointed the body with ambrosia to preserve it from decay. Later there was a story that Thetis removed his body to the White Island at the mouth of the Danube. Sailors passing the island heard by day the incessant clashing of weapons and by night songs and the clinking of cups. And in the Elysian Fields Achilles is said to have married MEDEA, or Iphigenia, or Helen, or Polyxena. There is also a tale that, after Troy had been taken but before the Greeks had left, a voice from Achilles' tomb had been heard demanding that Polyxena should be sacrificed in his memory.

As depicted by Homer, Achilles was handsome, fair-haired, with flashing eyes and a powerful voice. He did not know the meaning of fear: his greatest passion was fighting, and he loved glory above all else. Yet he also had milder qualities: he was musical and could charm away care with lyre and song; he loved both his friend Patroclus, and his concubine Briseis. He could be cruel, as when he ordered the execution of the captured Trojans, and when, from beyond the grave, he demanded the sacrifice of Polyxena, but he was also hospitable and wept with Priam when the latter came to recover his son's body. In the Elysian Fields he rejoiced to learn that his son Neoptolemus was a man of courage. He revered his parents, and, when he knew the gods' will, lost no time in carrying it out. Despite all these civilized characteristics, Achilles was taken by many Hellenistic philosophers for the archetype of the man of violence, a slave to his emotions, and they were very ready to contrast him with Odysseus, the man of judgement.

The cult of Achilles was widely practised in the islands, as well as on the Asiatic mainland. We also know of the cult consecrated to Achilles by Alexander the Great who took him as his pattern. Both of them died young.

Achilles was the inspiration behind many works of literature, from the *Iliad* to the *Achilleid* of Statius. He plays a part in many tragedies, notably Euripides' *Iphigenia in Aulis*.

Acis (Ἄκις) The god of the river of the same name, near Etna. He was the son of Pan or Faunus (in the Latin tradition) and the Nymph Symaethis. Before becoming a river he had loved GALATEA (I).

Acontius (Ἀκόντιος) A young man from Chios who belonged to an affluent though not noble family. One year he went to the festivals in Delos, where he saw an Athenian girl called CYDIPPE who had also come to worship there. Acontius instantly fell in love with her. Acontius followed her to the temple of ARTEMIS, where she sat down while the sacrifice was taking place. Then Acontius picked a quince and on it scratched 'I swear by the temple of Artemis that I will marry Acontius'. Then he threw the quince towards Cydippe who innocently read the writing on it out loud. On realizing the meaning of the words she threw the fruit away, but she had uttered a form of words which bound her to Acontius. Moreover, the goddess

Artemis was a witness of the oath. Acontius returned to Chios, consumed by love for the girl, whom he regarded as his betrothed. Cydippe's father, however, was preparing for her engagement to a husband of his choice, but Cydippe fell so suddenly and seriously ill that the engagement had to be postponed. The girl immediately recovered, but three times, at each attempt to arrange the betrothal, her mysterious illness returned. News of this reached Acontius, who hurried to Athens and constantly asked about Cydippe's health, to the point where he became the talk of the town. People began to think that he had bewitched the girl. Her father went to consult the oracle at Delphi and discovered that Cydippe was bound by an oath and that she was punished by the anger of Artemis each time she was on the point of committing perjury. Her father therefore made enquiries about the family of Acontius, which seemed to him to be entirely suitable, and soon a happy marriage rewarded the young man's trick. (See also HERMOCHARES.)

Acrisius (*Ἀκρίσιος*) ABAS (2) was the father of twin sons, PROETUS and Acrisius (Table 7). The two children fought each other while they were still in their mother's womb, and their antagonism continued into adulthood. They declared war on each other to find out which of them should succeed to the throne of Argos, bequeathed to them by their father at his death. It is said that during this war round shields, which were destined to be widely used in warfare in antiquity, were first invented. Eventually victory went to Acrisius, who expelled his brother; the latter went to Lycia where he married Anteia (see STHENEBOEA). Her father, King Iobates, restored Proetus to the Argolid and set him up at Tiryns, which the CYCLOPES had fortified for him. At this point the brothers decided to come to an agreement whereby Acrisius reigned at Argos and Proetus at Tiryns, thus dividing the kingdom of the Argolid into two equal parts.

Acrisius had a daughter, DANAE. He wanted to have a son and consulted the oracle, which told him that his daughter would bear a son who would kill him. In order to thwart the prediction, Acrisius had an underground room built of bronze, where he kept Danae under guard, but this did not prevent Danae from being seduced. Some think that Proetus was the culprit, but most say that Zeus seduced her in the form of a shower of gold which fell through a crack in the roof into her womb. When Acrisius heard of this he put her and her baby into a chest which he left to its fate on the sea. The child was PERSEUS. DICTYS rescued him from the beach at Seriphos, where the tide had cast him up. Later, Perseus wanted to see his grandfather again and returned to Argos. When Acrisius learned that Perseus was preparing to come he was afraid that the oracle would be fulfilled and left for Larissa in the land of the Pelasgians, at the furthest point of Greece, equally far from Seriphos and Argos. When he arrived at Larissa he found that King Teutamides was holding games and that Perseus had come there to compete. At the moment of Perseus throwing the discus a violent wind sprang up and the discus struck Acrisius a fatal blow. Perseus, realizing that the prediction had in spite of everything come true, buried Acrisius outside the city and returned to Argos.

Acron King of the Sabine town of Caenina. After the rape of the Sabines he took up arms against ROMULUS. He accepted the latter's challenge and their duel took place before the two armies. Acron was killed by Romulus, who stripped him of his armour and dedicated it to Jupiter Feretrinus on the Capitol. This was the origin of the ceremony of the Spolia Opima.

Actaeon (*Ἀκταίων*) ARISTEUS had a son named Actaeon; he was brought up by the Centaur CHIRON who taught him the art of hunting. One day Actaeon was devoured by his own dogs on Mount Cithaeron. There are differing accounts of his death: some say that this was his punishment from ZEUS for having tried to rob him of the love of SEMELE, but most authors ascribe it to the wrath of the goddess ARTEMIS, incensed at having been seen naked by Actaeon when she was bathing. She incited his hounds to fury and set them on him. They ate him without recognizing him, and then hunted for him in vain throughout the forest. Finally their search brought them to the cave where Chiron lived, and he made a statue of Actaeon to calm them.

Actor (*Ἄκτωρ*)

1. A Thessalian hero, sometimes said to be the son of MYRMIDON and Pisidice (3) and sometimes said to be a Lapith, the son of Phorbas (1) and Hyrmine. In the latter version Actor was the father of Augias. The traditions about his descendants vary: sometimes he is regarded as the father of Menoetius (1), and the grandfather of Patroclus, and sometimes as the father of the Molionidae (see THALPIUS). Actor reigned at Pherae in Thessaly, and Peleus came to him when, having killed Phocus (3), he was searching for someone to purify him. Actor agreed to do so and on his death bequeathed his kingdom to Peleus. According to this version of the legend, Actor had a son, EURYTION (3).
2. A son of Hippasus. One of the Argonauts.

Admete (*Ἀδμήτη*) A priestess of Hera at Argos. One version of the legend of the Amazons says that it was for her that Heracles went to fetch the girdle of the Amazon queen. On the death of her father Eurystheus, Admete fled to Samos, taking Hera's cult statue with her. She discovered an ancient shrine of the goddess, founded by the Leleges and the Nymphs, and put the statue there. The Argives commissioned some pirates to search for the statue, and, as the shrine in Samos had no door, they easily removed it. However, when they tried to set sail and were unable to cast off, they realized that the goddess wanted to remain in Samos, so they placed the cult statue on the shore and offered a sacrifice to her. When the Samians found the statue abandoned on the shore by the departing pirates, they assumed that the goddess had come there of her own accord. They bound the statue in rushes, and when Admete arrived she unfastened it, purified it, consecrated it afresh, and brought it back to its temple. An annual fesstival was instituted in which the Samians carried the statue of Hera to the shore and gave it offerings.

Pausanias claims that the Argive statue of Hera was brought to Samos not by Admete but by the Argonauts.

Admetus (*Ἄδμητος*) Son of Pheres, founder of Pherae in Thessaly, and Periclymene. He took part in the Calydonian boar hunt and the Argonauts' expedition. He succeeded his father as king, and fell in love with Alcestis, the daughter of Pelias, who would give his daughter only to a man whose chariot was drawn by wild beasts. Apollo, who was Admetus' drover at this time, harnessed a lion and a wild boar for him. However, when Admetus failed to offer a sacrifice to Artemis during the wedding celebrations, she filled the bridal chamber with snakes, and Apollo had to appease her. Apollo also asked the Fates that Admetus should not die on the day fixed by Destiny, if he found someone to take his place. To do this Apollo made the Fates drunk (or persuaded Artemis). Admetus was unable to find anyone to take his place except his wife, who died on his behalf. According to the tradition followed by Euripides in his *Alcestis*, she was saved by Heracles, who went down to the Underworld, wrestled with Thanatos, the god of Death, and brought her back; another tradition holds that Persephone returned her spontaneously. Admetus had three children: Eumelus, Perimele and Hippasus (Table 6).

Adonis (*Ἄδωνις*) A Greek hero of Syrian origin, Adonis is mentioned by Hesiod, who considers him the son of Phoenix (4) and Alphesiboea; Apollodrous calls him a son of Cinyras and Metharme, but the generally accepted version is that Smyrna (2) was impelled by Aphrodite to commit incest with her father, Theias. With the help of her nurse Hippolyta (2) she tricked Theias and became pregnant, but when Theias discovered the trick he pursued her with a knife. The gods changed Smyrna into a myrrh tree, which later burst open, allowing the child Adonis to emerge. Aphrodite, moved by the child's beauty, sheltered him and entrusted him to Persephone. Persephone was so taken with his beauty that she refused to give him back. In some versions the dispute was settled by Zeus, in others by Calliope on Zeus' behalf: Adonis was to spend one third of each year with each goddess and the remaining third wherever he chose. He always spent two thirds with Aphrodite. However, at an early age he was fatally wounded by a wild boar.

The reason often given for the curse of Aphrodite upon Smyrna is that Cenchreis the wife of Cinyras (who here takes the place of Theias) had offended the goddess by claiming that her daughter was more beautiful; Smyrna's desire for an illicit love was a punishment for this. As soon as she realized the nature of her passion, Smyrna wanted to hang herself but her nurse advised her to satisfy her love. Once incestuous intercourse had taken place, the girl hid herself in a forest where Aphrodite, taking pity on her victim, changed her into a tree. Smyrna's father struck the bark of the tree with his sword, thus bringing the baby Adonis into the world, but in another version it was a wild boar which freed the child from the tree by opening it up with its tusks, thus foretelling the young man's death. Hellenistic poets depicted Adonis as having been brought up by the Nymphs, hunting or leading his flocks. The tragedy which led to his death was sometimes said to have been caused not by Artemis but by the jealousy of Ares, Aphrodite's lover, or by the vengeance of Apollo on Aphrodite, who had blinded ERYMANTHUS (1), the god's son, because he had seen her bathing naked.

The Adonis legend is set sometimes on Mount Idalion, sometimes in Lebanon. A river called the Adonis flowed through Byblos, and its waters coloured red every year on the day when the death of Adonis was celebrated.

The story of Adonis provides a basis for myths such as that of the origin of myrrh (the tears of Smyrna) and that of the red rose, which was originally white. As Aphrodite ran to Adonis' assistance she pricked her foot on a thorn and the flowers dedicated to him were coloured by her blood. Anemones too were said to be born of the blood of the wounded Adonis. The poet Bion tells that the goddess shed as many tears as Adonis shed drops of blood; from each tear sprang a rose, and from each drop of blood an anemone.

In honour of Adonis, Aphrodite established a funeral feast, celebrated each spring by the followers of his cult. They nurtured green plants, called 'gardens of Adonis', which grew unnaturally quickly and died equally rapidly, thus symbolizing the fate of Adonis, for which the women uttered ritual laments.

Adonis is found depicted on Etruscan mirrors, and his cult spread throughout the Mediterranean world in the Hellenistic period.

Adrastus (*Ἄδραστος*) An Argive king, leader of the Seven against Thebes. During a riot Amphiaraus killed Talaus, Adrastus' father, wherupon Adrastus fled to Sicyon, whose king, Polybus (2), died without male children and left him the kingdom. Adrastus then made peace with Amphiaraus, to whom he gave the hand of his sister ERIPHYLE, and returned to the throne of Argos. There, Polynices, forced to leave Thebes by Eteocles, and TYDEUS, exiled by his father, Oeneus, because of a murder, appeared together to seek asylum. They quarrelled and awoke Adrastus, who, realizing that they fought like lion and wild boar (or perhaps seeing the two animals depicted on their armour), remembered an oracle that he would marry his daughters to a lion and a wild boar: he gave Argia to Polynices, and Deipyle to Tydeus.

Adrastus' promise to restore the heroes to their rights in their countries was the start of the expedition of the Seven against Thebes. The seven chiefs were: Adrastus (their leader), Amphiaraus, Capaneus, Hippomedon, Parthenopaeus, Polynices and Tydeus. They stopped at Nemea, where they instituted the Nemean Games in honour of Opheltes (see AMPHIARAUS), then pressed on to Thebes where, after an initial success, their whole army was exterminated. Adrastus alone escaped on his horse, Areion. One tradition holds that after this Adrastus persuaded the Thebans to hand over the bodies of the dead, another that he fled to Athens, whose king, Theseus, regained the bodies by force and buried them at Eleusis.

Ten years later Adrastus undertook a fresh war against Thebes with the EPIGONI, the sons of those who had died in the earlier venture. They were successful, but Adrastus' son Aegialeus was killed by Laodamas, son of Eteocles. The aged Adrastus died of grief at Megara. Hyginus relates, however, that, in obedience to an oracle of Apollo, he cast himself into a fire.

Adrastus had six children by his wife, Amphithea. His four daughters Argia, Hippodamia (2), Deipyle and Aegiale married Polynices, Pirithous, Tydeus and Diomedes (2) respectively.

Aeacus (*Αἰάκός*) Son of Zeus and the Nymph Aegina. He was born on the island of Oenone. Aeacus wanted some companions, so Zeus changed the numerous ants on the island into human beings. The people were named Myrmidons by Aeacus, from the Greek (*μύρμηξ*) meaning 'ant'. Aecus subsequently married Endeis and fathered Telamon and Peleus (see also CYCHREUS). Some writers, however, cite only Peleus as the son of Aeacus.

Later, Aeacus had a son by the Nereid Psamathe (1). Psamathe had turned herself into a seal to escape from Aeacus, but this was to no avail, and the resulting son was called Phocus (3), which recalled his mother's metamorphosis (Greek *φώκη* = 'seal'). The son was exceptionally athletic and this made his two brothers, Peleus and Telamon, so envious that they killed him by throwing a discus at his head. When Aeacus discovered this he exiled his sons. Such integrity resulted in his being chosen out of all the Greeks to pray to Zeus at a time when fields were barren as a result of Zeus being angry with Pelops for dismembering STYMPHALUS. Aeacus succeeded in placating Zeus.

After his death, Aeacus judged the spirits of the dead in the Underworld, although this belief is comparatively late: Plato is the first source to cite Aeacus in this context. Another legend claims that Aeacus took part in building the walls of Troy together with Apollo and Poseidon. After the walls had been built, three serpents climbed up them. When two of the serpents approached the sections built by the two gods, they died but the third was able to slide over the section built by Aeacus. Apollo interpreted this as forecasting that Troy would be taken twice, first by a son of Aeacus (meaning the capture by Heracles – see HERACLES, III) and secondly, three generations later, by NEOPTOLEMUS, the great-grandson of Aeacus.

Aechmagoras (*Αἰχμαγόρας*) Phialo, the daughter of Alcimedon of Arcadia, had a son, Aechmagoras by Heracles. Alcimedon told his daughter to expose him to die, and abandoned them both on a mountain. A nearby jay heard the infant's cries and tried to imitate them. Heracles heard echoes of the jay's cries, came to the place and saved his lover and his son. A neighbouring spring took the name of Cissa ('the spring of the jay').

Aedon (*Ἀηδών*) In the *Odyssey*, Aedon envied the number of children born to her sister-in-law NIOBE (2). She tried to kill Niobe's eldest son, Amaleus, in his sleep, but by mistake she killed her own son, Itylus. In her grief she begged the gods' pity and they transformed her into a nightingale (*ἀηδών* in Greek). In an alternative legend about the nightingale Aedon was the wife of the artist Polytechnus. They had a son, ITYS. In their good fortune they boasted that they were more closely united than Hera and Zeus, whereupon Hera punished them by filling them with the desire to outdo each other. Both set to work, he building a chariot, she weaving, the first to complete their task having to give the other a serving-maid. With the help of Hera, Aedon won.

The resentful Polytechnus went to Ephesus and asked his father-in-law to allow him to take Chelidon, Aedon's sister, to stay with her. On the journey he raped her, gave her the clothes of a slave, cut off her hair and threatened her with death if she told her sister who she was. On his return, he gave Chelidon to Aedon as a serving-maid. One day when she was lamenting her misfortunes, Aedon overheard and recognized her and they resolved to take revenge. They killed Itys, served his body on a dish to his father, and fled. Polytechnus, learning the nature of the food he had eaten, left in pursuit but was stopped by the servants of Pandareus, the girls' father, who by now knew the whole story. Polytechnus was arrested, smeared all over with honey and laid out in a meadow. Plagued by flies, he aroused the pity of Aedon, who drove off the flies. Her brothers and sisters, enraged by this, wanted to kill her, but Zeus took pity on the family and changed them all into birds, Pandareus into a sea-eagle, Polytechnus into a green woodpecker, Aedon into a nightingale, and Chelidon into a swallow (*χελίδων* in Greek).

Aeetes (*Αἰήτης*) The son of Helios and Perseis. He was given the kingdom of Corinth by his father but soon left for Colchis on the coast of the Black Sea. His sisters were Circe and Pasiphae. The traditions about the name of Aeetes' wife, Eurylyte, vary: she has been named as the Nereid Neaera, Idyia and Hecate (see MEDEA).

Aeetes ruled over Aea in Colchis and his capital was the town of Phasis. When PHRIXUS arrived at Colchis, on a ram with a golden fleece, he was welcomed by the king, who gave him in marriage his daughter Chalciope (2). Phrixus sacrificed the ram to Zeus and gave the fleece to Aeetes, who nailed it to an oak tree in a wood dedicated to Ares. Jason, being ordered by Pelias to bring him the Golden Fleece, went with his companions in search of it (see ARGONAUTS), and the king promised them the fleece provided that Jason succeeded in accomplishing various feats, thinking by this means to get rid of him. But when Jason succeeded in overcoming the tests which were set him, Aeetes refused to let him have the fleece and tried to burn the *Argo*. Jason took the fleece by force and fled, taking Aeetes' daughter Medea with him. Aeetes pursued them, but Medea killed and dismembered her brother Apsyrtus, scattering the limbs on the sea, and Aeetes, by waiting to gather them up, allowed Jason to escape. At a later date Aeetes is said to have been dethroned by his brother Perses, and restored to his rights by Medea, who had returned without being recognized.

Aegaeon (*Aἰγαίων*) One of the HECATONCHEIRES was called Briareus by the gods and Aegaeon by mortals. Together with his brothers he fought with the Olympians against the Titans. Sometimes he is one of the warders of the Titans in their underground prison, and sometimes it is said that Poseidon rewarded him for his courage by giving him the hand of his daughter Cympolea and exempting him from keeping guard over the Titans. When Hera, Athena and Poseidon wanted to put Zeus in chains, it was to Aegaeon that Thetis turned for help, and fear of his prodigious strength was enough to deter them. However, a variant tradition claims that this faithful friend of Zeus was an ally of the Titans, with whom he fought against the Olympians.

Aegestes (*Aἰγέστης*)

1. The son of the Sicilian river-god Crimisus and a Trojan woman named Aegesta or Segesta, who received Aeneas and the Trojans on Sicily. There are a number of explanations of how she first arrived in Sicily. According to Servius, after Laomedon refused to pay Apollo and Poseidon for building the wall around Troy, the gods inflicted calamities on the country: Poseidon sent a sea-monster and Apollo caused a plague, and said that, to end the epidemic, the youngest generation of noble families must be given up to feed the monster. Many Trojans sent their offspring abroad, and Aegesta was evacuated to Sicily. There Crimisus coupled with her in the shape of a dog or a bear, and she gave birth to Aegestes who founded the town of Aegesta or Segesta. According to Lycophron, Aegesta was the daughter of Phoenodamas, who advised his fellow-Trojans to give Hesione (3), the daughter of Laomedon, to the monster. In revenge Laomedon gave Phoenodamas' daughters to some sailors with instructions that they should be left out in the open in Sicily where the wild beasts could eat them. Thanks to Aphrodite the girls escaped. Aegesta married Crimisus. In this version, her son, Segestes, founded the towns of Segesta, Eryx and Entella. According to one tradition Aegesta returned to Troy where she married Capys (1) and gave birth to Anchises. According to Dionysius of Halicarnassus, a grandfather of Aegesta who quarrelled with Laomedon was put to death by him, together with all the male members of his family. Laomedon was reluctant to have the females killed, and gave them to merchants. A young Trojan followed them to Sicily; there he married one of them and fathered Aegestes. After Troy was attacked, Aegestes returned to defend it, but when the city was lost he went back to Sicily, taking Elymus with him. Strabo says that the companions of

Philoctetes helped him to found Segesta.

2. A priest at Lanuvium. After the founding of the city of Alba the images of the Penates kept returning to Lanuvium. Aegestes was sent from Alba to Lanuvium to practise the worship of the Penates at the place where the gods wished to remain.

Aegeus (*Αἰγεύς*) A king of Athens and father of Theseus. He was the son of Pandion (2). Pandion was forced to leave Athens for Megara where he ultimately became King. At Megara, Pandion's four sons, Aegeus, Pallas (7), Nisus and Lycus (6) were born. After Pandion's death his sons marched on Athens and regained power, Aegeus exercising the largest share. Another tradition makes Aegeus only the adopted son of Pandion; this lay behind the argument between the descendants of Pallas and those of Theseus, the legitimacy of whose power was disputed.

Aegeus married first Meta and then Chalciope (3), but he was unable to have a child, a fact which he put down to the anger of APHRODITE Urania, whose cult he introduced into Athens. Then he sought the advice of the Delphic oracle, which replied as follows: 'Do not, thou most excellent of men, unloose the opening which causes wine to gush out from the wine bottle before you have reached the highest point in the city of Athens.' Aegeus went out of his way to consult Pittheus, the king of Troezen. Pittheus understood the oracle and made haste to make Aegeus drunk and to leave him with his own daughter Aethra. When he left, Aegeus instructed Aethra that should she give birth to a son she must not tell him the name of his father, but he left his sandals and his sword under a rock, saying that when the child was big enough to move the rock he would have the means to trace his father. The child was THESEUS.

Medea promised Aegeus that if he married her his sterility would end. He did so and she gave him a son, Medus (1). When Theseus returned to Athens, Medea tried to poison him, but Aegeus recognized the boy and drove Medea out. Theseus arrived just in time; the sons of Pallas were in revolt against Aegeus and were trying to dethrone him, but they were crushed by Theseus.

Aegeus was responsible for the death of ANDROGEOS, as a result of which Minos invaded Attica, imposing the annual tribute of young men and young girls which gave rise to Theseus' expedition against the Minotaur. Theseus promised to change the sails of his ship from black to white if he returned victorious, but forgot to do so. Aegeus, led to believe that his son was dead, threw himself into the sea, which ever since has been called the Aegean Sea after him.

Aegialea (*Αἰγιάλεια*) The daughter of Adrastus, she married Diomedes (2), who shortly afterwards left to fight against Thebes and Troy. Aegiale remained faithful to him for a long time but later had intrigues with various heroes including Cometes (1). One explanation for this is that Aphrodite, who was wounded by Diomedes at Troy, sought her revenge by inplanting uncontrollable passions in Aegiale: alternatively, Aegiale's behaviour was attributed to the slanders of Nauplius (2), who, to avenge the stoning of his son Palamedes, went from town to town saying that the husbands were preparing to bring back from Troy concubines who would take the places of their legitimate wives.

When Diomedes returned from Troy he had to extricate himself from the traps set for him by Aegiale and her lover, and escaped to Hesperia.

Aegimius (*Αἰγιμιός*) The son of Dorus, the mythical ancestor of the Dorians, to whom he gave a legal system. When the Dorians were driven out by the Lapiths, Aegimius appealed to Heracles, whose assistance ensured their victory. Aegimius adopted Hyllus, Heracles' son, and gave him an equal share of the country with his own sons, Dymas and Pamphylus, after whom the three Dorian tribes, Hylleans, Dymanes and Pamphylians, were named.

Aegina (*Αἴγινα*) The daughter of the river-god Asopus. She was abducted by Zeus. Her father looked all over Greece for her and discovered the truth from SISYPHUS. Asopus gave him the Spring of Pirene as a reward but Sisyphus later paid for this treachery in the Underworld. When Asopus returned to his original bed Zeus struck him with lightning, and later still, lumps of coal could be found on the river bed. Zeus took Aegina to the island of Oenone and fathered AEACUS. The island subsequently took her name. Later Aegina went to Thessaly, where she married Actor and gave birth to Menoetius (1).

Aegisthus (*Αἴγισθος*) The son of Thyestes and his daughter Pelopia (1) (Table 2). Thyestes was banished and his sons killed by his brother Atreus, but an oracle told him that he would find an avenger in the form of a son by his own daughter. Accordingly he raped Pelopia by night. Then he disappeared, but during the rape Pelopia stole his sword. Later, Atreus married Pelopia without knowing who she was. Pelopia abandoned Aegisthus at birth, but Atreus discovered the child among shepherds who had taken him in and fed him with goat's milk (the source of his name, since *αἴξ* means 'goat'). When he became a young man Atreus told him to go to Delphi, capture Thyestes and bring him back. (Another version of this story says that Agamemnon and Menelaus, Atreus' two sons by Aerope (1), were charged with this mission.) Aegisthus brought back Thyestes and was ordered to kill him. Aegisthus was wearing a sword which Pelopia had given him, the same sword which had been stolen on the night of the rape. Thyestes learned of this, begged for Pelopia to be summoned, and then disclosed the secret of Aegisthus' birth. Pelopia seized the sword and stabbed herself; Aegisthus pulled it out, went to find Atreus, who thought that his brother was already dead, killed him and thereafter ruled jointly with Thyestes at Mycenae.

When Agamemnon and Menelaus were at Troy, Aegisthus seduced Clytemnestra and lived with her. When Agamemnon returned, he was received with great demonstrations of friendship and happiness. A great feast was prepared for him, during which he was murdered by Clytemnestra. Aegisthus subsequently reigned for seven more years over Mycenae before he was killed by Orestes, Agamemnon's son. Aegisthus had two children, Aletes (2) and Erigone (2).

Aegyptus (*Αἴγυπτος*) The eponym of Egypt, the son of Belus (Table 3). He had a brother DANAUS. Belus established Danaus in Libya and gave Arabia to Aegyptus, who also conquered the land of the Melampodes (meaning, literally, 'black feet') which he renamed Egypt. Aegyptus had fifty sons, and his brother Danaus had fifty daughters (see DANAIDES). The brothers quarrelled and Danaus fled to Argos. Aegyptus' sons went to meet Danaus there and asked permission for his daughters to marry them; Danaus agreed, but on the eve of this marriage he contrived for all the sons to be killed by their intended wives, with the exception of Lynceus (1) who was spared by Hypermestra (1). Aegyptus, his sons all dead, became afraid of his brother and he retired to Aroe, where he died.

Aeneas (*Αἰνείας*) A Trojan hero, the son of Anchises and Aphrodite (Table 4). For the circumstances of his birth, see ANCHISES. Aeneas was initially brought up in the mountains; when he was five he was taken to the city by his father and entrusted to his brother-in-law Alcathus, who took charge of his education. Later Aeneas stood out as the bravest of the Trojans after Hector. He was not a member of the reigning house, but when Aphrodite revealed her identity to Anchises, after he had coupled with her, she said: 'You will have a son, who will rule over the Trojans, and sons will be born to his sons, and so on for all eternity.'

In the Trojan War Aeneas encountered Achilles during raids on Mount Ida, but Aeneas was driven to Lyrnessos, where he was rescued by Zeus when Achilles sacked the city. Aeneas was also wounded by Diomedes (2): in trying to save him Aphrodite was herself wounded, but Apollo hid Aeneas in a cloud and removed him from the battlefield. He later returned to slay Crethon and Orsilochus, attack the Achaean camp, confront Idomeneus, kill a large number of Greeks, and fight at Hector's side when the latter put the Achaeans to flight. He was among those fighting around Patroclus' body, and again fought with Achilles: Aeneas was saved by Poseidon, who caused a mist to rise before Achilles' eyes, removed the spear which was stuck in Aeneas' shield, and transported the hero behind his own lines. Poseidon's motive in saving a Trojan was that he had remembered Aphrodite's prophecy that Aeneas would one day rule over the Trojans, and that his descendants would keep this position of supremacy; it was also perhaps that Aeneas was not one of the immediate descendants of Laomedon, but was directly linked with Tros, through Anchises, Capys and Assaracus (see Table 4, POSEIDON and LAOMEDON). Thus Homer's Aeneas was a hero protected by the gods (whom he obeyed with due respect) and destined for a great role: in him lay the future of the Trojan race. These elements were combined by Virgil in his *Aeneid*.

After the death of Hector, Aeneas assumed his role in the defence of the city, and after the fall of Troy his importance increased still further. Following the death of LAOCOON, he realized that the fall of the city was imminent, and made his escape with Anchises, Creusa (4) and his son Ascanius. One version of the legend claimed that Aeneas was taken by surprise by the Greek attack on the city and made his escape with old Anchises on his back and Ascanius in his arms, carrying the PENATES and the PALLADIUM. He then withdrew to Mount Ida where he gathered together the surviving Trojans and founded another city over which he reigned, thus fulfilling the prediction of Aphrodite – who, it was said, had instigated the Trojan War to strip Priam of the throne and give it to her own descendants.

The story which formed the basis for Virgil's *Aeneid* was that of Aeneas' travels. After a short stay on Mount Ida (see OXYNIUS), he left for Hesperia. He called at Samothrace, Thrace, Macedonia, Crete (via Delos), Cythera, Laconia and Arcadia; from there he went to Zacynthus, Leucas, Epirus, and finally reached southern Italy. He then sailed round Sicily, avoiding SCYLLA (1) and CHARYBDIS, and stopped at Drepanum, where Anchises died. When he set sail again a storm drove him to Carthage (see DIDO). From there he resumed his journey at the order of the gods, who did not want him peacefully to establish himself in the city destined to be Rome's enemy, and landed at Cumae, the scene of his visit to the SIBYL and his descent into the Underworld. After leaving Cumae he landed for the burial of his old nurse at Caieta, which was named in her honour, avoided Circe's island, and finally reached the mouth of the Tiber, where he became embroiled in a series of battles with the Rutuli. Aeneas went up the Tiber to Pallanteum, which was later to become the site of the city of Rome (the Palatine), and there sought an alliance with King Evander (3), a one-time guest of Anchises. Evander welcomed Aeneas and sent a body of troops to his aid, led by his own son Pallas (4). On Evander's advice Aeneas went to Agylla, in Etruria, to incite the subjects of King Mezentius to rebel, but in his absence the troops of Turnus, the Rutulian king, attacked the Trojan camp. Only Aeneas' timely arrival with the allied troops reversed the situation. Aeneas ultimately killed Turnus in single combat.

Virgil's *Aeneid* ends with the death of Turnus and does not directly mention later events recorded by the historians – the founding of Lavinium, struggles against local tribes, the disappearance of Aeneas in a storm. In these traditions the founder of Rome was ROMULUS; Aeneas' son Ascanius (or IULUS) founded Alba Longa. For versions of the legend before Virgil, see LATINUS. Some traditions make Aeneas the direct founder of Rome (see ODYSSEUS, IV); others give him four sons – Ascanius, Euryleon, Romulus and REMUS.

Virgil's version set the tradition for all later writers. The legend of Aeneas gave Rome the stamp of respectability by tracing its founders' race back to the beginnings of history, and attributing divine ancestors (Zeus and Aphrodite) to it. Furthermore, Rome's grandeur seemed to have been foretold by Homer himself.

Aeolia (*Aἰολία*)

1. In the *Odyssey* the island of Aeolia is the home of Aeolus (2), the Lord of the Winds. It was a rocky floating island, surrounded by a wall of bronze. It was sometimes identified as the island of Strongyle (today's Stromboli), and sometimes as the island of Lipari.
2. The daughter of Amythaon and wife of Calydon (1) (Table 1).

Aeolus (*Aἴολος*)

1. The son of Hellen and Orseis (Table 5). His descendants became known as the Aeolians. Aeolus was king of Magnesia, in Thessaly. He married Enarete, by whom he had seven sons and five daughters (Table 5). This Aeolus was sometimes identified with the Lord of the Winds, but this title is more often given to Aeolus (2). Aeolus played a part in the tragic affair of his daughter CANACE with Macareus (1).
2. The grandson of Aeolus (1). His mother was Arne, or, in the tradition followed by Euripides in two lost tragedies, Melanippe (1). Melanippe (or Arne) had twins, Aeolus and Boeotus, by Poseidon. At their birth Melanippe's father blinded and imprisoned her, and ordered the twins to be exposed. A cow fed them with its milk until some shepherds took them in. Now King Metapontus, being unable to have a child by his wife Theano (2), had threatened to divorce her. She asked the shepherds to provide her with infants which she could pass off as her own, and they gave her Aeolus and Boeotus. Theano convinced Metapontus that they were his sons, but when she herself bore twin sons she became anxious to get rid of the strangers and she told her sons the secret of Aeolus and Boeotus' birth. The four youths fought, and with Poseidon's help Aeolus and Boeotus killed Theano's sons and fled to the shepherds who had taken them in. Poseidon then told them that he was their father and that their mother was still a prisoner, whereupon they hastened to her rescue. Poseidon restored her sight, and her sons took her back to Metapontum, where they revealed Theano's crimes to King Metapontus. The king married Melanippe, and the young men left to found cities abroad.

In other versions of the myth, Arne/Melanippe, pregnant by Poseidon, was not imprisoned but handed over to an inhabitant of Metapontum who subsequently adopted the two children, Aeolus and Boeotus. When they grew up they seized the throne of Metapontum, slew their adoptive father's wife (Autolyta or SIRIS), and fled, Boeotus to Aeolis, later known as Thessaly, Aeolus to the Aeolian Islands, where he was welcomed by King Liparus, who gave him both his daughter Cyane (1) in marriage and his throne. Aeolus and Cyane had six sons: Astyochus, Xuthus, Androcles, Pheraemon, Iocastus and Agathyrnus.

Aeolus (2) was often identified with Aeolus the Lord of the Winds (see 1 above). In the *Odyssey* he received Odysseus on his island, and when Odysseus left he gave him an oxhide bottle containing all the winds except the one which would take him back to Ithaca. But Odysseus' companions opened the bottle while he was asleep, so the winds escaped, causing a storm which drove the ship back to Aeolia, where Aeolus, regarding Odysseus as the victim of divine wrath, drove him away.

Aepytus (*Αἴπυτος*)
1. An Arcadian who attempted to force his way into the temple of Poseidon at Mantinea where he was blinded by the god and died.
2. The great-grandson of Cresphontes and Aepytus (1), son of Merope (2). During a riot his father and his brothers were killed. Aepytus managed to escape and took refuge with his grandfather Cypselus. When he had grown up he returned with the help of the sons of Aristodemus and Isthmius, and slew Polyphontes, the leader of the riot, who, after the death of Cresphontes, had forcibly taken MEROPE (2) as his wife. Aepytus freed his mother and reigned over the country. His reputation for virtue and wisdom was so great that his descendants, who till then had called themselves the Heraclids, were given the name of Aepytidae.
3. The son of Elatus (1) or, in some versions, of Arcas. He ruled over the whole of Arcadia. He was bitten by a snake while hunting and died. His tomb was not far from Mount Cyllene. He brought up as his daughter Evadne (1), the daughter of Poseidon, whom Pitane (1) had entrusted to him.

Aerope (*Ἀερόπη*)
1. A daughter of Catreus. An oracle had told Catreus that he would die at the hands of one of his children, so he gave Aerope and her sister Clymene (4) to the traveller Nauplius (2), who took them to Argos. There Aerope married Atreus and gave birth to Agamemnon and Menelaus (Table 2). She was seduced by her brother-in-law, Thyestes, causing the feud between the two brothers. ATREUS kept his throne, however, and punished Aerope by throwing her into the sea.

Sophocles says that Catreus gave Aerope to Nauplius with orders to drown her because she had had an affair with a slave. Another tradition holds that Aerope married Pleisthenes, king of Argos. It has also been suggested that Atreus was either the son or the father of Pleisthenes, and that Aerope married Pleisthenes first and Atreus after his death.
2. A daughter of Cepheus (1), who was loved by Ares and died while giving birth to a son. But Ares ensured that the child could continue to suck at his mother's breast.

Aesacus (*Αἴσακος*) The son of Priam and Arisbe, and grandson of Merops, from whom he inherited the gift of interpreting dreams (see CILLA and PARIS). Aesacus' wife died from a snake-bite, and he threw himself into the sea. In pity Thetis changed him into a bird.

Aesculapius See ASCLEPIUS.

Aeson (*Αἴσων*) A son of Cretheus (Tables 1 and 6). By marrying Polymede he became the great-uncle of

Odysseus, though other traditions made him marry Alcimede, daughter of Phylacus. He was half-brother to Pelias and the father of Jason. Pelias robbed him of his kingdom of Iolcos and sent Jason to win the Golden Fleece. During Jason's absence Pelias forced Aeson to commit suicide; Aeson poisoned himself with bull's blood. In Ovid's version Aeson saw Jason again and was restored to youth by Medea's magic.

Aethalides (*Αἰθαλίδης*) An excellent archer who took part in the Argonauts' expedition, in which he acted as herald. He had inherited from his father Hermes an exceptionally good memory, which he retained even after his death. Moreover he did not always stay among the dead but came back to live among men for short periods.

Aether (*Αἰθήρ*) The personification of the upper sky, where the light is clearer than it is in the lower levels nearer the earth. According to Hesiod Aether was the son of Erebus and Nyx and the brother of Hemera. According to other traditions, when united with Day he begot not only Earth, Sky and Sea, but a number of abstract qualities, among them Grief, Anger and Falsehood, as well as Oceanus, Themis, Tartarus, Briareus, Gyges (1), Steropes, Atlas, Hyperion, Saturn, Ops, Moreta, Dione and the Three Furies. According to Cicero, Aether was the father of Jupiter and Caelus and grandfather of the Sun.

Aethra (*Αἴθρα*) Daughter of Pittheus, king of Troezen, and the mother of Theseus (Table 2).

Aethra was first wooed by Bellerophon. But when AEGEUS arrived at Troezen from Delphi, Pittheus arranged to bring together his daughter and his guest without the latter's knowledge. From their union Theseus was born. It is also said that on the eve of the day on which Aegeus was to arrive Athena inspired Aethra in a dream to go to a neighbouring island and offer a sacrifice to the hero Sphaerus. There she was raped by Poseidon. The same night she slept with Aegeus, so that Theseus could pass as the son of both god and man.

When Aegeus returned to Athens, Aethra remained at Troezen where she brought up Theseus. Later, having become king of Athens, Theseus entrusted to his mother the care of Helen, whom he had abducted. The girl's brothers, the Dioscuri, came to rescue her and took Aethra prisoner. She followed Helen to Troy as a slave, and some authors hold that she advised Helen to leave Menelaus and follow Paris. When the city was taken she was recognized by her grandsons Demophon (2) and Acamas (3), who secured her release.

It is said that at the death of Theseus, Aethra killed herself for grief.

Aetna (*Αἴτνη*) Aetna, whose name eventually became that of the volcano Etna, was the daughter of Uranus and Gaia or, by some accounts, of Briareus. When Hephaestus and Demeter were quarrelling over the ownership of Sicily (land of volcanoes and corn) Aetna stepped in to act as arbitrator. She is sometimes regarded as the mother of the Palici.

Aetolus (*Αἰτωλός*) A king of Elis,

son of Endymion. To decide which of his sons should succeed him, Endymion made them run a race at Olympia. Epeius (1) won, but Aetolus later succeeded to the throne on his brother's death. At some funeral games Aetolus accidentally ran over Apis in his chariot and killed him. He went into exile and was hospitably received at the mouth of the River Achelous by Dorus (2), Laodocus and Polypoetes (1). However, he killed them, seized the throne, drove out the Curetes, and called the land Aetolia. He married Pronoe, daughter of Phorbas, who bore him Pleuron and Calydon.

Agamedes (*Ἀγαμήδης*) A mythical architect whose son by Epicaste, Cercyon (2), and stepson Trophonius were equally talented architects. The marriage chamber of Alcmene at Thebes and the temples of Apollo at Delphi and of Poseidon at Mantinea are all attributed to them. Agamedes and Trophonius also built a treasury for King Hyrieus, in which they placed a stone that could easily be removed, allowing them to steal the king's treasures. Hyrieus commissioned Daedalus to arrange a trap in which Agamedes was caught. Trophonius cut off his head, so that he could not give him away, but the earth swallowed up Trophonius near Lebadeia. In the wood of Lebadeus there was a hole and a stele bearing the name of Agamedes, and there stood the oracle of Trophonius.

In a different version the king in question was Augias. Cercyon, who took part in the theft, fled with Trophonius to Orchomenus, but when they were pursued by Daedalus and Augias, Cercyon sought refuge in Athens, and Trophonius at Lebadeus.

According to another version, when Agamedes and Trophonius had built the temple to Apollo, the god promised to pay them at the end of a week and advised them to lead a happy life in the meantime. On the eighth night the two architects died peacefully, this being the best payment the god could make them.

Agamemnon (*Ἀγαμέμνων*) In the *Iliad*, the supreme commander of the Achaean army. He is variously described as a descendant of Atreus, of Pelops (1) or of Tantalus (1) (Table 2), and as King of Argos (as in the *Iliad*), of Mycenae, or of Lacedaemon. For his ancestry see AEROPE (1) and ATREUS.

Agamemnon married CLYTEMNESTRA after slaying her husband Tantalus (2). Agamemnon and Clytemnestra had three daughters, Chrysothemis (2), Laodice (3) and Iphianassa (2), and a son, Orestes. Subsequently there appeared Iphigenia (not the same person as Iphianassa) and, in place of Laodice, Electra (3).

When a crowd of suitors were trying to win Helen, her father, Tyndareus, bound them on oath not only to respect her decision but also to come to the aid of the man she chose, should he be attacked. Thus when Paris abducted Helen and Menelaus sought Agamemnon's help, Agamemnon reminded the former suitors of their oath, and they formed the nucleus of the army which later attacked Troy. Agamemnon was unanimously chosen as commander-in-chief.

According to a poem later than

the *Iliad*, the Greeks, who did not know their way to Troy, landed first in Mysia, but were scattered by a storm and forced back to their homes (see ACHILLES). Eight years later they reassembled at Aulis, but could not sail because of a persistent calm. Calchas (1) said this was due to the anger of Artemis, either because Agamemnon had compared himself with the goddess as a hunter, or because ATREUS had not sacrificed the golden lamb to her, or because Agamemnon had promised to sacrifice the most beautiful produce of the year to Artemis in the year when IPHIGENIA was born, and had not carried out his promise. Only the sacrifice of Iphigenia would appease the goddess, and Agamemnon ultimately agreed to this.

Once under way, the expedition called in at Tenedos, where Agamemnon quarrelled with Achilles for the first time, and Lemnos, where Agamemnon abandoned PHILOCTETES, before reaching Troy.

During a raid in the tenth year of the siege of Troy Achilles captured Briseis, and Agamemnon took Chryseis, the daughter of Chryses (1). When Agamemnon refused to ransom Chryses' daughter Apollo caused a plague in the Greek army. At this point the *Iliad* begins. Agamemnon later gave up Chryseis, but demanded that Achilles should give him Briseis, whereupon Achilles retired to his tent in anger and refused to fight. Agamemnon performed some remarkable feats in battle, but was wounded and was forced to withdraw. After the Trojan attack on the camp he realized that defeat was imminent unless Achilles returned; he therefore restored Briseis to Achilles, promised him the hand of one of his daughters, and gave him rich gifts. From this point Agamemnon fades from prominence in the *Iliad*.

Other epics speak of Agamemnon's involvement in the events following Hector's and Achilles' deaths (see AJAX (2)). The *Odyssey* tells how, after the capture of Troy, Agamemnon took Priam's daughter Cassandra, who bore him twins, Teledamus and Pelops (2).

The return of Agamemnon also features in epic. The *Odyssey* refers to a quarrel between him and Menelaus, who wanted to leave as soon as the war was over, while Agamemnon wanted to stay to win the favour of Athena by giving her gifts. Poems about Agamemnon's return tell how the ghost of Achilles tried to make him stay by predicting his future misfortunes.

When Agamemnon arrived home, Aegisthus, his wife's lover, invited him to a feast and, assisted by twenty men, killed him. Other versions implicate Clytemnestra in the murder of Agamemnon and Cassandra. Pindar adds that Clytemnestra hated Agamemnon's family so bitterly that she wanted to kill her own son Orestes as well. The accounts given by the tragedians also differ: sometimes Agamemnon is struck down while at table; sometimes he is killed in his bath, hampered either by a net or by a shirt with sewn-up sleeves which Clytemnestra had given him. For another variant see OEAX.

Eventually Agamemnon was avenged by his son ORESTES.

Agapenor (*Ἀγαπήνωρ*) Mentioned

in the *Iliad's* Catalogue of Ships as the leader of the Arcadian contingent. As a former suitor of Helen, Agapenor took part in the Trojan expedition (see AGAMEMNON). On his way back his ship was wrecked and he was cast up on Cyprus, where he founded the town of Paphos and built a temple to Aphrodite. While Agapenor lived at Tegea, Agenor and Pronous met at his house the two sons of Alcmaeon (1), who killed them in revenge for their father's murder.

Agave (*Ἀγαυή*) The daughter of Cadmus and Harmonia (1). She married Echion (1) and had a son, Pentheus. After her sister Semele had been killed by a thunderbolt when she rashly asked her lover Zeus to show her how powerful he could be, Agave alleged that Semele had had a liaison with a mortal and that Zeus had punished her for having claimed that she was pregnant by him. Later Dionysus, Semele's son, punished Agave for her slander. When Dionysus returned to Thebes, where Agave's son Pentheus was ruling, he ordered all the women in the town to assemble on Mount Cithaeron to celebrate his mysteries. Pentheus, who was opposed to the introduction of the ritual, tried to spy upon the Bacchantes. He was glimpsed by Agave, who took him for a wild beast and tore him limb from limb. When she had returned to her senses she fled to Illyria, to Lycotherses, the king of the country, whom she married. But later she killed him, to ensure that her father Cadmus should possess the kingdom.

Agdistis (*Ἄγδιστις*) In Pausanias' version, Zeus spilt some semen on the earth which begot Agdistis, a hermaphrodite. The other gods castrated Agdistis and from his/her penis sprang an almond tree. Nana, the daughter of Sangarius, picked an almond from the tree, placed it in her lap, became pregnant, and gave birth to ATTIS. She abandoned him, but he was cared for by a goat. When Attis grew up Agdistis (by this time purely female) fell in love with him, but he was sent to Pessinus to marry the king's daughter. Agdistis appeared after the marriage hymn had been sung, whereupon Attis castrated himself and died. Agdistis was so upset that she was granted that Attis' body should not decay.

In another version Zeus, having tried in vain to marry Cybele, let some of his semen fall on a nearby rock. This begot the hermaphrodite Agdistis. Dionysus made Agdistis drunk and castrasted him/her. From the blood grew a pomegranate tree. Nana became pregnant by inserting one of the fruits in her womb, and gave birth to Attis. At Sangarius' wish she abandoned him, but he was taken in by some passers-by and reared on honey and billy-goat's milk (*sic*), hence his name (Attis = 'he goat' (*attagus*) or 'beautiful' in Phrygian). Attis grew very handsome, and King Midas of Pessinus determined he should marry one of his daughters, but during an argument between Agdistis and Cybele, Attis and his attendants became frenzied. Attis castrated himself beneath a pine tree and died. Cybele buried him, but violets grew round the pine tree from the blood which had fallen from his wounds. Cybele also buried Midas' daughter, who had killed herself in despair, and violets grew from her blood and also an almond tree over her tomb. Zeus granted Agdistis that Attis' body should not decay, his hair should continue to grow, and his little finger should move. Agdistis founded a community of priests and a festival in Attis' honour at Pessinus.

Agenor (*Ἀγήνωρ*) Poseidon and Libya had twin sons, Agenor and Belus (Table 3). Belus ruled Egypt, while Agenor ruled Tyre or Sidon. Agenor's children were Europa (5), Cadmus, Phoenix (2) and Cilix. When Zeus abducted Europa, Agenor sent his sons to find her with orders not to return until they had done so, and as their search was futile they settled abroad. Traditions about the names of the sons vary: Euripides and Pausanias also mention Thasos, while Herodotus speaks of Phoenician colonies established on the island of that name. The name of Agenor's wife also varies: sometimes it is Telephassa, sometimes Argiope, sometimes Antiope, the daughter of Belus.

Aglaurus (*Ἄγλαυρος* or *Ἄγραυλος*)
1. The daughter of Actaeus, first King of Athens, and the wife of Cecrops by whom she had Erysichthon, Aglaurus (2), Herse and Pandrosus.
2. The daughter of Aglaurus (1), she was loved by Ares, by whom she had Alcippe. Aglaurus later went mad and threw herself off the Athenian Acropolis (see ERICHTHONIUS). Ovid tells a different story, saying that Aglaurus was not struck with madness. Some time later Ovid shows her to be jealous of her sister, Herse, who was loved by Hermes. The god finally changed her into a stone statue (see CERYX).

Aius Locutius This name embraces the idea of speech (*aio* and *loquor*) and belongs to a god who revealed himself only at the time of the Gallic invasion in 390 BC, in the form of a voice announcing the approach of the enemy. No one took any notice of it, but after the Gauls had been put to flight the dictator, Camillus, in order to make amends, built a shrine to him at the place where the voice had been heard.

Ajax (*Αἴας*)
1. Ajax of Locri is called the son of Oileus or the Lesser Ajax to distinguish him from Ajax (2). He fought beside his namesake the son of Telamon at Troy, but whereas the latter was heavily armed, the son of Oileus was armed only with a breastplate of linen and a bow. He took part in all the great battles of the *Iliad*, as well as in the drawing of lots for the intended duel with Hector; he fought in the battles around the ships, and around the body of Patroclus, and competed in the funerary games given in honour of Patroclus.

He is said to have been a man of bad character, being arrogant, cruel to his enemies, quarrelsome, and impious. He committed sacrilege against Athena when, during the capture of Troy, Cassandra had sought refuge near Athena's altar. Ajax used force to carry off both girl and statue. The Achaeans wanted to stone him for this act of impiety, but Ajax in his turn sought safety near the altar of Athena and so escaped death. But on the return journey

Athena sent a storm which wrecked a large number of Achaean ships, including the one in which Ajax was travelling. Nevertheless he was saved by Poseidon. Ajax boasted that he had survived in spite of the goddess's wrath, whereupon Athena insisted that he should be destroyed, so Poseidon took his trident and broke the rock on which Ajax had taken refuge and drowned him. There is also a story that Athena herself destroyed him with a thunderbolt.

But the sacrilege committed by Ajax continued to oppress his countrymen, the Locrians: epidemics broke out in Locris and there was a series of bad harvests. The oracle replied that these calamities were a sign of the divine wrath, and that Athena would be appeased only if the Locrians sent two girls to Troy each year, for a thousand years, to expiate the rape of Cassandra. This was done. The Trojans killed the first pair and scattered their ashes on the sea. Their successors were pursued by the populace, armed with sticks and seeking to put them to death. If they escaped they repaired barefooted to the shrine of Athena and there they stayed, unmarried, to a very advanced age. Thus the sacrilege against Cassandra was expiated, long after Ajax's death.

2. Ajax son of Telamon is the Great Ajax. In the Achaean camp at Troy he commanded the left wing. Next to Achilles he was the most powerful hero in the army. Strong, large, handsome, calm and self-controlled, he was heavily armed with a remarkable shield, made of seven layers of oxhides, the eighth and outermost coating being a sheet of bronze.

The son of Telamon was taciturn, benevolent and god-fearing, but he lacked the sensitivity, love of music, and kindness of Achilles. He was first and foremost a man of war.

Ajax was chosen by lot to fight Hector in single combat. He struck him to the ground with a stone, but the heralds then intervened to stop the fight. During the Achaean defeats he tried again to stop Hector but was wounded and had to leave the field. When Hector launched his attack on the ships Ajax was at the heart of the Achaean defence. He wounded Hector once more with a stone but the latter forced him to defend himself on his own ship. When Hector broke his spear on him he acknowledged the will of the gods and took flight. Ajax returned to the battle after the death of Patroclus; Hector was about to attack him and would have done so had not Zeus, in deference to the fate which ordained that Hector should fall under Achilles' blows, enveloped them both in a cloud.

Legends later than the *Iliad* put Ajax nearly on a par with Achilles. He was, like Achilles, made out to be the grandson of Aeacus (see TELAMON). In Attica his mother was said to be Periboea (5).

When Heracles came to invite Telamon to take part in his expedition against Troy, he found Telamon in the middle of a banquet. Heracles stretched his lion-skin beneath him and begged Zeus to grant Telamon a son as brave as himself and as strong as the lion to whose skin he pointed. Zeus granted his prayer. According to another legend Ajax had already been born at the time of the visit of Heracles, and the hero wrapped him in his lion-skin, asking Zeus to make him invulnerable. The child grew up to be so, except for those parts which on the body of Heracles supported the quiver: armpit, hip and shoulder.

Gradually Ajax' character as portrayed in the *Iliad* acquired new features. When he left for Troy his father advised him to fight first of all with the spear, but also with the help of the gods. Ajax replied that 'the coward as well could be victorious with the help of the gods'. Then he seems to have removed the picture of Athena from his shield, thereby incurring the goddess's wrath.

Ajax played an important part in the preliminary expeditions. He was appointed to command the fleet together with Achilles and Phoenix (3). He replaced Agamemnon as commander-in-chief when the latter was removed from that position for having killed the sacred doe of Artemis. After the landing in Mysia Ajax killed Teuthranius, the brother of Telephus.

During the first nine years of the fighting before Troy Ajax attacked the town of the Phrygian king, Teleutas, and carried off his daughter Tecmessa. He also laid waste the Thracian Chersonese of which Polymestor was king. Polymestor surrendered Polydorus (2), one of his father-in-law Priam's children, of whom he had custody.

After Achilles' death, during the final stages of the war, Ajax is described as welcoming Achilles' son, Neoptolemus, treating him as his own son and fighting alongside him. He also fought beside the archer Philoctetes, just as, in the *Iliad*, he fought beside the archer Teucer. Once the city had been captured, he demanded that Helen should be put to death, but Odysseus secured her return to Menelaus. Then Ajax demanded the Palladium as his share of the spoils, but Odysseus, under pressure from Menelaus and Agamemnon prevented him taking it. Ajax threatened to take vengeance but the Atrides surrounded themselves with guards and on the following morning Ajax was found stabbed with his own sword.

The account of his death better known to the tragic poets tells how Ajax was refused the arms of Achilles. These arms had been destined by Thetis for whoever had inspired most fear in the Trojans. The Trojan prisoners were questioned and they named Odysseus, who received the arms. During the night Ajax went mad, slaughtered the Greek flocks and killed himself when he realized the state of distraction into which he had fallen.

Ajax was not cremated but placed in a coffin and buried. The Athenians offered him divine honours every year at Salamis.

Alalcomeneus (Ἀλαλκομένευς) Founder of Alalcomenae in Boeotia. He also founded the Hieros Gamos, the religious ceremony symbolizing the marriage between Zeus and Hera. When Hera complained to Alalcomeneus, who had been made responsible for bringing up Athena, about Zeus' infidelities, he advised her to have a statue of herself made of oak and to have it wheeled through the streets attended by a retinue, as was done for a marriage. The ritual was supposed to revive and renew the divine marriage (cf. CITHAERON).

Alcathous (*Ἀλκάθοος*)
1. Son of Pelops (1) and Hippodamia (1) (Table 2).

King Megareus had a son who had been killed by a lion, and had promised the hand of his daughter Evaechme to anyone who could kill the beast. Alcathous did so, gained the reward, deserted his wife, Pyrgo (1), and simultaneously gained the throne of Onchestus.

With Apollo's help Alcathous rebuilt the walls of Megara. The stone on which Apollo laid his lyre while working on the wall would give out a musical sound when struck with a pebble.

Alcathous' son Ischepolis was killed in the Calydonian boar hunt. In his haste to give Alcathous the news, his other son, Callipolis, interrupted a sacrifice to Apollo. Alcathous, angered and thinking that his son wanted to offend the gods, killed him with a blazing log (see POLYIDUS(1)).

Alcathous also had a daughter, Iphinoe, whose tomb could be seen at Megara.
2. Son of Porthaon and Euryte. He was either murdered by his nephew Tydeus or put to death by Oenomaus when he became a suitor of Hippodamia (1) (see TARAXIPPUS(1)).

Alcestis (*Ἄλκηστις*) Daughter of Pelias and Anaxibia (Table 6). She was the most beautiful and pious of women, and the only one of Pelias' children who had no hand in his murder when Medea brought about his death at the hands of his own sons (see JASON). When Admetus asked for the hand of Alcestis, Pelias forced him to accept certain conditions which, with the help of Apollo, he met. Euripides tells us that their marriage was a model of connubial bliss, to the extent that Alcestis agreed to die in place of her husband. But after her death Heracles plunged into Hades and he brought her back more beautiful and younger than ever. There was also a story that Persephone, moved by Alcestis' devotion, had spontaneously returned her to the land of the living.

Alcinous (*Ἀλκίνοος*) King of an island which Homer refers to as Scheria (see PHAEACIANS). Alcinous was the grandson of Poseidon and the son of Nausithous (1). Alcinous had five sons and one daughter, NAUSICAA. Alcinous' wife was called Arete. She lived in the palace with her husband and children, held by all in honour and respect. Their palace was surrounded by a wonderful orchard, where fruit of every kind ripened all the year round. Arete and Alcinous were beloved by their people, hospitable to strangers and especially to victims of shipwreck. One of these victims was Odysseus. Having refreshed Odysseus and listened to the long tale of his adventures, Alcinous gave him a ship on which to return to Ithaca and loaded him with gifts. But Poseidon changed the boat into a rock and surrounded Alcinous' city with mountains.

In the *Argonautica*, Medea and the Argonauts landed in Alcinous' country and found, at his court, a group of envoys from Medea's father, Aeetes, with orders to bring Medea back. Alcinous was chosen to arbitrate and decided that if Medea was still a virgin, she should be sent back to her father; if not she should be left with Jason. Faced with this decision, Arete hastened to marry the young couple. Not daring to appear before their king, the Colchian envoys settled in Scheria, while the Argonauts made their way back home.

Alcmaeon (*Ἀλκμάιων*)

1. Son of Amphiaraus (see Table 1) and elder brother of Amphilochus (1). When Amphiaraus, under pressure from his wife, Eriphyle, had to leave for the war against Thebes, knowing from his powers of divination that he must die there, he charged his children to avenge him. To achieve this they were to undertake an expedition against Thebes and also kill their mother. Alcmaeon therefore took part, as a follower of ADRASTUS, in the campaign of the EPIGONI. An oracle had promised the Epigoni that they would be victorious if they were led by Alcmaeon.

Alcmaeon showed no enthusiasm for leaving to fight against Thebes. He was finally persuaded to do so by his mother, who had been lured by the gift of the robe of Harmonia (1) (see ERIPHYLE). In the fighting Alcmaeon killed Laodamas, king of Thebes. The Thebans fled during the night on the advice of their soothsayer, Tiresias, and on the following day the victorious troops entered the town. They dedicated part of the booty to Apollo and put Thersandrus (2) in charge of the town.

After the battle Alcmaeon went to the Delphic oracle to ask about the murder of his mother. The oracle replied that he must do this without fail, and Alcmaeon killed Eriphyle, either with the help of his brother Amphilochus (1) or, more probably, by himself. After this the avenging Furies pursued him. In his distraction he went to his grandfather Oecles and then to the protection of Phegeus. The latter purified him, brought him back to health and gave him his daughter Arsinoe (or in other accounts Alphesiboea (2)) in marriage. Alcmaeon gave her the necklace and the robe of Harmonia. But Phegeus' land was struck by barrenness and the oracle directed that Alcmaeon must be purified again, this time by the river-god Achelous. Alcmaeon was welcomed by Oeneus at Calydon, then driven out by the Thesproti in Epirus. Eventually he found at the mouth of the Achelous a piece of ground 'created after his mother's murder' and there the river-god purified him and gave him his daughter Callirhoe (2) in marriage. But Callirhoe demanded the robe and necklace of Harmonia as a condition of their living together. In order to comply with her wishes Alcmaeon set off again to Phegeus and demanded that his first wife should return the presents, on the grounds that he had to dedicate them to Apollo to gain final pardon for the murder of his mother. Phegeus permitted his daughter to return the gifts, but one of Alcmaeon's servants disclosed Alcmaeon's true purpose. In his indignation Phegeus ordered his sons Pronous and Agenor (sometimes said to be Temenus (2) and Axion) to set a trap for Alcmaeon and kill him.

Alcmaeon's sons, however, lost no time in avenging their father (see ACARNAN). A tradition, mentioned by Propertius, had it that this revenge was carried out by Alcmaeon's first wife herself (who, in this version is called Alphesiboea (2)).

A tradition used by Euripides has it that when he was being pursued by the Furies, Alcmaeon had two children, Amphilochus (2) and Tisiphone (2), by Manto, the daughter of Tiresias. Subsequently he brought them both to Corinth and entrusted them to Creon (1) to bring up. Tisiphone became so beautiful that the queen, fearing that the king might make her his wife, had her sold as a slave. The girl was bought by her true father, Alcmaeon, who did not recognize her. When Alcmaeon returned to Corinth Creon could give back only his son, but it was later realized that the slave that Alcmaeon had bought was Tisiphone and in this way Alcmaeon regained his two children.

2. The son of SILLUS.

Alcmene (*Ἀλκμήνη*) The wife of AMPHITRYON and mother of Heracles (Table 7). She would not allow Amphitryon to consummate the marriage until he had avenged the murder of her brothers by the Teleboeans. While he was away, Zeus seduced her by assuming the appearance of Amphitryon, since Alcmene's chastity was well known. One tradition has it that Zeus caused the nuptial night to last for three full days. Alcmene was said to have been the last of the mortal women with whom Zeus was united. To deceive her, Zeus made her a present of a gold cup which had belonged to Pterelaus, and told her of the feats accomplished by the real Amphitryon on the expedition. When Amphitryon returned and began to tell Alcmene of his campaign, she replied that she already knew all the details of it. Tiresias was consulted and told Amphitryon of his extraordinary misfortune. Amphitryon first decided to punish his wife by burning her on a pyre, but when Zeus caused a downpour which put the flames out, Amphitryon forgave her. Alcmene gave birth to twins, Heracles, the son of Zeus, and Iphicles, the son of Amphitryon.

Hera, as goddess of childbirth, out of jealousy for her mortal rival made every effort to make Alcmene's pregnancy as long as possible. She had another reason for doing so: an oracle of Zeus allowed her, by arranging the moment when the birth should take place, to make Heracles a slave of EURYSTHEUS.

Later on Alcmene became a widow and she went with Heracles, Iphicles and the latter's son Iolaus to try to recapture Tiryns, their original native land. They were thwarted by Eurystheus, but even so, at the time of the apotheosis of Heracles, Alcmene was settled in Tiryns with some of her grandchildren. Once Heracles was dead, Eurystheus forced Alcmene to leave Corinth and persuaded Ceyx (1), the king of Trachis, to undertake to expel the descendants of Heracles who were in his realm. All of them fled to Athens. Eurystheus demanded that the Athenians should also expel the descendants of Heracles; they refused, and in the war which followed, Eurystheus was killed. His head was carried to Alcmene, who tore out his eyes with spindles. Thereafter Alcmene lived at Thebes. When she finally died Zeus sent Hermes to take her body to the Islands of the Blessed, where she married Rhadamanthys. Other accounts say that she was raised to Olympus, where she shared in the divine honours of her son. It is also sometimes asserted that after the death of Amphitryon Alcmene married Rhadamanthys, at that time in exile, and lived with him at Ocaleus in Boeotia.

Alcon (*Ἄλκων*)
1. A Cretan archer and a companion of Heracles. His arrows never missed: he could make them go through rings placed on a man's head and could split an arrow in half by striking a blade set up as a target. One day, when his son had been attacked by a snake, Alcon put an arrow through it, without hurting the child.
2. The father of Phalerus, one of the Argonauts. The same story is told of him as of Alcon (1), and the two heroes were frequently confused.

Alcyone (*Ἀλκυόνη*)
1. The daughter of Aeolus (1). She married Ceyx (2). They were so happy that they compared themselves to Zeus and Hera. Annoyed at such pride, the divinities changed them into birds, a diver and halcyon respectively. Since Alcyone made her nest on the edge of the sea and the waves continually destroyed it, Zeus commanded that the waves should be calm during the seven days when the halcyon was hatching her eggs. Sailors call these the halcyon days, when storms are unknown.

In Ovid's version, Ceyx died in a shipwreck. Alcyone found his body washed up on the shore and in her despair she was changed into a halcyon, as was her husband.
2. One of the PLEIADES.

Alcyoneus (*Ἀλκυονεύς*)
1. A son of Gaia and Uranus, Alcyoneus was exceptional for his height and strength. He played a leading part in the battle between the Giants and the Gods (see GIANTS), and attacked Heracles as he returned from Erythia with Geryon's cattle. Alcyoneus was invulnerable as long as he fought on the land where he had been born. Every time he was felled he drew strength from merely touching the earth from which he had sprung, so Heracles took him far away from Pallene and shot him dead with an arrow after Alcyoneus had crushed twenty-four of Heracles' companions to death with an enormous rock. In despair at Alcyoneus' death, his daughters threw themselves into the sea and were changed into Halcyons.
2. When the monster Lamia (3) or Sybaris (1) was terrorizing the area near Delphi, Apollo told the inhabitants to offer a young man as a sacrifice to the monster. Alcyoneus was chosen, crowned, and led in procession towards the monster. A young nobleman named Eurybatus saw this, fell in love with Alcyoneus, and offered himself in his place. His offer was accepted. On reaching the monster's lair Eurybatus shattered its head on the rocks, and henceforth a spring called Sybaris gushed forth in its place.

Alebion (*Ἀλεβίων*) A son of Poseidon. He and his brother Dercynus lived in Liguria. When Heracles passed through their country with the cattle of Geryon they tried to steal the oxen from him, but he killed them both (see also LIGYS).

Alectryon (*Ἀλεκτρυών*) During his love affair with APHRODITE, Ares stationed Alectryon (the cock) with orders to warn him when day was breaking. One morning the sentry went to sleep, and thus the Sun took the two lovers by surprise and lost no time in telling Hephaestus, Aphrodite's husband.

Aletes (*Ἀλήτης*)

1. A descendant of Heracles (Table 7). His name, which means 'wanderer', had been given him by his father HIPPOTES because he was born at the time when Hippotes had been banished for murder and was travelling from town to town (see HERACLIDS). When Aletes reached manhood he decided to seize Corinth. He went to consult the oracle of Dodona, which promised that he would succeed if someone should give him a lump of Corinthian earth, and if he attacked the town 'on a day when crowns were being worn'. The first condition was fulfilled when Aletes, having asked a Corinthian for a piece of bread, was given, as a gesture of scorn, only a clod of earth. To satisfy the second condition he marched against the town on a day when the inhabitants were celebrating a festival in honour of the dead and were all wearing crowns. Aletes persuaded the daughter of Creon (1), the king, to open the gates of the town to him on that very day by promising to marry her. The girl agreed to the bargain and duly surrendered the town to him.

Subsequently Aletes undertook an expedition against Athens. The oracle promised that he would be victorious if he spared the life of the king. But the Athenians persuaded their king, Codrus, to sacrifice himself for his people, and so Aletes failed in his undertaking.

2. Son of Aegisthus. See ORESTES and ELECTRA (3).

3. A son of Icarius (2) and brother of Penelope.

Alexander See PARIS.

Alexandra (*Ἀλεξάνδρα*) See CASSANDRA.

Aloadae (*Ἀλωάδαι*) The sons of Poseidon by IPHIMEDIA (Table 5). Iphimedia had fallen in love with Poseidon, and it was her custom to walk along the seashore scooping up the waves in her hand and emptying the water into her bosom. Eventually Poseidon succumbed to her love and gave her two sons, Otus and Ephialtes, who were giants; when they were nine years old they were four metres broad and seventeen metres tall. They decided to make war on the gods, put Ossa on Mount Olympus, and Pelion on top of both, threatening to climb up to the sky. Next they announced that they would fill the sea with the mountains to make it dry and put the sea on what had hitherto been dry land. In addition Ephialtes declared his love for Hera, and Otus his for Artemis. Finally they shut Ares in a brazen cauldron, having first bound him with chains. All these outrageous actions brought the wrath of the gods on the two brothers. Some accounts tell that

Zeus struck them with lightning; others have it that Artemis changed herself into a doe and rushed between them when they were hunting, and in their haste to hit her they killed each other. When they reached Hades they were bound with snakes to a pillar where an owl, perpetually screeching, came to torment them.

Their presence on Naxos at the time of their death was explained by an errand for which their foster-father Aloeus had made them responsible (see IPHIMEDIA).

Alope (*Ἀλόπη*) Daughter of Cercyon (1). She had a child by Poseidon which she exposed in a forest. A mare suckled the child, who later was found by shepherds. They argued over possession of the child and its magnificent swaddling clothes, and referred their dispute to Cercyon, who recognized Alope's handiwork. Alope was put to death, but Poseidon changed her into a spring. The child was again exposed, and again he was suckled by a mare and found by a shepherd, who called him Hippothoon. Later Hippothoon became the eponym of the Attic tribe Hippothoontis. When Theseus had killed Cercyon, Hippothoon came to him to ask for the return of his grandfather's kingdom, which Theseus readily gave him.

Alphaeus (*Ἀλφαιός*) Son of Sangarius. A Phrygian who instructed Athena to play the flute. He was struck down by a thunderbolt from Zeus when he tried to assault his pupil.

Alphesiboea (*Ἀλφεσίβοια*)

1. A Nymph from Asia who was seduced by Dionysus. Medus (2) was the result of this union.
2. Daughter of Phegeus, otherwise known as Arsinoe.

Alpheus (*Ἀλφειός*) The god of the river of that name, which runs between Elis and Arcadia in the Peloponnese. He is the son of Oceanus and Tethys. His children are said to be Orsilochus, the king of Phere in Messenia and, in some accounts, PHEGEUS of Arcadia. Alpheus loved Artemis. One day when she and her Nymphs were celebrating a festival at Letrinoi he tried to approach her, but she smeared her face with mud and he failed to recognize her. Another version says that Alpheus pursued Artemis as far as Ortygia, which lies off the coast of Sicily. Alpheus also loved Arethusa (1) the Nymph, and he turned himself into a hunter in order to follow her. She fled to Ortygia, and Alpheus went after her. Arethusa was changed into a spring and for love of her Alpheus mingled his waters with hers. (See another version of this legend under NAIADS.)

The Alpheus was also the river which Heracles used to flush out the stables of Augias.

Alpos (*Ἄλπος*) A giant from Sicily. He had many arms and his head was covered by a hundred vipers. He used to lie in wait for travellers, crush them beneath the rocks and then eat them. When Dionysus came into the district, Alpos attacked him, protected by a breastplate of a lump of rock, while his weapons of attack were whole trees. Dionysus hurled his thyrsus against Alpos, hitting him in the throat. Alpos fell into the sea.

Althaea (*Ἀλθαία*) The wife of Oeneus and mother of Deianeira and Meleager. When Meleager was seven days old the Fates predicted that he would die if the log which was then burning on the hearth was burnt to ashes. Althaea immediately put it out and hid it in a chest. According to other traditions this log was an olive branch to which Althaea had given birth at the same time as her son.

During the hunt in Calydon Meleager killed Althaea's brothers. In her anger she threw on the fire the log on which her son's life depended. Meleager instantly died, and in her despair Althaea hanged herself.

A variant story says that the children of Althaea were not the sons of Oeneus, but that Meleager was the son of Ares and Deianeira, the daughter of Dionysus. The latter had fallen in love with Althaea, and Oeneus, who had become aware of it, lent him his wife. In gratitude the god gave him a plan of a vineyard and showed him how to use it for cultivation of the vine.

Amalthea (*Ἀμάλθεια*) The nurse who brought up Zeus in secrecy on Mount Ida in Crete when Cronus wanted to eat him. In some sources, Amalthea is the she-goat who suckled the child, in others she is a Nymph. Amalthea hung the baby in a tree to prevent his father from finding him 'in heaven, or on earth, or in the sea', and she gathered the Curetes round him so that their songs and noisy dances should drown his cries. The goat that gave its milk was called Aix (a she-goat). She was a terrifying beast, descended from Helios, and the Titans were so frightened by her mere appearance that Gaia, at their request, had hidden her in a cave in the Cretan mountains. Later, when Zeus was fighting the Titans, he made himself armour from her skin. This armour was called the aegis. There is also a story that Zeus took one of the goat's horns and gave it to Amalthea, promising her that it would he filled with all the kinds of fruit she wanted. This is the Horn of Amalthea or the Cornucopia (see ACHELOUS).

Amata The wife of LATINUS and the mother of LAVINIA. Amata had chosen Turnus, the young king of the Rutuli, to marry Lavinia. So when Latinus decided to give his daughter's hand to Aeneas, Amata tried to prevent the marriage by rousing the women of Laurentium against the Trojans. When she heard of the Trojan victory and the death of Turnus she hanged herself.

Amazons (*Ἀμαζόνες*) A race of warrior women. Their kingdom was in the north on the boundaries of the civilized world. They conducted their own government; they were ruled by a queen; they could not stand the presence of men except as servants; at certain times they had intercourse with strangers to preserve their race, keeping only the baby girls. They removed one of the breasts of the infant girls so that they should be able to shoot with the bow or to handle a spear, and it was from this custom that the Greeks often derived their name from *ἀ-μαζών* (having no breasts).

Bellerophon fought the Amazons at the command of Iobates. Heracles received the mission of taking the girdle of Hippolyta (1), the queen of the Amazons. Hippolyta would have been willing to give him the girdle, but Hera incited the Amazons to mutiny and Heracles was forced to kill Hippolyta. On this expedition he was accompanied by Theseus, who abducted an Amazon called Antiope (2). In revenge the Amazons marched against Athens. They were defeated by the Athenians led by Theseus. There was also a story that the Amazons had sent a contingent commanded by their queen, Penthesilea, to help Priam. Achilles killed her, though her last look aroused his love for her.

The goddess worshipped above all by the Amazons was Artemis, whose myths have so much in common with their lifestyle. They were sometimes regarded as the founders of Ephesus and the builders of the great Temple of Artemis.

Ampelus (Ἄμπελος) A youth beloved by Dionysus. His name means vine stick. The god presented him with a vine laden with grapes which hung from the branches of an elm tree.The youth climbed the elm, but fell while he was picking the grapes and was killed. Dionysus changed him into a constellation.

Amphiaraus (Ἀμφιάραος) Son of Oecles and Hypermestra (3) (Table 1). His sons were Alcmaeon (1) and Amphilochus (1), to whom other traditions add Tiburtus, Coras and Catillus.

Amphiaraus was a seer beloved of Zeus and Apollo, and a warrior. He was renowned for his integrity, courage and piety. At the beginning of his reign at Argos he had killed Talaus and driven out Adrastus, but later tried to patch up the quarrel. Adrastus gave him his sister ERIPHYLE in marriage, stipulating that she should settle any dispute between them. When Adrastus promised to restore Polynices to the throne of Thebes he asked Amphiaraus to join the expedition. Being a seer, Amphiaraus predicted the disastrous outcome of the expedition, and tried to dissuade Adrastus, but Polynices bribed Eriphyle with the necklace of Harmonia (1) (see CADMUS), and she pronounced in favour of the war. Bound by his promise, Amphiaraus marched on Thebes, but made his sons swear to avenge him by killing Eriphyle and raising a second expedition against Thebes (see ALCMAEON (1) and EPIGONI).

On the road to Thebes they witnessed the uncanny death of the infant Opheltes (see HYPSIPYLE). Amphiaraus explained that this was an omen that the expedition would fail and that the chiefs would die, but, after founding the Nemean Games in honour of Opheltes, whom they called Archemorus, they continued on their way. Amphiaraus won prizes for jumping and throwing the discus in these games.

At Thebes Amphiaraus killed MELANIPPUS(2) (see also TYDEUS). In the rout which marked the end of the campaign, Amphiaraus fled to the banks of the Ismenus. Just as he was about to be attacked by Periclymenus (1), Zeus caused the earth to swallow Amphiaraus up. Zeus granted Amphiaraus immortality, and he continued to utter oracles at Oropus in Attica.

Amphictyon (*Ἀμφικτύων*) The second son of Deucalion (1) and Pyrrha (1) (Table 5). He had married one of the daughters of Cranaus, King of Athens, and expelled his father-in-law in order to reign in his stead (see also COLAENUS). He was himself banished by Erichthonius. Some traditions say that it was he who gave Athens its name and dedicated the city to Athena. During his reign Dionysus came to Attica, where he was the king's guest. The foundation of the Amphictyonic League, the religious association in which envoys of all Greek cities met periodically at Delphi, is sometimes attributed to him. Before he assumed the throne of Athens, he is said to have been king of Thermopylae, the other place where the association met.

Amphilochus (*Ἀμφίλοχος*)

1. Son of AMPHIARAUS and brother of ALCMAEON (Table 1). He was one of the suitors of Helen, and therefore took part in the Trojan War after his return from the war of the EPIGONI against Thebes. He inherited his father's gift of prophecy and at Troy he helped the seer Calchas (1), and with him established a number of oracles on the Asia Minor coast.
2. Nephew of Amphilochus (1), many of whose later accomplishments are attributed to him, and son of Alcmaeon and Manto (2). He founded Argos in Aetolia (not to be confused with the better-known Argos in the Argolid). He also went to Troy, and with Mopsus (2) he founded Mallos in Cilicia. When he went to revisit Argos he left Mopsus in charge at Mallos. He returned after finding out the state of affairs at Argos, but Mopsus refused to return Mallos to his control, whereupon the two seers fought in single combat. Both of them were killed.

Amphion (*Ἀμφίων*) The son of Zeus and Antiope (1), and the twin brother of Zethus. The twins were exposed at birth but were rescued by a shepherd. Zethus applied himself to fighting, agriculture and animal husbandry, Amphion, who had been given a lyre by Hermes, to music. They frequently quarrelled over the merits of their respective pursuits.

Their mother, ANTIOPE (1), was a prisoner of her uncle Lycus (3) and his wife, Dirce, who was jealous of her beauty. One day her shackles miraculously fell off and she escaped to her sons' cottage. They did not recognize her and handed her over to Dirce, but when the shepherd who had rescued the twins told them that Antiope was their mother, they took revenge: Dirce was tied to a bull which dragged her across the rocks and tore her to pieces; Lycus too was killed. The brothers ruled at Thebes in Lycus' place and built walls round the town, Zethus carrying the stones, Amphion charming them into place with his music.

Amphion later married NIOBE (2). Some say he was killed along with his children by Apollo, others that he went mad and tried to destroy a temple of Apollo, and that the god shot him with an arrow.

Amphisthenes (*Ἀμφισθένης*) A Lacedaemonian, whose grandsons Astrabacus and Alopecus discovered the long-lost statue of Artemis Orthia which Orestes and Iphigenia had brought from Tauris. As a punishment for having set eyes on the sacred statue the two children went mad. This was the statue in front of which the young Spartans were beaten every year until their blood flowed.

Amphitrite (*Ἀμφιτρίτη*) The Queen of the Sea. She was either a Nereid or a daughter of Oceanus and Tethys. Poseidon was in love with her but she hid from him in the depths of the Ocean beyond the Pillars of Hercules. She was discovered by dolphins and brought back by them to Poseidon, who married her.

Amphitryon (*Ἀμφιτρύων*) The son of Alceus, son of Perseus, and either Astydamia (Tables 2, 7), Laonome, Lysidice or Hipponome, daughter of Menoeceus (1). He took part in the war between Electryon, king of Mycenae, and PTERELAUS of Taphos, in which he recovered Electryon's herds from Polyxenus (3). When Electryon determined to avenge his sons, all of whom except Licymnius had died in the war, he entrusted his kingdom and his daughter Alcmene to Amphitryon, who swore to respect her until the king returned. But Electryon never set off. As Amphitryon was returning the herds, a cow went mad, and when he threw his staff at it, it bounced off the cow's horns, hit Electryon and killed him. Sthenelas of Argos, to whom the kingdom of Mycenae ultimately belonged, banished Amphitryon, who fled to Thebes, where he was purified of the murder by Creon (2). Amphitryon was still bound by his oath, and so could not marry Alcmene; she refused marriage while her brothers were unavenged. So Amphitryon mounted an expedition against Pterelaus. Creon agreed to help, on condition that Amphitryon should rid Thebes of the fox of Teumessa, which was laying the country waste. The fox could not be caught by running, so Amphitryon asked for the hound of PROCRIS, but when this could not outpace the fox Zeus changed both animals into stone.

Amphitryon, Creon and other contingents, including those led by Cephalus, Panopeus and Heleius, laid waste the island of Taphos. But so long as Pterelaus was alive Taphos could not be captured. Pterelaus was invincible as long as his head bore the golden lock of immortality which Poseidon had planted in his hair. His daughter Comaetho (1), however, fell in love with Amphitryon and cut off the fatal hair, assuring victory for her father's enemies. Amphitryon did not yield to her advances and had her put to death.

For the events following Amphitryon's return, and the birth of Iphicles and Heracles, see ALCMENE and HERACLES, I.

In one tradition Amphitryon met his death fighting at Heracles' side in the struggle which the Thebans were conducting against the Minyans of Orchomenus (see ERGINUS (1)); in another he did not die until later, after leading a successful expedition with Heracles against Chalcodon (1).

Amulius The fifteenth king of Alba Longa, the son of Procas and brother of NUMITOR. Procas divided the royal inheritance into two parts: one consisted of the treasure, the other of the kingdom. Numitor chose the latter but Amulius, relying on his wealth drove him out and usurped his place. However despite all his precautions he was unable to prevent his niece Rhea Silvia (1) from giving birth to Romulus and Remus, who eventually dethroned him, put him to death and restored power to their grandfather Numitor.

Amycus (*Ἄμυκος*) A giant, a son of Poseidon and king of the Bebryces in Bithynia. Savage by nature, he used to force strangers to box with him. He invariably killed his opponents. When the Argonauts landed in his country, Amycus challenged them to fight. Pollux took up the challenge. Despite his huge height and brute strength, Amycus was defeated by the skill and suppleness of Pollux. In Apollonius Rhodius Amycus was killed, in Theocritus he was knocked out, and Pollux was satisfied with making the giant promise that he would refrain from harming strangers in future.

Amymone (*Ἀμυμώνη*) One of the Danaides. Her mother was Europa (4). When DANAUS left Libya with his children, Amymone went with him to Argos. But the country had no water owing to the wrath of Poseidon. After Danaus had become king he sent his daughters in search of water. Tired out by walking, Amymone went to sleep at the wayside; a Satyr came upon her and tried to rape her. The girl called on Poseidon, who with one blow from his trident drove the Satyr away. Amymone then granted Poseidon what she had refused the Satyr. But the trident had struck the rock, and a stream with three springs gushed from it. Another version of the story is that after Poseidon, who was in love with Amymone, had come to her rescue he showed her the existence of the spring of Lerna. Amymone had a son, Nauplius (1), by Poseidon.

Ananke (*Ἀνάγκη*) Necessity, the personification of absolute obligation and of the constraining force of the decrees of destiny, she appears in the Orphic theogony where, with her daughter Adrasteia, she is the nurse of the little Zeus. She herself was a daughter of Cronus. Her children were Aether, Chaos and Erebus. Ananke also occurs in the philosophers. For example, in Plato's *Republic*, Ananke is the mother of the Moirae. Gradually, and particularly in popular tradition, Ananke became a goddess of death, but in the works of the poets, particularly the tragedians, she remained the incarnation of the ultimate Force which even the gods must obey. In Rome, Ananke became *Necessitas*.

Anaxagoras (*Ἀναξαγόρας*) The son of Megapenthes (2). According to Pausanias and Diodorus it was during Anaxagoras' reign at Argos, and not that of his grandfather PROETUS, that all the Argive women were struck with a madness which was cured by MELAMPUS. As a reward Anaxagoras gave Melampus a third of his kingdom, giving another third to Melampus' brother Bias, and keeping the remaining third for himself. His descendants, the Anaxagorides, ruled under this system until the son of Sthenelus (3), Cylarabes, reunited the whole kingdom of Argos under his own sway.

Anaxarete (*Ἀναξαρέτη*) A young Cypriot called Iphis (3) fell in love with Anaxarete, but she was cruel to him. In his despair Iphis hanged himself at her door. She was unmoved by the sight, and merely wanted to watch the funeral procession as it passed beneath her window. Aphrodite, angered by Anaxarete's lack of feeling, changed her into a stone statue in the position she had taken up in order to look out of the window. This statue was placed in a temple in Salamis in Cyprus.

Anchemolus The son of Rhoetus (4), king of the Italian tribe of the Marruvians. Anchemolus had been the lover of his stepmother Casperia. When Rhoetus came to hear of it he wanted to kill his son, who fled to Daunus, the father of Turnus. He fought beside Turnus against Aeneas and died in the thick of the fighting.

Anchises (*Ἀγχίσης*) The father of Aeneas and son of Capys and Themiste (Table 4) or Aegesta (see AEGESTES). He was loved by Aphrodite who approached him claiming to be the daughter of Otreus, king of Phrygia. By this device she married him. Later, she told Anchises who she really was and predicted that she would bear him a son (Aeneas), but begged him not to tell anyone that his son was the child of a goddess. But Anchises drank too much wine one feast day and boasted of his love affairs. Zeus punished him by making him lame with a blast from a thunderbolt or, in other traditions, blind. Anchises is also said to have been the father of Lyrnus. The *Iliad* also gives Anchises a mortal wife named Eriopis, by whom he had several daughters, including Hippodamia (4).

When Troy had been captured Aeneas snatched his father from the carnage and made him his companion on his wanderings. The place of Anchises' death (he was eighty years old when he left Troy) is sometimes said to be on Ida where he had once looked after the flocks; alternatively it is placed near the peninsula of Pallene in Macedonia, in Arcadia, in Epirus, in southern Italy, or on Cape Drepanum in Sicily. Aeneas, according to Virgil, established in his honour the funeral games that were the origin of the Trojan Games held in Rome until the beginning of the Empire. Other writers make Anchises live on until Aeneas arrived in Latium (see also AEGESTES).

Anchurus (*Ἄγχουρος*) The son of Midas. When a chasm opened near his capital and threatened to engulf the town an oracle was asked how to end the threat. The oracle replied that Midas had to cast into it whatever he held most dear. Gold and jewels were thrown into it without any result. At last Anchurus threw himself in and the chasm immediately closed up.

Androclus (*Ἄνδροκλος*) The leader of the Ionian colonists who drove the Leleges and the Carians from the area round Ephesus. He himself was supposed to have founded the city. He also conquered Samos. An oracle had foretold that the site of Ephesus would be revealed to the colonists by a wild boar and a fish. One evening a fish that they were cooking jumped off the fire, taking with it a burning piece of charcoal which set light to a thicket out of which ran a wild boar, which Androclus killed. Realizing that the oracle had been proved accurate, Androclus founded the town on that spot.

Androgeos (*Ἀνδρόγεως*) A son of Minos and Pasiphae. A brilliant athlete, he took part in the meeting held by Aegeus at Athens, and beat all the other competitors. Out of jealousy, Aegeus sent him to fight the bull of Marathon, which killed him. In other versions Androgeos was on his way to compete at Thebes, after his victories at Athens, when he was attacked on the road by his unsuccessful competitors and killed. News of his death was brought to Minos as he was celebrating a sacrifice to the Charites on Paros. Although he did not interrupt the festival he wished to show some sign of grief, and threw his crown off his head, asking his flute-players to stop playing. This is said to be the origin of the ceremony, peculiar to Paros, which banned crowns of flowers and ritual flute music in sacrifices to the Graces. As soon as the festival was over Minos left to attack Athens. He took Megara thanks to the treachery of Scylla (2) and from there he marched on Athens. When the war dragged on, Minos prayed to Zeus to avenge him on the Athenians, and plague and famine struck the city. The Athenians consulted the oracle, which replied that if they wanted the calamities to cease they would have to concede to Minos' demand of an annual tribute of seven girls and seven young men to be handed over as food for the MINOTAUR.

One tradition claims that Androgeos had been brought back to life by Asclepius (this is possibly a mistake for GLAUCUS (5)). Androgeos had two sons, Alceus and Sthenelus (2), who settled in Paros (see NEPHALION).

Andromache (*Ἀνδρομάχη*) The daughter of Eëtion, the wife of Hector and daughter-in-law of Priam. By Hector she had an only son, Astyanax. After the death of her husband and the sack of Troy Andromache fell, as part of his share of the Trojan booty, to Neoptolemus. He brought her to Epirus, of which he was king. There Andromache bore him three sons, Molossus, Pielus and Pergamus. When Neoptolemus was killed he bequeathed his kingdom and his wife to Helenus, brother of Hector (see MOLOSSUS).

During Aeneas' travels in Epirus Andromache reigned peacefully with Helenus. On the latter's death she was said to have gone with her son Pergamus as far as Mysia, where he founded Pergamum. Tradition has it that Andromache was a tall, dark woman with a dominating character.

Andromeda (*Ἀνδρομέδη*) The daughter of Cepheus (2) and Cassiopia who claimed to be more beautiful than all the Nereids put together. In jealousy the Nereids asked Poseidon to avenge this insult, and he sent a monster to lay waste the country of Cepheus. An oracle predicted that Ethiopia would be freed from this scourge if Cassiopia's daughter were to be abandoned as a victim in expiation. The inhabitants of the country forced Cepheus to agree to this, and Andromeda was bound to a rock. Here PERSEUS, on his way back from his expedition against the Gorgon, saw her, fell in love with her and promised Cepheus to free her if she could become his wife. Cepheus agreed and, with the aid of his miraculous weapons, Perseus killed the monster and married Andromeda. But Phineus (2), a brother of Cepheus who had been betrothed to Andromeda, plotted against Perseus, who realized what was happening and held the Gorgon's head before him and his accomplices, turning them to stone. When Perseus left Ethiopia he took Andromeda first to Argos and later to Tiryns, where they had several sons and a daughter (Table 7).

According to Conon, Cepheus ruled over the country later to be called Phoenicia and had a very beautiful daughter called Andromeda, who was wooed by Phoenix (2) and her uncle Phineus (2), the brother of Cepheus. Cepheus decided to marry Andromeda to Phoenix but, unwilling to give the impression that he was refusing his brother, pretended that she had been abducted. Phoenix carried her off on a boat called the *Whale*, but Andromeda, having no idea that this was merely a device to deceive her uncle, shouted for help. At that very moment Perseus happened to be passing by. He saw the girl being abducted, took one look at her and fell in love with her. He leapt forward, upset the boat, left the sailors 'turned to stone' with astonishment and carried off Andromeda, whom he married, and thereafter reigned peacefully in Argos.

Anius (*Ἄνιος*)

1. A king of Delos. He was the son of Apollo (or Zeus) and RHOEO. By Dorippa he had three daughters who had been granted the power to make corn, oil and wine spring from the earth. Anius offered their services to the Greeks during the Trojan War, since he had the gift of prophecy and knew the war would last ten years. As the war dragged on Odysseus and Menelaus went to Delos to look for them. The girls went readily, but then grew weary and departed. When the Greeks pursued them they begged Dionysus to give them his protection, and he changed them into doves.
2. The father of LAVINIA.

Anna Perenna A Roman goddess worshipped in a sacred wood on the Via Flaminia. She had the features of an old woman. When the plebs seceded to the Sacred Mountain she made cakes which she sold to them, thus averting famine. That is why she received divine honours when Rome's political troubles had abated.

Another tradition made Anna the sister of DIDO. After Dido's suicide Anna was driven from Carthage by IARBAS. Eventually she arrived on the shores of Latium at the time when Aeneas was ruling Laurentium. Aeneas was walking by the sea with Achates, who recognized Anna. Aeneas wept as he welcomed her, bewailed Dido's death, and set Anna up in his palace, to the displeasure of his wife Lavinia. Anna was warned about Lavinia's hostility in a dream and fled. She met Numicus, the god of a nearby stream, who carried her off. Anna's servants followed her tracks to the stream, where a shape rose from the water and told them that Anna had become a water nymph, whose new name, Perenna, signified eternity. Thereupon the servants celebrated the first annual festival of Anna Perenna.

Mars chose Anna as an intermediary between himself and Minerva, whom he loved. Anna knew that the virgin goddess would never succumb, so she put herself in Minerva's place at a night-time meeting. When Mars was shown into the bridal chamber she lifted her veil; Mars recognized her and spoke angrily. This is what is said to lie behind the obscenities which were sung at the Festival of Anna.

Antaeus (*Ἀνταῖος*) A giant, son of Poseidon and Gaia. He lived in Libya and made all travellers fight with him. After he had defeated and killed them he decorated his father's temple with their corpses. Antaeus was invulnerable so long as he kept in touch with his mother (that is, the earth), but Heracles fought with him and choked him to death by hoisting him on his shoulders.

Anteia (*Ἄντεια*) see STHENEBOEA.

Antenor (*Ἀντήνωρ*) A companion and adviser of Priam. Before the Trojan War he was friends with Menelaus and Odysseus, who tried to negotiate a friendly settlement with him before the siege. In the *Iliad* Antenor urged moderation: he tried to get the war decided by a duel between Paris and Menelaus. While the city was being sacked the Greeks hung a leopard skin over Antenor's door to show that his house should be spared.

With the development of the Trojan cycle Antenor appears as a traitor: he helped the Greeks steal the PALLADIUM and let the soldiers out of the Wooden Horse. After Troy was captured he went to northern Italy.

Antheias (*Ἀνθείας*) A hero from Patras (see TRIPTOLEMUS).

Antheus (*Ἀνθεύς*) A native of Halicarnassus, of royal stock, who lived as a hostage at the court of Phobius, the tyrant of Miletus. Phobius' wife Cleoboea (sometimes called Philaechme) fell in love with him, but he would not yield to her. Cleoboea took her revenge by throwing a golden cup into a deep well. When Antheus went down to look for it she threw an enormous stone on him which crushed him. In remorse at the murder she hanged herself (see also PHRYGIUS).

Anticleia (*Ἀντίκλεια*) The mother of Odysseus and wife of Laertes. When Sisyphus went to her father, Autolycus, to recover his cattle, Anticleia secretly gave herself to Sisyphus before marrying Laertes. Hence Odysseus is sometimes regarded as Sisyphus' son. During Odysseus' absence Anticleia, tired of waiting for him to come back and consumed with worry, killed herself.

Antigone (*Ἀντιγόνη*)

1. The daughter of Oedipus. The earliest legends call her the daughter of Eurygania (1), but the version, used by the tragic writers says that she was the daughter of Jocasta.

When Oedipus blinded himself and exiled himself from Thebes, Antigone made herself his companion. After her father's death Antigone returned to Thebes, where she lived with her sister Ismene (2). During the War of the Seven Against Thebes her brothers, Eteocles and Polynices, found themselves on opposite sides. In the course of the fighting each brother died at the other's hands. Creon (2) the king, the uncle of Eteocles, Polynices and the girls, granted a funeral for Eteocles but forbade anyone to bury Polynices, who had called in strangers against his own country. But Antigone, believing that it was a sacred duty to bury the dead and especially her close kin, broke Creon's ban and scattered a handful of dust over Polynices' body, a ritual gesture which was enough to fulfil the duty imposed by religion. For this she was condemned to death by Creon and walled up in the tomb of Labdacus, from whom she was descended. In her confinement she hanged herself, and Haemon (1), son of Creon and her betrothed, killed himself on her corpse while Creon's wife Eurydice (5) hanged herself in despair.

2. Priam's sister. She was very proud of her hair, which she claimed was more beautiful than Hera's. In a fit of rage the goddess turned Antigone's hair into snakes. But the gods took pity on her and turned her into a stork, the enemy of snakes.

3. Daughter of Eurytion (3) and wife of PELEUS (see also POLYDORA and STEROPE (5)).

Antilochus (*Ἀντίλοχος*) The son of Nestor. Being handsome and a swift runner he was loved by ACHILLES, second in his affection only to Patroclus. It was he who told Achilles of the death of Patroclus. But Antilochus himself was soon to die, either, according to varying sources, at the hands of Memnon, or Hector, or at the same time as Achilles, killed by Paris. A variant of this legend describes Antilochus coming to his father's rescue when he was on the point of being overwhelmed by his enemies. He saved his father, but was himself killed. His ashes were laid to rest beside those of Patroclus and Achilles. The three heroes were said to pass their time after death in fighting and feasting on the White Island.

Antinoe (*Ἀντινόη*)

1. A daughter of Cepheus (1). On the advice of an oracle she followed a snake and led the inhabitants of Mantinea to a spot where they founded a new town on the banks of the Ophis (which means 'snake' in Greek).

2. One of the daughters of Pelias. After the unintentional murder of her father (see PELIAS and MEDEA) she fled to Arcadia.

Antinous (*Ἀντίνοος*)

1. The leader of the suitors who invaded Odysseus' palace. Antinous was notorious for his violence, brutality, pride and hard-heartedness. He tried to cause Telemachus' death, led his companions in the scramble for Odysseus' possessions, insulted Eumaeus when the old swineherd admitted Odysseus into the palace, and incited the beggar Irus (2) against Odysseus, whom he did not recognize. He was killed by the first

arrow loosed by Odysseus, at the very moment when he was raising a cup to his lips. (See also CALCHAS (1).)

2. The favourite of the Emperor Hadrian. After he was accidentally drowned he was deified and cults were established in his honour.

Antiochus (*Ἀντίοχος*) A son of Heracles and ancestor of Hippotes (1) (see PHYLAS 3 and 4).

Antiope (*Ἀντιόπη*)

1. A daughter of Asopus or, according to others, Nycteus. Zeus wooed her in the form of a Satyr, and by him she had Amphion and Zethus. Before the twins were born she fled, fearing her father's wrath, to King Epopeus (1) (see LAMEDON). Nycteus killed himself in despair at Antiope's departure, but asked his brother Lycus (3) to avenge him. Lycus took Sicyon, killed Epopeus and took Antiope to Thebes. On the journey she gave birth to the two children (for subsequent events see AMPHION). In the end Antiope was driven mad by Dionysus, who was angered at Dirce's death. She wandered all over Greece until she was cured by PHOCUS (2), who married her. Variations of the myth can be found under LYCUS (3).

2. An Amazon queen. See HIPPOLYTA (1).

Aphrodite (*Ἀφροδίτη*) The goddess of love, identified in Rome with Venus. There are two accounts of her birth: sometimes she is the daughter of Zeus and Dione, and sometimes a daughter of Uranus, whose sexual organs, cut off by Cronos, fell in the sea and begot the goddess. Aphrodite had scarcely emerged from the sea when she was carried by the Zephyrs to Cythera and then to Cyprus. There she was welcomed by the Horae. Lucian records that she was first brought up by Nereus (compare HERA). Plato formulated the idea of there having been two Aphrodites, Aphrodite Urania, the goddess of pure love, and Aphrodite Pandemos, goddess of common love. This distinction is a philosophical concept, unknown in the early forms of the myths about the goddess.

Aphrodite was married to Hephaestus, but she loved Ares. The *Odyssey* tells how the two lovers were caught by surprise one morning by the all-seeing Helios, who told Hephaestus. The latter set a trap in the form of an invisible net which only he could handle. One night when the two lovers were both in Aphrodite's bed, Hephaestus closed the net over them and summoned all the Olympian gods, much to their delight. At Poseidon's request, Hephaestus drew the net back and Aphrodite, covered with shame, fled to Cyprus. The affair resulted in the birth of Eros and Anteros, Deimos and Phobos (1) and Harmonia. To these names is sometimes added Priapus.

Aphrodite had other love affairs, notably with ADONIS and ANCHISES, by whom she had two sons, Aeneas and, in some traditions, Lyrnus.

Aphrodite's outbursts of anger were famous. She inspired Eos with an irresistible love for Orion, in order to punish her for having yielded to Ares. She vented her anger on the women of Lemnos for not honouring her by making them smell so horribly that their husbands abandoned them for Thracian slave girls. The women then killed all but one of the men on the island and established a community of women, until the Argonauts arrived and enabled them to beget sons (see THOAS (1)). Aphrodite also punished the daughters of CINYRAS by compelling them to become prostitutes for strangers (see also PHAEDRA, PASIPHAE). It could, however, be equally dangerous to be in Aphrodite's favour, as the example of the Judgement of PARIS shows.

Throughout the Trojan War she granted her protection to the Trojans, and to Paris in particular. When Paris took on Menelaus in single combat and was about to yield, she snatched him from danger. Later she protected Aeneas when he was on the point of being killed by Diomedes (2), who actually wounded her. But the protection offered by Aphrodite could not avert the fall of Troy and the death of Paris. Nevertheless she succeeded in preserving the Trojan race, and it was thanks to her that AENEAS escaped from the burning city to seek a new fatherland. This was how Aphrodite-Venus became the special protectress of Rome. She was regarded as the ancestress of the Julii, who claimed descent from Iulus, his father Aeneas, and consequently the goddess. For this reason Julius Caesar built a temple in her honour under the protection of Mother Venus or Venus Genetrix.

Apis (*Ἆπις*) According to Apollodorus, Apis was the son of Phoroneus and the Nymph Teledice. From Phoroneus he inherited power over the whole Peloponnese, which was called Apia after him. But he acted like a tyrant and was killed, according to some by Aetolus, according to others by Thelxion and Telchis. He was subsequently deified and worshipped under the name of Sarapis.

According to Aeschylus, Apis was a physician with the gift of prophecy, a son of Apollo, who had come from Naupactus to purify the Peloponnese.

Pausanias records that Apis is said to be the son of Telchis of Sicyon and father of Thelxion.

Apollo (*Ἀπόλλων*) An Olympian god, son of Zeus and Leto and brother of Artemis. In her jealousy of Leto, Hera pursued her all round the world. Leto searched for a place to give birth to the children with whom she was pregnant; and the whole world refused to welcome her for fear of Hera's wrath. Only a floating island called Ortygia or later Asteria (1) agreed to shelter her. That was where Apollo was born; in gratitude the god named it Delos 'the brilliant'. There Leto waited nine days and nights for the birth, but Hera kept Eilithyia, the goddess who presided over happy deliveries, away. Eventually the other goddesses sent Iris to ask Hera for permission for the birth to take place, offering her a necklace of gold and amber, nine cubits thick. This gift was large enough for Hera to agree to Eilithyia's coming down from Olympus and going to Delos. At the foot of a palm tree Leto gave birth to Artemis and Apollo. Zeus at once gave his son gifts – a golden mitre, a lyre and a chariot drawn by swans – and bade him go straight to Delphi.

But the swans first took Apollo to the land of the Hyperboreans. After a year Apollo returned to Greece and made his way to Delphi. Even Nature was in festive mood for him: cicadas and nightingales sang to honour him, and the springs were clearer. Each year at Delphi the arrival of the god was celebrated with hecatombs.

At Delphi Apollo slew a dragon called either Python or Delphyne (2), which had the task of protecting the oracle of Themis but terrorized the neighbourhood. There is a story that Hera had bidden the monster to pursue Leto before Apollo and Artemis were born. Apollo rid the country of it and founded funerary games in its honour, which took the name of the Pythian games and were held at Delphi. He then took possession of the oracle and dedicated a tripod in the shrine. The tripod is one of Apollo's symbols, and the Pythian was seated on one when she uttered her oracles. The inhabitants of Delphi celebrated the god's victory and instituted the singing of the Paean, which is essentially a hymn in honour of Apollo. Apollo had to cleanse himself of the pollution resulting from slaying the dragon. Every eight years a festival was held at Delphi in memory of the killing of the Python and the purification of Apollo. The god had to defend his oracle against Heracles, who had come to question it and, when it refused to give him any answer, tried to ransack the temple, carry off the tripod and establish an oracle of his own elsewhere. Apollo confronted him, but Zeus separated the opponents (who were both his sons) by hurling a thunderbolt between them. But the oracle remained at Delphi.

Apollo was depicted as a god of outstanding beauty and great stature, especially distinguished for his long, curling, black hair. He had a great many love affairs, with both Nymphs and mortal women.

He fell in love with the Nymph DAPHNE, with whom he was unable to satisfy his desires. He fared better with the Nymph Cyrene by whom he begot the demigod Aristaeus. He also had love affairs with the Muses, whose cult was closely linked with his own. He is said to have been, through Thalia (1), the father of the Corybantes. By Urania he fathered the musicians Linus (2) and Orpheus, though other versions ascribe them to Oeagrus and Calliope. One of his most famous love affairs is that relating to the birth of ASCLEPIUS, in which he was the victim of the unfaithfulness of Coronis (1). He suffered a similar misfortune with Marpessa. Apollo loved her but she was carried off by Idas to Messina, where he and Apollo fought. Zeus parted them and Marpessa was given the right to choose between them. She chose Idas, fearing that she would be deserted in her old age if she married Apollo. His love for Cassandra, had equally unhappy results. In order to seduce her, he promised to teach her the art of divination. She learned the skills, but still refused to yield to him. Apollo took his revenge by ensuring that none of her predictions were believed. Apollo was loved by Hecuba, Cassandra's mother, and she presented him with a son, Troilus. At Colophon, in Asia, Apollo had a son by the soothsayer Manto (1); this was the seer Mopsus (2). Also in

Asia, Apollo had a son called Miletus by a woman variously called Aria, Acalle or ACACALLIS.

In Greece itself Apollo was generally regarded as the lover of Phthia, who gave her name to the eponymous area of Thessaly, and three children were born to them – Dorus, Laodocus and Polypoetes (1). By Rhoeo he begot Anius, who ruled over Delos. Tenes is sometimes said to be the son of Apollo.

Apollo loved young men. The best known are the heroes Hyacinthus and Cyparissus (2), whose metamorphoses (the former became a hyacinth, the second became a cypress) distressed the god very deeply.

On two occasions Apollo had to put himself in the position of a slave in the service of mortal masters. The first followed a conspiracy in which he had joined Poseidon, Hera and Athena to bind Zeus in iron chains and hang him in the sky (see AEGAEON). After the failure of this plot Apollo and Poseidon were compelled to work for Laomedon, king of Troy, on the task of building the walls of the city though, according to some writers, Apollo looked after the king's flocks on Mount Ida. When the time of their servitude was up Laomedon refused to pay the two gods their agreed wages, and when they protested he threatened to cut off their ears and sell them as slaves. When Apollo regained his divine power he sent a plague to Troy. (See HESIONE (3) and HERACLES, III.)

The motif of Apollo as herdsman recurs in the story that when Apollo's son Asclepius had advanced so far in the art of medicine that he could bring corpses back to life, Zeus struck him with lightning. Apollo could not exact revenge from Zeus himself so he killed the Cyclopes who made the lightning. As his punishment, Zeus commanded that Apollo should serve a mortal master as a slave for a year. In compliance Apollo made his way to the court of King Admetus, and served him as a herdsman. Thanks to him the cows produced two calves at a time, and he brought general prosperity to the family (see ALCESTIS).

Apollo also appears as a cowherd working for himself. His oxen were stolen by the young Hermes. Apollo recovered his possessions on Mount Cyllene, but the infant Hermes had invented the lyre and Apollo was so delighted with it that in exchange for it he let Hermes keep his cattle. When Hermes subsequently invented the flute Apollo bought it from him for a golden staff (the Caduceus of Hermes) and instructed him in the art of soothsaying. See MARSYAS for another legend about Apollo in which the flute has a role.

Apollo was the god of music and poetry and he presided over the pastimes of the Muses on Mount Parnassus. His oracular pronouncements were generally in verse and he provided inspiration for seers as well as for poets. He shared this office with DIONYSUS.

Apollo's love affairs with Nymphs and young people who became flowers and trees linked him intimately with plant growth and Nature. Apollo was also a warrior god, like his sister Artemis. Together they massacred Niobe's children to avenge the honour of Leto. Apollo brought down on the Greeks before Troy a plague, in order to compel

Agamemnon to return Chryseis to his priest Chryses. He also slew the Cyclopes, the snake Python and the giant Tityus. He fought on the side of the Olympians in their struggle against the Giants. In the *Iliad* he fought for the Trojans against the Greeks and protected Paris, and it was his involvement which led to the death of Achilles.

Certain animals were especially dedicated to Apollo: the wolf, which was sometimes sacrificed to him, and which is often depicted with him on coins; the roebuck or hind, which also plays a part in the cult of Artemis; the swan, the kite, the vulture and the crow, whose flight could convey omens. There was also the dolphin, whose name (δελφίς) recalls that of Delphi, home of the main shrine of Apollo. The bay laurel was the plant of Apollo above all others. It was a bay leaf that the Pythia chewed during her prophetic trances.

Apollo gradually became the god of the Orphic religion, and with his name was associated a whole system of thought which promised safety and eternal life to its initiates (see ZAGREUS and ORPHEUS). Apollo was believed to be the father of Pythagoras, to whose name similar doctrines were often attached. Apollo was often seen as ruling over the Isles of the Blessed, in Orphism and neo-Pythagoreanism. It is by virtue of this that myths of Apollo are to be found on the walls of the Basilica of the Porta Maxima in Rome, as well as on carved Roman sarcophagi. Augustus, the first Roman Emperor, took Apollo as his personal guardian and ascribed to him the naval victory which he had won over Antony and Cleopatra at Actium in 31 BC. Augustus built a temple of Apollo beside his own house on the Palatine, and established a private cult in his honour. It was largely in Apollo's honour that the Ludi Saeculares, at which the *Carmen Saeculare* of Horace was sung, were celebrated in 17 BC.

Apsyrtus (*Ἄψυρτος*) See ARGONAUTS.

Arachne (*Ἀράχνη*) A Lydian girl who gained such a great reputation for weaving and embroidery that the Nymphs from the countryside around used to come to gaze at her work. Her skill gained her the reputation of having been Athena's pupil, for she was the goddess of spinners and embroiderers. But Arachne would not attribute her talent to anyone but herself. She challenged the goddess, who first appeared to her in the guise of an old woman and advised Arachne to behave with greater modesty. Arachne replied with insults, at which point the goddess threw off her disguise and the contest began. The design of Athena's tapestry showed the twelve Olympian gods in all their majesty, and, as a warning to her rival, in each of the corners she depicted the defeat of mortals who had dared to defy the gods. Arachne's theme was the least creditable love affairs of the gods: Zeus and Europa (5), Zeus and Danae, and so on. Her work was perfect, but Athena was so angry that she tore it up and struck her rival with the shuttle. At this abuse Arachne lost heart and hanged herself, but Athena would not let her die and changed her into a spider, which continues to spin and weave until it has no more thread.

Arcas (*Ἀρκάς*) The son of Zeus and CALLISTO (1). When Callisto died or was changed into a bear, her child was entrusted to Maia (1). Arcas was the grandson of LYCAON (2), who, in order to test Zeus' perspicacity, cooked and served him the limbs of Arcas. Zeus, who was not fooled, punished Lycaon and reassembled Arcas' limbs and restored him to life.

When Arcas was grown up, he went hunting and met his mother in the shape of a bear. He pursued her into the temple of 'Lycian' Zeus, thereby committing a sacrilege punishable by death. Zeus, however, took pity on them both and changed them into the constellations of Ursa (the Bear) and its guardian Arcturus.

Arcas succeeded his uncle Nyctimus as ruler of the Pelasgians, who were called Arcadians after him. He taught them how to grow corn, make bread and spin wool. He married Meganira, daughter of Amyclas or Crocon, by whom he had Elatus (1) and Aphidas (for a different version see CHRYSOPELIA). By Erato (2) he had Azan. He divided Arcadia between these three sons.

Archelaus (*Ἀρχέλαος*) Son of Temenus (3). Banished from Argos, he went to King Cissseus in Macedonia. Cisseus was under siege and promised Archelaus his daughter and his throne in return for deliverance, but following Archelaus' victory he revoked his promise and plotted to kill him. As a trap he prepared a pit filled with glowing coals, covered with a layer of branches, but Archelaus was forewarned of this and threw Cisseus into the pit. He then left the town, and, on Apollo's orders, followed a she-goat to a place in Macedonia where he founded a town called Aege (Greek *αἴξ* = goat).

Archemorus (*Ἀρχήμορος*) See HYPSIPYLE.

Areion (*Ἀρείων*) Adrastus' horse in the first expedition against Thebes. After the defeat of the Argive army Areion, whose speed had already been demonstrated in the funeral games of Opheltes (see AMPHIARAUS), carried his master away from the battlefield and left him near Colonus in Attica.

The following story was told about Areion's breeding. When Demeter was searching for her PERSEPHONE, Poseidon followed her everywhere she went. Demeter had the idea of changing herself into a mare and hiding among the horses of King Oncus, in Arcadia. But Poseidon assumed the likeness of a horse and in this guise mated with her. From this union was born a daughter whose name could not be uttered (known as the Lady or the Mistress) and a horse, Areion. This horse belonged first to Oncus, and then to Heracles, who used it in the expedition against Elis and the struggle against Cycnus (3).

Ares (*Ἄρης*) The Greek god of war, the equivalent of MARS. He was the son of Zeus and Hera (Table 8) and is one of the twelve Olympian deities. From the Homeric period Ares was pre-eminently the god of war. In the fighting at Troy he was generally on the side of the Trojans, but had little regard for the justice of the cause he was backing. He is represented wearing armour and a helmet, and carrying a shield, spear and sword. He was of more than human height, uttered terrible cries, and normally fought on foot, although he could sometimes be found in a chariot. He was attended by Deimos and Phobos (Fear and Terror), his children, and also sometimes by Eris (Strife) and Enyo.

Ares lived in Thrace, traditionally the home of the Amazons, who were his daughters. In Greece he was the object of a special cult in Thebes, where he had a spring, guarded by a dragon of which he was the father. When CADMUS wanted to draw water from the spring, the dragon tried to stop him. Cadmus killed it and, in expiation of the murder, had to serve Ares as a slave for eight years. At the end of that time the gods married Cadmus to Ares' daughter Harmonia (1).

Most myths featuring Ares are about fighting. But the brute strength of Ares is often restrained or deceived by the wiser strength of Heracles or the wisdom of Athena. On the battlefield at Troy, Ares found himself confronting Diomedes (2). Ares' spear deflected and he was wounded by Diomedes. The god uttered a terrible cry and fled back to Olympus, where Zeus had his wound dressed. On another occasion, in the fighting between the gods which took place before Troy, Athena again got the better of Ares by stunning him with a stone.

The antagonism between Ares and Athena was not confined to the Trojan cycle. When Ares defended his son Cycnus against Heracles, Athena had to intervene directly in order to turn aside Ares' spear. Heracles took advantage of Ares' failure to protect himself and wounded him in the thigh. Ares fled to Olympus. This was the second time that Heracles had wounded Ares: the first was at Pylos where Heracles had even stripped him of his weapons. When PENTHESILEA, Ares' daughter, was killed before Troy, Ares wanted to rush headlong to avenge her without any regard to the Fates, and Zeus had to stop him with a thunderbolt. Another misfortune of Ares was to be imprisoned by the ALOADAE, who kept him for thirteen months chained up in a bronze vessel.

For Ares' association with the Areopagus, the hill in Athens which was the meeting place of the court responsible for trying crimes of a religious character, see HALIRRHOTHIUS.

There are many legends about Ares' love affairs. The best known is his affair with APHRODITE. He also had many children by mortal women. Most of them turned into violent men who attacked travellers and killed them or committed various acts of cruelty. By Pyrene (2) he had three sons, Cycnus (3), Diomedes (1), whose mares ate human flesh, and Lycaon (3). Ares was also the father of Meleager and of Dryas. Ares was also said to have given his son Oenomaus the weapons with which he slaughtered his daughter's suitors (see PELOPS and HIPPODAMIA (1)).

Arethusa (*Ἀρέθουσα*)

1. A nymph of the Peloponnese and of Sicily (see ALPHEUS and NAIADS).
2. One of the HESPERIDES.

Argennus (*Ἄργεννος*) A youth of great beauty, son of Pisidice. One day when he was bathing in the Cephissus, Agamemnon caught sight of him and fell in love with him. Argennus fled and Agamemnon pursued him. Eventually Argennus threw himself into the river and drowned. Agamemnon arranged a splendid funeral for him and founded a temple of Artemis Argennis in his honour.

Argonauts (*Ἀργοναῦται*) JASON's companions in his search for the Golden Fleece. They were so called after the *Argo*, the name of the ship they sailed in (see ARGOS (4)).

I. THE ARGONAUTS. A number of catalogues of names of the Argonauts have been preserved. Two of them are especially interesting: those of Apollonius of Rhodes and of Apollodorus. The number of the Argonauts is fairly constant at fifty to fifty-five. The ship was built for forty oarsmen. A certain number of names occur in both lists: Jason was in command of the expedition; Argos (4) built the ship, and Tiphys was the helmsman. He had taken on this duty on the orders of Athena who had taught him the art of navigation, previously unknown. When Tiphys died in the land of the Mariandyni (see below) his place was taken by Erginus (2) or by Ancaeus. Then there was Orpheus, the music-maker, whose task it was to set the rhythm for the oarsmen. The crew numbered several soothsayers – Idmon, Amphiaraus and, in Apollonius, Mopsus (1). Then there were Zetes and Calais, Castor and Pollux, and their two cousins Idas and Lynceus (2). The herald of the expedition was Aethalides, a son of Hermes, whose name does not occur in Apollodorus. All these heroes played an active part in the *Argo*'s adventures. The following generally played minor parts: Admetus; Acastus; Periclymenus (2); Asterius (or Asterion), the son of Cometes; Polyphemus (1); Caeneus, or sometimes his son Coronus; Eurytus (3) and (according to Apollonius) his brother Echion (2); Augias; Cepheus (1) and (only in Apollonius' account) his brother Amphidamas; Palaemonius; Euphemus; Peleus and his brother Telamon; Iphitus (2); Poeas is mentioned by Valerius Flaccus and Hyginus. There were also Iphiclus (2) and his nephew, Meleager; Butes (3) and, in Apollonius only, Eribotes. Apollonius and Apollodorus both include Heracles and Anceus, son of Lycurgus (1).

The following names are not mentioned by Apollodorus: Talaus, Areius and Leodocus (Table 1); Iphiclus (1); Eurydamas, son of Ctimenus; Phalerus, Phlias or Philius, son of Dionysus (Apollodorus records instead two other sons of Dionysus, Phanus and Staphylus (3)); Nauplius (2); Oileus. Among the relatives of Meleager, Apollonius adds Laocoon (2), who is not mentioned by Apollodorus. There were also Eurytion (3); Clytius and Iphitus (1); Canthus, the son of Canethus; and Asterius and Amphion, the sons of Hyperasius.

Apollodorus names the following heroes who are not mentioned by Apollonius besides Phanus and Staphylus (3) (see above); Actor (2); Laertes, and his father-in-law Autolycus; Euryalus (1), Peneleus, Leitus, then Atalanta, the only female member of the expedition, Theseus, Menoetius (1), the son of Actor (1), and finally Ascalaphus (2) and Ialmenus.

Differing scholars and later poets included among the Argonauts names which were not accepted by either Apollonius or Apollodorus: for example Tydeus, Asclepius, Philammon, Nestor, who is mentioned only by Valerius Flaccus, Pirithous, Hyllus, together with Iolaus, Iphis (2) and even, but only in Hyginus, Iphicles, the twin brother of Heracles. Valerius Flaccus gives the name of a certain Clymenus, uncle of Meleager, generally thought to be one of his brothers (see PERICLYMENUS). Hyginus is the only writer to mention Hippalcimus, the son of Pelops and Hippodamia (1), Deucalion (2), and a hero whose name seems to be Thersanor, son of the Leucothoe (2) (see CLYTIA).

II. THE VOYAGE. The ship was built at Pagasae by ARGOS (4) with the help of Athena. The wood came from Pelion save for the prow, which was a piece of the sacred oak of Dodona. Athena herself had cut it and given it the power of speech, to such a degree that it could prophesy.

The *Argo* was launched by the heroes at Pagasae. They sacrificed to Apollo and the omens were good; they were interpreted by Idmon, who disclosed that everyone except himself would return safe and sound.

The first port of call was the island of Lemnos, at that period inhabited only by women (see APHRODITE, HYPSIPYLE, THOAS (1)). They then visited Samothrace where, on the advice of Orpheus, they were initiated into the Orphic mysteries. Next they made their way into the Hellespont; they reached the island of Cyzicus. For the ensuing events see CYZICUS. Before they left, as a storm prevented them from putting to sea again, the Argonauts erected a statue of Cybele on Mount Dindymus, which overlooks Cyzicus.

The next stage of their voyage took them further east to the coast of Mysia. The inhabitants welcomed them and gave them gifts. It was here that the Argonouts abandoned Heracles and Polyphemus (1). See HYLAS.

The *Argo* arrived next at the country of the Bebryces, ruled by King AMYCUS. According to some traditions, after Amycus had been defeated by Pollux, the fighting between the Argonauts and the Bebryces became general. Many of the latter were killed before they finally fled.

On the following day the Argonauts departed and put in on the coast of Thrace, where they found themselves in the land of the seer Phineus (3). They liberated him from the Harpies who were tormenting him (see PHINEUS (3)), and once his curse had been lifted Phineus revealed that part of the Argonauts' future which they were allowed to know. He warned them against the danger of the Cyanean Rocks also also known as the Symplegades, meaning 'Clashing Rocks', moving reefs which collided with each other. To ascertain whether they would be able to pass between them, Phineus advised them to get a dove to fly in front of them. If it succeeded in passing through the straits in safety they would be able to follow it without danger. After hearing this oracle the Argonauts went on their way. When they arrived at the Symplegades they let loose a dove which managed to get through the channel. But the rocks, closing up again, gripped the longest feathers of its tail. The heroes then made the passage in their turn. The ship got through safe and sound, but the stern was slightly damaged, like the tail of the dove. Ever since then the Symplegades have remained motionless, for fate had decreed that once a ship passed them safely they could move no more.

Having thus made their way into the Black Sea, the Argonauts reached the land of the Mariandyni whose king, Lycus (6), received them favourably. It was there, during a hunt, that the seer Idmon was wounded by a boar and died. There too their steersman Tiphys, died. His place at the helm was taken by Ancaeus or Erginus (2). Then the Argonauts passed the mouth of the Thermodon, skirted the Caucasus and arrived at the mouth of the River Phasis, which was the goal of their voyage.

Jason presented himself to King Aeetes, to whom he explained his mission. The king granted the Golden Fleece, on condition that he should yoke, unaided, two bulls with brazen hoofs which breathed fire from their nostrils. When he had finished this test Jason would have to plough a field and sow the teeth of a dragon. These were the rest of the teeth of Ares' dragon at Thebes, which Athena had given to Aeetes (see CADMUS and ARES).

Jason was wondering how he could yoke these monstrous beasts when MEDEA, the king's daughter, who had fallen in love with him, came to help him. She began by making him promise that he would marry her and take her to Greece if she helped him perform the tasks which her father had set him. Medea then gave him magic balsam (for she was very skilled in all the occult arts) with which he was to cover his body and his shield before he attacked the bulls. This balm made anyone covered by it invulnerable for a whole day to harm from iron or fire. Furthermore, she showed him that the dragon's teeth would give birth to a crop of armed men who would try to kill him, but he had only to throw a stone into their midst from a distance and the men would start to attack and kill each other. Jason, thus forewarned, managed to yoke and harness the oxen, plough the field and sow the dragon's teeth. Then he concealed himself and from a distance stoned the warriors who had sprung up. They began to fight each other and, taking advantage of their failure to notice him, Jason slew them.

Aeetes, however, did not keep his promise: he tried to burn the *Argo* and kill her crew. But before he had time to do so, Jason, acting on Medea's advice, secured the Fleece (Medea had put a spell on the dragon which was guarding it) and made his escape.

Aeetes gave chase, but Medea, who had foreseen that this would happen, killed her brother, Apsyrtus, whom she had taken with her, and scattered his limbs along the way. Aeetes spent some time picking them up, which gave the fugitives time to escape. But before he returned to Colchis he sent out several groups of his subjects in pursuit of the *Argo*, warning them that if they returned without Medea they would be put to death. Another version of the story says that Apsyrtus had been sent by Aeetes in pursuit of his sister but that Jason, with the help of Medea, had killed him in a temple dedicated to Artemis which lies at the mouth of the Danube. The Argonauts went on their way towards the Danube and followed the river upstream until they reached the Adriatic (at the date of this story the Danube, or Istros, was thought to link the Black Sea with the Adriatic). Zeus, angered by the murder of Apsyrtus, sent a storm which blew the ship off course. At this point the ship itself began to speak, and explained Zeus' anger, adding that this would not cease before the Argonauts had been purified by Circe. Accordingly the ship sailed, by a complicated route, to Circe's home on the island of Aeaea. There the sorceress, who was the aunt of Medea, purified the hero and had a long conversation with Medea, but refused to offer Jason hospitality. The ship set forth again and, guided by Thetis, at Hera's bidding, it crossed the sea of the SIRENS. At this point Orpheus sang so sweetly that the heroes had no wish to respond to the Sirens' call. Only one of them, Butes (3), swam to their rock, but Aphrodite saved him by extracting him and settling him at Lilybaeum in Sicily.

Thereafter the *Argo* passed through the straits of Scylla (1) and Charybdis, then the Wandering Isles above which hung a cloud of black smoke. Finally it arrived at Corcyra in the land of the Phaeacians, where Jason and Medea were married in order to escape the pursuit of a band of Colchians (see ALCINOUS), and the Argonauts took to the sea once again.

They had hardly departed before a storm drove them towards the Syrtes, on the Libyan coast. There they had to carry the ship on their shoulders until they reached Lake Tritonis. Thanks to Triton, the spirit of the lake, they found a channel to the sea and continued their voyage towards Crete. But during this phase they lost two of their company, Canthus and Mopsus (1), though they are not mentioned in all the lists of the Argonauts traditionally recorded (see above).

Just as they were disembarking in Crete, the Argonauts came into conflict with a giant named TALOS (1). Medea got the better of him by means of her spells. So the Argonauts reached land and spent the night on the beach. On the following day they built a shrine to Minoan Athena and went on their way.

On the Cretan Sea, they were suddenly overtaken by a black night which caused them to run into the greatest dangers. Jason prayed to Phoebus, who in response threw out a shaft of flame which showed them that the boat was very close to a small island of the Sporades where they could cast anchor. They called the island Anaphe (the Isle of Discovery) and raised on it a shrine to Phoebus. But the offerings for celebrating the inaugural sacrifice were lacking and they had to make their ritual libations with water rather than wine. When the female Phaeacian servants given by Arete to Medea as a wedding present saw this, they began to laugh and made robust jokes about the Argonauts. The latter responded in kind and the custom was repeated every time a sacrifice in honour of Apollo was made on this tiny island.

The Argonauts finally arrived back at Iolcos, having accomplished their round voyage in four months, bringing the Golden Fleece with them. Jason then sailed the *Argo* to Corinth where he dedicated it to Poseidon.

The legend of the Argonauts is best known to modern readers through the epic *Argonautica* by Apollonius Rhodius. It became extremely popular in the ancient world and it was possible to extract from the adventures of the *Argo* plots for plays and poetry of every description. The story of Medea, in particular, caught the imagination of the poets (see MEDEA and JASON).

Argos (*Ἄργος*)

1. The son of Zeus and Niobe (1). Argos received the sovereignty of the Peloponnese, which he called Argos. He married Evadne (3), the daughter of Strymon and Neaera (or alternatively of Peitho (2)) and had four sons, Ecbasus, Piras, Epidaurus and Criasus. Another tradition makes him father of Peirasus, Phorbas (2) and Tiryns. Argos was supposed to have introduced the practice of tilling the soil and planting corn into Greece.
2. The great-grandson of Argos (1), generally known by the Latinized form of his name, Argus. Some traditions give him a single eye, others four, two looking backwards and two forwards, others ascribe to him a large number of eyes all over his body. He freed Arcadia from a bull which was devastating the area, flayed it and clothed himself in its hide. Then he killed a Satyr which was terrorizing the Arcadians and their flocks. Then he killed ECHIDNA by overcoming her in her sleep. Hera then appointed him to watch over the heifer IO. Argos tethered Io to an olive tree, and thanks to his many eyes was able to keep a permanent watch on her. But Zeus got Hermes to free her. Sometimes Hermes is said to have killed Argos by throwing a stone; sometimes he lulls Argos to sleep with the Pan pipes; sometimes he sends him to sleep with his divine wand. To give immortality to her faithful servant, Hera moved his eyes to the tail of the peacock.
3. The son of Phrixus and Chalciope (2). He was born and brought up in Colchis, but left to go and claim his inheritance from his grandfather, Athamas. He was shipwrecked on the island of Aria, where he was sheltered by the Argonauts. Another version says that he met Jason at the house of Aeetes. It was he who brought about the first meeting between Jason and Medea. He came back with the Argonauts. In Greece he married Perimele (1) and by her he had a son, Magnes.
4. The hero who built the *Argo* (see ARGONAUTS). He took part in the expedition in search of the Golden Fleece. He is sometimes regarded as being the son of Arestor, a relationship also claimed for Argos (2), and sometimes confused with Argos (3).

Argynnus A variant spelling of ARGENNUS.

Argyra (*Ἀργυρᾶ*) A Nymph of an

Arcadian spring. She loved a handsome young shepherd called Selemnus, but when he grew older she abandoned him. In his despair Selemnus died and was turned into a stream by Aphrodite. But as he still suffered from his love in spite of undergoing this change, Aphrodite granted him the gift of oblivion. That is why all who bathed in the Selemnus were able to forget the sorrows of love.

Ariadne (*Ἀριάδνη*) The daughter of Minos and Pasiphae. When Theseus arrived in Crete to do battle with the MINOTAUR Ariadne fell in love with him; to enable him to find his way in the Labyrinth where the Minotaur was confined she gave him a ball of thread, which he unwound to show him the way to return. She then fled with him to escape the wrath of Minos, but Theseus abandoned her while she slept on the shore of Naxos. Sometimes Theseus is said to have left her because he was in love with another woman; other versions say that Theseus acted on the command of the gods because fate would not allow him to marry her. Ariadne woke up in the morning to see the sails of her lover's ship vanishing over the horizon, but Dionysus soon appeared on the scene. Overcome by her youthful beauty, Dionysus married her and carried her off to Olympus. As a wedding present he gave her a golden diadem, made by Hephaestus, which later became a constellation. Ariadne had four children by Dionysus, named Thoas (1), Staphylus (3), Oenopion and Peparethus. Another tradition tells how Ariadne was killed on the island of Dia (later identified with Naxos) by Artemis at the bidding of Dionysus (for alternative versions of the legend about Ariadne, see THESEUS, III).

Arion (*Ἀρίων*) A musician from Lesbos who had been given leave by his master, the tyrant of Corinth, Periander, to travel and earn money from his singing. When he wanted to go back to Corinth the crew of the ship in which he was travelling conspired to kill him and appropriate his money. Apollo appeared to Arion in a dream and warned him of the plot. When Arion was attacked by the conspirators he asked to be allowed to sing once more. They granted this request and when the dolphins heard his voice, they gathered round and Arion, putting his trust in the god, leaped into the sea. A dolphin carried him safely to the shore. The musician dedicated an *ex voto* to Apollo and made his way to Corinth where he told his story to Periander. When the ship containing the would-be assassins arrived at Corinth Periander asked the sailors where Arion was and they replied that he had died on the voyage. Arion then appeared in person and the conspirators were executed. To commemorate the story, Apollo changed Arion's lyre and the dolphins into constellations.

Aristaeus (*Ἀρισταῖος*) One day when Apollo was hunting in a valley of Pelion, he saw the Nymph Cyrene and transported her to Libya where she bore him a son named Aristaeus. Apollo placed him in the care of his great-grandmother Gaia and of the Horae. According to another tradition, Aristaeus was brought up by Chiron, the Centaur. The Muses completed his education by teaching him the arts of medicine and divination. They entrusted him with the care of their sheep. The nymphs also taught him the arts of dairy farming, bee-keeping, and viticulture. In his turn, he taught men the skills that the goddesses had taught him.

Aristaeus married Autonoe, the daughter of Cadmus, and fathered Actaeon. He is also credited with a whole range of discoveries about hunting, notably the use of pits and netting. Virgil tells how Aristaeus pursued Eurydice (1). In her flight, Eurydice was bitten by a snake and died. The gods punished Aristaeus by causing an illness among his bees. In despair he called for help on his mother, Cyrene, who referred him to the sea-god Proteus. Aristaeus went off to question Proteus and, taking advantage of the fact that Proteus was asleep, tied him up and forced him to answer, for Proteus did not like questioners. He told Aristaeus that the gods were punishing him for Eurydice's death and gave him advice on how to get new swarms of bees.

There is also a story that Aristaeus took part in the conquest of India with Dionysus. During a plague which caused much damage to the Cyclades the inhabitants asked Aristaeus for help. He settled in Ceos and there built a great altar to Zeus. Zeus, moved by his prayers, sent the Etesian winds, which cooled the atmosphere and blew away the unhealthy air. Ever since then, each year these winds rise at the hot season and purify the air of the Cyclades. Aristaeus was held in honour in Arcadia, where he had introduced bee-keeping. He was also honoured in Libya, whither he was said to have followed his mother and where he planted the precious herb called Silphium, which produced both a cure and a spice.

Aristeas (*Ἀριστέας*) The poet of Proconnesus, who died in a fuller's workshop, though his body could not be found. Seven years after his supposed death Aristeas returned and wrote his poem, the *Arimaspes*. During his absence he was said to have gone with Apollo to the land of the Hyperboreans. Once his poem was finished, he disappeared again.

Aristodemus (*Ἀριστόδημος*) Son of Aristomachus and a descendant of Heracles. His brothers were Temenus (3) and Cresphontes, who conquered the Peloponnese. When he was at Naupactus preparing for this campaign, Aristodemus was struck by a thunderbolt at the request of Apollo, as a punishment for not having first consulted the Delphic oracle. Another tradition says that he was killed by Medon (3) and Strophius (2). In another version he was not killed but took part in the successful campaign and was awarded Laconia as his share. For his descendants see THERAS.

Artemis (*Ἄρτεμις*) Identified by the Romans with Diana. She is sometimes said to have been the daughter of Demeter, but is generally regarded as the twin sister of Apollo, their parents being Zeus and Leto. Artemis, the elder twin, was born in Delos and helped her mother to give birth to her brother. Artemis was always a virgin and eternally young, an untamed girl with few interests beyond hunting. Like her brother, her weapon was the bow, which she used while she was hunting stags as well as mortals, and she inflicted pain on women who died in childbirth. She was vindictive and there were many who suffered from her anger. One of her actions was to join Apollo in killing the children of NIOBE (2). They did this out of love for their mother, who had been insulted by Niobe, and it was in defence of Leto again that Artemis and Apollo, though scarcely born, killed the dragon which had come to attack them; in the same way they killed Tityus, who was trying to violate Leto.

Artemis took part in the battle against the Giants, where she killed Gration. She also destroyed the ALOADAE and is said to have killed the monster BOUPHAGUS. Other victims of Artemis included ORION and ACTAEON who, like Orion, was a hunter. He owed his death to the wrath of Artemis, and she was the instigator of the hunt for the wild boar of Calydon, which was fated to lead to the death of the huntsman MELEAGER. Artemis is sometimes said to have been responsible for the death of CALLISTO (1). All these myths relate to hunting, giving a picture of a ferocious goddess of the woods and mountains, who usually kept company with wild beasts.

An account of the Labours of HERACLES (II) tells how Eurystheus ordered him to bring back the Ceryneian hind which was sacred to Artemis. When he finally killed it Artemis and Apollo appeared before him, asking for an explanation. Heracles appeased them by blaming Eurystheus. A similar theme recurs in the story of IPHIGENIA (see also AGAMEMNON, and for the long-standing hatred of Artemis against his family, ATREUS).

Artemis was held in honour in all the wild and mountainous areas of Greece, in Arcadia and in the country of Sparta, in Laconia on Mount Taygetus and in Elis. Her most famous shrine was at Ephesus. She was closely associated with the Moon as Apollo was with the Sun, but not all the Artemis cults had lunar significance. Artemis absorbed some cults which involved human sacrifice, such as that practised in Tauris (see AMPHISTHENES). Artemis was also the protecting deity of the Amazons who, like her, were warriors and huntresses and independent of men. For her relationship with magic, see HECATE.

Ascalabus (*Ἀσκάλαβος*) When Demeter was searching for Persephone she passed through Attica. She was very thirsty, and a woman called Misme gave her a drink; she swallowed so eagerly that Misme's small son Ascalabus burst out laughing. Demeter was so annoyed that she threw the rest of the water over him and he became a spotted lizard.

Ascalaphus (*Ἀσκάλαφος*)

1. A son of a Nymph and the river-god Acheron; he was in the garden of Hades when PERSEPHONE was eating a pomegranate seed, thus breaking her fast and unknowingly destroying any hope of returning to the light of day. Ascalaphus saw this and revealed the fact. Demeter in her anger changed him into an owl. In a

different version Ascalaphus was first made to lie under a large stone, which Heracles moved when he descended into Hades, whereupon Ascalaphus was changed into an owl.
2. A son of Ares, see IALMENUS.

Ascanius (*Ἀσκάνιος*) Son of Aeneas and Creusa (4). Another tradition makes Lavinia his mother after the arrival of Aeneas in Italy. In the oldest version of the story Ascanius was taken away by Aeneas after the fall of Troy and sent to the Propontis, where he ruled until he refounded the city of Troy with Scamandrius (1) (see ASTYANAX). In another tradition Ascanius lived with Aeneas in Italy. In his old age Aeneas was said to have returned to rule in Troy and on his death to have left the kingdom to his son. The tradition related to the Roman legend of Aeneas depicts Ascanius as settled in Italy, where he was the first of his line.

Ascanius is clearly characterized in Virgil's *Aeneid*. He is on the verge of manhood, competes in the Trojan Games, goes hunting in the forests of Latium, is loved by Aeneas and by his grandmother Venus, and embodies many of the Trojans' hopes for the future.

After Aeneas' death Ascanius defeated the Etruscans on the shores of Lake Numicus. He founded the city of Alba Longa on the spot where Aeneas had sacrificed a white sow and her thirty piglets. He was forced to do so by the Latini, who sided with his stepmother Lavinia against him. Lavinia, pregnant after Aeneas' death, had fled, fearing that Ascanius would kill her unborn child. She took refuge with a shepherd called Tyrrhus, and her child SILVIUS was born in his home. When Ascanius died Silvius succeeded to the throne of Alba.

Ascanius is often referred to as Iulus.

Asclepius (*Ἀσκληπιός*) In Latin Aesculapius. The god of medicine. He was the son of Apollo. In the account given by Pindar, Apollo loved Coronis (1) and fathered a son, but before the child was born, Coronis yielded her love to a mortal, Ischys, the son of Elatus (1). Apollo killed her, but just as her body was lying on the funeral pyre, Apollo tore the child, still alive, from her womb. That is how Asclepius was born. According to another tradition a thief named Phlegyas came to Epidaurus to discover the wealth it contained and how he could appropriate it. His daughter Coronis (1) accompanied him but was seduced by Apollo, and secretly gave birth to a son in Epidaurus, at the foot of Mount Myrtion. She abandoned the child but a she-goat came to suckle the infant and a dog protected him. The shepherd Aresthanas who owned both animals found the child and was astounded by the brilliant light in which he was bathed. Another version makes Arsinoe, the daughter of Leucippus (1), the child's mother, although the child was brought up by Coronis.

Asclepius was entrusted by his father to the Centaur Chiron, who taught him medicine, in which Asclepius developed exceptional skill. He was given the blood which had flowed in the Gorgon's veins by Athena, and while the blood from its left side spread a fatal poison, that from the right was beneficial, and Asclepius knew how to use it to restore the dead to life. Capaneus, Lycurgus, Glaucus (5) and Hippolytus (1) (see PHAEDRA) are all said to have been revived by him. Zeus, feared that Asclepius might upset the natural order of things and struck him with a thunderbolt. To avenge him APOLLO killed the Cyclopes. After his death Asclepius was changed into a constellation and became the plant serpentaria. Several late pieces of evidence show Asclepius taking part in the Calydonian hunt and the Argonauts' expedition, but he usually stands outside the legendary cycles.

He is said to have had two children, Podalirius and Machaon, whose names are found in the *Iliad*. Other traditions give him a wife, Epione, and five daughters, Aceso, Iaso, Panacea, Aglaea and Hygieia. The cult of Asclepius was centred on Epidaurus in the Peloponnese, where a school of medicine flourished. This art was practised by the Asclepiadae or descendants of Asclepius, the best known of these being Hippocrates. The usual symbols of Asclepius were snakes twined round a staff, together with pine-cones, crowns of laurel and sometimes a nanny-goat or a dog.

Asia (*Ἀσία*) The daughter of Oceanus and Tethys (Table 8) who gave her name to the Asian continent. She was married to Iapetus and had four children, Atlas (1), Prometheus, Epimetheus and Menoetius (2).

Asopus (*Ἀσωπός*) The god of the river of the same name, either the son of Poseidon and Pero, of Zeus and Eurynome, or of Oceanus and Tethys. He married Metope (1), the daughter of Ladon (1), and fathered two sons, Ismenus (1) and Pelagon, and twenty daughters. Diodorus gives the names of only twelve: Corcyra, Salamis, Aegina, Pirene, Cleone, Thebe (3), Tanagra, Thespia, Asopis, Sinope, Oenia (or Ornia) and Chalcis. Asopus is also said to be the father of Antiope and Plataea, after whom the city is named (see ISMENE (1) and AEGINA).

Aspalis (*Ἀσπαλίς*) See MELITEUS.

Assaon (*Ἀσσάων*) The father of Niobe (2) in one version of the legend. See NIOBE (2).

Asteria (*Ἀστερία*)

1. The daughter of Coeus and Phoebe (1). She was Leto's sister. Zeus loved her but she changed herself into a quail to escape him and threw herself into the sea, where she became an island called Ortygia (Quail Island) which was subsequently called Delos. (See APOLLO). She was the mother of Hecate by Perses.
2. Asteria (or Asteropia) was the daughter of Deion and Diomede. She was the mother of Panopeus and Crisus by Phocus (3).
3. The daughter of Teucer (2) and Eune.

Asterion (*Ἀστερίων*) (or Asterius) The son of Tectamus or Dorus (1) and a daughter of Cretheus, was a king of Crete who married Europa (5) after she had been seduced by Zeus. Asterion adopted their children, Minos, Sarpedon (2) and Rhadamanthys.

Astraea (*Ἀστραία*) The daughter of Zeus and Themis. She spread the feelings of justice and virtue among mankind in the Golden Age, but after wickedness took possession of the world, Astraea returned to heaven, where she became the constellation Virgo. (See also IUSTITIA.)

Astyanax (*Ἀστυάναξ*) The son of Hector and Andromache. His father called him Scamandrius (1), after the river which flowed by Troy, but the common people called him Astyanax (Prince of the City). After the fall of Troy Astyanax was seized by the Greeks led by Odysseus, who put him to death by throwing him from a tower. According to a later tradition Astyanax was not killed, but founded a new Troy (see ASCANIUS).

Atalanta (*Ἀταλάντη*) A mythical huntress. Sometimes she is regarded as the daughter of Iasus (1) (or Iasius), sometimes (e.g. in Euripides) as the daughter of Menalus, the eponym of Mount Menalus, or most commonly as the daughter of Schoeneus (1). Since her father wanted only sons, Atalanta was exposed at birth on Mount Parthenon. A she-bear fed her until she was found and taken in by some huntsmen. When she reached girlhood Atalanta devoted herself to hunting. She took part in the Calydonian boar hunt (see MELEAGER). At the funeral games held in honour of Pelias she won the prize, either for the race or for wrestling with Peleus.

Atalanta was unwilling to marry, either because she was devoted to the virgin goddess Artemis or because an oracle had told her that if she did marry she would be changed into an animal. So she made it known that she would marry only a man who could beat her in a race. If she won she would put the suitor to death. She was so fast that she would give her opponent a start, catch him and kill him. This happened frequently until Hippomenes, son of Megareus (or her first cousin Melanion or Milanion, son of Amphidamas) arrived with three golden apples which had been given to him by Aphrodite. They came either from a shrine of the goddess in Cyprus or from the garden of the Hesperides. In the race he threw them one by one in front of her. She stopped to pick them up, allowing him to win the race and the prize. However, he failed to give due honour to Aphrodite, and some time later, at Aphrodite's instigation, he entered a shrine of Zeus or Cybele with Atalanta and made love with her. Furious at the sacrilege, the enraged deity changed them both into lions. Thus Aphrodite's revenge was very subtle: it was believed that lions do not mate with each other, but with leopards.

A Spring of Atalanta could be seen near Epidaurus where Atalanta, searching for water, had struck the rock with her spear and a spring had gushed forth.

Atalanta had, either by her husband, or by Meleager, or by Ares, a son called PARTHENOPAEUS.

Ate (*Ἄτη*) The personification of Delusion, the goddess of rash actions. A goddess whose feet rested on the heads of mortals without their knowing it. When Zeus pledged to give pre-eminence to the first descendant of Perseus, and in this way exalted Eurystheus above Heracles, it was Ate who deceived him. Zeus took his revenge by casting her down from Olympus. Ate fell to earth in Phrygia, on the hill which took the name of the Hill of Error. That was the spot where Ilus (2) built the fortress of Ilium (Troy). Zeus forbade Ate ever to stay on Olympus, and that is why Delusion is the sad lot of mankind.

Athamas (*Ἀθάμας*) A king of Thebes in Boeotia. He was the son of Aeolus (1) (Table 5). Athamas was married three times, first to Nephele (1), who bore a son, PHRIXUS, and a daughter, HELLE. Later he discarded Nephele and married Ino, the daughter of Cadmus, by whom he had Learchus and Melicertes (see LEUCOTHEA (1)). Ino was jealous of the children of Athamas' first marriage and wanted to kill them. She persuaded the women of the country to roast the seeds of corn which were to be sown. The men sowed the seed, but none of it came up. Athamas sent messengers to the Delphic oracle. Ino bribed them to report that the god required the sacrifice of Phrixus. The ruse almost succeeded, but Phrixus was rescued by a ram with a golden fleece (see PHRIXUS). Hyginus relates a tradition which claims that the messenger who had been bribed by Ino pitied Phrixus and revealed the plan to Athamas who, when he learned of the plot of which his wife had been guilty, gave orders that she should be sacrificed in place of Phrixus, along with her son, Melicertes. When they were being led to the altar, however, Dionysus had pity on his former nurse (see below) and enveloped her in a cloud which made her invisible and allowed her to escape with Melicertes. He then caused Athamas to go mad and kill his younger son, Learchus, by throwing him into a cauldron of boiling water. Ino, in turn, killed herself together with Melicertes (see LEUCOTHEA (1)).

Euripides' tragedy *Ino* deals with the third marriage of Athamas with Themisto, the daughter of Hypseus. In this play Ino departed to the mountains to join Dionysus. Athamas, who believed that she was dead, married Themisto, and fathered two children, Orchomenus and Sphingius, but Ino returned secretly. She made herself known to Athamas, who brought her into the palace in the guise of a servant. Themisto discovered that her rival was not dead, but could not learn where she was hiding. She set about killing Ino's children and took the new servant as her confidante. She ordered her to make Ino's children wear black clothes and her own children white so that they could be recognized in the dark. The servant changed the clothes round so that Themisto killed her own two sons. When she discovered her mistake Themisto killed herself. The more common story was that the wrath of Hera had fallen on Athamas after the sacrifice of Phrixus because he agreed to bring up Dionysus who had been entrusted to Ino, the sister of SEMELE. Struck with madness by the goddess, he killed Learchus. At this, Ino killed Melicertes and then threw herself into the sea with his body (see LEUCOTHEA (1)).

Athamas was banished from Boeotia because of this crime, so he asked the oracle where he should settle, and was told to stop at the place where the wild beasts would feed him. When he reached Thessaly he found wolves eating a sheep's carcass. When they saw him they ran off, leaving the carcass behind, and thus the oracle was fulfilled. Athamas settled in that region. There he was said to have married Themisto, by whom he had four sons: Leucon, Erythrius, Schoeneus (3) and Ptous. According to Herodotus, Athamas was on the point of being sacrificed by his subjects as a scapegoat, but he was saved by his grandson CYTISSORUS. This episode was dramatized by Sophocles in his lost tragedy *Athamas Crowned*.

Athena (*Ἀθηνᾶ*) A goddess identified at Rome with MINERVA. She was the daughter of Zeus and Metis. When Metis became pregnant, Gaia and Uranus told Zeus that after giving birth to a daughter, she would then have a son by Zeus who would later dethrone him. On Gaia's advice Zeus swallowed Metis. When the time came for the child to be born, Hephaestus split Zeus' head open with an axe. A girl in full armour sprang forth from his head: it was Athena.

Athena, the warrior goddess, armed with spear and aegis (a goatskin shield or short cloak surrounded by Fear, Strife, Force and Pursuit, with a Gorgon-head in the centre and fringe of snakes), played a key role in the struggle against the Giants. She killed Pallas (6), flayed him, and used his skin as a breastplate for the rest of the battle; Enceladus fled, but she immobilised him by throwing the island of Sicily on top of him. In the *Iliad* she fought on the Achaean side (she was hostile to the Trojans since the Judgement of PARIS), supporting Diomedes (2), Odysseus, Achilles and Menelaus. She also looked after Heracles during his Labours: she gave him the bronze castanets with which he scared the Stymphalian birds, and in return he gave her the Golden Apples of the Hesperides and fought beside her against the Giants.

In the *Odyssey* Athena helped Odysseus to return to Ithaca. She sent a dream to NAUSICAA to give her the idea of doing her washing at the river on the day that Odysseus landed at Phaeacia; she gave him supernatural good looks to ensure that Nausicaa would obtain a boat for him to return home; she begged Zeus to show Odysseus his favour; she caused CALYPSO (1) to release Odysseus and give him the means to put to sea again.

Athena also presided over the arts and literature, though she was more closely linked with philosophy than with poetry and music (cf. the MUSES). She was the patroness of spinning, weaving, embroidery and similar household activities practised by women (see ARACHNE). Her combination of ingenuity and warlike spirit led her to invent the war chariot, help DANAUS build the first two-prowed ship, Argos (4) to build the *Argo*, and Epeius (2) to build the Trojan Horse. In Athens and Attica she was blessed for the discovery of olive oil and the introduction of the olive tree. Poseidon disputed the sovereignty of Attica with her. Each deity tried to give Attica the best present they could: Poseidon caused salt-water to spring up on the Acropolis by throwing his trident into the ground (this sea-water was, according to Pausanias, a well of salt-water within the precincts of the Erechtheum); Athena summoned Cecrops (1) as a witness, planted an olive tree (which was still being pointed out in the second century AD, in the Pandroseion), and demanded possession of the land. The dispute was referred to Zeus, who named the arbitrators. In one tradition they were Cecrops and Cranaus, in another the Olympian gods. The tribunal decided in favour of Athena because Cecrops testified that she had been the first to plant an olive tree on the Acropolis. The furious Poseidon flooded the plain of Eleusis.

Athena was patroness of many towns apart from Athens: Megara, Argos, Sparta and others all had temples to her on their citadels. At Troy she was worshipped in the form of the PALLADIUM.

Athena was a virgin goddess, though she had a 'son' in the following way. She went to Hephaestus to get some weapons. He fell in love with her, and, though lame, caught up with her. While she resisted him he ejaculated on her leg. In disgust she wiped his semen off with a piece of wool which she threw on to the ground. In this way Mother Earth was fertilised and ERICHTHONIUS was born. Athena regarded him as her son and brought him up without the other gods knowing (see AGLAURUS (2)).

Athena's attributes were the spear, the helmet and the aegis. She attached the Gorgon's head, which Perseus had given her, to her shield, and this turned to stone every living thing that looked at it. Her favourite animal was the owl, and her favourite plant the olive tree. She was tall with calm features, majestic, and was traditionally described as 'the goddess with the grey eyes'. (For her name of Pallas see PALLAS (1), (2) and (3)).

Atlantis (*Ἀτλαντίς*) Plato, in his *Timaeus* and *Critias*, tells that Solon was told by an Egyptian priest of very ancient traditions relating to a war between the Athenians and the people of Atlantis, an island lying beyond the pillars of Hercules, in the Atlantic Ocean. In Atlantis dwelt Clito, daughter of Evenor and Leucippe (4), who was loved by Poseidon. She lived on a mountain in the middle of the island. Poseidon constructed walls and moats around her dwelling and lived there with her for a long time. They had five pairs of twin sons, the eldest of all being Atlas (2), to whom Poseidon gave the supremacy. The whole island was divided into ten areas, and Atlas reigned on the mountain in the centre. The island was rich in minerals and vegetation, and its kings built magnificent cities with many vaults, bridges, canals and passages to ease defence and trade. In each of the ten districts reigned the descendants of the ten original kings, the sons of Poseidon and Clito, all in their turn subject to the descendants of Atlas. The kings ruled benevolently at first, but became more tyrannical with each succeeding generation, until they tried to conquer the world. They were defeated by the Athenians 9,000 years before Plato's time. Later the island and its inhabitants disappeared for ever, submerged by a disastrous flood.

According to a different tradition, the people of Atlantis were neighbours of the Libyans and were attacked by the Amazons (see MYRINA).

Atlas (*Ἄτλας*)

1. A giant, the son of Iapetus and Clymene (1) (or in some versions of ASIA). According to some traditions he was the son of Uranus and thus the brother of Cronus. He belongs to the generation of monstrous divinities which preceded the Olympians. He took part in the stuggle between the Gods and the Giants, and Zeus sentenced him to carry the vault of the sky on his shoulders as a punishment. His dwelling was generally regarded as in the far West, in the country of the Hesperides, though it was sometimes said to be 'among the Hyperboreans'. Herodotus was the first writer to refer to Atlas as a mountain in North Africa. In Ovid's *Metamorphoses* PERSEUS turned Atlas into a rock on returning after slaying the Gorgon, by confronting him with Medusa's head. For Atlas' encounter with Heracles see HERACLES, II, *The Golden Apples of the Hesperides*.

Atlas had several children: the Pleiades and the Hyades by Pleione, and the Hesperides by Hesperis. Dione was also regarded as his daughter, and his sons were Hyas and Hesperus.

2. The eponym of ATLANTIS.

Atreus (*Ἀτρεύς*) The son of Pelops and Hippodamia (1) whose younger brother was Thyestes (Table 2). The underlying theme of the myths about him is the hatred between the two brothers and the appalling forms of revenge they took on each other. This hatred is sometimes said to have its origin in a curse of Pelops, since Atreus, Thyestes and Hippodamia killed their half-brother Chrysippus, whom the Nymph Axioche bore to Pelops. Pelops banished and cursed the two youths. They took refuge in Mycenae, with Eurystheus or, according to the most usual version, with Sthenelus (4), the father of Eurystheus. Sthenelus entrusted the city and land of Midea to Atreus and Thyestes, and when Eurystheus died childless an oracle advised the inhabitants of Mycenae to take a son of Pelops as their king. They summoned Atreus and Thyestes, and the two brothers stated their claim to the kingship: this was the moment when their hatred showed itself. Atreus had previously found a lamb with a golden fleece in his flock, and although he had vowed that year to sacrifice the finest produce of his flock to Artemis, he kept the lamb back for himself and hid the fleece in a chest, but his wife, Aerope (1) who was Thyestes' lover, had secretly given the fleece to Thyestes. In the debate at Mycenae, Thyestes proposed that the throne should go to whoever could display a golden fleece. Atreus accepted, knowing nothing of Thyestes' theft. Thyestes produced it and was chosen, but Zeus advised Atreus to propose that if the sun were to change its course, it would be Atreus who would rule Mycenae. Thyestes accepted and the sun immediately set in the east. Accordingly, Atreus, who was clearly favoured by the gods, finally reigned over Mycenae. He banished Thyestes. Subsequently, learning of Aerope's affair with Thyestes, he pretended to make up the quarrel and recalled him, secretly killed his three sons, Aglaus, Callileon and Orchomenus, or two sons, Tantalus and Pleisthenes, and had the children cut up, boiled and served in a dish to their father during a feast. After Thyestes had eaten, Atreus showed him the heads of his children, making clear the true nature of the meal, and hounded him out of the country. Thyestes took refuge in Sicyon. There, he begot a son named AEGISTHUS who ultimately killed Atreus and then gave the kingdom to Thyestes. For details see AEGISTHUS.

Atreus had two sons, Agamemnon and Menelaus, though these children are sometimes attributed to PLEISTHENES.

Atrides (*Ἀτρεῖδαι*) 'The sons of Atreus', a patryonymic given to AGEMEMNON and MENELAUS. See also ATREUS.

Attis (*Ἄττις*) A Phrygian god, the companion of Cybele, who was regarded as the son of Agdistis and Nana, the daughter of the river-god Sangarius. For the circumstances of his birth, self-castration and death see AGDISTIS. Ovid tells a different version of the Attis legend. According to him, Attis, who lived in the Phrygian woods, was so handsome that he was loved by Cybele. She resolved never to let him leave her and to make him the guardian of her temple, but she laid down a condition, that he should retain his virginity. Attis however, succumbed to the love of the Hamadryad Sagaritis. Cybele in her rage felled the tree to which the Nymph's life was closely bound, and she struck Attis with madness. During a violent fit, he castrated himself. After his self-inflicted injury Attis seems to have been once more taken into Cybele's service. He was generally portrayed with Cybele in her chariot crossing the Phrygian mountains.

Aucnus (or Ocnus) An Etruscan hero. Aucnus was a native of Perusia but left the city in order not to overshadow his brother Aulestes who had founded it, crossed the Apennines and was the founder of Felsina, the Etruscan town which was later to be Bologna.

Auge (*Αὔγη*) The daughter of Aleus the king of Tegea, and Neaara, daughter of Perseus.

According to epic traditions Auge lived at the court of Laomedon, king of Troy, where she was loved by Heracles when he came to capture the city. After the birth of her son, TELEPHUS, she was abandoned at sea by Aleus in a chest which drifted to the shore of Mysia. Other versions claim that Aleus ordered Nauplius (1) to drown Auge, but he gave her to merchants who sold her to King Teuthras of Mysia. Telephus was brought up at his court.

Another version goes back to Euripides' *Auge* and Sophocles' *Mysians* and *Aleadai*. In this an oracle warned Aleus that his daughter would have a son who would kill his uncles and reign in their stead. The king accordingly dedicated his daughter to Athena and forbade her to marry, on pain of death, but Heracles, who was passing through Tegea, was welcomed by Aleus. While he was there, he became drunk and raped Auge (who he did not know was the king's daughter) either in the shrine of Athena or beside a neighbouring stream. When the king learned that his daughter was pregnant he wanted to kill her, and he either put Auge and her child in a chest which he cast into the sea or entrusted them to Nauplius (1) with orders to throw them into the sea. But Nauplius sold them both to slave merchants who carried them off to Mysia. The king of the country, who was childless, married Auge and adopted her son, Telephus. Another version says that Auge was sold before her son was born and that he stayed in Arcadia, where he had been put out to die on Mount Parthenion, and was suckled by a doe. Later, after taking the advice of the Delphic oracle, Telephus came to the court of Teuthras in Mysia and met his mother again.

Augias (*Αὐγείας*) The king of Elis in the Peloponnese. He was generally regarded as the son of Helios, although he is also said to be the son of Phorbas (1), or of Poseidon, or of Eleius, the eponym of Elis. His mother was Hyrmine. All these genealogies say that Actor (1) was his brother. He took part in the expedition of the Argonauts with the purpose of getting to know his half-brother, Aeetes, whom he had never seen. Augias was the owner of very important herds inherited from Helios, but through his carelessness, he let the dung pile up in his stables. This neglect deprived the soil of manure and damaged the fertility of his lands. Accordingly, when Eurystheus ordered Heracles to clean his stables, Augias readily agreed. According to some authors Heracles demanded by way of payment a tenth of his herds if he managed to finish the task in a single day, and Augias thought this was impossible; according to others he promised him a tenth of his kingdom on the same terms. Heracles made an opening in the wall surrounding the stables and diverted the Rivers Alpheus and Peneus through them. The water washed away all the dung. In his anger at seeing the hero perform the task, Augias refused to pay the agreed price. On being called as a witness, Augias' son Phyleus swore that his father had indeed promised a tenth of his herds to Heracles, but before the verdict was pronounced, Augias banished both Heracles and Phyleus. Later, however, Heracles mustered an army, marched against Augias, killed him and his sons, and set Phyleus on the throne (see HERACLES, III, and MOLIONIDAE). In another tradition, Augias died naturally in extreme old age, and his people gave him divine honours. (For the story of the treasure of Augias, see AGAMEDES.)

Aura (*Αὖρα*) whose name means 'breeze', was as swift as the wind, and was one of Artemis' companions. Dionysus loved her and tried to catch her. She always escaped until, at Dionysus' request, Aphrodite struck her with madness so that she yielded to him. She had twin sons by Dionysus but destroyed them in her madness and threw herself into the river Sangarius. Zeus changed her into a stream. One of her twin sons was IACCHUS.

Aurora See EOS.

Auson (*Αὔσων*) A son of Odysseus by either Circe or Calypso (1). He was a brother of Latinus and had a son called Liparus. Auson gave his name to the Ausones, who were the first inhabitants of Italy, itself then known as Ausonia. He was the first ruler of the country (see also LEUCARIA).

Autoleon (*Αὐτολέων*) When the Locrians went into battle they used to leave a gap in the ranks in honour of their compatriot Ajax (1). One day one of the adversaries, named Autoleon, sought to pass through this gap, but he was wounded in the thigh by a ghost and the wound would not heal. The oracle directed him to go to the White Island, at the mouth of the Danube (see ACHILLES), and there to offer sacrifices to Ajax of Locri. There he saw Helen, who entrusted him with a message to the poet Stesichorus, who had been struck by blindness for having spoken evil of her in one of his poems. Helen told him to tell Stesichorus that he would regain his sight if he sang a recantation: he did, and his sight was restored. This is the version given by Conon, but Pausanias calls the hero of the story Leonymus.

Autolycus (*Αὐτόλυκος*) The son of Hermes and Chione (3) or Stilbe (2) (see DAEDALION). He was the grandfather of Odysseus through his daughter Anticleia. He inherited from Hermes the gift of stealing without being caught. He stole a leather helmet from Amyntor, and gave it to Achilles; he stole some flocks from Eurytus (2); he also stole some beasts from Sisyphus, although Sisyphus later recovered them (see SISYPHUS). He excelled in disguising his thefts, for example, by dyeing the skins of the oxen. According to some writers he had the gift of transforming himself, and he taught Heracles the art of fighting.

Autolycus took part in the Argonauts' expedition. He was in some accounts said to be the grandfather of Jason since his daughter, Polymede, had married Aeson.

Automedon (*Αὐτομέδων*) Achilles' charioteer. After Achilles' death, he continued to serve under his son, Neoptolemus, and took part in the capture of Troy.

Auxesia (*Αὐξησία*) Auxesia and her companion Damia were two Cretan girls who were stoned to death by the mob at Troezen. As an act of atonement they were made the objects of a cult and a festival was held in their honour. Auxesia and Damia were identified with Demeter and Persephone.

Avillus The son of Romulus and HERSILIA.

Azan (*Ἄζαν*) An Arcadian, the son of Arcas and Erato (2). He was betrothed to the daughter of Dexamenus. The Centaur Eurytion tried to abduct his wife on their wedding day. See CENTAURS.

B

Babys (*Βάβυς*) The brother of MARSYAS, who wanted to compete with Apollo in music. Babys played a flute with only one pipe, while his brother played the double flute. Babys played so badly that he was spared the god's anger.

Bacchus (*Βάκχος*) See DIONYSUS.

Baios (*Baîos*) A pilot of ODYSSEUS whose name does not occur in the *Odyssey* but who gave his name to several places, such as a mountain on the island of Cephalonia and the town of Baiae. While piloting Odysseus' vessel he met his death in Italian waters.

Balius (*Βαλίος*)
1. One of Achilles' immortal horses, offspring of Zephyr and the Harpy Podarge. Achilles' other horse was called Xanthus.
2. One of the dogs of Actaeon (1).

Basileia (*Βασίλεια*) Basileia was, according to Diodorus Siculus, the daughter of Uranus and Titaia and a sister of Rhea and the Titans, whom she brought up. She married her brother Hyperion, and bore Selene and Helios. But the other Titans killed Hyperion and immersed Helios in the River Eridanus, and in her grief Selene cast herself from the roof of her house. Helios and Selene were then made into the sun and the moon. Basileia learnt of what had happened, became deranged and began to scour the country banging on the tambourine and clashing the cymbals which had belonged to Selene, until she was restrained. Then a storm broke and Basileia vanished. A cult was established in her honour, under the name of the Great Goddess, which identifies her with Cybele.

Baton (*Βάτων*) The chariot-driver of AMPHIARAUS. Fighting before Thebes, Baton shared the fate of his master and was swallowed up by the earth just as Amphiaraus was about to be struck by an enemy. He was given divine honours. A different tradition claims that Baton withdrew to Illyria after the death of Amphiaraus.

Battus (*Βάττος*)
1. When Apollo was absorbed by his love for Hymenaeus, he neglected his flocks, and Hermes stole some beasts from him and removed them to the outskirts of Menale in the Peloponnese. There, meeting an old man called Battus, he promised him a heifer if he agreed to keep silent about the theft. The old man gave his promise but Hermes changed his shape and returned to Battus, pretending that he was looking for his cattle, and promising him a reward if he would help him to find them. Battus broke his promise and told him, and Hermes in anger changed him into a rock.
2. The founder of Cyrene on the

coast of Libya. His father was Polymnestus and his mother was Phronime, and he belonged to the race known as Minyans who were descended from the Argonauts (see MINYAS). In the commonest tradition Battus was only a nickname given to a hero because he stammered (Greek *βάττος* = 'stammerer'); however, Herodotus tells us that Battus means 'king' in the language spoken in Libya. Battus' real name is said by some to be Aristoteles, by others, Aristaeus. According to Pausanias, Battus regained the power of speech after the foundation of Cyrene.

Baubo (*Βαυβώ*) The wife of Dysaules who lived at Eleusis. When Demeter was searching for her daughter she arrived at Eleusis, accompanied by her small son, Iacchus. Dysaules and Baubo welcomed them and Baubo offered Demeter some soup, which the goddess in her grief refused. Then Baubo tucked up her clothes and showed her buttocks. When Iacchus saw this, he began to cheer. The goddess began to laugh and accepted the soup. Dysaules and Baubo had two sons, Triptolemus and Eubouleus (1), and two daughters, Protonoe and Nisa.

Baucis (*Βαύκις*) A Phrygian woman, the wife of Philemon, a very poor peasant. They welcomed Zeus and Hermes to their cottage one day when the two gods were making their way through Phrygia. Baucis and Philemon were the only ones in the area to offer hospitality. In their anger, the gods sent a storm over the whole country but left the cottage with the two old people unharmed. The place became a shrine and, because Baucis and Philemon had asked to end their days together, Zeus and Hermes turned them into two trees which stood side by side in front of the temple.

Bellerophon (*Βελλεροφόντης*, *Βελλεροφῶν*) Son of Glaucus (3) and Eurymede or Eurynome (2). He accidentally killed his brother Deliades, or Piren (1), or Alcimenes or Bellerus (*Βελλεροφῶν* = 'killer of Bellerus') and went into exile to King Proetus at Tiryns. Proetus purified him. His wife, Stheneboea (called Anteia by Homer), asked Bellerophon to meet her secretly, but when he refused she claimed he had tried to seduce her. Proetus then sent Bellerophon to his father-in-law, Iobates, king of Lycia, and gave him a letter which demanded that its bearer be put to death. Proetus was unwilling to kill Bellerophon himself, since he was his guest, so he ordered Bellerophon to kill the CHIMAERA, which was ravaging the country. Bellerophon mounted PEGASUS, the winged horse, and swooped down on the Chimaera and killed it. There is also a story that Bellerophon fitted the point of his spear with a piece of lead which melted when exposed to the flames breathed out by the Chimaera and killed it. Iobates then sent Bellerophon to fight his ferocious neighbours the Solymnes, whom he defeated. Next Iobates sent him to fight the Amazons; he killed many of them. Finally Iobates organized an ambush, but Bellerophon killed all his attackers. After this Iobates showed Bellerophon the letter, gave him his daughter Philonoe, Cassandra, Alcimene or Anticleia in marriage, and bequeathed him his kingdom. For Bellerophon's revenge see STHENEBOEA. Bellerophon had two sons, Isandros and Hippolochus (1), and a daughter, Laodamia (1). Later Bellerophon tried to ride on his winged horse up to the domain of Zeus, but Zeus hurled him back to earth, where he was killed. He was honoured as a hero in Corinth and Lycia.

Bellona The Roman goddess of war, who was for a long time regarded as a personification of mere force, but gradually became identified with the Greek goddess, ENYO. She was sometimes portrayed as the wife of Mars and was depicted as driving her own chariot, holding a torch, sword or spear in her hand.

Belus (*Βῆλος*) One of Poseidon's twin sons by Libya. The other was Agenor (Table 3) and while the latter went to Syria, Belus remained in Egypt, where he was king, and married Anchinoe, the daughter of the god Nile. He had twin sons, Egyptus and Danaus and is sometimes said to have fathered Cepheus (2) and Phineus (2). His name is also found in the genealogy of Queen Dido of Carthage.

Bia (*Βία*) The personification of violence. She was the daughter of Pallas (2) and the Styx. In the struggle between the Gods and the Giants she fought on the side of Zeus. Her sister was Nike (Victory) and her brothers, Zelus (Ardour) and Cratos (Strength), and with them she was the constant companion of Zeus. She helped to tie down Prometheus in Aeschylus' *Prometheus Bound*.

Bias (*Βίας*) The son of Amythaon and Idomene. His brother was Melampus (Tables 1 and 6). When Bias wanted to marry Pero, he had to perform a task imposed by her father Neleus, namely, to steal the herds of Phylacus (1). Melampus agreed to steal them on behalf of his brother and, when he had been granted the hand of Pero, he gave her up to Bias. Subsequently, after Melampus had cured the daughters of Proetus of their madness, he secured a third of the latter's kingdom for Bias (see ANAXAGORAS and PROETIDES). When married to Pero, Bias fathered Talaus, and possibly (Table 1) Perialces, Laodocus, Areius and Alphesiboea. Later, when he was settled in Argos, he married one of Proetus' daughters. She was perhaps the mother of his daughter Anaxibia.

Bona Dea An ancient Roman divinity. Her real name was Fauna, Bona Dea being a title meaning 'the Good Goddess'. In one version Bona Dea was the daughter of Faunus, who fell in love with her and had intercourse with her in the form of a snake. In another version Bona Dea was Faunus' wife. She was extremely skilled in the domestic arts and was very chaste. One day she found a jug of wine, drank it and became drunk, whereupon Faunus beat her to death with switches of myrtle. In remorse he granted her divine honours. Bona Dea had a shrine on the Aventine at Rome and her mysteries were celebrated by women only. Hercules, who had been excluded from these, in revenge founded ceremonies, in which no women could take part, at his Great Altar.

Boreades (*Βορεάδαι*) Zetes and Calais, the twin sons of BOREAS by Orithyia. They had wings, and like their father were spirits of the winds: Calais was 'he who blows gentle', Zetes 'he who blows strongly'. They were born in Thrace and their main characteristic was speed. They took part in the expedition of the Argonauts and played an important part during their stay with PHINEUS (3). They took part in the funeral games for Pelias (see JASON) and won the prize for running, but when returning they were killed on the island of Tenos by Heracles for advising the Argonauts to leave him in Mysia when he was searching for HYLAS. He erected two pillars to them, which shook every time the north wind blew on the island.

Boreas (*Βορέας*) The god of the north wind. He lived in Thrace. He is depicted as winged, extremely strong, bearded and normally clad in a short pleated tunic. He was the son of Eos and Astraeus, and the brother of Zephyrus and Notus, and belonged to the race of the Titans. Among other violent acts he abducted Orithyia while she was playing on the banks of the Ilissus. She gave birth to Calais and Zetes (see BOREADES), Cleopatra (1) and Chione (1) (see BUTES). Another tradition says that the abduction took place during a procession which was heading for the temple of Athena Polias on the Athenian Acropolis. Sometimes the punishment of PHINEUS (3) is ascribed to Boreas. In the shape of a horse Boreas sired by the mares of Erichthonius twelve colts which could gallop over a field of wheat without bending the heads of the wheat, or over the sea without causing ripples. Boreas also sired swift horses by one of the Furies and by a Harpy.

Botres (*Βότρης*) Son of a devotee of Apollo called Eumelus (2). Eumelus killed Botres with a firebrand for not performing a sacrifice correctly. To console Botres' parents Apollo changed him into a bird called the Aeropus.

Boucolos (*Βουκόλος*) See EUNOSTUS.

Bounos (*Βοῦνος*) The son of Hermes and Alcidamia. When AEETES left Corinth for Colchis, he gave Bounos the throne of Corinth.

Bouphagus (*Βουφάγος*) The son of Iapetus and Thornax. During the war against Augias, he sheltered Iphicles who had been wounded by the MOLIONIDAE (see HERACLES, III). Bouphagus cared for Iapetus until his death. Later, he was killed by Artemis when he pursued her on Mount Pholoe in Arcadia.

Branchus (*Βράγχος*) The son of Smicrus. Before Branchus was born, his mother had a vision in which she saw the sun sink into her mouth, pass through her body and come out of her belly. When the boy, who was very handsome, was looking after the flocks on the mountain one day, Apollo fell in love with him. Branchus raised an altar to Apollo the Friendly, and, inspired by the god who endowed him with the gift of divination, he founded an oracle at Didyma, which was regarded until historical times as almost equal in prestige to that of Delphi. It was served by the Branchides (descendants of Branchus).

Briareus (*Βριάρεως*) See AEGAEON.

Briseis (*Βρισηίς*) Briseis, whose real name was Hippodamia (3), was the daughter of Brises. She was called Briseis after her father, and was married to Mynes. He was killed by Achilles, who carried off Briseis. Achilles married her, and in effect she became Achilles' favourite slave, dearly loved by him. When the Greeks compelled Agamemnon to return CHRYSEIS to her father and Agamemnon demanded in return that Achilles should hand over Briseis, Achilles refused to fight, and it was she alone whom Achilles accepted at the time of his reconciliation with Agamemnon. She offered the tributes at the funeral of Achilles.

Brises (*Βρίσης*) The father of BRISEIS. In some accounts he was the king of the Leleges in Caria, but generally, like his brother CHRYSES, he was the priest of Apollo in the town of Lyrnessos, which was looted by the Greeks in the Trojan War. As well as his daughter, he had a son who was named Eëtion (not to be confused with Eëtion the father of Andromache). Brises hanged himself when his house was destroyed by Achilles.

Britomartis (*Βριτόμαρτις*) A Cretan goddess. She was the daughter of Zeus and Carme. Minos was in love with her and pursued her for nine months throughout the island of Crete. When she realized that she was about to be caught she threw herself from the top of a cliff into the sea, where she fell into the fishermen's nets and was saved, which was why she acquired the name of Dictynna, 'the daughter of the net'. Another version explains the same epithet by attributing to Britomartis the invention of the nets used for hunting. In yet another story, Britomartis was caught by accident in a net and, after being rescued by Artemis, she was accorded divine honours under the name of Dictynna. Like Artemis, she was portrayed as surrounded by hounds, dressed as a huntress, eschewing male company and very fond of solitude.

Bryte (*Βρύτη*) A daughter of Ares and an attendant of Artemis. She was loved by Minos and threw herself into the sea where her body was recovered in a fisherman's net. A plague broke out, and the oracle pronounced that to bring it to an end she must be accorded divine honours under the name of Diana Dictynna (Artemis of the net). (Cf. BRITOMARTIS).

Busiris (*Βούσιρις*) The son of Poseidon and Lysianassa (Table 3), and a king of Egypt. Busiris was very cruel, and the harshness of his rule forced PROTEUS to flee from Egypt. He sent a band of pirates to abduct the Hesperides, but Heracles, while on his journey to get the golden apples, met and killed the pirates. A run of bad harvests fell on Egypt, and the seer Phrasius advised the king to sacrifice a stranger to

Zeus each year to restore prosperity. When Heracles was passing through Egypt, Busiris captured him and led him to the altar as a victim, but Heracles burst his bonds, and killed Busiris, his son and all the spectators.

Butes (*Βούτης*)
1. A son of BOREAS and the half-brother of Lycurgus (2). They had different mothers, neither of them being Orithyia, the god's legitimate wife. Butes sought to kill Lycurgus, but he was exiled. He established himself on Naxos, where he lived by piracy. On Naxos he encountered the female worshippers of Dionysus; most of them escaped, but the god's nurse, Coronis (3), was carried off and given to Butes. In answer to her prayers, Butes was struck with madness by Dionysus. He threw himself into a well and died.
2. The son of Pandion (1) and Zeuxippe (1). On the death of Pandion, his estate was divided between his sons: Erechtheus received the kingship, and Butes the priesthood of Athena and Poseidon. He married the daughter of ERECHTHEUS, Chthonia (2).
3. An Argonaut, the son of Teleon, who founded the town of Lilybaeum in Sicily (see ERYX). Butes was carried away by Aphrodite when he had yielded to the Sirens' songs.

Buzyges (*Βουζύγης*) Buzyges, or 'he who puts oxen under the yoke' was the mythical inventor of the yoke who had the idea of taming and harnessing bulls for work. He was also believed to have been one of the first legislators, and is said to have banned the killing of oxen or bulls since they were so useful in cultivation (see also PALLADIUM).

Byblis (*Βυβλίς*) By her father MILETUS Byblis was the great-granddaughter of Minos (see ACACALLIS) or, in some traditions, his granddaughter. She had a twin brother, Caunus, and she loved him with an incestuous passion. Filled with horror for his sister, Caunus fled and went to found the town of Caunus in Caria. Byblis went mad. The Nymphs, who pitied her, turned her into an inexhaustible stream, like the girl's own tears. There is another contrasting tradition: according to this Caunus conceived a guilty passion for his sister, and this was why he fled from his father's house and why Byblis hanged herself. Her name was given to two towns: Byblis in Caria and Byblus in Phoenicia.

Byzas (*Βύζας*) Son of Poseidon and Ceroessa. He founded the city of Byzantium and fortified it with the help of Apollo and Poseidon. When Haemus (2) attacked the city, Byzas defeated him in single combat and pursued his enemies back into Thrace. While he was away Odryses of Scythia besieged the city, but Byzas' wife, Phidalia, saved it by throwing snakes into the enemy camp. She also saved it from attacks by her brother-in-law, Strombus.

C

Caanthus (*Κάανθος*) A son of Oceanus. After his sister, Melia (1), had been abducted by Apollo his father sent him to look for her. He found them but could not induce them to part. Enraged by this, he set fire to the shrine of Apollo, whereupon the god slew him with an arrow.

Cabiri (*Κάβειροι*) Divinities whose main shrine was at Samothrace. Their numbers vary: some traditions maintain that there were three; another names four: Axierus, Axiocersa, Axiocersus and Cadmilus; others give seven; and one commentary also cites, in addition to the names mentioned above, a 'pair' of Cabiri, Alcon and Eurymedon.

The Cabiri could not be named with impunity; they were generally referred to as the 'great gods'. They are said to have been present at the birth of Zeus at Pergamum. They were servants of Rhea and because of this were often confused with the CORYBANTES and CURETES. After the Classical era they were regarded as protectors of navigation with similar functions to those of the DIOSCURI, with whom they had some affinities.

Cabirides (*Καβειρίδες*) Three nymphs, sisters of the three CABIRI in some traditions.

Cabiro (*Καβειρώ*) Daughter of Proteus and Anchinoe. According to some traditions she was the mother of the CABIRI and CABIRIDES by Hephaestus.

Caca A Roman goddess, the sister of CACUS. She betrayed her brother by disclosing to Hercules the place where Cacus had hidden the stolen oxen. In return Caca became the object of a cult, and a flame was kept perpetually alight in her honour.

Cacus A three-headed, fire-breathing giant, son of Vulcan. When Hercules drove the cattle he had stolen from Geryon through Italy, Cacus stole four cows and four oxen, and hid them in his cave. In order to leave no clues, Cacus pulled the beasts backwards by their tails, so that their tracks seemed to lead from, not to, his cave. Hercules discovered the trick when the cattle lowed, or when Cacus' sister Caca betrayed him. In the ensuing fight Hercules either got the better of Cacus with his club, or, when Cacus piled rocks in front of his cave, tore away the top of the mountain to reveal his hiding place and killed him. The local king, EVANDER (3), welcomed Hercules and purified him after the murder. For a variant version of this myth see RECARANUS.

Cadmus (*Κάδμος*) The son of Agenor and Telephassa or, in another tradition, of Argiope (Table 3); he was the brother of Cilix, Phoenix (2) and Europa (5), though sometimes Phoenix is said to have been the father of Cadmus and Europa. A Boeotian tradition claims that Cadmus was the son of Ogygus (1).

After Europa was abducted, Agenor sent Telephassa and his sons to find her, ordering them not to reappear without her. They soon realized that their quest was a vain one, however, and Cadmus and Telephassa went to Thrace, where they were kindly received by the inhabitants. When his mother died Cadmus consulted the Delphic oracle which told him to found a town; in order to choose its site he should follow a cow until it collapsed with fatigue. As Cadmus was crossing Phocis he saw a cow among the herds belonging to Pelagon which led him to the place that later became Thebes. Cadmus saw that the oracle had been fulfilled and wanted to sacrifice the cow to Athena. He sent some of his companions to look for water from the Spring of Ares, but a dragon, which in some accounts is said to be a descendant of Ares himself, was guarding the spring and killed most of them. Cadmus came to the rescue and killed the dragon. Athena then appeared and advised him to sow half of its teeth (the other half she gave to Aeetes. See ARGONAUTS). Cadmus did so, and at once, armed men sprang out of the ground; these became known as the Spartoi, or 'Sown Men'. The miraculous men threatened Cadmus, who threw stones into their midst. The Spartoi did not know who was attacking them; they first accused and then slaughtered each other. Only five survived, namely Echion (1) (who subsequently married Agave, one of Cadmus' daughters), Oudaeus, Chthonius, Hyperenor and Pelorus. Cadmus admitted them into his city; with their help he built the Cadmeia, the citadel of Thebes. To atone for killing the dragon, Cadmus served as Ares' slave for eight years, but when his sentence ended he became king of Thebes, through the protection of Athena, and Zeus gave him as a wife Harmonia (1). The gods and the Muses took part in their wedding. The principal wedding gifts, a wonderful robe, woven by the Charites, and a golden necklace, fashioned by Hephaestus, were for Harmonia. This necklace and robe would later play a large part in the episode of the expedition of the Seven against Thebes (see AMPHIARAUS, ALCMAEON (1) and ERIPHYLE). Cadmus had four daughters by Harmonia: Autonoe, Ino (who took the name of Leucothea after her deification), Agave and Semele, and one son, Polydorus (1).

Cadmus and Harmonia later left Thebes under mysterious circumstances, giving the throne to their grandson, Pentheus. They went to live among the Encheleans who had been promised victory in battle by an oracle if Cadmus and Harmonia would lead them. They were indeed victorious, and Cadmus then ruled over the Illyrians and had another son, named Illyrius. But later Cadmus and Harmonia were turned into serpents and reached the Elysian Fields. A legend recorded by Nonnus tells how Cadmus followed the tracks of the bull which had carried off Europa, and was enlisted by Zeus in the expedition against TYPHON. After Typhon had removed the sinews of Zeus, Cadmus bewitched him by playing the lyre, and retrieved Zeus' sinews by saying that he needed them to make strings for the instrument. Cadmus returned them to Zeus, thus enabling him to win the struggle. As his reward Cadmus received Harmonia as a wife.

Caeculus The Roman legend of Praeneste ascribes the foundation of the town to Caeculus. There lived in this country two brothers called the Depidii, who were shepherds. One day when their sister was sitting near the hearth, a spark flew out of the fire and jumped into her bosom. She conceived a child who was regarded as a son of Vulcan, but she abandoned him near the temple of Jupiter. Some young women found the infant beside a lighted fire and took it to the Depidii. They brought the child up, and called him Caeculus (from *caecus*, 'blind') when they first saw him, for the smoke of the fire had made his eyes water and he seemed to be blind. After he had grown up, he and some companions founded the village which was destined to become Praeneste. On the day of the inauguration of the new town he asked his father Vulcan to produce a wonderful spectacle: Vulcan sent down flames, which encircled the crowd and extinguished themselves as soon as Caeculus bade them. A great many people came to settle there, to be under the protection of the god and his son. Caeculus later fought alongside Turnus against Aeneas.

Caelus The personification of the Sky; this was a Latin translation of the name of the Greek god URANUS.

Caeneus (*Καινεύς*) Originally a girl named Caenis, the daughter of Elatus (2), who was raped by Poseidon. She asked the god to change her into a man; Poseidon granted this request and made Caeneus invulnerable. Caeneus took part in the stuggle against the Centaurs, but when they could not kill him, they beat him with the trunks of fir trees and finally buried him alive. It is said that after his death Caeneus became a woman again, or, according to Ovid, a bird.

A different tradition tells that after he had become a man, Caeneus grew extremely proud: he set up his spear in the market place and ordered the populace to worship it. To punish him, Zeus roused the Centaurs against him and they finally killed him. His name appears in some of the lists of the Argonauts. He had a son called CORONUS.

Caieta One legend about this town (the modern Gaeta) tells how it had been founded in memory of Caieta, the nurse of Aeneas. Some versions say that she was buried there and others that she had quelled the fire which was threatening to burn Aeneas' ship.

Calais (*Κάλαϊς*) See BOREADES.

Calamus (*Κάλαμος*) The son of the river-god Meander, his name means 'reed'. He was in love with a youth named Carpus. One day they were both bathing in the Meander and Calamus wanted to show his friend that he was the better swimmer, but in the competition which ensued Carpus was drowned. In his grief Calamus withered to such an extent that he became a reed by the river bank.

Calchas (*Κάλχας*)
1. A seer of Mycenae or Megara, the son of Thestor. He could interpret the meaning of the flight of birds and knew the past, present and future: his grandfather Apollo had given him this gift of prophecy. When Achilles was nine years old, Calchas announced that Troy could not be taken without him. At Aulis, after a sacrifice to Apollo, according to the *Iliad*, a snake lept from the altar towards a nearby tree and swallowed eight birds and their mother, and then turned to stone. Calchas interpreted this as meaning that Troy would fall after ten years. In Aeschylus, a pregnant hare was torn to pieces by two eagles. Calchas said this signified that Troy would be destroyed but Artemis would be hostile to the Greeks. When TELEPHUS agreed to lead the Greek fleet to the Troad, Calchas confirmed that Telephus' directions were correct. Just as the fleet was about to leave Aulis for the second time, Calchas disclosed that the calm which prevented its departure was due to the wrath of Artemis, who would be appeased only by the sacrifice of IPHIGENIA. After Achilles and Ajax (2) had died, Calchas said that Troy could not be captured without the bow of Heracles (see PHILOCTETES). Finally, it was Calchas who suggested building the Wooden Horse, and he was one of the warriors inside it. He also foretold that the return journey would be difficult because of the wrath of Athena, who was displeased with the injustice suffered by her protégé, Ajax (2). Accordingly Calchas left Troy with Amphilochus (1). They arrived at Colophon where they met the seer Mopsus (2). An oracle had predicted that Calchas would die when he met a seer better than himself. Near Mopsus' home was a fig tree, and when Calchas asked, 'How many figs does it bear?' Mopsus replied, 'Ten thousand and one bushels and one fig more', the exact figure. Mopsus then asked Calchas how many piglets would be born to a certain pregnant sow, and how soon. Calchas replied that there would be eight, but Mopsus correctly predicted that there would be nine, all males, born at the sixth hour of the next day. Calchas was so vexed that he died or committed suicide. He was buried at Notion near Colophon.

There is also a story which tells how Calchas had planted a vine in a grove sacred to Apollo. A seer who lived nearby forecast that he would never drink wine from it. The vine grew, bore grapes out of which wine was made, and on the day when the new wine was to be tasted Calchas invited the people who lived nearby as well as the seer who had made the prophecy. At the very moment when Calchas was about to drink, his rival repeated that he would never taste the wine. Calchas began to laugh so heartily that he choked to death and died before the cup had reached his lips (see ANTINOUS (1)).

2. South Italian legends speak of a diviner called Calchas, whose tomb could be seen at Siris on the gulf of Tarentum.

3. Another Calchas had a shrine where people used to sleep in order to learn of the future through their dreams; this shrine was in the neighbourhood of Mount Garganon, on the Adriatic coast.

Calchus (*Κάλχος*) King of the Daunii of south Italy; he loved Circe, but she was in love with Odysseus and turned Calchus into a pig; she then shut him up in her pigsty. When the Daunians came to look for him Circe agreed to give him back to them, in human form, but on the condition that he would not set foot on her island again.

Callidice (*Καλλιδίκη*) A queen of the Thesproti, who married Odysseus when he was forced to leave Ithaca again to comply with the prophecy of Tiresias. Odysseus fathered a son by her named Polypoetes (3).

Calliope (*Καλλιόπη*) One of the Muses. From the Alexandrian period she was regarded as Muse of lyric poetry. Calliope is said to have been the mother of the Sirens, Orpheus, Linus (2) and Rhesus. She also appears as the arbitress in the quarrel over Adonis between Persephone and Aphrodite.

Callipolis (*Καλλίπολις*) The son of ALCATHUS.

Callirhoe (*Καλλιρρόη*)

1. The daughter of Oceanus and Tethys. By Chrysaor she gave birth to Geryon and Echidna. She had other children: Minyas by Poseidon, Chione by Nilus and Cotys by Manes.
2. The daughter of Achelous. She married Alcmaeon (1), who fathered her two sons, Amphoterus and Acarnan (Table 1). After the murder of her husband she was loved by Zeus; she asked him to make her two sons grow up immediately and to give them the strength to avenge their father. Zeus did as she asked and in this way Alcmaeon was avenged.
3. A Nymph loved by Paris at the time when he looked after the flocks on Mount Ida. Paris later left her for Helen, and Callirhoe is said to have wept bitterly for her lost love.
4. The daughter of the river-god Scamander. She married Tros and by him had four children: Cleopatra (4), Ilus (2), Assaracus and Ganymede (Table 4).
5. A daughter of LYCUS (8).
6. A girl who had rejected the advances of a priest of Dionysus, called Coresus; he complained to Dionysus, who spread an outbreak of madness throughout the land. The inhabitants consulted the oracle of Dodona, which disclosed that, to appease the god, the girl would have to be sacrificed at the altar attended by Coresus. Just as he was about to sacrifice her, Coresus, overcome by his love, lost his resolve and killed himself. Callirhoe committed suicide beside a spring which thereafter bore her name.
7. The daughter of PHOCUS (1).

Callisto (*Καλλιστώ*)

1. According to some writers, a wood-nymph; to others she was a daughter of Lycaon (1) or of Nycteus. She was a companion of Artemis and had vowed to remain a virgin. Zeus fell in love with her, assumed the guise of Artemis or Apollo, and raped her. She became the mother of ARCAS. One day Artemis and her companions were bathing in a spring; Callisto had to undress and her pregnancy was revealed, whereupon Artemis changed her into a she-bear. Variants of the story attribute the metamor-

phosis to Hera, or to Zeus' desire to conceal his love. Nevertheless, either Hera persuaded Artemis to kill Callisto with an arrow, or Artemis killed her for having lost her virginity. Callisto was sometimes said to have been the mother of PAN. See also HELICE (2).
2. The sister of Odysseus.

Calydon (*Καλυδών*)
1. The eponym Calydon in Aetolia; he was the son of Aetolus and Pronoe. He married Aeolia (2) and fathered two daughters, Epicaste and Protogenia (3).
2. A son of Thestius. The latter returned from a stay at Sicyon to find Calydon lying near his mother. Believing that their relationship was incestuous, he killed them. When he later realized his mistake he threw himself into a stream called the Axenus, and it was thereafter called the Thestius, until it was finally renamed the Achelous.
3. The son of Ares and Astynome, who saw Artemis bathing and was changed into a rock.

Calypso (*Καλυψώ*)
1. One of the PLEIADES, or, in other versions, a daughter of Helios and Perseis, and so the sister of Aeetes and Circe. She lived on the island of Ogygia. She welcomed the shipwrecked Odysseus, loved him, and kept him there (for ten years in the *Odyssey*, one or seven in other traditions), but Odysseus yearned to return to Ithaca, and, in response to Athena's request, Calypso let him depart. She gave him food, a raft, and navigational instructions.

According to some legends Calypso and Odysseus had a son, Latinus (more usually said to be a son of CIRCE) but some writers say they had two sons, Nausinous and Nausithous (3). They were also said to have had a son called Auson.
2. A daughter of Tethys and Oceanus.

Cambles (*Κάμβλης*) A king of Lydia, who was so greedy that he ate his own wife (see IARDANUS).

Camenae Nymphs of springs in Rome. Their shrine was in a wood not far from the Camenean Gate. They were identified with the Muses from an early period.

Camers The king of Amyclae. He was the son of Vulcens. His town vanished after it was visited by a plague of snakes.

Camesus A very early king who ruled over Latium at the time when the god Janus landed there after he had been exiled from Thessaly. Camesus welcomed him and shared his kingdom with him; they ruled together and when Camesus died, Janus ruled by himself.

Camilla The daughter of Metabus, king of the Volsci. Metabus was driven out of his town and fled with Camilla, who was still a little girl. When they reached the River Amisenus in Latium he tied Camilla to a pike, vowed that he would dedicate her to Diana if she reached safety, and hurled her over the river. Diana granted his prayer and both Camilla and Metabus safely reached the far bank. They lived in solitude in the woods; Camilla used to hunt and engage in warfare. She fought against

Aeneas and was killed by the hero Arruns.

Campe (*Κάμπη*) A female monster appointed by Cronus to guard the Cyclopes and the Hecatoncheires, whom he had imprisoned in Hades. When an oracle promised Zeus that he would defeat Cronus and the Titans if he had the assistance of the Cyclopes, he killed Campe and freed them.

Canace (*Κανάκη*) One of the daughters of Aeolus (1) (Table 5). Ovid tells that she gave birth to a son fathered by her brother Macareus (1). Aeolus threw the child to the dogs and sent a sword to his daughter, ordering her to kill herself. According to another tradition Canace had Hopleus, Nireus, Epopeus (1), Aloeus and Triopas by Poseidon.

Canens A Nymph of Latium, the daughter of Janus. She was married to King PICUS. One day during a hunt Circe fell in love with Picus; to separate him from his attendants she changed him into a wild boar. Picus, parted from his wife, grieved deeply; when Circe declared her love for him he repulsed her, and in her anger she changed him into a green woodpecker. In the meantime Canens despaired; she wandered in search of Picus and finally collapsed on the banks of the Tiber where she sang for the last time and then vanished into thin air.

Canopus (*Κάνωπος*) The eponym of Canopus or Canobus in Egypt and of one of the rivers of the Nile delta (Canope). He acted as pilot for Menelaus when the latter came with Helen to Egypt after the capture of Troy. Theonoe (1) loved Canopus, but he did not return her love. One day he was bitten by a snake and died. Menelaus and Helen buried him, building him a tomb on the island of Canope. Another tradition claims that Canopus was the pilot of Osiris, the Egyptian god. He is also said to have steered the *Argo*, and both pilot and ship were placed among the constellations.

Capaneus (*Καπανεύς*) One of the Seven against Thebes (see AMPHIARAUS and ADRASTUS). He was the son of Hipponous. He had no fear of the gods, but in the first attack on Thebes Zeus killed him with his thunderbolt just as he was about to scale the Theban walls. His wife Evadne (2) threw herself on his funeral pyre. Sthenelus (3) was his son.

Caphaurus (*Κάφαυρος*) In Apollonius Rhodius a Libyan shepherd, the son of Amphithemis (also known as Garamas) and a Nymph of Lake Tritonis. Canthus, one of the Argonauts, tried to steal some of his sheep. Caphaurus killed him but was himself killed by the Argonauts (see CEPHALION).

Caphene (*Καφένη*) A girl from Cryassus, a Carian town which felt threatened by a nearby settlement of Greeks from Melos, led by Nymphaeus. The people of Cryassus invited the Greeks to a feast, intending to kill them, but Caphene was in love with Nymphaeus and told him of the plan. The Greeks accepted the invitation, but insisted that their wives should also attend. At the feast the men were unarmed, but the women all carried concealed weapons, and when the Carians fell upon them the Greeks killed them all. They demolished and rebuilt Cryassus, naming it New Cryassus. Caphene married Nymphaeus.

Caphira (*Καφείρα*) A daughter of Oceanus. She helped the Telchines bring up Poseidon, who had been entrusted to her by Rhea.

Capys (*Κάπυς*)
1. The *Iliad* mentions a Capys who was the grandfather of Aeneas (Table 4). Other legends give Aeneas a companion of the same name who founded Capua in Campania, but there is also a story that Capua had been founded by Aeneas' son Rhomus, and that is was called this in memory of his great-grandfather (see AEGESTES (1)). Capys was sometimes also regarded as the founder of Caphyes in Arcadia.
2. Some writers say that the founder of Capua was not a Trojan but a Samnite of the same name.

Carmanor (*Καρμάνωρ*) A Cretan priest who welcomed Apollo and Artemis after the murder of Python and purified them. He also allowed the intrigue between Apollo and ACACALLIS to take place in his house.

Carme (*Κάρμη*) The mother of Britomartis. She is said to have been the daughter of Eubouleus, the son of Carmanor. Other writers make her the daughter of Phoenix (2) (Table 3). She is said to have been taken to Megara as a prisoner in her old age and to have been made nurse to Scylla (2).

Carmenta Daughter of Ladon (1) and mother of EVANDER (3) whom she accompanied when he was exiled from Arcadia. In Arcadia she was identified with Nicostrate, Themis, Timandra, Telpousa or Tyburtis; she was called Carmenta at Rome because she had the gift of prophecy (Latin *carmen* = 'prophecy', 'incantation'). She chose the most favourable site on which to establish Evander. When Hercules came to Pallantium she told him of the fate which lay ahead of him (see CACUS). She lived to the age of one hundred and ten; her son buried her at the foot of the Capitol, close to the Porta Carmentalis, so called in her memory.

In other traditions Carmenta was Evander's wife. When she refused an invitation from Hercules to attend the sacrifice he was offering at the Ara Maxima, he forbade women to be present at the ceremony thereafter. Carmenta was also regarded as a divinity of procreation: she was invoked by two names, Prorsa (head first) and Postversa (feet first), the two positions in which a child can be born.

Carna A nymph who lived in a sacred wood on the banks of the Tiber. Ovid says she was originally called Crane and had dedicated herself to virginity. When a suitor approached her she would make him promise to follow her into the woods, where she would immediately disappear. The god Janus fell in love with her, followed her, saw her as she was trying to hide behind a rock, and raped her. To make amends he gave her power over the hinges of doors and entrusted her with a branch of flowering hawthorn, which had the power of excluding all evil spells from the openings of houses. Carna had a special responsibility for warding off vampires: according to Ovid she saved a son of King Procas, even after the vampires had left their mark on the baby's body.

Carnus (*Κάρνος*)

1. A seer who joined the army of the Heraclids. Hippotes took him for a spy and killed him (see HERACLIDS).
2. Carnus or Carneus was a son of Zeus and Europa (5), who was loved by Apollo.

Cassandra (*Κασσάνδρα*) The daughter of Priam and Hecuba and twin sister of Helenus. According to one tradition, the children acquired the gift of prophecy after their sensory organs were licked by serpents in the temple of Apollo Thymbrius. According to Aeschylus, however, Cassandra had been given this gift by Apollo. The god, who was in love with her, had promised her the power to foretell the future if she would yield to his advances. Cassandra agreed, but once she had received the gift of prophecy she slipped away. Apollo then spat in her mouth, and henceforth nobody believed her prophecies.

Cassandra was generally regarded as an 'inspired' prophetess like the Pythian oracle and the Sibyl: the god would take possession of her and she uttered her oracles in a trance. Cassandra's prophecies played a part in many important moments during the history of Troy. She foretold that Paris (whose identity was at the time unknown) was fated to cause the downfall of Troy. She was on the point of obtaining his execution when she realized that he was one of Priam's sons, and this recognition saved his life. When Paris returned to Troy with Helen, she predicted that this abduction would lead to the loss of the city. She was the first person to know that Priam would return from Achilles with Hector's body. She and Laocoon (1) fought against the idea of bringing the Wooden Horse into the city, and she declared that it was full of warriors, but Apollo sent snakes which ate up Laocoon and his sons and the Trojans paid no heed to her. Cassandra also made prophecies about the fate of the Trojan women who had been captured after the fall of Troy and about the fate of the line of Aeneas. During the sack of Troy, she took shelter in the temple of Athena but was abducted by AJAX (1). When the booty was shared out Cassandra was given to Agamemnon, who fell in love with her. Up to that point Cassandra had remained a virgin, although there had been no lack of suitors for her hand, notably Othryoneus, who promised to rid Troy of the Greeks if he could be rewarded with her hand; he, however, was killed by Idomeneus.

Cassandra had twin sons, Teledamus (2) and Pelops (2), by Agamemnon. When Agamemnon returned to Mycenae he was murdered by his wife who, at the same time, killed Cassandra.

Cassandra was sometimes called Alexandra, and it was under this name that the Hellenistic poet Lycophron made her the leading character in his *Alexandra.* In Lycophron's poem, Priam, who was unhappy about the prophetic gifts of his daughter and feared the ridicule of the Trojans, shut her up and placed over her a keeper with orders to report to him what she said. The poem was supposed to reproduce the girl's prophecies.

Cassiopia (Κασσιέπεια, Κασσιόπεια, Κασσιόπη) Mother of ANDROMEDA. She boasted that her, or Andromeda's, beauty outshone that of the Nereids or Hera, so Poseidon sent a sea-monster to lay waste the land. Andromeda had to be sacrificed to the monster to appease the god, but PERSEUS rescued her. Cassiopia was turned into a constellation.

Traditions about Cassiopia's origin vary. She is said to have belonged to the family of Agenor. She is also said to have been the wife of Phoenix (2) (see CILIX) and the mother of Phineus (2) (Table 3). She was the daughter of Arabus, eponym of Arabia. Her husband is sometimes said to be Epaphus, by whom she bore Libya, Agenor's mother. She is also said to have been the wife of Cepheus (2) of Ethiopia. In all these cases the myth is associated with countries of the extreme south – Arabia, Ethiopia or southern Egypt.

Castalia (Κασταλία) A girl from Delphi. She was pursued by Apollo and threw herself into the spring which was sacred to Apollo. Thereafter it bore her name. In another version, Castalia was the daughter of Achelous and wife of King Delphus. By him she had a son, Castalius, who ruled over Delphi after the death of his father.

Castor (Κάστωρ) One of the DIOSCURI.

Cathetus (Κάθητος) He was in love with the daughter of the Etruscan king Annius (2), who was called Salia. When Cathetus abducted her and brought her to Rome Annius tried unsuccessfully to catch them. In his despair, he cast himself into the nearest river which was thereafter called the Anio. Cathetus married Salia and by his marriage had Salius, who gave his name to the *Collegium* of the Salii which annually in Rome performed a sacred dance during a ritual procession.

Catillus A hero associated with the foundation of the town of Tibur. Roman historians regarded him as a Greek; alternatively Catillus might have come with Evander (3), whose fleet he commanded, or he might have been the son of Amphiaraus, who after his father's death went to seek his fortune in Italy on the orders of Oecles. There Catillus is said to have had three sons, Tiburnus, Coras and Catillus the younger, who were supposed to have founded the town of Tibur.

Catreus (Κατρεύς) Son of Minos and Pasiphae. An oracle had warned that Catreus would die at the hands of one of his four children, Areope, Clymene (4), Apemosyne and Althaemenes. The latter two fled to Rhodes to avoid fulfilling the oracle, and Catreus gave Aerope and Clymene to Nauplius (2) to be sold as slaves abroad. In his old age Catreus wanted to leave his kingdom to

Althaemenes and went to Rhodes to find him, but on landing there he and his crew were mistaken for pirates and Althaemenes killed him. When he realized his mistake Althaemenes was, by his own prayer, swallowed up by the earth.

It was when Menelaus was attending the funeral of Catreus – his grandfather (Table 2) – that Paris abducted Helen.

Caucon (*Καύκων*)
1. One of the sons of LYCAON (1). He gave his name to the Caucones, who lived in the west of the Peloponnese. Together with all his brothers, he was struck by lightning by Zeus in retribution for the impiety of Lycaon.
2. The son of Celaenus and grandson of the Athenian Phylus. He was the first to introduce the mysteries of Demeter into Messenia.

Caulon (*Καυλών*) The son of the Amazon Clete. He came to Italy with his mother and founded Cautonia near Locri.

Caunus (*Καῦνος*) The twin of BYBLIS. There is also a story that in Lycia he married the Nymph Pronoe and fathered a son called Aegialus who is said to have founded Caucus.

Caystrus (*Κάυστρος*) A Lydian river-god, the son of Achilles and Penthesilea. His son Ephesus founded the city of the same name. Caystrus was also the father of SEMIRAMIS by Derceto.

Cecrops (*Κέκροψ*)
1. A mythical king of Attica, often regarded as the first. He was born of the earth and the upper part of his body was human, the lower took the form of a serpent. He married Aglaurus (1), the daughter of Actaeus the king of Acte. He succeeded Actaeus and renamed the land (subsequently called Attica) Cecropia. Cecrops fathered four children, ERYSICHTHON (2), Pandrosus, AGLAURUS (2) and Herse. During his reign Poseidon and Athena quarrelled over the possession of Attica: Poseidon struck the ground with his trident and a salt-water spring burst forth on the Acropolis; Athena planted an olive tree on the hill. In some accounts Cecrops was the judge of the contest, and ruled in favour of Athena. Cecrops' reign was peaceful: he taught mankind how to build cities and how to bury the dead, and is sometimes credited with the invention of writing and the census.
2. The roll of the kings of Attica includes another Cecrops, the son of ERECHTHEUS and Praxithea.

Cedalion (*Κηδαλίων*) After Hephaestus was born his mother Hera placed him in the care of Cedalion who lived at Naxos, and Cedalion taught him the art of metalwork. Cedalion also helped ORION to regain his sight when he became blind.

Celaeno (*Κελαινώ*)
1. One of the Pleiades. She married Poseidon and bore, in varying traditions, Lycus (1), Nycteus, Eurypylus (5) and Triton. She was also said to be the mother of Deucalion (1) by Prometheus (see Table 8).
2. One of the Harpies.

Celbidas (*Κελβίδας*) A native of Cumae who left Italy to found Triteia in Achaea. According to other authors, Triteia was said to have been founded by Melanippus (1).

Celeus (*Κελεός*) The son of Eleusis and the first ruler of the district of that name (see RARUS). He was ruling over Eleusis when Persephone was abducted. Demeter arrived at Eleusis in search of Persephone in the guise of an old woman. The daughters of Celeus led her to their father's house where she was offered the position of a serving-woman. Demeter accepted and was put in charge of Demophon, the king's youngest son (see DEMOPHON (1)). She finally disclosed her divine nature, but before returning to Olympus she told Celeus the rules of her cult and helped him to build a temple (see also TRIPTOLEMUS and DEMETER). Some versions of the story claim that Celeus was not a king, but a peasant of Eleusis.

Celmis (*Κέλμις*) A divinity who was one of the companions of Zeus when he was a child, but he offended Rhea and as a result was changed into a lump of diamond (or steel) by Zeus.

Celtus (*Κελτός*) The eponym of the Celts. When Heracles was passing through Britain with the cattle of GERYON, Celtine, the king's daughter, concealed the herds and refused to give them back unless Heracles married her. He assented and Celtus was born. In other traditions Celtus was the son of Heracles and Sterope (1).

Centaurs (*Κένταυροι*) Mythical creatures, half man and half horse. The upper parts of their bodies were human, as were sometimes the front parts of their legs, but the rear part was that of a horse and in the Classical era, they had four horses' hooves and two human arms. They lived in the mountains and forests and their food was raw flesh. They were descended from Centaurus, the son of Apollo and Stilbe (1), or of IXION and Nephele (2). The Centaurs Chiron and Pholus were of a different descent: Chiron was the son of Philyra and Cronus; Pholus the son of Silenus and a Nymph. Unlike their fellows, they were hospitable and non-violent.

When Heracles was hunting the Erymanthian boar, he visited Pholus, who received him hospitably, giving him cooked meat whereas Pholus himself ate exclusively raw food. When Heracles asked for wine, Pholus told him that there was only one jar, which either belonged communally to the Centaurs or had been a gift from Dionysus who had advised them to open it only if Heracles should be their guest. Heracles told Pholus to open it and not be afraid. When the Centaurs smelled the wine they rushed from the mountains armed with rocks, fir trees, and torches to attack the cave. The first two Centaurs to attack were Anchius and Agrius, whom Heracles killed, but Pholus was killed in the fight: while burying one of his fellow-Centaurs he drew one of Heracles' poisoned arrows from a wound, accidentally dropped it on his foot, and died. Heracles drove off the other Centaurs and pursued them to Cape Malea where they took refuge with Chiron. In the ensuing battle Heracles shot Elatus in the elbow, but Chiron either dropped one of Heracles' arrows on his foot or was shot in the knee by Heracles. The wounds of Heracles' arrows could not be healed (see PHILOCTETES), and the immortal Chiron begged to be made mortal: Prometheus agreed to take on his immortality, and Chiron died. Most of the other Centaurs took refuge in Eleusis. Their mother, Nephele (2), came to their aid by causing a rain storm, but in the battle Heracles killed Daphnis, Argeius, Amphion, Hippotion, Oreius, Ispoples, Melanchaetes, Thereus, Doupon, Phrixus and Homadus.

The Centaurs also fought against the LAPITHS. Pirithous invited the Centaurs, who regarded themselves as his parents, to his wedding feast. Unused to drinking wine, the Centaurs became drunk and one of them tried to rape Hippodamia (2), Pirithous' bride. A violent brawl broke out. Ultimately the Lapiths drove the Centaurs out of Thessaly. This 'Centauromachy' became a popular theme in art.

Centaurs appear in other legends concerning abductions. Eurytion (2) attempted to rape Hippolyta or Mnesimache, the daughter of Dexamenus. In one version Dexamenus had betrothed his daughter to Azan, an Arcadian. Eurytion tried to kidnap her at the wedding feast, but Heracles arrived in time to kill him, and return her to Azan. In another version, Heracles, on his way to Augias, seduced the girl and promised to marry her on his return. While he was away she was forcibly betrothed to Eurytion. Heracles returned just as the wedding was about to start, killed the Centaur and married the girl. A variant of the legend makes Mnesimache identical with Deianeira, and sets the scene at Calydon, where a similar struggle for possession of the young girl took place between Heracles and ACHELOUS. In other legends the Centaur NESSUS tried to violate Deianeira, and Hylaus and Rhoecus (2) tried to rape Atalanta.

Centimani Giants with a hundred hands (see HECATONCHEIRES).

Cephalion (*Κεφαλίων*) A shepherd in Libya who, according to Hyginus, killed two Argonauts, Eribotes and Canthus, who tried to rob him of some of his flock (see also CAPHAURUS).

Cephalus (*Κέφαλος*) The commonest account of his origin makes him the son of Deion, son of Aeolus (1). His mother was Diomede, the daughter of Xuthus and Creusa (2) (Table 5). Other writers claim that he was an Athenian, the son of Herse.

Cephalus was abducted by Aurora (see EOS) who loved him; he fathered her son Phaethon in Syria, but abandoned her and returned to Attica, where he married PROCRIS. One day Cephalus began to doubt whether his wife was faithful and decided to test his suspicions. He disguised himself and got into her presence when she thought he was away and offered her more and more valuable gifts if she would yield to his advances. She held out for a long time but finally gave way. At this point Cephalus revealed who he was. In her shame and anger Procris fled into the mountains. Cephalus was filled with remorse, went after her and they were eventually reconciled. Then Procris became jealous in her turn. She often saw her husband leave to go hunting, and she wondered whether the mountain Nymphs were attracting him. She questioned a servant who said that after the hunt Cephalus would stop and call for a cloud (*Nephele*) or breeze (*Aura*). Procris assumed this ambiguous name was that of his lover and decided to catch Cephalus by surprise: she followed him when he went hunting and Cephalus, hearing some movement in the thicket, launched his spear which had the property of never failing to hit its target. Procris was mortally wounded, but on her deathbed she saw that she had been mistaken.

Cephalus was tried for murder before the Areopagus and sentenced to exile. He went with Amphitryon on his expedition against Taphos. After their victory the island of Cephalonia was named after Cephalus. There he married Lysippe (2) and fathered four children. The origin of the race of Laertes is also ascribed to him as Arcesius, the father of Laertes, is sometimes regarded as either Cephalus' son or grandson.

Cepheus (*Κηφεύς*)

1. The king of Tegea in Arcadia and one of the Argonauts. When Heracles undertook an expedition against the son of Hippocoon he called for an alliance with Cepheus. As an inducement, Heracles entrusted him with a lock of the Gorgon's hair in a bronze vase. This had been given to him by Athena. Heracles told Cepheus that if his enemies attacked the town while he was away, his daughter Sterope (4) had only to shake the lock of hair over the town walls three times. Provided that she took care not to look behind her, the enemy would be put to flight. Cepheus went to war with Heracles and his brother Iphicles. During the fighting, however, Iphicles, Cepheus and his sons lost their lives, but Heracles emerged the winner.

2. The father of ANDROMEDA and husband of CASSIOPIA. He was the son of Belus (Table 3).

Cerambus (*Κέραμβος*) A shepherd from Othrys, in Thessaly. During the great flood in Deucalion's time he had taken shelter on the mountains to escape the waters, and the Nymphs gave him wings, transforming him into a beetle (see also TERAMBUS).

Ceramus (*Κέραμος*) An Attic hero who gave his name to a quarter of Athens called the Ceramicus. He was said to have invented the art of pottery.

Cerberus (*Κέρβερος*) The dog of Hades. He watched over the realm of the dead and forbade living people to enter it, and prevented the dead from leaving it. Cerberus is generally described as having three dogs' heads, a serpent for a tail, and on his back innumerable snakes' heads. He is sometimes said to have had fifty, or a hundred heads. He was chained up in front of the gate of the Underworld and filled souls with terror as they were entering. One of the labours of Heracles was to go to the Underworld to find Cerberus and bring him back to earth (see HERACLES, II). Cerberus also succumbed to the charms of Orpheus. Cerberus was believed to be the son of Echidna and Typhon, brother of Orthrus, the monstrous dog of Geryon, of the Hydra of Lerna, and of the Nemean lion.

Cercaphus (*Κέρκαφος*) One of the HELIADES (2).

Cercopes (*Κέρκωπες*) Two brothers, named in some versions Eurybates and Phrynondas, and in others Sillus and Triballus. They were huge and exceptionally strong, and robbed passers-by and killed them. Their mother, the Oceanid Theia, had warned them against a hero called Melampygus ('the man with the black buttocks'). One day they came on HERACLES, who had gone to sleep by the side of the road, and tried to rob him, but the hero woke up, easily overcame them and hung each of them by the feet at the end of a long stick. While they were hanging in this position, they could see that Heracles had black buttocks and they understood what their mother had prophesied, but Heracles was so amused by their jokes that he agreed to let them go. Despite this adventure, the Cercopes persisted with their life of plundering and armed robbery until Zeus, enraged by their behaviour, changed them into monkeys and removed them to the islands at the mouth of the bay of Naples, Proscida and Ischia.

Cercyon (*Κερκυών*)

1. A bandit who had his lair on the road between Eleusis and Megara; he used to stop travellers and make them fight with him. Then, when he had defeated them, he killed them. At last Theseus came past the spot; he was more expert at fighting than Cercyon, lifted his enemy in the air, hurled him to the ground and crushed him (see ALOPE and RARUS).
2. The son of AGAMEDES.

Cercyra (*Κέρκυρα*) Cercyra or Corcyra was one of the daughters of Asopus and Metope. She was abducted by Poseidon, who married her on the island of Corcyra (the modern Corfu) which came to be called after her. She bore Poseidon a son, Phaeax (1).

Ceres The Roman name for DEMETER, with whom she is identical. There is a story that when the Etruscans under Porsenna were attacking Rome the city was threatened with famine. The Sibylline Books (see SIBYL) were consulted, and they advised the introduction to Rome of the cults of Dionysus and Demeter. This advice was followed in 496 BC and the two gods were established on the Aventine Hill. For the legends about Ceres see DEMETER.

Ceryx (*Κῆρυξ*) The son of Eumolpus. His name in Greek means 'the herald'. On the death of his father Eumolpus took over responsibility for the cult of Demeter, and it was his 'descendants' who were the 'heralds' (Ceryces) involved in the ritual. Some sources have it that Ceryx was the son of AGLAURUS and Hermes.

Cetes (*Κέτης*) A king of Egypt who was able to change himself into every kind of animal or tree, or element such as fire and water.

Ceto (*Κητώ*) The daughter of Pontus and Gaia. Her name is the generic Greek name for any large sea monster. She married her own brother Phorcys, by whom she had the GRAEAE, the Gorgons, the dragon which guarded the Apples of the Hesperides, and the Hesperides themselves.

Ceyx (*Κήυξ*)

1. King of Trachis in Thessaly and a relation of Heracles. Heracles took refuge with him after he had accidentally killed EUNOMUS, and after Heracles' death his children, pursued by the hate of Eurystheus, took refuge with Ceyx, until Eurystheus made them leave. The daughter of Ceyx, Themistonoe, was the wife of Cycnus (3), who was killed by Heracles. Ceyx offered funerary honours to Cycnus after his death. Ceyx had two sons, Hippasus, who went with Heracles on his expedition against Oechalia and died there, and HYLAS.
2. The son of Eosphorus. He was married to ALCYONE (1) and became a bird.

Chalciope (*Χαλκιόπη*)

1. The daughter of Eurypylus (3). By her union with Heracles she had Thessalus.
2. The daughter of Aeetes. She married Phrixus, by whom she had four children, Argos (3), Melas (2), Phrontis and Cytissorus.
3. The daughter of Rhexenor (or Chalcodon (1)). She was the second wife of AEGEUS, king of Athens. Because Aegeus could not have any children by her he went to Delphi and, while passing through Troezen on his way back, he fathered Theseus by his union with Aethra.

Chalcodon (*Χαλκώδων*)

1. The son of Abas (1) and the father of ELEPHENOR. Chalcodon died at the hands of Amphitryon. Besides Elephenor, Chalcodon had a daughter Chalciope (3).
2. A companion of Heracles on his expedition against Elis.
3. One of the suitors of Hippodamia (1). He was killed by OENOMAUS.
4. One of the defenders of Cos against Heracles during his attack on Eurypylus (3). He inflicted a wound on Heracles, who was saved only by the intervention of Zeus.

Chalcon (*Χάλκων*)

1. An oracle had advised Nestor to give Chalcon to his son Antilochus to be his armour-bearer and adviser. During the fight between Achilles and Penthesilea, Chalcon, who was in love with Penthesilea, went to her help. He was killed by Achilles and his corpse was crucified by the Greeks to punish his treachery.
2. The son of Metion.

Chaon (*Χάων*) The hero who gave his name to the Chaones, a tribe of Epirus. After Chaon was killed in a hunting accident his brother or friend HELENUS named part of his kingdom after him. Sometimes it is said that Chaon had offered his life to the gods voluntarily for his countrymen during an epidemic.

Chaos (*Χάος*) The embodiment of the primeval Void which existed before Order had been imposed on the universe. Chaos begot Erebus and Nyx and then Hemera and Air. In a different version of the myth, Chaos is said to have been the son of Chronus and the brother of Air.

Chariclo (*Χαρικλώ*)
1. A daughter of Apollo (in other versions, of Oceanus), who married Chiron. She brought up Jason and Achilles.
2. The daughter of CYCHREUS (see also SCIRON).
3. A Nymph, the mother of Tiresias. She was a companion of Athena, who often allowed her to ride in her chariot. One day when Athena and Chariclo were bathing in the Hippocrene fountain on Mount Helicon, TIRESIAS came upon the spring and saw Athena naked. The goddess blinded him and when Chariclo reproached her for her cruelty, Athena explained that every mortal who saw a deity against his or her wishes must lose his or her sense of sight. In reparation she gave Tiresias a dogwood stick, with which he could guide himself as well as if he could see, then she refined his sense of hearing so effectively that he could understand what the birds were saying. Moreover, she promised him that after his death he would retain all his intellectual faculties in Hades and especially his gift of prophecy.

Charila (*Χαρίλα*) During a famine at Delphi an orphan girl called Charila went to the king to beg for corn. But he kicked her in the face, and in despair she hanged herself. The drought worsened, and the oracle said that Charila's death must be expiated. Accordingly a nine-yearly festival was instituted at Delphi in which corn was distributed and a doll, named Charila, ritually buried.

Charites (*Χάριτες*) The Charites, called the GRATIAE (Graces) in Latin, were personifications of grace and beauty. They spread the joy of Nature and lived on Olympus. Their names, number and parentage vary, but after Hesiod they are generally said to be three sisters named Euphrosyne, Thalia (2), and Aglaea, the daughters of Zeus and Eurynome (1) or Hera.

They influenced artistic and imaginative works and wove the robe of Harmonia (1) (see CADMUS). They often accompanied Athena, Aphrodite, Eros, Apollo and Dionysus. In art they are frequently represented as naked girls with their hands on each other's shoulders, the two outer figures looking one way and the middle one looking the other.

Charon (*Χάρων*) The ferryman of the dead, who transported the spirits over the marsh of Acheron. Every soul had to pay him one obol, hence the custom of putting a coin in the mouth of corpses at burial. In Aristophanes' *Frogs* and Euripides' *Alcestis* he is a miserable old man; in Virgil's *Aeneid* VI he is a sordid, awkward minor deity; on Etruscan tomb paintings he is a winged demon with snakes in his hair and a mallet in his hand. When he refused Heracles access to the Underworld, Heracles beat him into submission with his boathook; Charon was subsequently placed in chains for a year for allowing a living being to enter.

Charops (*Χάροψ*) A Thracian who warned Dionysus of the harm which

LYCURGUS (2) was planning to inflict on him. After punishing Lycurgus, Dionysus placed Charops on the throne of Thrace and initiated him into the Dionysiac mysteries. Charops handed down the knowledge of the Dionysiac religion to his descendants.

Charybdis (*Χάρυβδις*) A monster, the daughter of Gaia and Poseidon, she lived on the rock near Messina which lies just beside the straits between Italy and Sicily. During her life on earth Heracles passed through her region, bringing with him the flocks of Geryon. Charybdis stole some beasts from him and ate them. Zeus punished her by striking her with a thunderbolt and casting her into the sea, where she became a monster. Three times every day Charybdis drank great quantities of sea water swallowing everything that was floating. When ODYSSEUS passed through the straits for the first time he escaped Charybdis, but later he was caught clinging to the mast of his shipwrecked vessel by the current of Charybdis. He succeeded in grasping a fig tree which was growing at the entrance to her cave, and when she spewed the mast out, Odysseus grasped it and continued on his voyage. On the other side of the strait, another monster lay in wait for sailors; this was SCYLLA (1).

Chelidon (*Χελιδών*) The sister of AEDON.

Chelone (*Χελώνη*) When the wedding of Zeus and Hera took place, Hermes invited not only the gods, but also all the humans and even the animals to attend. Chelone was the only person who stayed at home, and this was by mistake. Hermes noticed that she was not there; he came down to earth again, took hold of the house with the girl inside it and cast them both into a river. Chelone was changed into a tortoise which, like her, is inseparable from its house.

Chimaera (*Χίμαιρα*) A beast which took its shape from both a goat and a lion. In some versions it is said to have had the hindquarters of a snake and the head of a lion on the body of a goat, and in others it is claimed that it had two heads, one of a goat and one of a lion; it breathed fire. It was the offspring of Typhon and Echidna. Iobates commanded BELLEROPHON to kill it since it made many raids on his kingdom.

Chimaereus (*Χιμαιρεύς*) One of the sons of the Prometheus and Celaeno (1) (Table 8). He was buried at Troy. When a plague broke out in Lacedaemon the oracle of Apollo said that it would not cease until a noble Lacedaemonian had offered a sacrifice on the tomb of the son of Prometheus. Menelaus offered up the prescribed sacrifice. While staying at Troy he was the guest of Paris, and this was how they first came to meet.

Chione (*Χιόνη*)
1. The daughter of Boreas and Orithyia. She bore Poseidon a son named EUMOLPUS and threw him into the sea; he was saved by his father.
2. The child of Callirhoe (1) and Nilus. Chione was raped by a peasant but Hermes carried her off and placed her among the clouds.

3. A daughter of Daedalion, whom both Apollo and Hermes loved at the same time. She was the mother of Autolycus and Philammon.
4. The mother of Priapus.

Chiron (*Χείρων*) The most famous and wisest of all the Centaurs; he was the son of Cronus and the Oceanid Philyra. Cronus coupled with Philyra in the shape of a horse, and this accounts for Chiron's twofold nature. Chiron was born an immortal and lived in a cave on Mount Pelion in Thessaly. He was very friendly with humans and was judicious and kindly. He gave protection to PELEUS during his adventures at the court of ACASTUS by defending him against the savage treatment given by the other Centaurs. Chiron also advised Peleus to marry Thetis and showed him how to force her into marrying him by preventing her from assuming another form; at their marriage Chiron gave Peleus a spear of ash wood. Peleus entrusted his son ACHILLES to Chiron after his separation from his wife. He also brought up Jason, Asclepius and others; Apollo himself is said to have had lessons from him. His knowledge covered music, the martial arts, hunting, ethics and medicine. Chiron was a famous doctor; when ACHILLES as a child had had his ankle burned as a result of magical practices used on him by his mother, Chiron replaced the missing bone with one taken from the skeleton of a giant. For Chiron's death see CENTAURS

Choricus A king of Arcadia whose two sons, Plexippus and Enetus, devised the art of wrestling. Their sister Palaestra told her lover Hermes of the new skill. Hermes taught it to mankind, saying he had first thought of it. The young men complained to Choricus, who told them to take revenge on Hermes. They found the god asleep on Mount Cyllene. The two young men cut off his hands. Hermes complained to Zeus, who flayed Choricus and made a leather bottle out of his skin. Hermes gave the new-found art the name of his beloved, Palaestra (*Παλαίστρα* in Greek means 'wrestling-school').

Chrysanthis (*Χρυσανθίς*) A woman from the Argolid who, in one version of the Demeter legend, told the goddess, when she came to Argos in search of her daughter, how Persephone had been abducted.

Chrysaor (*Χρυσάωρ*) Chrysaor, like Pegasus, was born from the neck of Medusa, one of the GORGONS, who was killed by Perseus. Chrysaor was born brandishing a golden sword. From his marriage to Callirhoe (1), Geryon and Echidna were born.

Chryseis (*Χρυσηίς*) The daughter of Chryses (1). Her real name was Astynome. She was abducted by the Greeks when she was staying at Thebes in Mysia with Iphinoe, the sister of King Aetion. She was given to Agamemnon as part of the spoils. Chryseis prayed to Apollo to send a plague on the Greeks. The god did so and the Greeks forced Agamemnon to return her to her father, but Agamemnon demanded BRISEIS from Achilles in return (see ACHILLES, AGAMEMNON). There is a tradition that Chryses subsequently returned Chryseis to Agamemnon of his own free will. She had two children by Agamemnon (see IPHIGENIA and CHRYSES (2)). Traditions subsequent to Homer describe Chryseis as fair, slender and small in stature; Briseis was a tall, dark, well-dressd woman with sparkling eyes, a clear complexion and eyebrows that nearly met. The two girls represent two different types of womanly beauty.

Chryses (*Χρύσης*)
1. A priest of Apollo Smintheus, who lived in the town of Chryse in the Troad. He was the father of CHRYSEIS, and the grandfather of Chryses (2).
2. Son of Chryseis and Agamemnon. According to Hyginus, when Chryseis was returned to her father by Agamemnon she was pregnant, but when she gave birth to a son whom she called Chryses, she asserted that the child was Apollo's. When Orestes, Pylades and Iphigenia, fleeing from Thoas (3), arrived at the home of Chryses (1), Chryses (2) wanted to hand them over. At that point Chryseis disclosed that Agamemnon was the real father of Chryses (2). Because of this the two dynasties were linked by family connections, and Chryses (2) not only refused to hand over Orestes and Iphigenia, but also helped them kill Thoas.
3. Son of Poseidon and Chrysogenia. He succeeded to his uncle PHLEGYAS' kingdom.
4. Son of Minos and the Nymph Paria.

Chrysippus (*Χρύσιππος*) The son of Pelops (1) and the Nymph Axioche. When Laius arrived as an exile at the court of Pelops, he received a warm welcome; he then fell in love with Chrysippus and abducted him. Pelops then ritually cursed Laius, and this was the beginning of the curse of the Labdacidae (see OEDIPUS). Chrysippus committed suicide in shame. In another version Chrysippus was killed by his half-brothers ATREUS and Thyestes at the instigation of his stepmother HIPPODAMIA (1).

Chrysopelia (*Χρυσοπέλεια*) A HAMADRYAD who lived in an oak tree in Arcadia. One day Arcas saw that the oak tree was about to be swept away by a flood. Chrysopelia begged him to save her, and Arcas built a dyke to divert the water. In gratitude Chrysopelia married him, and bore him two sons named Elatus (1) and Aphidas.

Chrysothemis (*Χρυσόθεμις*)
1. The daughter of CARMANOR; she is said to have introduced musical contests, and is supposed to have won the prize in the first competition. She was also the mother of Philammon.
2. A daughter of Agamemnon and Clytemnestra.

Chthonia (*Χθονία*)
1. The daughter of Phoroneus. She founded a temple of Demeter at Hermione. An Argive tradition makes Chthonia the daughter of Colontas. Colontas refused to restore a cult in Demeter's honour, and Chthonia reproached her father for his impiety. The house of Colontas was burned down by the goddess, who then removed Chthonia to

Hermione. There the girl founded a shrine of Demeter Chthonia.

2. One of the daughters of ERECHTHEUS. She married Butes (2), her uncle, though in another version she was offered as a sacrifice at the time of the struggle between Eumolpus of Eleusis and Erechtheus. In another account she killed herself and her sisters after the eldest, Protogenia (4), had been sacrificed.

Cicones (*Κίκονες*) A Thracian tribe recorded in the *Iliad* as being allies of Priam. In the *Odyssey* Odysseus made his first stop in their country after leaving Troy. He sacked Ismarus, sparing only MARON, a priest of Apollo, and his wife. Odysseus' soldiers stayed on to plunder the town, giving the local population time to come in strength and attack them. They lost six men from each ship before they escaped.

The Cicones derive their name from Cicon, the son of Apollo and Rhodope. Orpheus is said to have lived in their country and was initiated there into the mysteries of Apollo, and it is said Ciconian women tore him to pieces.

Cilix (*Κίλιξ*) One of the sons of Agenor; he was the brother of Cadmus, Thasos and Europa (5) (Table 3). He accompanied his brothers in their search for Europa and stopped when he arrived at Cilicia, which took his name. Other authors make him the son of Cassiopia and Phoenix (2), who, in an alternative version, was his brother. Cilix joined forces with Sarpedon (2) in an expedition against the Lycians, and after their victory he gave up a part of Lycia to Sarpedon.

Cilla (*Κίλλα*) Sister of Priam (Table 4). She bore THYMOETES a son called Munippus whilst Hecuba was pregnant with PARIS. When Hecuba dreamt that she gave birth to a blazing brand which set Troy on fire, the people asked Aesacus what this meant. He explained that the forthcoming child would destroy Troy. Although Aesacus meant Paris, Priam misinterpreted the prophecy and had his sister's child put to death. Sometimes Cilla is said to be Hecuba's sister, and Priam to have fathered her son.

Cillas (*Κίλλας*) The charioteer of Pelops (1). He drowned during a voyage with Pelops from Lycia to the Peloponnese, where Pelops was to have a chariot race with Oenomaus (see SPHAERUS).

Cimmerians (*Κιμμέριοι*) A mythical race who lived in a country where the sun was never seen. Odysseus went there to conjure up the dead and to question Tiresias. Ancient writers hold different views on where this country was located: some say it was in the extreme West and others that it lay to the north of the Black Sea. Accordingly, the Cimmerians are regarded as the ancestors of the Celts or as the forefathers of the Scythians of southern Russia. Occasionally they are said to live near Cumae; it was believed that one of the gates of the Underworld was there, and the Cimmerians were supposed to live near the Country of the Dead. They are also said to have lived in underground dwellings, linked with each other by passages, and never to have left their city except at night.

Cinyras (*Κινύρας*) Traditionally the first king of Cyprus, although he was not a native. His origin and parentage are uncertain: in some traditions he was a son of Apollo and Paphos (1) (see PYGMALION (2)), in others the son of the Syrian Sandocus by Pharnace. Some say he arrived in Cyprus and founded Paphos after marrying Metharme, daughter of Pygmalion (2). They had two sons, Adonis and Oxyporus, and three daughters. The daughters were victims of the wrath of Aphrodite, and were made to serve as prostitutes to passing strangers. Another version claims that Cinyras committed incest with his daughter Smyrna (2) and fathered Adonis.

Cinyras was said to be the first to introduce the cult of Aphrodite to Cyprus. He had the gift of prophecy, was a good musician, introduced copper-mining to the island, and invented bronze. He was loved by Aphrodite and she allowed him to live to be one hundred and sixty.

At the time of the Trojan War, Odysseus and Talthybius sought his support. He promised them fifty ships, but he fitted out only one: the others were made of earth and dissolved in the sea. After the war TEUCER sought refuge with Cinyras, who gave him some land and the hand of his daughter Eune.

Cipus Returning at the head of his victorious Roman army at a very early date, Cipus noticed his head had sprouted horns. Omens were taken which showed that he would become king if he entered the city at once, but as a loyal Republican he went into exile. In gratitude the Senate offered him as much land as he could plough in a day, and his portrait was carved on the Raudusculan Gate.

Circe (*Κίρκη*) The daughter of Helios and of Perseis or, in some accounts, of Hecate. She was the sister of AEETES and Pasiphae. She lived on the island of Aeaea. Odysseus arrived at Aeaea on his way home from Troy. He sent half his force to spy out the land. The expedition made its way into a forest and came to a valley where its members saw a gleaming palace; they all entered except for Eurylochus who stayed on guard. The Greeks were welcomed by the mistress of the palace, who was Circe. She invited them to a banquet. They accepted but they had scarcely tasted the food and wine when Eurylochus saw Circe touch the guests with a wand. They were all instantly changed into animals – pigs, lions and dogs – each in accordance with his fundamental character and disposition. Then Circe propelled them towards the stables, which were already full of animals. Eurylochus rushed back to Odysseus and described what had happened. Odysseus had decided to go and find the witch himself to save his companions when he saw the god Hermes appear. Hermes told him that if he were to throw a magic plant called moly into the drink which Circe gave him he would have nothing to fear; then he had only to draw his sword, and Circe would free his friends from the enchantment. Hermes also gave him some moly. Accordingly, Odysseus sought out Circe who welcomed him and offered some wine. Odysseus mixed the moly with the contents of the cup. Then, when Circe touched him with her wand, he remained unaffected by her spell. He drew his sword and threatened to kill her but she swore by the Styx to do no harm either to himself or to his men and changed the sailors back to their original shapes. Odysseus spent a very pleasant month in her company, some sources say a year. During this period he fathered a son called TELEGONUS, a daughter called Cassiphone and, in some versions, a son called Nausithous (3).

In other traditions Circe is also said to have borne a son called Latinus (see CALYPSO) or in other versions, three sons, Romus, Antias and Ardeas. Circe is also said to have been involved in intrigues with Picus (see CANENS) and with Jupiter, who fathered the god Faunus.

Circe plays a part during the return voyage of the ARGONAUTS. She was also responsible for the metamorphosis of SCYLLA (1) who was her rival for the love of the sea-deity GLAUCUS (4).

Cithaeron (*Κιθαιρών*) A king of Plataea who gave his name to the nearby Mount Cithaeron. He preceded Asopus on the throne. During Cithaeron's reign Zeus quarrelled with Hera. Zeus was upset and went to Plataea, where Cithaeron advised him to make a statue of a woman, cover it in a big cloak and put it in a cart drawn by oxen. When Hera saw this she made enquiries and was told that Zeus was abducting Plataea, the daughter of Asopus, and was to make her his wife. Hera rushed up and tore the cloak off the statue, realized the trick and began to laugh. She and Zeus were reconciled. In memory of this a festival celebrating the marriage of Zeus and Hera was held annually at Plataea (cf. ALALCOMENEUS).

Other legends allude to the name of Cithaeron. According to one the violent Cithaeron killed his father and his gentle brother Helicon by hurling them from a rock, killing himself in the fall. Two neighbouring mountains came to be called Cithaeron and Helicon, the former in memory of the brutal hero because it was the home of the Erinyes, the latter after the kindly hero because it was the home of the Muses. For another legend concerning Cithaeron see TISIPHONE.

Cleomedes (*Κλεομήδης*) A hero from Astypalaea who during the Olympic Games killed his opponent, Iccus of Epidaurus. He went mad when he was not declared the winner. He returned to his own country and knocked down the pillar which supported the roof of a school, and some sixty children were killed. Then he took refuge in the temple of Athena. His pursuers decided to capture him there but failed to find him, dead or alive. They questioned the oracle which replied that Cleomedes was the last hero to live and that his cult should be established, and this was carried out at the seventy-second Olympic Games.

Cleopatra (*Κλεοπάτρα*)

1. The daughter of Boreas and Orithyia. She was married to Phineus (3), who fathered two sons, Plexippus (2) and Pandion. Cleopatra was imprisoned by her husband and her children were blinded when

Phineus married a second wife, Idaea (2), but the Argonauts came to her rescue and (in at least one version of the story) killed Phineus.

2. The daughter of Idas and the wife of Meleager. After her husband's death she hanged herself.

3. A girl who was sent to Troy by the Locrians (see PERIBOEA 3).

4. The daughter of Tros and Callirhoe (4).

Cleostratus (*Κλεόστρατος*) A Theban who rid his country of a dragon which demanded as a tribute the life of a young man every year. Cleostratus had been chosen by lot as the victim, but his friend Menestratus made him a metal breastplate studded with iron hooks. Cleostratus put it on and allowed himself to be eaten, but the dragon died from the effects.

Cleothera (*Κλεοθήρα*) A daughter of PANDAREOS and Harmothoe and the sister of Aedon and Merope (3). After they had lost their parents the three sisters were brought up by Aphrodite, Hera and Athena. When they became young women the eldest, Aedon, married Zethus, but Cleothera and Merope were abducted by the Erinyes.

Clesonymus (*Κλησώνυμος*) The son of Amphidamas of Opontus. In his childhood he used to play with PATROCLUS but he was accidentally killed by his playmate.

Clete (*Κλήτη*) The nurse of PENTHESILEA and an Amazon herself. After Penthesilea died, Clete was cast up by a storm on the south coast of Italy where she founded the town of Clete. Some time later she died fighting against the people of Croton, who annexed her town. She had a son called Caulon.

Clinis (*Κλεῖνις*) A Babylonian who was loved by Apollo and Artemis. He often used to visit the land of the Hyperboreans with Apollo and there he saw that asses were sacrificed to the gods. He wished to do the same in Babylon but Apollo forbade him to do so, telling him to sacrifice only animals which were generally used, such as sheep, oxen and goats. Despite this command, two of his sons, Lycius and Harpasus, disobeyed, but Apollo made the donkey become deranged. It killed the two young men, their father and the rest of the family, who arrived, drawn by the noise. Apollo and the other gods took pity on them, however, and changed them into birds.

Clite (*Κλείτη*) The daughter of Merops, the prophet of Percotus, in Mysia. She was the wife of CYZICUS.

Clitor (*Κλείτωρ*)

1. One of the sons of Azan. Clitor founded the town which subsequently bore his name and he was the most powerful prince in the whole of Arcadia. He died childless and his kingdom was inherited by Aepytus (3).

2. One of the fifty sons of Lycaon (2). He may be identical with Clitor (1).

Clitus (*Κλεῖτος*)

1. The son of Mantius. He was abducted by Eos because of his

beauty and set by her among the immortals. He had a son called Coeranus (1) and a grandson, Polyidus (1).
2. See PALLENE (1).
3. The son of Polyidus (1).

Clymene (*Κλυμένη*)
1. A daughter of Oceanus and Tethys. By her marriage to Iapetus she gave birth to Atlas (1), Prometheus, Epimetheus and Menoetius (2) (Table 8). In some versions she is regarded as the wife of Prometheus and the mother of Hellen. According to other accounts she is said to have married Helios and to have borne him a son, Phaethon, and the HELIADES (2).
2. The daughter of Nereus and Doris.
3. One of the daughters of Minyas. She married Phylacus (1) and had two sons, Iphiclus (1) and Alcimedes. In other accounts she is said to have been the wife of Cephalus whom she married after the death of Procris, but is also supposed to have married Iasus (1) and to have had a daughter, Atalanta.
4. One of the daughters of Catreus of Crete. She married Nauplius (2) and was the mother of Palamedes, Oeax and Nausimedon.

Clymenus (*Κλύμενος*)
1. A native of the town of Cydonia, in Crete. He came to Olympia about fifty years after Deucalion's flood and founded the Games there; he also built an altar there to the Curetes and to his ancestor Heracles. Clymenus reigned over the country until ENDYMION stripped him of his power.
2. A Boeotian hero; he was the son of Presbon and ruled the town of Orchomenus. He was stoned to death by the Thebans in the wood which was sacred to Poseidon, and in revenge for his death his son ERGINUS (1) forced the Thebans to pay tribute; they were freed from this by Heracles.
3. An Arcadian, the son of Schoeneus (1), or of Teleus, king of Arcadia; he fell in love with his daughter, Harpalyce (2) and had an incestuous relationship with her. Later, he married her to Alastor but then abducted her from her husband. In revenge the girl killed either her young brothers or the son Clymenus had fathered, served them up to Clymenus and made him eat them. When he realized what a strange dish his daughter had given him, Clymenus killed first her and then himself. He is also said to have been turned into a bird or to have committed suicide.
4. A son of Oeneus of Calydon.

Clytemnestra (*Κλυταιμνήστρα*)
Daughter of Tyndareus and LEDA, and twin sister of Helen, although Helen was the daughter of Zeus, who coupled with Leda in the form of a swan.

She was first married to Tantalus (2), but Agamemnon killed him and her children. Her brothers, the Dioscuri, then forced him to marry her. She had several children by AGAMEMNON. When Menelaus was at Troy attempting to recover Helen, Clytemnestra looked after Helen's daughter Hermione. After the Greek army gathered at Aulis, the seer Calchas (1) declared that Clytemnestra's daughter IPHIGENIA had to be sacrificed. After the sacrifice Agamemnon sent Clytemnestra back to

Argos, where she fostered plans for revenge.

Clytemnestra was initially faithful to Agamemnon while he was at Troy. He had left Demodocus (2) with her with instructions both to act as her adviser and to report back to him. But AEGISTHUS fell in love with her and Demodocus could not prevent her yielding to him. She may have been influenced by NAUPLIUS (2), by desire to take revenge for the sacrifice of Iphigenia, or by jealousy of Agamemnon's liaison with Chryseis. In the epic poets Clytemnestra played no part in Agamemnon's murder on his return from Troy, but the tragedians maintain that she was an accomplice, and indeed that she killed him with her own hands: she made a robe for him, sewing up the neck and sleeves, so that he was encumbered and rendered helpless. She also killed Cassandra, of whom she was jealous. Tragic writers say that she visited her hatred on Agamemnon's children: she had Electra (3) incarcerated, and would have killed Orestes had the child not been taken away by his tutor. Later Clytemnestra was killed by ORESTES to avenge the death of his father.

Clytia (*Κλυτία*) A young girl loved by Helios who then spurned her for love of Leucothoe (2). Clytia told Leucothoe's father, and for this was buried in a deep ditch, where she died. Helios never visited Leucothoe again. She wasted away with love and turned into a heliotrope, the flower which keeps its face turned always towards the sun. A son called Thersanor was born from the liaison between Leucothoe and Helios. His name appears in some lists of the Argonauts.

Cnageus (*Κναγεύς*) A Laconian who had been taken prisoner by the Athenians at the battle of Aphidna. He was sold as a slave in Crete and placed in the service of Artemis. He eventually escaped, taking with him the priestess, a young girl, and the statue of the goddess. After his return to Laconia, he established the cult of Artemis Cnagia.

Cocalus (*Κώκαλος*) King of Camicos in Sicily. Daedalus took refuge with him after his escape from Crete (see ICARUS). Minos went looking for Daedalus, and wherever he went he offered rewards to anyone who could insert a thread into a spiral shell. When Cocalus brought the threaded shell to Minos he knew that Daedalus, the man of ingenuity above all others, must be close at hand. Cocalus then promised to hand Daedalus over after a banquet, but instructed his daughters to scald Minos to death in his bath. Thus Minos met his end.

Cocytus (*Κωκυτός*) The Cocytus or the 'River of Groans' was one of the rivers of Hades. It was an extremely cold watercourse which ran parallel to the Styx. It had to be crossed by the souls of the dead before they could reach the kingdom of Hades (see CHARON).

Codrus (*Κόδρος*) The son of MELANTHUS whom he succeeded as king of Athens. During his reign the Peloponnesians declared war on the Athenians, and the Delphic oracle promised them victory if they refrained from killing the king of Athens. When this pronouncement became known to the Athenians, Codrus resolved to sacrifice his life for his country: he left Athens dressed as a beggar and sought out two of the enemy, with whom he picked a quarrel. He killed one of them, and was himself slain by the other. The Athenians then demanded his body from the Peloponnesians in order to bury it. The Peloponnesians realized they had lost all hope of conquering Athens and returned to their own country. Codrus' tomb was erected at the place where he died, on the right bank of the Ilissus; it became one of the show-places of Athens. After his death Codrus was succeeded by his elder son, Medon. His younger son, NELEUS (2), went into exile at Miletus.

Coeranus (*Κοίρανος*)
1. The son of CLITUS (1) and father of POLYIDUS (1).
2. A charioteer who was slain by Hector.
3. A Milesian who saw a fisherman with a dolphin he had caught; Coeranus bought the animal and returned it to the water. Some time later, when he was shipwrecked, Coeranus was saved by dolphins. After his death, when his funeral cortège passed near the port of Miletus, a school of dolphins appeared and accompanied the mourners.

Coeus (*Κοῖος*) One of the Titans. By his own sister, Phoebe (1), he sired Leto, the mother of Apollo, Artemis and Asteria (1) (Table 8).

Colaenus (*Κόλαινος*) Reputedly the first king of Attica. He was overthrown by his brother-in-law Amphictyon; driven out of the city, he settled in the district of Myrrhina, where he consecrated a shrine to Artemis Coelanis; he died there (see CRANAUS and CECROPS for varying traditions).

Comaetho (*Κομαιθώ*)
1. The daughter of Pterelaus (Table 7). See AMPHITRYON.
2. A priestess of Artemis at Patras. She was loved by Melanippus (6), and she returned his love, though their parents were opposed to this match. The two young lovers used to meet in the priestess' sanctuary, and Artemis, angered by this sacrilege, sent a plague upon the land. The oracle of Delphi revealed the cause of Artemis' anger; the sacrifice of the guilty couple was pronounced to be the only means of appeasing her. This was carried out, and furthermore, each year the handsomest youth and the most beautiful girl in the land were sacrificed to Artemis. This custom continued until the arrival of EURYPYLUS (2).

Comatas (*Κομάτας*) A shepherd from Thurii, on the gulf of Tarentum, who used frequently to make sacrifices to the Muses. His master (from whose herds Comatas used to select the victims) shut him up in a sarcophagus of cedar-wood, telling him that the Muses would no doubt find a way to save him. Three months later the sarcophagus was opened, and the young man was found still alive: the goddesses had sent him bees which had nourished him with their honey.

Combe (*Κόμβη*) Daughter of Asopus. Traditions vary as to the number of her children, although seven is the usual number, the seven Corybantes or Curetes of Euboea. She was married to the god Socus or Saocus, but he was so violent that she fled with her children via Crete to Phrygia, where they were taken in by Dionysus. They later went to Athens where Cecrops (1) helped them take revenge on Socus. After Socus died she returned to Euboea, where she was metamorphosed into a dove (see also CURETES). She was also called Chalcis because she was believed to have introduced bronze weapons (Greek *χαλκός* = bronze); her sons used to dance and clash their weapons, hitting their shields with their spears (see also PYRRHICUS).

Cometes (*Κομήτης*)

1. The son of Sthenelus (3). When DIOMEDES (2) left for the Trojan War, he entrusted Cometes with the care of his house, but Cometes seduced his wife AEGIALE. In doing this, Cometes was the instrument of the anger of Aphrodite, who had been wounded by the hero. On returning to his fatherland, Diomedes was forced into exile by Cometes and Aegiale.
2. The son of TISAMENUS (1).

Condyleatis (*Κονδυλεᾶτις*) A statue of Artemis, called Artemis Condyleatis, stood in a sacred wood near Caphyes in Arcadia. One day, a group of children playing there found a length of cord which they wound round the neck of the image as if they were going to strangle her. Some of the townsfolk happened to pass by and, in an excess of piety, they stoned the children to death. However, after this the babies of the women of Caphyes were all still-born. The oracle of Delphi said that the goddess was angered by the slaughter of the children and ordered that they be buried reverently and be paid the honours due to heroes. This was done, and thereafter this Artemis was called 'The Strangled Artemis' (*Ἀπαγχομένη*).

Consentes The Etruscans acknowledged the existence of six gods and six goddesses, who formed Jupiter's privy council and who assisted him when important decisions had to be taken, notably the hurling of certain types of thunderbolt. Their statues stood beneath a portico at the side of the road running from the Forum to the Capitol.

Consus A Roman god who had an underground altar in the middle of the Circus Maximus. This altar was disinterred on each of the god's feast-days, during the *Consualia* and during the horse-races. Draught animals, horses, asses and mules were spared from work on these days and garlanded with flowers; horse-races and even mule-races were held. The rape of the Sabine women took place during the first feast-day of Consus.

Copreus (*Κοπρεύς*) Son of Pelops (1). After slaying Iphitus (3) he had to leave Elis, and he took refuge with EURYSTHEUS. He became Eurystheus' herald. When Eurystheus sent him to Athens demanding that the Heraclids be expelled, he behaved so insolently that the Athenians killed him. In expiation for this crime Athenian youths wore dark-coloured tunics on certain festal days.

Cora (*Κόρα*) Cora, whose name means 'young girl', was DEMETER's daughter, better known as PERSEPHONE.

Corcyra (*Κέρκυρα*) See CERCYRA.

Corinnus (*Κόριννος*) A legendary Trojan poet who is said to have written the *Iliad* before Homer, at the actual time of the Trojan war, and to have learnt the art of writing from Palamedes. He was also said to have composed an epic poem on the war waged by Dardanus against the Paphlagonians.

Corinthus (*Κόρινθος*) Corinthus, the eponym of Corinth, was said by the Corinthians to be one of the sons of Zeus. The rest of Greece laughed at this claim until the phrase 'Corinthus, son of Zeus' became the proverbial expression for a monotonous catch-phrase. He was said to be the son of MARATHON. He fled to Attica with his father, and on the death of EPOPEUS both father and son returned to Corinth. When Marathon died, Corinthus became king. According to one tradition, he was assassinated by his subjects (see also GORGE (2)), and his death was avenged by Sisyphus, who reigned over Corinth after him.

Coroebus (*Κόροιβος*)

1. Apollo sent a monster called Poene to devour the children of the inhabitants of Argos because of the action of CROTOPUS. Eventually a young countryman called Coroebus slew Poene, but another scourge was visited upon the Argives. Coroebus then went to Delphi, where he offered to make whatever amends Apollo might demand for his having slain Poene. The oracle instructed him to take a sacred tripod from the temple at Delphi and set out bearing it upon his back. When the tripod fell from his shoulders he was to stop and found a city; thus the site for the city of Megara was selected. His tomb was to be seen in the central square of this city.
2. A Phrygian, the son of MYGDON (1), who came to offer help to Priam, if the latter would agree to give him CASSANDRA's hand in return; but he was killed at the fall of Troy.

Coronides (*Κορωνίδες*) The Coronides were two young sisters called Metioche and Menippe, the daughters of Orion. They were sacrificed during a plague which had been visited upon Orchomenus in Boeotia. Their bodies were duly interred, but Hades and Persephone took pity on them and transformed their dead bodies into stars.

Coronis (*Κορωνίς*)

1. The daughter of Phlegyas, king of the Lapiths. She was the mother of Asclepius. According to a sacred tradition she was really called Aegla and had been given the surname Coronis (the Crow) because of her beauty. In this tradition Phlegyas was an ordinary inhabitant of Epidaurus who had married a Thessalian girl, Cleomene, the daughter of Malus and Erato (1). For her legend see ASCLEPIUS and compare MARPESSA.
2. The daughter of Coronus, who was changed into a crow by her protectress Athena to enable her to escape the attentions of Poseidon who was in love with her.

3. One of the Nymphs who were Dionysus' nurses. See BUTES (1).

Coronus (*Κόρωνος*) The son of Caeneus who reigned over the Lapiths. King Aegimius appealed to Heracles for help against Coronus, and Heracles slew him. Coronus had taken part in the expedition of the Argonauts.

Corybantes (*Κορύβαντες*) Sons of Apollo and Thalia (1). They were attendants of Cybele, Dionysus and Rhea. Like the CURETES, with whom they are often confused, they celebrated their rites with armed dances in which they clashed their spears and shields. The priests of Cybele, also known as Corybantes, celebrated her festivals by dancing to the sound of cymbals, drums and flutes. Some writers say that they took their name from Corybas, son of Iasus and Cybele, who first introduced Cybele's rites into Phrygia.

Corythus (*Κόρυθος*)
1. The son of Zeus and Electra (2). In one legend Iasion and DARDANUS were his sons but according to others they were actually sons of Zeus and Electra (see Table 4). Corythus reigned over the Tyrrhenians of Italy, the ancestors of the Etruscans, and founded the city of Cortona in Italy.
2. A king of Tegea in Arcadia who rescued and reared TELEPHUS after his mother Auge exposed him.

Cranaus (*Κραναός*) One of the first kings of Attica, who succeeded CECROPS. During his reign the population called themselves Cranaeans and the town of Athens, Cranae. When his daughter Atthis died unmarried, her name was given to the country: thus Cranae became Attica. Cranaus was overthrown by his son-in-law, AMPHICTYON.

Crantor (*Κράντωρ*) Peleus' favourite squire. He was at his side at the battle between the Lapiths and the Centaurs. He was killed by a tree hurled by the Centaur Demeleon; his death was avenged by Peleus.

Creon (*Κρέων*)
1. A king of Corinth, and the son of Lycaethus. ALCMAEON entrusted him with the upbringing of Amphilochus and Tisiphone (2), his children by Manto. For Creon's death see MEDEA.
2. A king of Thebes, and the son of Menoeceus (1). After Laius died at the hands of Oedipus, Creon succeeded him as king; but the city fell victim to the SPHINX. Creon offered a reward for whoever could rid the city of this scourge. OEDIPUS killed the Sphinx, and Creon, in accordance with his promise, gave up the throne to him. He also gave JOCASTA to Oedipus in marriage. Later, when Thebes was ravaged by a plague, Oedipus sent Creon to consult the Delphic oracle. Once Oedipus' incest with Jocasta was revealed Creon took his place as king. In another legend Oedipus went to Colonus in Attica, but Creon tried to make him return to Thebes because the Delphic Oracle had declared that Thebes' prosperity would not be assured until Oedipus returned there. When Oedipus refused, Creon tried to have him brought back by force, and Theseus had to intervene on Oedipus' behalf.

During the war of the Seven against Thebes (see ADRASTUS) Creon offered his own son Megareus as a sacrifice to Ares at the order of Tiresias, and thus saved the city. He then decreed that POLYNICES, who had borne arms against his own city, should remain unburied (see also ANTIGONE). Theseus forced Creon to return the bodies of the dead to the Argives: some versions say that Theseus slew Creon during this incident.

Creon purified AMPHITRYON when the latter took refuge in Thebes; he also required Amphitryon to slay the Teumessian fox before he would accompany him on his expedition against the Teleboeans. Creon was also ruler of Thebes when Heracles rid the city of the tribute imposed by ERGINUS (1).

Creontiades (*Κρεοντιάδης*) A son of Heracles and Megara (1). He was killed together with his brothers by his own father, who had gone mad.

Cres (*Κρής*) The eponym of the Cretans. He reigned over the first inhabitants of the island, the 'Eteocretans', and is also said to have provided asylum in the range of Mount Ida to the child Zeus who was threatened with death by his father Cronus. He gave the Cretans a code of laws before the time of Minos. He is sometimes presented as the father of Talos (1).

Cresphontes (*Κρεσφόντης*) One of the Heraclids. With his brothers Aristodemus and Temenus (3) he conquered the peninsula of the Peloponnese, at the head of the Dorians. After the conquest the three brothers divided the country up by drawing lots. Each brother had to put a pebble into an urn full of water, and the portions were to be allotted in the order in which each of the pebbles was drawn out. Cresphontes wanted Messenia, the richest of the portions, and he put a lump of earth into the water, which disintegrated. Thus the two other pebbles were drawn out first and Cresphontes became ruler of Messenia, while Temenus received Argos and Aristodemus got Lacedaemon. Each brother built an altar to Zeus and on these altars each found a sign in keeping with the character of the people over whom he had been chosen to rule: on the altar of the ruler of Argos, a toad; on that of Lacedaemon, a snake; and on that of Messenia, a fox.

Cresphontes divided Messenia into five regions, granted the indigenous population rights equal to those of the Dorians, and chose Stenyclarus as his capital; but the Dorians criticized this choice, and Cresphontes changed his system of government accordingly. He assigned Stenyclarus for occupation exclusively by the Dorians, but then the rich land-owners became discontented, rose in rebellion and killed him.

Cretheus (*Κρηθεύς*) A son of Aeolus (1) and Aenarete (Table 5). His marriage to his niece Tyro produced three sons: Aeson, Pheres (1) and Amythaon (Table 6). He adopted Neleus and Pelias, Tyro's children, fathered by Poseidon before her marriage. He is said to have sired Talaus (more commonly said to have been the son of Bias); a daughter, Hippolyta, surnamed

Cretheis, who married ACASTUS; and Myrina, wife of Thoas (1). Cretheus founded the city of Iolcos.

Creusa (*Κρέουσα*)
1. A Naiad who was loved by the River Peneius. She had two children, Hypseus, king of the Lapiths, and Stilbe (1). Andreus is sometimes cited as a child of hers.
2. A daughter of ERECTHEUS and PRAXITHEA (1). She was raped by Apollo in a grotto on the Acropolis at Athens and had a son, Ion. She exposed the child at the spot where she had been surprised by the god. Creusa married Xuthus. For a long time she was childless, but after a pilgrimage to Delphi where she met her son again, she presented her husmand with Diomede and Achaeus (Table 5).
3. The daughter of Creon (1), sometimes called Glauce (2).
4. Aeneas' wife. She was the daughter of Priam and Hecuba. In the great paintings in the Lesche at Delphi, Polygnotus showed her among the Trojan captive women, but she is more frequently considered to have escaped when Troy fell. In Virgil's version, Creusa was carried away by Aphrodite while Aeneas left the city with Anchises and Ascanius. Aeneas came back into the city to rescue her; but her shade appeared to him and foretold his travels in search of a new country. The oldest epics call Aeneas' wife Eurydice (7).

Crimisus (*Κριμισός*) See AEGESTES. Virgil and Hyginus refer to him as Crinisus.

Crisus (*Κρίσος*) The founder of the city of Crisa on Mount Parnassus. His father was Phocus and his mother was called Asteria (Table 5). Crisus had a twin brother, PANOPEUS, with whom he quarrelled. However, another tradition maintains that Crisus and Panopeus sprang from different stock: while the latter was the son of Phocus, the former was the son of Tyrranus and Asterodia. Crisus married Antiphatia, daughter of Naubolus, and they had a son, Strophius (1) (Table 2).

Critheis (*Κριθηίς*) A Nymph who was said to have been the mother of the poet Homer by the River Meles.

Another legend identifies her as the daughter of Apelles, an inhabitant of Cyme. On his death-bed, Apelles entrusted her to his brother Maeon (2), but Critheis escaped and gave herself to Phemius, who lived at Smyrna. One day, as she was washing her linen in the River Meles, she gave birth to a son who became the poet Homer.

A third version makes Critheis a young maiden of Ios. Captured by pirates, Critheis was taken to Smyrna where Maeon (2) married her. She gave birth to Homer on the banks of the Meles, and died immediately afterwards.

Crocon (*Κρόκων*) An early king of Eleusis. He was the son of Triptolemus. Crocon and his brother, Coeron, were the ancestors of the priestly families, the Croconides and the Coeronides, who played a part in the cult of Demeter.

Crocus (*Κρόκος*) A young man who was changed into a saffron plant after an unhappy love affair with the Nymph Smilax.

Cronus (*Κρόνος*) A Titan, the youngest son of Uranus and Gaia. By his own sister Rhea he was father of Hestia, Demeter, Hera, Pluto (Hades), Poseidon and Zeus (see URANUS, GAIA and ZEUS). He was also the father of the Centaur CHIRON by Philyra. Other myths identify him as the father of Hephaestus by Hera. In some traditions Aphrodite is his daughter, rather than that of Uranus (Table 8).

In the Orphic tradition Cronus appears reconciled with Zeus and living in the Islands of the Blessed. In this tradition Cronus is regarded as a good king, the first to rule over both Heaven and Earth (see GOLDEN AGE). In Greece he was said to have reigned on Olympus; in Rome, where he was identified with Saturn, his throne was located on the Capitol. He is also said to have reigned in Africa, Sicily and the whole of the western Mediterranean. Later, when mankind had become wicked during the ages of bronze and iron, Cronus was relegated to Heaven. Cronus is sometimes identified with Chronus (Time personified: the Greek *Κρόνος* and *Χρόνος* sound similar).

Croton (*Κρότων*) When HERACLES returned from his quest for Geryon's cattle, Croton welcomed him, and Heracles became his guest; but Lacinius, a neighbour of Croton's, tried to steal the cattle. Heracles killed him, but also accidentally killed Croton during the fight. In expiaton, Heracles built him a tomb and prophesied that a famous city would rise which would bear the name of Crotona. Croton is sometimes claimed to be the brother of Alcinous. This legend is connected with that of LACINIUS.

Crotopus (*Κρότωπος*) Son of Agenor, and the father of Sthenelas and Psamathe (2). Psamathe was loved by Apollo and he fathered her child, Linus (1). Linus was exposed by his mother and was brought up by shepherds. Some say that Crotopus heard of the incident and caused the child to be eaten by dogs; others that the shepherd's dogs killed him by mistake. Crotopus also had Psamathe put to death – buried alive according to some authors. Apollo was angered by the death of his son and mistress and punished the Argives (see COROEBUS (1)). The oracle instructed the Argives to introduce the custom of singing dirges to Psamathe and Linus. At this ceremony any dogs found in the street or square were killed. Crotopus was exiled. Ovid relates that on Crotopus' death he was dispatched to Tartarus, to be with the major criminals.

Cteatus (*Κτέατος*) One of the MOLIONIDAE.

Ctimene (*Κτιμένη*)

1. The sister of ODYSSEUS and wife of EURYLOCHUS.
2. The wife of PHYLEUS.

Curetes (*Κούρητες*) Also known as CORYBANTES. Traditions speak of a people called the Curetes who once lived in Aetolia; but they also relate how they were driven out by AETOLUS (see MELEAGER).

More commonly the Curetes

were *daemons* (spirits), companions of Zeus during his childhood on Crete. Traditions about their origin vary: sometimes they are identified with the Curetes of Aetolia; more often they are the sons of COMBE and Socus: Prymneus, Mimas, Acmon, Damneus, Ocythous, Idaeus (5), and Melisseus (2). They are also said to be the sons of Mother Earth, or, variously, sons of Zeus and Hera, Apollo, or the Nymph Danais. Their number also varies from two to seven to nine to unspecified.

When Rhea gave birth to Zeus in a cave on Mount Ida in Crete, she entrusted him to the Nymph AMALTHEIA. In order that his cries should not reveal his existence to Cronus, who would have devoured him, she asked the Curetes to perform their noisy dances around him. This they did, and Zeus grew up safely.

Some myths give the Curetes the gift of prophecy, and tell how they showed Minos how to bring his son GLAUCUS (5) back to life. They abducted Io's son EPAPHUS at Hera's insistence, for which Zeus, Epaphus' father, killed them with a thunderbolt.

Curtius During the early days of the Republic, the ground opened in the middle of the Forum; the Romans tried to fill the gulf by pouring earth into it, but their efforts were in vain. An oracle told them to throw the most prized of their possessions into it. Marcus Curtius, realizing that Rome's most prized possessions were its youth and its soldiery, decided to sacrifice himself for the salvation of all: clad in his armour, and mounted on his horse, he rode into the abyss. It closed above him, leaving only a little lake, to which the name Lake Curtius was given, and round its shores a fig-tree, an olive-tree and a vine sprang up. Under the Empire, it was customary to throw coins into the lake as an offering to Curtius, the genius of the place.

According to another tradition, Curtius was a Sabine who, during the war between Tatius and Romulus, was almost swallowed up in the marshes near the Comitium and had to abandon his horse. This episode gave Lake Curtius its name.

Cyane (*Κυανή*)

1. Cyane, whose name evokes the blue colour of the waters of the sea, was the daughter of LIPARUS (see AEOLUS (2)).
2. A water-nymph of Syracuse, who tried to prevent the abduction of Persephone by Hades. In his anger, Hades transformed her into a pool of a deep blue colour, like that of the sea.
3. A young girl who was raped by her father Cyannipus (3). This took place in the dark of night, and Cyanippus hoped that he had not been recognized; but Cyane had pulled a ring off his finger during the assault and realized who had been involved. A plague broke out in the city, and the oracle declared that it would be brought to an end only by the sacrifice of a human victim – one who had committed incest. Cyane and her father then killed themselves.

Cyanippus (*Κυάνιππος*)

1. A grandson of Adrastus, who ruled over Argos. According to another tradition, he was the son of Adrastus (Table 1). He took part in

the Trojan War, and was one of the heroes inside the Wooden Horse.
2. A Thessalian who married a girl called Leucone. Cyanippus would go out hunting in the morning and come back in the evening so tired that he usually went straight to bed. Leucone felt neglected and bored. One day she decided to follow her husband, hoping to discover what he found so attractive in the woods. She slipped out of the house and before long found herself deep in the thicket, where her husband's hounds discovered her and tore her to pieces. When he discovered her body Cyanippus was driven to despair. He built a funeral-pyre and laid his wife upon it; then he slew his hounds, threw them on to the pyre and, finally, he slew himself.
3. The father of CYANE 3.

Cyathus (*Κύαθος*) See EUNOMUS.

Cybele (*Κυβέλη*) A Phrygian goddess, often called 'the Mother of the Gods', or 'the Great Mother': she governed the whole of Nature. Her cult spread over the whole of the Greek world, and, later, into the Roman world as well.

Cybele was often identified by the Greek mythographers with RHEA. The Rhea worshipped on Mount Cybele in Phrygia was said to be Cybele. She figures little in myth; in the story of AGDISTIS and ATTIS, Attis appeared sometimes as her lover but more often as her companion. It is also possible that her personality was concealed behind that of the hermaphrodite Agdistis, the lover of Attis after his emasculation.

Cybele's major importance lay in the orgiastic cult which grew up around her and which survived to a fairly late period under the Roman Empire. She was generally portrayed wearing a crown of towers and accompanied by lions, or riding in a chariot drawn by these animals. She had as her servants the CURETES, also known as the CORYBANTES.

Cychreus (*Κυχρεύς*) Son of Poseidon and Salamis. Cychreus killed a serpent which was ravaging the island of Salamis, after which the islanders made him their king. In other versions Cychreus raised the serpent, which was later driven out to Eleusis where it became an attendant of Demeter. During the naval battle of Salamis a serpent was said to have appeared among the Greek ships: the Delphic oracle revealed that this was Cychreus.

Cychreus had a daughter, Chariclo (2), the mother of Endeis and mother-in-law of Aeacus. Cychreus left his kingdom to his great grandson Telamon, Aeacus' son. In another tradition Cychreus' daughter was Glauce (3), who bore Telamon by Actaeus.

Cyclopes (*Κύκλωπες*) Ancient mythographers recognized three different kinds of Cyclopes: the Uranian Cyclopes, sons of Uranus and Gaia, the Sicilian Cyclopes, and the 'master-mason' Cyclopes.

The Uranian Cyclopes had only one eye in the middle of the forehead and they were distinguished by their strength and manual dexterity. There were three of them, Brontes, Steropes (or Asteropes) and Arges, names which corresponded to Thunder, Lightning and Thunderbolt, respectively. They were imprisoned by Uranus and released by Cronus, but only to be confined once more by him in Tartarus, until Zeus finally released them, warned by an oracle that he could achieve victory only with their aid. They provided Zeus with thunder, lightning and thunderbolts; to Hades, they gave a helmet which made him invisible, and to Poseidon, they gave a trident. Thus armed, the Olympian gods defeated the Titans and threw them into Tartarus.

As manufacturers of divine thunderbolts the Cyclopes incurred the wrath of APOLLO, whose son ASCLEPIUS had been slain by Zeus with a thunderbolt for having brought the dead back to life. Unable to revenge himself on Zeus, Apollo slew the Cyclopes.

In Alexandrine poetry, the Cyclopes appear as smiths and craftsmen who made every type of weapon for the gods. They fashioned the bows and arrows used by Apollo and Artemis. They lived in the Aeolian Islands, or perhaps in Sicily, where they owned an underground forge: their panting breath and the clanging of their anvils could be heard reverberating deep in the volcanoes of Sicily. The fire of their forge reddened the evening sky at the top of Mount Etna.

In the *Odyssey*, the Cyclopes were a race of gigantic, savage beings, with one single eye and tremendous strength, who lived in the Phlegraean Fields near Naples. They were devoted sheep-breeders, cannibals by choice, and were strangers to the practice of drinking wine. They lived in caves, and had not learnt how to build cities (see POLYPHEMUS 2).

Cyclopes who came from Lycia were credited with the construction of all the prehistoric monuments to be seen in Greece, Sicily and elsewhere, made of huge blocks of stone. The Cyclopes in this account were a whole new race, one which had put itself at the service of such heroes as Proetus, in the fortification of Tiryns, and Perseus, in the fortification of Argos, and so on.

Cycnus (*Κύκνος*)

1. A son of Poseidon and Calyce. Cycnus took part in the games given before the Trojan War in honour of PARIS, who at that time was believed to have died. He came to the aid of the Trojans with a fleet when the Greeks landed; he held the invaders up for a long time, until he encountered Achilles. Cycnus was invulnerable, so Achilles had to strike him in the face with the pommel of his sword, and drive him backwards with his shield, until Cycnus stumbled and fell. Achilles then strangled him; but through his father's intercession, Cycnus was transformed into a swan.

2. The son of Poseidon and Scamandrodice. He ruled over a city called Colonae, which lay opposite the island later known as Tenedos. His mother had exposed him at birth on the sea-shore, and a swan had taken care of him. Later, he married Proclea, one of Laomedon's daughters, and fathered two children by her: a boy, TENES, and a girl Hemithea (2). Proclea died, and Cycnus then married Philonome, the daughter of Tragasus. For subsequent events see TENES.

Cycnus is said to have been killed in Tenedos by Achilles. This Cycnus, the father of Tenes, seems not always to have been clearly distinguished from Cycnus (1), and doubtless this is the explanation for this later variant.

3. The son of Ares and Pelopia (2). He was a brigand who used to waylay travellers and kill them and then offer sacrifices to his father from the ransom he took from them. He preyed in particular upon travellers to Delphi; this earned him the hatred of Apollo, who incited the hero Heracles against him. Heracles very soon despatched Cycnus; but then Ares came forward to avenge his death. However, Athena deflected Ares' javelin and Heracles wounded the god in the thigh. So runs the Hesiodic version.

This fight was generally considered to have taken place at Pagasae in Thessaly, but Apollodorus places it in Macedonia. According to him Cycnus was the son of Ares and Pyrene (2); as in the other version, Cycnus was slain, but Appollodorus claims that when Ares intervened, Zeus parted the combatants with a thunderbolt. Apollodorus wrote of another Cycnus, the son of Ares and Pelopia, who was killed at Itonus, but there is no mention of divine intervention in the fight.

A version given by Stesichorus and Pindar states that when Heracles found himself opposed by both Cycnus and Ares during the first engagement, he withdrew. Later, he met Cycnus alone, and slew him.

4. A king of Liguria, and a friend of PHAETHON. Cycnus mourned Phaethon's death so bitterly that he was transformed into a swan. Apollo had given this Cycnus a beautiful voice, and from this account springs the supposition that swans sing when on the point of death.

5. The son of Apollo and Thyria, the daughter of Amphinomus. This Cycnus lived in Aetolia, between Pleuron and Calydon. He was very handsome, but harsh and capricious – so much so that one after another all his friends and lovers grew disheartened. Of all those who paid court to him, only Phylius remained in the end. Cycnus then imposed a series of tasks on him: he killed a lion without using iron weapons; captured man-eating vultures; and led a wild bull to the altar of Zeus with his own hands. After this, his patience exhausted, he threw himself over a cliff. Cycnus, dishonoured and completely alone, threw himself into a lake. Out of pity, Apollo transformed Cycnus and his mother into swans.

Cydnus (*Κύδνος*) The son of the Nymph Anchiale; he gave his name to the river in Cilicia. There was a popular legend in Cilicia which told the love story of Cydnus, half man, half river, and Comaetho: Comaetho fell in love with the river, and ended up by marrying Cydnus.

Cydon (*Κύδων*) The son of Hermes and ACACALLIS. He was reputed to be the founder of the Cretan city of Cydonia. The inhabitants of Tegea in Arcadia believed that he was one of the sons of their hero Tegeates; but there were also those who said that Apollo was his father, though his mother was the same Acacallis.

Cylabras (*Κυλάβρας*) A shepherd of Lycia from whom Lacius bought the land on which the town of Phaselis was built, paying for it in salted fish. The inhabitants built a sanctuary to Cylabras, where they offered up salted fish in his honour.

Cyllarus (*Κύλλαρος*) A young Centaur who was loved by the she-Centaur Hylonome. He was killed during the fight between the Lapiths and Centaurs. Not wishing to live without him, Hylonome took her own life with the same arrow that had killed him.

Cyllene (*Κυλλήνη*) An Arcadian Nymph, who gave her name to Mount Cyllene, where Hermes is said to have been born. Sometimes she is said to have brought Hermes up during his infancy.

Cynortas (*Κυνόρτας*) A king of Sparta, the son of Lacedaemon and the elder brother of HYACINTHUS. Cynortas had a son called Perieres, or perhaps Oebalus, though Perieres was generally considered to have been the son of Aeolus (1). One version omits this generation completely, and makes Tyndareus the son of Cynortas.

Cynosura (*Κυνόσουρα*) A Nymph on Mount Ida in Crete, and in some legends she and Helice (2) were said to have brought up the infant Zeus (see AMALTHEA). When Cronus pursued them, Zeus turned them into two constellations, the great Bear and the Little Bear. Cynosura gave her name to a place in Crete, near the town of Histoi.

Cyparissus (*Κυπάρισσος*)

1. A son of Telephus who lived on Ceos, and was loved by Apollo (and according to some accounts, by the god Zephyrus, and possibly by the Roman god Silvanus). His favourite companion was a sacred stag which he had tamed, but one summer's day Cyparissus inadvertently killed it with his javelin. Racked by his grief, he besought heaven to let his tears flow for all eternity. The gods turned him into a cypress, the tree of sadness.

Cypselus (*Κύψελος*)

1. The son of Aepytus (1). He was ruler of Arcadia when the HERACLIDS attacked Peloponnese for a second time. Cypselus appeased them by giving his daughter Merope (2) to Cresphontes. Later he brought up AEPYTUS (2), the son of Cresphontes and Merope, and allowed him to avenge his father's death. Cypselus had raised a temple and an altar to Demeter of Eleusis at Basilis in the land of the Parrhesians. During this goddess's annual festival, a female beauty contest was held; Herodice, Cypselus' own wife, carried off first prize.
2. A Corinthian, one of the Seven Sages. Among the votive offerings at Olympia was a chest, which Cypselus had offered: this was the chest in which his mother had hidden him at birth to conceal him from the Bacchiadae. As the Corinthian for a chest at that time was 'cypsela', the infant was named accordingly. This chest, described by Pausanias, carried archaic inscriptions and pictures of mythical scenes.

Cyrene (*Κυρήνη*) A Thessalian Nymph, daughter of Hypseus, the king of the Lapiths. According to Pindar, Cyrene lived in the forests of

Mount Pindus and looked after her father's flocks. One day, unarmed, she attacked and overcame a lion. Apollo saw her do this and fell in love with her. After enquiring of the Centaur Chiron who she was, he abducted her to Libya and gave her the land of Cyrene. She had a son, ARISTAEUS, by Apollo.

In the Hellenistic era it was said that after Cyrene's arrival in Libya she was given the kingdom of Cyrene by Eurypylus (5), since she was able to kill a lion which was ravaging the country.

The myth of Cyrene has many variants. Some say that she came to Libya straight from Thessaly, others that she came via Crete. Others say that Apollo mated with her in the form of a wolf (there was a cult of Lycian Apollo in Cyrene). Virgil describes Cyrene as a water-nymph who lived beneath the River Peneus. She is also said to be the mother of Idmon.

Cytissorus (*Κυτίσσωρος*) The son fathered by Phrixus after his arrival in Colchis, on one of King Aeetes' daughters, either Chalciope (2) or Iophassa. When he grew up, he went to his grandfather ATHAMAS to receive his inheritance. He arrived at the very moment when Athamas' subjects were preparing to sacrifice him to propitiate Zeus. Cytissorus saved him. This earned both him and his descendants Zeus' wrath. In each generation, the eldest son had to avoid the Prytaneum; for if he were found within the council hall, he would have been sacrificed.

Cyzicus (*Κύζικος*) A hero of the Propontis, on the Asiatic coast. He played a part in the legend of the ARGONAUTS. Cyzicus is said to have come from northern Greece. He was the son of Aeneas and of Aenete, a daughter of Eusorus, the king of Thrace. Cyzicus reigned over the Doliones, who traced their origins back to Poseidon. When the Argonauts arrived in his country, he had just married Clite, daughter of the soothsayer Merops. Cyzicus welcomed the sailors, gave them a banquet, and replenished their supplies, but after the Argonauts had set sail a storm came up at night and forced them back to shore at the place which they had just left. The Doliones thought they were being attacked by pirates, and fell upon the Argonauts. Cyzicus came to the aid of his men and was slain by Jason. On the next morning, everyone discovered the mistake. The Argonauts mourned for three days over the king's corpse and then gave him a great funeral in the Grecian style and held funeral games. Clite was overcome by despair and hanged herself. The city over which Cyzicus had reigned then took his name.

D

Dactyls (*Δάκτυλοι*) The Dactyls of Mount Ida were daemons, Cretan or Phrygian in origin, who formed part of Rhea's or Cybele's retinue. Their name means 'the fingers'. They were so called either on account of their skill at working with their hands because when their mother (Rhea, or one of the Nymphs of Mount Ida) was giving birth to them she pressed her clenched fingers into the soil to ease her pain, or because they sprang from the dust that Zeus' nurses scattered behind them through their fingers.

They were related to the Curetes, and were said, like them, to have watched over Zeus during his infancy. They were said to have numbered five, ten, or sometimes even a hundred. An Elean tradition names the males as follows: Heracles (not Alcmene's son), Epimedes, Idas (or Acesidas), Paeonius, and Iasus.

The Dactyls were credited with the spread, and sometimes the invention, of the Mysteries. To amuse the infant Zeus, they organized the first Olympic Games. They were also believed to have taught Paris music on Mount Ida in the Troad.

Daedalion (*Δαιδαλίων*) The brother of Ceyx (2) and the son of Eosphorus. He loved hunting and fighting, and made many conquests. He had a daughter called Chione (3) who attracted many suitors. One day Hermes and Apollo both fell in love with her. She gave them two children from this encounter. The one by Hermes was called AUTOLYCUS and the one by Apollo Philammon. But Chione had the audacity to set her beauty above that of Artemis, who killed her with an arrow. Daedalion's grief was so intense that Apollo transformed him into a sparrow-hawk, a bird which retained the violent instincts he had had as a man.

Daedalus (*Δαίδαλος*) An Athenian descended from Cecrops. Daedalus was a skilled artist, architect, sculptor and inventor. In antiquity he was credited with archaic works of art and such inventions as the animated statues mentioned in Plato's *Meno*. According to some legends, Daedalus' father was Eupalamus or alternatively METION.

Daedalus worked in Athens, where his nephew Talos (2) was his pupil. Talos proved so talented that Daedalus became jealous, and when Talos, drawing his inspiration from the jaw-bone of a serpent, invented the saw, Daedalus threw him from the top of the Acropolis. Daedalus was tried before the Areopagus and sentenced to exile. He fled to the court of King Minos at Crete. When Minos' wife PASIPHAE became enamoured of a bull, Daedalus constructed a wooden cow for her. He also built the Labyrinth for Minos – a building with a maze of corridors in which the MINOTAUR was confined – and then in due course suggested to Ariadne the trick which saved Theseus when he went to fight the Minotaur (see THESEUS, III). When Minos learnt of Theseus' success he imprisoned Daedalus in the Labyrinth, as Theseus' accomplice, together with his son ICARUS. But Daedalus made wings for himself and his son, which he attached with wax, and they both flew off. Daedalus reached Cumae and subsequently took refuge at Camicos in Sicily, under the protection of King Cocalus (for the ruse by which Minos discovered Daedalus, see COCALUS). Once Minos had been killed, Daedalus showed his gratitude to his host by erecting many buildings.

Damaethus (*Δάμαιθος*) See PODALIRIUS.

Damasen (*Δαμασήν*) A giant, born of Gaia, and brought up by Eris. He was born bearded, and immediately after his birth Eilithyia gave him weapons. He grew to a prodigious size and strength. At the request of the Nymph MORIA, he slew the snake which had killed Tylus, Moria's brother.

Damastes (*Δαμάστης*) A giant, more commonly known as PROCRUSTES.

Damysus (*Δάμυσος*) Damysus had been the swiftest runner of all the giants. When entrusted with the infant ACHILLES, Chiron disinterred Damysus and took his heel-bone to replace the child's, which had been damaged by fire; this was why Achilles was so swift a runner. According to one legend about his death, his heel-bone came off as he was being pursued by Apollo. Achilles fell, thus giving the god a chance to kill him.

Danae (*Δανάη*) The daughter of Acrisius (2) and Eurydice (Table 7). An oracle warned Acrisius that he would be slain by the son of Danae (see ACRISIUS), and after the birth of the child, Perseus, Danae was put into a wooden chest with him and thrown into the sea. For the ensuing events, see PERSEUS. Danae ultimately went back to Argos to live with her mother, while Perseus went off to hunt down Acrisius.

In an Italian version of the legend, Danae and the infant Perseus in the chest were washed up on the coast of Latium. There Danae married Pilumnus (2) and the two of them founded the city of Ardea.

Danaides (*Δαναΐδες*) The fifty daughters of King DANAUS, who accompanied him when he fled from Egypt fearing the fifty sons of his brother Aegyptus, with whom he had quarrelled. Once established in Argos, he invited his fifty nephews to visit him. They asked him to forget their quarrel and announced their intention of marrying his fifty daughters; and although he had no faith in this reconciliation, Danaus accepted their proposals. He gave a great feast to celebrate the weddings, but presented each of his daughters with a dagger and made them all swear to kill their husbands during the night. This they did, except for HYPERMESTRA (1), who spared LYNCEUS (1) because he had spared her virginity. The murderesses cut off the heads of their victims, gave their bodies full funeral honours at Argos, and buried the heads at Lerna. At Zeus' order, they were purified of their murders by Hermes and Athena. Danaus later confirmed the union of Hypermestra and Lynceus, and tried to marry off the other daughters, but there were few suitors. He then decided to hold games with his daughters as prizes; would-be suitors were excused the requirement of providing the customary gifts. His daughters thus married young men from their own country; and with them they produced the race of the Danaans. Together with their father they were later killed by Lynceus, who thus avenged his brothers' deaths. The Danaides were also said to have been punished in Hades by being compelled everlastingly to refill leaking water-pots (see AMYMONE).

Danaus (*Δαναός*) One of the two sons of BELUS and Anchinoe (see AEGYPTUS, and Table 3). By different wives he had fifty daughters (see DANAIDES). His father had given him Libya as his kingdom, but he fled the country, either after a warning from an oracle or from fear of his brother Aegyptus' fifty sons. He travelled in a ship with fifty banks of oars, which Athena had advised him to build, via Rhodes to Argos. Gelanor was king of Argos at that time; according to some he yielded his throne to Danaus spontaneously, but other stories hold that Danaus obtained the throne only after a rhetorical battle with Gelanor in the presence of the people of Argos. As the two contestants met to present their final arguments, a wolf came out of the forest and fell upon a herd of cattle that was passing the city walls. The wolf attacked the bull, overcame it, and killed it. The Argives were struck by the analogy between this wolf that had come out of its solitude, far from mankind, and Danaus, and chose Danaus as their king. Danaus built a shrine to Lycian Apollo (Wolfish Apollo).

For the way in which Danaus procured water for the land of Argos, which had been deprived of it as a result of Poseidon's anger, see AMYMONE and INACHUS. For the murder of Aegyptus' fifty sons, see DANAIDES.

Danaus was said to have founded the citadel of Argos. He was buried there.

Daphne (*Δάφνη*) A Nymph loved by Apollo; her name means 'laurel' in Greek. She is sometimes said to be the daughter of the River Ladon, sometimes of the Thessalian River Peneus. Apollo's love for her was fired by Eros, angered by the taunts of Apollo who had derided him for practising archery. Daphne fled to the mountains, and just as Apollo was about to catch her she begged her father to transform her so that she might escape. She became a laurel, the tree sacred to Apollo.

A Laconian version of the myth made Daphne the daughter of Amyclas. She spent her time among the mountains and was a favourite of Artemis. Leucippus (2) fell in love with her, disguised himself as a girl, and joined her companions. Daphne became fond of him, but Apollo became jealous and inspired Daphne and her companions with the wish to bathe. Leucippus hesitated to remove his clothing, but his companions forcibly undressed him. On discovering his identity they attacked him, but the gods made him invisible. Apollo tried to seize Daphne but she ran off, and in answer to her prayer, Zeus turned her into a laurel.

Daphnis (*Δάφνις*) Son of Hermes and a Nymph. Daphnis was born in Sicily in a thicket of laurel, and this gave him his name (Greek *δάφνις* = 'laurel'). He was brought up by the Nymphs, who taught him the herdsman's art. He was very beautiful, and was loved by many Nymphs, mortals and gods. Pan taught him music, and Daphnis played the syrinx (Pan pipes) and sang songs in the bucolic mode, which he invented. The Nymph Nomia the Shepherdess loved him, and he loved her. He had sworn to remain eternally faithful, and did so until a daughter of the king of Sicily made him drunk and slept with him. In her anger Nomia blinded or killed him. The blind Daphnis sang sad songs until he threw himself off a high rock, was transformed into a rock, or was taken up to Olympus by Hermes.

In another version Daphnis loved a Nymph called Pimplea, or Thalia (1), who was abducted by pirates. He found her in Phrygia (see LITYERSES).

Dardanus (*Δάρδανος*) The son of Zeus and Electra. His country of origin was Samothrace, where he lived with his brother IASION. After a flood in which Iasion drowned, Dardanus set out to sea on a raft, which took him to the coast of Asia. Here reigned King Teucer. Teucer received Dardanus hospitably, and gave him part of his kindgom, together with his daughter Batieia. Dardanus built the city that carried his name, and on Teucer's death he called the whole country Dardania. Batieia gave him sons – Ilus (1), Erichthonius and (some say) Zacynthus, and a daughter, Idaea (2) named after her mother's grandmother (Table 4). Dardanus built the citadel of Troy and reigned over the Troad. He was said to have initiated the Trojans into the mysteries of the CABIRI (sometimes he was even thought to be one of them) and to have introduced the cult of Cybele into Phrygia. According to one legend Dardanus stole the PALLADIUM and brought it over to Troy.

According to an Italian tradition Dardanus came from the Etruscan city of Cortona. He won a victory over the Aborigines and then founded the city. Later he emigrated to Phrygia, thereby creating a bond between Italy and the Troad. It was in memory of these earliest origins of his race that Aeneas went to Italy after the fall of Troy.

Another tradition has it that Dardanus was a connection of Evander (3) and of Pallas (4).

Dares (*Δάρης*) A Phrygian who was given to Hector as an adviser, to stop him from fighting Patroclus (for the Fates had decreed that if Hector were to slay Patroclus, he himself would be slain by Achilles). Dares deserted to the Greeks, but he was put to death by Odysseus.

Daunus (*Δαύνιος* or *Δαῦνος*) One of the three sons of Lycaon (2). Together with his brothers, he invaded southern Italy at the head of an Illyrian army, threw out the Ausonians, and divided the land into three kingdoms.

When DIOMEDES (2) came to Italy he was given a warm welcome by Daunus, who gave him land and the hand of his daughter. A later tradition tells of dissension between Daunus and Diomedes, the latter being slain by the former.

This Daunus (or a figure with the same name) was the father of TURNUS.

Decelus (*Δέκελος*) The eponym of the Attic city of Decelea. When the Dioscuri were looking for Helen, it was Decelus who showed them where she was being held prisoner. It was sometimes held that the revelation was made by ACADEMUS.

Deianeira (*Δηιάνειρα*) The daughter of King Oeneus of Calydon. According to another legend her father was Dionysus, who had been Oeneus' guest. Her mother was ALTHAEA. Deianeira knew how to drive a chariot and understood the art of war. When her brother Meleager died, she and her sisters were transformed into guinea-fowl; but at Dionysus' pleading, she and one sister, Gorge (1), resumed their human forms.

When Heracles went down to Hades in search of Cerberus, he encountered the spirit of Meleager, who asked him to marry Deianeira, left without support since Meleager's death. As soon as he returned to earth, Heracles hastened to Calydon where he found Deianeira, who was being wooed by the river-god ACHELOUS. In the ensuing struggle Heracles overthrew his rival. For events after their marriage, see HERACLES, VI.

Deion (*Δηιών*)

1. Son of Aeolus (1) and Enarete. He was king of Phocis. He married Diomede, daughter of Xuthus, and fathered Cephalus, Phylacus, Actor, Aenetus and Asterodia.
2. An alternative spelling for DEIONEUS.

Deioneus (*Δηιονεύς*) The father of Dia, and the father-in-law of IXION. Also known as DEION (2).

Deiphobus (*Δηίφοβος*) A son of Priam and Hecuba. It was in the likeness of Deiphobus that Athena appeared to HECTOR at his meeting with ACHILLES, and urged him to fight, thus causing his death. It was also Deiphobus who recognized Paris at the funeral games where Paris defeated all his brothers. After the death of Paris, Deiphobus won the hand of Helen in competition with his brother HELENUS, even though the latter was the elder. After the sack of Troy, Odysseus and Menelaus seized his house, and Menelaus killed him and mutilated his body. His shade appeared to Aeneas in Hades.

Deiphontes (*Δηιφόντης*) One of the HERACLIDS. He married Hyrnetho, daughter of Temenus (3). When the Heraclids seized the Peloponnese, Temenus received Argos, and Deiphontes joined him there. Temenus' sons feared that they would be disinherited in favour of Deiphontes, and so all of them, except Agrius, the youngest, attacked Temenus while he was bathing. Temenus died of his wounds, but had time to leave the kingdom to Deiphontes and reveal his sons' crime. Temenus' sons were banished, but later regained power in Argos with external help; Deiphontes went to Epidaurus, along with Hyrnetho and Agrius, and obtained the throne of King Pityreus. While Deiphontes was at Epidaurus his brothers-in-law, Cerynes and Phalces, carried off his wife. Deiphontes pursued them and killed Cerynes, but Phalces slew Hyrnetho and escaped. She was buried on the spot, in an olive grove, and divine honours were paid to her.

Deipylus (*Δηίπυλος*) Son of POLYMESTOR and Priam's daughter Ilione. Priam entrusted his son Polydorus (2) to Ilione to bring up, and she exchanged the two children, passing her own son Deipylus off as her young brother. This was to ensure that if one of them should die, the other would retain his right to the throne. After the fall of Troy, Agamemnon wanted to destroy Priam's race completely, and promised Polymestor his daughter Electra (3) if he would agree to murder Polydorus. Polymestor accepted and killed his own son Deipylus, thinking he was Polydorus. Later the Delphic oracle informed Polydorus that his mother and father were dead and his native land ruined. He questioned Ilione, who told him the truth. On Polydorus' advice Ilione blinded Polymestor and put him to death.

Delphus (*Δελφός*) The hero who gave his name to Delphi. He is said to have been the reigning king of the country when APOLLO arrived to take possession of it. He was sometimes said to be the son of Poseidon and Melantho; Poseidon coupled with her in the shape of a dolphin (whence the name of the child. The Greek *δελφίς* = 'dolphin'). Sometimes he was held to be the son of Apollo, either by Celaeno (or Melaenis), or by Thyia, or yet again by Melaena (Table 5). Delphi owed its original name of Pytho either to Delphus' son, King Pythes, or to one of his daughters called Pythis (see also PYTHON).

Delphyne (*Δελφύνη*)

1. A dragon, half woman, half serpent, who was charged by TYPHON with keeping watch over Zeus' sinews and muscles, which Typhon had hidden in a cave in Cilicia. But Hermes and Pan outwitted Delphyne and restored Zeus to his former shape and strength.
2. The dragon at Delphi, which watched over the fountain near which lay the old oracle taken over by APOLLO. See also PYTHON.

Demeter (*Δημήτηρ*) One of the Olympian deities, the Mother Goddess of the Earth. She was the second daughter of Cronus and Rhea (Table 8). Her personality is distinct from that of GAIA, who was the Earth viewed as a cosmogonic element. Demeter, the divinity of agriculture, is essentially the Corn Goddess.

Both in myth and in cult, Demeter was closely linked to her daughter PERSEPHONE, and together they formed a couple known simply as the Goddesses. Initiation into the Eleusinian Mysteries revealed the profound significance that lay behind the myth. Persephone was the daughter of Zeus and Demeter and – at least in the traditional legend – the goddess' only child. She grew up among the Nymphs, in company with Athena and Artemis, Zeus' other daughters, and gave little thought to marriage. But her uncle Hades fell in love with her, and, possibly with Zeus' help, abducted her. The abduction is said to have taken place at Enna in Sicily, or on the plain of Mysa, or along the River Cephissus at Eleusis, or in Arcadia at the foot of Mount Cyllene, or in Crete, near Cnossus, and so on. While Persephone was picking a narcissus (or a lily) the ground opened, Hades appeared, and dragged her down into the Underworld. Persephone cried out as she disappeared into the abyss. Demeter heard her, and ran towards the sound, but there was no sign of Persephone. For nine days and nine nights, without eating, drinking, bathing or changing her clothes, Demeter wandered over the world, a lighted torch in either hand. On the tenth day she met Hecate, who had also heard Persephone's cry but had not recognized her abductor. Only Helios, who sees everything, could tell her what had happened, although according to local tradition, it was the people of Hermione in the Argolid who revealed the culprit to her. Demeter decided to abandon her divine role until her daughter was returned to her. She assumed the shape of an old woman and went to Eleusis. First she rested on a stone, which was known thenceforth as the Joyless Stone. Then she went to see King Celeus, the ruler of the country, and fell in with some old women (see IAMBE). The goddess then entered the service of Metanira, Celeus' wife, and was taken on as a wet-nurse to DEMOPHON (I) (or, in certain versions, TRIPTOLEMUS). The goddess tried to make him immortal, but was unsuccessful (see DEMOPHON (I)). Other legends show the goddess playing the role of wet-nurse for Plemnaeus, king of Sicyon (see ORTHOPOLIS).

Demeter's self-imposed exile had made the earth sterile, so Zeus ordered Hades to return Persephone. But that was no longer possible. During her stay in the Underworld Persephone had eaten a pomegranate seed, in this way binding herself for good to Hades. So compromise was reached: Demeter would return to Mount Olympus, and Persephone would divide the year between the Underworld and her mother. This was why each spring, when the first shoots appeared in the furrows, Persephone would escape from below the ground, and make her way towards the sky, only to return to the shades at seed-time. And for as long as she remained separated from Demeter, the ground stayed sterile and winter gripped the land.

Various local variants were incorporated into the story of Demeter's search. At Sicyon, the goddess was credited with the invention of the mill; elsewhere she is associated with the raising of vegetables (see PHYTALUS). Demeter's sanctuaries were to be seen throughout Greece, and it was invariably claimed that these had been built by those who had been her hosts: at Argos, one Mysius and his wife Chrysanthis; at Pheneus in Arcadia, Trisaules and Damithales, and so on. Poseidon's amorous pursuit of Demeter was also woven into the story of her search for Persephone. To escape from Poseidon, the goddess was said to have assumed the form of a mare; but it was in vain, for she gave birth not only to a horse called AREION but also to a daughter, who was known only as the Mistress (Despoina). For another love story involving Demeter see IASION.

Demeter battled with Hephaestus for possession of Sicily (see AETNA), and with Dionysus for Campania. (See also ERYSICHTHON and EUBOULEUS.) Demeter is often portrayed seated, with torches or a serpent.

Demodice (*Δημοδίκη*) The name of PHRIXUS' aunt in one version of this legend. She was the wife of Cretheus (Table 5). Demodice fell in love with Phrixus, who did not respond to her advances, whereupon she made false accusations about him to Cretheus, who persuaded his brother ATHAMAS to have him put to death. But Phrixus' mother, Nephele (1), saved him by giving him a wonderful ram, which flew away with Phrixus on its back.

Demodocus (*Δημόδοκος*)
1. The bard who sang at the court of Alcinous during the banquet at which Odysseus recounted his adventures. He was loved by the Muses, who had deprived him of his sight, but in return had given him the power of song.
2. The bard whom Agamemnon left to look after his wife CLYTEMNESTRA on his departure for the Trojan War.

Demophon (*Δημοφών*)
1. The son of Celeus and Metanira, and the younger brother of Triptolemus. In her search for Persephone Demeter had entered Metanira's service, and was entrusted with Demophon's upbringing. Wishing to make him immortal, she held him over the fire at nights, to burn away his mortal elements. As the child seemed to be growing in miraculous fashion his mother – or perhaps his nurse PRAXITHEA (3) – kept watch on Demeter, and one night saw her starting her magical treatment. She uttered a cry, and Demeter dropped the child to the floor; then she revealed her true identity. According to some, Demophon was burnt up in the fire. According to others he survived, but as a mortal. This episode is sometimes attributed to Triptolemus (see TRIPTOLEMUS, ELEUSIS, and CELEUS).
2. The brother of ACAMAS (3), and hence the son of Theseus and Phaedra (or, as some said, of Theseus and Ariadne). With Acamas he took part in the Trojan War in order to recover their grandmother, AETHRA, who was one of Helen's slaves. While Theseus was in the Underworld rescuing Persephone, the Dioscuri drove Acamas and Demophon from the throne of Athens, and installed MENESTHEUS in their place. Acamas and Demophon withdrew to Scyros, where they were joined by their father (see THESEUS, VII); and it was from here that they left for the Trojan War, with Elephenor. They played a part in the fall of the city, being among the heroes inside the Wooden Horse.

During the journey back from Troy, Demophon (or Acamas) had an amorous adventure in Thrace with PHYLLIS as a result of which he subsequently died.

The Athenians were indebted to Demophon for the PALLADIUM.

During Demophon's reign

ORESTES came to Athens, pursued by the Eumenides. In this same period the HERACLIDS came seeking help against Eurystheus.

Dendritis (*Δενδρῖτις*) This was the name that Helen used in Rhodes (from *δένδρον* tree). See POLYXO (2).

Dercynus (*Δέρκυνος*) The brother of ALEBION.

Deucalion (*Δευκαλίων*)

1. The son of Prometheus and Clymene (1) or Celaeno (1) (Table 8). His wife was Pyrrha (1), the daughter of Epimetheus and PANDORA. When Zeus felt that the people of the Bronze Age were so steeped in vice that he had best destroy them, he decided to unleash a great flood and drown them. He decided to spare only two decent people, Deucalion and his wife. On Prometheus' advice, Deucalion and Pyrrha built a big chest and got inside. For nine days and nine nights they floated on the waters, and finally ran ashore on the mountains of Thessaly. When the flood had abated Zeus sent Hermes down to tell them they could make one wish, and it would be granted. Deucalion wished that they could have some companions. Zeus then told both of them to throw their mother's bones over their shoulders, meaning stones – the bones of the Earth, the great Mother of all. So Deucalion threw stones over his shoulder, and from the stones he threw sprang men. Pyrrha followed suit, and from her stones sprang women.

   Deucalion and Pyrrha had many descendants (Table 5).
2. The son of Minos and Pasiphae, and brother of Catreus, Glaucus (5), and Androgeos. He was a friend of Theseus, and took part in the Calydonian hunt and was one of the Argonauts, according to Hyginus.

Dexamenus (*Δεξαμενός*) A king of Olenus in Achaea. Heracles sought refuge with him after his defeat by Augias (see HERACLES, III), and was promised the hand of Dexamenus' daughter Mnesimache. Heracles then went off on an expedition, and on his return he found her forcibly betrothed to the Centaur Eurytion (1) (see CENTAURS).

Dexamenus gave two of his daughters, Theronice and Theraephone, in marriage to the MOLIONIDAE.

Dexicreon (*Δεξικρέων*) A merchant from Samos. While in port in Cyprus, he was advised by Aphrodite to load his boat solely with water and to leave as quickly as possible. Then when he got out to sea a flat calm occurred, and he was able to sell his water to the becalmed ships at a handsome profit. As a token of his gratitude he put up a statue to the goddess.

Diana The Italo-Roman goddess identified with ARTEMIS. The two oldest of her shrines were the one at Capua, where she went by the name of Diana Tifatina, and the one at Aricia (on the shores of Lake Nemi, near Rome), where she was called Diana Nemorensis, Diana of the Woods. It was said that the Diana of Nemi was Taurian Artemis, brought to Italy by ORESTES. It was also said that Artemis had given sanctuary to HIPPOLYTUS (1) after his death and his resurrection at the hands of Asclepius. She had brought him to Italy, and hidden him under another name in her sanctuary at Aricia, where she had made him priest in charge. Hippolytus was identifed with VIRBIUS. At Capua, there was a legend about a hind that was sacred to Diana, an incredibly long-lived animal, whose fate was bound up with the preservation of the city.

Dicte (*Δίκτη*) Another name for BRITOMARTIS. Dicte was loved by Minos, leapt into the sea and was saved by fishermen's nets.

Dictys (*Δίκτυς*) The brother of POLYDECTES, and the protector of DANAE and PERSEUS. It was he who, on the shore of Seriphos, caught the chest in which Perseus and his mother were floating. He was sometimes portrayed as a simple fisherman. After Polydectes' death, he ruled over Seriphos.

Dido The queen and founder of Carthage. Mutto, the king of Tyre, had a son Pygmalion (1) and a daughter Elissa (Elissa was Dido's Tyrian name). When Mutto died he left his kingdom to his children, and Pygmalion was recognized as king, even though he was still a minor. Elissa married her uncle Sicharbas, the priest of Heracles, but Pygmalion had Sicharbas assassinated so that he could seize his treasure. However, Elissa secretly had Sicharbas' treasure loaded on to boats and fled with some disaffected nobles. She visited Cyprus, where a priest of Zeus slept with her, and there her companions carried off twenty-four maidens consecrated to Aphrodite and made them their wives. On reaching Africa, Dido asked the local inhibitants for some land. They allowed her to take 'as much as they could enclose in the hide of a bull', so Dido had the hide cut into thin strips which, when tied together, enabled her to surround a large plot of land. Soon the citizens of Utica encouraged the newcomers to found a city. When work commenced on the first site that was chosen, the head of an ox was dug up. This was considered inauspicious, so the site was changed, and this time a horse's head was dug up: this seemed to augur well for the warlike valour of the future city. The city prospered and attracted colonists, and a neighbouring king, Iarbas, expressed a wish to marry Dido, threatening war if she refused. Dido dared not refuse, so she asked for three months' delay to placate her first husband's spirit with expiatory sacrifices. At the end of that time she mounted a funeral pyre and killed herself.

This was the theme on which Virgil based the story of Dido and Aeneas. Aeneas was driven by a storm to Carthage, the city founded by Dido. He was welcomed, and, at a banquet in his honour, related his adventures and told of the fall of Troy. He became Dido's guest and she fell in love with him. During a hunting party, through the will of Venus and at Juno's instigation, they were brought together by a storm which forced them to take shelter in a cave, where she became his mistress. King Iarbas, angered at seeing a stranger preferred to himself, asked Jupiter to send Aeneas away. Jupiter, aware that Aeneas' destiny was to establish the future of Rome in Italy, commanded Aeneas to leave. Aeneas obeyed his instructions. When Dido learned the truth, she built a funeral pyre on which she took her own life. In Virgil's version Dido had been married previously, to Sychaeus. Her sister Anna also appeared in the story, though apparently no mention of her had been made before (see ANNA PERENNA).

Diomedes (*Διομήδης*)
1. A king of Thrace, the son of Ares and Pyrene (2). He used to have strangers who came into his land eaten by his mares. Eurystheus charged Heracles to put an end to this and bring the mares back to Mycenae. Heracles killed Diomedes, in one tradition, by feeding him to his own mares. (See HERACLES, II.)
2. An Aetolian hero, son of Tydeus and Deipyle (see ADRASTUS and Table 1). He took part in the Trojan War and in the expedition of the Epigoni against Thebes. His first exploit was to take revenge on the sons of Agrius, who had ousted his grandfather Oeneus from Calydon and given it to their own father. Diomedes came from his adopted country Argos (see TYDEUS) with Alcmaeon, and killed all Agrius' sons except Onchestus and Thersites, who fled to the Peloponnese. As Oeneus was an old man, Diomedes gave his kingdom to Andraemon, who had married Oeneus' daughter Gorge (1). When Oeneus was murdered by Agrius' surviving sons, Diomedes gave him a magnificent funeral. Diomedes then married Aegiale, his aunt or his cousin (Table 1).

Diomedes set out for Troy as one of Helen's former suitors. In the tales of the Trojan cycle he was Odysseus' companion in many of his undertakings: in some legends he was at Odysseus' side in Scyros, trying to secure Achilles' support; he helped Odysseus persuade Agamemnon to sacrifice Iphigenia at Aulis, and accompanied him on his mission to Achilles when he was seeking to appease the hero's anger and persuade him to return to the fighting; he took part in Odysseus' excercise the night after the mission to Achilles; with Odysseus he killed DOLON and also RHESUS. Then there was Diomedes' meeting with GLAUCUS (2). Diomedes competed in the funeral games held in honour of Patroclus. In legends subsequent to the *Iliad* he accompanied Odysseus to Lemnos to fetch PHILOCTETES. Diomedes was a formidable fighter, who wounded the goddess Aphrodite in battle. He was a fluent speaker and figured in various war councils of the Achaean chiefs. When Achilles killed Thersites after the latter's remarks about Penthesilea, Diomedes lost his temper, reminded Achilles that Thersites was a relative of his, and demanded that the Amazon's body be thrown into the Scamander.

Of all the return journeys from Troy, Diomedes' was considered to have been the happiest, but his wife AEGIALEA had been unfaithful to him, and on his arrival at Argos he only just escaped the traps she set for him. He took refuge at Hera's altar, and then fled to Italy to the court of King Daunus. Diomedes fought against Daunus' enemies, but, in a later tradition, Daunus denied him the reward he had promised. Diomedes cursed the country, and doomed it to sterility every year it was not cultivated by his fellow-countrymen, the Aetolians. He then took possession of the country, but Daunus eventually killed him.

Diomedes was credited with founding a whole series of cities in southern Italy.

Dione (*Διώνη*) One of the goddesses of the first divine generation. Sometimes she was a daughter of Uranus and Gaia; sometimes she was a daughter of Oceanus and Tethys; sometimes she was numbered among Atlas' daughters. She had children by Tantalus – Niobe (2) and Pelops – and one tradition claimed that she was the mother of APHRODITE.

Dionysus (*Διόνυσος*) Also called Bacchus (*Βάκχος*), and identified in Rome with the Italic god Liber Pater, Dionysus was essentially the god of the vine, of wine and of mystic ecstasy. Dionysus also absorbed several similar cults from Asia Minor, and these partial identifications gave rise to various episodes in his mythology.

Dionysus was an Olympian deity, the son of Zeus and Semele (Table 3). Semele asked Zeus to show himself to her in all his majesty. This he did, but Semele was unable to endure the sight of the lightning which flashed about her lover, and was struck dead. Zeus took the unborn child, which was still only in its sixth month, from her womb and sewed it up inside his thigh. In due course it was born alive and perfectly formed. This was Dionysus, the 'twice-born' god. The child was given to King Athamas and his wife Ino to rear, with instructions to dress Dionysus as a girl in order to deceive Hera, who wanted to destroy the child as the fruit of her husband's adultery. But Hera was not deceived, and she sent Ino and Athamas mad (see LEUCOTHEA (1), PALAEMON (3) and ATHAMAS). Therefore Zeus entrusted Dionysus to the Nymphs of Nysa (see HYADES). To avoid Hera recognizing him again, Zeus transformed him into a kid.

When he grew to manhood, Dionysus discovered the vine and its uses, but Hera drove him mad, and he wandered throughout Egypt and Syria. From there he went up the Asian coast until he reached Phrygia, where Cybele initiated him into the rites of her cult. Cured of his madness, Dionysus went to Thrace where he encountered the hostility of LYCURGUS (2). From Thrace he went to India, which he conquered by force of arms (he had an army with him) and also by enchantments and mystic powers. Here originated his triumphal train, which thereafter accompanied him everywhere. This consisted of a chariot drawn by panthers and bedecked with vine-branches and ivy; the Sileni; the Bacchantes; the Satyrs; and all sorts of minor deities such as Priapus.

Returning to Greece, Dionysus reached Boeotia, his mother's native land. In Thebes, where PENTHEUS reigned, he introduced his revels in which the whole populace – and especially the women – were seized with mystical ecstasy and went out of the city into the wild countryside. Pentheus opposed the introduction of rites as subversive as these; he was duly punished for his opposition, as was his mother AGAVE. Dionysus demonstrated his power in a similar fashion at Argos, driving King Proetus' daughters mad (see PROETIDES).

On one occasion Dionysus decided to go to Naxos and hired some Tyrrhenian pirates to take him there. However, the pirates headed for Asia, intending to sell their passenger as a slave. When Dionysus realized this he turned their oars into serpents, filled the ship with ivy, made it echo with the sounds of invisible flutes, and immobilized it with garlands of vine. The pirates went mad and threw themselves overboard, where they became dolphins.

Once Dionysus' power had won world-wide recognition and his cult had been widely established he retired to Olympus. Subsequently he decided to seek out the shade of his mother, Semele, in the Underworld and restore her to life. He went by way of Lake Lerna, a bottomless lake which offered the quickest access to Hades, but as he did not know the way had to ask Prosymnus (or POLYMNUS). Down in the Underworld Dionysus persuaded Hades to release Semele in exchange for something that he held very dear. From among his favourite plants Dionysus gave up the myrtle, and this is said to be why initiates into Dionysus' mysteries wore crowns of myrtle.

It was as a god, after his ascent to Olympus, that Dionysus rescued Ariadne from Naxos (see ARIADNE and THESEUS, III).

Dionysus also took part in the war of the Gods against the Titans; he killed Eurytus (I) with a blow from his thyrsus (a long staff entwined with ivy), which was his usual emblem.

Dionysus, god of wine and inspiration, was worshipped with tumultuous processions in which the spirits of the earth and of fecundity appeared, their likenesses evoked by masks. From these revels evolved the more ordinary representations of the theatre, comedy, tragedy and satyric drama. From the second century BC, the mysteries of Dionysus made their way into Italy, where they took root very quickly among the people of southern and central Italy. In 186 BC, the Roman Senate prohibited the celebration of the Bacchanalia. But various mystic sects still retained the Dionysiac tradition. In all probability, Caesar authorized the Bacchic ceremonies once again, and Dionysus still played an important part in the religion of the Imperial Age.

Diopatra (*Διόπατρα*) See TERAMBUS.

Dioscuri (*Διόσκουροι*) Castor and Pollux, the 'Sons of Zeus'. They were the brothers of Helen and Clytemnestra (Table 2). Their mother, Leda, was married to Tyndareus, and in Homer Castor and Pollux are both sons of Tyndareus and are known as the Tyndarides. In other traditions, on the night when Zeus mated with Leda in the form of a swan, Leda also slept with Tyndareus; of the two pairs of twins that resulted, Pollux and Helen were attributed to Zeus, Castor and Clytemnestra to Tyndareus. One version holds that each pair of twins was born from an egg laid by Leda after her union with Zeus. They were born on Mount Taygetus in Sparta. They were pre-eminently Dorian heroes and became engaged in strife with Theseus, the Athenian. When Theseus and Pirithous went to the

Underworld to win Persephone's hand, the Dioscuri successfully attacked Attica (see THESEUS, VI).

The Dioscuri took part in the expedition of the ARGONAUTS (see AMYCUS). They were also present in the Calydonian boar-hunt (see MELEAGER) and helped JASON and Peleus lay waste Iolcus.

The Dioscuri became divine after the following adventures. Tyndareus' brothers were Icarius, Aphareus and Leucippus (1). Aphareus had two sons, Idas and Lynceus (2). In one version Leucippus' daughters, Hilaera and Phoebe (2) (the Leucippidae), married Castor and Pollux, but at a festival in Sparta given by the Dioscuri in honour of Aeneas and Paris, who were visiting Meneaus intending to kidnap Helen, the sons of Aphareus got drunk and reproached their cousins, Castor and Pollux, for having married their wives without paying the usual dowry. A fight ensued in which one of the Dioscuri was killed, along with Idas and Lynceus. In later versions, such as Theocritus' *Idyll* XXII, the Leucippidae were engaged to Idas and Lynceus but were kidnapped by the Dioscuri at the wedding. A struggle ensued in which Lynceus killed Castor but was himself killed by Pollux. Idas was about to kill Pollux when Zeus killed Idas with a thunderbolt and took Pollux up to Olympus. In another tradition Castor and Lynceus decided to settle the issue by single combat: Castor killed Lynceus and Idas was on the point of felling Castor in revenge when he was killed by a thunderbolt from Zeus. Hyginus said that Lynceus was killed by Castor, but when Idas wanted to bury him Castor tried to stop him on the pretext that Lynceus had not shown courage in the fight and had 'died like a woman'. Enraged, Idas stabbed Castor. In another account he attacked him under the column which he was building on Lynceus' tomb, and was in turn killed by Pollux. There is another episode, however, where the emnity between the Dioscuri and their cousins is not on account of their wives. They mounted an expedition with Lynceus and Idas to steal cattle in Arcadia. Idas was appointed to divide the spoils. He killed a bull and divided it into four pieces; whoever ate his portion first was to have half the booty; the second to finish was to have the rest. Idas immediately ate his portion, then that of his brother, and took all the booty. The Dioscuri then set up an ambush for their cousins, but Lynceus saw Castor hidden in the crack of a chestnut tree and pointed him out to Idas, who killed him with his spear. At this point Zeus killed Idas with a thunderbolt and took Pollux up to Olympus. But Pollux refused to accept the immortality offered him by the god if Castor remained in the Underworld. At this Zeus allowed each of them to spend one day in two among the gods.

In Roman legends the Dioscuri appeared as participants in the battle of Lake Regillus alongside the Romans; it was they who came to the city to announce the victory, and they watered their horses at the Lacus Juturnae in the Forum Romanum. Juturna, the Nymph of this spring was said to be their sister. The Temple of Castor stood near this spring.

Dirce (*Δίρκη*) The wife of Lycus (3). See AMPHION.

Dis Pater A god of the Underworld in Rome. At a very early date, he was identified with Pluto, the HADES of the Greeks.

Dolius (*Δολίος*) The old gardener who looked after Odysseus' domain during the latter's absence. He helped Odysseus defeat the suitors.

Dolon (*Δόλων*) A Trojan who was a very swift runner. When Hector suggested that a spy should be sent into the camp of the Achaeans, and promised to give the man who accepted this mission Achilles' chariot and his two divine horses, Dolon agreed to undertake it. He donned a wolf's pelt and set off at night. But he ran into Diomedes (2) and Odysseus, who captured him. They forced him to tell them how the Trojan army was positioned, and then Diomedes killed him.

Doris (*Δωρίς*) The daughter of Oceanus and the wife of Nereus. She was the mother of the NEREIDS.

Dorus (*Δῶρος*)

1. The hero who gave his name to the Dorians. Dorus was the son of Hellen and Orseis (Table 5) and the brother of Aeolus (1), the eponymous hero of the Aeolians. In this version Dorus and his descendants lived in the region of Phthiotis, in Thessaly, then emigrated to the area round Mount Olympus and Ossa, then moved westward into the interior, towards the range of the Pindus, later withdrawing to the area around Mount Oeta, before finally settling in the Peloponnese.
2. The son of Apollo and Phthia, and the brother of Laodocus and Polypoetes (1). The three brothers were said to have been slain by AETOLUS who seized their kingdom of Aetolia, to the north of the Gulf of Corinth.

Drimacus (*Δρίμακος*) In myth the people of Chios were the first people to buy slaves, but a number of them escaped to the mountains, from where, under Drimacus' leadership, they raided their former masters' territory. The Chians eventually agreed to pay an annual tribute if the slaves would not attack them, but they still put a price on Drimacus' head. Drimacus persuaded a young man whom he loved to cut his head off and collect the reward. This was done, after which the slaves resumed their brigandage. The Chians built a shrine to Drimacus and initiated a cult in his honour. Whenever anyone was being plotted against by the slaves, Drimacus would appear in a dream and warn him or her.

Dryas (*Δρύας*)

1. A son of Ares who took part in the Calydonian hunt. He can perhaps be identified with the Dryas who was a brother of TEREUS. When Tereus found out that his son Itys was fated to be slain by a near relation, he believed Dryas to be planning this. He killed Dryas, but Dryas was innocent: it was Procne who soon slew Itys (see PHILOMELA).
2. See PALLENE (1).

Dryope (*Δρυόπη*)

1. According to Antoninus Libera-

lis, a daughter of Dryops; she looked after her father's flocks near Mount Oeta. The Hamadryads made her their companion and Apollo fell in love with her. To come closer to her he turned himself into a tortoise. The girl played with him as though he were a ball. When he found himself in Dryope's lap he took the shape of a serpent, and coupled with her. Dryope ran home, but said nothing to her parents. Soon she married Andraemon, and gave birth to a son, Amphissus. One day when Dryope had gone to sacrifice to the Hamadryads, near a temple to Apollo built by her son, the Hamadryads carried her off and made her one of themselves. A tall poplar sprang up at the place where she was kidnapped, and a spring gushed forth from the ground.

Ovid relates a slightly different version. When Amphissus was still quite small, Dryope went up into the mountain to make a sacrifice to the Nymphs, but she saw a tree with beautiful shining flowers and picked some of them. She was unaware that this tree was the transformed body of the Nymph Lotis. Blood ran from the branches, and in her anger the Nymph changed Dryope into a tree like herself.

2. In the *Aeneid* Dryope was a Nymph beloved of the god Faunus.

Dryops (*Δρύοψ*) Dryops gave his name to the Dryopians, who were said to have been one of the first peoples to occupy the Hellenic peninsula. He is sometimes portrayed as the son of River Spercheius by POLYDORA, and sometimes as the son of Apollo by Dia. His descendants, who originally inhabited the region round Mount Parnassus, were expelled by the Dorians. Some settled in Euboea, others in Thessaly, still others in the Peloponnese, and even in Cyprus. In the Arcadian version of his legend, which made him a descendant of Lycaon (2), Dryops had a daughter who was loved by Hermes and became the mother of Pan. In the Thessalian version, his daughter DRYOPE coupled with Apollo, and give birth to Amphissus.

E

Ecbasus (Ἔκβασος) According to Apollodorus, the son of Argos (1) and Evadne (3), and brother of Piren (2), Epidaurus and Criasus.

Echemus (Ἔχεμος) The son of Aeropus and husband of TIMANDRA (Table 2). Echemus succeeded Lycurgus (1) on the Arcadian throne, and he defended the Peloponnese against the HERACLIDS' first invasion. Echemus agreed to fight Hyllus, the Heraclids' leader, in single combat: if Echemus were to win, the Heraclids would not invade the Peloponnese again for fifty, or a hundred, years. Echemus killed Hyllus, and the Heraclids withdrew. Echemus' tomb is said to have been at Megara, beside Hyllus', but his grave is also supposed to be at Tegea. According to one account, Echemus participated in the expedition led by the Dioscuri against Attica to release Helen from Theseus.

Echetlus (Ἔχετλος) An Attic hero. During the battle of Marathon he is supposed to have appeared on the battlefield wearing peasant's clothes and to have killed many Persians. After the victory he disappeared: an oracle ordered that a sanctuary should be dedicated to Echetlus.

Echetus (Ἔχετος) A hero of Epirus and an archetypal tyrant. In the *Odyssey* the beggar Irus was threatened with being handed over to Echetus, who would then have had Irus' nose and ears cut off and thrown to his dogs. Echetus' daughter Metope (2) had an intrigue with a lover; as a punishment Echetus mutilated the lover and blinded Metope with bronze needles. He then incarcerated her and gave her grains of bronze, promising that she would regain her sight when she had ground them into flour.

Echidna (Ἔχιδνα) A monster with the torso of a woman and a serpent's tail instead of legs. According to Hesiod she was the daughter of Phorcys and Ceto; other versions claim that she was descended from Tartarus and Gaia, or from Styx, or from Chrysaor. Echidna inhabited a cave either in Sicily or in the Peloponnese. She used to devour passers-by until eventually she was killed by Argos (2). Many monstrous offspring were attributed to her: by Typhon she is said to have given birth to ORTHRUS, CERBERUS, the HYDRA OF LERNA and the CHIMAERA. The dragons guarding the Golden Fleece and the Garden of the Hesperides are said to have been Echidna's offspring, as was the eagle of PROMETHEUS.

In a quite different tradition related by Herodotus, when Heracles visited Scythia he left his horses to graze while he slept, and when he awoke he found they had disappeared. As he searched he came across Echidna in a cave; she promised to return his horses if he agreed to couple with her. He consented, and as a result Echidna gave birth to Agathyrsus, Gelonus and Scythes.

Echion (*'Εχίων*)
1. One of the five Spartoi, or men born from the dragon's teeth sown by CADMUS, who were still surviving at the foundation of Thebes. He married Agave. She gave birth to PENTHEUS.
2. One of the Argonauts, the twin brother of Eurytus (3).
3. For another Echion, see PORTHEUS (2).

Echo (*'Ηχώ*) A Nymph of the trees and springs. In one account Echo was loved by Pan but loved a Satyr instead, who shunned her; in revenge, Pan sent some shepherds mad, who tore her to pieces. In another account Echo loved Narcissus unrequitedly and pined away; when she died her voice alone remained – this repeated the last syllables of spoken words.

Eëtion (*'Ηετίων*) A king of Thebes in Mysia and the father of Andromache. He was killed by ACHILLES. Achilles admired Eëtion's courage to such an extent that he did not strip him of his arms but buried them with his body, giving him lavish funeral rites. The Nymphs planted an elm tree on his grave.

Egeria A Roman Nymph who formed part of the cult of DIANA at Nemi. Egeria also had a cult at the Porta Capena. She was the adviser (and in some accounts wife or lover) of King NUMA POMPILIUS, prescribing the religious practices which he followed. When he died she wept so much that she became a spring.

Elatus (*"Ελατος*)
1. The eldest son of ARCAS. When Arcas divided up his lands Elatus was given the area around Mount Cyllene; he later added Phocis to this, assisting the natives against the Phlegyans; he then founded the town of Elatea.
2. A Thessalian counterpart of ELATUS (1). This Elatus, from Larissa, was sometimes linked with CAENEUS (see POLYPHEMUS (1)).

Electra (*'Ηλέκτρα*)
1. One of the daughters of Oceanus and Tethys, who married Thaumas and then gave birth to Iris and to the Harpies. Electra was one of Persephone's companions, and was present when she was carried off by Hades.
2. One of the PLEIADES. Zeus fathered her child Dardanus (Table 4), who left Samothrace and went to the Troad, where he founded the royal dynasty of Troy.

Electra had another son, IASION. Electra is also said to have had a third son, named Emathion, who ruled over Samothrace, but more frequently this third child of hers by Zeus is named as Harmonia (2). In the Italian version of Electra's legend, she was the wife of the Etruscan king Corythus (1), and Dardanus and Iasion were born in Italy.

Electra is also linked to the legend of the PALLADIUM. She was later transformed with her sisters into the constellation of the Pleiades.
3. Daughter of Agamemnon and Clytemnestra (Table 2). After Agamemnon was murdered by Aegisthus and Clytemnestra, Electra was treated as a slave; she was spared only on the intervention of her mother. In

some accounts Electra saved her brother, the young Orestes, by entrusting him to their old tutor, who took him away from Mycenae. To prevent her giving birth to a son who might avenge her father, Electra was either married to a peasant who lived far from the city, or, having been betrothed to Castor and then Polymestor, was imprisoned at Mycenae.

On Orestes' return, she recognized him at Agamemnon's tomb and played an active part in the assassination of Aegisthus and Clytemnestra. When the Erinyes pursued Orestes for this crime, she devoted herself to his welfare. In Euripides' *Orestes* she fought at her brother's side against the local populace, who wanted to condemn the murderers to death. Electra was the main character in Sophocles' *Aletes* (now lost): when Orestes and Pylades went to Tauris, rumours started at Mycenae that they had died, and that Electra's sister Iphigenia had killed Orestes. Aegisthus' son Aletes assumed the throne and Electra went to Delphi, where she met Iphigenia who had gone there with Orestes. Electra was about to blind her when she saw her brother. Electra and Orestes returned to Mycenae and killed Aletes. Electra married Pylades and went with him to Phocis; their children were Medon (3) and Strophius (2).

Electryon (*'Ηλεκτρύων*) One of the sons of Perseus and Andromeda, and the father of ALCMENE (Table 7). For his death see AMPHITRYON and PTERELAUS.

Elephenor (*'Ελεφήνωρ*) Grandson of ABAS (1) whom he succeeded on the Euboean throne. One day Elephenor saw his grandfather being ill-treated by a servant: he aimed a blow at the servant's head, but his club struck Abas and killed him. Elephenor then went into exile. As one of Helen's suitors he took part in the Trojan War, to which he led the Abantes. Since he could not set foot on Euboean soil he mustered the troops from a rock just off the shore. In the *Iliad* he was killed at Troy by Agenor, but in other traditions he survived the war and settled on Othronus, an island off Sicily, from which he was driven by a serpent. He then went to Epirus in the area of Abantia or Amantia.

Eleusis (*'Ελευσίς*) The eponymous hero of Eleusis. According to certain accounts he was married to Cothone; their son was TRIPTOLEMUS. Demeter tried to make Triptolemus immortal by plunging him into a fire. On seeing this, Eleusis cried out, which enraged Demeter and she killed him. See also DEMOPHON (1).

Elis (*'Ηλις*) The son of Eurypyla and Poseidon. Elis succeeded his grandfather Endymion to the throne and then founded the city to which he gave his name.

Elissa See DIDO.

Elpenor (*'Ελπήνωρ*) One of Odysseus' companions; he was changed into a pig by Circe, who later restored his human form. When Odysseus was about to leave Circe's island, Elpenor was asleep on the terrace of her palace; when his name was called he started up, half-asleep, and fell to his death from the terrace. Later Odysseus met the shade of Elpenor in the Underworld and was asked to carry out Elpenor's funeral rites, which he did on his return to the upper world.

Elymus (*"Ελυμος*) The bastard son of Anchises and the companion of AEGESTES (1), with whom he founded several Sicilian cities.

Empusa (*"Εμπουσα*) One of the creatures in Hecate's entourage: she belonged to the Underworld and filled the night with terrors. Empusa could assume various shapes and appeared particularly to women and children. She fed on human flesh, and often assumed the form of a young girl to attract her victims.

Enarophorus (*'Εναροφόρος*) One of HIPPOCOON's sons; when he tried to rape Helen, Tyndareus entrusted her to Theseus.

Endymion (*'Ενδυμίων*) Endymion is most frequently depicted as the son of Aethlius and Calyce, though sometimes his father is said to have been Zeus. He led the Aeolians from Thessaly to Elis, and ruled over them. Then he married (his wife's name varies) and had three sons – Paeon, EPEIUS (1) and AETOLUS – and a daughter, Eurycyde.

Selene saw Endymion, depicted in the legend as a young shepherd of great beauty, fell violently in love with him and seduced him. At Selene's request Zeus promised to grant Endymion one wish; he chose the gift of eternal sleep, remaining young forever. Some versions claim that it was during this sleep that Selene saw him and fell in love with him. Sometimes the Peloponnese is the location of the legend, sometimes Caria (see also HYPNUS). Endymion is said to have given his lover fifty daughters. The hero NAXOS is sometimes said to have been born of their union.

Enipeus (*'Ενιπεύς*) A Thessalian river-god. See TYRO and Table 6.

Entoria (*'Εντωρία*) When Saturn lived in Italy (see GOLDEN AGE) a peasant named Icarius gave hospitality to the god, who slept with his host's daughter, Entoria, and fathered four children: Janus, Hymnus (2), Faustus and Felix. Saturn also taught his host the art of cultivating the vine and making wine; and he advised him to share these skills with his neighbours. Icarius invited his neighbours and gave them wine; this made them all fall asleep. When they awoke they thought they had been poisoned, and stoned Icarius to death. His grandsons hanged themselves in grief. An epidemic then broke out among the Romans which the oracle at Delphi declared was the result of Saturn's anger. To appease the god, Lutatius Catulus founded the temple of Saturn at the foot of the Capitol and built an altar decorated with four faces (Entoria's four children); he also gave the month January its Roman name Januarius (the month of Janus). Saturn transformed Icarius' whole family into a constellation. Compare the myth of ERIGONE (1).

Enyo (*'Ενυώ*)

1. A goddess of war, most frequently depicted as daughter of ARES,

though sometimes as his mother or his sister. She appears covered in blood, and striking attitudes of violence. In Rome she was identified with BELLONA

2. One of the GRAEAE.

Eos (*'Ηώς*) The personification of the Dawn. She belongs to the generation of the Titans. She was the daughter of Hyperion and Theia and the sister of Helios and Selene, or, according to other traditions, the daughter of PALLAS (3). By Astraeus she was the mother of the Winds: Zephyrus, Boreas and Notus; and also of Heosphorus and the Stars. She was depicted as a goddess whose rosy fingers opened the gates of heaven to the chariot of the Sun.

Her legend consists almost entirely of her intrigues. She first slept with Ares; this earned her the wrath of Aphrodite who punished her by turning her into a nymphomaniac. Her lovers were ORION, whom she abducted and carried off to Delos; then CEPHALUS, whom she carried off to Syria, where she bore him a son, PHAETHON (more commonly held to be the son of Helios). Finally she abducted TITHONUS. She bore him two sons, Emathion and MEMNON.

Eosphorus (*'Εωσφόρος*) See HEOSPHORUS.

Epaphus (*"Επαφος*) After Io was transformed into a cow, she wandered, pursued by the wrath of Hera, until she found asylum on the banks of the Nile. Here she regained her human form and gave birth to a son, Epaphus. Hera transferred her hatred to Io's son, and ordered the Curetes to hide him. Zeus killed the Curetes and Io continued her search. She learnt that Epaphus was being brought up by the wife of the king of Byblos in Syria, went there and took him back to Egypt. When Epaphus became a man he succeeded his adoptive father, Telegonus, as ruler. Epaphus married Memphis, daughter of the river-god Nile, and fathered LIBYA, Lysianassa and THEBE (4). Sometimes his wife is said to be CASSIOPIA.

Epeius (*'Επειός*)

1. Son of Endymion whom he succeeded as king of Elis (see AETOLUS). For a time part of the Elean race bore the name of Epeians after him.

2. Son of Panopeus. He was one of the Phocian leaders in the Trojan War and distinguished himself by his boxing during the funeral games for Patroclus. With Athena's help he built the Wooden Horse with which to capture Troy. Returning from Troy, Epeius became separated from his party and landed in southern Italy, where he dedicated the tools with which he had built the Wooden Horse to Athena. In another tradition he was cast up on the Italian coast by a storm; when he disembarked, the Trojan captives whom he left aboard set fire to his ships, whereupon he founded the city of Pisa, calling it after the Elean city of the same name.

In Callimachus' *Iambi* Epeius was said to have made a statue of Hermes before he made the Wooden Horse. The statue was swept away when the River SCAMANDER flooded in an attempt to halt Achilles; it came ashore at Ainos, where some fishermen caught it in their nets. Displeased with their catch, they tried to chop it up for firewood, but could only make a small cut in one shoulder. They then put the whole statue in the fire, but it would not burn. Finally they threw it back into the sea, but when it again became caught in their nets they realized it was a divine image and raised a shrine for it.

Ephialtes (*'Εφιάλτης*) One of the ALOADAE. See also GIANTS.

Epidius A hero from Nuceria in Italy. One day he disappeared into the River Sarno; later he reappeared with bulls' horns on his forehead, a sign that he had been transformed into a river-god.

Epigeus (*'Επειγεύς*) The king of Budeion in Thessaly. He killed a kinsman, was exiled, and fled to the court of Peleus. He accompanied Achilles to Troy, where he was slain by Hector.

Epigoni (*'Επίγονοι*) Ten years after the failure of the expedition of the Seven against Thebes (see ADRASTUS and ALCMAEON (1)), the sons of the heroes who had fallen decided to avenge their fathers. The oracle promised them victory if they took Alcmaeon (1) as their leader. Alcmaeon reluctantly accepted at the bidding of his mother, ERIPHYLE. Those who took part in the war were Alcmaeon (1); AMPHILOCHUS (1); Aegialeus; DIOMEDES (2); PROMACHUS (2); STHENELUS (3); THERSANDRUS (2); and EURYALUS (1) (Pausanias also mentions Timeas and Adrastus, both brothers of Thersandrus). The Epigoni began their campaign by ravaging the villages around Thebes. The Thebans advanced to meet them, led by Laodamas, son of Eteocles, and the two sides met at Glissas. Laodamas slew Aegialeus, but was himself killed by Alcmaeon; the Thebans were forced to retreat. During the night, on the advice of the seer Tiresias, the inhabitants of the city fled. The Epigoni entered Thebes the next morning and pillaged it; they devoted a large part of the spoils to Pythian Apollo.

Epimelides (*'Επιμηλίδες*) Nymphs who watched over sheep. One day some shepherds saw the Nymphs dancing near their shrine. The shepherds jeered at them and pretended that they could surpass them. The Nymphs accepted the challenge; and the shepherds, who were unskilled in dancing, were easily beaten. As punishment the Nymphs turned the shepherds into trees.

Epimetheus (*'Επιμηθεύς*) One of the four children of Iapetus and of either Clymene (1), or of Asia (Table 8). He belonged to the race of Titans; his brothers were Atlas (1), Menoetius (2), and PROMETHEUS. Epimetheus ('Hindsight') formed a pair with Prometheus ('Foresight'). He was the tool used by Zeus to deceive the highly skilled Prometheus; after the latter had outwitted Zeus on two separate occasions he forbade Epimetheus to accept even the smallest of presents from Zeus. However Epimetheus could not resist when Zeus offered him PANDORA. In this way, Epimetheus became responsible for all the miseries of mankind. Epimetheus and Pandora were the parents of Pyrrha (1).

Epione (*'Ηπιόνη*) The companion of ASCLEPIUS. Their children were generally considered to have included the daughters IASO, PANACEA, Aglaea, HYGIEIA and Aceso (the latter being an Athenian addition), and the sons MACHAON and PODALIRIUS. At Epidaurus, her statue stood beside the image of Asclepius. On Cos she was consideered to be Asclepius' daughter. She is sometimes described as Merops' daughter.

Epopeus (*'Επωπεύς*)
1. A hero of Sicyon. In some accounts he is said to have been the grandson of Canace and Poseidon; in others he is considered to have been their son. He reigned over Sicyon as Corax's heir; but upon the death of Bounos (who had inherited the throne of Corinth from Aeetes after the latter's departure for Colchis) Epopeus succeeded him, thus uniting the two cities under his rule. Epopeus played a role in the legend of ANTIOPE. Antiope's uncle Lycus (3) came and attacked Sicyon, and during the fall of the city Epopeus was slain. Epopeus had a son named Marathon who took refuge in Attica while his father was alive. He returned to Corinth after Epopeus' death.
2. A king of Lesbos, who had an incestuous relationship with his daughter, NYCTIMENE.

Erato (*'Ερατώ*)
1. The Muse of lyric poetry, and especially of love poetry.
2. An Arcadian Dryad, the mother of Azan by Arcas. She was a prophetess, inspired by Pan.

Erebus (*"Ερεβος*) The infernal Shades personified and given a genealogy as the son of Chaos and the brother of Nyx.

Erechtheus (*'Ερεχθεύς*) An 'earthborn' Athenian hero who was reared by Athena. He is often indistinguishable from ERICHTHONIUS. Euripides depicted him as Erichthonius' son, but in the chronology of the first kings of Athens he is the son of PANDION (1) and Zeuxippe (1), and hence Erichthonius' grandson. He had a brother, BUTES (2), and two sisters, PHILOMELA and Procne. When Pandion died Erechtheus took the throne, and Butes became the priest of Athena and Poseidon, the city's protecting deities.

Erechtheus married PRAXITHEA (1). Their sons were CECROPS (2), Pandorus, Metion and (in some accounts) Alcon, Orneus, Thespius and Eupalamus. Their daughters included Protogenia (4), Pandora, Procris, CREUSA (2), Chthonia (2), Orithyia and Merope (6).

During a war between the Athenians and the Eleusinians, the latter had EUMOLPUS, the son of Poseidon and Erechtheus' great-grandson, as their ally. Erechtheus asked the Delphic oracle how he could assure himself of victory. The oracle replied that he would have to sacrifice one of his daughters. Accordingly he sacrificed either CHTHONIA (2) or Protogenia (4). Erechtheus and the Athenians were victorious; Eumolpus was killed in battle but Poseidon was so angry at his son's death that he persuaded Zeus to kill Erechtheus with a thunderbolt. Erechtheus is sometimes credited with the introduction of the festival of the Panathenaea, as well as with the invention of the chariot, under Athena's inspiration.

Erginus (*'Εργῖνος*)

1. The king of the Minyans of Orchomenus, in Boeotia, and the son of Clymenus (2). When his father was killed by a Theban called Perieres (2), Erginus marched on Thebes. After slaying many Thebans he concluded a treaty with the king of the city, under which Thebes would pay him an annual tribute of a hundred cattle for twenty years. When Heracles was on his way home after his successful hunt for the lion of Cithaeron, he met Erginus' heralds as they went to collect the tribute. He mutilated them by cutting off their ears and noses, which he hung round their necks; he told them to take this tribute back to Erginus. The outraged Erginus marched again on Thebes. Creon (2), the king of the city, was prepared to surrender, but Heracles called the youth of Thebes to arms. He received a suit of armour from the hands of Athena, took command of the force, and joined battle with Eriginus. Heracles flooded the plain to prevent the enemy's cavalry from advancing and won the battle, but during the fighting his adoptive father, Amphitryon, was killed; in revenge, Heracles himself slew Erginus. To reward him for his victory Creon gave him the hand of his daughter, Megara (1).

According to one tradition Erginus did not die in this battle but concluded a treaty with Heracles, who imposed on the Minyans a tribute which was twice as large as the one imposed on the Thebans before. He then set out to rebuild his fortune from his ravaged kingdom. When he had amassed a sufficient sum, he married a young woman on the advice of the oracle and fathered two children, the architects AGAMEDES and TROPHONIOS.

2. A son of Poseidon and one of the ARGONAUTS. Sometimes he is identified with Erginus (1). When the *Argo*'s pilot, Tiphys, died, Erginus took his place. Although he was quite young his hair was white, and this provoked derision from the women at Lemnos. In the games they held at Lemnos, he won the prize for running.

Erichthonius (*'Εριχθόνιος*) One of the first kings of Athens. His genealogy varies: sometimes he is described as the son of Atthis, the daughter of Cranaus; sometimes he is portrayed as the child of Athena, fathered by Hephaestus. See ATHENA. Athena hid Erichthonius in a basket, which she entrusted to one of the daughters of Cecrops (1). Filled with curiosity, the girls opened the basket and there they saw the child, with two snakes guarding him. According to certain versions the body of the child terminated in a serpent's tail, as was the case with most of Mother Earth's children. Others claim that when he saw the basket opened Erichthonius escaped in the form of a snake and hid behind the goddess's shield. The girls were terrified by this sight: they went mad and killed themselves by throwing themselves off the Acropolis.

Athena brought up Erichthonius in the sacred precincts of her temple on the Acropolis, and Cecrops later yielded the throne to him. An alternative version claims that Erichthonius expelled AMPHICTYON, who held the throne of Athens at the time.

Erichthonius then married a Naiad named Praxithea (2) and by her had a son named Pandion (1), who succeeded him on the Athenian throne. Erichthonius is generally credited with the invention of the four-horse chariot, the introduction into Attica of the use of silver, and the organization of the Panathenaea, the annual festival in celebration of Athena. Some of these innovations were also attributed to ERECHTHEUS.

Eridanus (*'Ηριδανός*) A river-god, one of the sons of Oceanus and Tethys. He is generally considered as a river of the West. He featured in Heracles' journey to the Garden of Hesperides (see HERACLES, II), and he also played a part in the voyage of the ARGONAUTS. He was said to have guided the *Argo* to the land of the Celts and out into the Adriatic. The River Eridanus was identified sometimes with the Po, and sometimes with the Rhône.

Erigone (*'Ηριγόνη*)

1. The daughter of Icarius (1), who welcomed Dionysus when he came down to earth. The god presented Icarius with a goat-skin bottle full of wine, telling him to let his neighbours taste it. Icarius shared the wine with some shepherds, who became drunk and suspected that Icarius had poisoned them. They beat him to death and abandoned his body. The howling of his dog, Maera, showed Erigone where her father's corpse lay unburied at the foot of a tree: the sight so shocked Erigone that she hanged herself from the tree. Dionysus afflicted the young girls of Athens with madness so that they hanged themselves. The oracle at Delphi explained that this was the god's way of avenging the deaths of Icarius and Erigone. The Athenians then punished the shepherds and instituted a festival in honour of Erigone. During this festival young girls swung from trees on swings; later the girls were replaced by masks in the shape of human faces. This was the legendary origin of the rite of the *oscilla*, performed throughout Italy at the Liberalia, the festival of Liber Pater, who was the Italian Dionysus. Compare the myth of ENTORIA.
2. The daughter of Aegisthus and Clytemnestra and the sister of Aletes (2). It is sometimes claimed that ORESTES was brought to trial for his double murder because of Erigone's intervention. When he was acquitted Erigone committed suicide. According to other authorities, Orestes wanted to kill her with her parents, but Artemis took her to Athens, where she made Erigone her priestess. Another tradition claims that she married Orestes and gave him a son, Penthilus.

Erinyes (*'Ερινύες*) Goddesses, whom the Romans identified with their Furies. They were also known as the Eumenides, which means the 'kindly ones', a name intended to flatter them, and thus to avoid bringing down their wrath upon the speakers. They were engendered by the drops of blood that were spilt on the earth when URANUS was castrated. The Erinyes were analogous with the PARCAE, or MOIRAE, who had no laws other than their own, which even Zeus had to obey. There was originally an indeterminate number of Erinyes, but later it was generally accepted that there were three – Alecto, Tisiphone (1), and Megaera. They were depicted as winged spirits, with their hair entwined with snakes, and they held whips or torches in their hands. They tortured their victims and sent them mad. They lived in Erebus, the darkest pit of the Underworld.

Their essential function was to avenge crime and particularly offences against the family. Althaea's crime against MELEAGER was instigated by the Erinyes as a punishment for Meleager's murder of his uncles; they caused the misfortunes that plagued AGAMEMNON's family after the sacrifice of IPHIGENIA (see also CLYTEMNESTRA and ORESTES); they were equally responsible for OEDIPUS' curse. As protectresses of the social order, the Erinyes punished all crimes likely to disturb this order: they punished overwhelming pride, or *hubris*; they forbade seers and soothsayers to foretell the future too precisely; they punished murderers, since murder endangered the stability of the social group in which it was committed. Murderers were usually banished and wandered from place to place until someone agreed to purify them; often they were struck with madness by the Erinyes (see ORESTES and ALCMAEON (1)). In the *Aeneid*, Virgil depicted the Erinyes in the deeps of Tartarus, tormenting the souls of the dead with their whips and snakes.

Eriphyle (*'Εριφύλη*) The daughter of Talaus, and the sister of ADRASTUS. After Adrastus had been reconciled with his cousin AMPHIARAUS, the reconciliation was sealed by the marriage of Eriphyle to Amphiaraus (Table 1). Four children were born of this marriage: two sons, ALCMAEON (1) and AMPHILOCHUS (1), and two daughters, EURYDICE (4) and Demonassa.

The legend of Eriphyle is linked with the Theban cycle and the expeditions of the Seven and of the Epigoni. When Amphiaraus was asked by Adrastus to take part in the first of these expeditions on behalf of POLYNICES, he refused, because his gift of prophecy told him that he would perish there. But when he married, he had agreed to accept his wife, Eriphyle, as arbitress of any disagreement between himself and Adrastus. The dispute was submitted to her for settlement, but Eriphyle allowed herself to be influenced by Polynices' present – the necklace of HARMONIA (1). When he set out for Thebes, Amphiaraus made his sons swear to avenge him. When the expedition of the EPIGONI, was being prepared Eriphyle accepted a bribe, as she had done before, and forced Alcmaeon to accept the command. On this occasion it was Polynices' son Thersandrus who bribed her, by giving her Harmonia's robe. When ALCMAEON returned from this expedition he killed Eriphyle and dedicated the necklace and the robe to Apollo at Delphi.

Eris (*"Ερις*) The personification of Strife. In Hesiod's *Theogony* she is a daughter of NYX and herself gives birth to Work, Forgetfulness, Hunger, Pain, Battles, Fights, Murders, Killings, Quarrels, Lies, Stories, Disputes, Lawlessness, Ruin and the Oath. In the *Works and Days*,

Hesiod postulates two separate Strifes: one a daughter of Nyx, the other a spirit of emulation, placed by Zeus within the world to give it a healthy sense of competition. Eris was generally portrayed as a female winged spirit. She threw the apple intended for the fairest of the goddesses, which PARIS had the task of awarding; this was the origin of the Trojan War.

Eros (*Ἔρως*) The personification of Love. His personality evolved considerably between the Archaic era and the age of Alexandria and Rome. In the oldest theogonies Eros was considered to be a god born directly from primitive Chaos; and he had an early cult at Thespiae, in the shape of an amorphous stone. Other legends claim that Eros was born from the primordial egg, which was born to Night and then split into two halves, one forming the Earth, and the other the Sky. Eros always remained a fundamental world force, ensuring the continuity of the species and the internal cohesion of the cosmos. Authors of cosmogonies, philosophers and poets speculated on this theme. In Plato's *Symposium* Diotima, a priestess from Mantinea, describes Eros as a demon half-way between god and man. He was born from the union of Expediency (Poros) and Poverty (Penia), and owed some characteristics to his parents: he was always busy in search of his objective, like Poverty, and he could always think of some way of attaining it, like Expediency; but far from being an all-powerful god, he was a perpeteually dissatisfied and restless force.

Different myths gave Eros different genealogies. He is sometimes said to be the son of Eilithyia or of Iris, or of Hermes and Artemis, or – the generally accepted tradition – of Hermes and Aphrodite. One Eros was the son of Hermes and Uranian APHRODITE; another, called Anteros (Reciprocal Love), was born to Ares and Aphrodite. A third was the son of Hermes and Artemis; and this Eros in particular was the winged god well known by poets and sculptors. Cicero, at the end of the treatise on *The Nature of the Gods*, argued that these various theories were invented belatedly to resolve contradictions contained in the primitive legends.

Eros gradually assumed his traditional appearance under the influence of the poets. He was depicted as a child, often winged, but also wingless, whose occupation was to trouble the hearts of humans. He either inflamed them with his torch or wounded them with his arrows. He also attacked Heracles, Apollo (who had poked fun at him for playing the archer), even Zeus and his own mother. The Alexandrine poets loved to portray him playing at knucklebones (antiquity's equivalent of dice), notably with Ganymede. Furthermore, they invented scenes that fitted Eros' new childlike character; these depicted Eros punished by his mother, wounded while plucking roses, and so on; the paintings at Pompeii exemplify this concept of him. Invariably beneath the apparently innocent child could be seen the powerful god capable of inflicting cruel wounds as his whims dictated.

One of the most celebrated

legends in which Eros plays a part is the romantic adventure of PSYCHE.

Erylus A hero of Praeneste. He was the son of the goddess Feronia, and had three separate lives and three bodies. When EVANDER (3) came to settle in Latium he fought with Erylus and defeated him in single combat.

Erymanthus (Ἐρύμανθος)
1. A son of Apollo, who was smitten with blindess by Aphrodite, because he had seen her bathing before she went to couple with ADONIS.
2. The god of the river of the same name in Psophis.

Erysichthon (Ἐρυσίχθων)
1. A Thessalian, either the son or brother of King Triopas. He decided to cut down a grove dedicated to Demeter. Divine warnings failed to divert him from his act of sacrilege. To punish him, Demeter condemned him to suffer perpetual hunger; he quickly devoured all the wealth of his household. Erysichthon's daughter Mestra, who possessed the gift of metamorphosis, conceived the idea of selling herself as a slave. Once she was sold she assumed another form, escaped, and then sold herself again to procure funds for her father. Erysichthon eventually became insane and ate himself.
2. A hero of Athens, the son of Cecrops (1) and Aglaurus. He died young, without leaving descendants. He went to Delos, where he carried off a statue of Eilithyia, and died on his way home.

Erytus (Ἔρυτος) See EURYTUS (3).

Eryx (Ἔρυξ) The hero who gave his name to Mount Eryx in Sicily where he was responsible for constructing the Temple of Aphrodite Erycina. He was the son of Aphrodite and BUTES (3), or, in other traditions, of Aphrodite and Poseidon. When Heracles was returning home with the cattle of Geryon, Eryx challenged him to a fight. Heracles accepted, and killed Eryx. He handed Eryx's kingdom over to its inhabitants, telling them that his descendants would come to take possession of it in due course. This was fulfilled when the Lacedaemonian Dorieu founded a colony on that site in the historical era.

Eteocles (Ἐτεοκλῆς) The son of Oedipus and JOCASTA or in other traditions of Oedipus and EURYGANIA (1), and the brother of POLYNICES.

Eubouleus (Εὐβουλεύς)
1. A brother of TRIPTOLEMUS, and the son of Trochilus. Certain traditions, however, claim that Triptolemus and Eubouleus were the sons of Dysaules and Baubo.
2. A swineherd who was with his pigs at the place where Hades dragged Persephone down into the Underworld; some of his animals were engulfed with the two divinities. This incident was the origin of the rite carried out in the Thesmophoria festival at Eleusis, in which a number of young pigs were sacrificed in Eubouleus' honour, in an underground chamber.
3. The name Eubouleus (meaning 'Good Counsellor' or 'Benevolent') was one of the epithets of Hades; it

was sometimes applied to a divinity born to Zeus and Persephone, and worshipped at Athens conjointly with Tritopatreus and Dionysus.

Euchenor (*Εὐχήνωρ*) A son of the soothsayer Polyidus (1) who told him that he could choose between an easy death at home, or a violent death if he went to fight at Troy. He chose to die gloriously and fell smitten by an arrow from Paris' bow.

Eudorus (*Εὔδωρος*) A son of Hermes and Polymela (1), the daughter of Phylas (2). He was brought up by his grandfather; and during the Trojan War he followed Achilles. When Achilles was sulking in his tent and Patroclus wished to continue fighting without him, Achilles gave him Eudorus as his companion in battle.

Eumaeus (*Εὔμαιος*) The son of Ctesius, ruler of Syris in the Cyclades. Eumaeus was entrusted to a Phoenician slave girl when still a child, and became Odysseus' swineherd. He remained loyal to Odysseus during his absence and tried to safeguard Odysseus' assets in Ithaca. When Odysseus returned, the first person he approached, on Athena's advice, was Eumaeus, who acted as his intermediary for his reconquest of the palace.

Eumelus (*Εὔμηλος*)
1. The son of Admetus and Alcestis. He fought at Troy, taking the horses which had formerly been looked after by Apolllo when he was in bond service to Admetus. These horses won him a victory at the funeral games of Patroclus.
2. The father of BOTRES.

Eumenides (*Εὐμενίδες*) The 'gracious goddesses', a euphemism for the ERINYES.

Eumolpus (*Εὔμολπος*)
1. According to the most common tradition, the son of Poseidon and Chione (1). Fearing the wrath of her father Boreas, Chione threw the child into the sea. Poseidon rescued him, took him to Ethiopia, and entrusted him to his daughter Benthesicyme. When Eumolpus grew up Benthesicyme's husband gave him one of his daughters as his wife. She bore him a son, Ismarus; but Eumolpus tried to rape his sister-in-law, and was banished. Eumolpus and Ismarus went to Thrace, to the court of King Tegyrius. Eumolpus then took part in a plot against Tegyrius. This was discovered and he fled to Eleusis. After Ismarus' death Eumolpus made his peace with Tegyrius, who recalled him to Thrace and left him his throne. War subsequently broke out between the Eleusinians and the Athenians. Eumolpus came to the aid of the Eleusinians but was killed in the fighting (see ERECHTHEUS).

Various traditions credit Eumolpus with the foundation of the Eleusinian Mysteries. Eumolpus purified Heracles after the murder of the Centaurs, and the priestly family of the Eumolpidae considered themselves to be his descendants. After his death his son CERYX was given a role to perform in the Mysteries. Some traditions link Eumolpus with MUSAEUS; others make Eumolpus the founder of the Mysteries distinct from Chione's son and claim that he was son of Deiope and grandson of Triptolemus.

2. The son of Philammon and nephew of Autolycus. He taught Heracles music after the death of Linus (2).

3. See MOLPUS.

Euneus (*Εὔνεως*) The son of Jason and HYPSIPYLE. Although he was not with the Achaean army at Troy, he maintained friendly relations with the Greeks, and provided them with wine. He bought Lycaon (1) from Patroclus, in return for a richly engraved drinking-bowl. When Hypsipyle was sold as a slave to Lycurgus (3), Euneus rescued her and brought her back to Lemnos.

Eunomus (*Εὔνομος*) When Heracles was living at the court of his father-in-law Oeneus, he accidentally killed a child called Eunomus. Eunomus poured the warm water with which he was supposed to be washing the hero's feet over his hands instead. Heracles gave him what he intended to be a slap, but the force of the blow killed the boy. Eunomus' father, Architeles, forgave the hero, but Heracles nevertheless went into exile at Trachis with his wife, Deianeira, and his son, Hyllus. Eunomus was sometimes called Cyathus.

Eunostus (*Εὔνοστος*) A hero from Tanagra in Boeotia. He was the son of Aelieus and Scias and was brought up by the Nymph Eunosta. Ochna, the daughter of Colonus, loved Eunostus but was rejected by him. She accused him in front of her brothers of having tried to assault her. They killed him, but then in remorse Ochna confessed the truth. The brothers fled before the threats of Eunostus' father; Ochna committed suicide.

Euphemus (*Εὔφημος*) One of the ARGONAUTS, and the son of Poseidon, who had given him the gift of walking on water, and Europa (1). When the Argonauts were passing through the Symplegades, Euphemus launched the dove whose fate was to inform them of the destiny awaiting them. At Lake Tritonis, Euphemus received a lump of earth from the god Triton, as a portent of his descendants' arrival in Cyrenaica. Euphemus threw his sacred lump into the sea, causing the island of Thera to spring up. Euphemus married Heracles' sister, Laonome (1).

Euphorbus (*Εὔφορβος*) A Trojan hero, who gave Patroclus his first wound. He was slain by Menelaus, who carried off Euphorbus' shield and laid it in Hera's temple at Argos. Pythagoras claimed to have been Euphorbus in a previous life.

Euphorion (*Εὐφορίων*) According to Ptolemy Hephaistion, a winged son of Achilles and Helen. Zeus killed him with a thunderbolt when he did not reciprocate his love.

Euphrates (*Εὐφράτης*) A man named Euphrates found his son Axurtus asleep next to his mother one day; mistaking him for a stranger, he killed him. When he realized his mistake he threw himself into the River Melos, which thereafter bore the name of Euphrates.

Europa (*Εὐρώπη*)

1. The daughter of Tityus and mother of EUPHEMUS by Poseidon.

2. One of the daughters of Oceanus and Tethys.
3. The mother of Niobe (1) and the wife of Phoroneus.
4. The daughter of Nilus, and one of Danaus' wives.
5. The daugher of Agenor and Telephassa (Table 3), although her father is in some accounts said to have been Agenor's son, Phoenix (2). Zeus saw Europa on the beach at Sidon, or Tyre, where her father was king. Filled with love for her, he transformed himself into a bull of a dazzling whiteness, with horns like a crescent moon, and lay down at Europa's feet. After she had overcome her initial fright, Europa sat upon the bull's back. The bull immediately made for the sea, plunged into the waves and swam away from the shore. They reached Crete and at Gortyna, beside a spring, Zeus lay with Europa beneath some plane trees.

Europa had three sons by Zeus: Minos, Sarpedon (2) and Rhadamanthys. She is also said to have given birth to Carnus (2) – and perhaps Dodon. Zeus gave her three gifts: the bronze automaton TALOS (1); a dog which never let any prey escape it; and a hunting-spear which never missed its mark. Zeus then married her to Asterius, the king of Crete. The marriage proved childless, and Asterius adopted Zeus' sons. After her death, Europa received divine honours; the bull whose form Zeus had taken became a constellation. For the saga of Europa's brothers when they went in search of their sister, see AGENOR and CADMUS.

Eurus (*Εὖρος*) The south-west wind, the son of Eos and Astraeus, or perhaps Typhon.

Euryalus (*Εὐρύαλος*)
1. The son of Mecisteus (Table 1). He took part in the expeditions of the Argonauts and the Epigoni, and in the Trojan War.
2. One of Odysseus' sons, whose mother was EVIPPE (1).
3. One of Aeneas' companions. A youth of great beauty, whose friendship with NISUS (2) was widely known. He died in the fighting against the Rutuli.

Eurycleia (*Εὐρύκλεια*) Odysseus' nurse.

Eurydice (*Εὐρυδίκη*)
1. The Dryad who was the wife of ORPHEUS (see also ARISTAEUS).
2. The daughter of Lacedaemon and Sparte, upon whom ACRISIUS fathered Danae (Table 7).
3. In Euripides' lost tragedy *Hypsipyle*, Eurydice was the wife of Lycurgus (3) and the mother of Archemorus.
4. The daughter of Amphiaraus and Eriphyle (Table 1).
5. The wife of Creon. See ANTIGONE (1).
6. The daughter of Adrastus and the mother of LAOMEDON by ILUS (2) (Table 4).
7. See CREUSA (4).
8. The daughter of Clymenus (2) and wife of Nestor (according to the *Odyssey* (see NESTOR)).

Eurygania (*Εὐρυγάνεια*) Eurygania, Eurygane or Euryanassa are the names of OEDIPUS' wife in some versions of the legend. Eurygania was the daughter of Hyperphas, Periphas

(1) or Teuthras. According to these accounts Oedipus had his four children, Eteocles, Polynices, Antigone and Ismene, by Eurygania and not Jocasta.

Eurylochus (*Εὐρύλοχος*) Odysseus' companion. He married Odysseus' sister, CTIMENE. On Circe's island, he was chosen to reconnnoitre; he did not enter the enchantress' palace, but returned to tell Odysseus of the transformation of his companions. Eurylochus also advised landing on the island where the cattle of the Sun were grazing, and assumed the blame for the curse which followed the sacrilege committed by Odysseus' companions, who had no hesitation about slaughtering the cattle and eating them. Eurylochus died with them.

Eurymachus (*Εὐρύμαχος*)

1. One of the suitors of PENELOPE in the *Odyssey*. He insulted Odysseus when the latter appeared disguised as a beggar, and threw a stool at him. When Theoclymenus warned the suitors of the doom that threatened them, Eurymachus accused him of being insane. When given the test of the bow, Eurymachus was unable to bend it, much to his shame. After the death of Antinous, he tried in vain to make his peace with Odysseus; he was killed by an arrow from Odysseus' bow.
2. See THEANO.

Eurymedon (*Εὐρυμέδων*)

1. A Giant, who reigned over a race of Giants at the far end of the earth. His violent deeds led to his downfall. While he was still a child he raped Hera and fathered PROMETHEUS on her; this earned him the wrath of Zeus.
2. A son of Minos and the Nymph Paria. During his expedition against the Amazons, Heracles landed on Paros. Since two of his companions had been killed by Minos' sons, who lived on this island, Heracles attacked these sons and slew them. He then laid siege to the city; to appease him, the inhabitants begged him to take two of their princes to replace his two companions. Heracles took Alceus and Sthenelus (2), the sons of Androgeos and grandsons of Minos. On their return from the expedition Heracles landed on Thasos, evicted the Thracians, and gave the island to the two brothers as their kingdom.
3. Agememnon's charioteer.

Eurynome (*Εὐρυνόμη*)

1. A daughter of Oceanus and Tethys (Table 8). She reigned with Ophion over Olympus until they were expelled by Cronus and Rhea. She and Ophion took refuge in the sea, where, with Thetis, she welcomed HEPHAESTUS when he was thrown from Olympus. She was loved by Zeus, who fathered the CHARITES and the river-god Asopus. A temple on the outskirts of Phigalia was dedicated to Eurynome. The cult statue which represented her had the torso of a woman, but from the waist downwards had the form of a fish.
2. A daughter of Nisus, king of Megara, and the mother of BELLEROPHON. She was also known as Eurymede.

Eurynomus (*Εὐρύνομος*) A demon

who ate the flesh from buried bodies, leaving only the bones.

Eurypylus (*Εὐρύπυλος*)

1. A Thessalian chief who took part in the Trojan War. He was wounded by Paris, but was rescued by Patroclus.
2. The inhabitants of Patras used to make an annual sacrifice to Artemis of the most beautiful boy and girl in the city (see COMAETHO (2)). As part of his share of the spoils of Troy, Eurypylus had been given a chest; upon opening it he had gone mad. The oracle told him he would be cured when he came across 'an unusual sacrifice', and that he must settle in the land where he found it. On reaching Patras he saw the sacrifice to Artemis and realized that the oracle had been fulfilled. The inhabitants of Patras had also been told that the sacrifice could cease once it had been witnessed by a leader from another land; when Eurypylus arrived they knew that Artemis had been appeased. Eurypylus settled in Patras and died there. He is often identified with Eurypylus (1).
3. A king of the island of Cos, the son of Poseidon and Astypalaea (see HERACLES, III).
4. The son of TELEPHUS. Telephus had promised that neither he nor his descendants would ever fight against the Greeks; but Eurypylus' mother, Astyoche, having been bribed with the golden vine which Zeus had once offered to Ganymede, was persuaded to send Eurypylus to Troy, where he was killed by Neoptolemus.
5. A son of Poseidon. He ruled Cyrene in Libya. He gave EUPHEMUS a present of a lump of earth, when the Argonauts were passing through Lake Tritonis. According to Pindar, Eurypylus was the incarnation of the god Triton; other authors depict him as Triton's brother, with his mother being Celaeno (1). During his reign Apollo brought the Nymph CYRENE into the country.
6. One of the sons of Thestius.

Eurysaces (*Εὐρυσάκης*) Son of Ajax (2) and TECMESSA. Before committing suicide, Ajax entrusted Eurysaces to his half-brother, TEUCER (2). After the fall of Troy, Eurysaces returned to Salamis, his father's homeland, but was not allowed to travel in Teucer's ship. This angered Telamon, Eurysaces' grandfather, who banished Teucer and made Eurysaces his heir. On Telamon's death Teucer tried to return, but Eurysaces sent him away. Eurysaces and his brother Philaeus handed over Salamis to the Athenians, though in some traditions Philaeus was Eurysaces' son, not his brother, and he, rather than Eurysaces, handed the island over. Miltiades, Cimon, Alcibiades and Thucydides the historian claimed Eurysaces as an ancestor.

Eurystheus (*Εὐρυσθεύς*) Perseus' grandson, son of Sthenelus (4) and Nicippe (Table 7). He ruled Tiryns, Mycenae and Midea. When Heracles was about to be born, Zeus declared that Mycenae would be ruled by the descendant of Perseus who was about to see the light of day. The jealous Hera persuaded Eilithyia, the goddess of childbirth, to hold back the birth of Heracles (see ALCMENE) and to hasten that of Eurystheus, who was still only in his seventh month. So Eurystheus was born first and reaped the benefit of Zeus' promise.

In the legend of Heracles, despite being a physical and moral weakling, Eurystheus made Heracles undertake the Twelve Labours (see HERACLES, II). Out of fear he refused to allow Heracles within the walls of Mycenae; nor would he show himself to the hero, but instead sent orders to him through his herald, Copreus. Eurystheus instructed Heracles to leave whatever he had brought back from each of his Labours outside the gates of the city. He had a big bronze jar made for himself to serve as a place of refuge should Heracles attack him. When Heracles had accomplished the Labours, Eurystheus offered a sacrifice to which he invited the hero; but Eurystheus' sons offered Heracles a portion of the meat that was smaller than the rest; Heracles took offence and killed three of them. Heracles then wished to settle in Tiryns, but Eurystheus refused permission. After Heracles' death, Eurystheus tried to persuade CEYX (1) to hand the hero's descendants over to him; but they found protection in Attica. When Eurystheus marched against the Athenians he was killed in battle. His head was brought to Alcmene, who tore out his eyes.

An Alexandrian tradition related by Diotimus asserts that Heracles and Eurystheus were lovers, and that the hero undertook the Twelve Labours for love.

Eurytion (*Εὐρυτίων*)

1. One of the Centaurs who tried to carry off HIPPODAMIA (2); this caused the battle between the CENTAURS and the Lapiths.

2. A Centaur who was killed by Heracles when he tried to rape Mnesimache, the daughter of Dexamenus (see CENTAURS).

3. A hero from Phthia, who took part in the Calydonian hunt. His father was Actor, or, in other traditions, Irus (1). PELEUS took refuge at his court after the murder of Phocus (see AEACUS). Eurytion purified him and gave him his daughter Antigone (3) in marriage, together with a third of his kingdom. Peleus accidentally killed his father-in-law during the Calydonian hunt.

4. GERYON's herdsman.

Eurytus (*Εὔρυτος*)

1. One of the Giants who revolted against the gods. Dionysus killed him with his thyrsus.

2. King of Oechalia. He was the son of Melaneus and Stratonice, and an archer whose skill had won him the reputation of being a son of Apollo, the divine archer. He was married to Pylon's daughter Antioche, and he had four sons, Deion (or Molion), Clytius, Toxeus (1) and Iphitus (1), and one daughter, Iole. According to the Homeric version of the legend, he challenged Apollo himself, who slew Eurytus before he attained old age, to punish him for his presumption. Eurytus taught Heracles how to use a bow. Iphitus gave Odysseus this bow as a present. This was the bow with which Odysseus killed the suitors.

Eurytus suggested an archery contest, with the hand of his daughter as the prize for the archer who managed to defeat him. Heracles accepted the challenge, and won; but Eurytus' sons would not let him have the prize. They were afraid that if Heracles had children by their sister, he might kill them in a fit of madness, as he had done to his children by Megara (1) (see HERACLES, I). Only Iphitus took the hero's side. According to some versions, Eurytus accused Heracles of stealing some cattle, which had in reality been stolen by Autolycus. Iphitus offered to help Heracles look for them; whereupon Heracles was seized with another attack of madness, and threw Iphitus off the ramparts of Tiryns. In other versions, Heracles had stolen the cattle himself, and when Iphitus came to recover the booty, Heracles killed him. Eurytus refused to accept the price Heracles was prepared to pay him as compensation for the death of his son (see OMPHALE). Subsequently Heracles mounted an expedition against Oechalia, captured the city, killed Eurytus and his sons, and carried Iole off into captivity.

3. Eurytus or Erytus was the son of Hermes and Antianira, the twin brother of Echion (2), and one of the Argonauts.

4. One of the MOLIONIDAE.

Euthymus (*Εὔθυμος*) A demon named Alybas was the spirit of Odysseus' companion Polites (2). When Odysseus landed at Temesa, Polites raped a local girl. The inhabitants stoned him to death. Polites' spirit persecuted them and insisted that they dedicate a shrine to it, and offer up the most beautiful maiden each year. This tribute was paid until the arrival of Euthymus, a famous boxer from Locri, who challenged the demon, beat it and forced it to leave the country. He married and lived to an old age. Instead of dying he disappeared under mysterious circumstances.

Evadne (*Εὐάδνη*)

1. The daughter of Poseidon and Pitane (1). Her 'mortal' father was AEPYTUS (3). Evadne was loved by Apollo and bore him a son named IAMUS.

2. The daughter of Iphis (1). She was married to Capaneus, and on the death of her husband she threw herself into the flames of his funeral pyre.

3. The daughter of Strymon and Neaera. She married Argos (1) and bore Ecbasus, Piras (or Piren (2)), Epidaurus and Criasus.

Evander (*Εὔανδρος*)

1. Son of Sarpedon (3).

2. One of Priam's sons.

3. The founder of Pallantium on the Palatine Hill, before Romulus founded Rome. Evander came from Pallantium in Arcadia. According to some traditions he was the son of Hermes and an Arcadian Nymph (see CARMENTA); in others he is said to have been the son of Echemus of Tegea and Timandra, the daughter of Tyndareus and Leda. The reasons given for his leaving Arcadia vary: some say he left of his own free will; others that he had to go into exile after the murder of his father, whom he had killed to protect his mother; others say that he had killed his mother.

Evander settled on the Palatine Hill. He was welcomed by FAUNUS, king of the Aborgines, but had to fight the Giant ERYLUS. Evander was a benevolent ruler who taught the inhabitants of the land the hitherto unknown arts of writing and music, and other useful skills. He is also said to have introduced the cults of Ceres (Demeter), Neptune (Poseidon) and Lycian Pan (in whose honour he initiated the festival of the Lupercalia) into Latium. When Heracles came to Pallantium, Evander welcomed him and purified him of the murder of Cacus. He recognized Heracles' divine origin, and instituted the cult of the Ara Maxima in his honour, between the Palatine and Aventine Hills. Evander arrived in Latium 60 years before the Trojan War; thus he was an old man when AENEAS came to seek his help against the Rutuli. Remembering that in former days he had been a guest of Anchises, Evander welcomed Aeneas and gave him a contingent of troops under the command of his son PALLAS (4). Evander also had two daughters, Rhome and Dyne, or Dauna. An altar was dedicated to Evander at the foot of the Aventine Hill. This altar was symmetrical with the one dedicated to Carmenta at the foot of the Capitol.

Evenus (*Εὔηνος*) A king of Aetolia, the son of Ares and Demonice. He had a daughter, Marpessa, and he used to kill her suitors and then decorate the temple of Poseidon with their skulls. For the abduction of Marpessa and the death of Evenus, see MARPESSA.

Evippe (*Εὐίππη*)

1. After he had killed Penelope's suitors, ODYSSEUS went to Epirus to consult the oracle. There he was welcomed by King Tyrimmas. He seduced the king's daughter, Evippe, and fathered a son called Euryalus (2). When Euryalus reached manhood, Evippe sent him to Ithaca, with some tokens which would ensure that Euryalus would be recognized by his father. Euryalus reached Ithaca while Odysseus was away. Penelope knew of Odysseus' affair with Evippe; when Odysseus returned, she persuaded him to kill Euryalus, pretending that the young man had come to Ithaca with the intention of assassinating him. Odysseus killed him himself. According to other traditions, the son of Evippe and Odysseus was called Leontophron.
2. A granddaughter of Athamas.

F

Fama According to Virgil, Earth gave birth to Fama ('the Voice of the Multitude') after Coeus and Enceladus. Fama possessed a great number of eyes and mouths, and moved by flying very swiftly through the air. Ovid depicted her as living in a palace at the centre of the world, within the limits of Earth, Heaven, and Sea – an echoing palace with a thousand openings, through which even the lowest voice could penetrate. This palace, made entirely of bronze, was always open and every word that entered it was broadcast again, much amplified. Fama lived surrounded by Credulity, Error, Unfounded Joy, Terror, Sedition, and False Rumour, and from her palace she kept watch over the whole world. This creature is clearly a late allegory rather than a true myth.

Fames The allegory of Hunger. Her name was a translation of LIMOS. Virgil portayed her in the entrance-hall of Hades, alongside Poverty; Ovid depicted her as living in Scythia, a desolate land, where she nibbled ceaselessly at what scanty vegetation she could find. At the demand of Ceres, she destroyed ERYSICHTHON (I).

Fatum The god of Destiny. Originally this word meant the word of god, and was applied to an irrevocable divine decision. Under the influence of Greek religion, Fatum came to include the divinities of Destiny, such as the MOIRAE, the PARCAE, and even the SIBYLS. Near the Rostra in Rome stood three statues, which were called the three Fata: these were statues of the Sibyls. The word Fata was in time mistaken for a feminine singular, and became the origin of the word for fairies in Roman folklore. The lower classes even invented a god Fatus (by making Fatum masculine), who was a personal demon, symbolizing individual destiny and analogous to the GENII. Feminine destiny was personified by a Fata, feminine, a later equivalent of the primitive JUNO.

Fauna The sister and wife of FAUNUS. She was a divinity of women, identified with BONA DEA, for whom she was perhaps originally merely an epithet: the *favourable* goddess in Latin (*quae favet*). As Bona Dea she appeared in the cycle of Hercules, in which she was the wife of the Latin King Faunus. Hercules loved her and gave her a son, the future King LATINUS. Another tradition depicted Fauna as a young Hyperborean girl who bore Hercules' child Latinus, and then married Faunus after Hercules had left her.

Faunus An ancient Roman deity. From his name he was apparently a benevolent god (in Latin *qui favet*), particularly the protector of shepherds and their flocks. He was identified with the Arcadian god PAN. He also became associated with the Arcadian King EVANDER (3) (Εὐ-ἀνήρ = 'the Good Man'), and in this way myths about the Arcadians and their migration to the Palatine Hill took root on Roman soil. Faunus came to be regarded as one of the first kings of Latium, ruling before the arrival of Aeneas. He is sometimes described as the son of CIRCE and Jupiter. He succeeded King Picus and was himself succeeded by his son Latinus (see FAUNA). Faunus' divine personality lived on as the Fauns (Fauni) of the Classical Age, who were rustic demons equivalent to the Greek SATYRS.

The cult of Faunus originally included the procession of the Luperci, during which boys ran about clad in goat skins whipping any women they met with lashes of rawhide; this flagellation was said to bring fertility to the victims. For other legends of Faunus see BONA DEA and FAUNA.

Faustinus A companion of EVANDER (3) and the brother of FAUSTULUS. While Faustulus was a shepherd to Amulius, whose flocks he tended on the Palatine Hill, Faustinus looked after Numitor's on the Aventine. For a version of the Romulus legend in which Faustinus plays a peculiar role, see NUMITOR. Both Faustinus and Faustulus died in the struggle between Romulus and Remus. The rivalry between two hills, the Aventine and the Palatine, is echoed by the locations of the two shepherds in this legend, as it is by the strife between Romulus and Remus.

Faustulus The shepherd who sheltered ROMULUS and Remus on the banks of the Tiber, and then entrusted them to his wife Acca Larentia (2) to bring up. Faustulus was considered to be a good and charitable man; he was sometimes described as King Amulius' head shepherd. When Amulius ordered Romulus and Remus to be exposed, Faustulus was on the same road as the servants who were taking the children away. He waited until the servants had started back but discovered that some shepherds had already found the two infants. He persuaded them to hand the children over to him, on the grounds that his wife had just lost a son and would be happy to have some nurslings. According to another version, Faustulus found the children as they were being suckled by a she-wolf. For another tradition see NUMITOR.

During the strife between Romulus and Remus, Faustulus tried to intervene and was killed. He was buried in the Forum. Later, the statue of a lion was raised above his tomb. In Classical days, Faustulus' hut was still to be seen on the Palatine Hill preserved as a relic of these mythical times. Certain authors refer to him as Faustus, the diminutive of which was Faustulus.

Febris The goddess of Fever. She was much feared at Rome, where the low ground and even the upper parts of the valleys stayed damp and unhealthy for a long time. She was a maleficent power who had to be conciliated. She had an archaic altar on the Palatine Hill, one on the Esquiline Hill and another at the head of the Quirinal Valley.

Februus The god to whom the month of February was sacred. In later days he was identified with DIS PATER. During February the city was purified by appeasing the dead with sacrifices and offerings. These festivals bore the name of Februalia.

Ferentina A Latin Nymph, the goddess of a spring and a sacred wood. Her shrine was common to the whole of the Latin confederacy.

Feronia A goddess of springs and woods, whose cult was widespread in Central Italy. Slaves were freed in her temple at Terracina, which explains why she is sometimes identified with Libertas. She is said to have been the mother of ERYLUS.

Fides The Roman personification of Good Faith. She was portrayed as an old woman with white hair, older than Jupiter himself. Aeneas' granddaughter Rhome is said to have dedicated a temple to her on the Palatine Hill.

Flora The power that makes the trees blossom. She presided over everything that blooms. According to the legends, she was introduced to Rome by Titus Tatius. She was honoured by every race in Italy. The Sabine people dedicated a month to her corresponding to April in the Roman calendar.

Ovid suggests that Flora was a Greek Nymph called Chloris. He relates how Zephyr, the god of the wind, fell in love with her and carried her off. He married her and, to show his love, he granted her dominion over the flowers. Honey is said to have been one of her gifts to mankind, as well as the seeds of countless varieties of flowers. Ovid's version of this legend probably used Orithyia's abduction by Boreas as the model for the account of Flora's abduction; but Ovid also attributed the birth of Mars to Flora in the following way. Juno, incensed by Minerva's springing spontaneously from Jupiter's head, wished to conceive a child without recourse to any male assistance. Flora gave her a flower which would make a woman pregnant by touching it. Juno then gave birth to Mars without prior sexual relations with Jupiter.

Flora had her own priest at Rome. The Floralia were celebrated in her honour; these were marked by games in which courtesans took part.

Fons A god associated with springs; he is also known as Fontus. He had a temple at Rome, perhaps adjacent to the Porta Fontinalis, and an altar at the foot of the Janiculum, not far from the so-called tomb of Numa. His festival bore the name of the Fontinalia.

Fornax The goddess of the oven in which bread is baked.

Fors A divinity of chance who was associated with FORTUNA in the phrase *Fors Fortuna*, which eventually came to be regarded as a single divinity.

Fortuna The Roman personification of Chance, identified with the Greek TYCHE. She was portrayed with the cornucopia and with a rudder, to symbolize that she steered the course of people's lives. She was sometimes shown seated, sometimes standing, and sometimes blind. The introduction of her cult was credited to Servius Tullius. She was said to have loved him, although he was a mortal, and to have gained access to his chamber through a little window. A statue of Servius stood in the temple of the goddess.

Fortuna was invoked under many different names, such as *Redux* (when safe return from a voyage was being sought), *Publica* and *Huiusce Diei* (the special Fortuna of that particular day). During the Imperial period, each Emperor had his own personal Fortuna. Under the influence of Greece, Fortuna gradually became assimilated with other divinities, notably Isis and Nemesis.

Furies Roman demons of the Underworld. They became assimilated with the Greek ERINYES, whose myths they borrowed.

Furrina The Nymph of a spring and a sacred wood that were located at the foot of the Janiculum in Rome.

G

Gaia (*Γαῖα*) Gaia, or Ge, was the earth conceived as the primordial element from which sprang the divine races. According to Hesiod, Gaia was born immediately after Chaos and just before Eros. Without the aid of any male, she gave birth to URANUS, the Mountains, and PONTUS. After the birth of Uranus, she coupled with him, and bore the six Titans – Oceanus, Coeus, Crius, Hyperion, Iapetus and Cronus – and the six Titanesses – Theia, Rhea, Themis, Mnemosyne, Phoebe (I) and Tethys. CRONUS was the youngest of this line (Table 8). Gaia then gave birth to the CYCLOPES and finally the HECATONCHEIRES. All these children lived in terror of their father, who forced them to remain entombed in the depths of Gaia's body. She was determined to free her children, and asked them to exact vengeance on Uranus; but none of them was willing except Cronus. Gaia then entrusted him with a sickle, and when Uranus came to lie with Gaia that night, Cronus cut off his father's testicles, and threw them over his shoulder. The blood from the wound fell upon Gaia and fertilized her once again. As a result Gaia gave birth to the ERINYES, the GIANTS, the Ash Nymphs and other divinities also associated with trees.

After Uranus' castration, Gaia coupled with another of her children, Pontus. She gave birth to five marine divinities: Nereus, Thaumas, Phorcys, Ceto and Eurybia. Cronus now ruled the world, and he showed himself to be as brutal a tyrant as his father. When he too imprisoned his brothers in Tartarus, Gaia started planning a second revolution. Cronus' wife Rhea had seen all her children eaten by Cronus, who had been warned he would be overthrown by one of them. When she was pregnant with Zeus, she went to Gaia and Uranus and asked them how to save the child. They then revealed the secret of the Fates to her, and showed her how to cheat Cronus. Gaia concealed him at birth and hid him in a deep cave. In place of the child she gave Cronus a stone wrapped in swaddling-clothes, which the god devoured. In this way ZEUS was able to escape and grow to manhood. Later, when Zeus began openly resisting Cronus, Gaia told him he could achieve victory only with the Titans as his allies (see ZEUS, II). Nevertheless, Gaia did not completely throw in her lot with Zeus. Displeased by the defeat of the Hecatoncheires, she coupled with Tartarus, and gave birth to TYPHON, a monster of prodigious strength, who declared war on the gods and held them at bay for a considerable time. She had another monstrous child by Tartarus, ECHIDNA.

In other theogonies she was said to have been the mother of TRIPTOLEMUS by Oceanus. The giant ANTAEUS was also said to have been her son, by Poseidon. Other monsters considered by various mythographers as the children of Gaia include: CHAR-

YBDIS, the HARPIES, PYTHON, the dragon that guarded the Golden Fleece in the land of Aeetes, and FAMA.

Earth, the power and inexhaustible reserve of fecundity, gradually became known as the Universal Mother and the mother of the gods. Mother Earth became incarnated as divinities such as Demeter or Cybele, while speculations about Earth as an element passed from the realm of mythology into that of philosophy. Gaia was credited with being the inspiration of numerous oracles, for she possessed the secrets of the Fates, and her oracles were reputedly older and more accurate than those of Apollo.

Galaesus When Aeneas' son Iulus (or Ascanius) killed a tame hind, almost starting a war between the Latins and the Trojans, Galaesus tried to intervene and restore peace. He failed in his attempt and was killed.

Galatea (*Γαλάτεια*)
1. A daughter of Nereus and a sea-goddess who featured in the myths of Sicily. The milk-white maiden (*γάλα* = 'milk') Galatea lived in the sea and was loved by Polyphemus (2), the Sicilian Cyclops. She did not return his passion, however, and was instead in love with Acis. One day when Galatea was lying beside the sea with her lover, Polyphemus saw them. Although Acis tried to flee, the Cyclops threw an enormous boulder at him which crushed him to death. Galatea turned Acis into a stream with sparkling waters.
2. A Cretan girl who was married to Lamprus. When Lamprus discovered that Galatea was pregnant he told her he wanted only a son; if she gave birth to a girl she would have to expose it. Galatea gave birth to a girl, but she could not bring herself to expose it. On the advice of soothsayers she dressed the child as a boy and called him Leucippus (6). However, as time went by, Leucippus became very beautiful, and it became impossible to continue the masquerade. Galatea went to Leto's shrine, where she asked the goddess to change her daughter's sex. Leto granted her request (compare IPHIS).

Galates (*Γαλατής*) When Heracles passed through Gaul on his way back from stealing Geryon's cattle, he founded the city of Alesia. The daughter of a local prince loved him; he fathered a son called Galates, whose bravery earned him rule over the whole of Gaul. Later, Galates gave his name to Galatia, the land of the Galatians (compare also CELTUS).

Galeotes (*Γαλεώτης*) A Hyperborean who was the ancestor of a race of Sicilian soothsayers. With Telmissus, another Hyperborean, Galeotes went to consult the oracle at Dodona. They were instructed to travel, one East and the other West, until an eagle robbed them of the meat and the offering made during a sacrifice. At that place they were to raise an altar. Galeotes went to Sicily and Telmissus stopped in Caria.

Galinthias (*Γαλινθίας*) Daughter of Proetus and friend of Alcmene. Hera had ordered the Moirae and Eilithyia, the divinities of childbirth, to stop Alcmene delivering her child Heracles. For nine days and nights they sat on the threshold of Alcmene's house, with their arms and legs crossed, holding back the birth. However, Galinthias (or Historis) tricked the goddesses by telling them that despite their efforts, Alcmene had given birth to a boy, at Zeus' command. The goddesses rose to their feet in indignation, abandoning the position which had been holding Alcmene in bondage. She immediately gave birth. In revenge the divinities turned Galinthias into a weasel (γαλῆ = weasel), and since it was her mouth that had deceived them, they condemned her to give birth through her mouth. Hecate, however, took her as her own servant and her sacred animal. When Heracles reached manhood, he raised a shrine to Galinthias. The Thebans used to bring offerings on the feast of Heracles (see also HISTORIS).

Ganges (*Γάγγης*) The god of the River Ganges in India. While drunk, he unwittingly coupled with his mother, Calauria. When he came to his senses, he threw himself into the river which had hitherto been called Chliarus, and which was henceforth known as Ganges.

Ganymede (*Γανυμήδης*) A descendant of Dardanus (Table 4). He is generally said to have been the youngest son of Tros and Callirhoe (4). Other versions, however, make him variously the son of Laomedon, Ilus (2), Assaracus, or Erichthonius. When Ganymede was barely adolescent, he was guarding his father's flocks in the mountains near Troy. Zeus fell in love with him and carried him off to Olympus. Ganymede was said to have been the most beautiful of mortals. On Olympus Ganymede served as a cup-bearer. He used to pour nectar into Zeus' cup and he replaced Hebe, the goddess of Youth, in this service.

Traditions differ as to the details of his abduction. Sometimes Zeus himself is said to have carried the boy off; sometimes the god is said to have entrusted the mission to an eagle; other accounts say that Zeus himself had taken on the form of an eagle. Still other versions suggest that the abductor was Minos, or Tantalus, or even Eos. The place of the abduction varies equally with different authors. While the generally accepted location is Mount Ida in the Troad, some versions place it in Crete, Euboea, or in Mysia. In compensation for this abduction, Zeus presented the boy's father with some divine horses, or a golden vine, the work of Hephaestus. The eagle that carried off Ganymede became a constellation.

Gavanes (*Γαυάνης*) According to Herodotus, Gavanes was expelled from Argos with his brothers Aeropus and Perdiccas. They went to Macedonia via Illyria, and became herdsmen for the king of Lebaea. Every time the queen baked bread for Perdiccas, the bread rose to twice its proper size. The king was so disturbed that he discharged the three brothers; and instead of paying them the wages he owed them he pointed to a patch of sunlight that came down the 'chimney' (smoke-hole). Perdiccas drew his knife, scratched a line round the sunlight and made as if to collect it in his tunic. The brothers left. When the king sent horsemen to kill the brothers, a river rose miraculously to prevent them. They settled in Macedonia, where

Perdiccas founded the country's royal line.

Ge (*Γῆ*) A common variant of GAIA.

Gelanor (*Γελάνωρ*) In the genealogy of the kings of Argos, as set out by Pausanias, Gelanor, the son of Sthenelas, was the last of Phoroneus' line to rule. He was dethroned by DANAUS when the latter arrived from Egypt.

Genii Spirits that represented the inborn power of individuals, localities, and corporations (such as societies, colleges, and cities). The genius was born at the same time as the person or thing to which it was linked, and its essential function was to keep its charge alive. It played a part in the conception of the individual, and also presided at marriage. There was a genius of the marriage bed, which brought fertility to the couple. As a personification of the being, the personal genius was an interior force that generated optimism. A Latin proverb, *indulgere genio*, 'to yield to one's genius', applied to every act of compliance with one's personal taste, in particular over-indulgence in drink. Oaths were sworn on one's personal genius or on the genius of others. The genius gradually became identified with the MANES (2) and was considered an immortal element in Man. The tendency to allot a separate genius to every entity was so strong that even the gods had their own genii. Sacrifices, for example, were offered to the genius of Mars and to that of Jupiter. For women, the genius was replaced by the JUNO.

Gerana (*Γέρανα*) A Pygmy woman who held the gods in comtempt. To punish her, Hera turned her into a crane. When she became a bird she tried to rejoin her son Mopsus (3) in her former home, but the cranes were at war with the PYGMIES (through Hera's will); the Pygmies made it impossible for Gerana to reach her former home, thus unwittingly adding to her torment.

Geryon (*Γηρυονεύς*) The three-headed giant, who also had a triple body down as far as his hips, was the son of CHRYSAOR and Callirhoe (1). He lived on the island of Erythia, and his wealth consisted of herds of cattle, guarded by a herdsman, Eurytion (4), and a dog, Orthus (or Orthrus). At Eurystheus' command, Heracles stole Geryon's cattle from him (see HERACLES, II). Heracles brought the cattle back in stages to Greece. Antiquity allotted various sites to the island of Erythia; the name Erythia was supposed to be eponymous with one of the HESPERIDES, whose garden lay near the island. Another tradition, however, places it in Epirus, in the region of Ambracia.

Giants (*Γίγαντες*) The children of GAIA, born from the blood of her husband Uranus when he was castrated by Cronus. Although of divine origin they could be killed if they were slain simultaneously by a god and a mortal. There was a magic herb produced by the Earth which could protect them from the blows of mortals; but Zeus acquired this herb for himself by forbidding the Sun, the Moon and the Dawn to shine so that nobody could see well enough to find the herb before he did. Other traditions claim that some Giants (Alcyoneus (1), for example, or Porphyrion) were immortal as long as they remained on Earth, where they had been born. The legend of the Giants is dominated by their revolt against the gods. Gaia gave birth to them to avenge the Titans, whom Zeus had imprisoned in Tartarus. The Giants were enormous beings of invincible strength and terrifying appearance. They had thick shocks of hair, bristling beards, and their legs were the bodies of great snakes. Their birthplace was Phlegrae on the peninsula of Pallene in Thrace. They began threatening heaven by bombarding it with enormous rocks and flaming trees. The Giants' main adversaries were initially Zeus and Athena. Zeus was armed with his aegis and his thunderbolts, brought to him by his eagles. Athena also had an eagle and launched thunderbolts. Their chief assistant was Heracles, the mortal whose help was needed to kill the Giants. Heracles stationed himself on Zeus' chariot, and fought from afar with his arrows. Dionysus is sometimes said to have taken part in the struggle, armed with his thyrsus and with firebrands, and supported by the Satyrs. Various other deities also came to be included, such as Ares, Hephaestus, Aphrodite, Eros and Poseidon.

During the struggle ALCYONEUS (1) was slain by Heracles with the assistance of Athena. Porphyrion attacked Heracles and Hera, but Zeus filled him with lust for Hera, and while he was trying to tear her garments off Zeus smote him with a thunderbolt and Heracles killed him with an arrow. Ephialtes was slain by an arrow from Apollo in his left eye and another from Heracles in his right; Eurytus (1) was killed by Dionysus with a blow from his thyrsus. Hecate killed Clytius, using firebrands, and Hephaestus dispatched Mimas by throwing lumps of red-hot iron at him. Athena destroyed Enceladus and Pallas (6) (see ATHENA). Polybotes was chased by Poseidon as far as Cos. There the god broke off the part of the isle called Nisyrus and crushed the Giant beneath it. Hermes wore Hades' helmet, which made him invisible; he killed Hippolytus (2) while Artemis slew Gration. The Moirae, armed with their bronze clubs, killed Agrius and Thoas (7). Zeus stunned the rest of the Giants with his thunderbolts and Heracles finished them off with his arrows. The site of this battle was generally thought to be on the peninsula of Pallene, but a local tradition placed it in Arcadia, on the banks of the River Alpheus.

Later traditions name even more Giants, but these are generally TITANS wrongly included in the category of Giants, or other monsters such as TYPHON, AEGAEON and the ALOADAE, whose immense size and strength entitled them to be called 'giants'. The Gigantomachy, or the revolt of the Giants against the gods, was a favourite theme of plastic art in the Classical and Hellenistic periods.

Glauce (*Γλαύκη*)

1. A Nereid and also an Arcadian Nymph.
2. Daughter of Creon (1): she was also called CREUSA (3).
3. Daughter of Cychreus, king of Salamis, and the mother of Telamon by Actaeus in some traditions.

Glaucia (*Γλαυκία*) The daughter of the River Scamander. When Heracles undertook his expedition against Troy he was accompanied by Deimachus, the son of Eleon. Glaucia and Deimachus loved each other, and Glaucia became pregnant; but Deimachus was killed before their son's birth. When the child was born Glaucia called him Scamander, in memory of his grandfather. Heracles took Glaucia and her son to Greece, where he entrusted them to Eleon. Glaucia's name was given to a stream not far from Tanagra. Scamander's three daughters by Acidusa had a cult consecrated to them under the name of the Three Virgins.

Glaucus (*Γλαῦκος*)
1. The son of ANTENOR: he helped Paris to abduct Helen, and because of this his father drove him out. He fought against the Greeks, and is sometimes said to have been slain by Agamemnon; but it is more generally thought that he was saved by Odysseus and Menelaus, as the son of Antenor, who was bound to them by ties of friendship.
2. Son of Hippolochus and grandson of Bellerophon. With his cousin SARPEDON (3) he commanded the Lycian contingent at Troy. In the fighting around the city he found himself face to face with Diomedes (2), but both recalled that their families were bound by ties of friendship. Diomedes gave Glaucus his own weapons which were bronze, and Glaucus gave him his, which were gold. Later, when Sarpedon (3) was wounded, he went to assist him, but was stopped by Teucer, wounded, and forced to leave the fray. Apollo cured Glaucus in time to recover Sarpedon's body, though he was unable to stop the Greeks stripping the corpse of its arms. Glaucus was killed during the fight for the body of Patroclus by Ajax (2). At Apollo's orders, Glaucus' body was carried back to Lycia by the winds.
3. The great-grandfather of Glaucus (2). He was the son of SISYPHUS, and succeeded his father to the throne of Ephyra, which later became Corinth. Glaucus took part in the funeral games of Pelias, but was beaten in the four-horse chariot-race by IOLAUS; after this his mares ate him alive (see TARAXIPPUS (2) and (1)). They had been maddened either by the water of a magic well, or as a result of Aphrodite's anger, for in order to make his mares run faster Glaucus refused to let them breed, and so offended the goddess. In another legend, this Glaucus drank from a fountain which conferred immortality. No one would believe that he had become immortal, however, so he threw himself into the sea, where he became a sea-god. Every sailor who saw him was assured of an early death.
4. A sea-deity. He was originally a fisherman who was born mortal but ate a herb that made him immortal. The sea goddesses cleansed him of his remaining traces of mortality and he assumed a new form: his shoulders grew broader and his legs became a fish tail, while his cheeks developed a thick beard, tinted green like the patina of bronze. He also received the gift of prophecy. Virgil makes him the father of the Cumaean Sibyl. Glaucus appeared to Menelaus when the latter was returning from Troy. In some traditions he is said to

have built the *Argo* and to have accompanied the ship on its voyage.

Glaucus courted SCYLLA (1) unsucessfully, and also tried to win the favours of Ariadne when Theseus abandoned her on Naxos. He failed, but Dionysus included him in his train when the god took her away and made her his wife.

5. The son of Minos and Pasiphae. While still a child he was chasing a mouse when he fell into a jar of honey and drowned. When Minos finally found his son's corpse, the Curetes told him that Glaucus could be restored to life by the man who could best describe the colour of a certain cow among his herds which changed its colour three times a day. It first became white, then it turned red, and finally became black. Minos asked all the cleverest men in Crete to describe the colour of the cow. Polyidus answered that the cow was mulberry-coloured, for the fruit is first white, turns red, and finally goes black when ripe. Minos felt that Polyidus had solved the problem, and told him to bring Glaucus back to life, shutting him up with Glaucus' body. Polyidus was at his wits' end, until he saw a snake make its way into the room and go over towards the body. He killed the animal, but soon a second snake came in and saw the first one lying dead, went out, and finally returned carrying in its mouth a herb with which it touched its companion. The snake immediately returned to life. Polyidus rubbed this herb on Glaucus, who revived at once. Minos, however, was still not satisfied. Before allowing Polyidus to return to his fatherland he demanded that the soothsayer should teach Glaucus his art. This Polyidus did, but when he was finally allowed to go, he spat into his pupil's mouth, and Glaucus immediately lost all the knowledge he had just acquired. In other versions of the legend, it was Asclepius, not Polyidus, who brought Glaucus back to life.

Golden Age In his *Works and Days* Hesiod describes the different races which had followed each other since the beginning of humanity. Originally, he says, there was a 'golden race' at the time when Cronus was still ruling in heaven. People in those days lived free from worries and safe from grief and distress. They remained eternally young, and spent their time in banquets and festivals. When the time came for them to die, they went peacefully to sleep. They had no need to work; every good thing came to them spontaneously. The soil needed no labour to produce large crops, and men lived in peace in the countryside. This race vanished from the earth in the reign of Zeus, but they still remain as good spirits, protectors of mankind and distributors of wealth.

Very soon the myth became a commonplace of morality, depicting the beginnings of humanity as the reign of Justice and Honesty. In Rome, where Cronus was identified with Saturn, the Golden Age was the era when Saturn ruled in Italy, then still called Ausonia. The gods lived in close association with mortals. Doors had not yet been invented, for there was no such thing as theft, and people had nothing to hide. The only food was vegetables and fruit, since killing had not been thought of. Civilization was in its earliest stages. Saturn introduced the use of the sickle (which was an attribute in representations of the god); he taught people to exploit the natural fertility of the soil. It was said in Rome that he reigned on the Capitol, the very spot where the temple of Jupiter Optimus Maximus stood later. Saturn had been welcomed to Italy by the god Janus, who ruled with him and agreed to share his kingdom with the newcomer.

Poets embroidered this theme. They told of wool colouring itself on the sheeps' backs, brambles bearing delicious fruits, and the earth rejoicing in a perpetual spring. The myth of the Golden Age also formed an element in neo-Pythagorean mysticism.

Gordias (*Γορδιάς*) A mythical king of Phrygia who founded the city of Gordium. He kept his chariot in the citadel, and the chariot-pole was attached by a knot so complicated that nobody could untie it. The empire of Asia was promised to whoever could undo it. Alexander the Great, who was familiar with the oracle, drew his sword and cut through the knot. Gordias had been the lover of Cybele, who bore him a son, Midas.

Gorge (*Γοργή*)

1. The daughter of Oeneus, king of Calydon, and the sister of Meleager. She had a son named TYDEUS by her own father; and by Andraemon she had another son, THOAS (4). She and her sister Deianeira escaped the metamorphosis which their sisters underwent (see MELEAGRIDS).
2. The wife of Corinthus, the founder of Corinth. When her children were slaughtered, she threw herself in her despair into a lake, which thereafter took the name of Lake Gorgopis.

Gorgons (*Γοργόνες*) There were three Gorgons, called Stheno, Euryale and Medusa, all daughters of Phorcys and Ceto. Medusa, was mortal; the other two were immortal. The name Gorgon was generally applied to Medusa, who was particularly considered as the Gorgon. They lived in the far West. Their heads were entwined with snakes and their necks were protected by dragons' scales; they had huge tusks, like those of a boar, hands of bronze, and golden wings. Their gaze was so penetrating that anyone who encountered it was turned to stone. Poseidon alone was not afraid of them, for he had coupled with Medusa and fathered a child. For the death of Medusa see PERSEUS. From the stump of Medusa's neck, two beings sired by Poseidon issued forth: PEGASUS, the winged horse, and CHRYSAOR. Athena fixed Medusa's head to her shield, or the centre of her aegis. In this way she could turn her enemies to stone. Perseus also gathered up the blood that flowed from the wound, for it had magic properties. The blood which flowed from the vein on the left was a mortal poison, while that from the vein on the right was a remedy capable of restoring the dead to life (see ASCLEPIUS). Furthermore, a single lock of her hair, when held up in the face of an attacking army, would put the enemy to flight (see CEPHEUS (1)).

By the Hellenistic era, the legend

of Medusa had evolved considerably. At the start, the Gorgon was a monster which belonged to the pre-Olympian generation. Then she came to be considered as the victim of a metamorphosis. It was said that the Gorgon had originally been a beautiful girl, who had dared to set her beauty against that of Athena. She was especially proud of her beautiful hair; so to punish her, Athena changed her hair into a mass of snakes. In other versions, Athena unleashed her wrath against the girl because Poseidon had ravished her in a temple sacred to the goddess; Medusa had to suffer punishment for this sacrilege.

Gorgophone (*Γοργοφόνη*) The daughter of Perseus and Andromeda (Table 7). She married Perieres (1) and bore two sons, Aphareus and Leucippus (1). Her other two sons, Icarius (1) and Tyndareus, were sometimes thought to have been fathered by Perieres and sometimes by Oebalus (1), who became her second husband after Perieres' death. Gorgophone was the first Grecian widow to remarry. Until then, it was considered that widows should not enter into a second marriage.

Gorgophonus (*Γοργοφόνος*)
1. A grandson of Perseus (Table 7).
2. A king of Epidaurus, who had been expelled from his kingdom and instructed by the oracle to found a city at the place where he found part of a sword. Gorgophonus found this object in the Peloponnese where it had been dropped by Perseus as he fled back after slaying Medusa. He founded the city of Mycenae at the spot.

Gouneus (*Γουνεύς*) Son of Ocytus. Having been one of Helen's suitors, he fought at Troy, leading the Aenians and Perrhaebi. On his return he was shipwrecked in Libya, where he settled on the banks of the river Cinyps.

Graces See CHARITES.

Graeae (*Γραῖαι*) The 'Old Women', who had never been young, and were born old. Their parents were Phorcys and Ceto (they were sometimes known as the Phorcides), and their sisters were the GORGONS. They were three in number (only two, in certain traditions), and were called Enyo (2), Pephredo and Dino; they had only one eye and one tooth between them, and they shared these in turn. They lived in the far West, in the land of night, where the Sun never shone.

When PERSEUS set out to slay Medusa, the Graeae barred the road that led to the Gorgons. As they had only one eye, they kept watch in rotation, and the two who did not have the eye slept while awaiting their turn. Perseus managed to steal this eye; this enabled him to pass them and carry out his task. He threw the eye into Lake Tritonis.

In another tradition, the Graeae were trustees of an oracle: they knew that Perseus had to obtain three things in order to kill the Gorgon: some winged sandals from certain Nymphs, a sort of bag called a *kibisis*, and Hades' helmet, which made the wearer invisible. Under the coaching of Hermes and Athena, Perseus, deprived them of their eye and their tooth, and forced them to reveal their secret to him. They told him where to find the Nymphs, who supplied him with the things he needed.

Gratiae See CHARITES.

Griffins (*Γρῦπες*) Fabulous birds with powerful wings, lions' bodies and eagles' beaks. They were sacred to Apollo, whose treasures they guarded in the land of the Hyperboreans. Other authors place them among the Ethiopians, still others in India. The griffins were associated with Nemesis, and also with Dionysus as the guardians of his ever-flowing bowl of wine. Later fables relate that the griffins resisted any search for gold in the deserts in the north of India, either because they were guardians of the precious metal or because their nests lay in the mountains in which it was mined, and they wished to defend their young against every danger.

Gyas (*Γύας*)

1. One of Aeneas' companions, who took part in the funeral games held in honour of Anchises.
2. One of Aeneas' opponents, who was slain by the hero together with his brother Cisseus. Gyas was a Latin who had accompanied Heracles on his expedition against GERYON and had settled in Latium on his return.

Gyges (*Γύγης*)

1. One of the HECATONCHEIRES. He was the brother of Briareus (AEGAEON) and Cottus. With Cottus he took part in the revolt against the Olympians, and was imprisoned by Zeus in Tartarus, where he was guarded by his own brother, Briareus.
2. A king of Lydia, whose story as told by Herodotus contains many elements of folk lore, such as the ring that confers invisibility, the amazing fortune, the discovery of treasure, and the love of a queen.

H

Hades (*Ἅιδης*) The god of the dead. Hades was the son of Cronus and Rhea (Table 8). With his brothers Zeus and Poseidon he shared the empire of the Universe after the defeat of the Titans: Zeus gained the sky, Poseidon the sea, and Hades the Underworld. The Greek Underworld, called 'the House of Hades' by Homer, came to be called simply 'Hades'.

Like his brothers, Hades had been swallowed at birth by Cronus, and later disgorged. He fought against the Titans and the Cyclopes armed with a helmet which conferred invisibility on the wearer. This helmet was subsequently worn by Athena and Perseus.

In the Underworld, Hades reigned over the Dead, allowing none of his subjects to return to the Living. His niece Persephone, the daughter of Demeter (Table 8), reigned at his side. For Persephone's abduction by Hades see PERSEPHONE and DEMETER.

Apart from the story of Persephone's abduction, Hades hardly appears in the legends. The main exception is related in the *Iliad*. Here Heracles went down into the Underworld and shot Hades in the shoulder with an arrow at the Gate of Hell. However, Hades found his way to Olympus where Paean the Healer applied magic ointments which healed his wound immediately. Other versions make Heracles the victor by stunning Hades with a huge boulder.

Hades, whose name means 'the Invisible', was not usually named out loud, for fear of arousing his anger. Euphemisms were used to describe him instead: he was most commonly called Pluton, 'the Rich' – an allusion to the wealth of the cultivated earth and the mines beneath it. Pluton was often depicted holding a horn of plenty, as a symbol of richness (see also PLUTON, PLUTUS, DIS PATER and ORCUS).

Haemon (*Αἵμων*)

1. The son of Creon (2). There are two different traditions about him: according to the first, Haemon was devoured by the Sphinx, and to avenge his death Creon had promised his kingdom to whoever should deliver Thebes from the monster. According to the second, Haemon was betrothed to ANTIGONE (1), and slew himself when Creon condemned the young girl to death. It was sometimes said that Haemon and Antigone had a son, called Maeon (1).
2. The eponymous hero of Haemonia, the old name for Thessaly. This Haemon was the son of Pelasgus and the father of Thessalus (4), who gave the country its new name. In another genealogy, Haemon was one of the fifty sons of Lycaon (2), who himself was the son of Pelasgus. In this tradition, Haemon was not the eponym of Haemonia the country, but the founder of the Arcadian city of Haemonia.

3. The grandson of Cadmus and the son of Polydorus (Table 3). This Haemon had accidentally killed one of his companions during a hunt, and had had to seek refuge in Athens.
4. The son of Thoas (4) and father of Oxylus (2).

Haemus (*Αἷμος*)
1. Haemus (or Hemus) was one of the sons of Boreas and Orithyia, and hence a brother of the Boreades. He married Rhodope, daughter of the river-god Strymon, and reigned over Thrace with her. They had a son called Hebrus, who gave his name to the River Hebrus. Haemus and Rhodope initiated a cult to themselves, calling themselves Zeus and Hera respectively. As punishment for this sacrilege they were transformed into mountains.
2. One of Telephus' companions before Troy. Like Telephus, he came from Mysia, and was said to be the son of Ares.

Hagno (*Ἁγνώ*) In the Arcadian legend of Zeus it was said that the god was born on Mount Lyceus, at a place called Cretea. He had been brought up by three local Nymphs: Hagno, Thisoa, and Neda. Hagno was the Nymph of a spring on Mount Lyceus which was noteworthy for always having water, both in winter and in summer. During a severe drought the priest of Lycian Zeus addressed solemn prayers to the god: and during a sacrifice he dipped a twig of oak into the spring. The water immediately started moving to and fro and a storm sprang up, which drenched the land with rain.

Halesus An Italian hero who gave his name to the Faliscans of Falerii. In some traditions he was a companion, or illegitimate son, of Agamemnon, and had come to Italy at the time of the Trojan War, in other traditions he was a son of Neptune, and as such was respected by Morrius, king of Veii, who initiated the *carmen Saliare* in his honour.

As a descendant of Agamemnon, Halesus was hostile to Aeneas when the latter landed in Italy. Halesus fought alongside Turnus, and was slain by Pallas (5).

Halia (*Ἁλία*)
1. A Rhodian heroine, the sister of the Telchines. Married to Poseidon, she had six sons, and a daughter called Rhodus, who gave her name to Rhodes. Aphrodite struck Halia's sons with madness, and they tried to rape their own mother; but Poseidon thrust them underground with blows from his trident, whereupon Halia threw herself into the sea. The inhabitants of Rhodes worshipped her under the name of Leucothea (2).
2. A Nereid. The name *Halia* was connected with one of the names of the sea, the 'salty element' (*ἅλς*).

Haliacmon (*Ἁλιάκμων*) A river in Macedonia, the god of which was the son of Oceanus and Tethys.

Haliae (*Ἁλίαι*) The name (meaning Women of the Sea) given to some women whose tomb lay in Argos. They were said to have come from the Aegean Sea to fight alongside Dionysus against PERSEUS and the Argives.

Haliartus (*Ἁλίαρτος*) He and his

brother Coronus were the sons of Thersandrus (1) and grandsons of Sisyphus (see PRESBON).

Halirrhothius (*Ἁλιρρόθιος*) The son of Poseidon and the Nymph Euryte. Near Asclepius' spring in Athens he tried to rape Alcippe, the daughter of Ares. Ares slew Halirrhothius, and Poseidon accused his son's murderer before a tribunal of the gods, which met on a hill thereafter known as the Areopagus (the hill of Ares).

Another version claimed that Halirrhothius was outraged when Attica was allotted to Athena and denied to his father. He tried to cut down the olive tree which the goddess had presented to Attica; but his axe flew out of his hands and chopped off his head.

Halmus (*Ἅλμος*) A son of Sisyphus. Eteocles, king of Orchomenus, gave Halmus a portion of land on which he founded the city of Halmones.

Hals (*Ἅλς*) Hals (the Sea) was the name of an enchantress, companion of Circe. When Odysseus paid his second visit to Circe (in the legends which described a sequel to the *Odyssey*) he visited Hals, who transformed him into a horse. She kept him until he died of old age. This legend was intended to explain a verse in the *Odyssey*, which foretold that death would come to Odysseus 'from the Sea'.

Hamadryads (*Ἁμαδρυάδες*) Tree Nymphs who were born with the trees they protected, and shared their fate. Callimachus, in his *Hymn to Delos*, told of an oak Nymph's anguish for her tree, which had been struck by lightning. It was maintained that the Hamadryads died at the same time as their trees. They lived for a very long time – ten 'palm tree lives', or nine thousand seven hundred and twenty years.

Some legends preserve the memory of Hamadryads who had entreated some hero or another to save their trees (see RHOECUS (1), and CHRYSOPELIA). Other legends told of the punishments visited on men who had shown contempt for a Nymph's prayers and cut down her tree (see ERYSICHTHON (1)). For a later legend concerning the origin of the Hamadryads, see OXYLUS (3).

Harmonia (*Ἁρμονία*)

1. In the Theban tradition, Harmonia was the daughter of Ares and Aphrodite. Zeus married her to Cadmus; the wedding took place on the Cadmeia, the citadel of Thebes, and the gods attended. They brought presents including a robe woven by the Charites (a present from Athena or Aphrodite) and a necklace (from Hephaestus). In some versions the robe and necklace were given to Harmonia by CADMUS himself. He had obtained them from Europa (5) and had been given them by Zeus. Another tradition asserts that the robe had been made by Athena and Hephaestus, who impregnated it with a philtre which poisoned Harmonia's children. Their hatred was due to Harmonia being the love-child of Ares and Aphrodite. The robe and necklace play an important role in the legend of the Seven Chiefs (see ALCMAEON (1), AMPHIARAUS, and ERIPHYLE).

2. In the Samothracian traditions, Harmonia was the daughter of Zeus and Electra (2); she was therefore the sister of Dardanus and Iasion (Table 4). In these versions Cadmus met her when he went in search of his sister Europa (5) who had been carried off by Zeus. Harmonia's marriage to Cadmus took place in Samothrace, in the same way as in the Theban tradition. It was also said that Cadmus had carried Harmonia off with Athena's help. Cadmus and Harmonia had several children (Table 3). At the end of their lives, they abandoned the throne of Thebes and went to Illyria, where they were eventually transformed into snakes.
3. The name Harmonia was also applied to the abstract concept of harmony and concord.

Harmonides (*Ἁρμονίδης*) The shipwright who built the ship in which Paris sailed to carry off Helen.

Harpalion (*Ἁρπαλίων*) The son of Pylaemenes, king of Paphlagonia. He fought alongside the Trojans and was killed by Meriones.

Harpalyce (*Ἁρπαλύκη*)
1. Daughter of the Thracian King Harpalycus (1). Her mother died while she was still a child, and Harpalycus fed her on cow's and mare's milk and taught her how to fight. Harpalyce became a skilled warrior. When Thrace was attacked by the Getae, Harpalycus was surrounded by the enemy and seriously wounded; he was saved by his daughter. Harpalycus was later dethroned, and withdrew into the woods, accompanied by Harpalyce, who provided for their needs by hunting and raiding until the local shepherds eventually caught her in their hunting nets and killed her. When the shepherds caught her she had a kid with her, and they argued over this so violently that many of them were killed. A tomb was built for Harpalyce and a cult grew up around her. At the feast held in her honour worshippers engaged in mock battles, in memory of the brawls which marked her death.
2. A girl who committed incest with her father CLYMENUS (3).
3. A girl who fell in love with Iphicles. When he spurned her advances she killed herself.

Harpies (*Ἅρπυιαι*) The Harpies ('the Snatchers') were winged demons, the daughters of Thaumas and Electra (1). Hesiod names two of them, Aello (sometimes called Nicothoe) and Ocypete, but a third, Celaeno (2) was sometimes mentioned. Homer also mentions a Harpy called Podarge. Their names reflected their nature: Aello (wind-squall); Ocypete (fast flyer); Celaeno (obscure, like the sky covered with storm-clouds); Podarge (fleet foot). They were depicted as winged women, or as birds with women's heads and sharp claws. They are said to have lived in the Strophades, islands in the Aegean sea; later, Virgil placed them at the entrance to the Underworld.

The Harpies carried off children and souls. They are sometimes depicted on tombs, carrying the soul of the deceased in their claws. They figure prominently in the myth of King PHINEUS (3) and also in that of PANDAREOS. They were said to have coupled with the wind-god Zephyrus and given birth to two pairs of horses: Xanthus and Balius (1), the horses of Achilles, and Phlogeus and Harpagus, the horses of the Dioscuri.

Harpinna (*Ἅρπιννα*) One of the daughters of the river-god Asopus. Harpinna was loved by Ares, who fathered her child OENOMAUS. She gave her name to the city of Harpina, founded by Oenomaus.

Hebe (*Ἥβη*) The personification of Youth. She was the daughter of Zeus and Hera (Table 8). Within the divine household her role was that of a serving-maid: she poured the nectar (until replaced in this function by GANYMEDE), prepared Ares' bath, and helped Hera to harness the horses to her chariot. She danced with the Muses and the Horae to the sound of Apollo's lyre. After Heracles became a god, he married Hebe; the gods celebrated the marriage as a symbol of his having attained the eternal youthfulness peculiar to the gods.

Hecale (*Ἑκάλη*) When THESEUS was on his way to fight the bull of Marathon, he spent the night in a village in Attica, where he was made welcome by an old woman called Hecale. They spent the evening together by the fire, and the following day, after Theseus' departure, Hecale sacrificed to Zeus to ensure the young man's safe return. After Theseus had killed the bull he went back to Hecale's cottage, only to find that she had died. Theseus then raised a shrine to Zeus Hecaleius in her honour and established the Hecalesian Rites.

Hecamede (*Ἑκαμήδη*) Arsinous' daughter. She was captured by Achilles when he took the island of Tenedos on his way to the Trojan War.

Hecate (*Ἑκάτη*) A goddess closely connectd with ARTEMIS. Hesiod portrays her as the offspring of Asteria (1) and Perses, and a direct descendant of the generation of Titans. She extended her goodwill towards all mortals: she could grant material prosperity, eloquence in political assemblies, and victory in battle and sporting events. She had the power to give fishermen big hauls of fish, and she made cattle grow fat or lean at will. She was most particularly invoked as the 'foster-mother goddess' of youth, as were Artemis and Apollo.

Hecate gradually came to be considered as the deity presiding over magic, and she was linked to the world of Shades. She appeared to magicians and sorceresses with a torch in each hand, or in the form of various animals, such as a mare, a bitch or a she-wolf. She was credited with the invention of sorcery, and legends linked her with magicians such as Aeetes and Medea (see PERSES). Later traditions even portray her as CIRCE's mother. As a magician, Hecate presided over crossroads, where statues were erected to her, in the form of a woman with three bodies or three heads. These statues were especially common in the countryside, and votive offerings were placed near them.

Hecatoncheires (*Ἑκατόγχειρες*) Giants who had a hundred arms and fifty heads. They were three in number: Cottus, Briareus (or

AEGAEON) and GYGES (1) (or Gyes). They were sons of Uranus and Gaia. They fought on the side of the Olympians in the war against the Titans.

Hector (*Ἕκτωρ*) The son of Priam and Hecuba – probably their eldest son, though certain traditions make him Apollo's son. Although Priam was king of Troy, Hector held the real power; he organized the Assembly debates and directed the war effort. He was much loved by the Trojans, and friends and enemies alike acknowledged him as the principal defender of the city. Agamemnon wished to kill Hector as quickly as possible, for he knew he would not take Troy while Hector was alive. Hector's personality is dealt with at considerable length in the *Iliad*. He was married to ANDROMACHE, and had one son by her, who was called Astyanax by the Trojans and Scamandrius (1) by his parents. One aberrant tradition gave Hector and Andromache another son, Laodamas; yet another version mentions a son called Oxynius.

Until the tenth year of the war, Hector avoided fighting in open country, since he knew that Achilles was among the Greeks. Achilles tried once to meet him face to face, but Hector retreated into the city. However, he created considerable carnage among the Greeks when Achilles was not present. He was protected by Ares, until Ares was wounded by Diomedes (2). Mnesthes, Anchialus, Teuthras (2), Orestes (not Agamemnon's son), Trechus, Oenomaus (not the father of Hippodamia (1)), Helenus (not Cassandra's twin brother) and Oresbius were prominent among those he killed. Hector then challenged any Greek hero to single combat; Menelaus came forward, but was held back by Agamemnon; finally Ajax (2) accepted the challenge. The fight went on till nightfall, whereupon Ajax and Hector exchanged presents.

Hector's most brilliant exploit was his attack on the Greek ships. The intervention of the gods was necessary to prevent him from killing such heroes as Nestor or Diomedes (2); Apollo, for his part, protected Hector; and Zeus instructed the gods and goddesses to let Hector be victorious as long as Achilles refused to join the fray. The situation had become critical for the Greeks when PATROCLUS came to their assistance. He was soon killed by Hector, who stripped him of his arms. Achilles rejoined the battle. When Achilles slew Polydorus (2), one of Hector's brothers, Hector tried unsuccessfully to avenge him. Hector was helpless against Achilles for he was fated to die at his hands. Apollo hid Hector in a cloud and Achilles sought him in vain; but when the Trojan army retreated behind the city walls, Hector stayed behind, alone, at the Scaean Gate. His father and mother urged him to take shelter; but he refused to listen and waited for Achilles. However when Achilles drew near, Hector fled from him. The two opponents circled the city three times, until Athena assumed the form of DEIPHOBUS and persuaded Hector to stand and fight. While Hector faced Achilles, Athena disappeared. Hector then realized his last hour had come. On Olympus, Zeus used Destiny's scales to weigh the fates of the two adversaries, and

Hector's proved the heavier. Apollo too abandoned Hector, and Achilles dealt him a mortal blow. As he lay dying, Hector begged Achilles to return his body to Priam, but Achilles refused. Then Hector foretold Achilles' own early death. Achilles attached Hector's body to his chariot and dragged it round the city, under the eyes of the Trojans. Then the corpse was exposed in the Greek camp and left for the dogs and birds of prey, till Zeus sent Iris to order Achilles to hand Hector's corpse over to Priam. For his part, Priam came to Achilles and ransomed his son's body at a heavy price. A twelve-day truce allowed the Trojans to perform their defender's funeral rites. Andromache, Hecuba and Helen were the chief mourners.

Hecuba (*Ἑκάβη*) Priam's second wife. According to one tradition about her genealogy, she was the daughter of Dymas, a king of Phrygia, and the Nymph Eunoe; in the other, she was the daughter of Cisseus, a king of Thrace, and Telecleia. In the first case, she was a descendant of SANGARIUS, and a variant of this tradition made Sangarius her father. In another variant, her mother was Glaucippe, Xanthus' daugher. The tradition linking Hecuba with Dymas and Phrygia was maintained in the *Iliad*. The Thracian lineage was preferred by the tragic poets, especially Euripides.

Hecuba was renowned for her fecundity. Apollodorus names fourteen children: Hector, the eldest; Paris, called Alexander, the second son; then four daughters, Creusa (4), Laodice (4), Polyxena, and Cassandra. The younger children were: Deiphobus, Helenus, Pammon, Polites (1), Antiphus, Hipponous, Polydorus (2), and TROILUS, the youngest. Hecuba is also said to have had a fifteenth child, Polydamas. Euripides said that she had fifty children.

In Homer's work, Hecuba plays only a modest role; in the epic cycles, and especially in the tragedies, she becomes a more significant figure. She had a dream just before giving birth to Paris: a torch emerged from her bosom, which set fire to the city of Troy and the forests of Mount Ida. The seers announced that the infant about to be born would bring about the ruin of the city. Hecuba had him exposed. The child was rescued and later returned to Troy (see PARIS). In another version the soothsayers (and especially AESACUS) merely warned Priam that the child to be born on a certain day would cause Troy's downfall. On the stated day, two births took place: that of Paris and that of Munippus, the son of CILLA and Thymoetes. Priam had Cilla and Munippus put to death.

When Troy fell, Hecuba had lost nearly all her sons. One of them, Polydorus (2), had been entrusted by Priam to Polymestor, king of the Chersonese. At the same time, Priam asked Polymestor to take care of some important treasures for his son. When Troy had fallen and Priam was dead, Polymestor decided to appropriate the treasures. He killed Polydorus and threw his body into the sea. (According to another version, he slew his own son DEIPYLUS by mistake. See also POLYDORUS (2) for variants.) The body was washed up on the coast of the Troad, just as

Hecuba – who had fallen to Odysseus when lots were drawn for the captured Trojan women – was about to leave Troy. The old queen plotted her revenge. She sent one of her serving-women with a false message for Polymestor, saying that a buried treasure had been found. Polymestor joined her, and after the captive Trojan women had slain the two children he had brought with him before his eyes, she tore his eyes out. As a punishment the Greeks decided to stone Hecuba to death; but beneath the mass of stones lay not her corpse, but a bitch with eyes of fire. In another version, Hecuba was transformed into a bitch as she was being pursued by Polydorus' companions, intent on avenging their king. Yet another tradition claims that Hecuba had been transformed aboard the ship that was taking her to Greece, and had thrown herself into the sea. For another version of her death, see HELENUS.

Hegeleus (*Ἡγέλεως*) A grandson of Heracles and the son of Tyrsenus. Tyrsenus is said to have invented the trumpet, and Hegeleus introduced the use of this instrument in war among the Heraclids and the Dorians. He built a temple in Argos to Athena Salpinx (Athena of the Trumpet) (see also MELAS (1)).

Heleius (*Ἕλειος*) The youngest son of Perseus and Andromeda (Table 7). He accompanied Amphitryon on the expedition to Taphos, and after the victory shared the sovereignty of the island with Cephalus. He was said to have founded the city of Helos in Laconia.

Helen (*Ἑλένη*) The wife of Menelaus and the woman for whom the Greeks fought at Troy. In Homer's epic work, she was the daughter of Zeus and Leda, with Tyndareus as her 'human' father (Table 2). The Dioscuri, Castor and Pollux, were her brothers, and Clytemnestra her sister. Helen was later said to be the daughter of Zeus and NEMESIS. The tradition that claims that Leda was Helen's mother recounts how Zeus lay with her in the form of a swan and how she laid an egg from which Helen issued. In a variant tradition, Leda laid *two* eggs; Helen and Pollux came from one, and Clytemnestra and Castor from the other. Yet another version claims that Helen, Castor and Pollux all came from the same egg, while Clytemnestra was born in the normal way. Still other traditions claim that Helen was the daughter of Oceanus or even of Aphrodite.

A legend not mentioned in Homer tells of Helen's abduction by Theseus and Pirithous. The two heroes decided to marry daughters of Zeus, since they were the sons of Poseidon and Zeus respectively, and began by abducting Helen. Some mythographers maintained that the abduction was carried out by Idas and Lynceus (2), or that Tyndareus handed her over to Theseus for protection, being afraid that one of the sons of Hippocoon wanted to abduct her. However, the most common version is that Theseus and Pirithous went to Sparta and kidnapped Helen while she was performing a ritual dance in the temple of Artemis Orthia. They drew lots for her and Theseus won. The Athenians were unwilling to welcome the young girl among them, so Theseus took her to Aphidnae, where he entrusted her to his mother AETHRA. Theseus and Pirithous then set off to the Underworld to bring Persephone back to earth. During their absence the Dioscuri arrived to rescue Helen. The people of Decelea showed the Dioscuri where Helen had been hidden (see DECELUS). Other versions attribute this role to ACADEMUS. Castor and Pollux attacked and captured Aphidnae and carried off their sister, taking Aethra back to Lacedaemon as a prisoner. They then installed MENESTHEUS on the Athenian throne. In some versions Theseus respected Helen's virginity; in others he gave her a daughter, IPHIGENIA.

On Helen's return to Lacedaemon Tyndareus thought that she should be married. A crowd of suitors appeared, including nearly every prince in Greece, although Achilles never appears in any of the lists. Tyndareus was afraid that by choosing one he would antagonize the others and so he took the advice of Odysseus, which was that he should make all the suitors take an oath to accept Helen's choice and support her betrothed, should need arise (see also ICARIUS (2)). It was this oath that Menelaus invoked some years later, compelling all the Greek leaders to take up arms against Troy. Helen chose Menelaus, and soon gave her husband a daugher, Hermione. According to some traditions, she also had a son called Nicostratus; but only after her return from Troy.

Helen was then carried off to Troy. She was then the most beautiful woman in the world, and had been promised to PARIS by Aphrodite. On her advice, he sailed to Sparta, where he was welcomed at Menelaus' court. When Menelaus had to go to Crete to attend CATREUS' funeral, Helen took his place among the guests. This is how she met Paris. Most authors believed that Helen was a consenting paraty in this abduction, though some asserted that she had yielded only to force. In some versions it is claimed that Tyndareus gave Paris Helen's hand while Menelaus was away. It was even said that Aphrodite had given Paris the face and figure of Menelaus, thus making it easy for him to seduce Helen. But the view generally held was that Paris' beauty and wealth were the significant factors. Helen took a wealth of treasure with her, and also her personal slaves, including the captive Aethra; however, she left Hermione in Sparta.

There are differing traditions about the voyage of the two lovers. One version says that favourable winds enabled Paris to reach Asia Minor in three days; another that Paris' ship was driven by a storm, raised by Hera, as far as Sidon in Phoenicia. Although the king welcomed him in friendly fashion, Paris plundered the palace before leaving, pursued by the Phoenicians, with whom he had a fierce battle. He finally reached Troy with Helen. A closely related traditions claims that Paris spent a considerable time in Phoenicia and Cyprus, and returned to Troy only when he was certain he would not be harassed by Menelaus. In all these differing versions, he kept Helen at his side. A different tradition claims that Hera, annoyed to see Aphrodite preferred to herself in the beauty contest, fashioned a cloud that looked exactly like Helen and gave it to Paris, while the real Helen was carried off to Egypt by Hermes and entrusted to PROTEUS. According to a variant tradition, Zeus himself sent a phantom Helen to Troy to provoke a war. According to Herodotus, when Helen and Paris went to Egypt on their way to Troy, Proteus initially made them welcome, until he found out how they came to be together. In his indignation he banished Paris and kept Helen prisoner in his palace until Menelaus could come to fetch her. Later authors added to the legend by claiming that Proteus was reluctant to send Paris off alone, so he used his magic arts to fashion a simulacrum of Helen to keep Paris company, and it was for this phantom Helen that the Trojan War was fought. The object of these legends may have been to free Helen from blame and present her as the instrument of fate. They probably derive from the poet Stesichorus' 'recantation' (see AUTOLEON).

According to the Homeric tradition, Helen was welcomed by Priam and Hecuba, who were enchanted by her beauty. Before long, however, ambassadors arrived from Greece seeking the fugitive's return: Odysseus and Menelaus, or Acamas (3) and Diomedes (2). These missions proved fruitless, and war broke out. Helen was universally looked upon as Paris' wife; but she was generally hated by the Trojan people, who regarded her as the cause of the war. Only Hector and Priam knew that the war had resulted from the wills of the gods, and they were well disposed towards her. In the *Iliad*, Helen is described as standing on the ramparts, helping the Trojans by pointing out the Greek leaders, but as a compatriot of the enemy she was sympathetic to their cause; the Trojans thus had good reason to distrust her. However, she faced her difficulties with courage, knowing her beauty would always get her out of trouble. A legend not included in the *Iliad* tells how Achilles was seized with a desire to meet Helen, and how Thetis and Artemis arranged a meeting for them. It is possible that Achilles fell in love with her at first sight and coupled with her immediately. This was the view of those mythographers who gave Helen five husbands, making Achilles the fourth, after Theseus, Menelaus and Paris. The fifth, whom she married after Paris' death, was DEIPHOBUS. As soon as Paris was slain, Priam offered Helen as a prize for the bravest man: Deiphobus and HELENUS put themselves forward, as did Idomeneus, another of Priam's sons. Deiphobus won her.

When Odysseus, dressed as a beggar, made his way into the city, Helen recognized him but did not betray him. Euripides claimed that she revealed his presence to Hecuba, who merely sent him out of the city, instead of handing him over to the Trojans. Later, Odysseus came back into Troy, accompanied by Diomedes (2) and intending to steal the PALLADIUM. This time Helen recognized him and actually helped him. Odysseus reached an understanding with her as to the necessary measures for the capture of Troy. On the fateful night, she waved a torch from the citadel, the signal for the return of the Greek fleet. She removed all arms from Deiphobus' house, and having thus proved her loyalty to the Greeks, she awaited the arrival of MENELAUS. After he had killed Deiphobus, Menelaus ran at her, intending to kill her as well, but she displayed herself to him half-naked, and the sword fell from his hand. It is also said that Helen took refuge in Aphrodite's temple, and made her peace with Menelaus from that inviolable ground. When the Greeks saw that Helen had survived, they wished to stone her to death. Once again she was saved by her beauty, and the stones fell from the hands of her would-be executioners.

Helen's return to Greece with Menelaus took eight years; she wandered over the eastern Mediterranean, especially Egypt, where her ship was wrecked. Various legends deal with her stay in Egypt: see CANOPUS, THON, POLYDAMNA and PHAROS.

According to Euripides, before Helen and Menelaus reached Sparta they landed at Argos, on the day that ORESTES had just slain Clytemnestra and Aegisthus. Neither Menelaus nor Helen knew what had just happened there. When Orestes set eyes on Helen, surrounded by the women of her train, and clad in Trojan dress, he wanted to kill her because he held her responsible for the disasters which had befallen his house; however at Zeus' command Apollo carried her away and made her immortal. This legend differs from the tradition generally accepted since the *Odyssey*, which shows Helen returning to Sparta at Menelaus' side, and thereafter setting an example of all the domestic virtues. There were many shrines to the deified Helen, in which Menelaus was honoured too. He had been deified in answer to the prayers of Helen, who was anxious to compensate him for the torments she had inflicted on him during their life together.

For a Rhodian myth, related by Pausanias, in which Helen meets a violent death, see POLYXO (2). In other traditions Iphigenia was said to have offered her as a sacrifice in Tauris ('poetic vengeance' for Iphigenia's sacrifice at Aulis); or again that Thetis, angered at the death of Achilles, who had fallen because of Helen, killed her during the return voyage. However, another legend portrays Helen as married to Achilles and enjoying an eternal life on the White Island at the mouth of the Danube. Poseidon and the other gods attended the wedding, and no mortal was allowed to set foot on this island (see, however, AUTOLEON). Achilles and Helen had a son, Euphorion, a winged being who was loved by Zeus.

Helen had several children from her various marriages. Only her marriage to Deiphobus was childless. She and Paris argued about what they should call their daughter: Alexandra, after her father, or Helena, after her mother. Finally, they decided to let the knucklebones make the choice for them, and Helen won. Helena is said to have been slain by Hecuba.

Helenus (*Ἕλενος*) Son of Priam and Hecuba, and Cassandra's twin brother. He acquired the gift of prophecy at the same time as she did (see CASSANDRA). Helenus was a favourite of Apollo, who presented him with an ivory bow, with which he wounded Achilles in the hand. Helenus predicted to Paris all the calamities that would occur as a result of his voyage to Greece in which he abducted HELEN. In the Trojan War Helenus fought alongside Hector; after Hector's death he replaced him as leader of the Trojans. He was wounded by Menelaus. After Paris' death Helenus' attitude changed completely. Priam refused him Helen's hand and gave her to Deiphobus; Helenus retired to Mount Ida. The Greek seer Calchas (1) had announced that only Helenus could reveal how Troy could be captured. Odysseus captured Helenus, and made him reveal these three conditions: Achilles' son Neoptolemus must be fighting with the Greeks; the Greeks must possess the bones of Pelops; the PALLADIUM must be stolen from the Trojans. Helenus is also said to have said that PHILOCTETES must return to the Greeks, bringing Heracles' bow and arrows with him. Helenus is also said to have advised the Greeks to use the Wooden Horse. For these and other services Helenus was spared and set free after the fall of the city. According to one tradition he then went to the Thracian Chersonese and settled there with Hecuba, Andromache and Cassandra. Hecuba is said to have been transformed into a bitch there, and to have died; Helenus buried her in the Bitch Tomb. Another tradition holds that he and Andromache were allotted to Neoptolemus as spoils of war. As a prophet Helenus advised Neoptolemus to make his way home by land; Neoptolemus thus escaped the disaster of Cape Caphareus, where most of the Greek fleet was wrecked. When NEOPTOLEMUS was slain by Orestes, Helenus married his widow ANDROMACHE; they had a son, Cestrinus.

Helenus was credited with founding Buthrotum and Ilium in Epirus. He gave Chaonia its name, after his brother CHAON. In the *Aeneid* Helenus is married to Andromache and welcomes any of his compatriots who pass through Epirus. A later tradition claims that when Deiphobus was preferred to Helenus, the latter left Troy for Greece, settled in Epirus and established himself as ruler of the Molossians.

Heliades (*Ἡλιάδαι* and *Ἡλιάδες*)
1. The daughters of Helios and Clymene (1). Their names were Merope (7), Helia, Phoebe (3), Aetheria, and Dioxippe (or Lampetia (2)). When their brother Phaethon was smitten by Zeus' thunderbolt, the Heliades wept for him on the banks of the river Eridanus, where they were transformed into poplars; their tears became drops of amber. It was also said that their metamorphosis was a punishment because they had given PHAETHON the chariot and horses of the Sun without Helios' permission.
2. The sons of Helios and the nymph Rhodus. There were seven of them: Ochimus, Cercaphus, Macareus (or MACAR), Actis, Tenages, Triopas and Candalus. They were all expert astrologers, but Macareus, Candalus, Actis and Triopas grew jealous of Tenages' skill and killed him. Then they fled to Lesbos, Cos, Egypt and Caria respectively. Ochimus and Cercaphus stayed in Rhodes. Ochimus, the eldest, seized power and reigned over the island. He married the Nymph Hegetoria and they had a daughter Cydippe.

Cydippe was married to her uncle, Cercaphus, who was his brother's heir and ruled after him. Cydippe had three sons – Lindos, Ialysus and Camirus, who in due course shared the country between them and founded the three cities that bore their names (see also TLEPOLEMUS). Another tradition recounts that Ochimus had engaged Cydippe to a man called Ocridion, but Cercaphus, who was in love with his niece, abducted her and fled abroad. He came back later when Ochimus was an old man.

Helicaon (*Ἑλικάων*) One of the sons of ANTENOR. He married Laodice (4). He was saved by Odysseus when the city fell, and accompanied Antenor and Polydamas to northern Italy.

Helice (*Ἑλίκη*)
1. Selinus' daughter; she married ION.
2. One of the two Nymphs who nursed Zeus. When Cronus wanted to punish them for bringing up the child, Zeus transformed them into constellations, the Great Bear and the Little Bear. Helice was sometimes identified with CALLISTO (1), who was changed into the constellation of the Great Bear by Zeus.

Helios (*Ἥλιος*) The Sun. He was the son of the Titan Hyperion and the Titaness Theia; he was the brother of Eos and Selene (Table 8), and a descendant of Uranus and Gaia. Helios' wife was Perseis, one of the daughters of Oceanus and Tethys. She bore Circe, Aeetes, Pasiphae, and a son, Perses, who dethroned his brother Aeetes, and was himself slain by his own niece, Medea. In addition, Helios coupled with the Nymph Rhodos, by whom he had the HELIADES (2); Clymene (1), who bore him daughters, the HELIADES (1); Leucothoe (2); and Eurynome (see also PHAETHON and CLYTIA).

Helios is portrayed as a young man of very great beauty: his head was surrounded with rays of light. He travelled across the sky in a chariot of fire drawn by swift horses called Pyrois, Eos, Aethon, and Phlegon. Each morning, preceded by the chariot of Aurora, Helios set out on his journey from the land of the Indians, crossing the centre of the sky, and reaching the Ocean in the evening. He rested in a golden palace, from which he set out again the next morning. His route then ran underground, or along the Ocean stream which encircled the world, in a boat fashioned out of a big hollow bowl (see HERACLES, II). His journey from west to east was much shorter than his daily passage along the vault of heaven. From the days of Homer, Helios was portrayed as the servant of the gods. He was unable to take any revenge himself for the insult done to him by Odysseus' companions, who killed and ate part of his herds. He sought redress by threatening to withdraw beneath the earth if the culprits were not punished as he requested. These cattle of the Sun, which were eaten by Odysseus' companions, were animals of immaculate whiteness, with gilded horns; they were tended by the HELIADES (1). Helios was often thought of as the eye of the world, who saw everything, and in this capacity he cured ORION's blindness.

For the quarrel between Helios and Poseidon, see POSEIDON.

Helle (*Ἕλλη*) See PHRIXUS.

Hellen (*Ἕλλην*) The hero who gave his name to the Greek race, the Hellenes. He was the son of Deucalion (1) (Table 5), though certain authors refer to him as Prometheus' son. He married a Nymph called Orseis, who bore him DORUS, XUTHUS, and AEOLUS (1), from whom sprang the principal groups of the Hellenes: Dorians, Aeolians, Ionians and Achaeans (Table 5). Hellen was the king of Phthia in Thessaly, which lay between the rivers Peneus and Asopus, the exact place where Deucalion and Pyrrha (1) had settled after the Flood. He was succeeded by Aeolus; his other sons emigrated and settled in different areas of Greece.

Hemera (*Ἡμέρα*) The personification of the Day. She was the daughter of Erebus and Nyx, and the sister of AETHER (see URANUS).

Hemicynes (*Ἡμίκυνες*) The 'Half-Dogs' were a legendary race who lived on the shore of the Euxine Sea (the Black Sea). They had the head and the bark of a dog.

Hemithea (*Ἡμιθέα*)

1. A heroine honoured at Castabus, in the Thracian Chersonese. She was the daughter of STAPHYLUS (3) (see PARTHENUS (1)).
2. The daughter of CYCNUS (2) (see also TENES). When the Greeks landed on Tenedos on their way to Troy, Achilles pursued Hemithea and would have raped her, had not the earth opened up and engulfed her.

Heosphorus (*Ἑωσφόρος*) Heosphorus or Eosphorus was the name of the Morning Star. He was the son of Aurora and Astraeus and the father of Telauge. He also had a daughter by Cleoboea, named Philonis (see PHILAMMON).

Hephaestus (*Ἥφαιστος*) The god of fire, the son of Zeus and Hera. Hesiod claimed that Hera produced him on her own, out of resentment for the birth of ATHENA, whom Zeus had brought into the world without the assistance of any woman. She then entrusted him to Cedalion so that he might learn metalworking. A tradition from Crete makes Hephaestus the son of TALOS (1).

Hephaestus was lame. The usual explanation is recounted in the *Iliad*. Hera was quarrelling with Zeus about Heracles, and Hephaestus took his mother's side. Zeus threw him down from Olympus. Hephaestus' fall lasted for a whole day: towards the evening, he hit the ground in the island of Lemnos, was rescued by the Sintians and restored to life, but he remained lame. Another legend about his infirmity is also found in the *Iliad*. Hephaestus was born lame, and in her shame his mother threw him down from Olympus. Hephaestus fell into the Ocean, where he was rescued by Tethys and Eurynome (1), who brought him up for nine years in a cave beneath the sea. Attempts have been made to reconcile the two versions. It was suggested that Hephaestus had been cast out by Zeus, but that he had fallen into the sea, where he had been rescued by the marine goddesses. (HERA herself was said to have been brought up by Oceanus and Tethys.)

To avenge himself on his mother for having thrown him from Olympus, Hephaestus fashioned a throne of gold, in which chains were concealed to bind anyone who sat in it. He sent it to his mother, who sat in it, only to find herself bound hand and foot. No one knew how to undo the chains except Hephaestus. The gods were thus compelled to recall him to Olympus, with the request that he should free the goddess. Dionysus was chosen to go to fetch him; to convince him, Dionysus made him drunk. Hephaestus made his entry to Olympus mounted upon an ass. Then he released his mother.

Hephaestus was master of fire. He used flame as his weapon in the Trojan War; during the Giants' Revolt he had slain Clytius with a mass of red-hot iron. He was also the god of metals and metallurgy. He ruled over the volcanoes, which were his workshops, where he worked with his assistants, the Cyclopes. Thetis turned to him when she wanted arms forged for Achilles. Hephaestus was an inventor for whom no technical miracle was impossible. Although he was deformed, Hephaestus was able to win the hearts of women of great beauty. In the *Iliad*, his name is linked with that of Charis, who was Grace personified. Hesiod portrays him as wedded to Aglaea, the youngest of the Charites. He was particularly famous for his amorous adventures, which are related in the *Odyssey* (see APHRODITE).

Tradition credits Hephaestus with several sons, among them Palaemon and Ardalus, a sculptor who, like Palaemon, inherited his father's manual dexterity. Periphetes (1) is also mentioned. ERICHTHONIUS was born of Mother Earth as a result of Hephaestus' lust for ATHENA. Hephaestus also played a part in the creation of PANDORA, whose body he fashioned out of clay. He also contributed to the punishment of PROMETHEUS by fettering him to the Caucasus Mountains.

Hera (*Ἥρα*) The greatest of all the Olympian goddesses. She was the daughter of Cronus and Rhea, and hence ZEUS' sister. She was swallowed by Cronus, but restored to life by METIS and Zeus. Hera was brought up by Oceanus and Tethys, to whom Rhea had entrusted her during the struggle between Zeus and the Titans. Other traditions credit the HORAE with Hera's upbringing, or Temenus (1), or the daughters of Asterion.

Hera married Zeus in a formal wedding ceremony. Hesiod says that she was Zeus' third wife: his first was Metis and the next was Themis. The love between Zeus and Hera was of long standing, however, and they had coupled secretly in the days when Cronus ruled the Universe. Four children were born of their marriage: Hephaestus, Ares, Eilithyia and Hebe (Table 8). One tradition places the site of their wedding in the Garden of the Hesperides. Some mythographers assert that the golden apples of the HESPERIDES were a present given to Hera by Gaia on the occasion of her marriage and that Hera found them so beautiful that she planted them in her garden on the shores of the Ocean. The *Iliad* says that Zeus and Hera were married on the summit of Mount Ida in Phrygia. Other traditions place the marriage in Euboea, where the god and goddess landed when they came from Crete. Festivals commemorating the marriage of Zeus and Hera took place almost everywhere in Greece. The statue of the goddess was dressed in the costume of a bride and carried in procession to a shrine where a marital bed had been made ready (see ALALCOMENEUS and CITHAERON). Hera was the protecting deity of wives. She is portrayed as jealous, violent, and vindictive, often angry with Zeus, whose infidelities she regarded as insults. She visited her hatred not only on Zeus' mistresses, but on the children he sired upon them. Among these, HERACLES was the greatest victim of Hera's wrath. Her vindictiveness cost her dear, however, for when Heracles returned after he had captured Troy, Hera raised a violent storm against his ship. This displeased Zeus, who hung her from Mount Olympus by her wrists with an anvil fastened to each foot. HEPHAESTUS tried to free his mother, which brought Zeus' wrath down upon him. Later, Hera made formal peace with Heracles.

Hera appears in many myths. She persecuted Io, and suggested to the Curetes that they should kill EPAPHUS, her rival's son. She was responsible for SEMELE's fate. She struck ATHAMAS and Ino with madness to punish them for having brought up DIONYSUS, Zeus' son by Semele. She urged Artemis to slay CALLISTO (I), whom Zeus had seduced, and she tried to stop the birth of Artemis and Apollo when LETO was in labour. Hera's anger and her acts of vengeance sometimes had other reasons behind them. Hera and Zeus were arguing one day as to whether the man or the woman derived greater pleasure from sex. Zeus said that women enjoyed it more, Hera that men did. The two deities consulted TIRESIAS, who had experienced sex both as a man and as a woman. Tiresias said that if the pleasures of love were divided into ten parts, the man felt one of those parts, while the woman felt the other nine. Hera was so annoyed that she deprived Tiresias of his sight.

Hera participated in the beauty contest with Aphrodite and Athena, with Paris acting as judge. In the Trojan War she sided against the Trojans in revenge for Paris' refusal to award her the prize, even though she had tried to bribe him by promising thim the sovereignty of the world. When Paris abducted HELEN, Hera raised a storm which drove them on to the Syrian coast. Hera became Achilles' protectress, since she had brought THETIS up, and this was the reason why Thetis spurned the advances of Zeus. Later, Hera extended her protection to MENELAUS, and gave him immortality.

Hera participated in the war against the Giants, in which she was attacked by Porphyrion (see GIANTS). Hera was attacked again later on by IXION, who wished to abduct her (see CENTAURS). Hera was also the protectress of the *Argo*, which she helped to pass unscathed between the Planctae, or Wandering Rocks (see ARGONAUTS) and through the narrows of Scylla (I) and Charybdis. Hera's usual symbol was the peacock, whose plumage was said to represent the eyes of ARGOS, whom the goddess had set over Io. In Rome, Hera was identified with JUNO.

Heracles (*Ἡρακλῆς*)

I. HERACLES' NAME, ORIGINS AND INFANCY

Heracles was originally called Alcides, a patronym formed from the name of his grandfather Alceus (Table 7), or even Alceus, like his grandfather. His name evokes the idea of physical strength (ἀλκή). When the hero went to Delphi to atone for the murder of the children he had by Megara (1), the Pythia instructed him to take the name of Heracles, meaning 'Hera's Glory' – perhaps because the Labours he was about to undertake would result in the goddess' glorification. His mortal father was AMPHITRYON and his mother ALCMENE; his grandfathers, Alceus and Electryon, were both sons of Perseus and Andromeda (Table 7). He therefore belonged to the Argive race and his birth at Thebes was quite fortuitous. He always considered the Argolid as his real fatherland and always wished to return there, and his descendants came back to settle there (see HERACLIDS). Heracles' real father was Zeus, who had profited by Amphitryon's absence on an expedition against the Teleboans (see ALCMENE).

Even before Heracles was born, Hera's wrath and her jealousy of Alcmene were apparent. Zeus had rashly stated that the first child to be born into the race of the Perseides would rule over Argos. Hera immediately arranged with Eilithyia, the goddess of childbirth, that the birth of Heracles should be held up, while that of his cousin EURYSTHEUS should be advanced. Eurystheus was born first (see also GALINTHIAS). While still a babe in arms, Heracles sucked at the breast of Hera, his bitterest enemy. This was the condition which had to be fulfilled for him to achieve immortality. Trickery was necessary in order to achieve it. Hermes put the babe to the goddess' breast as she lay asleep. When she woke up, she pushed the child away, but it was too late: the milk that spurted from her breast formed a trail of stars in the sky, the Milky Way. Another tradition tells that Alcmene, fearing Hera's jealousy, exposed Heracles as soon as he was born. Athena and Hera happened to be passing by; Athena asked Hera to give him the breast. Hera did so, but Heracles sucked so hard that he hurt the goddess. She flung him away, but Athena took him back to Alcmene, telling her to bring her child up without any further fear.

When Heracles was eight or ten months old, Hera tried to destroy him. Heracles and Iphicles were asleep in their cradle. Towards midnight, the goddess introduced two huge snakes into the room, which twined themselves around the babies. Iphicles started to cry, but Heracles grasped the animals, one in each hand, and strangled them. At Iphicles' screams, Amphitryon came running, but there was no need for him to take any action. It was clear that Heracles was indeed the son of a god. Heracles was given an education comparable to that of Greek children of the Classical era. His principal tutor was Linus (2), who taught him letters and music. Heracles was extremely undisciplined, so much so that Linus tried to beat him, but Heracles lost his temper, and killed his master (see LINUS (2)). Heracles was accused of murder. He defended himself successfully by quoting a judgement of Rhadamanthys, which entitled one to kill an aggressor in self-defence. Amphitryon feared further fits of rage from his adopted son; so he sent him off to the country and put him in charge of his herds of cattle. It is generally agreed, however, that he received his education from other masters: Amphitryon taught him how to drive a chariot and EURYTUS (2) showed him how to use a bow – although Rhadamanthys or a Scythian cowherd called Teutarus are also credited with this. He was taught how to handle arms by Castor (either one of the Dioscuri or a refugee from Argos, the son of Hippalus). After the death of his tutor his lessons were continued by Eumolpus (2).

Meanwhile, Heracles was growing up: he reached the extraordinary height of four cubits and one foot. When he was eighteen, he killed the lion of Cithaeron, a beast which caused havoc among the herds of Amphitryon and Thespius, who was ruler of a country close to Thebes (for subsequent events see THESPIUS). Some authors placed this first lion-hunt not on the slopes of Cithaeron but on Mount Helicon, or near Teumessus. Pausanias accepted a legend which claimed that the lion of Cithaeron was not slain by Heracles, but by ALCATHUS (who was more generally considered to have slain the lion of Megara).

For the events which occurred as Heracles was approaching Thebes on his return from hunting the lion, see ERGINUS (1). In some traditions Heracles' father Amphitryon died at this time; in others he did not die until after the successful expedition with Heracles against CHALCODON (1).

Creon (2), wishing to reward Heracles for defeating the Minyans of Orchomenus, gave him his eldest daughter Megara (1) in marriage, while IPHICLES was given the second daughter to marry. They had several children: according to different authors there were between three and eight of them. Their names differ and are given variously as Therimachus, Deiocoon, Creontiades, Oneites, Oxeus, Aristodemus, Clymenus, Glenus, Polydorus, Anicetus, Mecistophonus, Patrocles, Toxoclitus, Menebrontes and Chersibius. The various names are grouped according to the various traditions. The marriage had a tragic ending, however. The version recounted by Euripides in *Heracles Furens* is the standard one. Euripides tells how when Heracles had gone to the Underworld to find Cerberus, Lycus (4) had come to Euboea to dethrone Creon and had killed him. Lycus was on the point of murdering Megara and her children when Heracles returned. The hero began by killing Lycus and was about to offer a thanksgiving sacrifice to Zeus when he went mad and shot Megara and his children with his arrows, believing them to be Eurystheus' (in another tradition he threw them into the fire). He was on the point of doing the same with Amphitryon, who he thought was Eurystheus' father Sthenelus (4), when Athena hit him in the chest with a stone, which sent him into a deep sleep. When he awoke and realized what he had done, he wanted to commit suicide; but Theseus arrived, dissuaded him and took him to Athens.

Some mythographers claim that Megarus survived the massacre, and that Heracles then wanted to break up the marriage which he had stained with blood, and that he married Megara to his nephew Iolaus. Alternatively, after the killing, Heracles left Thebes for a year in exile. He was recalled by Iphicles and Licymnius, but did not wish to return. Iphicles, Licymnius and Megara went in search of him and found him at Tiryns. Yet another version claims that children of Heracles and Megara were killed by Lycus.

The usual explanation for the murders is an attack of madness induced by Hera. Hera wanted to force Heracles to put his services at the disposal of Eurystheus, by making him commit some defilement which would necessitate expiation. Despite Zeus' oracle, Heracles was reluctant to go to Argos and acknowledge Eurystheus as his master; but now Hera had sent him a warning.

II. THE TWELVE LABOURS

These were the exploits carried out by Heracles at the bidding of his cousin EURYSTHEUS. The traditions give different explanations of why the hero submitted to someone who was so far from being his equal. The *Iliad* describes the trickery of Hera, who turned Zeus' promise around to Eurystheus' advantage; but Heracles did not submit personally to his cousin, although the delaying of his own birth had in fact made him Eurystheus' 'subject'. According to Euripides, Heracles expressed his wish to return to Argos and Eurystheus agreed to this – but on the condition that Heracles should carry out for him certain Labours. This period of bondage was generally considered to be the expiation for Heracles' murder of his children. After the murder, Heracles went to consult the oracle at Delphi, where he was instructed to place himself at his cousin's disposal for twelve years. Apollo (and Athena) added that as a reward he would be granted immortality.

The mythographers of the Hellenistic age established an authoritative list of the Twelve Labours, dividing them into two series of six. The first six took place in the Peloponnese, while the other six took place in Crete, Thrace, Scythia; in the far West, in the land of the Hesperides; and in the Underworld. The established order of events is the one followed here. There are many variations on the order in which the Labours were carried out and on their number (Apollodorus, for example, recognized only ten).

Heracles' most distinctive weapon was his club, which he fashioned himself. In some versions he was said to have cut it in Nemea, and in others on Mount Helicon, or on the shores of the Saronic Gulf, from the trunk of a wild olive tree. The rest of his weapons were of divine origin – his sword was given to him by Hermes, his bow and arrows by Apollo, and his gilded breastplate was a present from Hephaestus. According to other traditions, Athena furnished him with all his weapons except for his club. Finally, his horses were a gift from Poseidon.

The Nemean Lion Heracles' first task was to kill the Nemean lion, a monster, the son of Orthrus and ECHIDNA. Hera (or perhaps Selene) brought it up and set it in the region of Nemea, where it ravaged the land. The lion lived in a cave with two exits and was invulnerable. Heracles shot at it with his bow, but this proved useless; then he threatened it with his club, drove it back into its cave, and blocked up one of the exits: then he seized it in his arms and strangled it. When the lion was dead, Heracles flayed it and clad himself in its skin, with the lion's head serving as a helmet. The lion's skin was impervious to both steel and fire, so Heracles used the monster's own claws to cut it. During the hunt for the Nemean lion Heracles met a peasant named MOLORCHUS. Heracles brought the lion's body back to Mycenae, where Eurystheus was so terrified by the courage of the hero who was able to slay such a monster that he forbade him to enter the city, and ordered him henceforth to leave the fruits of his Labours outside the gates. It is said that Zeus added the lion to the constellations to commemorate Heracles' exploit.

The Lernaean Hydra The Lernaean Hydra was a monster, the daughter of Echidna and Typhon. It was reared by Hera under a plane-tree near the source of the River Amymone, to serve as a test for Heracles. This Hydra was depicted as a snake with several heads; the number varies from five or six up to a hundred; sometimes they were said to be human heads. The breath that issued from its mouths was so venomous that anyone who approached it invariably died. It used to ravage the countryside. Heracles used flaming arrows against it, and was also said to have cut off its heads with a short curved sabre. He was helped in this by his nephew Iolaus, whose help was essential since every head he cut off immediately grew back again. To stop the heads growing back, Heracles asked Iolaus to set fire to the nearby grove of trees; he then used burning brands to cauterize the neck-stumps, making it impossible for heads to grow again. According to some authors, the central head was immortal; but Heracles cut it off, buried it, and then set a huge rock on top of it. He finally dipped his arrows in the Hydra's venom (or in its blood), and made them poisonous (see PHILOCTETES). In her spite against Heracles, Hera sent an enormous crab to help the Hydra; this crab nipped the hero on the heel, but he crushed it. According to Apollodorus, Eurystheus refused to count this Labour on the grounds that Heracles had been helped by Iolaus.

The Erymanthian Boar The third Labour was to bring back alive a monstrous boar that lived on Mount Erymanthus. Heracles' shouts forced the animal to leave its lair; then he drove it into the deep snow which covered the countryside, keeping it on the run until it was exhausted, thus enabling him to capture it. He brought it back to Mycenae across his shoulders. When Eurystheus saw it, he hid himself in a big jar he had had prepared for himself as a refuge in time of danger. During this Labour, Heracles had his adventure with the Centaur Pholus (see CENTAURS).

The Hind of Ceryneia The fourth

Labour was the capture of a hind that lived at Oenoe. Euripides says that it was an animal of enormous size, which ravaged the crops. Heracles killed it and consecrated its horns in the temple of Oenoetian Artemis. However, this version is an isolated one. In Callimachus' account, this hind was one of five which Artemis had seen in earlier days grazing on Mount Lycaeus. They all had gilded horns, and were bigger than bulls. The goddess captured four of them. The fifth, guided by Hera, took refuge on Mount Ceryneia. The animal was sacred to Artemis, and wore a collar round its neck with the inscription: 'Taygete has dedicated me to Artemis' (see TAYGETE). It was therefore an act of impiety to kill it. This hind was very swift; Heracles hunted it for a year without catching it. It finally grew tired and sought refuge on Mount Artemisium. When Heracles continued his pursuit, it tried to cross the river Ladon, in Arcadia. Heracles then wounded it with an arrow, after which he caught it quite easily. As he was returning he met Artemis and Apollo; the two deities sought to deprive him of the animal, which belonged to them. They accused him of wanting to kill it, but Heracles put the blame on to Eurystheus, arguing his case so well that they gave him back the hind and allowed him to continue. According to Pindar, Heracles hunted the hind towards the north, across the River Ister, into the land of the Hyperboreans, and as far as the Islands of the Blessed, where Artemis gave him a kindly welcome.

The Stymphalian Birds These birds lived in a forest on the shores of Lake Stymphalus in Arcadia, whither they had fled to avoid an invasion of wolves. They had become a plague to the surrounding territory; they ate the fruit of the fields and ravaged all the crops. Eurystheus ordered Heracles to destroy them. The difficulty lay in driving them out of the dense thickets; to achieve this the hero used castanets of bronze. Frightened by the noise of these castanets, the birds broke cover, and Heracles killed them with his arrows. Other traditions portray these creatures as birds of prey, which even devoured men. In some accounts their feathers were of sharp metal, and they shot them at their enemies like arrows.

The Stables of Augias Wishing to humiliate Heracles by ordering him to do menial labour, Eurystheus ordered him to clean these stables, which he did (see AUGIAS). Augias refused to pay the agreed reward, but Heracles waged a successful war against him (see HERACLES, III, and MOLIONIDAE). According to Apollodorus, Eurystheus refused to count this Labour on the grounds that Heracles had received, or at least asked for, a salary for cleaning the stables, and was therefore not in Eurystheus' service at the time.

The Cretan Bull The Cretan Bull, according to some versions, was the animal which abducted Europa (5), though this version does not agree that Zeus transformed himself into the bull; according to others, the Cretan Bull had been the lover of Pasiphae. Another account claims that it was a bull which rose from the sea after Minos had vowed to sacrifice to Poseidon anything which appeared on the waters. When Minos saw the beauty of the bull, he sent it to his own herd and sacrificed a much less valuable animal to Poseidon, who retaliated by making the animal untameable. Eurystheus ordered Heracles to bring this animal to him alive. Heracles went to Crete and asked Minos to help him; Minos refused but gave him permission to catch the bull. Heracles did so and returned to Greece with it. He presented the bull to Eurystheus, who wanted to dedicate it to Hera. However, the goddess refused to accept an offering in the name of Heracles; she freed the bull, which wandered until it eventually reached Attica (see THESEUS, II).

The Mares of Diomedes Diomedes (1), the king of Thrace, owned four mares, called Podargus, Lampon, Xanthus and Deinus, which fed on human flesh. They were tethered with iron chains to bronze mangers, and Heracles' task was to bring them back to Eurystheus alive. Heracles overpowered their grooms and led the animals away, but was attacked by the local inhabitants. Heracles entrusted the mares to Abderus, a son of Hermes, but they dragged him off and killed him. Heracles defeated the locals, slew Diomedes and founded a city called Abdera in Abderus' memory. He brought the mares back to Eurystheus who set them free, whereupon they were devoured by wild beasts on Mount Olympus. Another tradition claims that Heracles fed Diomedes to his own mares, which ate him. Then he brought the mares to Eurystheus, who consecrated them to Hera.

The Girdle of Queen Hippolyta At the order of ADMETE, the daughter of Eurystheus, Heracles set off to capture the girdle worn by the Amazon Hippolyta. This girdle had belonged to Ares, who gave it to Hippolyta as a symbol of his power over her people. When Heracles arrived in the Amazons' country, Hippolyta willingly agreed to give him the belt, but Hera, disguised as an Amazon, provoked a quarrel between Heracles' followers and the Amazons and a battle ensued in which Heracles killed Hippolyta. Other legends claim that hostilities began as soon as Heracles landed with his followers. Melanippe (3) was captured in the battle and Hippolyta agreed to hand over her girdle in exchange for Melanippe's freedom.

The Cattle of Geryon Geryon had an immense herd of cattle which grazed on the island of Erythia, attended by his herdsman, Eurytion (4) and an enormous dog, Orthrus. The island was situated in the extreme west. Eurystheus ordered Heracles to go there to collect the precious herds. The first difficulty was to cross the ocean: to overcome this Heracles borrowed the Cup of the Sun (see HELIOS). During his passage through the Libyan desert the hero had been so troubled by the heat that he had threatened to shoot the Sun with his arrows. Helios begged him not to shoot and Heracles agreed on condition that Helios lent him his Cup to enable him to cross the ocean and reach Erythia. Heracles had to threaten Oceanus with his arrows because he buffeted him with great waves. Oceanus became frightened and the waves subsided. At Erythia Heracles killed Orthrus with a single blow of his club and dealt with Eurytion in the same way. He then set off with the cattle. Menoetes, the herdsman of Hades, ran to warn Geryon, who met Heracles on the banks of the River Anthemus and was killed by the hero's arrows. Heracles then returned to Greece.

During his return Heracles had several adventures in the western Mediterranean. In memory of his passage to Tartessus he built two columns, one on each side of the strait which separates Libya from Europe, which became known as the Pillars of Heracles (the Rock of Gibraltar and the Rock of Ceuta). Heracles returned by the northern route, passing the coasts of Spain, Gaul, Italy and Sicily before arriving in Greece.

Heracles was attacked in Liguria by natives, and after he had killed many of them his supply of arrows ran out. The country was void of stones and Heracles appealed to Zeus who made stones rain from heaven. Using these missiles Heracles put his enemy to flight (see LIGYS). Similarly, in Liguria, two brigands, ALEBION and Dercynus, wanted to rob him and he killed them both. He then travelled on through Tyrrhenia and had to fight CACUS; there he was also entertained by EVANDER (3) (see HERCULES).

At Rheggium in Calabria one of his bulls escaped and swam across the strait to Sicily. Some accounts claim that Italy owes its name to this bull (the Latin word *vitulus* means 'calf'). ERYX wanted to take possession of the bull but he was killed by Heracles. During this episode the rest of the herd was in the charge of Hephaestus (see CROTON and LACINIUS). When they reached the Greek coast the herd was attacked by gadflies sent by Hera; the herd scattered. Heracles chased them but could only round up some. During his pursuit of the bulls Heracles was impeded by the River Strymon, so he cursed it and filled it with stones, transforming it from a navigable river into an impassable torrent. At last, the voyage complete, Heracles gave the surviving bulls to Eurystheus, who sacrificed them to Hera. Some variants of this story of the return of Heracles have been reported by various authors: Heracles is said to have crossed the Celtic countries, even Great Britain.

Cerberus Eurystheus instructed Heracles to descend to the Underworld and bring back Cerberus the dog. He first had to be initiated into the Mysteries of Eleusis. Guided by Hermes and perhaps by Athena, Heracles followed the path of Taenarum for his descent into the Underworld. When the Dead saw him, they all fled except Medusa and Meleager. Heracles drew his sword against Medusa, but Hermes told him that she was nothing but an empty shade. He drew his bow against MELEAGER, but Meleager described his death so movingly that Heracles wept and promised to marry Deianeira, the sister he had left behind. Further on Heracles met Theseus and Pirithous, who were both still alive but who had been put in chains by Pluto (see THESEUS, VI). Heracles then released ASCALAPHUS (1) and overpowered MENOETES, whom he would have killed if Persephone had not demanded mercy. Heracles finally reached the presence of Pluto and asked for permission to take Cerberus away. Pluto granted his request on condition that he mastered the dog without resorting to weapons. Heracles grasped the dog's neck with his hands and, although the dog had a forked tongue at the end of its tail, which stung Heracles several times, he overcame it. He returned to earth using the entrance at Troezen. When Eurystheus saw Cerberus he was so frightened that he hid himself in his jar. Because he did not know what to do with Cerberus, Heracles returned him to Pluto. An Olympian legend describes how Heracles brought the white poplar bark from the Underworld, the only wood allowed when sacrifices were being offered to Olympian Zeus.

The Golden Apples of the Hesperides When Hera married Zeus, Gaia gave her golden apples as a wedding present; Hera found them so lovely that she had them planted in her garden near Mount Atlas. The daughters of Atlas (1) used to come and steal from the garden, so Hera had it placed under the protection of an immortal dragon with one hundred heads, the offspring of Typhon and Echnida. Three Nymphs of the evening, the HESPERIDES, also guarded the apples. Eurystheus ordered Heracles to bring him these golden apples. He went north across Macedonia and on his way he first met CYCNUS (3). Then he reached the River Eridanus in Illyria where he met the river Nymphs who were the daughters of Themis and Zeus. They told him that the sea god Nereus was the only person who could tell him about the country he sought. Although Nereus repeatedly assumed different shapes, Heracles tied him up and would not release him until he had revealed the position of the garden of the Hesperides. Apollodorus describes how from the banks of the Eridanus the hero reached Libya where he fought the giant ANTAEUS; he then crossed Egypt where he barely escaped being sacrificed by BUSIRIS. He passed through Asia and into Arabia where he killed Emathion, the son of Tithonus. He embarked in Helios' cup and reached the other bank at the foot of the Caucasus. Whilst climbing the Caucasus he freed PROMETHEUS, who told Heracles that he himself would not be able to collect the apples: this must be done by Atlas. Heracles finally reached the country of the Hyperboreans where he found Atlas, the giant who bore the whole weight of the sky on his shoulders. He offered to relieve Atlas of his burden while he went to the garden of the Hesperides to collect three golden apples. Atlas agreed to do this but on his return he told Heracles that he himself would take the apples to Eurystheus if Heracles would continue to carry the weight of the vault of heaven. The hero pretended to agree to this but he asked Atlas to take the weight for a moment, while he put a cushion on his shoulders. Atlas agreed to do this but once relieved of the burden, Heracles picked up the apples and fled.

Other accounts claim that Heracles did not need Atlas' help but either killed the dragon of the Hesperides or put it to sleep and took possession of the golden fruit himself. The dragon was transported to the sky where it became the constellation of the Serpent. Heracles gave the golden apples to Eurystheus but he did not know what to do with them, so he gave them back to Heracles who presented them to Athena. She returned them to the garden of Hesperides.

III. THE CAMPAIGNS OF HERACLES

It is generally agreed by mythographers that the first of these great expeditions was against Troy. For the reasons behind Heracles' hostility towards Laomedon, king of Troy, see HESIONE (3). When Heracles had completed his Labours, he recruited a fleet and set sail for Troy. On his arrival, Heracles left Oecles to guard the fleet, while he attacked the city. Laomedon attacked Heracles' fleet and killed Oecles, but Heracles subsequently drove him back and besieged Troy. TELAMON was the first to enter the town: Heracles, angry to think that his bravery had been surpassed, was about to kill Telamon when the latter knelt down and filled his hands with stones. Heracles asked him what he was doing; Telamon replied that he was building an altar to Heracles the Conqueror. Heracles spared him, but killed Laomedon and all his children except Podarces and Hesione (see PRIAM).

As Heracles was returning from Troy, Hypnus was incited by Hera to make Zeus fall into a very deep sleep. Hera then raised a storm which drove Heracles' fleet on to the coast of Cos. The inhabitants thought they were being attacked by pirates and opposed the landing, but Heracles and his men landed, captured the town, and killed the king, Eurypylus (3). Heracles then had an intrigue with Eurypylus' daughter Chalciope (1), who bore a son Thessalus (2). A different account tells that Heracles was seriously wounded during the battle by Chalcodon (4) and that only the intervention of Zeus saved him. In another account Heracles lost all his fleet except his own ship in the storm. On Cos he met Eurypylus' son Antagoras. Heracles was ravenous, but when he asked Antagoras to give him a ram, Antagoras challenged him to a wrestling match with the ram as the reward for victory. During the contest, the locals thought Antagoras was being attacked, and rushed to his aid and overpowered Heracles. Heracles escaped to a woman's hut where he put on women's clothes to avoid being found. From Cos, Heracles went to Phlegra where he took part in the battle between the Gods and the Giants (see ALCYONEUS (1)).

The War against Augias When Augias banished Heracles from Elis (see HERACLES, II) Heracles gathered an army of Arcadians and marched against Elis. Augias put his two nephews the MOLIONIDAE in command of his army. They annihilated Heracles' army and mortally wounded his brother Iphicles. Much later, the inhabitants of Elis sent the Molionidae to represent them at the third Isthmian games. Heracles laid an ambush for them at Cleonae and killed them both. He mounted a second expedition against Elis, captured the town, killed Augias and made his son PHYLEUS king. After this expedition Heracles founded the Olympic Games and dedicated a sanctuary to Pelops.

The Expedition against Pylos Heracles was angry with Neleus (1) because after IPHITUS' murder Neleus refused to purify him. Neleus' son Periclymenus (2) had helped to drive him out of the country, whereas Nestor, alone among Neleus' children, advised that the hero should be granted his request. During the war against the Minyans of Orchomenus Neleus fought against Heracles and the Thebans, because Orchomenus was his son-in-law. According to another account Neleus tried to steal some of Geryon's herds from Heracles. Heracles turned against Neleus. The main event of the war was the fight between Heracles and PERICLYMENUS (2). During the same battle Heracles wounded several gods including Hera and Ares. According to Pindar, Poseidon and Apollo also took part in the fight. Heracles captured Pylos soon after Periclymenus' death. He killed Neleus and all his sons except for Nestor, because he had favoured Heracles. Pausanias claims that he put Nestor in charge of Pylos, asking him to look after it until the Heraclids came to claim it.

The War against Sparta Hippocoon ruled Sparta with his twenty sons the Hippocoontides after expelling the rightful ruling family, Icarius (2) and Tyndareus, who were half-brothers of Hippocoon. Heracles took action against the usurpers, either to reinstate Icarius and Tyndareus, or, alternatively, to avenge the death of his great-nephew Oeonus. This child was passing Hippocoon's palace when a mastiff dashed out and tried to bite him; Oeonus hit the dog with a stone. At once the Hippocoontides rushed out and beat him to death. According to another version the Hippocoontides had been Neleus' allies. Heracles asked CEPHEUS (1) and his twenty sons for help; they agreed to join him, but were killed in the course of the decisive battle. Heracles massacred Hippocoon and all his sons and gave the kingdom to TYNDAREUS. During the fight one of Heracles' hands was wounded. It was healed by Asclepius in the temple of Demeter in Eleusis. To celebrate his victory Heracles built two temples in Sparta, one dedicated to Athena and the other to Hera to thank her for having done nothing to make things difficult for him during the war.

The Alliance with Aegimius The three separate wars, undertaken as a result of Heracles' alliance with Aegimius, the king of the Dorians, took place in Thessaly. The Lapiths, led by Coronus, pressed Aegimius so closely that he was forced to fall back on his alliance with Heracles, promising him a third of his kingdom if victorious. Heracles defeated the Lapiths but refused his reward, asking Aegimius to set it aside for his heirs. Heracles then reopened his old dispute with a neighbouring race, the Dryopes. This had arisen when Heracles and Deianeira were forced to leave Calydon, taking Hyllus, their eldest son, with them. Hyllus became hungry. Heracles saw Theiodamas, the king of the Dryopes, working with a pair of oxen. He asked him for food for his son but Theiodamas refused; Heracles unyoked one of the oxen and killed it for food. Theiodamas retreated to the town and returned with an armed party. At first the fight went against Heracles and

Deianeira was forced to take part. Heracles eventually killed Theiodamas. After the war with the Lapiths, Heracles attacked the Dryopes because they had been their allies, and killed their king, Laogoras. Heracles took possession of the kingdom; the inhabitants split into three groups and fled: one group went to Euboea, the second group went to Cyprus and the third took refuge in the neighbourhood of Eurystheus who, because he hated Heracles, received them graciously. Finally Heracles captured the town of Orminion at the foot of Mount Pelion. The hero had been forbidden by its king, Amyntor, to cross his country but Heracles decided to seize the country and to kill the king. According to Diodorus, Heracles asked Amyntor for his daughter, Astydamia. When the king refused, Heracles captured the town and abducted Astydamia, who bore him a son called Ctesippus.

IV. THE MINOR ADVENTURES

Pholus and the Centaurs For the adventures concerning Pholus, see CENTAURS.

Eurytion For Heracles' fight with the Centaur Eurytion (2), see CENTAURS.

The Resurrection of Alcestis See ADMETUS and ALCESTIS.

Cycnus The fight against CYCNUS (3) took place during the journey to the Hesperides, according to Apollodorus.

Busiris Heracles' encounter with BUSIRIS was fitted into the story of the search for the golden apples.

Antaeus Heracles' clash with ANTAEUS took place on his journey through Libya in his quest for the golden apples. Heracles killed Antaeus and then lived with Antaeus' wife, Iphinoe; she bore him a son named Palaemon (1). The PYGMIES, a race of midgets, tried to take revenge on Heracles. They attacked him when he was asleep, but he awoke and laughed. He caught them all in one hand, imprisoned them in his lion skin, and took them all to Eurystheus.

Liberation of Prometheus While crossing the Caucasus Heracles freed PROMETHEUS.

The Fight with Lycaon LYCAON (3) was the son of Ares and Pyrene (2); he ruled over the Crestonians who lived in Macedonia on the border of Echedorus; this country was called Europe after Pyrene's grandfather, Europus. While he was looking for the golden apples, Heracles crossed a grove sacred to Pyrene. Lycaon attacked Heracles, who killed him.

The Battle with Alcyoneus See ALCYONEUS.

Slavery under Omphale Following the murder of Iphitus, Heracles had to sell himself as a slave and serve one owner for three years. He was bought by OMPHALE.

V. OTHER MYTHS

There are a number of other myths in which Heracles played a part. He was included among the Argonauts, for example. The myth of Heracles seems to have been conflated with numerous other myths. As an example, there is a story that Heracles had killed the Boreades as revenge for their advice to the Argonauts to abandon him. This later version may have been invented to unite the two originally independent cycles of Heracles and the Thessalian myths surrounding Boreas. Similarly, Heracles is supposed to have buried Icarus on the island of Doliche. In return Daedalus carved a statue of the hero which he consecrated at Pisa. Thus the myths of Heracles and Daedalus were conflated.

VI. LATER YEARS, DEATH AND DEIFICATION

The establishment of the myths concerning the events which led to Heracles' deification on Mount Oeta was particularly the result of the work of tragic poets, and the *Trachiniae* of Sophocles is the most important source for Heracles' end. The connecting thread is the love of Deianeira. The marriage with Deianeira was settled during Heracles' meeting with Meleager in the Underworld, but first Heracles had to win her in a savage fight with ACHELOUS. Heracles lived with Deianeira at Calydon, close to his father-in-law Oeneus, but fate made him accidentally kill Oeneus's cup-bearer, EUNOMUS. Although Architeles, the father of Eunomus, forgave him for the murder, the hero went into exile with his wife and son, Hyllus. During this journey he had to fight the centaur Nessus, who lived on the bank of the Evenus, where he was a ferryman. When Heracles arrived with Deianeira, Nessus ferried him over first and then returned for Deianeira, but while he ferried her, he tried to rape her. Heracles shot Nessus in the heart with an arrow as he landed; as he was dying, Nessus called Deianeira and told her that if Heracles ever stopped loving her, she could compel him to love her by giving him a love-potion made of the blood from Nessus' wound. Deianeira believed him and collected his blood. The myths about the composition of this so-called love-potion vary. Some versions say that it contained only Nessus' blood and others that it was mixed with the blood from the wounds of the Lernaean Hydra or with the sperm ejected by Nessus during his attempted rape. After Heracles captured Oechalia, he made IOLE his mistress. Deianeira was staying with Ceyx (1) and was told by Lichas, a follower of Heracles, that Iole might make Heracles forget her. Deianeira remembered the love-potion which Nessus had given her as he was dying and decided to use it. After his victory over Eurytus (2), Heracles wished to consecrate an altar to Zeus and he sent Lichas to Trachis to ask Deianeira for a new cloak for this ceremony. Deianeira dipped a tunic in Nessus' blood and gave it to Lichas. Heracles put the tunic on and started to make the sacrifice. As the tunic was warmed by his body the poison which it contained became active and attacked his skin. The pain quickly became so great that Heracles, beside himself, threw Lichas into the sea. At the same time he tried to force the garment off, but the cloth stuck to his body and tore off strips of skin. In this condition he was taken to Trachis in a boat. When she realized what she had done, Deianeira committed suicide. Heracles made his final arrangements: he gave Hyllus control of Iole, asking him to marry her when he was old enough; he then climbed Mount Oeta, not far from Trachis and built a funeral pyre and climbed on to it. When these preparations were finished he ordered his servants to set fire to the wood, but no one would obey him. PHILOCTETES finally obeyed him, and as a reward Heracles gave him his bow and arrows. There was a clap of thunder and the hero was raised to the sky on a cloud.

Once among the gods Heracles was reconciled with Hera and she assumed the role of immortal mother. He married Hebe, the goddess of Youth, and became one of the immortals thereafter.

Heraclids (*Ἡρακλειδαί*) Heracles' descendants, particularly the direct descendants of Heracles and Deianeira who colonized the Peloponnese. After the apotheosis of Heracles, his children, fearing Eurystheus' hatred, took refuge with Ceyx (1). However, when Eurystheus demanded their expulsion, Ceyx, who had always been afraid of Eurystheus, sent them away. They then went to Athens where Theseus, or his sons, agreed to protect them. Eurystheus declared war on Athens. In the battle Eurystheus' five sons were killed. Eurystheus fled but he was followed by Hyllus or IOLAUS and killed near the rocks of Sciron (see ALCMENE). The victory was ensured by the Athenians, who sacrificed one of Heracles' daughters, MACARIA.

When Eurystheus was beaten the Heraclids wanted to return to the Peloponnese, their father's country of origin. With HYLLUS in command they established themselves there. After a year, however, a plague broke out, and the oracle revealed that it was the result of divine anger at the return of the Heraclids before the time fixed by fate. The Heraclids went back to Attica, but they always hoped to be able to return. Hyllus went in their name to consult the oracle at Delphi, which told him that their wish would be granted after 'the third harvest'. The Heraclids looked on Hyllus as their leader and they asked him to lead them to their homeland. Hyllus entered the Isthmus of Corinth but there he ran into the army of ECHEMUS, the king of Tegea, who killed him.

Hyllus' grandson Aristomachus went to question the oracle again. The oracle replied: 'The gods will give you victory if you attack by the narrows' or 'by the narrow path'. The oracle's expression was ambiguous. Aristomachus thought this meant attacking by the narrow Isthmus, but this was wrong and he was killed. When Aristomachus' sons were grown up, Temenus (3) went to consult the oracle, which only repeated its two previous answers. Temenus remarked that his father and his grandfather had followed the advice of the god and that this had caused their deaths. The oracle replied that they did not know how to interpret the oracles; it added that 'third harvest' meant 'third generation' and that the 'narrow path' meant the straits between the coast of mainland Greece and the Peloponnese. To conform to the oracle's second reply Temenus built a fleet on the coast of Locri at a town which became named Naupactus (from two Greek words meaning 'to build a ship'). While there with his army, his youngest brother ARISTODEMUS died after being struck by lightning, leaving twin sons, Eurysthenes and Procles.

A short time later the Heraclids saw a soothsayer called CARNUS (1) approaching the camp. One of the Heraclids named HIPPOTES (1) pierced him with a javelin. A storm then arose which scattered and wrecked the fleet, and a famine visited the army which broke ranks and scattered. Temenus returned to the oracle, which told him that this was due to divine anger at the death of the soothsayer, adding that the murderer must be banished for ten years and that the Heraclids should take a being with three eyes as a guide. Hippotes was banished, and then a being with three eyes presented itself in the form of a man with one eye mounted on a horse. This man was OXYLUS (3). The Heraclids defeated the Peloponnesians and built an altar to Zeus, the father, to demonstrate their gratitude for the victory. They then divided the Peloponnese (see CRESPHONTES for details of the partition). An oracle had called upon the Heraclids in their conquest to spare 'those with whom they had shared a meal'. When the Heraclids approached Arcadia its king, Cypselus (1), sent ambassadors with presents. It happened that the ambassadors met Cresphontes' soldiers just as they were eating. They asked the Arcadians to share it with them. The Heraclids remembered the words of the oracle and made an agreement with the Arcadians, promising to spare their country. Another version claims that the Heraclids were struck by the abundance of crops on the Arcadian frontier. When Cypselus' envoys presented themselves the Heraclids refused to accept their presents because the oracle had forbidden them to make any alliance during the campaign. Cypselus pointed out that they had already received as a present the crops which they had seized, consequently the alliance was already concluded. The Heraclids recognized this and turned away from Arcadia. There is also a story that Cypselus, by giving his daughter in marriage to Cresphontes, succeeded in saving his country (see MEROPE (2)).

Hercules A latinized form of the Greek Heracles. This name was attached a whole collection of Roman legends which had been integrated into the account of Heracles' 'return from Geryon' (see HERACLES, II). One well-known episode was the fight between Hercules and CACUS. In its earliest form, the legend of Hercules respresents the reception of the hero as a guest by King FAUNUS, a king whose custom it was to sacrifice to the gods all strangers who visited him. When Faunus attempted to lay hands on his guest, Hercules killed him. After this, he continued his journey to Magna Graecia. The usual tradition made EVANDER (3) treat Hercules kindly. Evander was supposed to be the Greek form of Faunus.

The myth of the Good Goddess (see BONA DEA) is also part of the legend of Hercules. Propertius tells how, thirsty from his fight with Cacus, Hercules asked the Bona Dea (or Fauna), the goddess who performed sacred rites in the neighbourhood, for a drink. She refused to allow him to approach her sacred spring which was open only to women, and Hercules in anger then closed his shrine to women (see RECARANUS).

Hercyna (*Ἑρκύνα*) The Nymph who presided over a spring at Lebadea in Boeotia. One day while Hercyna played with Persephone, the goose belonging to the two young girls escaped and hid under a stone in a cave. Persephone chased after it and removed the stone. A spring immediately gushed out of the ground; this came to be known as the spring of Hercyna. It was situated near the oracle of Trophonius, and all who wanted to consult the oracle had to bathe in the spring.

Hermaphroditus (*Ἑρμαφρόδιτος*) The name given to all people with both masculine and feminine characteristics, and more particularly applied to a son of Aphrodite and Hermes. Hermaphroditus was brought up by Nymphs in the forests of Ida in Phrygia. He was remarkably handsome. One day when in Caria he came to a beautiful lake. The Nymph of the lake, Salmacis, fell in love with him. She made advances which the young man rebuffed. Hermaphroditus was attracted by the clearness of the water; he undressed and plunged into the lake. When Salmacis saw him in her domain and at her mercy, she joined him and embraced him. Hermaphroditus tried in vain to push her away. She prayed to the gods begging them to cause their bodies never to be separated; the gods granted this prayer and united them into one new being with a dual personality. At the same time Hermaphroditus also had a request granted by the gods: this was that anybody who bathed in the lake of Salmacis should lose his virility.

Hermes (*Ἑρμῆς*) The son of Zeus and Maia. He was born in a cave on Mount Cyllene in Arcadia on the fourth day of the month – a day which remained consecrated to him. He was wrapped in bandages as was customary for the new-born and was placed in a winnowing-basket instead of a cot. On the day of his birth he extricated himself from his bandages and went to Thessaly where his brother, Apollo, was shepherd in charge of the herds of Admetus. Apollo was absorbed by his love-affair with HYMENAEUS and neglected his duty as herdsman; Hermes was able to steal a dozen cows, a hundred heifers which had never known a halter, and a bull. He then tied a branch to each animal's tail (in some accounts he provided clogs for them all), and drove them across Greece to Pylos. He was seen by only one witness, an old man called BATTUS (1). Hermes sacrificed two of the stolen beasts to the twelve gods. Then, after concealing the remainder of the herd, he escaped to his cave on Cyllene. There he found a tortoise in front of the entrance; he cleaned it and stretched some strings made of the intestines of the cattle he had sacrificed across the hollow of the shell. In this way the first lyre was constructed.

Apollo, looking for his missing animals, finally came to Pylos where Battus showed him the hiding-place. (Some say, however, that Apollo was aware of the whole episode because of his powers of divination.) Apollo complained to Maia about the thefts, but showing him the child, wrapped in swaddling bands, Maia asked how he could possibly make such accusations. Apollo then called Zeus to the cave; Zeus ordered Hermes to return the animals. Apollo in the interim had seen the lyre in the cave and was so enchanted by the sounds it produced that he decided to give his beasts in exchange for the instrument.

A little later, Hermes invented the syrinx or Pan pipes. Apollo wanted to buy the new instrument, offering the golden crook which he used when looking after the herd of Admetus. Hermes agreed, but asked to be taught the art of soothsaying. Apollo accepted, and in this way the golden rod (the herald's wand) became one of Hermes' attributes. Hermes also learned how to foretell the future by using small pebbles. Zeus made him the herald with particular responsibilities towards him and the gods of the Underworld, Hades and Persephone.

Hermes usually played a secondary role as a divine agent and a protector of heroes. In the battle against the Giants he wore Hades' helmet which made the wearer invisible; this enabled him to kill the Giant Hippolytus (2). During the battle of the gods against the ALOADAE, he freed Ares from the bronze vessel in which the two giants had imprisoned him. He also saved Zeus during his fight with TYPHON. In all these adventures it was Hermes' skill which enabled him to intervene.

In other episodes Hermes simply interpreted divine will: it was to him that Deucalion (1) came after the flood, to ask him what he wanted; from Hermes Nephele (1) received the ram which saved her children PHRIXUS and ATHAMAS; Hermes gave Amphion his lyre, Heracles his sword, Perseus the helmet of Hades and the winged sandals. Hermes saved Odysseus, once when he gave CALYPSO (1) the order to release him and to help him to build a raft, and a second time, when Odysseus was with CIRCE, and Hermes showed Odysseus the magic plant which protected him from the transformation undergone by his companions. In Hades Hermes watched over Heracles (see HERACLES, II). Hermes also arranged Heracles' purchase as a slave by OMPHALE. Hermes was involved in the death of ARGOS (2) (see also IO). This murder was the explanation for the *cognomen* 'Argeiphontes' given to Hermes, meaning 'killer of Argos'. To help Zeus and to thwart Hera, he took the young DIONYSUS from one hiding-place to another on Mount Nysa and then to Athamas' estate. Hermes was instructed to take Hera, Aphrodite and Athena to Ida in Phrygia at the time of the Judgement of PARIS.

Hermes was also the god of commerce and flight, and the one who guided travellers along their way. His statue, known as a 'herm', used to be set up at crossroads in the form of a pillar of which only the top half was shaped as a human bust but which had very visible male organs. He was said to protect shepherds and was often shown carrying a lamb on his shoulders; it was this which earned him the title Hermes Criophorus, 'Bearing a Ram'. He also had the task of accompanying the spirits of the dead to Hades, and because of this he was given the name Psychopompus, 'accompanier of souls'. He was the father of AUTOLYCUS, who inherited Hermes' ability to steal without being caught, of Eurytus (3) and of Abderus – a favourite of Heracles who was devoured by the mares of Diomedes (1). Hermes was most frequently shown wearing winged shoes and a large-brimmed hat and carrying the winged staff, the symbol of his position as divine messenger.

Hermione (*Ἑρμιόνη*) The only daughter of Menelaus and Helen (Table 3). In the *Odyssey* Menelaus betrothed Hermione to NEOPTOLEMUS while he was away at Troy. When Neoptolemus returned to Lacedaemon, the marriage took place. According to the tragedians, however, Menelaus had initially betrothed Hermione to Orestes before the Trojan War. Yet, during the Trojan War, Menelaus had given his daughter to Achilles' son instead, since his co-operation was necessary if Troy was to be captured. Orestes was forced to give up Hermione to Neoptolemus. She thus became the source of contention between her two suitors. The marriage of Hermione and Neoptolemus produced no children, and during the visit he made to Delphi to discover the reason for the sterility, Neoptolemus was killed in a riot, either by Orestes himself or by another at Orestes' behest. Orestes then married Hermione, who bore him a son TISAMENUS (1).

Hermochares (*Ἑρμοχάρης*) A young Athenian who fell in love with a girl from Chios called Ctesylla when he saw her dancing at the altar of Pythian Apollo. He wrote an oath on an apple; Ctesylla saw the apple in the temple of Artemis and read the words aloud, thus becoming bound to him by the oath. Hermochares asked her father Alcidamas for permission to marry her; Alcidamas agreed and called on Apollo as witness, touching the sacred laurel. Time passed however, and Alcidamas forgot his promise and betrothed Ctesylla to another man. But, while she was sacrificing to Artemis to celebrate the engagement, Hermochares came to the temple. Following the wish of Artemis, Ctesylla fell in love with Hermochares and absconded with him to Athens, where they were married. They had a child, but Apollo caused Ctesylla to die in childbirth to expiate her father's perjury. At the funeral a dove flew away from the bier and Ctesylla's body disappeared. The oracle indicated that the girl had been deified and should receive her cult under the name of Aphrodite Ctesylla. (See also ACONTIUS).

Hermus (*Ἕρμος*) An Athenian noble who accompanied Theseus against the Amazons. On his way home, Theseus left Hermus and two of his companions to establish laws and regulations for the new town of Pythopolis.

Hero (*Ἡρώ*) The young girl whom LEANDER loved.

Herophile (Ἡροφίλη) The second SIBYL.

Herse (Ἕρση) One of the three daughters of Cecrops and Aglaurus (1). Her sisters were AGLAURUS (2) and Pandrosus. Athena entrusted the baby ERICHTHONIUS to them, but they opened the basket in which the baby was hidden. As a punishment, Athena sent Herse mad; she threw herself from the top of the Acropolis. There is another version which ascribed the blame to Aglaurus (2). In this account Herse escaped punishment and was seduced by Hermes, by whom she had a son called CEPHALUS.

Hersilia One of the highest born of the Sabine women abducted by Romulus' Romans; according to Plutarch, she was the only one who was married. Her husband was called Hostilius; he was killed during the war between the two peoples. It was also said that she was married to one of Romulus' followers, also called Hostilius, by whom she had a son called Hostus Hostilius, who was father of the king Tullus Hostilius. During the war between the Sabines and the Romans she intervened and brought about peace. Another legend made Hersilia the wife of Romulus, by whom she had two children: a daughter, Prima, and a son, Aollius, who was later called Avilius. After the apotheosis of her husband, Hersilia was in her turn deified with the name of Hora Quirini and associated with the cult of Romulus.

Hesione (Ἡσιόνη)

1. According to Aeschylus, one of the Oceanides and wife of Prometheus.
2. The wife of Nauplius (2). She was the mother of PALAMEDES, Oeax and Nausimedon.
3. The daughter of Laomedon, the king of Troy. She married Telamon by whom she had a son, Teucer (2). The circumstances of her marriage were peculiar. Since Laomedon had refused to pay Poseidon and Apollo the amount which he had promised for building the wall of Troy, Poseidon sent a sea monster against the country. A soothsayer explained that in order to calm the wrath of Poseidon, the king's own daughter must be sacrificed. Hesione therefore was roped to a rock to wait for the monster to devour her. Heracles arrived in the Troad at that time and offered to kill the monster on condition that the king would give him the horses he had received from Zeus in payment for GANYMEDE. Laomedon consented, but, as soon as his daughter was free, refused to keep to the agreed contract. Several years later Heracles organized an expedition in revenge, during which he captured Troy (see HERACLES, III). The first man to scale the wall was Telamon, and as a reward Heracles gave him the hand of Hesione. Among the captives the girl chose to have was her brother Podarces (see PRIAM).

Hesperides (Ἑσπερίδες) The Nymphs of the Setting Sun. In Hesiod's *Theogony* they were the daughters of Nyx, but later they were said to be daughters of Zeus and Themis, Phorcys and Ceto, and Atlas (1). Most often there were said to be three Hesperides: Aegle

('Brightness'), Erythia ('Scarlet') and Hesperarethusa ('Sunset Glow'), although the last name is often divided into two and applied to two distinct Hesperides: Hesperia and Arethusa (2). The Hesperides lived in the extreme west near the edge of the Ocean at the foot of Mount Atlas. Their main function, with the help of a dragon, the son of Phorcys and Ceto, or of Typhon and Echidna, was to guard the garden where the golden apples grew, a gift given to Hera when she married Zeus. They sang in chorus near springs which spurted forth ambrosia. The Hesperides were linked with the story of Heracles, who went to their dwelling place to find the golden apples (see HERACLES, II). The Hesperides were turned into trees, elm, poplar and willow, because of their despair at the loss of the apples.

Hesperus (*Ἕσπερος*) The evening star, the son or the brother of Atlas (1). He was the first to climb Mount Atlas to watch the stars; from there a storm swept him away, causing him to disappear without trace. People supposed that he had been transformed into the friendly evening star which every evening brought the peace of night. Thereafter they called the star Hesperus. Hellenistic authors identified Hesperus as the star Phosphorus, called Lucifer by the Romans.

Hestia (*Ἑστιά*) The goddess of the hearth. She was the eldest daughter of Cronus and Rhea, and the sister of Zeus and Hera. Although courted by Apollo and Poseidon, Zeus gave her permission to preserve her virginity. He granted her special honours, causing her to be worshipped in every household and in the temples of all the gods. Hestia remained on Olympus. In the same way that the domestic hearth was the religious centre of the household, so Hestia was the religious centre of the divine dwelling. Hestia's immobility meant that she played almost no role in myths, however.

Hierax (*Ἱέραξ*)

1. A gossip who prevented Hermes from snatching Io from Argos (2) and who thus caused the god to kill him. Hierax was transformed into a bird of the same name (a falcon).
2. A rich landowner of the country of the Mariandyni, a faithful servant of Demeter, who rewarded him by making his land fertile. When the wrath of Poseidon caused famine throughout the Troad, the Trojans turned to Hierax for help. He gave them large quantities of wheat and barley and saved them from starvation, but Poseidon punished him for his actions, turning him into a falcon.

Hilaera (*Ἵλαειρα*) One of the LEUCIPPIDAE.

Himalia (*Ἱμαλία*) The miller's wife, a Nymph of Rhodes with whom Zeus had intercourse, coming upon her as a shower of rain. She bore him three sons: Spartaeus (the sower); Cronius (the ripener); Cytus (literally 'the hollow', meaning possibly the container that stores grain). During a downpour which covered all Rhodes, the sons of Himalia saved themselves by taking refuge on the island's hills.

Himerus (*Ἵμερος*) The personification of sexual desire. He followed Eros in Aphrodite's train.

Hippe (*Ἵππη*) Chiron the Centaur's daughter, who was seduced by Aeolus (1). She fled to Pelion to give birth to the child without her father's knowledge – but her father followed her. Hippe besought the gods to let her bear the child in secret. The gods granted her request and transformed her into a constellation in the shape of a horse (see also MELANIPPE (1)).

Hippo (*Ἵππω*) Scedasus had two daughters, Hippo and Molpia, who were raped by two Spartans, Phrourarchidas and Parthenius, and, ashamed of what had happened, hanged themselves. Scedasus urged the Spartans to punish the guilty pair, but failed, and having cursed Sparta, he too committed suicide.

Hippocoon (*Ἱπποκόων*) The illegitimate son of Oebalus (1) and a Nymph called Batieia. He was a native of Sparta and the half-brother of Tyndareus and ICARIUS (1). When their father died, he banished them from Sparta and seized power. He himself had twelve sons, the Hippocoontides. Hippocoon and his sons were men of violence: they aroused the anger of Heracles, who declared war on them and killed them, restoring Tyndareus to the throne of Sparta (see HERACLES, III). (Some traditions maintain that Icarius helped Hippocoon to deprive Tyndareus of his kingdom.)

Hippocrene (*Ἱπποκρήνη*) The horse PEGASUS was on Helicon. He struck the rock with his hoof and a spring gushed from the ground. It was called Hippocrene, or the Horse's Spring, and it was round this spring that the Muses gathered to sing and dance, for its water was said to bring poetic inspiration.

Hippodamia (*Ἱπποδάμεια*)
1. The daughter of Oenomaus, king of Pisa in Elis. She was extremely beautiful and had many suitors, but Oenomaus refused to give her in marriage. Some versions maintain that an oracle had forecast that his son-in-law would kill him; others that he himself was in love with Hippodamia. To discourage the suitors he demanded that anyone who wanted to marry Hippodamia had to compete with him in a chariot race to the altar of Poseidon in Corinth. Each suitor had to take the girl in his own chariot while he, riding in his own chariot, strove to overtake them. Oenomaus made Hippodamia ride in the suitors' chariots, either to make the chariots heavier or to distract the drivers. Before setting off, Oenomaus would sacrifice a ram to Zeus while the suitor began the race. Oenomaus, though delayed by the sacrifice, speedily overtook his rival, whom he then slew. Oenomaus' horses had been given to him by Ares and were divine, so no ordinary chariot team could hope to win against them. The mythographers give the name of twelve (or thirteen) unsuccessful suitors: Mermnus, Hippothous, Eurylochus, Automedon, Pelops of Opus, Acarnan, Eurymachus, Lasius, Chalcon, Tricoronus, Alcathous (2), Aristomachus and Crotalus. Once he had won the race

Oenomaus would behead the suitor and nail the head to the door of the house to frighten future competitors.

When PELOPS (1) arrived to compete, Hippodamia fell in love with him. She enlisted the help of Myrtilus, her father's driver, who took the axle-pins out of Oenomaus' chariot-wheel and replaced them with wax pegs. These gave way during the race, causing an accident that was fatal to Oenomaus. Some sources say that in order to win Myrtilus' co-operation, Pelops promised him one night with Hippodamia; others that Hippodamia herself gave him this promise. Later Pelops killed Myrtilus by throwing him into the sea, either because he had tried to rape Hippodamia, or because he wanted to avoid paying Myrtilus the price agreed for his treachery. (Other sources, however, say that Hippodamia tried to seduce Myrtilus, but when he refused her advances, she invented the rape incident to relate to her husband.) As he died, Myrtilus cursed Pelops and all his descendants. This was the origin of the misfortune which struck the house of Pelops (see ATREUS, THYESTES, AGAMEMNON and Table 2).

Pelops, in honour of Hippodamia, founded the quinquennial festival of Hera at Olympia. There are various accounts of their children. Sometimes six sons are listed: Atreus, Thyestes, Pittheus, Alcathous (1), Peisthenes and Chrysippus. Another tradition gives them Atreus, Thyestes, Dias, Cynosurus, Corinthus, Hippalmus, Hippasus, Cleon, Argeus, Alcathous, Heleius, Pittheus and Troezen, together with three daughters: Nicippe, Lysidice and Astydamia, all of whom were said to have married sons of Perseus (Table 7). However, CHRYSIPPUS is more commonly said to be Hippodamia's son-in-law, whom she had murdered by Atreus and Thyestes. In revenge Pelops was said to have had her put to death. In a different version Hippodamia decided to murder Chrysippus herself, using the sword belonging to Laius, who was staying with Pelops. She left the weapon piercing Chrysippus' body in an attempt to ensure that suspicion would fall on Laius. But Chrysippus had time to reveal the facts before he died. Pelops banished Hippodamia from Elis. She took refuge at Midia in Argolis where she died. Later, as instructed by an oracle, Pelops had her ashes brought back to Olympia.

2. The wife of Pirithous. It was on her account that the battle between the LAPITHS and CENTAURS took place (see PIRITHOUS and Table 1).

3. Hippodamia was the real name of BRISEIS.

4. Mother of PHOENIX (3).

5. Daughter of ANCHISES.

Hippolochus (*Ἱππόλοχος*) The son of Bellerophon and Philonoe (or Anticleia). His son Glaucus (2) commanded the Lycians at the siege of Troy.

Hippolyta (*Ἱππολύτη*)

1. The queen of the Amazons, whose girdle Heracles attempted to seize (see HERACLES, II). Her father was Ares and her mother Otrera. Some claimed it was she who organized the expedition against Theseus (see THESEUS, V). She was even said to be the mother of HIPPOLYTUS (1). She was murdered by Heracles. She is also known as Antiope (2).

2. The nurse of Smyrna (2) (see ADONIS).

Hippolytus (*Ἱππόλυτος*)
1. Son of Theseus and the Amazon Antiope (2) (or Melanippe (3) or Hippolyta (1)). From his mother Hippolytus inherited a passion for hunting and exercise. He was devoted to the goddess Artemis, but scorned Aphrodite. Aphrodite took vengeance on him by making his stepmother, Phaedra, fall in love with him. Phaedra offered to sleep with him, but he rejected her advances. Fearing that he would tell Theseus about the incident she accused Hippolytus of trying to rape her. Theseus called on Poseidon to punish Hippolytus with death. Poseidon had promised Theseus that he would fulfil three requests, and so sent a sea-monster which appeared as Hippolytus was driving his chariot along the shore at Troezen. It frightened the horses, which flung him from the chariot and dragged him to his death. Phaedra hanged herself in despair. Another story tells how, at the request of Artemis, Asclepius brought Hippolytus back to life. Artemis then carried him to Italy to her sanctuary on the shore of Lake Nemi (see DIANA and VIRBIUS).
2. One of the GIANTS. He was killed by Hermes.
3. The son and successor of RHOPALUS.

Hippomedon (*Ἱππομέδων*) One of the Seven against Thebes (see ADRASTUS). He was the nephew of Adrastus and the son of Aristomachus, one of the sons of Talaus (Table 1). He was an enormous man, but he was killed during the assault on the town, by Ismarius. His son Polydorus was one of the EPIGONI.

Hippomenes (*Ἱππομένης*) The son of Megareus. Hippomenes married ATALANTA.

Hippotes (*Ἱππότης*)
1. One of the HERACLIDS (Table 7). He took part with Temenus (3) in the Heraclids' expedition against the Peloponnese. At Naupactus he killed a seer by mistake, thinking he was a spy. This aroused Apollo's anger against the army, and Hippotes was banished for ten years as a punishment. Hippotes had one son called ALETES.
2. The son of Creon (1) who welcomed Jason and Medea when they were banished by Acastus. When Medea murdered Creon and his daughter (see JASON), Hippotes indicted her before an Athenian Court, but she was declared innocent (see MEDUS (1)).

Hippothoe (*Ἱπποθόη*) The daughter of Mestor and Lysidice (Table 7). She was abducted by Poseidon and taken to the island of the Echinades. There she bore him a son Taphius.

Historis (*Ἱστορίς*) According to Pausanias, Historis, the daughter of Tiresias, worked out a scheme making it possible for GALINTHIAS to hasten the delivery of Alcmene, who had been prevented from giving birth to Heracles.

Homonoia (*Ὁμόνοια*) The personification of Harmony; she had an altar at Olympia. In Rome she was called Concordia. She also had a temple at the foot of the Capitol dedicated to her by Camillus, which symbolized the agreement finally reached between patricians and plebeians.

Honos The personification of morality. There were several temples dedicated to her in the city of Rome.

Hopladamus (Ὁπλάδαμος) One of the giants who escorted Rhea, carrying the baby Zeus in her arms, to protect her from Cronus.

Horae (Ὧραι) Daughters of Zeus and Themis. There were three – Eunomia, Dike and Eirene, meaning Discipline, Justice and Peace. However, the Athenians called them Thallo, Auxo and Carpo, names which denote budding, growth and ripening. As goddesses of nature they controlled the growth of plants; as goddesses of order they maintained the stability of society. On Olympus they guarded the entrance to the divine dwelling. By some they were said to have reared Hera, whose servants they were. They were responsible for unharnessing her horses and occasionally did the same for the god of the sun. They were followers of Aphrodite, and they appeared in the train of Dionysus and also among Persephone's companions. Pan was said to have enjoyed their companionship. They were customarily represented as three graceful girls, often holding a flower or a plant.

Horatius

1. The story of Horatius is linked to the war between the Romans and the Etruscans. After the battle it was not clear which country had won. The armies were camped on the battlefield near the forest of Arsia, from which suddenly a voice proclaimed: 'The Etruscans have lost one more man than the Romans; the Romans are the victors.' At this, the Etruscans fled. Horatius emerged from the forest as the hero, for it was his voice that had put the enemy to flight.

2. One-eyed Horatius (Horatius Cocles) single-handedly defended the only bridge connecting Rome with the opposite bank of the Tiber against the Etruscans. During the battle, however, he was wounded in the thigh and permanently lamed. In his honour a statue was erected at the Volcanal at the foot of the Capitol.

3. The conflict between the three Horatii and the three Curiatii, champions of Alba, is generally considered to be historic, but there is good reason to believe that this tale was a transposition of a very old initiation myth of which similar examples are found in Celtic legend.

Hostius Also called Hostus Hostilius, a Roman originally from the colony of Medullia. During the reign of Romulus he came and settled in Rome. After the removal of the Sabines he married HERSILIA by whom he had a son, who was the father of King Tullus Hostilius. During the Sabine war Hostius was the first to be killed. The Romans panicked momentarily until Jupiter Stator intervened to restore order. Hostius had already shown outstanding bravery at the capture of Fidenae, for which he was awarded a laurel wreath.

Hyacinthids (Ὑακινθίδες) According to one tradition they were daughters of the Lacedaemonian HYACINTHUS who had settled in Athens. There were four of them: Antheis, Aegleis, Lytaea and Orthaea. During Minos' war against Attica, plague and famine struck the country (see MINOS and ANDROGEOS). In accordance with an ancient oracle, the Athenians sacrificed the young girls. However these actions had no effect at all and the Athenians were forced finally to accept Minos' terms (see THESEUS, III). Other mythographers identified the Hyacinthids as the daughters of ERECHTHEUS – Protogenia (2) and Pandora (2) – who were offered in expiation to the gods when the Eleusinian army commanded by EUMOLPUS (1) approached Athens.

Hyacinthus (Ὑάκινθος)

1. Hyacinthus was so beautiful that Apollo fell in love with him, but one day while the two of them were practising throwing the discus, a gust of wind caught the discus, causing it to hit Hyacinthus on the head, killing him at once. (Some accounts relate that the discus hit a rock and rebounded.) Apollo was saddened, and to make the name of his friend immortal he transformed the blood which had flowed from the wound into a new flower, the 'hyacinth', of which the petals bore marks recalling either the god's cry of sorrow (Ai) or the initial of the Greek version of the young man's name. According to several authors, the one really responsible for the accident was Zephyrus, the unsuccessful rival of Apollo for Hyacinthus' affection, who made the discus change direction. Others declare that is was the action of Boreas, who was also supposed to be in love with Hyacinthus.

2. The father of the Hyacinthids of whom Apollodorus speaks.

Hyades (Ὑάδες) A group of stars whose appearance coincided with the season of spring rain (whence their name which recalls ὕειν, 'to rain'). They were originally Nymphs, daughters of Atlas (1), Melisseus (1), or HYAS, or even Erechtheus, or Cadmus. Their number varies from two to seven, and their names were no less variable. The most usual seem to have been Ambrosia, Eudora, Aesyle (or Phaesyle), Coronis (3), Dione, Polyxo and Phaeo. Before being transformed into stars they had, as the 'Nymphs of Nysa', nursed Dionysus, but for fear of Hera they were said to have passed their nursling over to Ino and fled to Tethys, their grandmother. There they were transformed into a constellation by Zeus. There was also a story which told that the death of their brother HYAS made them so sad that they committed suicide, after which they were changed into a constellation.

Hyamus (Ὕαμος) The son of LYCOREUS. He married one of the daughters of Deucalion (1), Melantheia. By her he had a daughter who bore DELPHUS, after whom the Delphians were named.

Hyas (Ὕας) A son of Atlas (1) and Pleione and brother of the PLEIADES and the HYADES. One day he was killed while hunting. Some of his sisters (traditions said five or seven) died of grief (or committed suicide). They were transformed into stars.

Hybris (Ὕβρις) The personification of lack of restraint and of insolence.

Hydne (Ὕδνη) The daughter of Scyllis, a native of Pallene. Both the father and daughter were skilled divers, and when Xerxes' fleet invaded Greece they cut the anchor cables while the ships were moored, so that many were wrecked. As a reward, the Amphictyons erected statues of them at Delphi.

Hydra of Lerna (Ὕδρα) The offspring of Typhon and Echidna, and the monster which Heracles killed (see HERACLES, II). Heracles used the Hydra's blood to poison his arrows. In some versions the Hydra's blood was also used in the so-called love-philtre which Nessus gave to Deianeira (see HERACLES, VI).

Hyettus (Ὕηττος) The first man to have taken revenge on an adulterer. He was a native of Argos and he killed Molourus, the son of Arisbas, when he caught him with his wife. After the murder Hyettus went into voluntary exile and found refuge with Orchomenus, Minyas' son.

Hygieia (Ὑγίεια) The personification of health. She was a daughter of Asclepius.

Hylaeus (Ὑλαῖος) One of the Arcadian Centaurs who tried to kidnap ATALANTA. He wounded Milanion, one of her suitors, but was killed by one of Atalanta's arrows. Another tradition has it that Hylaeus took part in the struggle between the Centaurs and the Lapiths and that he was killed by Theseus, or else by Heracles as a result of a fight at Pholus' home.

Hylas (Ὕλας) Heracles, while fighting the Dryopes, killed their king, Theiodamas, and abducted his son, Hylas, a very beautiful young man with whom Heracles fell in love. Hylas accompanied him on the Argonauts' expedition. During a landing in Mysia Heracles went to cut a tree to make an oar to replace the one he had broken, and in the meantime Hylas had been asked to draw water from a spring in the forest, or from the river (or lake) Ascanius. At the edge of the spring he met Nymphs, who, seeing his beauty, lured him to the spring, where he drowned. Polyphemus (I), who had landed with Hylas and Heracles, was the first to realize that the young man had disappeared. For a long time he called out for him in vain, as did Heracles. Meanwhile, however, the Argonauts raised anchor without waiting for their companions, perhaps on the advice of the BOREADES. Polyphemus founded on that spot the town of Cios. Heracles, suspecting that the Mysians had kidnapped Hylas, took hostages and ordered them to find the young man – this they continued to do in an annual ceremony in which the priests would march in procession towards the neighbouring mountain and call the name of Hylas three times.

Hyllus (Ὕλλος) The son of Heracles and Deianeira, at least according to the most generally accepted tradition. Heracles was said to have named him after a giant called Hyllus, whose skeleton had been brought to light by a flood. However, some mythographers said that Hyllus was the son of Heracles and Omphale. Apollonius Rhodius says that Hyllus was the son of Heracles and Melite, a Nymph with whom Heracles had an affair during his exile in Phaeacia after the murder of his sons (an exile usually ignored by mythographers in the traditional version). This Hyllus founded a settlement in Illyria, where he was killed in a dispute with the local inhabitants. But most often it was agreed that it was Deianeira who gave birth to Hyllus, at Calydon in the early days of her marriage to Heracles (see HERACLES, VI). He was already fully grown by the time of the exile to Ceyx (1). Heracles, as he was dying, asked him to marry IOLE, and when the Heraclids had to take refuge in Attica to escape the hatred of Eurystheus, they gathered round Hyllus who (according to some authors) killed Eurystheus. He then went to settle in Thebes with his grandmother (see ALCMENE). After that he tried to re-establish the children of Heracles in the Peloponnese, but because he misinterpreted a prophecy (see HERACLIDS) he died in single combat with ECHEMUS. After Heracles' death, Hyllus was adopted by AEGIMIUS, king of the Dorians, and by virtue of this he gave his name to one of the three Dorian tribes.

Hylonome (Ὑλονόμη) The wife of the Centaur CYLLARUS.

Hymenaeus (Ὑμέναιος) The god who led the wedding procession. The stories of his origin vary: sometimes he was said to be the son of a Muse (Calliope, Clio or Urania) and Apollo; sometimes Dionysus and Aphrodite; at other times his father was said to be Magnes or Pierus (2). Hymenaeus was a young Athenian of such beauty that he was generally thought to be a girl. Although he was of humble birth, he fell in love with a noble Athenian girl; as he had no hope of ever marrying her, he followed her everywhere at a distance. One day the girls of noble birth went to Eleusis to sacrifice to Demeter, but some pirates captured all the girls, and also Hymenaeus, whom they took for a girl. The pirates sailed to a deserted beach where they fell asleep. While they were slumbering, Hymenaeus killed them all. He then went alone to Athens, where he offered to return the girls on condition that he was given the hand of the one he loved. His terms were accepted. In memory of this episode, the name of Hymenaeus was invoked at every wedding, as a sign of good luck.

In a different tradition Hymenaeus was Magnes' son and a very skilful musician. He was singing during the wedding ceremony of Dionysus and Althaea when he died. In order to perpetuate his memory it was decided that, in future, his name would be brought into every wedding ceremony. Another legend told that Hymenaeus had been loved by HESPERUS. While he was singing at the wedding of Ariadne and Dionysus, he lost his voice. In memory of him, every wedding thereafter had its 'song of Hymenaeus'. In yet another version, Hymenaeus died on his wedding day, thus finally linking his name with the wedding ceremony.

Hymenaeus was loved by Apollo or by Thamyris or Hesperus. The attributes of Hymenaeus were a torch, a crown of flowers, and sometimes a flute.

Hymnus (Ὕμνος)
1. A Phrygian shepherd who was in love with NICAEA.
2. The son of Saturn and ENTORIA.

Hyperboreans (Ὑπερβόρειοι) A mythical race living in a region 'beyond the North Wind'. After Apollo's birth, he flew with his team of swans to the land of the Hyperboreans where he remained until he made his ceremonial entrance into Delphi. For nineteen years he returned to this land, each time when the stars had returned to their original positions. Each night between the vernal equinox and the rising of the Pleiades he could be heard singing hymns and playing his lyre.

After Apollo had massacred the CYCLOPES, he hid the arrow he had used in a temple in the main Hyperborean city. The arrow flew there of its own accord, before forming the constellation of Sagittarius. A Hyperborean called Abasis travelled throughout the world borne by this arrow, which also provided all his nourishment.

Leto was supposedly born in the land of the Hyperboreans, and the sacred objects pertaining to Apollo which were venerated at Delos were said to have come from there. Herodotus relates two different traditions concerning these objects. In one, the sacred objects were brought to Delos, wrapped in straw, by two girls, Hyperoche and Laodice (5), and five men. They died at Delos, where they were given divine honours. In the other version the sacred objects were entrusted by the Hyperboreans to the Scythians, who eventually brought them to Delos.

Two Hyperborean girls, Arges and Opis, came to Delos with offerings to Eilithyia, in order to obtain an easy birth of Apollo and Artemis for Leto.

The Delphic Oracle was reputedly established by a Hyperborean called Olen. When the Gauls attacked Delphi, two armed phantoms appeared to them; these were the Hyperborean heroes Hyperochus (1) and Laodocus (2), whose names recalled those of the girls in the Delian myth mentioned above.

The Hyperboreans also figure in the myths of Perseus and Heracles. Their country had a mild climate, inhabited by people with happy temperaments. The sun produced two crops a year; the inhabitants had civilized customs and lived in the fields and sacred groves to great ages. When the old people considered that they had had a good life they threw themselves into the sea from a high cliff with their heads garlanded with flowers, and found a happy end in the waves. The Hyperboreans knew of magic; they could travel in the air and find hidden treasure.

Hyperion (Ὑπερίων) One of the Titans, the son of Uranus and Gaia. He married his sister Theia and fathered Helios, Selene and Eos. Sometimes the name Hyperion was applied to the Sun himself since it means 'he who goes before' (the Earth).

Hypermestra (Ὑπερμήστρα)
1. Hypermestra or Hypermnestra was the only one of the DANAIDS who spared her husband, Lynceus (1); because she disobeyed the orders of Danaus she was handed over in judgement to him, but acquitted. She left the country with her husband and subsequently had a son, Abas (2).
2. The daughter of Thestius and Eurythemis, sister of Althaea, Leda and Iphiclus (2).
3. A daughter of Thespius and mother of Amphiaraus.

Hyperochus (Ὑπέροχος)
1. Hyperochus and Ladocus (1) were the two phantom defenders of Delphi against the Gauls (see HYPERBOREANS).
2. The father of OENOMAUS.

Hypnus (Ὕπνος) The personification of sleep. He was the son of Nyx and of Erebus (or perhaps the son of Astraea) and the twin of Thanatos (Death). Homer made him an inhabitant of Lemnos. Later his home became more remote; in the Underworld according to Virgil, or in the land of the Cimmerians according to Ovid, who described a magic palace where everything was asleep. It was often claimed that he had wings, travelling fast over land and sea and lulling humans to sleep. He fell in love with Endymion, to whom he gave the power of sleeping with open eyes, so that he could constantly watch the eyes of his lover.

Hypsicreon (Ὑψικρέων) A citizen of Miletus, as Theophrastus related, who had a friend from Naxos called Promedon. When Promedon was visiting his friend, Neaera, the wife of Hypsicreon, fell in love with him. One day, when Hypsicreon was away, she declared her love. Promedon rejected her advances, but Neaera ordered her servant to shut her up in the visitor's room, where she made him agree to her demands. Promedon was terrified by these events and returned to Naxos, but Neaera followed him. Hypsicreon demanded his wife back, but she took refuge at an altar. The Naxians advised him to use persuasion but they forbade the use of violence. Hypsicreon regarded this as an insult and persuaded the people of Miletus to declare war on Naxos.

Hypsipyle (Ὑψιπύλη) The daughter of Thoas (1) and Myrina; through her mother she was descended from Cretheus, and so from Aeolus (1) (Table 5 and 6). When the women of Lemnos neglected the cult of Aphrodite, the goddess punished them by making them all smell horrible; their husbands rejected them, seeking replacements among captives and foreigners. In revenge the women massacred all the men. Hypsipyle could not bring herself to kill her father, however, and saw to it that he was saved (see THOAS (1)). Hypsipyle was chosen to be queen around the time when the Argonauts arrived at Lemnos. According to some authors the Argonauts were given a friendly welcome; according to others, the women put up armed resistance. They softened, however, when the heroes undertook to unite with them, and Hypsipyle became

Jason's mistress. Then she gave the funeral games in honour of Thoas (who was officially dead) and all the massacred men of Lemnos. Hypsipyle had two sons by Jason: EUNEUS, and a second, sometimes called Nebrophonus (or Nephronius) and sometimes Thoas (2) (Table 6).

After the Argonauts had left, the women discovered that Hypsipyle had spared her father and they wanted to kill her, but Hypsipyle fled during the night and was kidnapped by pirates who sold her as a slave to Lycurgus (3), the king of the Spartans. She was ordered by him to look after his son, Opheltes. The Seven Chiefs passed through and asked her where they could get a drink of water. Hypsipyle momentarily put down the baby, whom an oracle had ordained she must not lay on the ground before he could walk, near a spring; the child was immediately suffocated by an enormous serpent (see AMPHIARAUS). Lycurgus wanted to put Hypsipyle to death, but in the meantime her sons Euneus and Thoas (2) arrived, trying to find their mother. Amphiaraus, one of the Seven, recognized them by the gold vine branch which they were wearing, which had earlier been given by Dionysus to Thoas (1). Further, Amphiaraus appeased Lycurgus' wife Eurydice (3) and obtained her agreement for Hypsipyle to return to Lemnos. This theme was used by Euripides in his *Hypsipyle*. In this play Hypsipyle came to be separated from her children when they had sailed off with Jason and the Argonauts a year after they were born (they were twins). Subsequently they had been taken to Thrace by Orpheus, who had brought them up. It was there that they had found their grandfather, Thoas (1).

Hyrieus (Ὑριεύς The father of Nycteus and Lycus (3) and, according to some traditions, of Orion, and the son of Poseidon and Alcyone (2). His wife was the Nymph Clonia. He entertained Zeus, Poseidon and Hermes once in his cottage. When they offered to fulfil a wish as a reward, he asked them for a son. The gods gave him one by urinating in the skin of the bull which the old man had sacrificed. This son was ORION. Some stories claim that it was for Hyrieus that TROPHONIUS and AGAMEDES built the treasury which was responsible for their deaths.

Hyrnetho (Ὑρνηθώ) The daughter of Temenus (3) and wife of DEIPHONTES.

I

Iacchus (*Ἴακχος*) The god who guided the initiated in the mysteries of Eleusis. 'Iacche' was the ritual cry uttered by the faithful; this cry simply became a name which was given to a god. Traditions vary as to his personality, but Iacchus, whose name recalls Bacchus, one of Dionysus' names, may be considered to be the go-between of the goddesses of Eleusis and Dionysus. Sometimes he is said to have been DEMETER's son (see BAUBO), but Iacchus was more often regarded as the son of Persephone, in which case he was the reborn ZAGREUS, Persephone's son by Zeus. Some stories made Iacchus Demeter's husband, others the son of Dionysus by the Nymph AURA. She had twins by the god, but in her madness she ate one. Iacchus was saved by another Nymph who was loved by the god. She entrusted the baby to the Bacchantes of Eleusis who brought him up. Athena is said to have breast-fed him. Sometimes Iacchus and Bacchus were said to be the same person. Iacchus is depicted in art as a child scarcely adolescent carrying a torch and dancing, and leading the procession of Eleusis.

Iaera (*Ἴαιρα*) According to Virgil, Iaera was a Phrygian Dryad. She bore Alcanor twins, Pandarus and Bitias, who were companions of Aeneas.

Ialemus (*Ἰάλεμος*) The son of Apollo and Calliope. He was the brother of Hymenaeus and ORPHEUS (according to one tradition). Ialemus is the personification of the funeral dirge, which he is said to have invented. Sometimes he was identified with Linus (1) about whom this sort of lament was sung.

Ialmenus (*Ἰάλμενος*) With his brother Ascalaphus (2), a son of Ares and Astyoche. They were kings of Orchomenus in Boeotia. During their reign the Minyans took part in the expedition against Troy, since Ialmenus had been one of HELEN's suitors. After the capture of Troy, Ialmenus sailed to the coast of the Euxine Sea where he founded a settlement whose inhabitants, at the time of Strabo, still claimed Orchomenus as their mother city. Ialmenus and his brother were also numbered among the Argonauts.

Ialysus (*Ἰάλυσος*) The eponym of Ialysus in Rhodes. Through his father, Cercaphus, he was descended from Helios. He married Dotis by whom he had a daughter called Syme, who gave her name to the island between Rhodes and Cnidus.

Iambe (*Ἰάμβη*) The daughter of Pan and Echo. She was a servant in the house of Celeus and Metanira, at the time when Demeter passed through on her search for Persephone. Iambe's jokes amused Demeter. This role was sometimes assigned to BAUBO.

Iamus (*Ἴαμος*) The son by Apollo of EVADNE (1), the daughter of Poseidon and Pitane. Ashamed of being seduced, Evadne abandoned her child. However, two snakes came and fed the child with honey. One day Evadne found him sleeping in the middle of some flowering violets. So she called him Iamus ('child of the violets'). The Delphic oracle told Evadne's husband AEPYTUS (3) that Iamus would be a famous prophet and would found a long line of priests (the Iamids). When Iamus was an adult Apollo led him to the site of Olympia and told him to settle there and wait for Heracles to come and found the Olympic games. Apollo also taught Iamus augury and divination.

Ianiscus (*Ἰάνισκος*) Descended from the Athenian Clytius. The latter had a daughter called Pheno, whom he gave in marriage to Lamedon, the king of Sicyon. Later, when ADRASTUS, one of Lamedon's successors, abdicated, Ianiscus was invited to become king. When he died he was succeeded by PHAESTUS.

Ianthe (*Ἰάνθη*)

1. One of the Oceanids, 'daughter of the violets'.
2. A Cretan heroine, the wife of IPHIS (6).

Iapetus (*Ἰαπετός*) One of the Titans, the son of Uranus and Gaia. According to Hesiod he married Clymene (1) by whom he had four children, Atlas (1), Menoetius, (2), Prometheus and Epimetheus (see Table 8). Other legends say that his wife was Asia; others maintained that his wife was Asopis, a daughter of Asopus. Together with the other Titans he was thrown down into Tartarus by Zeus.

Iapyx (*Ἰάπυξ*) The hero whose name was adopted by the Iapyges in southern Italy. Some authors claimed that he was the son of Lycaon (2) and the brother of Daunus (or Daunius) and Peucetius. Others said that he was a Cretan, the son of DAEDALUS and that he went to southern Italy as a result of the events which followed the death of MINOS. Iapyx was the leader of the Cretans who had followed Minos; after the latter's death they tried to return to Crete, but were caught in a storm and forced to land in the district of Tarentum. A variation of this story said that Iapyx was a Cretan who was the brother of ICADIUS. He went to southern Italy whereas his brother was carried off by a dolphin to the foot of Mount Parnassus.

Iarbas (*Ἰάρβας*) A native African king, son of Jupiter Ammon and a Nymph. He granted DIDO the land on which she founded Carthage, but being in love with the queen and jealous of Aeneas, he attacked the new city after Dido's death and drove out Dido's sister Anna (see ANNA PERENNA).

Iardanus (*Ἰάρδανος*) Sometimes called Iardanas, a king of Lydia, the father of Omphale. One tradition has it that he was a magician who by his spells caused Camblites or CAMBLES to eat his own wife by making him insatiably hungry.

Iasion (*Ἰασίων*) A son of Zeus and Electra (2) (Table 4). He lived with his brother, Dardanus, in Samothrace, though some legends said that he was a Cretan. A common thread in all these legends was his love for Demeter, but sometimes this love was unrequited, so he tried to hurt her. This aroused Zeus' anger and he killed him with a thunderbolt. It was more often claimed that his love was mutual, however, and that Iasion united with Demeter on a strip of fallow land which had been ploughed three times. She bore a son, PLUTUS. Diodorus claimed that Iasion was also the brother of Harmonia (2). Zeus taught him the secrets of Samothrace. After his sister had married Cadmus he met Demeter, who was attracted to him and gave him wheat-seed. Later Iasion married Cybele, by whom he had a son called Corybas, eponym of the Corybantes.

Iaso (*Ἰασώ*) The healer, said to be a daughter of Asclepius and a sister of Hygieia. Her sanctuary was at Oropus.

Iasus (*Ἴασος*) or **Iasius**

1. A king of Argos. In some accounts Iasus was one of the sons of Triopas; in others he was the son of Argos (2) and grandson of Agenor, the father of Io. In the legend which made him the son of Triopas he shared the Peloponnesian territory with his brothers. His share was in the west and included Elis. Pelasgus had land in the east and founded Larissa. However, Agenor inherited his father's cavalry, and drove out his two brothers.
2. A son of Lycurgus (1) and the grandson of Arcas. His daughter was ATALANTA.
3. The father of Amphion, king of Orchomenus. He was married to the daughter of Minyas.
4. Iasus or Iasius was often used instead of the name IASION.

Icadius (*Ἰκάδιος*) The son of Apollo and the Nymph Lycia. He gave his mother's name, Lycia, to the place of his birth. He there founded the town of Patara, where he set up Apollo's oracle. Later he sailed for Italy but was shipwrecked. A dolphin carried him to the foot of Mount Parnassus, where he founded Delphi in memory of the dolphin (in Greek, *δελφίς*). It was also said that Icadius was a Cretan and a brother of IAPYX.

Icarius (*Ἰκάριος*)

1. The father of ERIGONE (1), who was said to have spread the vine throughout Greece during the reign of King Pandion (1).
2. Son of Perieres (1). Alternatively Oebalus (1) was his father and Perieres his grandfather. Icarius and his brother, Tyndareus, were driven out of Sparta by HIPPOCOON and his sons. They took refuge in Pleuron near Thestius until Heracles killed Hippocoon (see CEPHEUS (1) and HERACLES, III). Tyndareus returned to Sparta while Icarius stayed in Acarnania, where he married Polycaste (2). They had three children: Penelope, Alyzeus and Leucadius. Another version says that Icarius returned to Sparta with Tyndareus and married Periboea (1). They had six children: Thoas (6), Damasippus, Imeusimus, Aletes (3), Perileus and Penelope. For Penelope's marriage see PENELOPE.

A Spartan tradition claimed that

Icarius turned against TYNDAREUS by taking sides with Hippocoon. He helped Hippocoon to expel Tyndareus from Sparta. As a result Tyndareus was said to have taken refuge in Pellene.

Icarus (*Ἴκαρος*) The son of DAEDALUS and one of Minos' slaves called Naucrate. When Daedalus explained to ARIADNE how Theseus could find his way out of the Labyrinth, Minos was so angry that he imprisoned Daedalus and his son in it. However, Daedalus made wings for Icarus and himself, and fixed them to their shoulders with wax. Daedalus advised Icarus not to fly too near the ground or too high in the sky. Icarus did not listen to his father's advice. He flew upwards so near to the sun that the wax melted and he fell into the sea, which was thereafter called the Sea of Icarus (it surrounds the island of Samos). According to another version, after killing Talos (2), DAEDALUS flew from Athens. At the same time Icarus was banished and set out to find his father. However he was shipwrecked and drowned off Samos, and the sea was given his name. His body was washed ashore on the island of Icaria, where he was buried by Heracles. It is also related that Icarus and Daedalus fled from Crete by boat. Daedalus had just invented the use of sails. Icarus, however, did not know how to control his sails and he capsized. Another version states that as he was approaching Icaria he jumped clumsily from his boat and was drowned. Daedalus erected two pillars, one in honour of his son and the other bearing his own name. These were in the Amber islands. Also, on the doors of the temple of Cumae he was said to have portrayed with his own hands the sad fate of his son. Icarus is occasionally said to have invented woodwork and carpentry.

Icmalius (*Ἰκμάλιος*) The craftsman who made Penelope's couch, which he decorated with ivory and silver.

Ida (*Ἴδη*)

1. One of Melisseus' daughters, who with her sister, Adrastea, fed the baby Zeus in Crete. Her name was also that of a mountain in Crete where ZEUS spent his childhood (see also AMALTHEA).
2. A daughter of Corybas. She married Lycastus (1) and bore him a son called Minos the Younger.

Idaea (*Ἰδαία*)

1. A Nymph from Mount Ida who from her union with the river-god Scamander gave birth to Teucer (1) (Table 4).
2. One of the daughters of Dardanus and so a great-granddaughter of Idaea (1). She married PHINEUS as his second wife.

Idaeus (*Ἰδαῖος*)

1. One of Priam's sons.
2. A son of Paris and Helen.
3. One of Priam's chariot-drivers.
4. A son of Dares, a Trojan hero.
5. One of the Curetes.
6. In one version of the legend of Dardanus, he had two sons by Chryse, Dimas and Idaeus. The latter settled on the Phrygian coast at the foot of the mountain which was to be called Ida after him. He introduced to that country the cult of CYBELE.

Idas (*Ἴδας*) According to the *Iliad*, the strongest and bravest man and, through his father, Aphareus, a member of the family of Perieres (1). His mother was Arena, a daughter of Oebalus (1). He had two brothers, Lynceus (2) and Pisus. Idas was a cousin of the Dioscuri as well as of the Leucippidae, Hilaera and Phoebe (2), and Penelope. Idas and Lynceus sailed with Jason and the ARGONAUTS. When they were with King Lycus (7) and the Mariandyni, the soothsayer Idmon was killed by a boar. Idas took revenge for the death of his companion by killing the boar. Then he tried unsuccessfully to seize the kingdom of Teuthras (1), the king of Mysia. He was defeated by TELEPHUS (see also AUGE). Idas and Lynceus both appear among the hunters of the boar of Calydon, Idas as father-in-law of Meleager (who had married his daughter, Cleopatra (2)). Idas abducted Marpessa, the daughter of Evenus, on a winged chariot given to him by Poseidon (see MARPESSA). Idas was also well known for his struggle with his cousins Castor and Pollux (see DIOSCURI).

Idmon (*Ἴδμων*) One of the Argonauts, the soothsayer whose duty was to interpret the forecasts for the expedition. He is said to have been a son of Apollo, but his mortal father was Abas (3) (Table 1). Sometimes Idmon was identified as Thestor, the son of Apollo and Laothoe, and the father of Calchas. His adventures with the ARGONAUTS were told in different ways. Some accounts agreed that he reached Colchis; others said that he was killed by a boar in the territory of the Mariandyni. Idmon had foreseen his own death but nevertheless had not hesitated to join the expedition.

Idomeneus (*Ἰδομενεύς*) A king of Crete, the son of Deucalion (2). He was a half-brother of Molus (1) who was the father of his brother-in-arms, MERIONES. As one of the suitors of Helen he took part in the Trojan War. He was one of the nine leaders who volunteered to fight Hector in single combat, and he killed numerous adversaries. His main opponent was Deiphobus, and then he faced Aeneas. In the fight round the body of Patroclus he intended to attack Hector, but fled when Hector killed Meriones' charioteer, Coeranus (2). After the events of the *Iliad*, Idomeneus won a victory for boxing at the funeral games of Achilles. He entered Troy in the Wooden Horse and was one of the judges who had to dispose of Achilles' arms. The *Odyssey* relates that his homecoming was a happy one.

Idomeneus' wife Meda was influenced by NAUPLIUS (2) to yield to the love of Leucus, son of Talos (1), who had been exposed by his father at birth. Idomeneus rescued him and brought him up. When Idomeneus went to the Trojan War he placed Leucus in charge of his kingdom and family, promising him the hand of his daughter Clisithera. Leucus seduced Meda, then killed her, along with Clisithera and all Idomeneus' children, and then usurped the throne. When he got back, Idomeneus blinded Leucus and regained his throne, but other versions say that Leucus drove Idomeneus into exile. In a different version Idomeneus' fleet was hit by a storm on the way back to Crete. He swore to sacrifice the first person he met in his kingdom if he returned safely; that person was his son. A plague broke out in Crete, and, to appease the gods, Idomeneus was banished. He went to Italy and established himself at Salentinum. In another story Thetis and Medea asked Idomeneus to adjudicate a beauty contest between them; he decided in favour of Thetis, whereupon Medea said, 'All Cretans are liars', and cursed the race of Idomeneus, condemning it to never telling the truth. This was the origin of the proverb 'All Cretans are liars'.

Idothea (*Εἰδοθέα*)
1. The daughter of Proteus. She advised Menelaus to question her father, in Egypt.
2. The second wife of PHINEUS (3). She was the sister of Cadmus. Phineus' second wife was sometimes called Eurytia or Idaea (2).

Idyia (*Ἰδυῖα*) An Oceanid who was the wife of AEETES and the mother of Medea and Chalciope (2). She was sometimes regarded as the mother of Apsyrtus.

Ilia (*Ἰλία*) The name frequently given to RHEA SILVIA (1), the mother of Romulus and Remus. Some ancient mythographers tried to distinguish between those myths where the mother of Romulus was called Rhea and others calling her Ilia. The name Ilia was reserved for the legends in which the mother of Romulus was the daughter of Aeneas and Lavinia. The legend remained the same whatever the heredity. Rhea/Ilia was loved by Mars, who was the father of the twins; and Amulius, king of Alba, who condemned her to be a Vestal Virgin, either kept her prisoner, or even had her thrown into the Tiber. It was also said that the river-god caused her to be made divine and married her.

Ilione (*Ἰλιόνη*) A daughter of Priam and Hecuba. She married POLYMESTOR (see also DEIPYLUS).

Ilioneus (*Ἰλιονεύς*)
1. The youngest son of Niobe (2) and Amphion.
2. The son of the Trojan Phorbas (5).
3. A companion of Aeneas.

Illyrius (*Ἰλλύριος*) The youngest son of Cadmus and Harmonia (1). He was born during their expedition against the Illyrians. It is from him that the country got its name.

Ilus (*Ἶλος*)
1. One of Dardanus' four children (Table 4). He died without issue.
2. One of the four children of Tros and Callirhoe (4) (Table 4). Ilus was the common ancestor of the family of Priam. He founded the town of Troy (Ilion). Being a native of the Troad, he had gone to Phrygia to take part in some games which the king of that country had organized. He won the prize which consisted of fifty young slaves of each sex. The king, under guidance of an oracle, added a dappled cow and advised Ilus to follow the cow and to found a city in the place where it stopped. The cow stopped on the Hill of ATE in Phrygia. Ilus built a town there which he called Ilion (the future Troy).

After the foundation of Ilion, Zeus, at the request of Ilus, sent a sign to confirm the choice of the site. One morning Ilus found outside his tent a statue, the PALLADIUM, which had miraculously fallen from the sky. Ilus built a temple to shelter the statue; this was the great temple of Athena at Troy. Another version maintains that during a fire in the temple Ilus saved the statue but was struck blind because it was forbidden to look upon this divine likeness. Nevertheless, Athena yielded to his prayers and restored his sight because his sacrilege had been justified.

According to some authors Ilus fought against Tantalus and Pelops (1) because of their abduction of Ganymede, and had them banished.

3. A member of Jason's family, generally said to be the son of Mermerus and the grandson of Pheres. In this version of the legend, Mermerus and Pheres are no longer the two sons of MEDEA, who were killed by her (or the Corinthians) after the murder of Glauce (2) (see also JASON and Table 6).

Ilus reigned at Ephyra. From Medea he inherited knowledge of deadly poisons. Odysseus went to ask him for a poison in which to dip his arrowheads to make them more lethal, but Ilus refused to give it to him.

Imbrasus (Ἴμβρασος)
1. A river on Samos of which the eponymous god was the son of Apollo and Ocyrrhoe (2).
2. A Thracian whose son Pirous played a part in the *Iliad*.

Inachus (Ἴναχος) A river deity of the Argolid, the son of Oceanus and Tethys. He was at one time king of Argos, and by Melia he had two sons, Phoroneus and Aegialeus. The Argives said that he lived before the human era and that Phoroneus was the first man. Other traditions claim that he was a contemporary of ERICHTHONIUS and EUMOLPUS (1), or that after the flood of Deucalion (1) he resettled people in the valley of the river which was named after him. Inachus, along with Cephissus and Asterion, adjudicated when Hera quarrelled with Poseidon for the possession of the country. When Inachus decided in favour of Hera, Poseidon made his river-bed dry out every summer. Inachus (or Phoroneus) built the first temple to Hera in Argos.

Inachus is also said to have been the father of IO, who was alternatively regarded as the daughter of Iasus. Inachus pursued Zeus, after he had raped Io, but Zeus sent Tisiphone (1) against him. She tormented him so much that he threw himself into the River Haliacmon. Another version says that Zeus struck him with a thunderbolt and dried up his river-bed.

Incubi Spirits which came out at night to sit on the chests of sleeping people, causing them to have nightmares. Sometimes they were said to have intercourse with sleeping women.

Indigetes Roman deities whose function was limited to the performance of a specific act and which normally did not exist apart from that act. Among them there were: Consevius (the god of conception); Nenia (the goddess of mourning at the funeral); Abeona, who directed a child's first steps away from its parents' home; Adeona who led it back home; and Potina, the goddess who made it drink. Similarly, there was a whole series of rural gods who watched over crops, including Segetia (from *Segetes* meaning harvests) and Lactarius who caused the 'milk' to rise in the ears of growing corn. Some of these deities, like FLORA and PROSERPINA, gradually acquired a more specific personality under the influence of Greek mythology. Others of the Indigetes had specific domains: Janus belonged to doors, Clivicola to sloping streets, and Cardea to door hinges. There were divinities of this sort everywhere.

Indus (*'Ινδός*)

1. The hero after whom India was named. He was the son of Earth, who was said to have been killed by Zeus. Another legend made him the husband of the Nymph Calauria, and the father of the River Ganges (see AEGYPTUS and NILUS).
2. A king of Scythia who invented silver, whose use was said to have been introduced into Greece by Erechtheus.

Ino (*'Ινώ*) See LEUCOTHEA (1).

Insula Tiberina After the expulsion of the Tarquins, the area of their lands immediately to the north of Rome was dedicated to Mars and became the Campus Martius. Since it was then harvest time and the area was covered with ripe wheat, it was decided to throw this wheat into the river, as it was dedicated to the god. The water was low and the sheaves became grounded on the sandbanks, forming the beginning of the Insula Tiberina at the foot of the Palatine. A different version maintained that the field of Mars did not belong to the Tarquins; it was voluntarily consecrated by its owner, the Vestal Tarquinia.

Io (*'Ιώ*) A priestess of Hera of Argos, with whom Zeus was in love. She was a princess of the royal family of Argos and a descendant of Inachus. Some said that her father was Iasus (1); others (and this was the story which the tragedians preferred) that he was Inachus himself. Alternatively her father was said to have been Piren (probably the brother of Bellerophon, Io thus being a member of the Corinthian royal family). If she was a daughter of Inachus, her mother was Melia. If her father was Iasus, Leucane was her mother.

Zeus' love for Io was either due to her beauty or to the spells of Iynx. In a dream Io was told to go to the Lernaean lake and to surrender to the embraces of Zeus. Io told her father about it, and he consulted the oracles of Dodona and Delphi. Both told him to obey. Zeus started an affair with the girl, and Hera became suspicious. To save Io from his wife's jealousy, Zeus transformed her into an exceptionally white heifer. He swore to Hera that he had never loved this animal. Hera demanded that he should give her the heifer. So Io found herself consecrated to her rival, who put Argos (2) in charge of her.

Io wandered to Mycenae and then to Euboea. Everywhere she went the earth produced new plants for her. Zeus felt pity for his love (he sometimes went to visit her in the shape of a bull) and he ordered Hermes to help her escape. Hermes killed Argos, but was of no avail to Io, for Hera sent a horsefly to torment her. The insect stuck to her flanks and made her mad. Io went along the coast of the gulf which became known as the Ionian gulf. She crossed the sea at the strait which divides Europe from Asia and she gave this strait the name Bosphorus ('cow crossing'). She finally arrived in Egypt, where she was well received and bore Zeus' son EPAPHUS (Table 3). She resumed her original form and, after a final attempt to find her son, who had on Hera's orders been abducted by the Curetes, she returned to rule in Egypt, where, under the name of Isis, she was worshipped.

Iobates (*'Ιοβάτης*) A king of Lycia who played an important part in the legends of ACRISIUS and of BELLEROPHON.

Iobes (*'Ιόβης*) One of Heracles' sons whose mother was Certhe, a daughter of Thespius.

Iocastus (*'Ιόκαστος*) The founder of Rhegium in Calabria; nevertheless another tradition recorded that it was founded by the people of Chalcis who set themselves up 'near the tomb of Iocastus', where there was a woman embracing a man, that is, a vine climbing a green oak. Iocastus was killed by a snake bite.

Iodama (*'Ιοδάμα*) The daughter of Itonus and the granddaughter of Amphictyon (Table 5). She was the priestess of Athena Itonia at Coronoea in Boeotia. One night the goddess visited her and she was turned to stone. In the temple she had an altar and every day a woman carrying the ritual fire repeated three times 'Iodama is alive and wants a burnt offering'. Zeus loved Iodama and had a child by her who was called THEBE (2).

Iolaus (*'Ιόλαος*) A nephew of Heracles; the son of Iphicles and Automedusa. He travelled with Heracles on his Labours and served as his chariot driver. He helped fight against the Lernaean Hydra and against Cycnus (3), went with Heracles to bring back Geryon's cattle, and was involved with the struggle against Troy (see HERACLES, II and III). He frequently appears in art at Heracles' side, for example, among the HESPERIDES, in the battle against ANTAEUS, or in search of Cerberus. Iolaus accompanied his uncle on the voyage of the ARGONAUTS and was one of the hunters of Calydon. He won the chariot prize at the first Olympic games, as well as the prize at the funeral games of Pelias (see GLAUCUS (3)). When Heracles married Iole he gave his wife Megara (1) to Iolaus; they had a daughter called Leipephile ('love of the abandoned', an allusion to Megara's state). Iolaus joined Heracles in the exile imposed by Eurystheus. He left Tiryns with him and took refuge with him in Attica. He also accompanied his uncle at his apotheosis on Mount Oeta.

After the death of Heracles Iolaus went to help the HERACLIDS. He took many of them to Sardinia. He founded several towns, notably Olbia, and commissioned Daedalus to build magnificent buildings. He either died in Sardinia or returned to Sicily. In his old age, or even after his death, he punished Eurystheus for attacking the Heraclids. Zeus and Hebe gave him one day of strength and youth and he killed Eurystheus.

Iole (*Ἰόλη*) Daughter of EURYTUS (2). Heracles won her in an archery competition, but had to seize her by force when Eurytus refused to give her to him. When she heard about this, DEIANEIRA sent Heracles the fatal tunic which caused his death. On his funeral pyre Heracles assigned Iole to his son Hyllus. In some traditions Iole resisted Heracles' advances and preferred to see her parents massacred rather than yield to him; in others she tried to commit suicide by throwing herself off the town walls, but her flowing clothes softened her fall. Heracles then sent her to Deianeira, but when Deianeira saw Iole she prepared the tunic, not realizing that it would prove deadly.

Ion (*Ἴων*) The hero who gave his name to the Ionians. He was of the family of Deucalion (1), the son of Xuthus and CREUSA (2) (Table 5). According to Pausanias, Xuthus was driven out of Thessaly by his brothers Dorus and Aeolus (1). He settled in Athens, but was driven out when his father-in-law, Erechtheus, died. He settled in Aegialus in the Peloponnese. After Xuthus' death his sons Ion and Achaeus separated: Achaeus went to Thessaly; King Selinus of the Aegialians gave Ion his daughter Helice (1) in marriage, and when Selinus died, Ion assumed power there. He named his subjects 'Ionians'. At this time the Athenians were at war with Eleusis. They called on Ion for help and made him their leader. He died in Attica. His descendants held power in Aegialus until Achaeus' descendants returned from Thessaly, drove them out, and renamed the country Achaea.

According to Strabo, Xuthus founded the Tetrapolis (Oenoe, Marathon, Probalinthus and Tricorynth) in Attica after he married Erechtheus' daughter. His son Achaeus committed an accidental murder and fled to Sparta, where he gave the people the name of Achaeans. Meanwhile Ion was made king at Athens after he defeated EUMOLPUS (1). Ion organized the country politically and when he died the area assumed his name. Later the Athenians colonized Aegialus and called the country Ionia. The colonists were subsequently driven out by the Achaeans who renamed it Achaea.

In Euripides' *Ion*, Ion was the son of Apollo and Creusa (2), conceived and born in a cave on the Acropolis. Creusa abandoned the child in a basket, thinking that Apollo would know how to look after it. Hermes took the baby to Delphi and put him in the cave of the temple priestess. Later Creusa married Xuthus, but the marriage proved to be childless. They consulted the Delphic oracle which told Xuthus to adopt the first child he saw when entering the temple. This was Creusa's son. Xuthus adopted him, but Creusa did not wish to welcome a child whom she did not know and even considered poisoning it. Finally, however, because of the basket in which the child had been found and which the priestess had kept, Creusa came to recognize her son in whom the blood of the Erechtheids was revived.

Ionius (*Ἰόνιος*) A son of Dyrrhachus, eponym of the town of Dyrrhachium. When Dyrrhachus was attacked by his own brothers, Heracles came to his aid, but killed his ally's son by mistake. The corpse was cast into the sea, which thereafter was called the Ionian Sea.

Ioxus (*Ἴωξος*) A grandson of Theseus, and a son of Perigoune, daughter of SINIS. Ioxus' descendants regarded the pimpernel as sacred because at the time Theseus was killing Sinis, Perigoune hid in clumps of this plant and swore that if they concealed her, she would never do them any harm.

Iphianassa (*Ἰφιάνασσα*)

1. A daughter of King Proetus of Argos, she went mad, with her sister, and was cured by Melampus (see PROETIDES and Tables 1 and 7).
2. One of AGAMEMNON's daughters (Table 2). At first there was a distinction between her and Iphigenia but as time went on they became confused.
3. According to Apollodorus she was Endymion's wife, the mother of Aetolus.

Iphicles (*Ἰφικλῆς*) Son of Amphitryon and Alcmene (Table 3) and a twin brother of Heracles, though the latter was fathered by Zeus (see HERACLES, I, and also ALCMENE). Iphicles joined Heracles on several of his Labours. He fought with him against the Orchomenians, and Creon (2) rewarded him by giving him his youngest daughter in marriage. Iphicles thus had to abandon his first wife, Automedusa, who had borne him his son IOLAUS In his madness Heracles killed two of Iphicles' sons, but Iphicles succeeded in saving the lives of Iolaus and also of Megara (1). According to a story in Hesiod, Iphicles voluntarily gave his services to EURYSTHEUS whilst Iolaus remained faithful to Heracles.

Iphicles went with Heracles on his expedition against Troy, and is included among the hunters of Calydon. He died in the war against HIPPOCOON's sons; in other accounts he died in the struggle against the MOLIONIDAE (see also BOUPHAGUS).

Iphiclus (*Ἴφικλος*)

1. The son of Phylacus (1) and a descendant of Deucalion (1) and Aeolus (1) (Table 5). As a young man he was struck with impotence. His father questioned the soothsayer MELAMPUS (see also BIAS) about a remedy. Melampus sacrificed two bulls, which he dismembered and left for the birds. The vultures said that at an earlier date, when he was castrating rams, Phylacus had put his knife beside Iphiclus; the child was frightened and stole the weapon, and then drove it into a sacred oak tree. The bark grew round the blade and covered it completely. The vultures said that if the knife were found and a drink prepared with the rust which covered it, Iphiclus would be cured, and would have a son. Melampus found the knife and prepared the liquid as prescribed, and Iphiclus had a son who was called Podarces (2). Iphiclus was famous for his speed of foot. He could run over a field without breaking the stalks. He also won

the running race at the funeral games in honour of Pelias. He took part in the voyage of the ARGONAUTS.

2. The son of Thestius and brother of Althaea. He participated in the hunt for the Calydonian boar and sailed with the ARGONAUTS.

3. A son of IDOMENEUS.

4. The leader of the Dorian invaders who put an end to Phoenician domination of Rhodes. Only one Phoenician garrison was left in the citadel of Ialysus under the command of Phalanthus. An oracle had promised Phalanthus that he would not be driven from his position as long as the crows were black and there were no fish in the well from which the garrison drew its water. Iphiclus learned of this oracle and bribed one of Phalanthus' servants (though others said that Dorcia, a daughter of Phalanthus, took part in the enterprise because of her love for Iphiclus), and with his help released crows whose wings were whitened with plaster. He then secretly had some fish put into the well. When he saw this, Phalanthus lost courage and surrendered.

Iphidamas (*Ἰφιδάμας*)

1. One of the children of the Trojan ANTENOR and Theano (1). He went to Troy with twelve ships and was killed by Agamemnon. His elder brother, Coon, tried to avenge him, but succeeded only in wounding the king, who temporarily withdrew from the battle. Coon was killed on the corpse of his brother.

2. A son of King BUSIRIS who was killed by Heracles.

Iphigenia (*Ἰφιγένεια*) One of the daughters of Agamemnon and Clytemnestra (Table 2). Agamemnon incurred the anger of ARTEMIS, who prevented the Achaean fleet from sailing from Aulis against Troy by inducing a prolonged calm. Calchas (1) explained that the goddess would be appeased only if Agamemnon sacrificed Iphigenia to her. Under the influence of public opinion, particularly that of Menelaus and Odysseus, Agamemnon gave in. He ordered his daughter to be fetched from Mycenae on the pretext that she was to be betrothed to Achilles, and then Calchas offered her to Artemis on the goddess's altar. However, the goddess spirited Iphigenia away in a cloud and put a deer in her place. She took her to Tauris, where she made her a priestess. There are a great number of variations of the story, however. In some accounts the place of sacrifice was an area called Brauron in Attica. It was also said that the goddess substituted a bear as victim in place of the deer, or that Iphigenia was changed into a bull, or a mare, or a she-bear, or even into an old woman, and disappeared in one of these forms. Her disappearance was explained by the fact that all the participants averted their eyes to avoid seeing such a horrible murder committed.

Iphigenia stayed for many years in Tauris in the service of the goddess; her duty was to sacrifice all foreigners. One day she recognized two strangers, who had been brought to her for sacrifice, as her brother Orestes and Pylades; they had been sent by the Delphic oracle to look for the statue of Artemis. She gave them the statue and fled with them to Greece. In Sophocles' tragedy *Chryses* (now lost) the fugitives landed at the town of Sminthion on the coast of the Troad, where CHRYSES (1) was the priest of Apollo. Chryses had a son of his daughter Chryseis and Agamemnon with him. This son had the same name as his grandfather and succeeded him as high priest. When the fugitives arived with Thoas (3), the king of Tauris, in pursuit, Chryses (2) arrested them. However, when his grandfather told him who his father was, Chryses killed Thoas and then accompanied his sister and brother to Mycenae. Another version made Iphigenia the daughter of Chryseis. In this account she was kidnapped by Scythian pirates on her return journey from Troy. Another variation claimed that Iphigenia was the daughter of THESEUS by HELEN. When she was rescued by her brothers the Dioscuri, Helen swore that she was still a virgin but in fact she had given birth to Iphigenia, whom she entrusted to her sister Clytemnestra, who brought her up.

It is sometimes said that Iphigenia died in Megara where she had a sanctuary, and at other times that Artemis immortalized her as the goddess Hecate.

Iphimedia (*Ἰφιμέδεια*) A daughter of Triops, who married her uncle Aloeus and bore two sons called the ALOADAE – Ephialtes and Otus – and a daughter, Pancratis. Iphimedia was in love with Poseidon and she frequently went into the sea and poured water on her breasts. He finally answered her prayers and gave her two sons. Other authors claimed that the Aloadae were the children of Gaia and that Iphimedia was only their nurse. One day when Iphimedia and Pancratis were celebrating the feast of Dionysus on Mount Drios in Achaea, they were kidnapped by two pirates from the island of Naxos (then called Strongyle). They were of Thracian descent and called either Scellis and Cassamenus or Sicelus and Hegetorus. Driven on by their love for these two women, they had a fight and killed each other simultaneously. The king of Naxos, Agassamenus, gave Iphimedia to one of his friends and kept Pancratis for himself. Aloeus sent his two sons to look for Pancratis and her mother. The two giants attacked the island of Naxos, drove out the Thracians who had settled there, and became rulers of the island.

Iphis (*Ἶφις*)

1. An Argive hero, the son of Alector. He was the father of Eteoclus and Evadne (2), the wife of CAPANEUS. According to another tradition, Iphis was the son of Alector and the brother of Capaneus. Eteoclus was killed outside Thebes, and Evadne threw herself on Capaneus' funeral pyre. He had been struck by lightning as he was starting to assault the wall. As Iphis had no more children he left his kingdom to STHENELUS (3) when he died.
2. The son of Sthenelus (4). Iphis was the brother of Eurystheus (Table 7), who took part in the Argonauts' expedition.
3. The lover of ANAXARETE.
4. One of the fifty daughters of Thespius, who slept with Heracles when he was a guest in their father's house.
5. A captive girl from Scyros who was loved by Patroclus.

6. The daughter of Ligdus and Telethousa. Ligdus had instructed Telethousa to abandon the child should it be a girl, but she had a vision in which Isis ordered her to rear her child whatever its sex. When she gave birth to a girl she decided to disguise it as a boy. She called her Iphis, a name common to both sexes, and dressed her in boys' clothes. But Iphis soon inspired the love of a girl called Ianthe (2) who thought Iphis was a boy. The two girls became engaged. Iphis' mother postponed the marriage for various reasons but finally could not defer it any longer. She then begged Isis to help her. The goddess turned Iphis into a boy, and the marriage took place (cf. GALATEA (2)).

Iphitus (*Ἴφιτος*)
1. The son of EURYTUS (2). At times he appears with Clytius among the Argonauts. He was a celebrated archer; the *Odyssey* relates that he inherited the divine bow used by his father, who had been given it by Apollo. Iphitus presented the bow to Odysseus when they met at Orsilochus' house in Messenia. Odysseus gave Iphitus a sword and a spear. Odysseus used the bow to kill Penelope's suitors. In this version Eurytus died before his son, killed by Apollo whom he had tried to rival in archery. Sometimes Heracles was said to have killed him along with his four sons (including Iphitus) at the capture of Oechalia (see IOLE). However, it was also said that Iphitus took Heracles' side and that he intended to give Iole, whom he had won in an archery competition, to Heracles: thus he survived the massacre; he was eventually killed by Heracles, however. When Odysseus met him in Messenia, Iphitus was searching for some animals which Heracles had stolen, or which Autolycus had stolen and entrusted to Heracles. The latter refused to give them up and killed Iphitus. Another version says that Heracles was only suspected of the theft and that Iphitus came to enlist his aid in finding his herd. Heracles promised to help but then had a fit of madness, and threw the young man from the walls of Tiryns. To atone for this murder Heracles had to be sold as a slave (see OMPHALE and SYLEUS).
2. The son of Naubolus, a prince of Phocis; he was the father of Schedius and Epistrophus who were leaders of the Phocian contingent in the attack on Troy. He went on the ARGONAUTS' expedition.
3. Another Iphitus was killed by COPREUS.
4. A king of Elis, a contemporary of Lycurgus, the Spartan lawgiver. He went to consult the Delphic oracle about a remedy for the plagues, epidemics and political quarrels which were destroying Greece, and was advised to reinstate the Olympic Games, which had not taken place since the death of Oxylus (2). At the same time he persuaded the people of Elis to initiate a cult of Heracles whom they had always regarded as their enemy. Through cordial relations with Lycurgus, Iphitus achieved the beginning of Panhellenic union.

Iris (*Ἶρις*) Daughter of Thaumas and Electra (1) and a sister of the Harpies. She was the goddess of the rainbow. She was usually portrayed with wings, dressed in thin silk.

Sometimes she was said to be the wife of Zephyrus and the mother of Eros. Iris was a messenger of the gods, particularly at the call of Zeus and Hera.

Irus (*Ἶρος*)

1. A son of Actor and the father of Eurydamas and EURYTION (3). When Peleus accidentally killed Eurytion he offered sheep and cattle to Irus as compensation, but Irus refused to accept them. An oracle then advised Peleus to leave the herds at liberty. A wolf attacked them, but divine intervention caused it to be turned into stone. The statue was displayed on the frontier between Locri and Phocis.
2. The beggar mentioned in the *Odyssey*, whom Odysseus fought to amuse the suitors.

Ischenus (*Ἴσχενος*) An inhabitant of Olympia, a son of Gigas. During a famine an oracle prophesied that it would come to an end if a noble man were sacrificed. Ischenus offered himself as the victim. He was buried on the hill of Cronus not far from the games stadium. Funeral games were held in his honour. After his death the Olympians gave him the name TARAXIPPUS (1) 'horse-frightener' because horses became uncontrollable near his tomb during races.

Ischys (*Ἴσχυς*) An Arcadian whose father was Elatus (see LAPITHS). He married Coronis (1) when she was already pregnant with ASCLEPIUS.

Isis (*Ἶσις*) An Egyptian goddess whose cult and myths were widespread in the Graeco-Roman world. She was the wife of Osiris and the mother of Horus. Seth, the god of darkness, killed Osiris and scattered his dismembered body throughout Egypt. Isis searched for Osiris (see NEMANUS) until Horus took revenge for her.

The story of IO was assimilated with Isis' myth and iconography (Isis was often shown as a cow carrying the lunar symbol). Isis was compared to Demeter who searched for her daughter, abducted by Hades, god of the Underworld. Isis represented the female principle: she ruled the sea, the fruits of the earth, and the dead. As goddess of magic, she controlled the transformation of things and beings, and the elements. The religious syncretism of the Imperial period developed around her.

Ismene (*Ἰσμήνη*)

1. The mother of Iasus (1) in the genealogy which made him a son of Argos (1). She was a daughter of Asopus.
2. The sister of Antigone and the daughter of Oedipus and Jocasta. According to Apollodorus, Ismene was loved by Theoclymenus (see TYDEUS).

Ismenus (*Ἰσμηνός*)

1. The god of the river Ismenus in Boeotia. He was the son of Oceanus and Tethys. Occasionally he was said to be a son of Asopus and Metope (1).
2. Ismenus (or Ismenius) was a son of Apollo and the Nymph MELIA (1). He had two daughters, Dirce and Strophia, two Theban springs.
3. The eldest son of NIOBE (2) and Amphion. He was killed by Apollo. As he was dying he threw himself

into a river, which consequently adopted his name.

Issa (*Ἴσσα*) According to Ovid, a Lesbian girl whom Apollo loved disguised as a shepherd.

Isthmiades (*Ἰσθμιάδης*) After the cult of the Cabiri was disrupted by the attack on Thebes by the Seven Chiefs, he and his wife, Pelarge, established it again in Boeotia. When Pelarge died, the oracle at Dodona ordered that she should be given divine honours because of her zeal for the gods.

Istrus (*Ἴστρος*) The personification of the river which is the modern Danube. Like all rivers, he was the son of Oceanus and Tethys.

Italus (*Ἰταλός*)

1. The hero who gave his name to Italy. He ruled the country with such justice and wisdom that in gratitude his kingdom was given the name of *Italia*.
2. An Italus also played a part in the epic of ODYSSEUS and CIRCE: he was a son of Penelope and Telegonus (1) (see also LEUCARIA).

Ithacus (*Ἴθακος*) The hero who gave his name to the island of Ithaca, he was the son of Pterelaus and Amphimede and a kinsman of Zeus. He had two brothers, Neritus and Polyctor, who emigrated with him from Corcyra and founded with him the town of Ithaca.

Ithome (*Ἰθώμη*) A Nymph of the mountain of the same name in Messenia. According to local legend she was given the task of rearing the infant Zeus. She was helped by another Nymph called Neda. Both Nymphs used to bathe him in the Spring Clepsydra. There was a sanctuary of Zeus Ithomas to which water was brought every day from the Clepsydra.

Itonus (*Ἴτωνος*) A son of Amphictyon (Table 5). By the Nymph Melanippe (2) he had three children: Boeotus, Chromia and Iodama. He was the founder of the cult of Athena Itonia. (See IODAMA.)

Itylus (*Ἴτυλος*) The son of Aedon and Zethus, in the Theban version of the legend of the nightingale (see AEDON).

Itys (*Ἴτυς*) The son of Procne in the version of the legend of the nightingale most commonly used by tragedians. His father was Tereus, the king of Thrace, who had married Procne, a daughter of Pandion (1), king of Athens. Itys was killed; his flesh was given as a meal to Tereus, and he was then transformed into a bird (possibly a pheasant). There was also a very similar Milesian legend of which AEDON was the heroine. See also ITYLUS.

Iulus Another name for ASCANIUS. The origin of this name was as follows: during the fighting which followed the disappearance of Aeneas, Ascanius took command and was victorious over the Rutulians and their Etruscan allies (see MEZENTIUS). As a reward he was given the surname of Iobum though perhaps it should read Iolum or Iovlum, the diminutive of Jupiter. This etymology was recorded as early as Cato's *Origins*. Sometimes Iulus was distinguished from Ascanius and was said to be the son of Ascanius himself. After his father's death he was driven from the throne of Alba by his uncle Silvius, a son of Aeneas and Lavinia, who made him a priest. See also APHRODITE.

Iustitia The Roman personification of Justice. She was not, however, the equivalent of Greek THEMIS, but of Dike and ASTRAEA. When mortal wrong-doing put Iustitia to flight and forced her to leave the earth, she took refuge in the sky and became the constellation of Virgo.

Iuventus (or *Iuventas* or *Iuventa*: the official form was *Iuventas*). The goddess of youth and in particular the protector of adolescents at the time when they started to wear adult clothes. She had an ancient shrine in the interior of the *cella* of Minerva in the temple of the Capitoline Triad. Later, Iuventus was more or less identified with HEBE but she always retained her Roman characteristics. Under the Empire, young men's associations were founded under the auspices of Iuventus. When a youth started to wear a man's toga, it was customary to give a coin as an offering to the goddess.

Ixion (*Ἰξίων*) Most often he was said to be the son of Phlegyas and therefore the brother of CORONIS (1), but sometimes he was said to be the son of Ares, Aeton, Antion, or Pision. His mother was Perimele (1). Ixion was a Thessalian king who ruled over the Lapiths. He married Dia, a daughter of King Deioneus, after making great promises to the king, but when the latter claimed the agreed presents after the wedding Ixion threw him into a ditch full of burning coal. The horror caused by this crime was so great that nobody would purify Ixion. Zeus alone took pity on him; he purified Ixion and delivered him from the madness which had come upon him. Ixion showed extreme ingratitude to his benefactor, however. He fell in love with Hera and tried to rape her; Zeus shaped a cloud which resembled the goddess and Ixion lay with this phantom, which bore him a son, Centaurus, the father of the Centaurs. Zeus decided to punish Ixion: he fastened him to a burning wheel which rotated continuously; Zeus also gave him a draught of magic liquor which made him immortal, so that Ixion had to suffer an eternal punishment, which is often said to have been inflicted in the Underworld, in Tartarus, alongside that of the worst criminals.

J

Janus One of the oldest of the gods in the Roman pantheon. He was represented as having two faces, one looking forwards and the other backwards. According to some mythographers, Janus was a native of Rome, where at some point he had ruled with CAMESUS. Others claimed that Janus was a native of Thessaly, who was exiled to Rome where he was welcomed by Camesus, who shared his kingdom with him. Janus was supposed to have built a city on a hill, which was consequently called Janiculum. He came to Italy with his wife Camise or Camasenea and they had children, the best-known being Tiberinus (2). After the death of Camesus, he ruled Latium alone. Janus received Saturn when he was driven from Greece by Jupiter (see CRONUS and ZEUS). While Janus ruled on the Janiculum Saturn ruled over Saturnia, a village situated on the heights of the Capitol. During the reign of Janus people were perfecly honest; there was plenty; and there was also complete peace. Janus was said to have invented the use of money. The oldest bronze Roman coins had the effigy of Janus on one side and the prow of a boat on the reverse. Janus was said to have civilized the first natives of Latium, although this was sometimes attributed to Saturn.

When Janus died he was deified. Other legends were attached to him: after Romulus and his companions had carried off the Sabine women, Titus Tatius and the Sabines attacked the city. One night TARPEIA delivered the citadel into the hands of the Sabines. They had already scaled the heights of the Capitol when Janus launched a jet of hot water which frightened them and put them to flight. To commemorate this miracle it was decided that in time of war the door of the Temple of Janus should always be left open so that the god could come to the aid of the Romans. It was closed only if the Roman Empire was at peace. Janus was also said to have married the Nymph Juturna and to have had a son by her, the god FONS or Fontus.

Jason (*Ἰάσων*) The son of AESON (Tables 6 and 1). He was a native of Iolcos. His mother was Alcimede, daughter of Phylacus (1), or, in other versions, Polymede, daughter of Autolycus. At Iolcos Aeson had been deposed by his half-brother Pelias, the son of Tyro and Poseidon. Another version says that Aeson had entrusted power to Pelias until Jason came of age. Jason was brought up by the Centaur Chiron, who taught him medicine. When he reached manhood Jason left Pelion, where the Centaur lived, and returned to Iolcos dressed in a tiger-skin with a lance in each hand, and no shoe on his left foot. He arrived in Iolcos just as his uncle Pelias was offering a sacrifice. Pelias was alarmed because an oracle had told him to 'mistrust a man who had only one shoe'. Jason stayed five days and nights at his father's house, and on the sixth day he called on Pelias and claimed the power which was his by right. Pelias ordered him to bring him the fleece of the ram which had carried Phrixus through the air: this was the Golden Fleece consecrated by Aeetes, king of Colchis, to Ares, and guarded by a dragon. Pelias was certain that Jason would never succeed. Another version claims that Pelias asked Jason what punishment he would give to somebody guilty of treason; Jason said that he would send him to fetch the Golden Fleece. The poets claim that the idea of this test was suggested to Jason by Hera who wanted to bring Medea to Colchis so that she could kill Pelias, with whom she was angry.

Jason sought the help of Argos, the son of Phrixus, and on the advice of Athena, Argos built a boat, the *Argo*, which was to take Jason and his companions to Colchis (see ARGOS (3) and (4) and ARGONAUTS).

When Jason came back from Colchis with the Golden Fleece, he married MEDEA, and gave the fleece to Pelias. In some versions he ruled instead of Pelias; in others he lived quietly in Iolcos, and fathered a son called Medeus; a third version claimed that Medea persuaded Pelias' daughters to boil him in a cauldron, telling them that this would rejuvenate him. The murder of Pelias was said to be Jason's revenge either for the usurpation which he had suffered or because of the death of AESON, who had been driven to commit suicide by Pelias. After Pelias' death Medea and Jason were driven out of Iolcos and took refuge in Corinth. Ultimately Jason grew weary of Medea and transferred his affections to Glauce (2) (or Creusa (3)) the daughter of Creon (1). Medea sent as a present to Glauce a wedding dress which made her veins burn violently. Medea murdered her two children by Jason and fled into the sky in a chariot given to her by the Sun. Jason then wished to go back to Iolcos where Acastus, the son of Pelias, was king. He made an alliance with PELEUS, and with the help of the Dioscuri laid the town waste. Thereafter either Jason or his son Thessalus (3) ruled over Iolcos. Jason was also among those who took part in the hunt of the Calydonian Boar.

Jocasta (*'Ιοκάστη*) The wife and mother of OEDIPUS. In the Homeric tradition, she was called Epicaste. She was the daughter of Menoeceus (1) and the sister of Hipponome and Creon (2). She was first married to Laius, by whom she had Oedipus. Later, without recognizing her son, or his recognizing her, she married Oedipus, by whom she had several children. When she discovered her incest she hanged herself. Another tradition says that Jocasta and Oedipus had two sons, Phrastor and LAONYTUS.

Juno The Roman equivalent of HERA. Originally she was one of the three divinities honoured on the Quirinal and then on the Capitol, namely Jupiter, Juno and Minerva. She also had other sanctuaries, notably under the name of Moneta 'the goddess who alerts people' or 'she who makes people remember'. She was worshipped in the citadel, or Arx. The saving of Rome at the time of the Gallic invasion in 390 BC was attributed to Juno Moneta. Geese which were reared in her sanctuary sounded the alarm and made it possible for Manlius Capitolinus to force the invaders to retreat.

Under the name of Lucina, Juno watched over childbirth. It was forbidden to take part in offerings to Juno Lucina unless all knots were untied, because the presence of a belt, knot or the like on any participant could hinder the delivery of the woman for whom the sacrifice was offered. In a general way Juno was the protector of women and particularly of those who were legally married. The *Matronalia* in her honour took place on the calends (first) of March. The date of this festival was sometimes said to be the birthday of Mars, the god of war and the son of Juno, and sometimes the anniversary of the end of the Roman–Sabine war. The festival recalled the part played by the Sabine women in throwing themselves between their fathers and their young husbands and re-establishing harmony between the two peoples.

While every man had his 'Genius' so every woman had her 'Juno' – a divine double which personified and protected her femininity. Inscriptions record a Juno of the goddess Dia and of the goddess Virtus, and so on.

Jupiter The Roman equivalent of ZEUS. He was the god of the sky, of daylight, of the weather, which he produced, and particularly of thunder and lightning. In Rome he ruled on the Capitol, which was consecrated to him. Virgil tells how at one time this area was covered with oak trees (oaks were sacred to Jupiter). The principal worship of the Latin confederation was always of Jupiter Latialis whose sanctuary was on the top of a wooded mountain which overlooks the lakes of Nemi and Albano. The Capitoline Jupiter was to a large extent the descendant of this older Jupiter (see LATINUS). On the Roman Capitol there were several cults of Jupiter in his different aspects, the best known being that of Jupiter Optimus Maximus. This cult was transferred comparatively late from the Quirinal to the Capitol at the same time as those of the other two divinities of the Triad, Juno and Minerva. Previously on the Capitol there had been a temple to Jupiter Feretrius where the Spolia Opima were consecrated – that is, the weapons of all enemy leaders killed by Roman commanders. Romulus was said to have been the first to consecrate Spolia Opima: those of King Acron. The memory of the second consecration was also preserved – A. Cornelius Cossus in 426 BC presented the spoils of Tolumnius, the king of the Veians. Romulus was also said to have built a temple to Jupiter Stator: during the battle between Romulus and the Sabines, the Sabines gained the advantage and drove the Romans back across the Forum. Then Romulus promised Jupiter that he would build a temple dedicated to him on that spot, if he stopped the enemy. The Sabines were driven off and Romulus kept his promise; the temple of Jupiter Stator (Jupiter who stays or halts) was situated at the bottom of the Palatine. It was also said that M. Atilius Regulus made a vow similar to that of

Romulus when he was fighting the Samnites in 294 BC.

Jupiter's place in Roman religion became increasingly important. He was seen as the supreme power, the 'president' of the council of gods, the source of all authority. This predominance of Jupiter was shown by the importance of the position given to his priest, the *flamen Dialis*, whose wife was *flaminica* of Juno. The marriage of the *flamen* and his wife operated as a symbol of the union of the divine couple. Under the Republic, Jupiter was the god to whom the consul first offered his prayers on entering office. The victors carried their triumphal crown and consecrated their ritual sacrifices to him. Jupiter guaranteed that treaties would be honoured; he oversaw international relations through the mediation of the college of priests.

During the Empire the emperors placed themselves under the protection of Jupiter. Augustus, the first emperor, claimed to have dreams sent directly by the god, and he related how he had been saved from a flash of lightning during a war in Spain: the slave who was walking in front of his litter was killed whereas he, inside the litter, was spared. In gratitude Augustus had a temple to Jupiter the Thunderer built on the Capitol. Later, Caligula arrogated to himself the two epithets of the Capitoline Jupiter, Optimus Maximus (Best and Greatest). He had his palace joined to the god's temple by a special passage. Every provincial city had a Capitol similar to the one in Rome; the Triad would be installed with Jupiter enthroned in the centre. Thus the god represented the political bond between Rome, the mother city, and the daughter cities which were each a small copy of her.

Juturna In earlier days her name was Diuturna. She was a Nymph who was originally worshipped on the bank of the Numicius not far from Lavinium. Later her cult was moved to Rome. The Spring of Juturna was situated in the Roman Forum not far from the temple of Vesta and very close to the temple of Castor and Pollux whose sister she was said to be (see DIOSCURI). Juturna was considered to be a healer. A temple dedicated to her was built on the Campus Martius in a marshy area which was waterlogged until it was drained in the reign of Augustus. See also LARA.

K

Keres (*Κῆρες*) The Keres were spirits which played an important part in the *Iliad*. They appeared in scenes of battle and violence and controlled the destiny of each hero. They were said to be horrible, black winged creatures, with big white teeth and long pointed nails. They tore corpses into pieces and drank the blood of the wounded and dead. Their garments were stained with blood. Some allusions made by Homer show that the Keres were Destinies co-existing with human beings and personifying what kind of life would fall to their lot and how they would die. For example, Achilles had two fates to choose from: one would give him a long and happy life, and the other, which he chose, would earn him eternal renown at Troy at the price of early death. Similarly, Zeus weighed the fates of Achilles and Hector on scales in front of the gods to determine which of them should die in the duel which faced them. The scale containing the fate of Hector descended towards Hades and therefore Apollo immediately abandoned the hero to his unavoidable destiny.

The Keres are given a genealogy in the *Theogony* of Hesiod. There they appear as 'daughters of Nyx'; but in the same passage, some verses later, the poet names a Fate, a sister of Thanatos and Moros (Death and Doom), and several Fates, sisters of the Moirae (in Latin, Parcae).

In the Classical era the Keres tend to be mixed with other similar deities, the Moirae and even the Erinyes, whom they resemble because of their savage character. In the *Laws* Plato considers that they are evil genii which, like the Harpies, sully everything which they touch in human life. Popular tradition identified them with the evil spirits of the dead which had to be appeased by sacrifices, such as, for example, took place at the festival of the Anthesteria.

L

Labdacus (*Λάβδακος*) Son of Polydorus (1) and grandson of CADMUS (Table 3) and on Nycteis, his mother's, side, the grandson of Chthonius (see also SPARTOI). Polydorus died when he was only one year old and his grandfather, Nycteus, became regent; when he too died, his brother Lycus (3) became regent. Labdacus finally obtained power. After his reign the title passed to his son LAIUS. The reign of Labdacus is notable for a war with King Pandion (1) of Athens over a question of the position of the frontier. During this war, Tereus, king of Thrace, came to help Pandion. According to a legend recorded by Apollodorus, Labdacus, like Pentheus, was torn to pieces by the Bacchantes because he had fought against the introduction of the cult of Bacchus.

Lacedaemon (*Λακεδαίμων*) The son of Zeus and TAYGETE. He married Sparta, the daughter of Eurotas. Eurotas bequeathed his kingdom to Lacedaemon, who gave the people his name – Lacedaemonians – and the capital of the country took his wife's name, Sparta. His children were Amyclas and Eurydice (2). In some versions Asine and Himerus were added. The latter was said to have assaulted his sister and in remorse he threw himself into the River Marathon, which was thereafter called the Himerus until its name was changed to Eurotas.

Lacestades (*Λακεστάδης*) When PHALCES took possession of Sicyon, Lacestades, the king of the town, reigned jointly with him.

Lacinius (*Λακίνιος*) The hero who gave his name to Cape Lacinium in southern Italy. In some accounts he was said to have been a king of the country, who came from Corcyra, and welcomed Croton when he arrived as a wandering exile; in others he was described as a brigand, a son of the Nymph Cyrene, who had tried to rob Heracles of the herds of Geryon (see HERACLES, II). After Heracles had killed Lacinius he built the temple of the Hera Lacinia on the promontory of the same name.

Ladon (*Λάδων*)

1. The god of the river of that name in Arcadia and the son of Oceanus and Tethys. He married Stymphalis and had two daughters, DAPHNE and Metope (1), wife of the river-god ASOPUS.
2. The dragon, the son of Phorcys and Ceto, which guarded the golden apples of the Hesperides. Other myths said that this dragon was the son of Typhon and Echidna or the son of Gaia. He had a hundred heads. After he had been killed by Heracles, Hera turned him into a constellation.

Laertes (*Λαέρτης*) The father of Odysseus. He was the son of Arcesius and Chalcomedusa. His family came originally from Cephalonia; his maternal grandfather was CEPHALUS. Laertes married ANTICLEIA, the daughter of Autolycus, though she had previously been married to Sisyphus, so that occasionally Odysseus was regarded as the son of Sisyphus. During Odysseus' absence Laertes had an unhappy old age. He withdrew to his estate in the country; his only company was an old maidservant, her husband, Dolius, and their children. Odysseus went to join him there when he returned. Athena gave him a magic bath which gave him the strength to help his son repulse the parents of the suitors who had been killed. He killed Eupithes, the father of Antinous (1), with a javelin. The marriage of Laertes and Anticleia produced a daughter called Ctimene (1), although in some accounts Odysseus was said to be the only child of Laertes.

Laestrygonians (*Λαιστρυγόνες*) Giant cannibals who devoured foreigners. The inhabited a town which was said to have been founded by Lamus (1). When Odysseus arrived there, he brought his ships into an apparently safe harbour where he anchored. He sent some of his men to explore the area. At the gate of a town they met the daughter of the king drawing water from a well. The girl took them to her home and called her father, Antiphates, who immediately consumed one of them. Then he called all his compatriots to gather together. They dashed to the harbour and bombarded the ships with enormous rocks. All the ships were wrecked except the one which held Odysseus, who managed to escape.

Laius (*Λάιος*) The son of Labdacus, the king of Thebes, and the father of Oedipus (Table 3). Labdacus died while Laius was still young. Lycus (3) became regent, but was killed by Zethus and AMPHION to avenge their mother, ANTIOPE (1); they then seized the kingdom of Thebes. Laius took refuge with Pelops (1). There he developed a passion for CHRYSIPPUS, a son of Pelops, so introducing, at least according to some writers, the practice of homosexual love. He abducted the young man and was cursed by Pelops. When Amphion and Zethus disappeared in their turn Laius was recalled as king by the Thebans. Laius married Jocasta (or Epicaste), Eurycleia (the daughter of Ecphas), EURYGANIA (1), Euryanassa, or Astymedusa (see OEDIPUS).

See OEDIPUS for the circumstances of his conception and birth. Laius could not escape what the oracle had predicted, namely that he would die at the hands of his son. He was killed by Oedipus not far from Delphi, at the crossing of the roads to Daulis and Thebes.

Lamedon (*Λαμέδων*) A king of Sicyon. Coronus was his father and Corax his brother. Corax died childless, and Epopeus succeeded him as king of Sicyon (see EPOPEUS (1) and ANTIOPE (1)). When Epopeus died Lamedon succeeded him. He gave his daughter Zeuxippe in marriage to SICYON, whom he had called in to help in his struggle with the Achaeans. He himself married an Athenian girl, Pheno, a daughter of Clytius, which explains why at a later date IANISCUS, an Athenian who was a descendant of Clytius, reigned over Sicyon.

Lamia (*Λαμία*)
1. A daughter of Poseidon, mother of the Libyan SIBYL.
2. A female monster who was said to steal children and was a terror to nurses. In one account Lamia was the daughter of Belus and Libya. Zeus had an affair with her, but every time she gave birth to a child, Hera arranged for it to die. Lamia hid herself in a cave; in despair she became a monster jealous of mothers more fortunate than herself, and she seized and devoured their children. In order to punish her yet more, Hera made it impossible for her to sleep, but Zeus gave her the power to take out her eyes and replace them when she wished. Female spirits which attached themselves to children in order to suck their blood were also called Lamiae.
3. The legend of ALCYONEUS (2) mentioned a monster called Lamia.

Lampetia (*Λαμπετίη*)
1. Helios and the Nymph Naera had two daughters, Lampetia and Phaethusa. They tended the flocks of their father in Thrinacia. They told Helios that Odysseus and his followers had killed and eaten his oxen.
2. One of the HELIADES (1), according to some traditions.

Lampsace (*Λαμψάκη*) The daughter of Mandron, king of the Bebryces. In the absence of the king, some settlers from Phocis whom he had established there were about to be massacred by the inhabitants. Lampsace warned the settlers and they succeeded in killing all the natives. At that point, Lampsace died; they gave her divine honours and thereafter called the town Lampsacus.

Lampus (*Λάμπος*) The son of Laomedon and the father of Dolops.

Lamus (*Λάμος*)
1. King of the LAESTRYGONIANS. The family of Aelii Lamii in Rome traced their origins back to Lamus.
2. A son of Heracles and Omphale. The Greek town of Lamia was called after him.

Laocoon (*Λαοκόων*)
1. The priest of Thymbrian Apollo at Troy; he had two sons, Ethron and Melanthus, sometimes called Antiphas and Thymbraeus. Laocoon aroused the god's anger because he lay with his wife before the sacred statue, which was sacrilege. Laocoon also opposed the introduction of the Wooden Horse into the town, and incurred Apollo's wrath again. The Trojans ordered Laocoon to sacrifice to Poseidon, asking him to cause storms on the route of the enemy fleet but, just as the priest was about to sacrifice a bull, two enormous serpents sent by Apollo came out of the sea and twined themselves round Laocoon and his two sons. All three were crushed by the creatures, which then coiled up at the foot of Athena's statue in the citadel temple. The Trojans, realizing that Laocoon had angered Apollo, dedicated the horse to the god, and that led eventually to the town's destruction. The names of the two snakes were Porce and Chariboea.
2. The brother of Oeneus of Calydon and son of Portheus (1) and a slave-girl. He joined the ARGONAUTS with Meleager.

Laodamas (*Λαοδάμας*) A son of

Eteocles, who belonged to the generation of the EPIGONI. After the regency of Creon (2), he became king of Thebes and sustained the attack of the second expedition against the city (see ALCMAEON). One legend told that he died in battle after he had killed Aegialeus, son of Adrastus. Another version claims that he escaped and took refuge in Illyria.

Laodamia (*Λαοδάμεια*)
1. A daughter of Bellerophon, who had a son, SARPEDON (3), by Zeus, according to the Homeric tradition. She died young, shot by Artemis, who was angry with her.
2. The daughter of Acastus and the wife of PROTESILAUS, the first Greek hero to be killed at Troy. When she learned of his death she begged the gods to allow her to have just three hours with him; Protesilaus had made the same request. When Protesilaus, brought back to life for the stipulated period, had to return once more to Hades, Laodamia killed herself in his arms. In another version Laodamia made a wax image of her dead husband which she used secretly to embrace. Her father discovered this and threw the image into the fire. Laodamia followed it, and was burned alive.

Laodice (*Λαοδίκη*)
1. The wife of ELATUS (1) and daughter of Cinyras.
2. A daughter of Agapenor, who on his return from Troy was shipwrecked off Cyprus, where he founded the town of Paphos. Laodice had sent a robe as an offering to Athena from Cyprus to Tegea, her birthplace. She also founded a temple to Aphrodite of Paphos at Tegea.
3. One of the daughters of Agamemnon and Clytemnestra, who in tragedies was renamed ELECTRA (3) (Table 2).
4. 'The most beautiful daughter of Priam and Hecuba.' She was married to Helicaon. Some authors recount that she fell in love with ACAMAS (3) when he came to Troy as ambassador to demand Helen's return. They had a son, Munitus. After the capture of Troy, Laodice, while escaping from the victors, was swallowed up by the earth.
5. A girl who brought sacred objects to Delos. See HYPERBOREANS.

Laodocus (*Λαόδοκος*)
1. One of the three sons of Apollo and Phthia. His brothers were Dorus (2) and Polypoetes (1). With them he ruled the country of the Curetes. The three brothers welcomed AETOLUS when he was driven from Elis, but he killed them all and seized the kingdom.
2. A Hyperborean hero (see HYPERBOREANS).

Laomedon (*Λαομέδων*) One of the first kings of Troy, the son of Ilus (2) and Eurydice (6) (Table 4). He had the walls of the fortress built with the aid of APOLLO and POSEIDON, who were helped by AEACUS. For Laomedon's perjuries leading to his death, see HESIONE (3) and HERACLES, III. Laomedon's tomb at Troy was in front of the Scaean Gate; a prophecy maintained that as long as the tomb was intact the town could not be captured. Sometimes Laomedon was regarded as the father of GANYMEDE, and it was to recompense Laomedon for the abduction of his son that Zeus gave him either a vine carved in gold or the divine horses, which he offered Heracles as a reward.

Laonome (*Λαονόμη*)
1. In one version of the Heracles legend the hero had a sister called Laonome, who was the daughter of Alcmene and Amphitryon. She married an Argonaut, sometimes called Euphemus and sometimes Polyphemus (1).
2. Amphitryon's mother was sometimes called Laonome. She was the daughter of Gouneus.

Laonytus (*Λαόνυτος*) In some accounts Oedipus and Jocasta had two sons, Laonytus and Phrastor; both were killed in the war between the Thebans and the Minyans and their king, ERGINUS (1). In this version Oedipus (1) had a second wife, Eurygania (1), who bore him Eteocles, Polynices, Antigone and Ismene (2).

Lapiths (*Λαπίθαι*) A Thessalian people who originally inhabited Pindus, Pelion and Ossa. They drove out the Pelasgians, who were the first inhabitants. Lapiths were also mentioned at Olenos, Elis, Rhodes and Cnidos. The Lapiths were said to have been descendants of Peneus (1) and Creusa (1) (or Philyra). Peneus had two sons, Hypseus and Andreus, and a daughter who, by Apollo, gave birth to Lapithes (the eponym of the Lapiths). He, in his turn, sired Phorbas (1), Periphas (1) and Triopas, and Lesbos (at least if the text of Diodorus Siculus is not corrupt). Periphas was supposedly the ancestor of IXION, but more often Ixion can be linked with the family of Phlegyas. The Lapiths were also related to CAENEUS and his son Coronus. Caeneus had a brother, Ischys, who was, like him, the son of Elatus. These names recur in the Arcadian legends (see CORONIS (1)). The main myth involving the Lapiths described their struggle against the CENTAURS. Heracles also fought them on behalf of their enemy AEGIMIUS (see HERACLES, III). Mythographers included Lapiths amongst the hunters of Calydon (see MELEAGER) and the Argonauts (notably Caeneus, Coronus, Mopsus (1), Pirithous, Asterion, Polyphemus (1), Leonteus, Polypoetes (2) and Phalerus).

Lara A Nymph of Latium, whose real name was Lala, 'the Gossip'. Jupiter loved JUTURNA, who sought to avoid him; therefore he requested the help of the Nymphs of the countryside. All gave their agreement except Lara, who warned Juturna and told Juno everything. Enraged, Jupiter tore out her tongue and gave her to Mercury, to be conveyed down to Hades where she would be the water Nymph in the kingdom of the dead. On the journey Mercury raped her and begot the LARES.

Larentia See ACCA LARENTIA.

Lares Roman tutelary gods, particularly charged with watching over crossroads and domestic property. Ovid (see LARA) claims that they were sons of Mercury and gives them duties similar to those of Mercury, the god of crossroads and posperity. It is also said that the Lar

Familiaris (protector of each household) was the father of King Servius Tullius. One day when a slave of Tarquin's wife, Tanaquil, was near the fire, a phallus made of ash rose from the hearth. King Servius was born from the union of this with the slave.

Larinus (*Λάρινος*) A herdsman of Epirus. When Heracles was travelling with the cattle of Geryon, Larinus was either given some as a present, or stole them.

Larissa (*Λάρισσα*) A heroine sometimes said to be from Argos and sometimes from Thessaly. She was the eponym of the cities in Thesaly called Larissa and of the fortress of Argos. In some versions she was the mother of Pelasgus (3) by Zeus, or by Poseidon, and in others she was the daughter of Pelasgus. In the first legend she had two other sons, Achaeus and Phthius.

Las (*Λᾶς*) A local hero of Taygete in the Peloponnese. The locals said that he was killed by Achilles (or Patroclus) when he entered the country to ask Tyndareus for the hand of Helen.

Latinus In Roman tradition, the king of the ABORIGINES and the eponym of the Latins. There are two distinct traditions regarding his origin. In the Greek version he was the son of Circe and either Odysseus or Telemachus; in the Latin one he was the son of Faunus and Marica. In a further genealogy, when Heracles was passing through Italy, he brought with him a young Hyperborean girl named Palanto. He gave her as a wife to Faunus (see also FAUNA and BONA DEA). When she married Faunus, she was already pregnant by Heracles. She bore Latinus. Other versions described Heracles as siring Latinus by the king's wife or daughter.

There are two principal accounts of Latinus' adventures. In one, when AENEAS landed in Italy, Latinus spontaneously gave him 680 hectares of land and the hand of his daughter Lavinia in marriage. But Trojan raids on the neighbouring countryside forced Latinus into an alliance with Turnus, king of the Rutuli. Both Latinus and Turnus were killed in a decisive battle. The capital of the Aborigines, here called Laurolavinium was captured, and Aeneas became its king. The Aborigines and Trojans subsequently united and named their land Latium after Latinus.

In the second tradition, Aeneas arrived on the coast of Latium and immediately started building a town. Latinus marched against the Trojans to oppose this. The night before the battle a native god warned Latinus in a dream that an alliance with the strangers would benefit him. Aeneas was also urged by his own gods, the Penates, to make a treaty with Latinus. In the morning an alliance was arranged. The Aborigines gave a piece of land to the Trojans; the Trojans helped the Aborigines in their war against the Rutuli. Aeneas married Lavinia and called his new town Lavinium. However, this was a cause of the war against Turnus, who was in this version an Etruscan, the nephew of Latinus' wife, Amata. Latinus and Turnus were both killed in this war, and Aeneas became king of the Aborigines, who adopted the name Latins.

In the *Aeneid*, Virgil united these two variants. Aeneas was well received by Latinus, who, in accordance with a prophecy, offered the hand of his daughter, Lavinia, to the 'heroic stranger'. But before the alliance could be concluded, Aeneas' son, Ascanius, killed a tame deer on a hunt. A fight broke out between the Trojans and the local herdsmen, who were annoyed at the murder. Amata, who wanted Lavinia to marry Turnus, king of the Rutuli, and Turnus himself urged Latinus to fight the Trojans. Latinus refused and retired to his palace. Juno herself opened the doors of the Temple of Janus (they were closed only in peace time) and Turnus called the people to arms. In the ensuing war Latinus kept apart, and merely requested a truce from the Trojans, so that they might bury their dead, and tried to prevent Turnus from challenging Aeneas to single combat. Latinus made peace after the death of Turnus. There are two sources in which Latinus disappeared during a campaign against Mezentius, king of Caere, and became the god Jupiter Latinus, who was worshipped on the mountain overlooking Lake Nemi.

Latinus Silvius The fourth king of Alba after Ascanius. His father was Aeneas Silvius. He reigned for fifty years and founded a number of cities which were members of the Latin confederation.

Lausus

1. A son of MEZENTIUS who was an ally of Turnus against Aeneas. He was killed by the latter.
2. A son of Numitor who was killed by Amulius.

Lavinia The daughter of King LATINUS and Amata. Before the arrival of AENEAS in Latium she was engaged to Turnus. Her father gave her to the Trojan. In her honour Aeneas named the town which he founded Lavinium. According to one legend her marriage with Aeneas resulted in the birth of Ascanius, but in the *Aeneid* Ascanius is her stepson, already a youth when Aeneas arrived. The mythographers said that after the death of Aeneas Lavinia gave birth to a posthumous son of the hero, SILVIUS (see also ASCANIUS), in the home of the herdsman Tyrrhus or Tyrrhenus, with whom she had taken refuge. Ascanius then handed over Lavinium to his half-brother and went to found Alba, but because he died without children he named Silvius as his sucessor.

Leagrus (*Λεάγρος*) An ally of the Heraclid Temenus (3). With the help of his friend Ergiaeus, and at the instigation of Temenus, he stole the PALLADIUM from Argos. After quarrelling with Temenus he offered the statue to the kings of Sparta who accepted willingly, since it ensured the safety of the town where it lay. They placed it by the sanctuary of the Leucippidae. As the Delphic oracle had advised them to give the Palladium, as a protector, the guardian-hero of those who had helped to steal it, they erected just by it a temple to Odysseus, because

PENELOPE had originally come from Sparta.

Leander (*Λέανδρος*) A young man of Abydos who was in love with a priestess of Aphrodite called Hero, who lived at Sestos on the other side of the Hellespont. Every night he swam across guided by a lamp which Hero placed on top of her house. One stormy night the lamp was blown out and Leander could not find the shore. The next day Hero discovered his corpse. Not wishing to survive her lover she threw herself off the balcony.

Learchus (*Λέαρχος*) A son of Ino and Athamas, his brother being Melicertes. When Athamas was driven mad by Hera, he killed Learchus with an arrow, mistaking him for a deer. According to another account he mistook him for a young lion and threw him off a rock. Another version maintains that Athamas learned of the crime which Ino had committed against Phrixus and Helle, his children by Nephele (1), and, intending to kill her, he killed Learchus by mistake.

Lebeadus (*Λεβέαδος*) Eleuther and Lebeadus were the only ones who did not take part in the blasphemy of their father, LYCAON (2). After the resulting disaster they fled to Boeotia where they founded the towns of Lebadea and Eleutherae.

Leda (*Λήδα*) A daughter of the king of Aetolia, Thestius, and his wife Eurythemis. Her sisters were Althaea, the mother of Meleager, and Hypermestra, though some legends quote her as having Clytia and Melanippe (4) as sisters. It was said that Glaucus (3), a son of Sisyphus, passed through Lacedaemon looking for horses which he had lost, and there had an affair with Pantidyia, who at the same time was married to Thestius; she had a daughter called Leda, whom she passed off as a daughter of Thestius (cf. the legend of the birth of ODYSSEUS). When Tyndareus was driven from Lacedaemon by Hippocoon and his sons he took refuge at the court of Thestius, who gave him his daughter Leda as wife. When Heracles restored Tyndareus as king of Sparta she went with him. By Tyndareus Leda had Timandra who married ECHEMUS; CLYTEMNESTRA, who married Agamemnon; HELEN and the DIOSCURI. Among all these children (to whom the tragic writers added Phoebe (4)), some were begotten by Zeus, who changed himself into a swan in order to unite with her. It was also said that Helen was the daughter of Zeus and NEMESIS. Nemesis laid an egg, which she abandoned. A herdsman found it and took it to Leda. When Helen emerged from it, Leda claimed that she was her child, because of her great beauty. More often it was accepted that Leda, because of her love for Zeus, laid an egg, or occasionally two eggs, from which emerged the two pairs of children: Pollux and Clytemnestra, Helen and Castor (see DIOSCURI). In Sparta at the temple of the Leucippidae fragments of an enormous shell were said to be part of the egg laid by Leda.

Leimon (*Λειμών*) When Apollo and Artemis wanted to avenge the rejections suffered by their mother when she had been pregnant, they came to the kingdom of Tegeates. There they were received by Scephrus, one of Apollo's sons, who spoke to the god secretly. He was seen by one of his brothers, Leimon, who imagined that he was slandering him to the god and in anger killed him; however, at the same time, Artemis shot him with an arrow. Tegeates and his wife Maera (1) offered sacrifices, but Apollo and Artemis would not relent; they departed, leaving a famine behind them. Tegeates consulted the Delphic oracle. It replied that they must give Scephrus full funeral honours. In consequence an annual festival was started at Tegea in his honour.

Leimone (*Λειμώνη*) A daughter of Hippomenes, an Athenian noble. When her father realized that she had had an affair before she was married, he shut her up with a horse in a lonely house and gave them no food or water. The horse grew mad with hunger and ate the young woman.

Leipephile (*Λειπεφίλη*) The daughter of Iolaus, a nephew of Heracles. Through her marriage to Phylas (4) she united two strands of Heraclean descent in her son HIPPOTES (1) (see also ALETES and Table 7).

Leitus (*Λήιτος*) A Theban chieftain, a son of Alectryon (or Alector). The *Iliad* describes his killing of the Trojan Phylacus (3) and his being wounded by Hector. He brought back the ashes of Archesilaus from Troy. He was one of the Argonauts.

Lelex (*Λέλεξ*)

1. The eponym of the Leleges. He was the first king of Laconia and a child of the sun. He had two sons, Myles and Polycaon (1); Myles succeeded him on the throne of Laconia, which he later bequeathed to his own son, Eurotas, the river-god. Polycaon married MESSENE and gained the kingdom which he called Messenia after his wife. Another legend made Lelex the father of Eurotas.
2. A son of Poseidon and Libya who came from Egypt to rule over Megara. He had a son, Cleson, whose daughters, Cleso and Tauropolis, received the body of Ino when it was brought to Megara by the sea after her suicide (see PALAEMON (3)).

Lemures The spirits of the dead which were exorcized annually at the Festival of the Lemuria in Rome on 9 May and the two following odd days, 11 and 13. This festival was celebrated at night. The father of the family came bare-footed out of the house and washed his hands in the water of a spring and threw into the darkness some kidney beans (or broad beans), turning his head and saying, 'By these beans, I redeem myself and my own.' He repeated this nine times without looking backwards, while, it was believed, the Lemures gathered the beans. The celebrant then purified his hands again and knocked on some bronze saying, 'Shadows of my ancestors, be gone.' He could then look behind himself. The Lemures had gone away satisfied for a year.

Leonteus (*Λεοντεύς*) A chief of the Lapiths, the son of Coronus and grandson of Caeneus. He went with Polypoetes (2) to the Trojan War. In the *Iliad* he is named among the warriors who manned the Wooden Horse. Myths also include him in the list of the suitors of Helen. After the capture of Troy, he followed CALCHAS (1) on the land road. After the death of the seer he returned to Troy, whence he returned to his own country.

Leontichus (*Λεόντιχος*) Rhadinea was a young girl of Triphylia in Samos. She was betrothed to a tyrant in Corinth but she loved a young fellow-countryman called Leontichus. When she sailed to Corinth to marry her fiancé, Leontichus took the land route. The tryant killed them both, and returned their bodies on a chariot. He then regretted his cruelty and buried them in an enclosure which he dedicated to them. Rejected lovers went there to ask for happiness in their love.

Leontophonus (*Λεοντοφόνος*) After the murder of the suitors, Odysseus, when accused by their parents, submitted the matter to the arbitration of Neoptolemus who condemned him to exile. Odysseus took refuge with Thoas (4), whose daughter he married. Leontophonus, 'the lion-killer', was born from this marriage.

Leonymus (*Λεώνυμος*) See AUTOLEON.

Leos (*Λέως*) The eponymous hero of the tribe of Leontis. He was a son of Orpheus, and he had a son, Clyanthus, and three daughters, Phasithea, Theope and Euboule. When Athens was suffering from a famine he sacrificed his three daughters because the Delphic oracle demanded human sacrifice to overcome the famine. The Athenians erected a shrine in the Ceramicus in memory of the girls.

Lepreus (*Λέπρεος*) The son of Astydamia, a sister of Augias. He advised Augias not to pay Heracles the money which he had promised for cleaning the king's stables. He further suggested that he should put Heracles into chains. When Heracles returned to take revenge on Augias, he intended also to punish Lepreus, but let himself be side-tracked by the entreaties of Astydamia, and contented himself with organizing a contest between himself and Lepreus of eating, drinking and discus-throwing. Lepreus, beaten at everything, took up arms. They fought until Lepreus was killed.

Lesbos (*Λέσβος*) The son of Lapithes. On the order of the oracle he went into exile in Lesbos (see MACAR). He gave his name to the island.

Lethaia (*Ληθαία*) The lover of Olenus. Over-confident in her beauty, she was turned to stone. Olenus was similarly transformed.

Lethe (*Λήθη*) Oblivion, the daughter of Eris, and according to one myth the mother of the Charites. She gave her name to the river of Oblivion in the Underworld. The dead drank from it to make them forget their earthly life. In the thinking of some philosophers, spirits drank this liquid before being reincarnated. This removed any memory of what they had seen when they were underground. Near the oracle of Trophonius at Lebadeia there were two springs which those consulting the oracle had to drink – the spring of forgetfulness (Lethe) and the spring of memory (Mnemosyne). Lethe became a personification of Oblivion, sister of Death and Sleep.

Leto (*Λητώ*) The mother of Apollo and Artemis by Zeus. Her father was the Titan Coeus and her mother the Titan Phoebe (1). Her sisters were Asteria (1) and Ortygia (Table 8). When Leto was about to produce her divine twins, Hera, being jealous, forbade every place in the world to offer her shelter. So Leto wandered without being able to find a resting-place. Finally Ortygia, which until then was a floating island, agreed to receive her. As a reward the island was fixed to the sea bed by four columns which kept it in position. Because Apollo, the god of light, first saw daylight on its soil it was named Delos, 'the Brilliant'. Another legend claimed that Hera had sworn that Leto could not give birth in any place which was reached by the sun's rays. On Zeus' order Boreas brought Leto to Poseidon, who, by raising waves, made a sort of liquid arch above the island. So, shaded from the sun, Leto was able to give birth. The birth pains lasted nine days and nights. All the goddesses came to help Leto except Hera and Eilithyia, the goddess of birth. Her absence hindered the event, so Iris was sent by the goddesses, and by promising Eilithyia a necklace in gold and amber, nine cubits long, persuaded her to help the suffering Leto. The two divine children were then born.

To escape Hera, Leto assumed the shape of a she-wolf and she fled from the land of the Hyperboreans where she usually lived. In Lycia Leto stopped by a spring or a pond to wash her children, but the neighbouring herdsmen hindered her from reaching it and the goddess turned them into frogs.

Leto later became a much loved mother of her children, who made every effort to defend her. They slaughtered the sons and daughters of NIOBE (2) for her. They killed TITYUS (2) because he tried to rape her; and because the PYTHON had threatened her, Apollo killed it at Delphi.

Leucadius (*Λευκάδιος*) Leucadius, Alyzeus and Penelope were all three children of ICARIUS (2) as was Polycaste (2) (see PENELOPE for a different legend). Icarius had been driven by Hippocoon from Lacedaemonia where he was ruling with his brother Tyndareus. But when Tyndareus was restored to Lacedaemonia by Heracles, Icarius stayed in Acarnania. Leucadius gave his name to the town of Leucas.

Leucaria (*Λευκαρία*) The mother of AUSON in one tradition. In another legend she was the mother of ROMUS. She was said to be the daughter of King Latinus and to have married Aeneas (consequently she is identified with LAVINIA).

Leucaspis (*Λεύκασπις*) A prince of Sicyon who fought Heracles when he crossed Sicily on his return from his time with Geryon. He was killed in the fight. He was given divine honours.

Leuce (*Λεύκη*)

1. A Nymph and daughter of Oceanus and Tethys. Hades fell in love with her and carried her off to the Underworld. Leuce died, but in order to make her immortal Hades changed her into a white poplar which he placed in the Elysian fields.
2. The White Island in the Black Sea at the mouth of the Danube. ACHILLES enjoyed with Helen (or Iphigenia or Medea) an after-life of feasting and fighting there.

Leucippe (*Λευκίππη*)

1. The wife of Laomedon and mother of Priam, according to Apollodorus (Table 4).
2. The wife of Thestius and mother of IPHICLUS (2).
3. Daughter of Thestor and sister of Calchas (1) and THEONOE (2).
4. Mother of Eurystheus in some versions.
5. The wife of Evenor of ATLANTIS.
6. One of the MINYADS.

Leucippidae (*Λευκίππιδαι*) Hilaera and Phobe (2), the daughters of Leucippus (1). They married Castor and Pollux, their first cousins (see DIOSCURI). According to a local legend recorded by Pausanias the Leucippidae were daughters of Apollo, and Leucippus was only their human father.

Leucippus (*Λεύκιππος*)

1. The father of the LEUCIPPIDAE. He was a son of Perieres (1) (or Oebalus (1)) and Gorgophone, and his wife was Philodice, a daughter of Inachus. He also had another daughter called Arsinoe, who, according to one legend, was a lover of Apollo, who fathered her child Asclepius (see CORONIS (1)). Leucippus was king of Messenia.
2. The son of Oenomaus. See DAPHNE.
3. The son of a king of Sicyon, Thurimachus. He had a daughter called Calchiaia, who had a son by Poseidon called Peratus. Leucippus adopted him and he succeeded him.
4. The son of Naxos. He had a son called Smerdius; it was during his reign that THESEUS abandoned ARIADNE.
5. Son of Xanthius. He was a formidable warrior whose reputation was well known throughout Lycia. Aphrodite's wrath fell on him, however, and he fell in love with his sister. He asked his mother to help him satisfy this desire. She agreed and Leucippus became his sister's lover, but the man she was to marry discovered the truth; he confronted Xanthius and, without mentioning Leucippus, told him that his daughter had a lover. Xanthius swore that he would punish his daughter's lover if he caught him in the act. He went to his daughter's bedroom. She hid, but Xanthius, thinking he had caught the culprit, without recognizing her, killed her. Leucippus dashed in not realizing that the attacker was Xanthius, and killed him. Leucippus went into exile in Crete and subsequently to near Miletus. Leucophryne, daughter of Mandrolytus, betrayed her city, Magnesia on the Meander, to Leucippus because she was in love with him.
6. Son of GALATEA (2).
7. Son of POEMANDRUS.

Leucon (*Λεύκων*) One of ATHAMAS' sons, whose mother was Themisto. His brothers were Erythrius, Schoeneus (3) and Ptous. Leucon had a son called Erythras, who founded the town of Erythrae in Boeotia, and two daughters, Evippe (2) and Pisidice, the mother of Argennus.

Leucosia (*Λευκόσια*) A siren who gave her name to an island opposite the gulf of Paestum.

Leucothea (*Λευκοθέα*)
1. The name of Ino, a daughter of Cadmus, after her transformation into a sea-goddess (Table 3). She was the second wife of ATHAMAS. After the death of her sister Semele, Ino persuaded Athamas to receive the child DIONYSUS and to bring him up with their children, LEARCHUS and MELICERTES. Hera, angry because they had received a son born of the adulterous affair of Zeus, made both Athamas and Ino mad. Ino threw Melicertes into a cauldron of boiling water, while Athamas killed Learchus with a spear, imagining that he was a deer. Ino threw herself into the sea with Melicertes' corpse. The sea-gods transformed her into a Nereid; the child became the young god PALAEMON (3). Ino became Leucothea, the White Goddess or the goddess of the spray. She and Palaemon guided sailors in storms. In Rome Leucothea was identified with Mater Matuta. Palaemon was identified with Portunus, the god of ports.
2. A sea-goddess who came from Rhodes (see HALIA (1)).

Leucothoe (*Λευκοθόη*)
1. The name sometimes given to LEUCOTHEA.
2. The rival of CLYTIA, the lover of HELIOS.

Leucus (*Λεῦκος*) A Cretan, son of Talos (1), who was exposed by his father at birth. IDOMENEUS rescued him and brought him up.

Liber The Italian equivalent of DIONYSUS. His name, which means 'Free' in Latin, was derived from one of Dionysus' nicknames, Lyaeus, or the Liberator. The Liberalia were celebrated in his honour. Liber had a female counterpart, Libera, who was often linked with Ceres. Latin mythograhers identified her with the deified Ariadne.

Libitina The Roman goddess concerned with supervising the rites that were paid to the dead. She had her shrine in a sacred wood where all the undertakers (Libitinarii) assembled. Libitina was confused with Libido (sensual passion): she was integrated with Venus and Libentina became a common name for her.

Libya (*Λιβύη*) The Nymph who gave her name to North Africa. She was a daughter of EPAPHUS, who was a son of Io and Zeus (Table 3). By Poseidon she bore two sons, AGENOR and BELUS. Sometimes, however, Libya was said to be Io's daughter. Besides Belus and Agenor, her children were Enyalius (which is only an epithet of Ares), Lelex (2), BUSIRIS, Phoenix (2) (though he was also considered to be her grandson) and even ATLAS (1). A late and 'rationalizing' tradition made Libya the daughter of Oceanus and sister of Asia, Europa and Thrace.

Lichas (*Λίχας*) A companion of Heracles. He served as Heracles' herald in the war against Oechalia. Lichas led Iole as a prisoner to Deianeira or told her that Heracles was in love with Iole. Deianeira gave him the tunic soaked in Nessus' blood (see HERACLES, VI). When Heracles put on the poisoned tunic he went to Lichas, seized one of his legs and threw him into the sky. Lichas was changed to stone and became the Lichadian Islands.

Licymnius (*Λικύμνιος*) A son of Electryon and Media, a Phrygian slave (Table 7), and therefore the half-brother of Alcmene, and uncle of Heracles. During the war which the Taphians fought against Electryon, Licymnius, who was still only young, was the only one of his children to escape massacre. When AMPHITRYON accidentally killed Electryon, Licymnius went with him in exile to Thebes. There he married Perimede, a sister of Amphitryon; they had several children: Oeonus, Argeius and Melas; the latter two accompanied Heracles against Oechalia and were killed in battle. Heracles had promised Licymnius to bring him back to his son, so he cremated the corpse of Argeius and returned the ashes in an urn.

After Heracles' death Licymnius shared the fate of the other HERACLIDS. He took refuge in Trachis and fought against Eurystheus. He later joined Hyllus in the disastrous expedition against the Peloponnese. The Argives invited Licymnius and Tlepolemus, one of Heracles' sons, to settle in their city. Licymnius was struck down in a quarrel or killed accidentally by Tlepolemus.

Ligys (*Λίγυς*) When Heracles on his return from the land of Geryon crossed southern Gaul, Ligys tried to get hold of the flock which the hero was bringing back with him. Heracles began to run short of arrows, and when he was on the point of being overpowered by his attackers he uttered a prayer to his father, who sent him piles of stones which he used to repulse his enemies.

Limos (*Λιμός*) The personification of hunger. She was said to have been a daughter of Eris.

Lindos (*Λίνδος*) A hero who gave his name to Lindos in Rhodes (see CERCAPHUS).

Linus (*Λίνος*)

1. The son, by Apollo, of Psamathe (2). See CROTOPUS and COROEBUS (1).
2. Son of Amphimarus or Apollo and a Muse (generally Urania but sometimes Calliope or Terpsichore). He was a remarkable musician who introduced gut strings on the lyre. But when he challenged Apollo as a singer, the god killed him. Linus also invented rhythm and melody. It is further said that he learned the Phoenician alphabet from Cadmus, but gave each letter its definitive name and shape himself. Linus is also named as the music teacher of Heracles and Iphicles. Heracles was unmusical and rebellious, however, and when Linus tried to beat him Heracles killed him, either with the plectrum or with a stool.

Later, Linus' name was linked to several philosophical and mystical treatises, and he was said to be the son of Hermes, because Hermes was the god of the science of language. At other times he was regarded as the son of Oeager and brother of Orpheus, with whom he became increasingly assimilated.

Liparus (*Λίπαρος*) One of the sons of Auson. He was driven out of Italy by his brothers and fled to an island which he called Lipara, off the Sicilian coast. There he established a community which prospered. Later he welcomed Aeolus (2) when he came to the island and gave him Cyane (1), his daughter, in marriage. In return Aeolus arranged for him to return to Italy. Liparus landed on the coast at Sorrento where he was made a king. When he died, his new subjects gave him divine honours.

Lityerses (*Λιτυέρσης*) A son of King Midas, and an accomplished harvester. He asked travellers who crossed his territory to go harvesting with him; if they refused he killed them or forced them to work for him. Then he beheaded them and put their bodies in a stook. Sometimes he forced them to compete with him to see who was the quicker harvester. He always won and would then behead his opponent. When Heracles was in the service of Omphale he passed Lityerses' estate, accepted Lityerses' challenge and, after making him drowsy by a song, cut off his head. Heracles killed him because Lityerses was keeping as a slave DAPHNIS, the herdsman who was searching for his lover, Pimplea or Thalia (1).

Locrus (*Λοκρός*) The figure who gave his name to Locri. Some say that he was a son of Physcus and a great-grandson of Amphictyon; others claim that he was the son of Amphictyon and the grandson of Deucalion (1) (Table 5). He ruled over the Leleges and gave them the name of Locrians. Opus, a king of Elis, had a daughter called Cabye of exceptional beauty. Zeus abducted her and took her to Mount Menalus. She became pregnant, and Zeus took her to Locrus, who had no children, and gave her to him as a wife. Locrus reared the child which she bore and called it Opus after his grandfather. In other versions Locrus was married to Protogenia (1). After an affair with Zeus, Protogenia gave birth to the hero Aethlius.

Locrus had a quarrel with Opus and decided to set himself up elsewhere. Locrus asked the oracle where he should go; the oracle told him to stop at a place where he was bitten by a 'bitch of the woods'. When he had reached the western slopes of Parnassus he stepped accidentally on the thorns of a wild rose (in Greek 'dog rose'). He realized that the oracle had been fulfilled and he settled in this country, which was also called Locris after him.

Lotis (*Λωτίς*) A Nymph loved by Priapus; she obstinately refused the god's advances. One night when she was sleeping among the Maenads, Priapus, who was one of the same band, tried to take her by surprise, but at that moment Silenus' donkey began to bray so loudly that everybody woke up; Lotis escaped, leaving Priapus abashed while everybody there laughed at his bad luck. Later Lotis asked to be changed into a plant and she became a shrub with red flowers called a Lotus (see also DRYOPE).

Lotophagi (*Λωτοφάγοι*) The Lotus-eaters, a people amongst whom Odysseus landed when he was driven off course by a violent north wind. They welcomed the hero and his men hospitably and gave them the fruit of the Lotus, which was their staple food. This fruit made people lose their memory. Odysseus' companions soon lost their desire to return to Ithaca, and Odysseus had to force them to put to sea again. Ancient geographers located the Lotophagi's country on the coast of Cyrene.

Lotus-eaters See LOTOPHAGI.

Lua A very old Roman goddess associated with Saturn, and connected with the *devotio* or offering of enemy spoils. She seems to have been a goddess of the plague or, more often, a magic defilement by which one hoped to see one's enemies struck.

Lucifer The Latin name for PHOSPHORUS.

Luna The Roman goddess of the moon. Her temple in Rome was on the Aventine. She was integrated with Diana, whose temple was adjacent to hers. In passages where she is alluded to in literature she is merely an equivalent of Selene.

Luperci Priests in Rome who celebrated the Lupercalia. This was a festival in honour of Faunus which took place every year on 15 February. During this ceremony they paraded naked round the Palatine and scourged any women they met on their way with the hide of a specially sacrificed goat. They believed that women would become fertile in this way. Before the procession the priest sacrificed the goat and with the bloody knife marked the foreheads of the Luperci. The marks were removed by being wiped with a wisp of wool soaked in milk; then the Luperci uttered a peal of ritual laughter. The sacrifice also included the immolation of a dog. The shrine of Faunus Lupercus was the cave of Lupercal situated on the Palatine. According to legend, the she-wolf suckled Romulus and Remus there (see ROMULUS).

Lycaon (*Λυκάων*)

1. One of the sons of Priam and Laothoe. He was captured by Achilles one night when he was cutting branches in Priam's orchard. Achilles sold him to Euneus of Lemnos but Eëtion of Imbros bought him back and returned him to Troy. Twelve days after his return he met Achilles on the banks of the Scamander. Although he offered a ransom, the Greek killed him mercilessly.
2. An Arcadian hero, a son of Pelasgus. His mother was either Meliboea (1) or the Nymph Cyllene. Lycaon succeeded his father as king of Arcadia. He had some fifty sons, but the mythographers do not agree on the names or the exact number of the sons. Pausanias and Apollodorus give remarkably different lists. It is said that generally the sons of Lycaon were the eponymous heroes of a great number of towns in the

Peloponnese. Like all genealogical legends this one is very complicated and seems to have changed with the times and the cities according to the needs of explanation and local data.

Lycaon was a very pious king like his father, Pelasgus, and was frequently visited by the gods. His sons wanted to know if the strangers who came to visit their father really were gods. So they murdered a child and mixed its flesh with that which had been prepared for the banquet. In horror the gods sent a tornado which destroyed the guilty. But more often, Lycaon, as well as his sons, was said to have been impious. One day Zeus came to ask the king for hospitality. The king received him but because he wanted to discover if his guest was a god, he gave him a child's flesh to eat, either that of a hostage whom he had held at court or even one of his own sons, Nyctimus, or indeed of his grandson ARCAS. Zeus, enraged by such a meal, turned the table over, and in his anger struck Lycaon and his children with lightning. Gaia intervened in time to save Nyctimus, who succeeded Lycaon as king. Other legends say that Lycaon was transformed into a wolf by Zeus.

3. A son of Ares and Pyrene (2) who was killed by Heracles (see HERACLES, IV).

Lycastus (*Λύκαστος*)

1. According to Diodorus, the father of Minos the Younger, whom he sired on Ida (2). In this version he was himself the son of Minos the Elder and Itone, the daughter of Lyctius.

2. The son of Ares and Phylonome. She was a daughter of Nyctimus; she gave birth to him and PARRHASIUS at the same time.

Lycius (*Λύκιος*)

1. The son of CLINIS, a Babylonian, who was turned into a crow by Apollo. The crow was originally white but it turned black because of his mistake (see also CORONIS (2)).

2. An epithet of Apollo.

Lycomedes (*Λυκομήδης*) King of the Dolopians who lived on the island of Scyros at the time of the Trojan War. See ACHILLES and THESEUS, VII.

Lycopeus (*Λυκωπεύς*) One of the sons of Agrius. With them he took part in an expedition against Oeneus. They captured the kingdom of Calydon from OENEUS, but Lycopeus was later killed by DIOMEDES (2).

Lycophron (*Λυκόφρων*) A son of Mestor. After committing a murder he had to leave Cythera, his home country. He accompanied Ajax (2) to Troy, where he was killed by Hector.

Lycoreus (*Λυκωρεύς*) The son of Apollo and the Nymph Corycia. He was the king and founder of a town called Lycoreia at the top of Parnassus. He had a son, HYAMUS, whose daughter had a son by Apollo, who was called DELPHUS.

Lycurgus (*Λυκοῦργος*)

1. A son of Aleus and Neaera. When his father died he followed him as king of Arcadia. Through his son, IASUS (2), he was the grandfather of Atalanta in one version of her story, and of Melanion, who suc-

ceeded in marrying her. His son Anceus was an Argonaut.
2. A king of Thrace. When the young Dionysus arrived in Thrace, Lycurgus frightened him so much that he jumped into the sea. Thetis rescued him. However, Zeus made Lycurgus blind. In the tragedies Lycurgus was the king of the Edones in Thrace. When Dionysus wanted to cross Thrace, Lycurgus refused permission. He captured the Bacchantes and the Satyrs in Dionysus' train. Dionysus took refuge with Thetis. The Bacchantes were freed miraculously from their chains and Lycurgus went mad; thinking he was cutting down a vine, Lycurgus cut his own leg, and his son's hands and feet. Then he regained his sanity; but the ground became barren and the oracle told the people that it would become fertile again only if Lycurgus was killed. On Mount Pangeus his subjects tied him to four horses which tore him to pieces.

Hyginus' version differs greatly from the previous one. Lycurgus drove Dionysus out of his kingdom, calling his divinity into question. Then, after drinking wine he tried to rape his own mother in his drunkenness. To stop a recurrence of such behaviour he tried to uproot all the vines, but Dionysus made him mad, and he killed his wife and son. Then Dionysus exposed him to the panthers on Mount Rhodope.

In Diodorus' opinion, Dionysus had decided to go from Asia to Europe with his army and made a treaty with Lycurgus to this end. The Bacchantes crossed the Hellespont and entered Thrace, but during the night Lycurgus ordered his soldiers to kill Dionysus and the Bacchantes. CHAROPS told the god about the plot. Dionysus retreated; then Lycurgus attacked the Bacchantes and put them to death, but Dionysus returned in force and routed the Thracian army. He captured Lycurgus and tore out his eyes. After much torture he crucified him. Diodorus says that this episode was sometimes set in Nysa in Ethiopia. Nonnus described a Bacchante called Ambrosia, who changed herself into a vine shoot so that she could throttle Lycurgus. Hera had to rescue him.
3. A king of Nemea, sometimes called Lycus. Either by Amphithea or by Eurydice (3) he had a child called Opheltes. The child was put in the charge of its nurse, Hypsipyle (see EUNEUS), but was strangled by a serpent near a spring (see AMPHIARAUS).

Lycus (*Λύκος*)
1. The son of Celaeno (1) and Poseidon. He was taken by his father to the Island of the Blessed.
2. The son of Celaeno (1) and Prometheus, and the brother of CHIMAEREUS (Table 8).
3. Grandson of Alcyone (2) and Poseidon. He was the son of Hyreius and the Nymph Clonia in some traditions, a son of Chthonius, one of the 'Spartoi' (the warriors born from the teeth of the dragon killed by CADMUS), in others. He is named as the uncle or father of ANTIOPE (1).

Apollodorus tells how Lycus and NYCTEUS had to flee from their native land, because they had killed Phlegyas. They ended up in Thebes where Pentheus welcomed them. Lycus either succeeded Pentheus or became regent, since Pentheus' son LAIUS was too young to become king. Hyginus records that Lycus was the husband of Antiope. He renounced her because she had an affair with Epaphus and was subsequently loved by Zeus. Lycus then married Dirce, but she was jealous of Antiope, so she had her imprisoned. Antiope was miraculously freed on the order of Zeus, and she fled to Cithaeron where she bore Amphion and Zethus, who later took revenge on Dirce and Lycus. See also ANTIOPE (1), AMPHION and NYCTEUS.

4. In *Heracles* by Euripides, a character also called Lycus seized the kingdom of Thebes and was on the point of exiling Megara when Heracles returned. The usurper had come from Euboea and was a descendant of the son of Nycteus who had the same name.

5. One of the TELCHINES. Lycus had a premonition that there would be a flood (at the time of Deucalion (1)), and took flight with his brothers. He landed in Lycia, where he introduced the worship of the Lycian Apollo in the valley of the Xanthus.

6. One of the four sons of Pandion (2). Shortly after Pandion's sons returned to Athens, Lycus was driven out by his brother Aegeus and took refuge in Messenia. He was a well-known priest and seer. The foundation of the cult of the Lycian Apollo was attributed to him. Another account says that he emigrated to Lycia and that the country owed its name to him.

7. A king of the Mariandyni. He succeeded his father, Dascylus. He received the ARGONAUTS hospitably, providing a magnificent funeral for Tiphys and Idmon and sending his son Dascylus to guide them. Lycus was grateful to the Argonauts for killing Amycus, the king of his hostile neighbours the Bebryces. Heracles, returning from his expedition to the Amazons, supported Lycus in a war against the Bebryces, killed Amycus' brother Mygdon (2), and gave Lycus part of the Bebryces' territory.

8. A king of Libya, who made a practice of sacrificing stangers to his father, Ares. Returning from Troy, Diomedes (2) was shipwrecked on the coast. Lycus took him prisoner and was about to sacrifice him when Callirhoe (5), his daughter, took pity on the prisoner and set him free. Diomedes did not reciprocate her love, however; he fled, and realizing that she was abandoned she hanged herself.

Lydus (*Λυδός*) The eponym of the Lydians of Asia Minor. Herodotus calls him the son of Atys, son of Manes (1). According to Dionysius of Halicarnassus, Manes was the son of Zeus and Gaia; by the Nymph Callirhoe (1) he had a son called Cotys who, by Halie (or Halia), had two sons, Adies and Atys. Atys married Callithea; their sons were Lydus and TYRRHENUS. Some versions claim that Lydus was one of the Heraclids, the son of Heracles and Omphale.

Lymphae Divinities of springs who were identified with the NYMPHS at an early stage. The Lymphae could make anyone who saw them become mad (hence Latin *lymphatus* = 'mad', 'crazy').

Lynceus (*Λυγκεύς*)

1. Son of Aegyptus, and husband of HYPERMESTRA (1), one of the

DANAIDES. She spared her fiancé at the time of the massacre. She was tried by her father, Danaus, for disobeying his orders but was acquitted with Aphrodite's help. Lynceus took refuge on a hill near Argos. Hypermestra let him know it was safe to return by waving a torch. In memory of this the Argives had a torchlight festival on the hill which was called Lyrceia (after LYRCUS (2), the son of Lynceus). Lynceus later became reconciled with Danaus and succeeded him as king. Lynceus and Hypermestra had one son, Abas (2) (Table 7). Another legend claimed that Lynceus killed Danaus.

2. The brother of IDAS and the son of Aphareus. He took part in the Calydonian boar hunt (see MELEAGER) and the ARGONAUTS' expedition, where he was distinguished by his keen sight. His most celebrated actions relate to his fight against the DIOSCURI on behalf of the Leucippidae.

Lyrcus (*Λύρκος*)

1. Son of Phoroneus. He was sent by Inachus to look for Io when she had been kidnapped by Zeus. He failed to find her and, afraid to return to Argos, settled in Caunus where Aegialus gave him the hand of his daughter Hilebia. The marriage was childless, so Lyrcus consulted the oracle at Dodona. It told him that the first woman he slept with would give him a son. On the way home Lyrcus stopped in the land of Staphylus (3). He became drunk at a banquet and during the night Staphylus, who knew of the oracle's prediction, put his daughter Hemithea (1) in the room with Lyrcus. (Staphylus' daughters Rhoeo and Hemithea, both finding Lyrcus attractive, had quarrelled over who should spend the night with him; Hemithea won). In the morning Lyrcus resented the incident, but he gave his belt to Hemithea as a token of recognition for their son, and returned to Caunus. Aegialus was angry and exiled Lyrcus. A civil war ensued in which Hilebia took her husband's side, helping him win. The son of Hemithea and Lyrcus, called Basilus, later came to Canus and succeeded his father.

2. A son of LYNCEUS (1); he established himself after his father's death in the village of Lynceia near Argos and changed its name to Lyrceia. Other accounts claim that Lyrcus was a bastard of King Abas (2).

Lysidice (*Λυσιδίκη*) The daughter of Pelops (1) and Hippodamia (1). She was the wife of Mestor and bore him Hippothoe. According to another myth she was the wife of Alceus and the mother of Amphitryon (Alceus' wife was more usually called Astydamia or Laonome (2)) (Table 7). Other versions say that she was the mother of Alcmene and the wife of Electryon.

Lysippe (*Λυσίππη*)

1. One of the PROETIDES.
2. The wife of CEPHALUS.

M

Macar (*Μάκαρ*) In the *Iliad*, a king of Lesbos. In some accounts he is one of the Heliades (2), who fled from Rhodes to Lesbos after the murder of his brother Tenages. Some authors call him Macareus. In other traditions he is a son of Crinacus. He was also said to have been a native of Olenus. After the flood associated with Deucalion (1), Macar came to Lesbos, founded a flourishing settlement, and assumed power over the neighbouring islands. At about the same time LESBOS came to Lesbos and married Macar's daughter Methymna (his other daughter was called Mytilene: they both gave their names to towns in Lesbos). Another tradition made Macar a son of Aeolus (1) (see MACAREUS (1)).

Macareus (*Μακαρεύς*)
1. The son of Aeolus (1), who had an incestuous affair with his sister CANACE. This Macareus has sometimes been confused with MACAR, king of Lesbos.
2. A priest of Dionysus at Mytilene. A stranger had deposited some gold in the temple. Macareus seized the treasure and when the stranger came to reclaim it, Macareus killed him in the sanctuary. Macareus' two sons were playing shortly afterwards. They amused themselves by imitating the sacrifice which their father had just offered. The elder took the sacred knife and stabbed his brother in the neck. Then in spite of his brother's screams he burned him on the altar. In anger his mother struck him down. Macareus killed his wife with a blow of a thyrsus.

Macaria (*Μακαρία*) The daughter of Heracles and Deianeira. Macaria slew her father's killer on Oeta. She later took refuge, with her brothers, in Trachis, and then in Athens, and when the oracle pronounced that victory over Eurystheus demanded a human sacrifice, Macaria offered herself, thus ensuring victory.

Macedon (*Μακέδων*)
1. Son of Zeus and Thyia.
2. Son of Aeolus (1).
3. Son of Lycaon (2).
4. Son of Osiris, who was established by his father as king of Macedonia when Osiris conquered the world. He was the brother of Anubis. He was dressed in a wolf-skin and wore the animal's head as a mask on his face.

Machaereus (*Μαχαιρεύς*) One of the priests of Delphi, a son of Daitas. He killed NEOPTOLEMUS.

Machaon (*Μαχάων*) A son of Asclepius. As one of Helen's suitors Machaon took part in the Trojan War. With PODALIRIUS his brother he ruled over three towns in Thessaly: Tricca, Ithome and Oechalia. At Troy he dedicated himself to the practice of medicine, a skill which he inherited from his father. The cure of TELEPHUS' wound was attributed to him, and also that of Menelaus, who was wounded by Pandarus. He himself was wounded by an arrow shot by Paris. He was nursed by Hecamede, the captive taken earlier by Achilles, though subsequently allotted to Nestor. He is principally known for curing a wound inflicted on PHILOCTETES by Heracles.

Machaon was one of the warriors who were in the Wooden Horse. He was killed either by the Amazon Penthesilea or by EURYPYLUS (4). He married Anticleia, a daughter of Diocles. Nicomachus, Gorgasus, Alexanor, Polemocrates, Sphyrus and Alcon are all mentioned as sons of Machaon.

Macris (*Μάκρις*) A daughter of Aristeus of Euboea. She and her father reared the baby Dionysus, who had been entrusted to them by Hermes. When Hera drove the god away, he took refuge in Corcyra (Corfu) which became known as Macris. There he lived in a cave where, later on, Jason and Medea were to celebrate their wedding (see ALCINOUS and MEDEA).

Maenads (*Μαινάδες*) The Maenads or Bacchantes were the female followers of Dionysus. They were depicted as being naked or dressed in thin veils; they wore wreaths of ivy on their heads and carried a thyrsus or sometimes a cantharus (two-handled urn) in their hands. They were also depicted as playing the double flute or striking a tambourine as they performed a hectic dance. The first Maenads were the Nymphs who nurtured DIONYSUS. Possessed by the god, they roamed about the countryside, drinking at springs and imagining that they drank milk or honey. Female followers of the cult of Dionysus sought to imitate their frenetic conduct. They had power over wild animals: they were depicted as riding panthers and holding wolf-cubs in their arms. The Maenads appear in a number of legends, such as those of LYCURGUS (2), ORPHEUS, PENTHEUS and the Minyads.

Maenalus (*Μαίναλος*) The eponym of the Arcadian mountain and of the city of Maenalon. He was the eldest son of LYCAON (2); it was he who advised his father to offer Zeus the limbs of a child cooked as if it were ordinary meat, as a way of testing the god. He and his father were both struck down by a thunderbolt. According to another tradition Maenalus was the son of ARCAS, and therefore the brother of ATALANTA.

Maeon (*Μαίων*)

1. A Theban, a son of Haemon (1), who fought against the Seven Chiefs. With Lycophontes he led the ambush against TYDEUS. Maeon was the only one of the ambush party who was not killed, as Tydeus spared him. When Tydeus died at the siege of Thebes Maeon buried him. A tradition used by Euripides made Maeon a son of Haemon and Antigone (1).
2. The poet Homer was often described as Maeonides, 'son of Maeon'. Maeon's relationship with the poet varied: some say he was Homer's father by CRITHEIS, others that he was his guardian, grandfather, or adoptive father.

Maera (*Μαῖρα*)

1. A heroine of Arcadia who was

the daughter of Atlas (1) and the wife of Tegeates, eponym of Tegea. Maera was the mother of LEIMON and Scephrus, as well as Cydon, Archedius and Gortys.

2. A dog owned by ICARIUS (1) was torn apart by drunken peasants. Maera's barking led ERIGONE (1) to her father's grave. After Erigone's suicide, the dog died of despair or committed suicide by throwing itself into the Onigrus spring. Dionysus turned this faithful dog into a constellation – 'the Dog'. In some accounts Maera was one of ORION's dogs.

Magnes (*Μάγνης*) A Thessalian hero who gave his name to Magnesia. He is thought most often to be the son of Aeolus (1) and Aenarete (Table 5). He married a Naiad and had two sons, Polydectes and Dictys. Other mythographers made him a son of Zeus and Thyia and the brother of Macedon (1). Hesiod, according to Antoninus Liberalis, claimed that he was a son of Argos (3) and Perimele (1). In that case he would be the father of Hymenaeus.

Maia (*Μαῖα*)

1. One of the PLEIADES, although another legend claims that her mother was Sterope (1). Maia was a Nymph of Mount Cyllene where, in an affair with Zeus, she conceived Hermes. She also appears as nurse of Arcas after the death of Callisto (1).

2. In very early times in Rome there was a goddess called Maia. She was the supporter of Vulcan, to whom the month of May was particularly dedicated. After the introduction of Hellenism she became identified with Maia (1) and was said to be the mother of Mercury.

Malcandrus (*Μάλκανδρος*) A king of Byblos in whose service Isis was a slave, as nurse to the queen of Byblos. This was at the time when Isis was searching for the body of Osiris.

Mamercus

1. A son of Pythagoras, nicknamed Aemilius ('the courteous') because of the sweetness of his manners. This Mamercus Aemilius is said to have been the ancestor of the Gens Aemilia. A variation claimed that he was the son of NUMA POMPILIUS, whose connections with Pythagoras and Pythagoreanism were well known.

2. Mars, disguised as a herdsman, had made Sylvia, the wife of Septimius Marcellus, pregnant. He gave her a lance, with a note setting out the destiny of the unborn child attached to it. This child was Mamers Mamercus. He fell in love with the daughter of Tuscinus. When Mamers Mamercus was out hunting he slew boar. He gave his lover the head and the feet, but his mother's two brothers, Scymbrathes and Muthias, were annoyed and snatched the trophies back. Mamercus then killed his uncles, but Sylvia burned the lance and Mamercus died.

Mamurius Jupiter sent a shield to king Numa as a pledge of victory for Rome. As a safeguard Numa had eleven copies made which he entrusted to the Salii. They were made by Mamurius, and in return his name was included in the song sung by the Salii at the festival of the shields. In Rome, at the festival of the Mamuralia, on 14 March, an old man, called for the occasion Mamurius, was ritually beaten with white sticks and driven out of the city.

Manes
1. A legendary Phrygian king (*Μάνης*). He was the son of Zeus and Ge. He married Callirhoe (1) and their children were Atys, Cotys and Acmon (see LYDUS and TYRRHENUS).
2. In Roman belief, the souls of the dead. Manes is an old Latin word meaning 'the Benevolent', and they were so called in the hope that flattery could make them well disposed. The Manes were offered wine, honey, milk and flowers. Two festivals were specially dedicated to them: the rose festival (or the violet festival) when graves were covered with roses or violets, and the Parentalia, celebrated from 18 to 21 February, said to have been introduced by Aeneas in honour of his father Anchises. It is also said that one year this festival of the dead was forgotten in Rome. The dead took revenge by invading the city and were appeased only when the ritual was carried out.

Mania (*Μανία*) The personification of madness.

Manto (*Μαντώ*)
1. A daughter of Tiresias. Like her father, she had the gift of prophecy. She led her blind father along the roads of Boeotia after the capture of Thebes by the Epigoni. The victorious Argives had promised Apollo, before capturing the town, that he should be given the finest piece of booty, and Manto was marked out as an offering for him. She stayed a long time in Delphi, perfecting her skill in prophecy, until the god sent her to Asia Minor, where she founded the town of Claros and married the Cretan Rhacius. By him she had one son (whose father, according to some mythographers, was Apollo), the prophet MOPSUS (2), famous for his rivalry with CALCHAS (1).
2. The wife of Alcmaeon, by whom she had a son AMPHILOCHUS (2) (Table 1). This Manto was the daughter of Polyidus (1).
3. Virgil refers to a Manto, after whom the Italian town of Mantua was named.
4. One of the daughters of MELAMPUS.

Marathon (*Μαραθών*) The son of EPOPEUS (1). He left Sicyon, driven away by Epopeus' violence, and took refuge in Attica where he introduced the first laws. When Epopeus died he returned to his own country and reunited Sicyon and Corinth. He had two sons who gave their names to the towns of Sicyon and Corinth. Marathon was the hero of the Attic deme of Marathon (see also MARATHUS).

Marathus (*Μάραθος*) An Arcadian who went on the expedition of the DIOSCURI against Attica. Marathus sacrificed himself since an oracle had demanded a human sacrifice to ensure the victory of the attackers. His name was given to the township called Marathon.

Mariandynus (*Μαριανδυνός*) The king who gave his name to the Mariandyni, a tribe who lived in Bithynia. He also ruled over part of

Paphlagonia and annexed the country of the Bebryces. He is said to have been a son of PHINEUS (3); his mother was said to be Idaea (2). He was also thought to be a son of Cimmerius, or Phrixus, or Zeus.

Marica A Nymph of Minturnae in Latium. Virgil described her as the mother of King Latinus and wife of Faunus. Marica was said to be Circe deified.

Marmax (*Μάρμαξ*) One of the suitors of HIPPODAMIA (1) He was killed by Oenomaus and buried with his two horses, Parthenias and Eriphas.

Maron (*Μάρων*) In the *Odyssey* he is the son of Evanthes. Since Odysseus defended him and his family, he presented him with some very strong and rare sweet wine. ODYSSEUS made the Cyclops POLYPHEMUS (2) drunk with this wine. According to Euripides, Maron was the son of Dionysus and companion of Silenus. In Nonnus, Maron was Silenus' son and he accompanied Dionysus on his expedition against India. He was a decrepit old man who only had the strength to drink and sing.

Marpessa (*Μαρπήσσα*) Daughter of Evenus. Her father used to kill her suitors and decorate the temple of Poseidon with their skulls (cf. PENELOPE and HIPPODAMIA (1)). Idas abducted her on a winged chariot given to him by Poseidon; Evenus gave chase but could not catch him, whereupon he slew his horses and threw himself into the River Lycormas which was thereafter called Evenus. Idas returned to Messenia. For the dispute over her between Idas and Apollo, see APOLLO and compare CORONIS (1). Idas and Marpessa had a daughter, Cleopatra (2) or Alcyone.

Mars The Roman god identified with the Greek ARES. The Roman myth of the love of Mars and Venus was based on Homer's account of the intrigue between Aphrodite and Ares. Mars was the son of Juno, just as Ares was the son of Hera. In a passage of Ovid, Juno conceived Mars without Jupiter's aid, using a flower with fertile properties which FLORA obtained for her. Mars' adventure with ANNA PERENNA is one of the genuinely Italian elements in his mythology.

In the Classical period Mars appeared in Rome as a god of war and agriculture. Mars supposedly guided the young to emigrate from the Sabine cities to found new towns. The Sabines used to consecrate to Mars a whole age-group of young people who emigrated, guided on their way by a woodpecker or wolf (both were dedicated to Mars: see PICUS). The she-wolf also plays a part in the legend of earliest Rome (see ROMULUS). Mars was the father of Romulus and Remus, whose mother was RHEA SILVIA (1). The twins were abandoned on the Palatine, nursed by a she-wolf, and sheltered by shepherds. Hence the twins were often called 'Children of the Wolf' or 'the Children of Mars'. Other people besides the Romans were supposedly descended from the god: the Marsians, the Marrucians, the Mamertines and others whose names indicated their connection with the god.

Marsyas (*Μαρσύας*) The inventor of the double-flute (as opposed to the Syrinx or Pan pipes). Marsyas was variously described as the son of Hyagnis, Olympus (2) or Oeager. In one version the flute was invented by Athena, but when she saw how distorted her face became whilst playing, she threw it away. A variant myth claims that Athena made the first flute out of deer's bones, but Hera and Aphrodite laughed so much at her appearance while blowing it that she went to Phrygia to look at her reflection in a stream. She saw that Hera and Aphrodite were right and threw the flute away. Marsyas picked it up and found he could make beautiful music with it. He challenged Apollo to produce equally beautiful music on his lyre. Apollo accepted, on condition that the winner could inflict any punishment he wished on the loser. The first trial was a draw but Apollo challenged his opponent to play his flute upside down as he could with his lyre. Marsyas was declared the loser. Apollo tied him to a pine (or plane) tree and flayed him alive. Marsyas was subsequently transformed into a river. The flaying of Marsyas was a popular theme in Hellenistic art. (See also BABYS).

Mater Matuta A Roman deity of growth, identified with the Greek LEUCOTHEA (1). Lucretius says she is a goddess of the dawn. She had a temple in the Forum Boarium near the Port of Rome. Her festival, the Matralia, was held on 11 June.

Mecisteus (*Μηκιστεύς*) One of the children of Talaus and Lysimache and consequently a brother of Adrastus (Table 1). His son was EURYALUS (1). He was one of the Seven Against Thebes. He was killed by Melanippus (2).

Medea (*Μήδεια*) The daughter of AEETES, king of Colchis, the granddaughter of Helios and the niece of Circe. Her mother was Idyia. In some accounts Hecate is said to have been her mother.

Without Medea, Jason would not have won the Golden Fleece; she gave him the ointment to protect him from the bulls of Hephaestus (see ARGONAUTS) and with her spells sent the dragon to sleep. A later legend, related by Diodorus, informs us that Medea was opposed to her father's policy of killing all foreigners. Annoyed by her mute opposition, Aeetes imprisoned her, but she easily freed herself. This happened on the day that the Argonauts landed in Colchis. She threw in her lot with theirs, persuading Jason to promise to marry her if she ensured the success of his enterprise. As soon as the fleece was gained, Medea took flight with Jason and the Argonauts. He had promised to marry her and all the subsequent crimes of Medea were explained by Jason's perjury. To give him victory Medea had not only betrayed her father but she had taken as a hostage her brother, Apsyrtus, whom she killed and cut into pieces to delay the pursuit of Aeetes (see ARGONAUTS).

Jason and Medea's marriage was postponed until the call on ALCINOUS: Alcinous had decided to give Medea up to Aeetes' envoys, but only if she was still a virgin. Alcinous' wife Arete told Medea secretly about the king's decision and Jason slept with her in the cave of MACRIS. In a much later legend Jason was married in Colchis, where he stayed for four years before carrying out the exploits for which he had come to the country. Medea, as priestess of Artemis/Hecate, was responsible for putting to death all foreigners who entered Colchis. When she saw Jason she was overcome with immediate love, inspired by Aphrodite, and the scene of the sacrifice was said to have ended with a wedding (cf. the story of Iphigenia and Orestes). Hesiod gave Jason and Medea a son called MEDEIUS. Other authors name a daughter, Eriopis; in the tradition used by the tragedians, Pheres (2) and Mermerus were said to have been their two sons. Diodorus named Thessalus (3), Alcimenes and Tisandrus.

While returning to Iolchus with JASON, Medea started her campaign of revenge against PELIAS. She persuaded the king's daughters that she could rejuvenate any living being if she wished to do so, by boiling it in a magic liquid. She demonstrated, using an old ram. Convinced by this, the daughters of Pelias cut him up and threw the pieces into a cauldron provided by Medea; Pelias, however, did not emerge. After this murder, Acastus, Pelias' son, banished Jason and Medea from his kingdom.

Corinth was the native city of AEETES. Jason and Medea lived for some time in Corinth, until CREON (1) wanted to marry his daughter Creusa (3) or Glauce (2) to Jason. He banished Medea but she obtained a day's delay, which she spent preparing her revenge. She dipped a dress in poison, together with ornaments and jewels. She had these delivered to Creusa; when Creusa put them on she was encircled by a mysterious fire, as was her father when he came to help her. Meanwhile Medea killed her own children in the temple of Hera. She then fled to Athens in a chariot driven by winged dragons which were a present from her ancestor, Helios. A different version claims that Medea's children were stoned by the Corinthians because they had brought the dress and jewels to Creusa (see MERMERUS).

It was said that Medea fled to Athens because, before she murdered her children, AEGEUS had promised to help her. After unsuccessfully trying to kill Theseus she was banished from Athens and made her way back to Asia, taking her son by Aegeus, MEDUS (1). She later returned to Colchis where Perses had dethroned Aeetes. She had Perses killed, and gave the kingdom back to her own father. In one legend Medea was transported to Elysium, where she was united with Achilles.

Medeius (*Μήδειος*) A son of Jason and Medea, who was brought up by Chiron.

Medon (*Μέδων*)

1. The natural son of Oileus and Rhene. He was a native of Phthiotis but had to go into exile after the murder of his parents by his mother-in-law, Eriopis. When PHILOCTETES was left on Lemnos, Medon took command of some of his troops. He was killed at Troy by Aeneas.
2. A herald of the suitors at Ithaca. When they decided to set a trap for Telemachus, Medon told Penelope about the plot; he was therefore

spared by Odysseus when the suitors were slaughtered.
3. A son of Pylades and Electra (3) and the brother of STROPHIUS (2).

Medus (*Μῆδος*)
1. Son of Medea and either Aegeus or an Asian king whom Medea married after being driven out of Athens on the return of Theseus. Medus gave his name to the Medes. Medus (son of Aegeus) fled with Medea from Athens but was captured in the country of his great-uncle Perses. Perses had been warned by an oracle to mistrust descendants of Aeetes; Medus, aware of this, said he was Hippotes (2) the son of Creon (1), who was searching for Medea to punish her for having murdered Creon and Creusa (3). Perses remained sceptical and imprisoned Medus. Meanwhile a famine hit the country. MEDEA arrived in a chariot drawn by dragons, claiming to be a priestess of Artemis who had come to alleviate the famine. Perses told her that he was holding Hippotes prisoner. Medea asked him to hand him over. When she saw that the prisoner was her son she drew him aside and gave him a weapon. He killed Perses and became king.
2. Son of ALPHESIBOEA (1).

Medusa (*Μέδουσα*) One of the GORGONS. See PERSEUS.

Mefitis An Italian goddess who presided over outbreaks of sulphurous fumes. It was claimed that these fumes were responsible for plagues, so sometimes Mefitis was said to be the goddess of plague. In Rome she had a temple on the Esquiline.

Megapenthes (*Μεγαπένθης*)
1. An illegitimate son of Menelaus. Megapenthes married the daughter of Alector of Sparta, but as he was illegitimate the Lacedaemonians would not let him succeed Menelaus. The throne went to Orestes. In a different tradition, after the death of Menelaus, and when Orestes was being pursued by the Erinyes, Megapenthes and his half-brother Nicostratus (the son of Menelaus and Helen; but see MENELAUS) drove HELEN out. She sought safety in Rhodes with Polyxo (2).
2. Son of Proetus. He was the father of ANAXAGORAS and Iphianira. He succeeded Proetus as king of Tiryns; but after Acrisius' death Perseus exchanged the kingdom of Argos for that of Tiryns.

Megara (*Μέγαρα*) Daughter of Creon (2) who gave her in marriage to Heracles in payment for his victory over the Minyans of Orchomenus. For her myths see HERACLES, I.

Megareus (*Μεγαρεύς*) Son of Poseidon and Oenope, or of Aegeus, or of Apollo. He was the father of Timalcus, Evippus, Evaechme (see ALCATHOUS) and Hippomenes (see ATALANTA). When Minos besieged King Nisus (1), he called on Megareus for help. Megareus was killed in the fighting. When his successor, Alcathous, rebuilt the citadel of Nisa he named it Megara. In a tradition of Megarian origin Megareus succeeded Nisus because Iphinoe was his wife and the daughter of Nisus. Alcathous succeeded Megareus because he was his son-in-law.

Meges (*Μέγης*) The son of PHYLEUS

and Ctimene (2) or Timandra. He appears among Helen's suitors; because of this, he took part in the siege of Troy, where he killed Pedaeus, Croesmus and Amphiclus. He was said to have been killed at Troy but this is not mentioned in the *Iliad*. The tradition followed by Polygnotus in the great fresco at Delphi depicted him among the Greeks who had returned from Troy, but it was accepted that he had been wounded, and perhaps he died during the voyage.

Melampus (*Μελάμπους*) 'The man with the black feet'. When he was born his mother had put him in the shade but had unintentionally left his feet in the sun. He was the son of Amphythaon and Idomene, and the grandson of Cretheus and Tyro (Tables 6 and 1). He married one of the daughters of Proetus, by whom he had Mantius, Antiphates, Abas (3), Pronoe and Manto (4). Diodorus claims that he married Iphianira, a daughter of MEGAPENTHES (2). In his childhood Melampus found a dead snake which he burnt on a pyre. The children of the snake were grateful to him because he took care of them and brought them up; so they purified his ears with their tongues, so that afterwards he could understand the language of birds and animals. Melampus was not only a prophet but also a doctor; he also knew about herbs, both magical and medicinal. Melampus and his brother Bias left Thessaly, their home country, and stayed with their uncle Neleus (1) at Pylos. There Bias wanted to marry Pero, a daughter of Neleus, but the latter would give his consent only if he brought as a wedding present the herds of PHYLACUS (1) (others said of IPHICLUS (1), but Iphiclus was the son of Phylacus and plays a definite part in the legend). These herds were at Phylace in Thessaly and they were guarded fiercely by a dog which neither man nor beast could approach. Bias asked Melampus for help. He agreed and forecast that he would succeed, but that he would be caught and would be imprisoned for a year. Then he went to Phylace and, as he had predicted, he was caught and incarcerated. He was in prison when he heard the worms which were in the roof beams ask each other how long the beam would hold before it collapsed. One of them said that the beam would break very soon. Melampus asked to be moved to a different prison and, very soon after, the roof collapsed. Phylacus realized that Melampus was a prophet and he asked for his help in curing his son, IPHICLUS, of impotence. As a reward he gave Melampus the herds he desired, which Melampus took back to Pylos, where Neleus gave Bias the hand of his daughter Pero. Another legend, recounted by Propertius, maintained that Melampus was in love with Pero (see also BIAS).

Later, Proetus, the king of Argos, called on Melampus to cure his daughters, who were suffering from collective madness (see PROETIDES).

Melampygus (*Μελάμπυγος*) 'The man with black buttocks', against whom the CERCOPES had been put on their guard by their mother. He turned out to be Heracles.

Melaneus (*Μελανεύς*) The son of Apollo; he was a famous archer. He had a son called EURYTUS (2). He is said to have founded the town of Oechalia in Messenia on land granted to him by Perieres (1).

Melanippe (*Μελανίππη*)

1. The daughter of Aeolus (1), the son of Hellen (Table 5). She had two sons by Poseidon, Boeotus and Aeolus (2). She was the heroine of two tragedies of Euripides, now lost: *Melanippe in Chains* and *Melanippe the Wise*.
2. A Nymph who married Itonus, the son of Amphictyon, and bore a son, Boeotus.
3. A daughter of Ares and a sister of Hippolyta (1). Melanippe was captured by Heracles but Hippolyta obtained her release by agreeing to the conditions of the captor. In the fight which followed the breakdown of the armistice Melanippe was killed by Telamon (see HERACLES, II).
4. The sister of MELEAGER (but see also LEDA).

Melanippus (*Μελάνιππος*)

1. A son of Ares and of the goddess Triteia. He founded the town of Triteia in Achaea.
2. A Theban, the son of Astacus, who was one of the warriors born from the teeth of the dragon of CADMUS. He fought in the war of the Seven against Thebes. He killed Mecisteus and mortally wounded Tydeus before he himself was killed by Amphiaraus. Amphiaraus beheaded his corpse and took the head to the dying Tydeus, who split the skull open and ate the brains. As a result Athena, who had decided to make Tydeus immortal, abandoned her idea. Amphiaraus, had foreseen what would happen and had given the head to Tydeus because he knew how savage he was. Amphiaraus was hostile to Tydeus because he had forced them to undertake this expedition, which Amphiaraus knew was doomed to be disastrous.
3. One of the sons of Agrius, who deposed Oeneus at Calydon (see DIOMEDES (2)).
4. The son Theseus had by Perigoune, daughter of SINIS. He was among the winners at the Nemean games in the time of the Epigoni.
5. Several Trojans with this name fell while fighting before Troy.
6. See COMAETHO (2).

Melanthius (*Μελάνθιος*) An Ithacan goatherd, a brother of MELANTHO (2). Like his sister, he betrayed the interests of Penelope and Odysseus. When Odysseus arrived in Ithaca disguised as a beggar, Melanthius insulted him and took the side of the suitors. During the massacre he tried to give arms to the suitors. He was locked in the room where the weapons were and when the servants had been hanged he was taken into the courtyard, where his nose and ears were cut off and given to the dogs to eat.

Melantho (*Μελανθώ*)

1. A daughter of Deucalion (1), according to one tradition. After an intrigue with Poseidon, who took the shape of a dolphin, she gave birth to DELPHUS, after whom Delphi was named. Other versions give the daughter of Deucalion the name of Melantheia, and make her the grandmother of Delphus. She also had by Cephissus, or by HYAMUS, a daughter called Melaena or Melaenis or Celaeno, who was the mother of Delphus (Table 5).

2. A serving-maid of Penelope, whom the latter had nursed as a child, but who took the side of the suitors. She was the mistress of Eurymachus (1). She was hanged after the slaughter of the suitors. She was the sister of MELANTHIUS.
3. The wife of Criasus and the mother of Phorbas and Cleoboea, according to Apollodorus.

Melanthus (*Μέλανθος*) A descendant of Neleus (1), the king of Messenia. Melanthus was driven out of Pylos by the Heraclids, and migrated to Athens. There the ruler of Attica was Thymoetes (1), the last descendant of Theseus, and the Athenians were at war with the Boeotians. They decided to settle the issue by single combat between the two kings, but Thymoetes was afraid of the Theban king, Xanthus (2), and said he would abdicate in favour of anyone who could defeat him. Melanthus accepted. Just before the battle he saw a warrior dressed in black armour behind Xanthus. This was Dionysus Melanaegis, but Melanthus took him for a combatant and accused the king of breaking the terms of the duel. When the king looked round to see who had come to help him Melanthus stabbed him. The Athenians built a sanctuary to Dionysus whose help had been so useful.

Athenaeus relates a different myth. When Melanthus was driven out of Pylos, the Pythian oracle advised him to settle where he was offered a head and feet to eat. At Eleusis the priests offered him the remains of a sacrifice – the head and the feet. Melanthus therefore settled in Eleusis. Melanthus also gave his name to an Attic Deme and was the father of CODRUS.

Melas (*Μήλας*)
1. A son of Heracles and Omphale and the counterpart of HEGELEUS. He introduced the use of the trumpet at the time of the expedition of the Heraclids.
2. Melas (*Μέλας*) was the son of PHRIXUS and CHALCIOPE (2).
3. A son of Porthaon.

Meleager (*Μελέαγρος*) Son of Oeneus of Calydon, and of Althaea. He was the hero of the Calydonian boar hunt. When Oeneus offered a sacrifice after the harvest to all the gods except Artemis, she sent an enormous boar to ravage the fields of Calydon. Meleager organized hunters from all the towns of the neighbourhood. The boar killed several of them but finally fell to Meleager. Artemis remained angry; she fomented a quarrel between the Aetolians and the Curetes over the division of the boar's skin and head. Meleager fought with his fellow-countrymen, the Aetolians, but when he killed his mother's brothers, she cursed him. Meleager, dreading his mother's words and fearing that the Erinyes would strike him, withdrew to his house. Without him, the Aetolians were driven back into Calydon and besieged. Meleager remained aloof from the conflict until the enemy were on the verge of sacking his house. His wife, Cleopatra (2), took refuge with him and explained the consequences which would follow an enemy victory. This moved Meleager to rejoin the battle; his people won, but he died in the fighting. In the *Iliad* Phoenix (3) told this tale to ACHILLES when he was sulking in his tent.

The hunt subsequently became the most important incident in the story. In this version Meleager was the son of Ares and Althaea, and his fate was said to be bound up with that of a log burning on the fire (see ALTHAEA). Meleager took it upon himself to rid the country of a monstrous boar which had been sent by Artemis. He assembled a large number of heroes: Dryas (1); Idas and Lynceus (2); the Dioscuri (Meleager's cousins); Theseus; Admetus; Anceus and Cepheus (1); Jason; Iphicles; Pirithous; Telamon; Peleus, who during the hunt killed his brother-in-law, Eurytion (3); Amphiaraus; the sons of Thestius (Meleager's uncles); and Atalanta. Ovid also mentions Caeneus, Leucippus, Acastus, Hippothous, Phoenix (3), Iolaus, Echion, Lelex, Panopeus, Hyleus, Hippasus, a contingent sent by Hippocoon, Nestor, Laertes, and the son of Ampycus. The hunters were feted by Oeneus for nine days; on the tenth they set off despite some opposition to the presence of the huntress Atalanta. However, Meleager, who was in love with Atalanta, managed to overcome this opposition.

During the hunt Hyleus and Anceus were killed and Peleus accidentally killed Eurytion (3) with a javelin. Atalanta was the first to wound the boar, then Amphiaraus shot it in the eye with an arrow; Meleager finally killed it with a knife and thus earned the spoils of the animal. He gave the spoils to Atalanta as a token of respect. This outraged his uncles, who said that they should have the remains, since they were his nearest relations on the hunt. Meleager then killed his uncles. Angered by this murder, Althaea threw the magic log on the fire and Meleager died. Later, she hanged herself in remorse, as did Meleager's wife, Cleopatra. It was also said that Meleager was invulnerable and that Apollo had to shoot an arrow to kill him. Among other exploits attributed to Meleager is a victory in the funeral games of Pelias. Diodorus presents him as fighting with the Argonauts at Colchis, where he killed Aeetes. For his meeting with Heracles in the Underworld see HERACLES, II and VI.

Meleagrids (*Μελεαγρίδες*)
Meleager's sisters: Gorge (1), Eurymede, Deianeira and Melanippe (4), who wept so bitterly at the death of their brother that Artemis turned them into birds. At the request of Dionysus, Gorge and Deianeira preserved their human form; or, alternatively, Dionysus restored it to them. The tears of the Meleagrids, like those of the Heliades, were said to have turned into drops of amber.

Meles (*Μέλης*) A young Athenian for whom Timagoras, a foreigner living in Athens, had a passion. Meles made Timagoras tolerate all his whims and when he finally challenged him to throw himself from the top of the Acropolis, Timagoras jumped without hesitation and killed himself. Horrified by what he had done, Meles threw himself from the top of the rock. An altar was built in honour of Anteros (Love Rejected) to commemorate the incident. According to the *Suda*, however, Timagoras was the beloved, and

Melitus (not Meles) the lover who was rejected. In despair Melitus threw himself from the top of the rock. Timagoras committed suicide on his body.

Melia (*Μελία*)
1. A daughter of Oceanus and a sister of Ismenus (2). After an affair with Apollo she gave birth to Ismenius and Tenerus. She was worshipped in the temple of Apollo Ismenius near Thebes, and at Thebes there was a spring called after her.
2. Another daughter of Oceanus. She married Inachus, by whom she had Aegialus, Phegeus and Phoroneus.

Meliads (*Μελίαδες*) Nymphs of the ash tree who were born from drops of blood spread by Uranus after he had been castrated by Cronus. In memory of their violent birth lances were made from ash trees. The warlike bronze age race supposedly sprang from ash trees. This was the third age of people who inhabited the earth.

Meliboea (*Μελίβοια*)
1. A daughter of Oceanus. She married Pelasgus, by whom she bore Lycaon (2).
2. One of the children of NIOBE (2). With her brother Amyclas she escaped the massacre of the Niobids. They took refuge in Argos, where they built a temple to Leto. During the massacre Meliboea turned pale with fear, so she adopted the surname Chloris (the green one).

Meliboeus (*Μελίβοιος*) A shepherd who found the infant OEDIPUS abandoned on the mountain.

Melicertes (*Μελικέρτης*) The younger son of Ino, who took him down with her when she drowned herself. Melicertes became the god Palaemon (3) (see LEUCOTHEA (1) and Table 3). In one tradition Athamas, Melicertes' father, threw him into a cauldron of boiling water from which his mother snatched him before committing suicide with him. According to another version, Ino threw him into the cauldron and then hurled herself into the sea with his dead body in her arms. In another version she fled with the still living child and drowned both him and herself together. At the place where Ino cast herself into the sea the body of Melicertes was retrieved by a dolphin, which hung it upon a pine tree. Sisyphus, found the body and had it buried. He instituted the worship of the boy under the name of PALAEMON, and founded the Isthmian Games as funeral games in his honour.

Melissa (*Μέλισσα*) The sister of Amalthea, who was nursemaid to the infant Zeus on Mount Ida in Crete (see MELISSEUS (1)).

Melisseus (*Μελισσεύς*)
1. The king of Crete at the time of Zeus' birth. Rhea entrusted the nurture of the infant god, whom she had hidden in a cave on Mount Ida, to his daughters AMALTHEA and Melissa. Melisseus was the first man to offer sacrifices to the gods. Melissa was the first priestess of Rhea.
2. One of the CURETES.
3. A king of the Chersonese in Caria, who purified Triopas of the murder of his brother Tenages.

Melissus (*Μέλισσος*) An Argive

who fled to Corinth because of the tyranny of Phidon, king of Argos. Archias, one of the Heraclids, killed Melissus' son whilst trying to abduct him. Melissus committed suicide after cursing his son's murderer. Plague and famine hit Corinth. After consulting the oracle to find the cause of these disasters, Archias went into voluntary exile. He founded the city of Syracuse.

Melite (*Μελίτη*) A Nymph of Corcyra, who had an intrigue with Heracles while he was in her country. She bore him HYLLUS.

Meliteus (*Μελιτεύς*) Son of Zeus and the Nymph Othreis. Fearing Hera's anger, Othreis abandoned him in the woods. Zeus had him fed by bees and, through an oracle, instructed a shepherd called Phagrus to bring up the child. Phagrus obeyed, and when Meliteus grew up he conquered the neighbouring peoples and founded a town called Melitaea in Thessaly. He ruled like a tyrant, abducting young girls. He was attracted to a girl called Aspalis, but when he ordered her to be brought to him, she hanged herself. Her brother, Astygites, put on her clothes, beneath which he hid a sword, and allowed himself to be taken away as if he were Aspalis. When he came into Meliteus' presence he killed him. Astygites became king. Meanwhile, Aspalis' body vanished and was replaced by a wooden statue, which became the object of cult.

Melpomene (*Μελπομένη*) One of the MUSES.

Membliarus (*Μεμβλίαρος*) A Phoenician who accompanied Cadmus in the search of Europa (5). Cadmus left him on the island of Thera (then called Calliste); he was placed in charge of a colony that Cadmus founded there. The island of Anaphe, close to Thera, is sometimes referred to as a Membliarus.

Memnon (*Μέμνων*) The son of Eos and Tithonus. He was brought up by the Hesperides and reigned over the Ethiopians. At the time of the Trojan War, Memnon came to Priam's aid. Memnon matched himself against Ajax (2) but there was no decisive outcome. He killed Nestor's son ANTILOCHUS but Achilles came swiftly up to avenge his friend's death. A battle began between Memnon, son of Eos, and Achilles, son of Thetis. The two goddesses, anxious over the fate of their offspring, hastened to Zeus, who weighed the destinies of the two heroes, and found that Memnon's weighed the heavier. Achilles was soon victorious, but Eos persuaded Zeus to grant her son immortality; she gathered up his body and carried it to Ethiopia. The tears that Eos shed are the drops of dew which we see each morning in the fields.

One tradition places the tomb of Memnon on the shore of the Hellespont. Every year birds gathered there to lament the hero's death; these birds, called the Memnonides, were supposed to be either the companions of Memnon transformed after his death or his ashes, which had acquired a sort of immortality. The birds divided into two groups and fought each other until half of them had been killed. The name

'Colossus of Memnon' was given to one of the huge statues raised by the Egyptian pharaoh Amenhotep III. When the first rays of the dawn struck this statue it was supposed to emit music as though to greet his mother's light (see TEUTAMUS).

Memphis (*Μέμφις*) The daughter of Nilus. She was married to Epaphus and gave birth to LIBYA (Table 3). The Egyptian city of Memphis was named in her honour.

Menelaus (*Μενέλαος*) The brother of Agamemnon and the husband of Helen. According to the *Iliad* Menelaus was the son of Atreus, king of Mycenae, and a member of the race of Pelops (Table 2). His mother was AEROPE (1), who was brought to Mycenae by Nauplius (2). A later tradition gives PLEISTHENES, one of the sons of ATREUS, as the father of Agamemnon and Menelaus, but Pleisthenes died young and Menelaus and his brother were brought up by Atreus.

When young Agamemnon and Menelaus were sent by Atreus to search for Thyestes, Atreus' brother, they found him and brought him to Mycenae. Atreus imprisoned him and tried to have him killed by AEGISTHUS, who recognized his father and killed Atreus instead. Agamemnon and Menelaus were then expelled from Mycenae by Aegisthus. They took refuge with Tyndareus in Sparta, where Agamemnon married Clytemnestra, and Menelaus HELEN. Menelaus was chosen from numerous suitors who had previously sworn to help whichever of their number was chosen, should any man dispute his possession of Helen. Tyndareus later bequeathed his kingdom to Menelaus. The children of this marriage were Hermione and a son, Nicostratus. During Helen's absence Menelaus had a son, MEGAPENTHES (1), by a slave girl. He also had another son, Xenodamus, by Cnossia.

Menelaus and Helen lived peacefully in Sparta until PARIS arrived, while Menelaus was in Crete attending the funeral of his grandfather, CATREUS, and abducted Helen. According to one tradition an epidemic and the curse of sterility had afflicted Sparta, and on the advice of the oracle Menelaus went to Troy to offer a sacrifice on the tombs of LYCUS (2) and CHIMAEREUS. At Troy he was the guest of Paris. As a result of an accidental killing, Paris was exiled from Troy and sought refuge with Menelaus; Menelaus repaid his hospitality but during the king's absence Paris abducted Helen.

Menelaus received news of his misfortune from Iris; he returned to Sparta, called together all the suitors who had sworn Tyndareus' oath and sought help from Agamemnon, Nestor, Palamedes and ODYSSEUS. Achilles was sent for and discovered in the harem of Lycomedes on Scyros. Hera aligned herself with Menelaus and united all the Greeks against Paris, her personal enemy. The supreme command of the expedition against Troy fell to AGAMEMNON. Although Menelaus was a valiant warrior, he was less violent than the other heroes assembled against Troy, and his enemies were quick to mock him, reproaching him with accusations of cowardice.

Menelaus and Odysseus went into Troy as ambassadors, to ask for the return of Helen and the treasures carried off by Paris. Antenor brought them before the Trojan assembly, but Paris and his supporters ensured that any attempt at compromise was rejected. According to the *Iliad*, Paris and Menelaus initially faced each other in single combat. Menelaus wounded Paris so heavily that Aphrodite had to cover Paris with a cloud and carry him off. Agamemnon pointed out to the Trojans who were watching that his brother was clearly the victor: he asked them to carry out the terms agreed before the fight, according to which Helen would belong to the winner. As the Trojans hesitated, Pandarus fired an arrow at Menelaus and grazed him; a general battle then broke out. Soon Menelaus killed Scamandrius (2) and had an indecisive encounter with Aeneas. That evening Hector issued a challenge to any Greek to face him in single combat. Menelaus was about to accept when he was restrained by the Greek chiefs. He distinguished himself in the fighting which took place around the ships, and after Patroclus' death he was the first to come forward and fight to regain his body. Menelaus sent Antilochus to Achilles with the news of his friend's death, and dragged Patroclus' corpse from the battlefield. He makes almost no appearance in the closing books of the *Iliad*, participating only in the chariot race during the funeral games held in Patroclus' honour.

Menelaus appeared again in the events subsequent to the *Iliad*. After Paris was killed, Menelaus had his corpse mutilated; he then figured among the warriors inside the Wooden Horse. During the capture of the city Menelaus ran to DEIPHOBUS' house, where he knew Helen was, since after Paris' death she had married Deiphobus. He killed Deiphobus and entered the house. For the meeting of Menelaus and Helen see HELEN.

After the victory Menelaus went to Tenedos, then Lesbos, then sailed over to Euboea and on towards Cape Sounion. Phrontis, his pilot, died there and Menelaus turned back to pay him his funeral honours while Nestor and Diomedes (2) continued homewards. When Menelaus set sail again, and reached a point level with Cape Malea, he was caught by a storm that carried him to Crete, where most of his ships foundered. He went on to Egypt, where he stayed for five years, acquiring great riches according to the *Odyssey*. See CANOPUS, THON, POLYDAMNA, PHAROS and IDOTHEA (1). Menelaus finally arrived in Sparta with Helen eight years after leaving Troy and eighteen years after the start of the war. According to another version, Menelaus found the real Helen in Egypt; she had been kept there by PROTEUS since the time when she and Paris had landed in that country.

At the end of his life, Menelaus was carried off alive to the Elysian fields, an honour bestowed on him by Zeus because he was his son-in-law. At the time of Pausanias, visitors to Sparta were shown the house where Menelaus had supposedly once lived. He was worshipped as if he were a god; men would come and ask him for strength in battle, while women appealed to Helen for beauty and grace.

Menestheus (*Μενεσθεύς*) The son

of Peteus, who was the grandson of Erechtheus. Menestheus was in exile at the time of the expedition of the Dioscuri against Attica when Theseus was in Hades with Pirithous (see HELEN). The Dioscuri brought him back and installed him on the throne of Athens. After Theseus' return Menestheus withdrew to Scyros. The Catalogue of Ships in the *Iliad* gives Menestheus as the leader of the Athenian contingent; he was also one of the warriors inside the Wooden Horse. After the fall of Troy he went to Melos, where he succeeded Polyanax on the throne.

Menesthius (*Μενέσθιος*) One of the warriors who fought at Troy under the command of Achilles, his uncle. He was the son of Polydora, the wife of Peleus or Peleus' daughter by the river-god Spercheius. According to another version, the human father of Menesthius was Borus.

Menoeceus (*Μενοικεύς*)

1. A grandson of Pentheus. He was the father of Creon (2) and Jocasta (see OEDIPUS).
2. The grandson of Menoeceus (1), the son of Creon (2). At the time of the expedition of the Seven against Thebes, Tiresias announced that Thebes would be assured of victory only if Menoeceus were sacrificed. Creon advised his son to flee, but Menoeceus discovered why his father wanted to send him away and volunteered himself to be sacrificed. This is the version recounted in the *Phoenician Women* of Euripides. According to other traditions, Menoeceus was eaten by the Sphinx, or sacrificed by Creon himself.

Menoetes (*Μενοίτης*) The herdsman whose task it was to guard the flocks of Hades on the island of Erythia. Menoetes warned Geryon of Heracles' theft. Menoetes also met Heracles when Heracles went down to Hades to bring back Cerberus. Menoetes tried to prevent Heracles from stealing one of his steers, but failed; his ribs were broken during the encounter. Persephone intervened and asked Heracles to release him.

Menoetius (*Μενοίτιος*)

1. The father of Patroclus and the son of ACTOR and AEGINA. Menoetius lived at Opus. He sent his son to stay with Peleus after Patroclus had accidentally killed Clesonymus (see PATROCLUS). The name of Patroclus' mother varies: Sthenele, Periopis and Polymela (2) are all mentioned. Menoetius was one of the Argonauts, but played no significant part in the expedition.
2. A giant who was the son of Iapetus by Clymene (1), or Asia, according to another tradition (Table 8). He was struck down by a thunderbolt from Zeus and plunged into Tartarus.

Menthe (*Μένθη*) A Nymph of the Underworld, beloved of Hades. She was ill-treated by Persephone and was changed into a mint plant on Mount Triphyle in Bithynia.

Mentor (*Μέντωρ*) The son of Alcimus. He was a faithful friend of Odysseus. The goddess Athena adopted the outward guise of Mentor on several occasions, notably when he accompanied Telemachus to help Odysseus during the battle with the suitors.

Mercury The Roman god Mercurius, or Mercury, was identified with the Greek HERMES; he protected merchants in particular, and travellers in general. He was depicted as the messenger of Jupiter and even as his servant in his amorous exploits (as in Plautus' *Amphytrion*). The first temple of Mercury in Rome was built not far from the port of Rome, where the commercial centre lay. The date traditionally assigned to the founding of this temple is 496 BC. The sanctuary was built outside the *pomerium*, the religious boundary of the city, which suggests that the cult was of foreign origin. Mercury's attributes are the caduceus (the wand), broad-brimmed hat, winged sandals and the purse, the symbol of the profit to be derived from trade. Mercury is the father of EVANDER (3) in some traditions. Mercury was also said to be the father of the LARES.

Meriones (*Μηριόνης*) The son of Molus, the illegitimate son of DEUCALION (2). At Troy Meriones was the most faithful of Idomeneus' companions and commanded the Cretan contingent with him. He is mentioned in the list of Helen's suitors. Meriones was present at the nocturnal council of war; he wounded Deiphobus, killed Adamas and Acamas (1), Harpalion, Moris, Hippotion and Laogone, and escaped from the blows of Aeneas. He participated in the skirmishes over the body of Patroclus, collected the wood for Patroclus' funeral pyre and competed in the chariot race, the archery contest, which he won, and the javelin-throwing in the funeral games given by Achilles. After the fall of Troy, Meriones accompanied Idomeneus back to Cnossos. Meriones was supposedly an outstanding dancer.

Mermerus (*Μέρμερος*) One of the two sons of Jason and Medea. He was killed with his brother, Pheres (2), in Corinth by MEDEA to punish JASON for his infidelity (Table 6). According to another tradition, Mermerus and Pheres were stoned by the Corinthians because they had brought poisoned gifts to Creusa (3), causing the death of her and her father Creon (1). Mermerus is also said to have died differently; after following his father into exile after Pelias' murder, he was killed by a lioness while hunting in Epirus.

Merope (*Μερόπη*)

1. One of the Pleiades, and married to Sisyphus, by whom she had a son, GLAUCUS (3). Merope was the only Pleiad to marry a mortal, and the star that she became in the constellation shines less brightly than those which represent her sisters.
2. Daughter of Cypselus (2), the King of Arcadia. Cypselus gave her in marriage to the Heraclid Cresphontes to seal his alliance with the HERACLIDS. In some traditions Cresphontes was killed by an uprising of his subjects, but in Euripides' lost tragedy *Cresphontes* he was assassinated by Polyphontes (2), another Heraclid, who also killed Cresphontes' two elder sons and married Merope against her will. Merope sent her youngest son Aepytus (2) to Aetolia, but Polyphontes knew he was alive, and offered a reward to anyone who

could kill him. Aepytus planned to avenge his father and brothers. Calling himself Telephontes, he went to Polyphontes and claimed that he had killed Aepytus. The king asked him to remain at his court while he made enquiries into this claim. Merope was convinced that 'Telephontes' was Aepytus' killer; she entered his room one night and was on the point of stabbing him when an old servant, recognizing him as Merope's son, prevented her. Mother and son then planned revenge. Merope went into mourning, as if Aepytus really was dead; Polyphontes was taken in by this and prepared to hold rites of thanksgiving. He invited 'Telephontes', asking him to perform the sacrifice himself, but Aepytus killed Polyphontes instead of the sacrificial victim. He then succeeded to the throne.

3. Daughter of PANDAREOS. See CLEOTHERA.

4. Daughter of OENOPION.

5. Wife of Polybus (3) of Corinth in the OEDIPUS myth.

6. Daughter of Erechtheus and mother of Daedalus.

7. One of the HELIADES (1).

Mesopotamia (*Μεσοποταμία*) The personification of the country of that name. Mesopotamia had three suitors, and to decide between them she deferred to the judgement of Bochorus. Mesopotamia gave gifts to the young men: to one she gave a goblet; to another her own crown; she embraced the third. Bochorus considered that this last gift was the most serious proof of love. The rivals rejected his decision; they fought until they were all dead, and Mesopotamia remained unmarried.

Messapus (*Μέσσαπος*) A hero who gave his name to Mount Messapion on the coast of Boeotia. He visited southern Italy where he gave his name to the territory of the Messapii. There was also an Illyrian hero named Messapus or Messapius, who according to another tradition was the man after whom the Messapian region was named.

Messene (*Μεσσήνη*) The daughter of Triopas or, according to another tradition, of Phorbas (2). She married Polycaon (1), the younger son of Lelex. Lelex' elder son Myles inherited his father's kingdom and Messene urged her husband to acquire a kingdom elsewhere. Polycaon conquered an area which he named Messenia after his wife. The capital of the region was established at Andania where Polycaon instituted the worship of Demeter and Persephone.

Mestra (*Μήστρα*) The daughter of ERYSICHTHON (1). Demeter had afflicted Erysichthon with an insatiable appetite, and Mestra used to sell herself as a slave to obtain food for her father. Mestra's lover Poseidon gave her the ability to change shape at will; each time she would escape from her master and return home, only to start again.

Meta (*Μήτα*) The first wife of Aegeus, who was unable to have children.

Metabus (*Μέταβος*) In the *Aeneid* Metabus was a king of the Volsci and ruler of the city of Privernum. He was the father of CAMILLA and was exiled with her by his subjects. (Servius associates him with METAPONTUS.) According to Greek legend Metabus was the son of Alybas.

Metanira (*Μετάνειρα*) The wife of CELEUS. She took DEMETER into her house when the goddess was looking for her daughter, and employed her as a servant.

Metapontus (*Μετάποντος*) The eponymous hero of the city of Metapontum or Metapontium, west of Tarentum (cf. METABUS). Metapontus is said to have been the son of Sisyphus and grandson of Aeolus (1), but he was more often said to be the adoptive father of Aeolus (2) and Boeotus. He took in Arne, the daughter of Aeolus (1), when she was pregnant and her father had sent her into exile. For Arne's sake Metapontus sent Siris, his first wife, to live in the city which took her name. Arne's sons killed Siris at their mother's instigation (see AEOLUS (2)).

Methymna (*Μηθύμνα*) The eponym of Methymna on Lesbos. She was the daughter of Macar, married Lepetymnus (or Lesbos), and bore Hicetaon and Helicaon, who were both killed by Achilles when he captured Lesbos.

Metion (*Μητίων*) He is generally listed amongst the sons of Erechtheus and Praxithea (2). His children by Alcippe drove Pandion (2) off the throne of Athens, and reigned in his stead (see PANDION (2)). According to this tradition Metion was the father of Eupalamus and the grandfather of DAEDALUS. In another legend Metion was the son of Eupalamus and the grandson of Erechtheus. He was married to Iphinoe and was the father of Daedalus. He is also credited with being the father of Musaeus. Metion is further said to have been the father of SICYON, who was summoned by Lamedon to succeed him on the throne of the city. See also ABAS (1) and CHALCON (2).

Metis (*Μῆτις*) Metis, whose name means 'cunning intelligence', was a daughter of Oceanus and Tethys. She is said to have been the first wife, or mistress, of Zeus; she gave him the drug which forced CRONUS to regurgitate all the children he had swallowed. Metis was the mother of ATHENA.

Metope (*Μετώπη*)

1. Daughter of Ladon (1) and mother of Thebe (3) by ASOPUS.
2. Daughter of ECHETUS.

Mezentius An Etruscan king who reigned at Caere and fought against Aeneas. In the oldest tradition Mezentius was summoned by Turnus after the latter's first defeat at the hands of Aeneas and Latinus. Turnus promised Mezentius half of all the wine produced that year in Latium and his own territory. Aeneas had made the same vow to Jupiter; this vow to the god carried the greater weight, and both Mezentius and Turnus were killed.

In the version given by Dionysius of Halicarnassus, after Aeneas' marriage to Lavinia, and the building of Lavinium, he and Latinus had to ward off the attack of the Rutuli led by Turnus. In the first battle Turnus and Latinus were killed. The Rutuli then called Mezentius to their aid. A battle of uncertain outcome took place during which Aeneas disappeared. Aeneas' son, Ascanius, asked for peace terms. Mezentius demanded all the wine produced in Latium. Ascanius vowed the same wine to Jupiter, then routed the Etruscans, killing Mezentius' son Lausus (1). Ascanius granted Mezentius lenient peace terms, and thereafter he remained a loyal ally of the Latins.

In Virgil's version, Mezentius had been driven out of Caere by his subjects because of his tyranny, and had taken refuge with Turnus. He fought at Turnus' side with Lausus (1), but both were killed by Aeneas. This account contains no reference to promises of wine, and only Mezentius is Aeneas' enemy; the Etruscans support the Trojans. (This can be explained by the fact that Virgil's patron Maecenas was an Etruscan and, at the time of writing, a close friend of Augustus.)

Midas (*Μίδας*) The mythical king of Phrygia. According to one tradition, he came across Silenus sleeping off the effects of heavy drinking. Midas asked him to teach him wisdom. Silenus then recounted the story of two cities, outside our world, called Eusebes or the city of piety, and Machimus, the city of war. The inhabitants of the first were always happy and died laughing, whereas the citizens of Machimus were born fully armed and spent their lives fighting. These two peoples were very rich. They decided to come and visit our world and they arrived in the land of the HYPERBOREANS. When they saw the miserable condition of the Hyperboreans and learnt that these were the happiest people in our world, they wanted to see no more and returned back to their own lands.

There is another version of the king's encounter with Silenus, told by Ovid in his *Metamorphoses*. Silenus had strayed away from the retinue of Dionysus and fell asleep in the mountains of Phrygia. Some peasants found him and brought him in chains to their king. Midas, who had once been initiated into the Mysteries, realized who his guest was. He received him with great honour and went off with him to rejoin Dionysus, who offered to fulfil any wish the king might make. Midas asked that anything he touched should turn to gold. The god granted his request, but when Midas wanted to eat, everything turned to gold; the wine, too, changed into metal. Midas begged Dionysus to take away his gift. Dionysus told him to wash in the spring at the source of the river Pactolus. Midas did so and was freed from his gift. The waters of the Pactolus were thereafter full of grains of gold.

A similar tale is recounted by Plutarch. Midas became lost in the middle of a desert. There was no water to quench his thirst but the earth sent forth a spring. This spring spouted gold instead of water and Midas begged Dionysus for his aid. The god changed the spring of gold into a fountain, which was accordingly called the Spring of Midas.

Midas plays a part in the myth of Pan, or MARSYAS, and Apollo. Midas happened to be present just as Tmolus had declared Apollo the winner; Midas complained that the judgement was unfair, whereupon Apollo made a pair of ass's ears grow out of his head. According to another version Midas was one of several judges and was the only one to decide in Marsyas' favour. Midas himself is credited with the invention of the so-called Pan pipes. Midas hid his ears under his head-dress, and only his barber knew the secret. He was forbidden to tell anyone, but weighed down under this secret, he could not contain himself and, digging a hole in the ground, he confided to the earth that Midas had monstrous ears. The reeds which grew in the area then whispered to the wind that ruffled them: 'King Midas has ass's ears.'

Miletus (*Μίλητος*) According to Ovid, the son of Apollo and Deione; Minos exiled him from Crete and he went to Asia Minor where he founded Miletus. There he married the daughter of the river-god Meander, and had two children, Caunus and BYBLIS. In another tradition he was the son of ACACALLIS or Aria and Apollo. His mother exposed him at birth, but he was either fed by a wolf and taken in by shepherds, or taken in by Aria's father Cleochus. Later Minos fell in love with him. On the advice of SARPEDON (2) Miletus fled to Caria, where he founded the city of Miletus. In one version he fled to Samos first, founding a city called Miletus there also.

Mimas (*Μίμας*) One of the GIANTS who fought against the gods.

Minerva The Roman goddess identified with the Greek ATHENA; she appeared first in Etruria and was then introduced into the Capitoline Triad, with Jupiter and Juno. One of her earliest temples was built on Mons Caelius. This temple bore the name Minerva Capta and it may have been built to house a statue of Minerva captured at Falerii during the Roman conquest of the city. According to one tradition Minerva was one of the gods brought to Rome by Numa. The festival of Minerva was celebrated in March at the Quinquatria. The attributes of the goddess are analogous to those of the Greek Pallas Athena. She presided over intellectual and, in particular, academic activity. On the Esquiline there was a shrine dedicated to Minerva Medica, Minerva the healer. Minerva plays no part in any specifically Roman legend (see, however, NERIO and ANNA PERENNA).

Minos (*Μίνως*) A king of Crete, said to have lived three generations before the Trojan War. He is regarded as the son of Europa (5) and Zeus, and was brought up by Asterion, king of Crete. He is also said to have been a son of Asterion (Table 3). Diodorus Siculus distinguishes between two bearers of the name Minos, the former the son of Zeus and the latter, grandson of the former, the subject of the rest of the legends. After Asterion's death Minos became the ruler of Crete. When his brothers raised objections, Minos replied that the gods meant the kingdom to be his. To prove it, he offered up a sacrifice to Poseidon, asking the god to make a bull emerge from the sea, and promising to sacrifice the animal to the god in return. Poseidon sent the bull, and Minos won his kingdom without opposition, but then refused to sacrifice the animal. Poseidon took his vengeance by sending the bull mad. Heracles subsequently dealt with it (see HERACLES, II). Pasiphae, Minos' wife, later fell in love with this bull and conceived the MINOTAUR.

Minos married Pasiphae, daughter of Helios and Perseis. His legitimate children were Catreus, Deucalion (2), Glaucus (5), Androgeos (also known as Eurygyes), Acacallis, Xenodice, Ariadne and Phaedra. He also had illegitimate children. The Nymph Paria conceived EURYMEDON (2), Chryses (4), Nephalion and Philolaus, and by another Nymph, Dexithea, Minos had Euxanthius. Minos is also said to have been the originator of homosexuality. In one tradition Minos rather than Zeus abducted GANYMEDE. He is also said to have been the lover of Theseus and was supposedly reconciled with him after Ariadne's abduction, and gave him his daughter Phaedra in marriage. Minos loved BRITOMARTIS. His mistresses were so numerous that Pasiphae cursed him. He was cured of this curse by PROCRIS.

Minos is said to have been the first man to civilize the Cretans and to rule them justly. Minos' laws were thought to have been inspired by Zeus: every nine years Minos consulted Zeus in the cave on Ida where Zeus had been brought up. Minos is often compared with his brother RHADAMANTHYS, whose work he supposedly imitated. In the Underworld both Minos and Rhadamanthys sat in judgement over the souls of the dead, assisted by AEACUS.

Mythographers credit Minos with dominion over a large number of islands around Crete, and as far away as Caria. He is said to have led several military expeditions, notably one against Athens to avenge Androgeos' death, in which he captured the city of Megara (see NISUS and SCYLLA (2)). He was victorious, and he demanded an annual tribute of seven young men and seven girls to be fed to the Minotaur.

Later Minos went to Sicily at the head of an army to recapture DAEDALUS, whom he found at the court of COCALUS. There Minos was killed in his bath by one of the king's daughters at the instigation of Daedalus.

At Heraclea Minoa there was a 'tomb of Minos', said to be the tomb built by Minos' companions in honour of their king. The ashes of Minos were preserved in an inner chamber. This tomb was knocked down at the time of the founding of Agrigentum, and Minos' ashes were then carried off to Crete.

Minotaur (*Μινώταυρος*) A monster with the body of a man and the head of a bull, whose real name was Asterius, or Asterion. He was the son of Pasiphae, the wife of MINOS, and of the bull sent to Minos by Poseidon. Minos commissioned Daedalus, who was then at his court, to build a vast palace (the Labyrinth) comprising such a maze of rooms and corridors that only the architect could find his way. Minos shut the monster in the Labyrinth, and every year he fed it with seven young men and seven girls, who were the tribute exacted from Athens. Theseus offered himself as one of the victims, and with the help of ARIADNE he succeeded not only in killing the beast but also in finding his way out of the Labyrinth. See THESEUS, III.

Minyads (*Μινυάδες*) The three daughters of king Minyas of Orchomenus; their names were Leucippe (5), Arsippe and Alcithoe, or Alcathoe. The three sisters remained at home during a festival of Dionysus, busily weaving and embroidering, while the women of Orchomenus were running over the mountains behaving like Bacchantes. In some versions ivy and vines began to grow around the stools where the girls were sitting, and milk and wine began to flow down from the roof. Mysterious lights appeared in the rooms, and the sounds of wild animals, flutes and tambourines rang out. The Minyads were seized with a divine madness; they tore the infant Hippasus, Leucippe's son, to pieces. Then they joined the other women in the mountains. In other accounts they were transformed into bats. Another version claims that Dionysus came to find them, in the guise of a young girl, and reproached them for their indifference. They made fun of him; then, before their eyes, Dionysus turned himself into a bull, a panther, and a lion. At the same time milk and wine flowed from the stools, and the Minyads went mad and tore Hippasus to pieces.

Minyas (*Μινύας*) Minyas from the Boeotian Orchomenus gave his name to the Minyans, the inhabitants of Orchomenus in the Homeric period. Minyas was either the son or the grandson of Poseidon; in the latter case his father was Chryses (3). By Euryanassa, the daughter of Hyperphas, he had a large number of children: his son Orchomenus, the successor to the throne (see CLYMENUS (2)), Cyparissus, the three MINYADS, Elara, who was the mother of TITYUS, Araethyrea, the mother of Phlias, and Clymene (3).

Misenus (*Μισηνός*)

1. One of Odysseus' companions who gave his name to Misenum in Campania.
2. A follower of Hector. After his death Misenus became Aeneas' trumpeter. Misenus challenged all the gods, claiming that he could play the trumpet better than any of the immortals. Out of jealousy the sea-god Triton tipped Misenus into the sea, where he drowned. He was buried on the shore of the headland in Campania which took his name.

Mnemon (*Μνήμων*) When Achilles went to the Trojan War his mother gave him a servant called Mnemon. An oracle had predicted that if Achilles should kill one of Apollo's sons, he would die at Troy. It was not known which of Apollo's sons the oracle referred to. Mnemon had constantly to remind Achilles to ensure his victim was not one of Apollo's descendants. On Tenedos, however, Achilles killed Tenes, a son of Apollo, and thereafter he could not escape his fate. To punish Mnemon, he killed him with his spear.

Mnemosyne (*Μνημοσύνη*) The personification of Memory. She was a Titaness, the daughter of Uranus and Gaia. Zeus coupled with her in Pieria for nine consecutive nights, and she later gave birth to the nine Muses. There was a spring dedicated to Mnemosyne before the oracle of Trophonius at Lebadea (see LETHE).

Mnestheus (*Μνησθεύς*) One of

Aeneas' companions who participated in the boat races organized by the hero and won second prize. Virgil claimed he was the eponym of the Roman *gens* of the Memmii.

Modius Fabidius During a festival of Quirinus a girl of noble lineage was dancing in honour of the god. She was inspired by the deity and went into the sanctuary, from where she emerged pregnant by him. She gave birth to a son who was named Modius Fabidius, who, when grown up, distinguished himself by his exploits in war. He gathered together a band of companions, and, after journeying some distance, he founded a city, naming it Cures; this etymology seems to derive from the Sabine word 'curis' meaning 'spear' (see QUIRINUS).

Moirae (*Μοῖραι*) The Moirae, also known as Fates or PARCAE, personified the individual's fate; originally each human being had his or her own *moira*, and this notion became transformed into deities who resembled the KERES. The Moirae embodied a law which even the gods could not break without endangering the equilibrium of existence. Gradually the idea of a universal Moira dominating the destiny of humanity as a whole seems to have developed. After the Homeric period three Moirae appeared, the sisters Atropus, Clotho and Lachesis, who regulated each individual's life by means of a thread which one Moira spun, the second wound up and the third cut when the life was at an end. The Moirae were daughters of Zeus and Themis and sisters of the HORAE.

Molionidae (*Μολιονίδαι*) Twin brothers named Eurytus (4) and Cteatus; their human father was Actor (1), and their divine father was Poseidon. Their mother was Molione, the daughter of Molus (2). The Molionidae are said to have been born from an egg. In the *Iliad* they appear as two separate men, of considerable size and strength, but human. Nestor fought them during the hostilities between Neleus (1) and the Epeioi. Nestor was on the point of killing them when Poseidon saved them by concealing them in a cloud. Augias called them to his aid when he was attacked by Heracles (see HERACLES, III). The Molionidae married Dexamenus' daughters Theronice and Theraephone, who bore them two sons named Amphimachus and THALPIUS.

Molorchus (*Μόλορχος*) A peasant who lived near Nemea. His son had been killed by the Nemean lion, and he welcomed Heracles when he came to fight the lion (see HERACLES, II). To honour his guest Molorchus proposed to slaughter his only ram. But Heracles persuaded him to wait thirty days; if he had not returned within that time Molorchus was to consider him dead and sacrifice the ram in his memory; if he returned victorious, the ram would be sacrificed to Zeus. On the thirtieth day, Molorchus was preparing to sacrifice the ram when Heracles arrived, clad in the lion's skin. He offered the ram to Zeus, and on that spot Heracles founded the Nemean Games (see also ADRASTUS).

Molossus (*Μολοσσός*) The son of Neoptolemus and the grandson of

Achilles, he was also known as Mollessus or Molottus. His mother was ANDROMACHE. In Euripides' *Andromache* the infant Molossus was left to die by Andromache but he survived, and while visiting Delphi Neoptolemus saw and recognized him. Hermione, the wife of Neoptolemus, was jealous since she herself was barren, and she persecuted both Andromache and Molossus. Hermione was on the point of killing mother and son when Peleus saved them. When Neoptolemus was killed by Orestes, Thetis, conscious that Molossus was the only surviving descendant of the race of Aeacus, instructed Andromache to take him to Epirus. Andromache did accordingly, and there married HELENUS; Molossus later succeeded his stepfather on the throne of Epirus. He gave his name to the inhabitants of the region, the Molossians.

Molpadia (*Μολπαδία*)
1. One of the Amazons who attacked Attica. She killed Antiope (2), the Amazon whom Thesus had married, but was then killed herself by Theseus.
2. The daughter of Staphylus (3) (see PARTHENUS (1)).

Molpus (*Μόλπος*) A flautist, also called Eumolpus (3), from Tenedos who gave perjured evidence against TENES. Thereafter on Tenedos flautists were not allowed into the temple dedicated to Tenes.

Molus (*Μόλος*)
1. A Cretan, the illegitimate son of Deucalion (2) and father of Meriones. During a festival on Crete a doll without a head was given the name of Molus and carried in procession. It is said that Molus attempted to rape a Nymph; his headless corpse was discovered some time later, and the rite was established to commemorate this.
2. The grandfather of the MOLIONIDAE.

Momus (*Μῶμος*) The personification of Blame. In Hesiod's *Theogony* she was a daughter of Nyx and a sister of the Hesperides. When Earth became exhausted by the weight that she was carrying, because the human race was multiplying too swiftly, she asked Zeus to reduce its numbers. Zeus accordingly sent down the Theban War, but it proved insufficient to deal with the problem. Momus then suggested that Zeus should marry Thetis to a mortal; she would in time give birth to a daughter (Helen) who would set Asia and Europe against one another. This was one of the accounts given to explain the origins of the Trojan War.

Moneta The Bringer of Warnings: this is the title under which Juno was worshipped on the Capitoline hill in Rome. When the Gauls attacked the city in 390 BC the sacred geese which were kept around the sanctuary of the goddess sounded the alarm by cackling when the enemy had attempted a surprise night assault. The temple of Juno Moneta stood on the site of the house of Manlius Capitolinus, the defender of the Capitol. In this temple coinage was minted, because during the war against Pyrrhus the Romans were afraid that they would run out of money. They asked Juno's advice and she replied that they would never be short of money if their wars were fought according to the principles of justice. It was therefore decided that the minting of coins would be placed under the auspices of the goddess.

Mopsus (*Μόψος*)
1. A Lapith, and the son of Ampyx and Chloris. He took part in the expedition of the Argonauts as a soothsayer. He competed at the funeral games held in honour of Pelias and is listed among the hunters of the Calydonian boar. He died of a snake bite during the Argonauts' expedition in Libya.
2. The son of Manto (1), and a grandson of Tiresias. He is often described as the son of Apollo. His human father is sometimes said to have been Rhacius, whom Manto met when leaving the temple at Delphi and who had thus been marked out by the god as her intended husband. According to another tradition Manto left for Claros, on Apollo's instructions, and was abducted on her way by Cretan pirates who took her to their leader, Rhacius. Mopsus was the fruit of this union.

Mopsus was credited with the founding of the city of Colophon where he competed against CALCHAS (1). After the death of Calchas, Mopsus joined forces with AMPHILOCHUS (1).
3. The son of GERANA or Oenoe (see PYGMIES).

Morges (*Μόργης*) Italus named as his successor a certain Morges, who reigned over the region bounded by Tarentum and Paestum, which was at that time called 'Italy'. His subjects took the name of the Morgetes. One day an exile from Rome named Sicelus visited Morges, who took him in and gave him part of his kingdom. Morges had a daughter, Siris. He was the founder of several cities including Morgantina.

Moria (*Μορία*) A Lydian woman. Her brother Tylus was walking along the banks of the River Hermos when a snake bit him on the face, and he died at once. Moria saw her brother's terrible fate and summoned Damasen, a giant. Damasen plucked up a tree by the roots, and crushed the snake; its mate then rushed off to a neighbouring wood and brought back in her mouth a herb which she placed in the corpse's nostrils. It came back to life and fled. Moria, learning from the snake, picked some of the herb and used it to bring back Tylus to life (cf. GLAUCUS (5)).

Mormo (*Μορμώ*) A female whose name was used to frighten small children. She was accused of biting naughty children in particular, and making them lame. She is sometimes identified with Lamia (2).

Mormolyce (*Μορμολύκη*) 'The She-Wolf Mormo', or Mormolyce, was, like MORMO, an evil spirit whose name was used to frighten children.

Morpheus (*Μορφεύς*) One of the thousand children of Hypnus. His name (derived from the Greek word for form) indicates his function: to take the shape of human beings and to show himself to people during their dreams. Morpheus had large, swift wings which beat silently and could carry him in seconds to the ends of the earth.

Mors The Roman personification of Death (cf. the Greek THANATOS).

Mothone (*Μοθώνη*) After the fall of Troy Diomedes (2) brought his grandfather Oeneus to Messenia. Mothone was the fruit of Oeneus' union with a local woman, and in honour of his daughter Oeneus changed the name of the city of Pedasos to Mothone.

Mucius Scaevola When Rome was besieged by the Etruscan King Porsenna, a man named Mucius decided to kill him. He slipped into the enemy camp but stabbed another of the enemy instead. He was arrested and brought before Porsenna. At this moment a brazier full of burning coals happened to be carried in: Mucius held his right hand on the flames and let it burn away. Filled with admiration Porsenna gave back to his enemy the sword that had been taken from him. Mucius then told him that three hundred Romans like himself were waiting for the chance to succeed in the enterprise in which he had just failed. This was untrue but Porsenna, much dismayed, at once concluded an armistice with Rome. Mucius, one-armed as a result of his sacrifice, took the name of Scaevola or 'the left-handed'.

Munichus (*Μούνιχος*) In Athens Munichus was the eponymous hero of Munichia, one of the military harbours. He is said to have been a king of Attica and son of Panteuces. He offered refuge to the Minyans when they were driven out by a Thracian invasion, and gave them land around the harbour, which they named after him.

Munitus (*Μούνιτος*) The son born of the clandestine relationship between Laodice (4), Priam's daughter, and Acamas (3), who had come with a deputation to Troy to recover Helen before the war started. The infant was entrusted to his grandmother Aethra. Munitus later died of a snake-bite during a hunting expedition in Thessaly.

Musaeus (*Μουσαῖος*) The friend, pupil, master, son, or simply contemporary of Orpheus. According to Attic legend his father was Antiphemus, or Eumolpus (1); these names indicate that they were singers, just as Musaeus' name suggests that he was the archetypal musician. His mother was Selene, and he was brought up by the Nymphs. Musaeus is said to have been a great musician, capable of healing the sick with his music. He was also a seer and he is sometimes credited with having introduced the Eleusinian mysteries into Attica. Various poems of mystic inspiration were attributed to him.

Muses (*Μοῦσαι*) The daughters of Mnemosyne and Zeus, the fruits of nine nights of love-making. Other traditions claim that they are the daughters of Harmonia, or the daughters of Uranus and Gaia. The Muses were not only divine singers, whose music delighted Zeus and other gods; they also presided over thought in all its forms: eloquence, persuasion, knowledge, history, mathematics, astronomy. Hesiod claimed that they accompany kings and inspire them with the persuasive words necessary to settle quarrels and re-establish peace, and give kings the gentleness which makes them dear to their subjects. Similarly, according to Hesiod, a singer (in other words a servant of the Muses) has only to celebrate the deeds of men of former days or to sing of the gods, and any man beset by troubles will forget them instantly. The oldest song of the Muses is the one sung after the victory of the Olympians over the Titans to celebrate the birth of a new order.

There were two main groups of Muses; the Thracians from Pieria, and the Boeotians from Mount Helicon. The former are often referred to in poetry as the PIERIDES. They are connected with the myth of Orpheus and with the cult of Dionysus, which was particularly strong in Thrace. The Muses of Helicon were placed directly under the control of Apollo who is said to have conducted their singing around the Hippocrene spring. There were other groups of Muses in other regions. Sometimes these groups contain only three figures, as at Delphi and at Sicyon. At Lesbos there was a cult of Seven Muses. From the classical period the number of Muses was standardized to nine, and the following list was generally accepted: CALLIOPE, Clio, POLHYMNIA (or Polyhymnia), Euterpe, TERPSICHORE, ERATO (1), Melpomene, THALIA (1) and Urania. Each came to be attributed with a specific function, but these vary from one author to another. Broadly speaking, Calliope was said to be the Muse of epic poetry, Clio of history, Polyhymnia of mime, Euterpe of the flute, Terpsichore of light verse and dance, Erato of lyric choral poetry, Melpomene of tragedy, Thalia of comedy and Urania of astronomy. The Muses took part as singers in all the great celebrations held by the gods and they were present at the marriages of Peleus and Thetis, and of Harmonia (1) and Cadmus.

Myceneus (*Μυκηνεύς*) The hero who founded the city of Mycene and gave it his name.

Mygdon (*Μύγδων*)

1. In the *Iliad*, the ruler of a part of Phrygia which lay on the banks of the River Sangarius. During an attack by the Amazons, Mygdon was helped by Priam; in return he came to the aid of Troy when the city was attacked by the Greeks. He was the father of Coroebus (2).
2. The brother of Amycus, and like him king of the Bebryces. He was defeated by Heracles, the ally of Lycus (7).

Myles (*Μύλης*) A Laconian hero, said to have invented the corn mill. Myles was the son of Lelex (1), the king of Lacedaemon, and of Peridia; he was the brother of Polycaon (1), Boumolchus and Therapne and the father of Eurotas. Other traditions, however, make Eurotas the son of Lelex.

Myrina (*Μύρινα*) In a euhemeristic version of the myth of the GORGONS, Diodorus Siculus speaks of an Amazon queen named Myrina who made war on the Atlantes. She captured and destroyed the city of Cerne, whereupon the rest of the Atlantes surrendered in terror. Myrina treated them generously, building the city of Myrina on the site of Cerne, and giving it to her prisoners. The Atlantes then asked for her help against a warlike people called the Gorgons, whom she eventually defeated. She raised a monument, known as the Tomb of the Amazons, to her subjects who died in the fighting. The Gorgons subsequently re-established their power, and later Perseus and then Heracles fought them. Myrina also conquered the greater part of Libya and later went to Egypt, where Horus reigned. She made a treaty with him, organized an expedition against the Arabs, ravaged Syria, received the voluntary surrender of the Cilicians, crossed the Taurus mountains, crossed Phrygia and reached the area of the River Caicus. She was eventually killed by the Thracian King Mopsus. This legend is not 'mythical' in the strict sense, since alongside the mythical elements the work of 'rationalist' Euhemerist mythographers, seeking to explain the myths in terms of historical events, is evident.

Myrina the Amazon Queen is mentioned in the *Iliad*: there her name Myrina is used only 'among the gods'; her human name was Batieia. She married Dardanus (Table 4) and was the daughter of Teucer.

Myrmidon (*Μυρμιδών*) The ancestor of the Myrmidons (a Thessalian people later ruled by Achilles) and the son of Zeus by Eurymedusa. He was the father of Actor (1) and Antiphus by Pisidice (3) (see Table 5). Through his daughter Eupolemia, he was the grandfather of the Argonaut Aethalides.

Myrrha (*Μύρρα*) The daughter of Cinyras, king of Cyprus. For her legend see ADONIS. She is also sometimes called Smyrna (2).

Myrtilus (*Μυρτίλος*) In the versions of the legend of Pelops (1) used by the dramatists Myrtilus is the charioteer who took the axle-pin out of Oenomaus's chariot-wheel and replaced it with a wax peg so that Pelops won the race (see HIPPODAMIA (1)). Myrtilus was the son of Hermes and Phaethusa, one of the daughters of Danaus, or of Clymene. After his death Myrtilus was changed by his father, Hermes, into a constellation, the Charioteer.

Myrto (*Μυρτώ*) A daughter of Menoetius (1) and the sister of Patroclus. She gave birth to a daughter fathered by Heracles, named Eucleia.

Myscelus (*Μύσκελος*) The founder of the city of Croton, in Italy. Apollo instructed him through the Delphic oracle to found Croton, but when he arrived in the country he saw the city of Sybaris and asked the god if it was necessary to found a new city in the same region. The oracle instructed Myscelus to accept the god's gift. Myscelus obeyed. A tradition recorded by Ovid says that Heracles had been given hospitality by Croton when on his way back from his encounter with Geryon. In return Heracles had promised Croton that a city would be built which would bear his name. Accordingly, he advised Myscelus in a dream to go and found a colony in Magna Graecia. However the laws of Argos forbade its citizens to go abroad, so Myscelus was brought to court and the judges all voted against him by each putting into an urn the black pebble which would condemn him to death. Myscelus begged Heracles to rescue him, and miraculously all the black pebbles turned white. Myscelus was acquitted and allowed to leave. He then founded his colony at Croton.

N

Naiads (*Ναϊάδες*) Water Nymphs. They lived for a very long time but were still mortal (see HAMADRYADS, NYMPHS). The Naiads incarnate the divinity of the spring or stream which they inhabit. A spring may have one or more Nymphs belonging to it.

Homer calls the Naiads 'daughters of Zeus'; elsewhere they are part of the race of Oceanus; often they are the daughters of the river in which they live (the daughters of Asopus were Naiads, for example). Every famous spring had its own Naiad. At Syracuse there was a beautiful Nymph, Arethusa (1), a companion of Artemis. One day when she was swimming in a river, thinking she was alone, she heard the voice of Alpheus, the god of the river, who had conceived a passion for her. Arethusa fled, pursued by the god. She called on Artemis to save her. The goddess enveloped her in a cloud, and in her fear (since Alpheus refused to leave the place where he had seen her disappear) she turned into a fountain. The earth opened up to prevent Alpheus mingling his own waters with those of the spring which Arethusa had become, and, guided by Artemis, Arethusa went through underground channels to Syracuse, on the Island of Ortygia, which is dedicated to Artemis. This version of the myth is a Hellenistic one. For a different account see ALPHEUS.

The Naiads were often said to have healing powers. The sick might drink or bathe in their springs, though bathing was sometimes considered sacrilegious. The Emperor Nero was attacked by a sort of paralysis and fever after bathing in the source of the Aqua Marcia: this was attributed to the displeasure of the Naiads. Another risk run by those who offended the Naiads was madness: whoever caught sight of the Naiads, for example, was 'possessed' by them and driven mad (see LYMPHAE).

Many genealogies feature a Naiad as foundress of a family, for example the wives of Endymion, Magnes, Lelex (1), Oebalus (1), Icarius (2), Erichthonius, Thyestes and others. Naiads are particularly numerous in the Peloponnese.

Nana In the legend of Attis Nana is the daughter of the river-god Sangarius (see AGDISTIS and ATTIS).

Nanas (*Νάνας*) The son of Teutamides, a king of the Pelasgians of Thessaly. During his reign before the Trojan War, the Pelasgians were driven out of Thessaly by the Greek invasions, crossed the Adriatic, captured the city of Croton and established themselves in Italy. They thenceforth called themselves Tyrrhenians. Herodotus distinguishes these Pelasgians from the Tyrrhenians who, according to him, orignally came from Asia Minor.

Nannacus (*Νάννακος*) A king of Phrygia. He had foreseen the flood associated with Deucalion (1) and organized public prayers to avert the catastrophe. These prayers were accompanied by the proverbial 'tears of Nannacus'. Nannacus lived for three hundred years, and, in accordance with an oracle, all his subjects died with him in the flood.

Nanus (*Νάνος*) The native ruler of Massilia whose daughter married Euxenus, the chief of the Phocian immigrants.

Narcissus (*Νάρκισσος*) A handsome young man who despised love. The best-known version is that of Ovid's *Metamorphoses*, in which Narcissus is the son of the god of Cephissus and of the Nymph Liriope. The seer Tiresias told them that the child 'would live to an old age if it did not look at itself'. Narcissus was the object of the passions of many girls and Nymphs but he was indifferent to all this. The Nymph Echo fell in love with him but she could get no more from him than the others. In despair she withdrew into a lonely spot where she faded away until all there was left of her was a plaintive voice. The girls rejected by Narcissus asked the heavens for vengeance. Nemesis heard them and arranged that one very hot day Narcissus bent over a stream to take a drink and saw his own face, which was so handsome that he immediately fell in love with it. Thenceforward he stayed watching his own reflection and let himself die, when he even tried to make out the beloved features in the waters of the Styx. On the spot where he died there later grew a flower which was given his name.

The Boeotian version of the legend was substantially different. Narcissus was an inhabitant of the city of Thespiae. He was very handsome but scorned the joys of love. He was loved by a young man called Ameinias, but did not love him in return, kept rejecting him and finally sent him a present of a sword. Ameinias committed suicide with this sword in front of Narcissus' door. As he died Ameinias called down curses upon Narcissus. Then one day when Narcissus saw himself in a spring he fell in love with himself and, made desperate by his passion, killed himself. The Thespians worshipped Eros, whose power this story illustrates. In the place where Narcissus killed himself there grew a flower which was named after him.

Pausanias records that Narcissus had a twin sister whom he closely resembled. Both were very attractive. The girl died; Narcissus was deeply upset and one day, seeing himself in a stream, thought he saw his sister, which allayed his sorrow. He fell into the habit of looking at himself in streams to console himself for her loss. This version is an attempt at a rationalizing interpretation of the pre-existing myth.

Nauplius (*Ναύπλιος*)

1. The son of Poseidon by Amymone, one of the Danaids. He was considered to have been founder of the city of Nauplion. His sons were Damastor, Polydectes, and Proetus (see Nauplius (2)).

2. Nauplius the younger was descended from Nauplius (1) as follows: Nauplius (1) – Proetus – Lernus – Naubolus – Clytoneus – Nauplius (2). He took part in the expedition of

the Argonauts, whose pilot he became after the death of Tiphys. Some of the mythographers name him as the father of Palamedes, but others, notably Apollodorus, take the father of Palamedes to be Nauplius (1), although this gives an implausibly long duration to the lifetime of Nauplius (1).

Nauplius (2) is notable principally for being the father of Palamedes, his wife being either Philyra or Hesione (2) or Clymene (4). His two other sons were OEAX and Nausimedon.

Nauplius was a remarkable navigator, and several kings had recourse to his services. In the myth of Telephus, his mother, Auge, was seduced by Heracles. Her father, Aleus, gave Nauplius instructions to drown her, but while he was conveying her to Nauplion she gave birth to Telephus. Nauplius took pity on her and gave her to some merchants, who took her off to Mysia. In a second legend CATREUS entrusted Nauplius with two of his daughters with orders to drown them. But Nauplius gave Aerope (1) to Atreus (or Pleisthenes, according to different traditions) and himself married Clymene (4).

Nauplius' son PALAMEDES joined the Greek army to fight against Troy but was stoned to death on a charge of treachery. Nauplius then devoted his life to avenging his son. He began by persuading the wives of the absent heroes to take lovers and was notably successful with CLYTEMNESTRA, the wife of Agamemnon, with Meda, the wife of IDOMENEUS, and with Aegiale, the wife of DIOMEDES (2). Later he even tackled Penelope, but to no avail. Furthermore, when the main convoy of the Greek army, on its way back from Troy, arrived level with the Gyroi (the Round Rocks near Cape Caphareus in the south of Euboea) Nauplius lit a fire on the reefs during the night. The Greeks, thinking they were near a harbour, headed for the light and their ships were wrecked. It was in this shipwreck that Ajax (1) died.

According to Apollodorus the death of Nauplius was caused by an act of treachery similar to that which he had inflicted on the Greek fleet. It is also said that on the occasion of his attempt to throw Penelope into the arms of the suitors Nauplius was deceived by Anticlea, the mother of Odysseus. She told him of the death of his sons, and in his grief Nauplius committed suicide.

Naus (*Ναός*) A great-great-grandson of EUMOLPUS (1), king of Eleusis. On the instruction of the Delphic oracle he introduced the mysteries of Demeter into Arcadia (though according to Arcadian traditions these mysteries were introduced by Demeter herself).

Nausicaa (*Ναυσικάα*) The daughter of King Alcinous of the Phaeacians, and of Arete. Odysseus had been shipwrecked and was thrown ashore on the coast of an island unknown to him. He fell asleep in a wood on the banks of a stream. Athena sent a dream to Nausicaa. The young girl dreamt that one of her friends chided her for her negligence and asked her to go and wash all the family linen in the river. In the morning Nausicaa asked her parents for permission to go and do this washing and went off with the female servants in a carriage drawn by mules. The girls washed the clothes, and while these were drying they began to play ball on the river bank. The ball went astray and rolled into the water. The girls gave a loud cry and woke Odysseus. He, being totally naked, covered himself with branches and made his appearance. The servants fled, but Nausicaa stayed where she was. Odysseus pretended to take her for a goddess or a Nymph of the stream; Nausicaa promised him her help. She gave him something to eat, lent him some clothes and scolded her servants for not having welcomed a guest sent by the gods. When evening fell Nausicaa returned to the city, having shown Odysseus the way to the palace; she herself rode in the carriage with her servants. There her role stops, but she expressly admitted to herself that she would like to marry Odysseus. Alcinous was ready to permit this but Odysseus had a wife in Ithaca. On this note the episode ends. The mythographers invented a later marriage between Telemachus and Nausicaa, by which she was said to have had a son named Persepolis.

Nausithous (*Ναυσίθοος*)

1. The son of Poseidon and of Periboea (2). He was king of the Phaeacians while they were still in Hyperia, and it was under his leadership that, driven out by the Cyclopes, they established themselves at Scheria. Nausithous was the father of Alcinous and of Rhexenor, and by the latter the grandfather of Arete, Alcinous' wife.
2. The pilot of the boat which took Theseus to Crete to fight the Minotaur (THESEUS, III).
3. One of the children of Odysseus and Calypso (1). He had a brother named Nausinous. One tradition makes him the son of Odysseus and Circe and the brother of Telegonus (1).

Nautes (*Ναύτης*) An elderly Trojan who accompanied Aeneas. In Sicily he advised Aeneas not to stay on the island but to go on to Latium. A tradition independent of the *Aeneid* says that it was he who received back the PALLADIUM from Diomedes (2) when the oracle ordered its return to the Trojans.

Naxos (*Νάξος*) The hero who gave his name to the island. According to one tradition he was a Carian, son of Polemon who had installed himself on the island at the head of a Carian colony. The island was then called Dia, and it was Naxos who gave it his own name. According to another legend he was the son of Endymion and Selene. A third version says that he was the son of Apollo and Acacallis.

Neda (*Νέδα*) After Rhea had given birth to Zeus she wanted to purify herself and bathe the child, but the river-beds were competely dry. In her distress Rhea struck the ground with her sceptre, calling on Gaia for help. A spring burst forth. Rhea gave it the name of Neda in honour of the Nymph, the eldest of the daughters of Oceanus after Styx and Philyra.

Neleus (*Νηλεύς*)

1. Son of TYRO and POSEIDON (Table 6). He was the twin brother of Pelias and the half-brother of Aeson, Pheres (1) and Amythaon. Neleus and Pelias were abandoned at

birth, but were fed by a mare sent by Poseidon. When the twins grew up they found their mother again when she was being badly treated by her stepmother, Sidero. They attacked Sidero, who took refuge in the temple of Hera, but Pelias murdered her at the altar. Later they fought each other to decide who should rule; Neleus was exiled and went to Messenia. There he founded Pylos and married Chloris, a daughter of Amphion, and had a daughter Pero, and twelve sons, including Nestor and Periclymenus (2).

For the war between Neleus and Heracles see HERACLES, III. In some traditions Neleus died in this war; in others he outlived his sons and died of illness in Corinth, where he was buried. For other wars waged by Neleus, notably against the Epeians, see NESTOR and MOLIONIDAE.

2. A descendant of Neleus (1) and a son of Codrus, king of Athens. He is credited with the foundation of Miletus. He headed a colony of Ionians who joined up with some Messenians who had been driven from their country by the Heraclids.

Nemanus (*Νεμανοῦς*) Wife of King Malcandrus who gave hospitality to Isis when she was searching for Osiris' body. Osiris' coffin had been cast up on the coast of Byblos and had landed in a tree which had grown and lifted it above the ground. Malcandrus had the tree cut down and used it as a column to hold up the palace roof. Thus Osiris' coffin was concealed in the palace roof. Isis arrived in Byblos disguised as a poor woman and Nemanus took her into her service as a nurse. At night Isis used to put the youngest child in the fire in order to rid him of his mortal elements. Meanwhile she would change into a swallow and circle round the column bearing Osiris' coffin. One night Nemanus appeared and let out a cry at seeing her son in the fire. Isis revealed her true identity, but warned that the child would never be immortal. She explained the reason for her presence and was given Osiris' body. When Isis opened the coffin she screamed so violently that Nemanus' youngest son died of shock. Nemanus' eldest son also died as a result of having seen Isis grieving for her husband.

Nemesis (*Νέμεσις*) Both a goddess and an abstract concept. She was one of the daughters of Nyx and was beloved by Zeus but tried to evade the god, assuming many different forms and finally changing herself into a goose. Zeus became a swan however and coupled with her. Nemesis laid an egg which some shepherds picked up and gave to LEDA. From this egg came Helen and the Dioscuri. Sometimes Nemesis is a goddess who punishes crime, but more often she is the power charged with curbing all excess, such as excessive good fortune, for example, or arrogant pride. This illustrates a basic concept in Greek thought: people who rise above their condition expose themselves to reprisals from the gods since they risk overthrowing the order of the world and must be punished. That is why Croesus, who was too wealthy and powerful, was enticed by Nemesis into his expedition against Cyrus, which ruined him.

At Rhamnus in Attica, Nemesis had a famous sanctuary. A statue of the goddess was carved by Agoracritus from a block of Parian marble acquired by the Persians, who intended to make it a trophy after they had captured Athens. In this they showed themselves too sure of their victory, and consequently their attempt to take Athens was unsuccessful.

Neoptolemus (*Νεοπτόλεμος*) Also known as the Young Warrior and as Pyrrhus, he was the son of Achilles and Deidamia, born when Achilles was concealed in Lycomedes' harem on Scyros. As Achilles was then disguised as a girl and called Pyrrha the name of Pyrrhus remained attached to his son. Neoptolemus was brought up by Lycomedes. After Achilles' death the Greeks discovered through Helenus that the city could never be captured unless Neoptolemus came to fight on the Greek side. The Greeks sent Odysseus, Phoenix (3) and Diomedes (2) to find Neoptolemus and bring him back. On the journey to Troy he accompanied the ambassadors to Lemnos to try to persuade PHILOCTETES to let them take the weapons of Heracles to Troy. Eventually he was successful.

Neoptolemus killed Eurypylus (4), and in his delight he invented the Pyrrhic war dance which is named after him. He was among the heroes who entered Troy in the Wooden Horse. During the decisive battles, he killed Elasus and Astynous, wounded Coroebus (2) and Agenos, then hurled ASTYANAX from the top of the tower. Thus Hector was killed by Achilles, and his son was killed by Neoptolemus. As part of his share of the plunder Neoptolemus was given Andromache. To honour his father's memory, he offered up POLYXENA to him as a sacrifice on his tomb.

Versions of his return from Troy diverge considerably. In the Homeric version Neoptolemus had a happy home-coming. Menelaus married him to his daughter Hermione, and Neoptolemus and Hermione went to live in Phthiotis. Other accounts say that Thetis advised Neoptolemus to return from Troy by land. That is why Neoptolemus went via Thrace, where he met Odysseus, to Epirus, and then to the area which later took the name of the 'Country of the Molossians' (see MOLOSSUS). Another tradition, recorded by Servius, says that it was Helenus who gave this advice to Neoptolemus, and that Helenus voluntarily accompanied him. This is supposed to be the origin of the friendship between the two men which led Neoptolemus on his deathbed to entrust Andromache to Helenus, asking him to marry her. This version supposes that during Achilles' absence Peleus had lost his throne to Acastus, so Neoptolemus went straight to Epirus. After disembarking in Thessaly on his return from Troy, Neoptolemus burnt his ships on the advice of Thetis and then settled in Epirus. Helenus had advised him to settle in a country where the houses had iron foundations, wooden walls and canvas roofs, and in Epirus the natives lived in tents with stakes that were tipped with iron, walls covered in wood and roofs of canvas.

Neoptolemus' marriage to Hermione was barren, whereas from his union with Andromache three sons were born, Molossus, Pielus and Pergamus. Jealous of the fertility of a mere concubine, Hermione summoned Orestes, whom she was to have married, to avenge her. Orestes killed Neoptolemus at Phthia, or in Epirus. In the account adopted by the tragedians Orestes carried out his revenge at Delphi, and his motive was not only to avenge Hermione, but also to punish his rival for having deprived him of his wife. Neoptolemus had gone to Delphi either to consult the oracle as to why his marriage with Hermione was still barren, or to dedicate part of the booty he had brought back from Troy, or to ask Apollo the reason for his hostility towards his father, Achilles (Apollo guided Paris' arrow which killed Achilles). Orestes is said to have fomented a riot, in the course of which Neoptolemus was killed.

There is a different version of Neoptolemus' death. It was the custom at Delphi for the priests to take the greater part of the meat of the animals offered up as sacrifices. Neoptolemus was angered by this custom and tried to prevent the priests from taking away the animal he had sacrificed. One of the priests named Machaereus killed him. A final version claims that the Delphians killed Neoptolemus on the instruction of the Pythia herself and that Apollo was carrying his anger against Achilles into the second generation. Neoptolemus was buried beneath the threshold of the temple of Delphi and divine honours were paid to him.

Nephalion (*Νηφαλίων*) One of the sons of Minos and the Nymph Paria. He settled in Paros at about the time when Heracles set off to look for the girdle of the Amazon queen, Hippolyta. Heracles stopped at Paros and Minos' sons killed two of his companions. Heracles retaliated by killing the sons: the island's inhabitants sent a deputation to him offering in compensation two of them to replace the two he had lost. The choice was to be his. Heracles took Nephalion's nephews Alceus and Sthenelus (2).

Nephele (*Νεφέλη*)

1. The first wife of Athamas, the mother of Phrixus and Helle. Athamas abandoned her and married Ino.
2. The Cloud (Greek 'nephele' = 'cloud') fashioned by Zeus to resemble Hera in order to frustrate IXION. Mating with him, the Cloud produced the Centaurs.

Aristophanes uses Clouds as characters in one of his comedies: they are the daughters of Oceanus; they sometimes live on the peaks of Olympus, sometimes in the gardens of Oceanus in the Hesperides, sometimes at the distant sources of the Nile, in the land of the Ethiopians.

In the myth of CEPHALUS it was sometimes the Cloud (Nephele), rather than the Breeze, who was summoned by the huntsman and it is over this name that Procris made her mistake.

Neptune The Roman god identified with POSEIDON. His festival was celebrated at the height of summer (on 23 July) during the season of the greatest dryness. He had a sanctuary between the Palatine and Aventine hills at the precise spot where a stream had once flowed. In Roman tradition Neptune was said to have had a companion spirit, whose name is sometimes given as Salacia, sometimes as Venilia.

Nereids (*Νηρεΐδες*) Sea-deities, daughters of Nereus and Doris, and granddaughters of Oceanus. Their number is usually set as fifty, but in some accounts they are thought to be as many as a hundred.

Some of the Nereids have more definitely drawn personalities than others: these include THETIS, AMPHITRITE, GALATEA (1), and Orithyia (see BOREAS). The Nereids lived at the bottom of the sea, seated on golden thrones in their father's palace. They were all very beautiful and they spent their time spinning, weaving and singing. The poets picture them playing in the waves, swimming to and fro amid the Tritons and dolphins. They wept for the deaths of Achilles and Patroclus with their sister Thetis; they told Heracles how to extract from Nereus the information he needed about the route to the land of the Hesperides; they were present at the freeing of Andromeda by Perseus.

Nereus (*Νηρεύς*) One of the so-called Old Men of the Sea and sometimes the archetypal Old Man of the Sea. He was a son of Pontus and Gaia and accordingly brother of Thaumas, Phorcys, Ceto, and Eurybia. His wife was Doris and by her he fathered the NEREIDS. Nereus ranks among the gods who represented the elementary forces of the world. Like many marine deities, he had the power to change himself into all sorts of animals and beings. In this way he tried to escape the questions put to him by Heracles, who wished to learn how to reach the land of the Hesperides (see HERACLES, II). In general Nereus was considered a benevolent and beneficent god as far as sailors are concerned. He was represented as bearded, armed with a trident and riding a Triton.

Nerio In Roman tradition Nerio was the wife of Mars. She was the personification of Valour. Sometimes the spoils taken from an enemy were dedicated to her. In certain traditions she seems to have been identified with Minerva, who was also a warrior-goddess like the Greek Pallas Athena. For the amorous escapades of Mars and Minerva-Nerio see MARS and ANNA PERENNA.

Nerites (*Νηρίτης*) The son of Nereus and Doris. He excited the love of Aphrodite in the days when she still lived in the sea. When the goddess flew off to Olympus, however, Nerites refused to follow her, even though she had given him wings. In anger Aphrodite changed him into a shell-fish, attached to a rock and incapable of moving. She then gave his wings to Eros, who agreed to be her companion.

Nessus (*Νέσσος*) A Centaur and, like all the CENTAURS, a son of Ixion and Nephele (2). He took part in the fight against Pholus and Heracles and, driven off by the hero, settled by the banks of the River Evenus, where he acted as ferryman. See HERACLES, VI.

Nestor (*Νέστωρ*) The youngest of the sons of Neleus (1) and Chloris (Table 6). He was the only one to survive the massacre by Heracles (see HERACLES, III). His mother, Chloris was one of the Niobids. Her brothers and sisters were killed by Apollo and Artemis, but to make restitution Apollo granted Nestor the right to live the number of years of which his uncles and aunts had been deprived.

In both the *Iliad* and the *Odyssey* Nestor is the archetypal wise old man, valiant on the battlefield but above all excellent in council. He reigned at Pylos and attacked the Epeians several times to punish them for their raids on his territory. During one of these battles he nearly killed the MOLIONIDAE. He also killed the giant Ereuthalion in Arcadia, after challenging him to single combat. He participated in the fight of the Lapiths and the Centaurs, in the hunting of the Calydonian boar, and, in certain late versions, in the expedition of the Argonauts. Above all he played an important role in the Trojan War. He accompanied Menelaus on his trip around Greece to assemble the heroes, and himself provided a fleet of ninety ships. He took part in the capture of Tenedos by Achilles before the events recounted in the *Iliad*. His share of the booty was Hecamede, the daughter of Arsinous. He acted as intermediary in the dispute between Achilles and Agamemnon. The epic poems also tell of how Nestor was attacked by Memnon and defended by his son Antilochus, who sacrificed his own life to save him. Achilles finally killed Memnon and avenged Antilochus. After the fall of Troy Nestor returned safely to Pylos. His wife (Eurydice (8) according to the *Odyssey*, but Anaxibia, daughter of Cratieus, according to Apollodorus) was still alive. Telemachus went to ask Nestor's advice when he was worried as to what had befallen his father.

Nicaea (*Νικαία*) A Naiad, the daughter of Sangarius and Cybele. She was devoted to hunting and spurned love, so when a Phrygian shepherd Hymnus (1) was attentive to her, she first rejected, and then killed him. Eros was indignant at this, so he inspired Dionysus, who had seen Nicaea bathing naked, with a passion for her. Nicaea threatened the god with the same fate as Hymnus, but Dionysus changed the water in the spring where she drank into wine and when she had become drunk he overpowered her. The fruit of their union was a daughter, Telete. Nicaea eventually made her peace with Dionysus and they had other children including a son called Satyrus. Dionysus later built the city of Nicaea in her honour.

Nicomachus (*Νικόμαχος*) A grandson of Asclepius, through his father, Machaon. Nicomachus and his brother Gorgasus became rulers of the city of Pherae in Messenia.

Nicostrate (*Νικοστράτη*) One of the names given in Greece to the mother of EVANDER (3). She is sometimes said to have been Evander's wife and the daughter of Hermes. In Rome she was known as CARMENTA.

Nicostratus (*Νικόστρατος*) The son of Helen and Menelaus. Since the Homeric poems affirm that Hermione was Helen's only child, Nicostratus is generally said to have been born after the return from Troy. He is sometimes presented as the son of Menelaus by a slave, in which case he would be the brother of Megapenthes (1).

Nike (*Νίκη*) The personification of Victory. She is represented as winged and flying at great speed. Hesiod makes her the daughter of Pallas (3) and Styx. Later traditions make her a companion of Pallas Athena instead. She is supposed to have been brought up by Palans, who consecrated a temple to her on the top of his hill, the Palatine, at Rome. This legend derives from accounts which at Athens combined the goddess Athena and Nike. It also derives from the homonymy of the two Pallases, the Titan and the goddess. At Athens Nike was an epithet of Athena.

Nileus (*Νειλεύς*) In the euhemerist tradition followed by Diodorus Siculus, Nileus was a king of Egypt. He gave his name to the River Nile, which had previously been called Aegyptus. This honour was awarded to him by his people in recognition of the substantial irrigation work he undertook.

Nilus (*Νεῖλος*) The god of the Nile. He was said to be a son of Oceanus, but a different legend grew up which associated the river with the myth of Io. Epaphus the son of Io was said to have married Memphis, the daughter of Nilus. From their union was born Libya, mother of the race of Agenor and Belus (see Table 3). The Greeks represented Nilus as a king who had made Egypt fertile (see NILEUS).

Ninus (*Νίνος*) The mythical founder of Nineveh and of the Babylonian Empire. He is said to have been the son of Belus, (the god Baal, who is identified with the Greek god Cronus). Ninus invented the art of warfare and was the first to assemble huge armies. With Ariaeus, king of Arabia, he conquered all Asia except for India. Bactria resisted him for a long time but he was finally able to conquer it thanks to a ruse of SEMIRAMIS. Herodotus gives a genealogy for King Ninus, which makes him a descendant of Heracles through his grandfather Alceus, who was the son of Heracles and Omphale.

Niobe (*Νιόβη*)

1. The daughter of Phoroneus by the Nymph Teledice (or Cerdo, or Electra (3), or Peitho (3)). She was the first mortal woman with whom Zeus mated, and by him she gave birth to Argos (1) and (according to Acousilaus) Pelasgus (1).
2. Daughter of Tantalus (1) and the sister of Pelops (1). She married Amphion and, according to most mythographers, bore him seven sons and seven daughters. In the Homeric tradition there were twelve children, six of each sex; in the tragedians' version there were ten sons and ten daughters; and Herodorus of Heraclea gave only five, two boys and three girls.

Happy and proud of her children, Niobe declared that she was superior to Leto who had only one son and one daughter. The goddess felt offended, and asked Apollo and Artemis to avenge her. The two deities slaughtered the children of Niobe with their arrows. Artemis killed the girls, Apollo the boys. Only one boy and one girl were saved. The latter became pallid with terror; she took the name Chloris ('Green') and later married Neleus (1). In the *Iliad* the children of Niobe remained unburied for ten days. On the eleventh, the gods themselves buried them. In the more recent version Niobe fled to Tantalus, at Sipylus (or to Mount Sipylis in Asia Minor), where she was changed into a rock by the gods. Her eyes continued to weep however, and people were shown the rock which had once been Niobe, from which a spring flowed.

There was another version of the Niobe legend in which Niobe was the daughter of Assaon, who had married her to an Assyrian named Philottus. The latter was killed during a hunt, and Assaon became enamoured of his own daughter. She refused to yield. Assaon then asked his grandchildren to a feast during which he set fire to the palace and burned them all alive. Stricken with remorse Assaon killed himself. Niobe was either changed into stone or threw herself from the top of a rock.

Nireus (*Νιρεύς*) One of the suitors of Helen. He was very handsome but of humble birth. He reigned over the island of Syme. During the battle between Achilles and Telephus in Mysia Nireus killed Hiera, the wife of Telephus, who was fighting at her husband's side. Nireus was killed by Telephus' son Eurypylus (4) before the walls of Troy. Another tradition includes him in the travels of Thoas (4) after the fall of Troy.

Nisus (*Nῖσος*)

1. One of the sons of Pandion (2). He was born at Megara while his father was in exile. His mother was Pylia, daughter of the king of Megara. After his father's death Nisus returned with his brothers to conquer Megara (see also SCIRON).

Some traditions attribute to Nisus a daughter named Iphinoe who married Megareus, son of Poseidon, but in the best-known tradition, Nisus' daughter was SCYLLA (2).

2. A companion of Aeneas famous for his friendship with Euryalus (3). At the funeral games of Anchises, Nisus ensured that his friend was the victor. During the war against the Rutuli, Nisus and Euryalus went into the enemy camp to reconnoitre during the night, but on their way back were pursued by a troop of cavalry. They sought refuge in the woods but became separated. Feeling that his friend was threatened Nisus left his hiding place and died trying to avenge the death of Euryalus.

Nixi Three kneeling female statues which could be seen at Rome, in front of the *cella* of the Capitoline Minerva. They represented the pains experienced by women at the moment when they bring a child into the world.

Notus (*Νότος*) The god of the South Wind, a warm and very moist wind. He was the son of Eos and Astraeus.

Numa Pompilius Numa, a Sabine by birth, was the second king of Rome. He was born on the day Romulus founded Rome, and married Tatia, the daughter of Titus Tatius. He was credited with creating most of the cults and sacred institutions. He began by paying divine honours to ROMULUS, under the title of Quirinus; then he created the colleges of the Flamines, the Augurs, the Vestals, the Salii, the Fetiales, and the Pontiffs, and introduced a large number of deities, for example the cults of Jupiter Terminus, of Jupiter Elicius, of Fides and Dius Fidius and of the Sabine gods. It was claimed that he was Pythagorean by persuasion, or, alternatively, that his religious policy was inspired by the Nymph EGERIA. All cultural and religious reforms are attributed to his name, such as the institution of a calendar based on the phases of the moon, and the distinction between *dies fasti* and *dies nefasti*.

Numa possessed magic powers. During a banquet over which he was presiding, the tables suddenly filled with costly dishes and delicious wines which nobody had brought in. He also captured Picus and Faunus on the Aventine by mixing honey and wine with the water of the spring at which they used to drink. They took on all manner of terrifying forms to escape from him, but in the end they revealed various secrets to him, such as charms against thunder. He is also said to have had a conversation with Jupiter during which he persuaded the god to content himself with turning thunder aside with onion heads, instead of using the heads of men, horses and fish. Numa had several sons, Pompo, Pinus, Calpus and Mamercus (1), each of whom was the ancestor of a Roman *gens*. He also had a daughter, Pompilia, either by Tatia or by Lucretia, whom he married after his accession to the throne. King Ancus Marcius was the grandson of Numa through Pompilia's husband Marcius. Numa died at an extremely old age and was buried on the Janiculum. The sacred books that he had written in his own hand were placed beside him, in a separate coffin. Later, under the consulate of P. Cornelius and M. Baebius, a violent rainstorm unearthed the two coffins. Numa's coffin was empty. The other contained the manuscripts; these were burnt in the Comitium in front of the Curia.

Numitor The elder son of Procas, king of Alba. His younger brother, AMULIUS, seized the throne on their father's death and expelled Numitor, killed Numitor's son and dedicated his daughter Rhea Silvia (1) to the service of Vesta, so that she would stay celibate beyond the age of childbearing. Rhea was loved by the god Mars, however, and gave birth to Romulus and Remus, who eventually re-established Numitor on the throne (see ROMULUS, REMUS, and FAUSTULUS).

Another version alleges that Numitor knew about his daughter Rhea's pregnancy and contrived to substitute two children for those of his daughter. Rhea's two sons were sent by him to the shepherd Faustulus on the Palatine. They were suckled by Faustulus' wife, Acca Larentia (2), who had once been a prostitute and thereby earned the title of 'she-wolf' (a term applied to women of easy virtue). Once they had been weaned, they were sent to Gabii to be educated. When they came back to the man they thought was their father, Numitor contrived a quarrel between them and his shepherds; he then complained to Amulius, who, without suspecting anything, summoned everyone to Alba to judge the trial. Numitor, helped by this crowd of young men, had no difficulty in overthrowing his brother and regaining the throne. Then he gave his grandsons a piece of ground on which to found a city, the precise spot where they had been brought up by Faustulus.

A number of variants of the legend of Amulius and Numitor exist. For example, both are said to have been sons of the hero Aventinus, or even his grandsons (Procas being their father). In one version their inheritance was shared; one chose power (Amulius), the other chose riches (Numitor). Or in an alternative account, Procas advised them to govern after the manner of the Roman Consuls, by forming a college of two equal kings, but Amulius took power into his hands alone.

Nycteus (*Νυκτεύς*) The father of ANTIOPE (1). He is generally considered to have been the brother of Lycus (3) and the son of Hyrieus and Clonia. However, the mythographers, confusing Lycus (1), the son of Poseidon and Calaeno (1), with Lycus (3), the son of Hyrieus, have sometimes made Nycteus the son of Poseidon and Celaeno. In other versions Lycus and Nycteus are said to have been the sons of Chthonius, one of the men born of the teeth of the dragon killed by CADMUS. In this version they fled to Euboea because they had killed Phlegyas, and there they became friendly with the king, Pentheus. They even acted as regents (see LAIUS and LABDACUS). When Nycteus' daughter ANTIOPE (1) fled to Sicyon to be with EPOPEUS, Nycteus killed himself and entrusted LYCUS (3) with the task of avenging his dishonour. A variant tradition given by Pausanias says that Nycteus was slain on the battlefield in an expedition against Epopeus, who had abducted Antiope. Epopeus was also wounded in the same battle and died soon after.

Nyctimene (*Νυκτιμένη*) The daughter of Epopeus (2). Her father fell in love with her and forced her into an incestuous relationship. In shame she fled to the woods, where Athena had pity on her and turned her into an owl. That is why owls do not like to be seen, and only come out at night.

Nyctimus (*Νύκτιμος*) The only one of the sons of LYCAON (2) whom the prayers of Ge saved from the vengeance of Zeus. He succeeded his father on the throne of Arcadia. The flood associated with Deucalion (1) occurred during his reign. Nyctimus was succeeded by ARCAS.

Nymphs (*Νύμφαι*) Female deities, the spirits of the fields and of nature in general. In the Homeric poems they are the daughters of Zeus. They lived in grottoes where they spent their time spinning and singing. They are often the attendants of a great goddess (particularly Artemis), or of another Nymph of higher status. Thus Calypso (1) and Circe had attendant Nymphs.

Nymphs could be categorized according to their habitats: the MELIADS, Nymphs of the ash trees, were daughters of Uranus, not Zeus; the NAIADS lived in springs and streams and were often considered to be the daughters of the appropriate river-god; the NEREIDS were usually believed to be the Nymphs of the calm sea; the Oreads lived in the mountains; Nymphs called Alseids lived in the groves (Greek *alsos* = 'sacred wood'); other Nymphs were attached to a specific spot or even a given tree, such as the HAMADRYADS. Nymphs are often found as wives of the eponymous hero of a locality or city (for example AEGINA and Aeacus, or TAYGETE). They also frequently occur in myths with a love motif (see DAPHNE, ECHO, CALLISTO (1)). Their usual lovers were deities such as Pan, the Satyrs and Priapus, although they also attracted the attentions of Zeus, Apollo, Hermes, Dionysus and others. In some accounts they fell in love with and abducted young boys such as HYLAS.

Nysa (*Νῦσα*) One of the Nymphs who brought up Dionysus as a child on Mount Nysa. With the god's other nursemaids she was, at his request, given back her youthfulness by Medea.

Nyx (*Νύξ*) The personification of the Night, and its goddess. She was the daughter of Chaos in the Hesiodic *Theogony*, and mother of Aether and Hemera, and also of a whole series of abstract forces: Morus (Destiny), the Keres, Hypnus (Sleep), the Dreams, Momus (Reproach), Oizys (Distress), the Moirae, Nemesis, Apate (Deceit), Philotes (Love), Geras (Old Age), Eris (Strife), and lastly the Hesperides. Her realm was in the far West beyond the land of Atlas (1). She was the sister of Erebus.

O

Oceanus (Ὠκεανός) The personification of the water that surrounded the world. Oceanus is represented as a river flowing around the flat disk of the Earth and marking its furthest limits. This provides an explanation of the topography of some stories, such as the legend of Heracles and the Hesperides and the account of his adventures with Geryon (see HERACLES, II). As knowledge of the world grew more precise, the name Oceanus came to refer to the Atlantic Ocean, the western boundary of the Ancient World.

Oceanus was the eldest of the Titans, and a son of Uranus and Gaia. As a deity, Oceanus was the father of all rivers. In the *Theogony* Hesiod names among his offspring: the Nile, the Alpheus, the Eridanus, the Strymon, the Meander, the Istrus, the Phasis, the Rhesus, the Achelous, the Nessus, the Rhodius, the Haliacmon, the Heptaporus, the Granicus, the Aesopus, the Simois, the Peneus, the Hermus, the Caicus, the Sangarius, the Ladon, the Parthenius, the Evenus, the Ardescus, and the Scamander. Hesiod himself warns us that this list is far from exhaustive. At least 3,000 other names would have to be added in order to list all the rivers that he fathered upon his sister Tethys. By Tethys he had as many daughters, the Oceanides, who were the lovers of a great many gods and some mortals, and gave birth to numerous children. They personify the rivers and springs. Hesiod gives the names of 41 of them, and other authors add further names.

Ochimus (Ὄχιμος) One of the HELIADES (2).

Ocnus (Ὄκνος)

1. Ocnus the rope-maker is a symbolic character, represented as being in Hades weaving a rope that a female donkey eats as fast as he can make it. This was sometimes interpreted as meaning that Ocnus was a hardworking man with a spendthrift wife.
2. See AUCNUS.

Ocrisia The daughter of the king of Corniculum. She was brought to Rome as a slave, becoming a maidservant in the house of old Tarquin. She saw a male sexual organ appear in the cinders of the hearth while she was taking the ritual offering to the household god. She recounted this vision to her mistress, Tanaquil, who advised her to put on bridal trappings and to shut herself in the room where she had seen the phenomenon. Ocrisia did this, and during the night her divine lover coupled with her; the child born of the union was Servius Tullius. Another version says that Ocrisia arrived in Rome pregnant and was the wife of the king of Corniculum. It was also said that Ocrisia's lover was not a god, but a hanger-on of the royal household.

Ocyrrhoe (Ὠκυρρόη)

1. One of the daughters of Ocea-

nus, who was said to have coupled with Helios and borne him a son called Phasis.

2. A Nymph of Samos, daughter of the Nymph Chesias and the River Imbrasus (1). Apollo fell in love with her and wanted to abduct her. Ocyrrhoe had asked a friend of her father, a sailor called Pompilus, to escort her. However Apollo appeared, took the girl, transformed Pompilus' boat into a rock and changed Pompilus into a fish.

3. The daughter of Chiron and the Nymph Chariclo (1). Her mother gave birth to her in a stream with swiftly flowing water (her name means 'swift-flowing'). At birth she received the power of divination, but she used it without discretion. Against the gods' orders she revealed to the little Asclepius and his father the secrets of the gods, so the gods changed her into a horse.

Odysseus (*'Οδυσσεύς*) Ulixes, or Ulysses, in Latin. His legend, the subject of the *Odyssey*, was continually reworked, added to and commented on.

I. BIRTH

His father was Laertes, his mother Anticleia. This is the parentage given by the *Odyssey*. On the paternal side, his grandfather was Arceisius (as given in the *Odyssey*) although Arceisius is sometimes said to be the son of Zeus and Euryodia, sometimes of CEPHALUS, or of Cileus, a son of Cephalus. On the maternal side, the *Odyssey* gives AUTOLYCUS as grandfather; but there is a tradition according to which Anticleia was seduced by SISYPHUS before her marriage to Laertes, and Odysseus was the son from his affair.

Odysseus was born in Ithaca, an island on the western coast of Greece. Anticleia is said to have given birth to him on Mount Neriton one day when she was caught by the rain and she found her path cut off by the water. (The name Odysseus can be interpreted as a fragment of the Greek phrase meaning 'Zeus rained on the road', *Κατὰ τὴν ὁδὸν ὗσεν ὁ Ζεύς*). But in the *Odyssey* Sisyphus named the child Odysseus because he was himself 'hated by many people' (Odysseus is similar to *ὀδύσσομαι*, 'to hate'). In the tradition which makes Odysseus the son of Sisyphus, Anticleia gave birth to him at Alalcomenae in Boeotia, while on her way to Ithaca with Laertes.

II. BEFORE THE TROJAN WAR

A late tradition maintains that Odysseus was one of the pupils of the Centaur Chiron, but the *Odyssey* only alludes to a boar hunt which he took part in while staying with Autolycus. During the hunt he was wounded in the knee, and the resulting scar was later to be the sign by which he was recognized on his return from Troy. Odysseus made journeys on Laertes' behalf. In particular, he went to Messenia to reclaim the sheep which had been stolen from him. At Lacedaemon he met IPHITUS (1) who gave him the bow of Eurytus (2), which he was later to use to kill the suitors.

On his reaching manhood, Laertes gave Odysseus the throne of Ithaca. In accounts later than the *Odyssey* it is at this period that his attempt to marry Helen took place. However, he gave up his claim to Helen in order to make a match that was almost as advantageous by marrying

PENELOPE, Helen's cousin, and daughter of Icarius (2). It was Odysseus who advised Tyndareus to demand that each of the suitors should swear to assist whoever was chosen to safeguard Helen, should anyone else lay claim to her. The grateful Tyndareus easily obtained the hand of Penelope for Odysseus. According to other authors, she was the prize in a race which Odysseus won.

There was one son of this marriage, TELEMACHUS. He was still very young when the news spread that Paris had abducted Helen. It was related by poets later than Homer that Odysseus feigned madness in order to avoid participating in the expedition, but PALAMEDES saw through this trick. Odysseus accepted the inevitable and set off for Troy. His father gave him an adviser, Myiscus, whose task was to watch over him during the war, but this Myiscus is not mentioned in the Homeric poems. From that moment, Odysseus enthusiastically embraced the cause of the Atrides. He accompanied Menelaus to Delphi to consult the oracle and went in search of Achilles, whose assistance was said by the Fates to be indispensable if Troy were to be taken. He found him finally at Scyros (see ACHILLES). During this preparatory period, we also find Odysseus as ambassador of the Atrides to the court of CINYRAS in Cyprus.

III. THE TROJAN WAR

The role of Odysseus in the first expedition which resulted in the landing in Mysia seems to have been limited to interpreting correctly the oracle which stated that TELEPHUS could be healed only by 'the person who caused the wound'. It was in the Trojan War itself, however, that Odysseus played a greater part. He acted as an intermediary for Agamemnon and made IPHIGENIA come to Aulis on a false pretext.

Odysseus commanded a contingent of a dozen ships on the voyage to Troy. He was one of the heroes who met in council, and was regarded as the equal of the greatest of them. On the way to Troy, he accepted the challenge made to him by PHILOMELIDES, the king of Lesbos, and killed him in the fight. During their stay on Lemnos, Odysseus, according to the *Odyssey*, quarrelled with Achilles during the banquet held for the leaders. Odysseus was praising prudence, Achilles, bravery. Agamemnon, to whom Apollo had predicted that the Greeks would take Troy when discord broke out among the assailants, saw this as an omen of quick victory. This episode was later transferred to Tenedos. It was on Lemnos, or on the neighbouring island of Chrysa, that PHILOCTETES was abandoned on Odysseus' advice. Another episode was introduced by poets writing later than Homer: the mission from Tenedos to demand the return of Helen. Odysseus and Menelaus had already made one trip to Troy, accompanied by Palamedes, to try to settle the matter peacefully. They renewed these negotiations, but in vain, and they were threatened by the Trojans, escaping only because of the intervention of Antenor (see MENELAUS).

During the siege, Odysseus proved to be a fighter of the greatest bravery, as well as a wise and effective adviser. In the *Iliad*, he was placed in charge of the mission to Achilles when Agamemnon wanted a reconciliation with the latter. By then he had already brought the prisoner Chryseis back to her father, concluded an armistice with the Trojans, organized the single combat between Paris and Menelaus, reduced Thersites to silence during the meeting of the soldiers, and persuaded the Greeks to remain in the Troad. Poets writing later than the *Iliad* added various other episodes: the mission to ANIUS (1) to persuade him to send his daughters and thus to ensure the replenishment of the army; the mission to PHILOCTETES when Helenus revealed that Heracles' arrows were needed to ensure the capture of Troy, and the mission to NEOPTOLEMUS.

Various espionage operations were also attributed to Odysseus. The *Iliad* shows him taking part in a night reconnaissance exercise with DIOMEDES (2), in the episode of the capture of DOLON, during which he killed Dolon and captured RHESUS' horses. There was also the later episode of the removal of the PALLADIUM. The intrigue which brought about the death of PALAMEDES was also attributed to Odysseus, as was the idea of building the Wooden Horse; the success of this trick was ensured by an expedition mentioned in the *Odyssey*. Odysseus had himself whipped by THOAS (4) to make himself unrecognizable and then, dressed in rags, he appeared in the city claiming to be a deserter. He made his way to Helen and persuaded her to betray the Trojans. Helen warned Hecuba of Odysseus' presence, but he had so touched the queen by his entreaties, tears and guileful speech that she swore to maintain secrecy. He escaped, killing the Trojan guards on the gate.

Odysseus' exploits during the war were numerous. He slew many Trojan warriors, protected Diomedes (2) when he was wounded, commanded the detachment inside the Wooden Horse, and warned his companions of Helen's trick of imitating the voices of their wives outside the horse. He was the first to leap out and accompanied Menelaus who wanted to seize Helen from Deiphobus as soon as possible. According to one version, he prevented Menelaus from killing his wife on the spot; in another version, he waited for the Greeks' anger to die down and saved Helen from being stoned, as the Greeks had wanted. He also saved HELICAON.

For Odysseus' role in the division of Achilles' arms, and his intrigues against Ajax (2), see AJAX (2). Odysseus was also responsible for the death of ASTYANAX and the sacrifice of POLYXENA. Hecuba fell to him in the sharing out of the captive Trojan women and, in the tradition according to which the old queen was stoned, it was Odysseus who threw the first stone.

IV. RETURN TO ITHACA

This part of Odysseus' adventures forms the subject of the *Odyssey*, although the legend has undergone later reworkings and additions.

MENELAUS and AGAMEMNON did not agree on the date of departure for Greece. Menelaus set off first with Nestor. Odysseus followed them, but quarrelled with them at Tenedos and returned to Troy to join Agamemnon. When the latter put to sea, Odysseus followed him, but was soon separated from him by a storm. He landed in the country of the Cicones where he took the city of Ismarus, sparing only MARON, a priest of Apollo. In gratitude, Maron gave him 12 earthenware jars of a strong, sweet wine, which were later to be extremely useful to him in the land of the Cyclopes.

Heading south, two days later, he arrived in sight of Cape Malea, but a violent north wind drove him out to sea and, two days later, he landed in the country of the Lotus-eaters. For the events here, see LOTOPHAGI.

Odysseus and his companions then replenished their food supplies and moved on to the land of the Cyclopes. Odysseus disembarked, accompanied by twelve men, and went into a cave. He had been careful to take with him goat-skins full of wine, as a gesture of hospitality towards the people whom he might encounter. In the cave, they found quantities of cheese, fresh milk and curds. Odysseus' companions urged him to take these and leave, but he was reluctant. At that point the inhabitant of the cave, the Cyclops POLYPHEMUS (2), returned, seized the strangers and shut them away. For subsequent events see POLYPHEMUS (2).

Having escaped from the Cyclopes, Odysseus reached the island of Aeolus, the Warden of the Winds (see AEOLUS (1) and (2)). He was received hospitably and given a cattle-skin bag containing all the winds except for a favourable breeze which would bring him straight back to Ithaca. They were already in sight of the fires lit by shepherds on the island when Odysseus fell asleep. His companions, thinking that Aeolus' bag contained gold, untied it. The winds escaped in a hurricane and drove the boat in the opposite direction. Again, the boat landed on Aeolus' island, and once more Odysseus went to see the king to ask for a favourable wind, but Aeolus replied that he could not do anything more for him. Odysseus then put to sea again, and heading north he reached the country of the Laestrygonians. The inhabitants stoned the Greeks, breaking up the ships and killing the men (see LAESTRYGONIANS). Odysseus narrowly escaped, and, with his fleet reduced to a single vessel and its crew, continued to sail north and soon landed on the island of Aeaea, where the sorceress CIRCE lived.

Circe sent him to consult the spirit of Tiresias. Tiresias informed him that he would return alone to his homeland on a foreign ship, that he would have to take revenge on the suitors and later set off again, with one oar on his shoulder, in search of a people who knew nothing about sailing. There he must offer an expiatory sacrifice to Poseidon; he would finally die during a happy old age, far from the sea. After encountering a number of heroes called up from the dead, Odysseus returned to Circe. He then set off again, and sailed along the coast of the island of the SIRENS; next he had to confront the Wandering Rocks, and the straits between SCYLLA (1) and CHARYBDIS. The ship escaped and reached Sicily where the white cattle belonging to Helios grazed. There the wind began to fail, and the food began to run out. The sailors killed some of the cattle to eat, despite being forbidden to do so by Odysseus. Helios saw this, and complained to Zeus. Accordingly, when the ship put to sea again, a storm sent by Zeus blew up and the ship was struck by lightning. Only Odysseus was saved, as he had refused to take part in the sacrilegious feast. He clung to the mast and was swept across the straits again, escaping Charybdis' whirlpool. He was tossed around by the sea for nine days and then he reached the island of CALYPSO (1). His stay with Calypso lasted for one, five, eight or ten years, depending on the source. Finally, at the request of Athena, the hero's protector, Zeus sent Hermes to order Calypso to release Odysseus. Reluctantly, Calypso provided him with enough wood to build a raft and Odysseus set off towards the east.

But Poseidon's anger at the death of his son, the Cyclops Polyphemus (2), had not yet abated: he whipped up a storm which broke up the raft, and clinging to a piece of wreckage, the naked hero was washed up on the shores of the island of the Phaeacians, called Scheria in the *Odyssey*. There Odysseus encountered NAUSICAA, who directed him to her father's palace, where he received a hospitable welcome from Alcinous and his queen, Arete. A banquet was held in his honour and Odysseus gave a full account of his adventures. He was then showered with presents and, since he declined the offer of the hand of Nausicaa and proclaimed his determination to return to Ithaca, a ship was put at his disposal. During the brief voyage, Odysseus fell asleep, and the Phaeacian sailors put him down on a remote spot on the island of Ithaca, with the treasures which he brought back as gifts from Alcinous. For the consequences for the Phaeacians of Alcinous' hospitality, see ALCINOUS.

Odysseus' absence had lasted twenty years. He was so transformed by age and dangers that nobody recognized him. However, PENELOPE was waiting faithfully for him, according to the version in the *Odyssey*. She had been exposed to the entreaties of the suitors who had moved into the palace and were squandering Odysseus' wealth in wild excesses. There were 108 suitors in all. They came from Dulichium, Samos, Zacynthos and Ithaca – the countries under Odysseus' rule.

Odysseus decided not to go immediately to the palace. First of all, he went to see Eumaeus, his head swineherd, whom he trusted totally. He disclosed his identity to him, and also met his son Telemachus. Father and son then went to the palace, Odysseus disguised as a beggar. No one recognized him except his old dog Argus, who leapt up, overcome with joy on seeing his master, and fell down dead.

At the palace, Odysseus asked the suitors for food. They insulted him, and the beggar Irus (2), who regularly attended the suitors' feasts, challenged this newcomer to a fight. Odysseus felled him with several blows and was subsequently further insulted by the suitors, notably by Antinous (1). Penelope, who had heard of the arrival of this foreign beggar, wanted to see him to ask whether he had any news of Odysseus. At nightfall, Telemachus, at his father's command, carried all the weapons in the palace to the armoury. Then the meeting between

Penelope and Odysseus took place, but he did not reveal his identity to her. She had dreamt that her husband would soon return, but she refused to believe it and proposed to arrange a competition among the suitors the next day, and to marry the victor. She would give them Odysseus' bow and the winner would be the man who was best able to use it. Odysseus encouraged her in this plan.

The competition took place the next day: the object was to shoot an arrow through rings formed by a number of axes placed side by side. The suitors each took the bow in turn but not one could bend it. Finally, the bow was handed to Odysseus, who accomplished the task at the first shot. Odysseus' servants shut the doors of the palace, Telemachus seized weapons, and the massacre of the suitors began. The servant girls, whose behaviour towards the suitors had not been totally appropriate, were hanged in the palace courtyard, along with the goatherd Melanthius, who had sided with the suitors. Odysseus revealed himself to Penelope and, to remove her doubts, described their nuptial chamber, which was known only to the two of them.

The next day, Odysseus went to the country, where his father lived, and disclosed his identity to him. The families of the suitors demanded recompense from Odysseus, but thanks to the intervention of Athena, disguised as MENTOR, peace soon returned to Ithaca.

Such is the story of the *Odyssey*.

After the massacre of the suitors Odysseus offered a sacrifice to Hades, Persephone and Tiresias, and went to the land of the Thesproti. The queen of the country, Callidice, urged him to stay with her and offered him her kingdom. Odysseus agreed, and they had a son, Polypoetes (3). Odysseus reigned jointly with Callidice, but when she died, he returned to Ithaca, where he found that Penelope had borne him a second son, Poliporthes. Meanwhile, Telegonus (1), the son of Odysseus and Circe, had set off in search of Odysseus. He landed in Ithaca, and plundered the herds. Odysseus came to the aid of his shepherds and was killed by his son in the fight. When Telegonus learnt who his victim was, he was grief-stricken. He returned to Circe with the body and with Penelope.

Other versions relate that Odysseus, accused by the kinsmen of the suitors, submitted the case to Neoptolemus the king of Epirus for judgement. Neoptolemus condemned Odysseus to exile. He later went to Aetolia, where he married the daughter of Thoas (4) and by her had a son, Leontophonus, and died of old age. Another tradition, related by Plutarch, maintains that after the judgement of Neoptolemus, Odysseus went into exile in Italy.

Tacitus records that Odysseus' voyage had taken him as far as the Rhine and that he had built an altar on the banks, which still existed at the time of the Roman conquest.

The list of Odysseus' children was very varied. It was modified at the whim of genealogists in order to give titles to all the Italian cities in the time of Cato. Thus, he and Circe were said to have had sons like Ardeas, eponym of the Latin city Ardea, and Latinus, eponym of the

Latins, etc. (See also ROMUS and EVIPPE (1).)

Oeager (*Οἴαγρος*) Father of Orpheus. He is sometimes said to have been the son of Ares, sometimes of Pierus (1) or of CHAROPS (see also LYCURGUS (2)). His wife was the Muse Calliope, Polyhymnia or Clio. Late authors claim that he was the father of Marsyas, Linus (2) and Cymothon.

Oeax (*Οἴαξ*) One of three sons of NAUPLIUS (2) by Clymene (4) or Hesione (2). His brothers were PALAMEDES and Nausimedon. When Palamedes was stoned to death by the Greeks, Oeax transmitted the news to Nauplius by writing an account of his brother's death on an oar and throwing it into the sea. It is also said that Oeax advised Clytemnestra to kill Agamemnon in order to avenge Palamedes' death. He may himself have died at the hand of Orestes or Pylades.

Oebalus (*Οἴβαλος*)

1. A king of Sparta, the son of Cynortas or Perieres (1). In various traditions his legitimate children were Arena, or Icarius (1), Arne and Tyndareus, with Hippocoon his illegitimate son by the Nymph Stratonice.
2. A Teleboean hero, the son of Telon and the Nymph Sebethis. Oebalus established a kindgom at Capri; his son went over to Campania and founded a kingdom between Sarno and Nola. Later, he is mentioned among the allies of Turnus against Aeneas.

Oecles (*Οἰκλῆς*) The son of Antiphates (Table 1), although some authors postulate Mantius as his father. He married Hypermestra (3), and had several children: Iphianira, Polyboea and Amphiaraus. Oecles accompanied Heracles on the Trojan expedition (see HERACLES, III). He had to withstand the counter-attack staged by Laomedon. He was killed during the first assault. Oecles is said to have given refuge to his grandson ALCMAEON (1) when the latter, to avenge his father, killed his mother, Eriphyle.

Oedipus (*Οἰδίπους*) Oedipus belonged to the race of Cadmus (Table 3). His great-grandfather was Polydorus (1), his grandfather was Labdacus, his father was Laius. All Oedipus' ancestors ruled Thebes – with some interruptions – during the time before Laius came of age (see LYCUS (3)).

Oedipus' mother is called Epicaste in the *Odyssey*; in the tragedies she is JOCASTA. In the epic version of the Oedipus cycle, the hero's mother was called Eurygania (1), or Euryanassa. Another variant gives her the name Astymedusa, the daughter of Sthenelus (4).

At his birth, Oedipus was already marked by a curse. In the tradition represented by Sophocles, the curse took the form of an oracle which had declared that the child Jocasta was bearing 'would kill his father'. According to Aeschylus and Euripides, the oracle told Laius not to father any children, predicting that if he had a son, this son would kill him and cause a terrible succession of misfortunes which would bring ruin upon his house. Laius took no notice of this advice and Oedipus was conceived. To avoid the fulfilment of the oracle, Laius exposed the child as soon as it was born. He had the boy's ankles pierced, so as to join them together with a strap. It was the swelling caused by this wound that won the child its name of Oedipus (swollen foot). It is sometimes said that Oedipus was put in a basket and thrown into the sea; he was found by Periboea (4), wife of King Polybus (3), who took him in and raised him. At other times the child is said to have been exposed in a pot on Mount Cithaeron near Thebes, in the middle of winter. Corinthian shepherds who happened to be in the area picked him up and took him to their king, who they knew was childless and wanted children. In the version followed by Sophocles, Laius ordered a servant to expose the child, but the servant gave it to the shepherds. The name of Oedipus' stepfather is always Polybus, though he is sometimes king of Corinth, sometimes of Sicyon, Anthedon or Plataea.

Oedipus stayed at the court of Polybus, under the impression that he was the king's real son, but when he reached manhood he left his adoptive parents. The oldest version seems to be that Oedipus left in search of stolen horses and in the process unwittingly came across his real father, Laius. According to the tragedians, a Corinthian revealed to Oedipus that he was not the king's son but a foundling, in order to insult him. Oedipus questioned Polybus, who confirmed that this was the case. Oedipus then went to ask the Delphic oracle who his real parents were. On his travels Oedipus met Laius; some say at Laphystion, on the road that took Oedipus to Orchomenus in pursuit of the horses; others place it at the Potniai crossroads, or in Phocis at a crossroads where the roads from Daulis and Thebes meet. When Laius' herald Polyphontes (3) (or Polypoetes (4)) ordered Oedipus to make way for the king, Oedipus in his anger slew both Polyphontes and Laius. In one version Oedipus was on his way back from Delphi, where the oracle had told him that he would kill his father and marry his mother. Frightened, and believing himself to be the son of Polybus, he decided to go into voluntary exile – which is why he was on the road to Thebes.

When he arrived at Thebes, Oedipus met the SPHINX, a monster, half lion, half woman, who asked riddles of those who passed and ate those who could not answer them. Oedipus solved the riddle and killed the Sphinx, and so, by freeing the Thebans of the monster, earned himself the favour of the whole city. In their gratitude the Thebans gave him the hand of Laius' widow and made him king. It is also sometimes said that Jocasta's brother Creon (2) had been acting as regent since the death of Laius and had voluntarily conceded the throne to Oedipus to thank him for having avenged the death of his son Haemon (1) who had been devoured by the Sphinx.

Soon, however, the secret of Oedipus' birth came to light. In one version the scars on his ankles gave away his identity. In Sophocles' tragedy *Oedipus Rex* a plague is ravaging the city of Thebes, and Oedipus has sent Creon to consult the Delphic oracle. Creon brings back the Pythia's reply: the plague will not cease before Laius' death is avenged. Oedipus then curses the author of this crime. He asks the seer Tiresias who the guilty man is. Tiresias, who knows the whole story through his seer's powers, tries to avoid giving a reply. Oedipus thinks that Tiresias and Creon must be responsible for the murder. A quarrel arises between Oedipus and Creon. Jocasta arrives, and to reconcile them throws doubt on Tiresias' powers. She gives as proof of his incompetence the oracle which he had once pronounced on the child she had by Laius, whom the king had exposed, fearing that it would kill him. And yet, she says, Laius was killed by brigands at a crossroads. At this mention of a crossroads Oedipus asks for a description of Laius and the carriage in which he was riding. He also asks for details of the spot where the murders took place, and recalls from the countryside one of the servants who had been with Laius and had seen the murder; this shepherd is the one who had exposed Oedipus on Laius' orders. In the midst of all this a messenger arrives from Corinth to tell Oedipus of the death of Polybus and to ask him to come back and take the throne. Polybus had died of natural causes. However, the second part of the threat remains. Does Oedipus run the risk of incest with the wife of Polybus? To reassure him the Corinthian envoy tells him that he is a foundling and that Polybus was not his father. The account that is given of the finding of the child leaves Jocasta with no doubts: her own son has killed his father and she has committed incest with him. She flees into the palace and kills herself. Oedipus then blinds himself.

Sophocles' version was modified by Euripides in a lost play. In this play, Creon sets up a conspiracy against Oedipus, whom he thinks a usurper. He arranges to have him convicted of the murder of Laius and then to have him blinded, but Periboea, Polybus' wife, arrives with the news of her husband's death. From her account of the discovery of the baby Oedipus on Cithaeron, Jocasta realizes that her second husband is her own son. As in the preceding version, she commits suicide.

In the epic versions of the Oedipus legend Oedipus stays on the throne and dies in the course of a war against Erginus (1) and the Minyans. But in the works of the tragedians Oedipus is banished from the city and is accompanied by his daughter Antigone, as his two sons have refused to intervene in his favour and have as a result themselves been cursed by him. Oedipus eventually comes to the village of Colonus in Attica, where he dies. An oracle has delcared that the land which contains the tomb of Oedipus will be blessed by the gods. Creon and Polynices have separately tried to persuade Oedipus to go back to Thebes but Oedipus, having been hospitably received by King Theseus, decides that his ashes should stay in Attica.

Oeneus (*Οἰνεύς*) King of Calydon. His name is cognate with the Greek word for wine (*οἶνος*). Dionysus presented the first vine planted in Greece to him (see ALTHAEA). For another version see STAPHYLUS (1).

Oeneus was the son of Porthaon, or Portheus (1), and Euryte, or of Phytius (see ORESTHEUS). Oeneus' first wife was ALTHAEA. By her he had Toxeus (2), Thyreus, Clymenus (4) and Meleager; then two daughters, Gorge (1) and Deianeira, to whom Eurymede and Melanippe (4) are sometimes added. After the death of Althaea, who committed suicide for having killed her son Meleager in a fit of rage, Oeneus remarried. His second wife was PERIBOEA (6). By Periboea Oeneus had one son, Tydeus, the father of Diomedes (2).

There are three main episodes among the adventures attributed to Oeneus. He was the unwitting cause of the scourge sent by Artemis upon Calydon because he forgot to name her during the sacrifices to celebrate the end of harvesting (see MELEAGER). Also Heracles spent several years of his life at his palace after carrying out his twelve Labours. He was driven from it as the result of involuntary murder (see HERACLES, VI). In old age Oeneus was dispossessed of his kingdom by his nephews, the sons of Agrius. His grandson, Diomedes (2), helped by Alcmaeon (1), killed them, gave the kingdom of Calydon to Andraemon, husband of Gorge (1), who was one of Oeneus' sons-in-law, and took the old man away with him as his great age made him incapable of defending his kingdom. During the journey two of Agrius' sons, who had survived, killed Oeneus as he was passing through Arcadia. Oeneus also plays a part in some versions of the legend of AGAMEMNON and MENELAUS. He was said to have given hospitality to the two princes in their youth when they were driven from their kingdom.

Oenoclus (*Οἴνοκλος*) King of the Aenians. He led his people as far as Cyrrha, where he was stoned to death because the oracle of Apollo pronounced his sacrifice necessary in order to end the famine afflicting the land.

Oenomaus (*Οἰνόμαος*) A king of Pisa, in Elis; he was the son of Ares by one of the daughters of the river-god Asopus, called Harpinna (or Eurythoe), or by Sterope (1). His father is sometimes given as Hyperochus (2). By Sterope (or Evarete, daughter of Acrisius) he had a daughter, Hippodamia (1). For Hippodamia's marriage to Pelops (1), and the death of Oenomaus, see HIPPODAMIA (1).

Oenone (*Οἰνώνη*) Daughter of the river-god Cebren. She was loved by Paris and they had a son, CORYTHUS (3). Paris later abandoned her for Helen. Oenone told him that if he were wounded he would have to come back to her, since she alone would know how to heal him (in exchange for her viginity Apollo had given her the knowledge of medicine). When Paris was wounded by one of Philoctetes' arrows he remembered Oenone's promise and asked her to heal him. Angry at having been abandoned she refused to help, and Paris died. Repenting of her harshness, she hastened to Paris, expecting to find him still alive; when she learned of his death she killed herself.

Oenopion (*Οἰνοπίων*) The wine-drinker, a son of Ariadne and Dionysus or Theseus. He was ruler of Chios, to which he introduced red wine. Oenopion had several children: Evanthes, Staphylus (but see

STAPHYLUS (3)), Maron, Talus and a daughter, Merope (4), whose hand in marriage was sought by ORION. Oenopion, who did not want to give Orion his daughter, made him drunk and blinded him in his stupor.

Oenotrus (*Οἴνωτρος*) One of the sons of Lycaon (2). Discontented with the lot that had fallen to him when the Peloponnese was divided up between him and his brothers, Oenotrus went to Italy with his brother Peucetius, where Oenotrus gave his name to the Oenotrians. Another tradition makes Oenotrus a Sabine king. He was also sometimes thought to be the brother of King Italus (1).

Oeonus (*Οἰωνός*) The son of Licymnius and therefore the cousin of Heracles whom he accompanied on his expeditions in the Peloponnese. He was the victor in the running race in the Olympic Games, which Heracles founded. He was killed by Hippocoon and his sons; it was to avenge Oeonus' death that Heracles undertook his expedition against Sparta (see HERACLES, III).

Ogygus (*Ὤγυγος*)

1. According to Boeotian tradition Ogygus was one of the original native kings of the area. Other authors made him the son of the hero Boeotus, who had given his name to Boeotia; others made him the son of Poseidon and Alistra. Ogygus was king of the Ectenians, who were the first inhabitants of the earth in the days before the flood of Deucalion (1). One of the gates of Thebes was named after him. He had three daughters, who gave their names to Theban villages: Alalcomenia, Anlis and Thelxinoia. During his reign there was a first flood which covered Boeotia. A tradition made Ogygus the father of Cadmus and Phoenix (2).
2. Another Ogygus in the Eleusinian tradition was the father of the hero Eleusis.
3. Ogygus was also the name given, in certain obscure traditions, to the Titan king who together with all his subjects, was defeated by Zeus.

Oileus (*Οἰλεύς*) King of the Locrians of Opus, known principally for being the father of Ajax (1). He took part in the expedition of the Argonauts, and was wounded by a feather of one of the Stymphalian birds. Oileus also had an illegitimate son, Medon (1), by a woman named Rhene. He is sometimes also associated with Alcimache, the sister of Telamon.

Olympus (*Ὄλυμπος*)

1. The Greek world contained many mountains called Olympus: in Mysia, Cilicia, Elis, Arcadia and (the best-known) on the borders of Macedonia and Thessaly. Olympus was considered to be the home of the gods, particularly Zeus. Gradually, however, the home of the gods became distinct from the Thessalian mountain itself, and the word 'Olympus' was applied in a general way to the 'heavenly dwelling place'.
2. A son of Cres, the eponymous hero of Crete. Cronus gave the infant Zeus to him to look after, but Olympus later suggested to the Giants that they should dethrone Zeus. He was struck down with a

thunderbolt, but Zeus afterwards repented of having killed him, and gave his own name to the tomb of Olympus in Crete.

3. The first husband of Cybele, whose second husband was Iasion, though this was probably part of a euhemerist interpretation of the legend of Cybele, which was associated with the Mount Olympus in Mysia.

4. A famous flautist, said to be the father (or, more often, the son) and pupil of Marsyas. When Apollo slew Marsyas, Olympus buried him.

Olynthus (*Ὄλυνθος*) The eponymous hero of the Macedonian city. According to one tradition he was the son of King Strymon. During a hunt he was killed by a lion and buried on the same spot by his brother Brangas. According to another tradition Olynthus was the son of Heracles by the Nymph Bolbe.

Omphale (*Ὀμφάλη*) A queen of Lydia and daughter of King Iardanus. In other traditions she was the daughter or widow of King Tmolus, who bequeathed his kingdom to her.

Following the murder of Iphitus, Heracles went to Delphi to ask what he should do to be purified. When the oracle refused to answer Heracles seized the prophetic tripod, claiming that he would set up his own oracle elsewhere. Apollo intervened and a fight took place. Zeus separated the combatants with a thunderbolt, and the Pythia told Heracles that to purify himself he had to sell himself into slavery for three years. The money from the sale was to go to Iphitus' father, Eurytus (2). Heracles was bought by Omphale for three talents. Eurytus refused to accept the money. Omphale ordered Heracles to clear her kingdom of robbers and monsters: he fought with the CERCOPES, SYLEUS, LITYERSES, and the Itones. The latter were ravaging Omphale's lands, so Heracles captured and destroyed their city and enslaved its inhabitants. Admiring Heracles' exploits, Omphale freed him and married him. They had son, Lamon. In a variant tradition, Omphale immediately became Heracles' mistress and the period of enslavement was spent in ease and indolence. Heracles dressed in Lydian clothes, particularly in women's long dresses and spun linen thread at the queen's feet; the queen took to wearing Heracles' lion-skin and brandishing his club.

Oneiros (*Ὄνειρος*) A demon in the form of a dream sent by Zeus to deceive Agamemnon. See also MORPHEUS.

Opheltes (*Ὀφέλτης*) See HYPSIPYLE.

Ophion (*Ὀφίων*) Ophion and his female companion, Eurynome, reigned over the Titans before Cronus and Rhea, who eventually seized power and cast Ophion and Eurynome into Tartarus.

Ops The Roman goddess of Plenty. Ops, who had a temple dedicated to her on the Capitol, was said to be one of the Sabine deities brought to Rome by Titus Tatius.

Opus (*Ὀποῦς*) The eponymous

hero of the Locrian Opus. See LOCRUS and Table 8.

Orcus In Roman popular belief Orcus was the spirit that presided over death, barely distinguishable from Hades itself as the realm of the dead. He appears in funerary paintings in Etruscan tombs as a bearded, hairy giant. Gradually this spirit was absorbed into the Greek pantheon and Orcus was used as another name for Pluto or Dis Pater.

Orestes (*Ὀρέστης*) The son of Agamemnon and Clyyemnestra (Table 2). By the period of the Homeric epics Orestes appears as the avenger of his father's death (although Homer does not mention the murder of Clytemnestra by her son). It is in the tragedians that Orestes became a major figure.

Telephus, having been wounded by ACHILLES, was told by an oracle that he could be healed only by the rust from Achilles' same lance. So he went to Aulis, where the Greek army had gathered. He was captured by soldiers and treated as a spy. To save himself he seized the little Orestes and threatened to kill him. In this way he managed to obtain a hearing, and his wound was healed.

When Agamemnon was assassinated by Aegisthus and Clytemnestra, Orestes was saved by his sister Electra (3), who secretly took him to Strophius (1), the child's uncle who lived in Phocis. Strophius brought up Orestes with his own son, Pylades. Thus began the friendship which bound Orestes and Pylades together. (There are other versions of Orestes' escape from massacre. Sometimes a nursemaid, a tutor or an old family retainer is credited with having rescued him.)

Orestes was ordered by Apollo to avenge his father's death by killing Aegisthus and Clytemnestra. (According to Sophocles, Electra urged him to avenge Agamemnon; Apollo said that this act of vengeance was permissible.) Orestes went to the tomb of Agamemnon at Argos and offered a dedicatory lock of his hair. Electra visited the tomb and recognized her brother's hair. Euripides substituted the intervention of an old man; Sophocles brought into the story a gold ring which once belonged to Agamemnon and which Orestes showed to his sister.

Orestes presented himself to Clytemnestra in the guise of a traveller charged by Strophius to bring news of the death of Orestes and to ask whether his ashes should be brought to Argos. Clytemnestra was overjoyed and sent for Aegisthus. As soon as Aegisthus arrived at the palace he was felled by Orestes. Clytemnestra ran to him and found her son, sword in hand. She begged him to spare the woman who suckled him, and Orestes was about to yield when Pylades reminded him of Apollo's instructions. Orestes killed her. In Euripides Orestes killed Aegisthus while the latter was offering a sacrifice to the Nymphs.

Orestes went mad. He was haunted by the Erinyes, who pursued him from the very day of Clytemnestra's funeral. He sought asylum and absolution. Aeschylus says that, on Apollo's instruction, Orestes fled to Delphi and was purified by Apollo himself. Purification did not free him from the Erinyes, however: that could happen only after a formal trial, which took place in Athens, on the spot where the Areopagus was later sited.

Traditions vary as to the identity of the prosecutor. Some say it was the Erinyes in person; others that it was Tyndareus, the father of Clytemnestra; others that it was Erigone (2); yet others that it was Perileus, a cousin of Clytemnestra. The judges were equally divided on the verdict. Consequently Orestes was acquitted, for Athene, who was presiding over the court, gave her casting vote to those advocating acquittal.

When Orestes was in Athens the 'Day of the Jugs' originated. During the Athenian festival of the Anthesteria King Demophon (2) (or Pandion (2)), was embarrassed by Orestes' arrival. The king did not want to let Orestes take part in the festival or enter the temple but on the other hand he did not want to insult him. So he closed the temple and served, on separate tables outside, a jug of wine for each of those present. This gave rise to the Festival of the Jugs.

There was another tradition which placed the trial of Orestes in the Argolid. Oeax and Tyndareus brought Orestes to trial before the citizens of Argos, who condemned him to death, leaving to him the choice of method, whereas the people of Mycenae merely condemned him to banishment. The Aeschylean version is far more widespread.

After Orestes' acquittal Apollo said that he would be rid of his madness if he went to Tauris in search of the statue of Artemis. This myth was used by Euripides in *Iphigenia in Tauris*. When they arrived in Tauris, Orestes and Pylades were imprisoned by the inhabitants, who sacrificed all strangers to their goddess. They were brought before Thoas (3), the king of the region, and then taken to IPHIGENIA, the priestess of Artemis. She realized who they were, and decided to help them to steal the statue of Artemis and then to flee with them. She persuaded Thoas that she could not sacrifice the strangers until she had purified both victims and statue in sea water. Iphigenia went to the seashore with Orestes and Pylades, induced the guards to withdraw, on the pretext that the purificatory rites must remain secret, and then boarded her brother's ship along with Pylades and the statue. But Poseidon cast the ship back on to the shore, and Thoas was about to recapture them when Athene manifested herself and ordered him to withdraw. Orestes, Pylades and Iphigenia all sailed to Attica, where they built a temple to Artemis. (See also CHRYSES (2).)

The last element in the Orestes legend concerns his settling in the Argolid and his marriage. He married his cousin Hermione after the death of her husband, NEOPTOLEMUS. They had a son called Tisamenus (1). Orestes reigned over Argos, where he succeeded Cylarabes, who died without an heir, and also at Sparta, as successor to Menelaus. He died at the age of ninety, after seventy years on the throne. He was paid divine honours.

Orestes' tomb was believed by some to be at Tegea; in Rome it was said that Orestes died at Aricia (one of the places where the cult of the Taurian Artemis was said to survive) and that his bones had been transferred to Rome and buried beneath the Temple of Saturn.

Orestheus (*Ὀρεσθεύς*) A king of Aetolia. One of his bitches gave birth to a piece of wood. Orestheus had it buried and from this stump there grew a vine bearing huge grapes. Impressed by this miracle, Orestheus gave his son the name Phytius (derived from the Greek verb 'to grow'). Phytius was the father of King Oeneus.

Orion (*Ὠρίων*) A giant huntsman, the son of Euryale and Poseidon or of Hyrieus. He was also said to be a son of Gaia. From Poseidon he received the gift of walking on the sea. He was very handsome and prodigiously strong. He married Side (2), who was so proud of her beauty that she claimed to outshine Hera; the goddess hurled her into Tartarus. Orion went to Chios, where Oenopion asked him to rid the island of wild beasts. There Orion fell in love with Oenopion's daughter, Merope (4). Her father was opposed to the match. Some versions of the myth say that Orion became drunk and tried to rape Merope, others that Oenopion got Orion drunk and put out his eyes while he was asleep. Orion then went to Hephaestus' forge and, taking a child called Cedalion on his shoulders, asked the boy to lead him in the direction of the rising sun. Immediately Orion's sight returned. He tried to take his revenge upon Oenopion but failed, for Hephaestus had made him an underground chamber, where he took refuge.

Aurora (EOS) fell in love with Orion, and carried him off to Delos. However Orion was killed by Artemis, either because he challenged her to a discus competition or because he tried to rape her attendant, Opis. In still other accounts Orion tried to rape Artemis herself, and the goddess set a scorpion on him, which bit him in the head. The scorpion was changed into a constellation, as was Orion.

Orithya (*Ὀρείθυια*) One of the daughters of Erechtheus, king of Athens. She was abducted by BOREAS.

Ornytus (*Ὄρνυτος*) An Arcadian hero (also called Teuthis) who led a contingent of Arcadians to join the Greek side at Troy. When the winds remained unfavourable at Aulis, Ornytus decided to return home. The goddess Athena asked him to stay. But he became angry and wounded the goddess in the thigh. Then he returned to his city. There the goddess appeared to him in a dream with her wounded thigh, and he was instantly struck down with a sickness; the city fell victim to a famine. The oracle at Dodona said that the remedy consisted in raising a statue to Athena, complete with the wound in her thigh dressed with a purple bandage.

Orontes (*Ὀρόντης*)

1. A Hindu hero. He commanded an army for the Hindu king, Deriades, at the time of Dionysus' expedition to India. He was a giant 20 cubits tall. He was wounded by Dionysus and killed himself. His body was carried away by the waters of the Orontes, which took the hero's name. In Roman times a long plaster

sarcophagus was found in the Orontes, containing a human skeleton of enormous size. The oracle at Clarus affirmed that this was the body of the hero Orontes.

2. The god of the River Orontes, who was a son of Oceanus and Tethys. He fell in love with the Nymph Meliboea (1), and the river overflowed its banks, flooding the countryside, until it was brought under control by Heracles.

3. A Lycian king who was shipwrecked with Aeneas.

Orpheus (*'Ορφεύς*) Orpheus was the son of Oeager. His mother is usually said to have been the Muse Calliope, occasionally Polhymnia or, more rarely, Menippe, daughter of Thamyris. Orpheus is Thracian in origin. He lived in a region bordering on Olympus, and is often depicted singing there in Thracian dress.

Orpheus is the 'type' of the singer, musician and poet. He plays the lyre and the cithara, which he is often said to have invented. If not given this distinction, he is said to have increased the number of strings on the instrument from seven to nine 'because of the number of the Muses'. Orpheus could sing so sweetly that wild beasts would follow him about; trees and plants would bow down to him and the wildest of men would become gentle.

Orpheus took part in the expedition of the ARGONAUTS. During a storm he calmed the crew and stilled the waves with his singing. As he alone was an initiate of the Samothracian Mysteries, he persuaded his companions to become initiates too. He sang while the Sirens were trying to seduce the Argonauts, and he managed to restrain the latter by surpassing the Sirens in sweetness.

The most famous myth about Orpheus is that of his descent into the Underworld to fetch his wife, Eurydice (1). Eurydice was a Nymph (a Dryad) or a daughter of Apollo. One day, as she was walking beside a river in Thrace, she was pursued by ARISTAEUS, who desired her. But she stepped on a snake which bit her, and she died. Orpheus, who was inconsolable, went down to the Underworld to bring her back. With the music of his lyre he charmed the monsters of Hades and the Underworld gods: IXION's wheel ceased to turn; SISYPHUS' stone remained poised without support; TANTALUS forgot his hunger and thirst; even the DANAIDES forgot about trying to fill their sieve. Hades and Persephone agreed to restore Eurydice to her husband because he had shown such proof of love. But they set a condition: Orpheus was to return to the light of day, followed by his wife, without looking back at her before they left the Underworld. Orpheus had almost reached daylight when a terrible doubt seized him. Was Eurydice really behind him? He turned around. Eurydice died a second time. Orpheus tried to rescue her again, but the entry to the Underworld was barred to him. He had to return to the human world unconsoled.

It was generally said that Orpheus was killed by the women of Thrace, who resented his fidelity to Eurydice as an insult to themselves. It was also said that Orpheus wanted nothing to do with women, and surrounded himself with young men: he was the inventor of pederasty and his lover was Calais, son of Boreas. Some authorities said that Orpheus instituted mysteries based on his experiences in the Underworld but forbade the admission of women. The men met him in a locked house, leaving their weapons outside. One night the women took the weapons and killed Orpheus. Another version says that when Aphrodite quarrelled with Persephone about Adonis, Orpheus' mother, Calliope, adjudicated; she decided that each goddess should keep Adonis for alternate parts of the year. Aphrodite was angered by this decision and made the women of Thrace fall in love with Orpheus, but as none was willing to stand aside in favour of any of the others they all tore him apart. When the Thracian women had torn his body to pieces they threw his remains into the river, which bore them down to the sea. The poet's head and his lyre arrived at Lesbos, whose inhabitants paid funerary honours to the poet. This is why the island of Lesbos excelled in lyric poetry. In other traditions his tomb was located at the mouth of the River Meles in Asia Minor, at Leibethra in Thessaly, or in Pieria.

After the murder of Orpheus a plague spread throughout Thrace. The oracle declared that the inhabitants would have to seek Orpheus' head in order to pay it due honour. Some fishermen found the head at the mouth of the Meles. It was bloody and still singing.

After Orpheus' death his lyre became a constellation. The soul of Orpheus was taken to the Elysian Fields where, dressed in a long white robe, it continued to sing for the benefit of the Blessed Ones. It was around this myth that Orphic theology formed. Orpheus was thought to have brought back from his descent into the Underworld information both about how to reach the land of the Blessed Ones and about how to avoid the obstacles which threaten the soul after death. A large number of poems are attributed to him, ranging from popular verses that people would inscribe on plaques and bury with the dead to hymns, a theogony and a long epic, the *Argonautica*. Orpheus was sometimes said to have shared with Dionysus the founding of the Eleusinian Mysteries.

A tradition recorded by various authors makes Orpheus the ancestor of Homer and Hesiod.

Orthopolis (*Ὀρθόπολις*) The son of Plemnaeus, the king of Sicyon. None of this king's previous children had survived birth: as soon as they gave their first cry they died. Demeter took pity on him, lifted the curse and reared the king's only surviving child. Orthopolis, the boy thus saved, had a daughter, Chrysorthe.

Orthrus (*Ὄρθρος*) Geryon's monstrous dog, which Heracles killed when he made off with Geryon's flocks. He was the offspring of Typhon and Echidna and therefore brother of Cerberus. By mating with Echidna, he fathered the Theban Sphinx. He also allegedly fathered Phix, a Boeotian monster, and the Nemean lion. Sometimes Orthrus is said to have several heads, sometimes a snake's body.

Osinius A prince of Clusium in Italy, and part of the contingent sent to Aeneas by Tarchon, king of the Etruscans, as an ally against Turnus.

Otreus (*Ὀτρεύς*) King of Phrygia, who came to Priam's aid against the Amazons. Aphrodite passed herself off as his daughter when she gave herself to Anchises.

Otus (*Ὦτος*) See ALOADAE.

Oxylus (*Ὄξυλος*)

1. A son of Ares by Protogenia (3).
2. The son of Haemon (4), the son of Thoas (4). Apollodorus, who makes him the son of Andraemon, says that his mother was Deianeira's sister Gorge (1). He is therefore related to the Heraclids, being the cousin of Hyllus, the son of Deianeira.

It is possible that Oxylus (1) and (2) are the same person. Both are descended from Aetolus and, through him, from Endymion.

Oxylus accidentally killed his brother, Thermus, with a discus and had to leave Aetolia. He took refuge in Elis. When his exile was over, he set out for Aetolia. At that time the Heraclids were expecting to find a guide 'with three eyes' who would lead them into the Peloponnese. Oxylus, who was either one-eyed himself (having lost the other as a result of an arrow wound) or riding a horse or mule which was one-eyed, rode towards them. They asked him to take them to their 'promised land' and Oxylus agreed. He brought them their victory but claimed as a reward the kingdom of Elis, which had belonged to his ancestors. Fearing, however, that if the Heraclids saw how beautiful Elis was they would be loath to give it to him, he led them through Arcadia. When the Heraclids had divided up the conquered lands among themselves Oxylus presented himself at the frontiers of Elis with his Aetolians. As the forces of the two parties were equal it was decided to settle the matter by single combat. The Eleans chose as their champion an archer called Degmenus. The Aetolians chose a sling-thrower, Pyraechmes, who won the contest.

Oxylus allowed the Eleans to retain their lands but installed Aetolian colonists, who intermarried with them. Under Oxylus' rule the city of Elis became strikingly beautiful, and usury was forbidden within his territories. He was also a protector of the Achaeans, who were ill-treated by the invading Dorians (the Heraclids). The Olympic Games, founded by Heracles, had fallen into abeyance. Oxylus restored them. In some traditions he was said to be their founder.

Oxylus married Pieria. His son Laias succeeded to the throne.

3. The son of Oreius. He married his own sister, Hamadryas, and fathered on her the tree Nymphs Carya, Balanus, Crania, Morea, Aeigirus, Ptelea, Ampelus and Syce, whose names evoke various trees.

Oxynius (*Ὀξύνιος*) Oxynius and Scamandrius (1) were two sons of Hector whom Priam had sent for safety to Lydia when Troy fell. After the destruction of Troy, Aeneas, who had taken refuge on Mount Ida, reigned over the country, but soon Oxynius and Scamandrius returned to claim possession of their grandfather's kingdom.

Oxyntes (Ὀξύντης) A king of Athens, the son of Demophon (2). His sons were Apheidas and Thymoetes (2). Apheidas inherited the crown, but was dethroned and murdered by his brother.

P

Pactolus (*Πακτωλός*) The god of the river of that name in Asia Minor. During the Mysteries of Aphrodite he unwittingly deflowered his own sister. When he realized what he had done he threw himself into the River Chrysorhoas (the 'golden stream', so called because its water has spangles of gold in it). In memory of this suicide the river afterwards took the name of Pactolus (see also MIDAS).

Paean (*Παιάν*) 'Paean' is frequently no more than the ritual epithet of Apollo the healer. In the Homeric poems, however, an independent god of healing named Paean or Paeon appears. It was he who took care of Hades when the latter was wounded.

Paeon (*Παίων*)

1. The eponym of the Paeonians. According to Pausanias he is one of the brothers of Endymion and therefore a brother of Aetolus, Epeius (1) and Eurycyde (1).
2. A son of Antilochus and a grandson of Nestor. His children were driven out of Messenia at the time of the return of the Heraclids. With his cousins he settled in Athens and from him was descended the Athenian clan of the Paeonids.
3. See PAEAN.

Palaemon (*Παλαίμων*)

1. 'The Wrestler', a son of Heracles, so called because of a wrestling match fought by his father.
2. One of the Argonauts in the list given by Apollodorus. Palaemon was the son of Aetolus (or of Hephaestus). He owed his name to the wrestling skills of his father.
3. The son of Ino-Leucothea (1). In his human childhood this Palaemon was called MELICERTES; his father was Athamas. On his mother's side Palaemon was the first cousin of Dionysus (Table 3). After the suicide of his mother, Melicertes became the sea-god Palaemon and Ino the goddess LEUCOTHEA (1). The Megarians said that though the body of the mother was cast up on to the shore near their city and buried by the daughters of Cleson, the body of the child was borne by a dolphin as far as the Isthmus of Corinth. There it was recovered by Sisyphus who buried it, raised an altar to the boy near a pine tree and paid divine honours under the name of Palaemon to mark the child's divine patronage of the Isthmian games.

At Rome Palaemon was identified with the god Portunus.

Palamedes (*Παλαμήδης*) One of the sons of Nauplius (2) and Clymene (4) or Hesione (4). His two brothers were Oeax and Nausimedon. He appeared among the pupils taught by the Centaur Chiron. At the time of the abduction of Helen he consoled Menelaus (to whom he was related: see Table 2). In certain accounts he took part in an embassy to Troy to try to negotiate a peaceful settlement of the war. He was even supposed to have carried a letter to Helen from Clytemnestra asking her to come back to her husband. In a second embassy, sent from Tenedos, Palamedes appears alongside Menelaus, Odysseus, Diomedes (2) and Acamas (3).

As Helen's former suitors were preparing to go to Troy, Odysseus tried to escape his obligation. When Menelaus and Palamedes came to fetch him he pretended to be mad: he harnessed his plough to an ass and an ox, yoked together, and started sowing salt. But to force Odysseus to reveal that he was quite sane, Palamedes placed Telemachus in front of the plough. Odysseus stopped his team before it killed the child. A variant of this tradition said that Palamedes threatened Telemachus with his sword. Odysseus never forgave Palamedes for seeing through his ruse and thus obliging him to join the expedition of Menelaus and Agamemnon.

Palamedes took part in the search for Achilles, who was hiding on Scyros at the court of Lycomedes. Similarly, Menelaus sent Palamedes as herald to summon Oenopion and Cinyras. He revealed the true identity of Epipole of Carystos, the daughter of Trachion, who had dressed up as a man in order to sail with the Greek army. She was stoned to death.

Palamedes raised the morale of the Greek soldiers when they were disquieted by an eclipse; he tried to avert the plague which threatened the Greek camp; and he foresaw the arrival in the camp of a wolf (Apollo's animal) which had come from the forests of Mount Ida. He also guarded against a drought by sending for the 'Vine-growers', the three daughters of Oenopion.

Eventually Odysseus contrived his revenge. In one version Odysseus, having captured a Trojan, forced him to write a letter, supposedly from Priam, alleging that Palamedes had offered to betray the Greeks. Then Odysseus bribed one of Palamedes' slaves to hide gold under his master's mattress. Finally, he dropped the letter in the camp. It was found by Agamemnon. Palamedes was arrested and stoned to death. Another version told how Odysseus and Diomedes (2) persuaded Palamedes to descend into a pit and then stoned him to death. The death was avenged, however, by Nauplius (2).

Tradition credited Palamedes with a great number of inventions, including one or more letters of the alphabet, the order of the alphabet, the invention of numbers, the use of coinage, the calculation of the lengths of months according to the movement of the stars, the game of draughts, the game of dice and the game of five-stones.

Palans A Roman hero, the son of Hercules and Dyna, the daughter of Evander (3). He died while still young, and his grandfather buried him on the hill to which he gave his name (see also PALLAS (5)).

Palici (*Παλικοί*) Twin gods, sometimes said to have been the sons of Zeus by Thaleia the daughter of Hephaestus, sometimes the sons of Zeus by Aetna. While she was pregnant Thaleia, fearing Hera's jealousy, hid in the earth, and when the time came the twin boys emerged from the ground, which explains their name 'the Returners' (from the Greek πάλιν, 'again'). Their place of worship was close to the Lago di Naftia, not far from Leontini, and was the site of various volcanic phenomena. The Sicilians swore their solemn oath by the Palici: the oath would be written on a tablet which was thrown into the lake. If the tablet floated, the oath was sincere; if it sank the oath was clearly invalid. It was said that the Palici struck blind all liars who falsely called upon their name.

Pales A guardian spirit of flocks who was worshipped at Rome. Sometimes Pales is male, sometimes female. In his or her honour the festival of the Parilia was celebrated on 21 April, when the shepherds lit huge straw and brushwood fires through which they leapt. The day of the Parilia was said to be the anniversary of the foundation of Rome by Romulus. The name of Pales was also said to be connected with that of the Palatine.

Palanto According to Varro, the daughter of a Hyperborean and beloved of Hercules. She bore him a son, who became King Latinus.

Palinurus (*Παλίνουρος*) Aeneas' pilot. When the Trojan fleet left Sicily for Italy Venus promised her son a successful voyage. Only one man's life would be lost, she said, and his death would ensure the safety of all the others. The man was Palinurus, who was steering the ship at night when, as Virgil describes it, the god of sleep afflicted him with an irresistible weariness. He fell into the sea. Everyone aboard was asleep: no one heard his cry as he fell. When Aeneas awoke he wept for him.

When he arrived in the Underworld, Aeneas saw on the banks of the Styx the crowd of the unburied dead. Among them was Palinurus, who told Aeneas that for three days and nights he had swum until he reached the Italian coast. But he was immediately murdered by the barbaric inhabitants of the area, who left his body at the sea's edge. Palinurus asked Aeneas, when he got back to the world above, to go to Velia and to pay him his due funeral honours. The Sibyl then promised Palinurus that the local inhabitants would collect up his body, pay it divine honours and give his name to a local headland.

Palladium (*Παλλάδιον*) A divine statue, endowed with magical properties, which was thought to represent the goddess Pallas (1). The Palladium does not appear in the Homeric poems. It was a standing deity, with the rigidity of the old *xoana* (idols from the archaic era). It had the power to guarantee the safety of the city which possessed it and worshipped it, and for ten years it preserved Troy. Several other cities then claimed to possess it, which conferred on them a reputation for inviolability.

Traditions all agree that the Palladium had a divine origin, but the details vary. In Apollodorus the goddess Athena was brought up as a child by the god Triton, who had a daughter named Pallas (2). The two little girls practised warfare together, but one day they quarrelled. Just as Pallas was about to strike Athena,

Zeus was afraid for his daughter and placed himself between them. He held the aegis before Pallas, who was frightened, failed to parry the blow that Athena was aiming at her and fell, mortally wounded. To make amends Athena carved a statue in the likeness of her friend, equipped it with the aegis which had indirectly caused her death, and placed her at Zeus' side, paying honours to her as to a goddess. The statue remained on Olympus until Zeus tried to rape Electra (2), who sought refuge by the statue. Zeus hurled the Palladium down from Olympus, and it fell in the Troad on the hill of ATE. At that time Ilus (2) was founding Troy (then called Ilion). The statue either fell immediately in front of his tent or into the unfinished temple of Athena, and of its own accord occupied the ritual position for the cult. This was taken as a sign that the gods approved of the foundation of the city. The Palladium was three cubits tall; its feet were joined together; in its right hand, which was raised, it held a spear, in its left a distaff and spindle. Other traditions say that the Palladium was carved out of the bone of the shoulder blade of Pelops (1), and that it was stolen from Sparta along with Helen.

Versions vary concerning the adventures of the statue. DARDANUS was said to have taken it with him to Samothrace, where he gave it to his father-in-law, Teucer (1). It was also said that the Trojans had a second Palladium made, identical with the first, to deceive robbers. They placed the false Palladium in the sanctuary, while the real one was kept in the temple treasury. In the epic cycles it was said that Helenus, when captured by Odysseus, had affirmed that Troy could be captured only if the Palladium was removed from the city. So, with the help of Diomedes (2) he got into the citadel by night. In some versions Odysseus left Diomedes on watch while he disguised himself as a beggar. Recognized by Helen despite his disguise, he succeeded, with her help, in carrying off the Palladium. The more common version states that, in order to scale the wall, Diomedes climbed on Odysseus' shoulders, but once on the top of the wall he refused to pull him up after him. On the return journey Odysseus tried to take the Palladium from Diomedes so as to receive all the credit for the theft. He walked behind Diomedes and was about to murder him when the shadow cast by his sword (it being full moon) warned Diomedes, who turned round and unsheathed his own sword just in time. Some traditions record that the two heroes got into the city through a sewer. Others say that Theano, the wife of the Greek sympathizer Antenor, handed the Palladium over to the Greeks. Other legends claim that the real Palladium stayed in Troy and that Aeneas rescued it just in time from the temple of Athena and carried it off to Ida, then later to Italy. This Palladium was taken to Rome and kept in the temple of Vesta. At Rome the safety of the city was linked with the safekeeping of the statue.

When AJAX (1) tried to abduct Cassandra, it was the Palladium to which she clung. Ajax pulled over the statue, which only priestesses had the right to touch. He thus drew down on himself the wrath of Athena. In this version the true Palladium stayed at Troy until the very end, Odysseus and Diomedes having stolen a false one. Both the statue, which Ajax also abducted, and Cassandra were restored to Agamemnon.

As for traditions where the Palladium was not in the keeping of Aeneas, some claim that Diomedes took it off to southern Italy and later gave it to Aeneas when he came to settle in Latium. Pausanias writes that the Argives claimed that Agamemnon took the Palladium with him to Argos (on the Argive Palladium, see also LEAGRUS).

Finally, the Athenians said that Demophon (2) was given the statue by Diomedes. Knowing that Agamemnon coveted it Demophon entrusted it to Buzyges, who took it back to Athens and had a copy of the statue made which he placed in his own tent. After the fall of Troy Agamemnon came to Demophon's tent and asked for the Palladium. After a prolonged struggle, Demophon appeared to capitulate and gave the king the worthless statue. Another version said that Diomedes went ashore at night at Phaleron in Attica but, not knowing precisely where he was, attacked the Athenians. Demophon came to his subjects' aid, killed many of Diomedes' men and captured the Palladium. But on his way back Demophon's horse knocked down an Athenian, who died. Demophon was brought before a special court which took the name of the Court of the Palladium and which, at a later date, continued to sit in judgement in cases of this kind.

Pallantidae (*Παλλάντιδαι*) The fifty sons of Pallas (7). They thought that their uncle Aegeus had no children (their cousin Theseus was not brought up in Athens), and hoped to share in his succession. When Theseus arrived from Troezen (see THESEUS, II) and was acknowledged by his father, they contested their cousin's legitimacy, but the Athenians overruled their objections and made Theseus king. The Pallantidae rebelled. They split into two groups: one attacked the city from the direction of the Sphettus; the other laid an ambush at Gargettus. But a herald called Leus revealed their plan to Theseus, who attacked and massacred the group waiting in ambush. The others scattered and the war was over.

Pallas (*Πάλλας*)

1. A stock epithet of Athena, who was frequently called Pallas Athena.
2. A daughter of the god Triton. Athena was brought up with her in childhood, and accidentally killed her (see PALLADIUM).
3. A Titan, son of Crius and Eurybia and brother of Perses and Astraeus (Table 8). According to Hesiod's *Theogony* he coupled with Styx, who bore him Zelos, Nike, Cratos and Bia (Zeal, Victory, Power and Force). Other traditions make him the father of Eos, who is usually considered to be the daughter of Hyperion and THEIA.
4. One of the sons of Lycaon (2). He is the eponym of the Arcadian city of Pallantion and is sometimes said to be the grandfather of Evander (3). According to Dionysius of Halicarnassus, Pallas had a daughter named Chryse, whom he gave in marriage to DARDANUS. Pallas gave his son-in-law the care of various

Arcadian deities, including the PALLADIUM. In this way the mythographers established a link between Rome and Troy, even before the foundation of Rome, since the eponymous hero of the Palatine (see PALLAS) was the nephew of the first queen of Troy (see DARDANUS).

5. In the *Aeneid* Virgil introduces Pallas, the son of Evander (3) and the eponym of the Palatine. Pallas was the companion of Aeneas in the war against Turnus. He was killed by Turnus. There was also a tradition that Pallas himself buried Evander on the Palatine and therefore died after his father. This Pallas can be compared with PALANS, who died young and gave his name to the Palatine.

6. A giant, the father of ATHENA (according to some authors), who tried to rape his own daughter. Athena killed him, removed his skin and dressed herself in it. This Pallas had wings, which Athena fixed to her feet.

7. The youngest son of Pandion (2). With his fifty sons, the PALLANTIDAE, he rebelled against Theseus. All fifty brothers were slain by Theseus.

Pallene (*Παλλήνη*)

1. The daughter of Sithon, king of the Thracian Chersonese, and of either Anchiroe (or Anchinoe) or of the Nymph Mendeis.

Sithon did not want to give Pallene in marriage to any of her numerous suitors. He forced them to fight against him and killed them. But finally he offered her as the prize in a contest to be fought by single combat between Dryas (2) and Clitus (2). Pallene was in love with Clitus, and wept bitterly. Her old teacher noticed her sorrow and succeeded in making her confess its cause. He bribed Dryas' charioteer to take out the axle-pin which secured his master's wheel. Dryas was killed. Sithon found out that Pallene was implicated in the treachery and decided to punish her with death. He had a funeral pyre built for the body of Dryas and persuaded his daughter to climb upon it. However, either Aphrodite appeared in person to forestall the murder, or heavy rainfall prevented the pyre from catching fire. The will of the gods having been made clear, Pallene was pardoned and she married Clitus. She gave her name to the peninsula of Pallene, in the Thracian Chersonese.

2. One of the daughters of ALCYONEUS (1).

Pamphos (*Πάμφως*) According to Pausanias Pamphos was a very early poet who wrote hymns for the Athenians.

Pamphylus (*Πάμφυλος*) One of the sons of Aegimius, who gave his name to a Dorian tribe, the Pamphylians. He fought on the Heraclid side against Tisamenus (1). He married Orsobia, daughter of Deiphontes.

Pan (*Πάν*) A god of shepherds and flocks. He was depicted as half-man half-animal, with a reed pipe, a shepherd's crook and a branch of pine or a crown of pine leaves. He had a wrinkled face with a very prominent chin. On his forehead were two horns. His body was hairy; the lower parts were those of a male goat. His feet had cloven hooves. He was a swift runner and climbed rocks with ease; he was adept at hiding in the bushes, where he crouched to watch the Nymphs or to sleep at midday. It was dangerous to disturb him at these times. He was fond of cool streams and woodland shade. Pan had considerable sexual energy; he pursued Nymphs and boys, but settled for solitary pleasures if his amorous ambitions were frustrated. Hellenistic poets often evoke him in pastoral idylls.

Pan is not mentioned in the Homeric poems, but a Homeric Hymn says that he was the son of Hermes by a daughter of Dryops. Pan's mother was frightened by her monstrous offspring, but Hermes wrapped him in a hare-pelt and carried him off to Olympus. The gods were delighted with the child, especially Dionysus (in whose company Pan frequently appears), and he was given the name Pan because he made them all feel happy (in popular etymology Pan is derived from the Greek *pan*, meaning 'all').

For the genealogy which claims that Penelope was the mother of Pan, see PENELOPE. Pan was also said to be either a son of Zeus and Hybris, or of Zeus and Callisto (1), and hence the brother of Arcas. Sometimes he is made out to be the son of Aether and the Nymph Oenoe; or of Cronus and Rhea, of Uranus and Ge, or of a shepherd called Crathis and a nanny-goat.

Pan loved the Nymph Echo and obtained the favours of the goddess Selene by giving her a herd of white oxen.

At Rome Pan is sometimes identified with the god FAUNUS or with SILVANUS.

Panacea (*Πανάκεια*) A goddess who symbolizes the power of healing through herbs. She is said to be one of the daughters of Ascelpius and EPIONE. She had two sisters, Iaso (the Healer) and Hygieia, and two brothers, MACHAON and Podalirius.

Pancratis (*Παγκράτις*) The daughter of Aloeus and Iphimedia and therefore a sister of the Aloadae (see IPHIMEDIA).

Pandareos (*Πανδάρεως*) When Rhea, fearing that Cronus would eat the baby Zeus, hid him in a mountain cave in Crete, she gave him a nanny-goat to suckle him and a magic golden dog to guard him. Once Cronus had been dethroned, the dog was assigned to guarding the sanctuary of Zeus on Crete. Pandareos stole the dog, took it to Mount Sipyle in Lydia, and entrusted it to Tantalus. When he asked Tantalus for his dog back, Tantalus swore on oath that he had never seen it. To punish them, Zeus changed Pandareos into a rock and buried Tantalus under Mount Sipyle.

In another version the dog had been entrusted to Tantalus, but it was Hermes who came to fetch it for Zeus. Tantalus swore that he had never seen the dog, but Hermes found the animal. Zeus then punished Tantalus as in the previous version. Pandareos was afraid when he learned what had happened to Tantalus and fled with his wife, Harmothoe, and his daughters. He went to Athens and then to Sicily. Zeus killed both him and his wife; his daughters were abducted by the Harpies.

The *Odyssey* refers to this myth. In her despair Penelope wished that she could die swiftly, like the daughters of Pandareos. After the death of their parents the gods were sorry for these girls: Aphrodite brought them food, Hera gave them wisdom and beauty, Artemis endowed them with elegance, and Athena equipped them with manual dexterity. However, when Aphrodite returned to Olympus to ask Zeus to find them suitable husbands, the Harpies carried the girls off and gave them as slaves to the Erinyes.

Traditions vary concerning the daughters of Pandareos; sometimes there are two: Camiro and Clytia, or Cleothera and Merope (3). Sometimes there are three: Cleothera, Merope (3) and Aedon. (For this legend see AEDON.)

Pandarus (*Πάνδαρος*) He came from the city of Zeleia. Apollo himself had taught him archery. Despite his father's advice, Pandarus went to Troy as a foot soldier, refusing to take a chariot and horses. When Paris and Menelaus were fighting in single combat, the goddess Athena incited Pandarus to fire an arrow at Menelaus. In this way the truce was broken and the war restored. Pandarus then fought Diomedes (2) but was killed. His death was thought to be punishment for his treachery in breaking the truce.

Pandion (*Πανδίων*)

1. The son of Erichthonius and Praxithea. He married his maternal aunt, Zeuxippe, and had four children by her: Erechtheus, Butes (2), Procne and Philomela. He was also credited with a bastard called Oeneus (not the same as the Calydonian hero). To his reign was dated the arrival in Attica of Dionysus and Demeter.

Pandion arranged Procne's marriage with Tereus, in exchange for which Tereus committed himself to helping Pandion in his battles with the Thebans. Pandion died of grief as a result of the misfortunes of his daughters (see PHILOMELA). After Pandion's death Erechtheus received the throne, Butes the priesthood.

2. The great-grandson of Pandion (1). His father was Cecrops (2), while his mother was Metiadusa. He inherited the throne from his father and was the eighth king of Attica. During his reign Orestes arrived there, having been purged of the stain of his mother's death, whereupon Pandion introduced the Festival of the Jugs during the Anthesteria. (This anecedote is sometimes assigned to the reign of Demophon (2). See ORESTES.) Pandion was driven from his throne by his cousins, the sons of Metion, and fled to Megara, to the court of King Pylas, who gave him his daughter Pylia in marriage. When Pylas was forced to leave Megara the throne passed to Pandion. (Some accounts date his marriage to Pylia to before the rebellion of Metion.) By Pylia Pandion had four sons: Aegeus, Pallas (7), Nisus (1) and Lycus (5).

3. One of the sons of PHINEUS (3) and CLEOPATRA (1).

Pandora (*Πανδώρα*)

1. The first woman, created by Hephaestus and Athena, on the instructions of Zeus. Each god and goddess endowed her with a special quality – beauty, grace, dexterity, cogency, etc. Hephaestus' bequests were lying and deceit. Pandora was

fashioned in the image of the goddesses, and Zeus designed her as punishment for the human race, to which Prometheus had just given fire. Pandora was designed to bring men misfortune.

In the *Works and Days* Hesiod recounts that Zeus sent Pandora to Epimetheus, who was seduced by her beauty and made her his wife. Pandora had hardly reached Earth when she lifted the lid of a great pot and released all the ills in the world. Hope, which was at the bottom, was trapped in the pot when Pandora replaced the lid. Other versions say that the pot contained every blessing, and that Pandora had brought it to Epimetheus as a wedding present from Zeus. By opening it she let all the good things escape and return to the heavens instead of staying among mankind. That is why men are afflicted with every form of evil.

2. The daughter of Erechtheus (see HYACINTHIDS).

Pandorus (*Πάνδωρος*) One of the sons of Erechtheus and Praxithea (1). He was said to have founded the city of Chalcis in Euboea.

Pandrosus (*Πάνδροσος*) One of the daughters of Cecrops (1) by Aglaurus (1). With her sisters she committed the crime of opening the basket in which Athena had hidden ERICHTHONIUS. Her punishment was death. Pandrosus was said to be the first woman to spin. She was worshipped on the Acropolis.

Panedes (*Πανήδης*) King of Chalcis in Euboea and brother to King Amphidamas, at whose funeral games Homer and Hesiod were supposed to have competed. Panedes wanted to give the prize to Hesiod, whose agricultural poetry he found more useful than Homer's. The public rejected Panedes' judgement, and the prize went to Homer. A decision showing lack of taste was commonly called 'a judgement of Panedes'.

Panopeus (*Πανοπεύς*) The eponymous hero of the city of Panopeus in Phocis. He was the son of Phocus and Asteria (2) and had a twin brother, Crisus, whom he hated; the two fought even at their mother's breast. Panopeus fought with Amphitryon against the Taphians. His son Epeius (2) built the Wooden Horse. In Sophocles' *Electra* (where he is called Phanoteus) Panopeus sided with Aegisthus, whereas his great-nephew Pylades was with Orestes. Thus the hatred between Panopeus and Crisus persisted among their descendants.

Panthous (*Πάνθοος*) One of the elderly Trojan companions of Priam. He had three sons, Hyperenor, Euphorbus and Polydamas. His wife was Phrontis or Pronome. Panthous came from Delphi and had been initiated into the worship of Apollo. When Troy was captured by Heracles, Priam consulted the Delphic oracle, and the deputation returned bringing Panthous to establish lasting relations between Troy and Delphi. In another version of the story Priam's envoy was one of the sons of Antenor, who fell in love with Panthous. He ravished him and abducted him to Troy. To recompense Panthous Priam made him high priest of Apollo at Troy. He was killed during the capture of the city.

Paraebius (*Παραίβιος*) Paraebius' father had cut down a pine tree sacred to the Hamadryads. The Nymphs punished him by condemning him and his son to poverty. King Phineus (3) told Paraebius that he could overcome the curse if he built an altar and made expiatory sacrifical offerings to the Nymphs. This Paraebius did, and the curse was brought to an end. Paraebius thereafter remained one of Phineus' most faithful servants.

Paralus (*Πάραλος*) An Athenian hero who supposedly invented warships. In his honour the official Athenian trireme was called the *Paralos*.

Parcae The three Roman goddesses of Destiny, identified with the Greek MOIRAE. The Parcae were originally the attendant spirits of childbirth. They were depicted as spinning thread and measuring out, at whim, the lifespan of all mortals. They were sisters; they presided over birth, marriage and death. In the Forum the statutes of the three Parcae were popularly called the Three Fates (the *tria Fata*).

Paris (*Πάρις*) The second son of Priam and Hecuba, who was also called Alexander. Hecuba saw herself in a dream giving birth to a torch which set fire to the citadel of Troy. The seer Aesacus warned that the child about to be born would cause the destruction of Troy and advised Priam to have it killed at birth. (For another tradition, see HECUBA.) Instead of killing the child Hecuba abandoned him on Mount Ida. Paris was reared by shepherds who found him and gave him the name of Alexander ('the Protector' or 'the Protected') because he had not died on the mountainside. A variant tradition claims that Paris was left out to die on the mountainside by a servant of Priam named Agelaus, and on the king's orders. A female bear came to suckle the child and when Agelaus found Paris still alive, he took the child in. Under Agelaus' care Paris developed into a young man of great beauty and courage. He protected his flocks against thieves, thus earning himself the name Alexander.

One day some of Priam's servants went to fetch a bull from the herd that Paris was guarding. Knowing that the animal was to be the prize at the funeral games which had been instituted in memory of Priam's son, who was supposed to have died at an early age (i.e. Paris himself), he followed the servants back to the city. He decided to take part in the games and to win back his favourite animal. He came first in all the events, in competition with his own brothers, who did not know who he was. In anger Deiphobus drew his sword on Paris, who sought refuge at the altar of Zeus, where his sister Cassandra recognized him; Priam welcomed him and restored to him his place in the royal household. In some versions Paris' identity was revealed though a deliberate move on his part. He brought with him the garments which he was wearing when he was abandoned, and proved who he was.

At the wedding of Peleus and Thetis, Eris (Strife) threw a golden apple into the midst of the guests, saying that it should be the prize 'for the fairest'. Athena, Hera and Aphrodite each claimed it. Zeus instructed Hermes to take them to Mount Ida so that Paris could judge. One after another each goddess promised him protection and special gifts if he declared in her favour: Hera guaranteed to make him ruler of all Asia; Athena promised him wisdom and victory in all combats; Aphrodite offered him the love of the most beautiful woman in the world, Helen of Sparta. Paris awarded the golden apple to Aphrodite. The episode is known as the Judgement of Paris.

Until the Judgment, Paris had loved a Nymph named OENONE. When Aphrodite promised him Helen's love he abandoned Oenone and left for Sparta. He was accompanied by Aeneas. Hecuba and Cassandra predicted the outcome of the escapade; no one believed them. Aeneas and Paris were welcomed at Sparta by Helen's brothers, the Dioscuri, who took them to Menelaus, her husband. Menelaus received them hospitably and introduced them to Helen. Then he himself left for Crete to attend the funeral of Catreus.

Aided by the presents that he lavished on her, by the oriental luxury with which he was surrounded, and by his beauty, which had been enhanced by Aphrodite, Paris won Helen's love. Helen eloped with Paris. (For their adventures on the voyage from Sparta to Asia Minor, see HELEN.)

When he got back to Troy, Paris was very well received despite the dark prophecies of Cassandra.

At the beginning of the *Iliad* the Greeks and Trojans agreed to settle the Trojan War by a single combat between Paris and Menelaus. Paris was only saved by Aphrodite, who hid him in a thick cloud. Later, Hector had to fetch him from Helen's side and order him to join the battle. Paris obeyed, killed Menestheus, wounded Diomedes (2), Machaon and Eurypylus (1), and took part in the attack on the Greek trenches. He killed Euchenor and Deiocus.

The *Iliad* sometimes depicts Paris as wearing heavy armour, but he is usually said to be an archer, and as an archer he killed Achilles (see ACHILLES and POLYXENA).

Paris himself was killed by one of Philoctetes' arrows which pierced his groin. He was carried off the battlefield and sent to Oenone, who had an antidote to the poison with which Philoctetes' arrows were tipped. But by the time she took pity on him it was too late (see OENONE).

Parnassus (*Παρνασσός*) The eponymous hero of Mount Parnassus. He was the son by Poseidon of a Nymph named Cleodora. He was also attributed a mortal father named Cleopompus. Parnassus founded the old oracle of Python, which was later occupied by Apollo. He also invented divination by birds.

Parrhasius (*Παρράσιος*) The son of Lycaon (2) or Zeus. He founded the Arcadian city of Parrhasia. Plutarch records that the Nymph Phylonome had twins by Ares, but, because she was afraid of her father, abandoned them. But a she-wolf suckled the two babies, who were later found and taken in by the shepherd Tyliphus. He gave them the names

Lycastus (2) and Parrhasius and brought them up as his own sons. Later the twins seized power in Arcadia.

Parsondes (*Παρσώνδης*) A Persian warrior and hunter, and the favourite of Artaeus, king of the Medes. He asked the king to give him the place of the satrap of Babylon, Nanerus, but Artaeus refused. Nanerus learned of this and decided to take his revenge. He promised a reward for the capture of Parsondes. One day Parsondes met some of Nanerus' retinue. They gave him too much to drink, chained him up and delivered him to his enemy. Nanerus handed Parsondes to his eunuchs, so that they could shave him and force him to live the life of a woman in the harem. Parsondes learned to play the cithara, dance and adorn himself, and became one of the satrap's wives. After seven years he got a message to King Artaeus, who had believed him dead. Artaeus demanded Parsondes' freedom. Nanerus eventually handed over Parsondes, who had become so like a woman that the king's envoy hardly recognized him among Nanerus' 150 wives.

Parsondes demanded vengeance, for he said it was the hope of revenge which had kept him going during his captivity. However, Nanerus corrupted the king with bribes, and Artaeus refused justice to Parsondes.

Parsondes fled, at the head of 3,000 men, to the land of the Cadusians, for his sister had married one of the most powerful lords of that region. War broke out. Parsondes was victorious, the Cadusians made him their king and from that time on there was constant warfare between the Medes and the Cadusians. This went on until Cyrus conquered the Cadusians.

Parthenopaeus (*Παρθενοπαῖος*) One of the Seven against Thebes. In some traditions he is an Arcadian, the son of Atalanta and Meleager or Melanion; in others he is an Argive, the son of Talaus and Lysimache (Table 1). According to Hyginus, he was abandoned as an infant with Telephus, accompanied him to Mysia, and took part in the expedition against Idas (see TELEPHUS and AUGE).

His name (reminiscent of *parthenos*, 'virgin') derived either from the long period during which his mother preserved her virginity, or from his having been abandoned in infancy on Mount Parthenion.

Handsome and brave, Parthenopaeus took part in the expedition of the Seven, contrary to the advice of Atalanta. At the games held at Nemea in honour of Archemorus-Opheltes (see AMPHIARAUS and HYPSIPYLE) he won the archery contest. He was killed at Thebes by Periclymenus (1) or by Asphodicus, Amphidicus or Dryas, the grandson of Orion.

Parthenope (*Παρθενόπη*) One of the SIRENS.

Parthenus (*Παρθένος*)

1. A daughter of Staphylus (3). Staphylus entrusted Parthenos and her sister Molpadia (2) with the task of looking after his wine. But the girls fell asleep, and some pigs found their way into Staphylus' cellar and broke all the wine jars. When the girls awoke they fled in fear and

threw themselves off the top of some rocks into the sea. Apollo, out of affection for them, gathered them up as they fell and bore them away to cities in the Chersonese. Parthenos went to Boubastos, where she received divine honours, and Molpadia to Castabos (see HEMITHEA (1)).

2. One tradition gives her as the daughter of Apollo and Chrysothemis. She died young and was changed into a constellation (Virgo) by her father. Another version makes her the daughter of Zeus and Themis and identifies her with Dike (Justice), who lived on earth during the Golden Age. In *Eclogue* IV Virgil sees in the return of the constellation of Virgo a presage of the coming of an age of justice. She was also said to be the daughter of Astraeus and Hemera or of Icarius (1) (in which case she was identified with Erigone (1)). Alternatively she was identified with Demeter or with Thespia, one of the daughters of the river-god Asopus.

Pasiphae (*Πασιφάη*) The wife of Minos and daugher of Helios and Perseis. Her brothers were Perses and Aeetes; her sister was Circe.

Minos, when reclaiming the Cretan throne, prayed to Poseidon to send a bull from the sea as a sign of the justice of his claim, promising in return that he would sacrifice it. But when Poseidon granted his prayer Minos refused to fulfil his part of the bargain. To punish him, Poseidon afflicted Pasiphae with an irresitible passion for the animal. But this passion was also said to be the revenge of Aphrodite either because Pasiphae had despised the goddess' cult or because Aphrodite was angered because Helios had disclosed to Hephaestus her affair with Ares.

Pasiphae sought the help of Daedalus, who constructed a life-like hollow wooden cow. Pasiphae wooed the bull in this disguise and the monstrous coupling took place. The fruit of their mating was the MINOTAUR. (For the standard version of the legend of Daedalus and the Labyrinth after the victory of Theseus, see DAEDALUS.)

Pasiphae was very jealous and possessed great skill as a sorceress, like her sister Circe and her niece Medea. She put a curse on Minos so that all the women to whom he made love were devoured by serpents which emerged from all over his body. He was cured of this curse by PROCRIS.

Patroclus (*Πάτροκλος*) In the *Iliad*, Patroclus was the friend of Achilles. The son of Menoetius (1), he was related to Achilles who was great-grandson of Aegina, Patroclus' paternal grandmother. (For the name of Patroclus' mother, see MENOETIUS (1).) When Patroclus was young he went to the court of Peleus. The standard explanation is that as a child, over a game of knucklebones, he killed one of his companions, Clitonymus (or Clesonymus), son of Amphidamus. He then had to go into exile and was given hospitality by Peleus, who accepted him as a companion to his own son, Achilles. The two were brought up together.

The friendship of Patroclus and Achilles was proverbial. Indeed, it was said that they were lovers. When Achilles left Mysia to fight Telephus, Patroclus was at his side. With Diomedes (2) he rescued the body of Thersandrus (2). He was himself wounded by an arrow but was cared for and healed by Achilles.

The exploits of Patroclus before Troy were numerous. It was he who sold Lycaon (1), the son of Priam taken prisoner by Achilles at Lemnos. He also took part in the capture of Lyrnessos and in the raid on Scyros. In the *Iliad* he restored Briseis to Agamemnon's heralds, and when the embassy of chiefs came to Achilles he stood by his friend. When the Greeks were in difficulty, Achilles sent Patroclus to Nestor for news. There he took care of Eurypylus (1), who had been wounded, and then told Achilles of the critical situation in the Achaean camp. He pressed Achilles to return to the fight or at least to let him, Patroclus, go back and take the Myrmidons with him. Achilles gave him permission to put on his own armour and to join battle. Patroclus wrought havoc among the Trojans. Then when they were in full flight, he killed Cebrion, Hector's charioteer, but with Apollo's aid Hector himself killed Patroclus. Battle was soon raging between Trojans and Greeks around the body of Patroclus, which his vanquisher stripped of the divine armour of Achilles. Antilochus told Achilles of the death of his friend, and Achilles in his grief went into the thick of battle without his armour. On hearing his battle-cry, the Trojans fled, leaving Patroclus' body behind.

The accounts of Patroclus' funeral and of the death of Hector comprise the whole of the end of the *Iliad*. The funeral is marked by the sacrifice of twelve young Trojans captured by Achilles beside the Scamander and by the funeral games in which all the Greek leaders took part. Achilles built a tomb to Patroclus on the site of the funeral pyre.

After the death of Achilles, the ashes of the two friends were mingled – though one tradition claimed that Patroclus had survived at Achilles' side, together with Helen, Ajax (2) and Antilochus, on the White Island in the Danube estuary.

Patron (*Πάτρων*)
1. A hero who appears in the *Aeneid* where he took part in the funeral games in honour of Anchises. He was an Acarnanian who joined Aeneas and who eventually settled in Sicily.
2. A companion of Evander (3) at Rome. Patron gave hospitality to people of limited means, so the Roman custom of patronage was named after him.

Pax The personification of Peace at Rome. She was given an altar by Augustus to sanctify the re-establishment of order after the Civil Wars. Later Vespasian, then Domitian, devoted a temple to her in the Forum, which was named the Forum of Peace.

Pegasus (*Πήγασος*) A winged horse. His name was derived from the Greek word for 'spring' (*πηγή*) and he was said to have been born 'at the springs of the Ocean' (i.e. in the extreme West). Some versions of the legend said that Pegasus had sprung from the Gorgon's neck when it was slain by Perseus, in which case he was the son of Poseidon and the Gorgon. In other versions he was born of the earth, which was fertilized by the Gorgon's blood. After his birth Pegasus flew to Olympus and placed himself at the disposal of Zeus, to whom he brought thunderbolts.

Versions of the meeting of BELLEROPHON and Pegasus vary. Either Athena brought the horse already broken in for Bellerophon to ride, or Poseidon gave him to the hero, or Bellerophon found him while he was drinking at the Pirenean spring. Thanks to Pegasus Bellerophon was able to kill the Chimaera and to defeat the Amazons.

After Bellerophon's death Pegasus returned to the gods. During the singing contest between the PIERIDES and the Muses, Mount Helicon swelled in pleasure. On Poseidon's order Pegasus struck the mountain with his hoof to instruct it to return to its normal size. Helicon obeyed, but at the spot where Pegasus had struck it there gushed a spring, the Hippocrene or Horse Spring. Eventually Pegasus was changed into a constellation.

Peitho (*Πειθώ*)
1. Persuasion, who usually appears in the train of Aphrodite. She is sometimes said to be the daughter of Ate, but other myths make her the sister of Tyche and Eunomia (Good Order) and the daughter of Prometheus.
2. One of the daughters of Oceanus and Tethys. She married Argos (1).
3. The wife of Phoroneus and the mother of Aegialeus and Apis.

Pelasgus (*Πελασγός*)
1. In Arcadian legend there were two distinct genealogies for Pelasgus. One made him the son of Niobe (1) and Zeus. By Meliboea (1), the Nymph Cyllene or by Deianeira he had a son, Lycaon (2), who in turn had fifty sons, founders of most of the cities in Arcadia, and one daughter, Callisto (1), on whom Zeus fathered Arcas, who gave his name to Arcadia. An Arcadian legend makes Pelasgus the first man to live in Arcadia: he was 'born to the soil' and was the first king of the area. He invented the use of houses, and distinguished between edible and poisonous plants.
2. The son of Triopas and Sosis (or Sois) and brother of Iasus (1) and Agenor. He is a descendant of Niobe (1) and Zeus. Pelasgus was Argive. He offerered hospitality to Demeter when she came in search of her daughter and built the temple of Demeter Pelasgis in her honour. His daughter Larissa gave her name to the citadel at Argos.
3. Thessalian legend tells of a Pelasgus who was Larissa's son by Poseidon. He had two brothers, Achaeus and Phthius, with whom he left the Peloponnese and took over Thessaly, which was then called Haemonia. They divided it into three parts, each named after the brother who appropriated it. Their descendants were ultimately driven out by the Curetes and the Leleges.

Peleus (*Πηλεύς*) King of Phthia in Thessaly, and the father of Achilles. He was the son of Aeacus and Endeis. In standard accounts he was the brother of Telamon and half-brother of Phocus (3), but sometimes Peleus and Telamon were said to be just friends, in which case Telamon was the son of Actaeus and Glauce (3).

Telamon and Peleus, who were

jealous of Phocus' physical skills, decided to kill him. Telamon slew him by throwing a discus at his head. (Other versions present the murder as accidental or claim that the culprit was Peleus.) Aeacus banished both Peleus and Telamon from Aegina. Telamon went to Salamis; Peleus went to the court of Eurytion (3) at Phthia in Thessaly. Eurytion purified him of the murder, gave him his daughter Antigone (3) in marriage along with a third of the kingdom. By Antigone Peleus had a daughter, Polydora.

Peleus was pursued by the anger of Phocus' mother, Psamathe (1), who sent a wolf to prey on his flocks, though at the request of Thetis she changed the wolf into stone.

Peleus took part in the hunting of the Calydonian boar but accidentally killed Eurytion. Again he had to go into exile. He sought refuge at the court of Acastus, who purified him. There he had an adventure which nearly cost him his life. See ACASTUS.

Peleus then married Thetis, the daughter of Nereus. Zeus and Poseidon had been rivals for her hand, but Themis (or Prometheus) warned them that the Parcae had ordained that the son of Thetis would be more powerful than his father. The two gods abandoned their courtship and plans were made for marrying Thetis to a mortal. A different version claims that Thetis refused to sleep with Zeus out of regard for Hera, who had brought her up, and that in his anger Zeus decided to marry her to a mortal as a punishment. Thetis refused at first. She had the gift of taking any shape she pleased, so she adopted a number of disguises: fire, water, wind, a tree, a bird, a tiger, a lion, a snake and finally a cuttlefish. Peleus, who had been advised by Chiron, held on to her firmly, and eventually she became a goddess and woman again. The marriage took place on Mount Pelion. The gods were present; the Muses sang the epithalamium and each brought a gift for the newly-weds. Among the presents were an ash-wood spear given by Chiron and two immortal horses, Balius (1) and Xanthus (7), donated by Poseidon. (These horses turn up again later, harnessed to the chariot of Achilles.)

The marriage was not a success. Thetis bore Peleus some children, but one after another perished as she attempted to make them immortal. When Peleus tried to save Achilles by snatching him from the fire into which Thetis was plunging him, she fled and refused to return.

In his old age, and while Achilles was at Troy, Peleus was attacked by Archandrus and Architeles, the sons of Acastus. He fled to Cos, where he met his grandson Neoptolemus. There he was given hospitality by Molon, and there he died. In another version, represented by Euripides' *Andromache*, Peleus outlived Neoptolemus and intervened on Andromache's behalf in the ploys of Hermione (see MOLOSSUS).

Peleus also plays a part in the adventures of the Argonauts, the expedition of Heracles against Troy (in which he accompanied his brother Telamon) and the Amazon War, which is connected with that expedition. He also appears among the contestants at the funeral games held in honour of Pelias. He was defeated in the wrestling competition by ATALANTA.

Pelias (*Πελιάς*) A son of Tyro by Poseidon or the river-god Enipeus whose shape Poseidon had assumed; his twin brother was Neleus (1). His 'human' father was Cretheus. His half-brothers were Aeson, Pheres (1) and Amythaon (Table 6). Tyro abandoned her twins at birth. Some horse dealers passed the spot where they lay and after a mare had accidentally kicked one of the babies, leaving a purple mark (*pelion*) on his face, they rescued and cared for the twins.

Other versions of the legend record that the twins were suckled by a mare. (The horse was sacred to Poseidon.) In Sophocles' lost tragedy *Tyro*, the twins were taken in by a shepherd and later recognized by Tyro. They then rescued Tyro from Sidero, her stepmother who was ill-treating her. Sidero took refuge at the altar of Hera but Pelias killed her there. His impiety towards Hera eventually brought about his downfall.

Pelias and Neleus fought each other to determine who should rule Thessaly. Pelias won, stayed in Thessaly, at Iolcos, and married Anaxibia, the daughter of Bias (or Philomache, the daughter of Amphion). By her he had a son, Acastus, and four daughters, Pisidice (5), Pelopia (2), Hippothoe and Alcestis.

Pelias decided to make a sacrifice to Poseidon and summoned his subjects to attend. His nephew Jason hurried to attend the ceremony, but in crossing a river he lost one of his sandals. Formerly Pelias had consulted the Delphic oracle and had been warned to beware of a man wearing only one shoe. Pelias remembered the oracle and asked Jason what he would do to a man who he knew was destined to overthrow him. Jason replied that he would send him off in quest of the Golden Fleece. Hera may have dictated the answer to him, since she planned to bring Medea to Iolcos in order to arrange the death of Pelias. Pelias took Jason at his word and sent him to find the Golden Fleece (see ARGONAUTS).

Pelias then killed his half-brother AESON. Alcimede, Jason's mother, put a curse on Pelias and hanged herself leaving a son, Promachus, whom Pelias also killed. At this point Jason returned. He went to Corinth, where he plotted with Medea how to punish Pelias. Medea went to the court of Iolcos and tricked Pelias' daughters into killing their father (see Medea). (According to tradition, only Alcestis refused to take part.) Overcome with horror at the crime they had committed, his daughters went into voluntary exile and fled to Arcadia. Another version records that they married: they were not considered guilty since they had merely been the instruments of Medea's crime.

Acastus, Pelias' son, gathered up his father's remains and gave him a solemn funeral, including the games which were to remain famous. The winners included Calais and Zetes, the Dioscuri, Telamon and Peleus, Heracles, Meleager, Cycnus (3), Bellerophon, Iolaus, Eurytus (3), Cephalus, Olympus, Orpheus (4), Linus (2) and Eumolpus (1). To this list is sometimes added the name of Atalanta, who was supposed to have beaten Peleus in the wrestling.

Pelopia (*Πελόπεια*)

1. The mother of Aegisthus,

whom Pelopia bore as the result of involuntary incest with her father, Thyestes. She lived at Sicyon, at the court of King Thesprotus. While pregnant with Aegisthus Pelopia married Atreus (see Table 2).

2. One of the daughters of Pelias and Anaxibia (see Table 6). She had a son, CYCNUS (3), by ARES.

3. The daughter of Niobe (2).

Pelops (*Πέλοψ*)

1. The son of Tantalus (1) (Table 2). Pelops was a native of Asia Minor, and emigrated to Europe because of the war waged by Ilus (2) against Tantalus.

Tantalus killed Pelops, cut him into small pieces and made him into a stew, which he served to the gods. Some mythographers claimed that Tantalus did this since there was a famine in his kingdom and he had no other victim to offer to the gods, but it was usually said that he wanted to test how perceptive the gods really were. All the gods recognized the meat and none of them touched it except Demeter, who was famished and ate a shoulder before realizing what it was (variants say that it was Ares or Thetis who was guilty of this). The gods reconstructed the body of Pelops and restored it to life. In place of the shoulder which had been eaten they made him an ivory one.

After his resurrection Pelops was beloved of Poseidon, taken to Olympus by him, and became his cup-bearer. Soon, however, he was sent back to earth because Tantalus had been using him to steal nectar and ambrosia from the gods. Poseidon remained his protector none the less, and made him a present of some winged horses. Poseidon also helped Pelops in his duel with Oenomaus for the possession of HIPPODAMIA (1).

Hippodamia and Pelops had a large number of children. All the authorities list Atreus, Thyestes and Pleisthenes. To these are sometimes added Chrysippus (also said to be the son of Pelops by Axioche), Astydamia, Copreus and Hippothoe.

The name of Pelops is associated with the Olympic Games. He was supposed to have been their first founder, the games having been later reintroduced by Heracles in his honour. They were sometimes thought to be funeral games dedicated to Oenomaus.

At the time of the Trojan War Helenus revealed that Troy could not be captured unless the bones of Pelops (or one of his shoulders) were brought to the city. These bones were therefore brought from Pisa to the Troad.

2. The son of Agamemnon by Cassandra.

Penates Roman deities who guarded hearth and home. They were often associated with Vesta, but they remained distinct from the LARES. Each home had its own Penates and so did the Roman state. These Penates, represented by two statues of seated youths, were brought to Italy by Aeneas; they had a temple known as the Velia at Rome.

Peneius (*Πηνειός*) A river-god of Thessaly and a son of Oceanus and Tethys; the founder of the race of Lapiths. He was married to Creusa (1) (or Philyra) by whom he had three children, Stilbe (1), Hypseus and Andreus. Two other daughters are attributed to him in later versions of the legend: Daphne and Cyrene.

Peneleos (*Πηνέλεως*) A Boeotian hero, listed among Helen's suitors. He was the son of Hippalcimus or Hippalmus. He is sometimes mentioned as one of the Argonauts. He led a Boeotian force to Troy, where he killed Ilioneus and Lycon and was himself wounded by Polydamas. He died at the hand of Eurypylus (4) (see TISAMENUS (2)). A different tradition names Peneleos as one of the captains who hid in the Wooden Horse and took part in the capture of Troy.

Penelope (*Πηνελόπη*) The wife of Odysseus, noted for her fidelity. Penelope was the daughter of Icarius (2) (or Icadius according to a tradition recorded by Aristotle), either by the Naiad Periboea (1), Polycaste (2), Dorodoche or Asterodia. The number of Penelope's brothers and sisters varies considerably (see e.g. LEUCADIUS), as do their names.

The mythographers give two main versions of the marriage between Odysseus and Penelope. In one version Odysseus was the winner of a race between her suitors organized by Icarius. It is also said that Penelope's uncle Tyndareus, who wanted to reward Odysseus for suggesting that the suitors of his daughter Helen swear an oath not to fight once Helen had made her choice, obtained his niece's hand for Odysseus. Icarius asked Odysseus to settle near him with his wife. Odysseus refused. Icarius persisted, however, so Odysseus asked Penelope to choose between her father and her husband. Penelope remained silent, blushed and covered her face with her veil. Icarius understood that she had made her choice, so he withdrew and built a sanctuary to Modesty on the site of this incident.

When Menelaus came to assemble the former suitors of Helen to go to Troy to avenge his dishonour, Odysseus pretended to be mad, since Penelope had just given him a son, Telemachus. His pretence was discovered by PALAMEDES, however, and he set off entrusting his house and his wife to his old friend Mentor. Penelope became the sole mistress of Odysseus' fortune. All the young men of the neighbourhood asked for her hand, and when she refused they moved into Odysseus' palace, hoping that their extravagant revels would force the young woman to give in by bringing about her financial ruin under her very eyes. Penelope thought of a trick. She told them that she would choose a husband from among them when she had finished weaving Laertes' shroud, and the work which she did by day she unravelled by night. After three years of this, however, she was betrayed by a maidservant.

Odysseus eventually returned and massacred the suitors (see ODYSSEUS, IV). Penelope hesitated but eventually recognized her husband, and Athena graciously lengthened the duration of the night that followed.

It was said in another tradition that NAUPLIUS (2) spread the rumour that Odysseus had died at Troy, that it was then that Odysseus' mother, Anticleia, committed suicide, and that Penelope threw herself into the sea but was saved by birds who brought her back to the shore. Among other post-Homeric traditions there is the legend that Penelope succumbed in succession to all of her 129 suitors and that during this orgy she conceived the god PAN. Another version said that Odysseus on his return realized that Penelope had been unfaithful to him and banished her. She fled via Sparta to Mantinea where she died. According to another version Odysseus killed Penelope to punish her for her adultery with the suitor Amphinomus.

According to some traditions Odysseus had a second son, Poliporthes, by Penelope after his return. Then he set off for the land of the Thesproti. On his return he was killed by another son, Telegonus (1), who did not recognize him. Telegonus then carried Penelope off to the island of his own mother, CIRCE, and there married her. Circe bore them both off to the Kingdom of the Blessed.

Penia (*Πενία*) The personification of Poverty. Socrates, reporting the words of Diotima in Plato's *Symposium*, says that after a feast among the gods Penia married Poros and by him gave birth to Eros.

Penthesilea (*Πενθεσίλεια*) An Amazon, the daughter of Ares and Otrere. She had a son named Caystrus and a grandson, Ephesus. After Hector's death Penthesilea went to Troy to help Priam, taking with her an army of Amazons. At Troy she made her mark in numerous exploits but was defeated by Achilles, who wounded her in the right breast and then fell in love with her as she died. Thersites made fun of this passion, and Achilles slew him.

Pentheus (*Πενθεύς*) A Theban descended from Cadmus. He was the son of Echion and Agave (Table 3). The standard version makes Pentheus the direct heir of Cadmus (see CADMUS), but a variant tradition places Polydorus on the throne between Cadmus and Pentheus, who dethroned him. According to another version, Pentheus was not king of Thebes.

Having conquered Asia, the god Dionysus decided to come back to his homeland, Thebes, to institute the worship of his cult and to punish his mother's sisters, particularly Agave, for having slandered Semele. At Thebes he inflicted madness on all the women, inducing them to go up into the mountains in Bacchant costume and celebrate the god's mysteries. Pentheus tried to prevent the spread of this cult, calling Dionysus a charlatan and an impostor. Despite several miracles, which he witnessed, Pentheus clapped Dionysus in chains, but the god freed himself and set the royal palace on fire. He suggested to Pentheus that he should climb the mountain to spy on the women and witness the excesses in which they indulged. Pentheus accepted this suggestion, disguised himself and hid in a pine tree. The women saw him, uprooted the tree and tore him to pieces. Agave impaled his head on a thyrsus and went back to Thebes, proudly carrying what she thought was a lion's head. When she came to her senses she saw that she had killed her own son. This myth, which was cast in theatrical form by both Euripides and Aeschylus, was very well known in classical art and literature.

Penthilus (*Πένθιλος*) An illegitimate son of Orestes by Erigone (2). Penthilus had two sons, Damasios and Echelas or Echelaus, who founded colonies at Lesbos and on the coast of Asia Minor. He supposedly founded the Lesbian city of Penthile.

Penthus (*Πένθος*) A deity personifying Grief. When Zeus allotted their functions to the various gods, Penthus could not be found. By the time he appeared Zeus had already distributed everything, and so had noting left to entrust to him except the task of presiding over the honours paid to the dead, mourning and tears. So Penthus favours those who weep for the dead and observe strict mourning. Because they are so good at weeping he sends them the most distressing experiences possible, and the surest way of keeping him at a distance is to moderate distress at misfortunes.

Peparethus (*Πεπάρηθος*) One of the four sons of Ariadne by Dionysus. He gave his name to the island of Peparethor.

Peratus (*Πέρατος*) A king of Sicyon, the successor to Leucippus (3). As Leucippus' only child was a daughter, he gave his kingdom to Peratus, a son of his daughter Calchiaia by Poseidon. Peratus' own son was Plemnaeus.

Perdix (*Πέρδιξ*) As a nephew of Daedalus, Perdix served an apprenticeship in his uncle's workshop and soon surpassed him in skill. In jealousy Daedalus pushed him from the top of the Acropolis. Daedalus was tried before the Areopagus. To Perdix was attributed among other things the invention of the saw; he was inspired by a snake's teeth. He is also said to have invented the potter's wheel. This young man is sometimes called Talos (2) or even Calus. He was given the name of Perdix because Athena, taking pity on him as his uncle pushed him off the Acropolis, turned him into a partridge. This bird joyfully attended the funeral of Icarus, son of Daedalus, who also died of a fall.

Pergamus (*Πέργαμος*) The eponymous hero of the city of Pergamon, he was the youngest son of Neoptolemus and Andromache. Pergamus came back from Asia with his mother and in a duel killed Areius, the king of the city of Teuthrania. He then took the throne and gave the city his own name.

Pergamus is also the name of the citadel of Troy, but the myth cited above is intended to explain the name of the Hellenistic city of Pergamon, the capital of the kingdom of the Attalids.

Periboea (*Περίβοια*)

1. The Naiad who bore Icarius (2) children, including Penelope.
2. The youngest daughter of Eurymedon (1) who, mating with Poseidon, gave birth to Nausithous (1), king of the Phaeacians.
3. One of the first pair of Locrian girls drawn by lot to be sent as slaves of the Athena at Ilion, in order to appease her wrath at the sacrilege committed by Ajax (1) (the other was Cleopatra (3)). This offering went on for a thousand years. The girls who were thus dedicated to the service of Athena simply cleansed the sanctu-

ary. They wore only a common tunic and went barefoot. If they were seen outside the sanctuary they could be put to death.

4. The wife of Polybus (3), king of Corinth, who took in OEDIPUS and brought him up.

5. Mother of Ajax (2) and wife of TELAMON. Her father was Alcathus, king of Megara (Table 2). Together with Theseus, she was sent as part of the tribute to Minos by Aegeus. Minos fell in love with her during the voyage. She called on Theseus to help her. Theseus claimed that, as a son of Poseidon, he was as noble as Minos, who was a son of Zeus. Minos prayed to Zeus, who sent down a flash of lightning. Then Minos threw a ring into the sea and ordered Theseus, if he really was a son of Poseidon, to retrieve it. Theseus dived after the ring and Poseidon handed it to him. Theseus was later said to have married Periboea (also known as PHEREBOEA).

6. The mother of Tydeus. There are several traditions concerning the marriage of Periboea and Oeneus. Some said that Oeneus obtained her as part of the booty after the sacking of Olenos. Others said that she had been seduced by Hippostratus, the son of Amarynceus, or by Ares, and that her father, Hipponous, had sent her to Oeneus to be put to death, but instead of killing her Oeneus married her. A third version claimed that the seducer was Oeneus himself and that Hipponous forced him to marry the girl.

Periclymenus (*Περικλύμενος*)

1. A son of Poseidon and of Chloris, the daughter of Tiresias. When the Seven attacked Thebes, he defended the city and killed Parthenopaeus by throwing a block of stone down on to his head from the city walls. Pursuing the enemy, he chased Amphiaraus and would have killed him had not Zeus made the earth open up and swallow Amphiaraus.

2. An inhabitant of Pylos and a son of Neleus (1), who took part in the expedition of the Argonauts. From his grandfather Poseidon (Table 6) he inherited the ability to change his shape. When Heracles attacked Pylos, Periclymenus changed himself into a bee to attack the hero, but, thanks to Athena's advice, Heracles recognized him in time and killed him. It was also said that Periclymenus changed into an eagle and was shot down by Heracles with an arrow.

Perieres (*Περιήρης*)

1. Usually a son of Aeolus (1) (Table 5), and the hero from whom the Aeolians of Messenia were descended. He reigned over Andania, married Gorgophone, daughter of Perseus (Table 7), and had by her Aphareus, Leucippus (1) and, in some versions, Tyndareus and Icarius (2). In this tradition Perieres is the common ancestor of the Tyndaridae (the Dioscuri, Helen and Clytemnestra), the Leucippidae (Phoebe (2) and Hilaera) and of Penelope, Lynceus (2) and Idas.

According to another tradition Perieres was the son of Cynortas and consequently directly related to Zeus and Taygete. The genealogies often give this Perieres the name of Oebalus (1).

2. A Theban, the charioteer of Menoeceus. At Onchestos he slew

the king of the Minyans, which led to a war betwen the Thebans and Minyans (for this war, see ERGINUS (1).

Periergus (*Περίεργος*) The son of Triopas and brother of Phorbas (1). After the death of Triopas he went to Rhodes.

Perigoune (*Περιγουνή*) The daughter of Sinis. She was beloved of Theseus and by him had a son, Melanippus (4).

Perimele (*Περιμήλη*)
1. The daughter of Amythaon and the mother of Ixion.
2. In Ovid's *Metamorphoses* Perimele is a girl beloved of the river-god ACHELOUS.

Periphas (*Περίφας*)
1. A Lapith, the husband of Astyagyia and the grandfather of Ixion.
2. An early king of Attica renowned for his justice and piety. He was a devoted worshipper of Apollo. His subjects built a temple to him under the name of Zeus. Zeus was angry at this, but he allowed himself to be moved by Apollo's prayers and merely paid Periphas a visit, then turned him into an eagle. Zeus made Periphas king of all birds and decreed that the eagle should thenceforth be linked with his own worship.

Periphetes (*Περιφήτης*)
1. The son of Hephaestus. He had weak legs and supported himself on a bronze crutch or club, with which he beat to death travellers on the road through Epidaurus. Theseus met him on his return journey to Attica and, having slain him, took his club and kept it for himself.
2. The son of COPREUS.

Pero (*Πηρώ*) A daughter of Neleus (1) and Chloris (Table 6). Being very beautiful she had many suitors, but Neleus, who did not want to part with her, demanded the flocks of Iphiclus as dowry. Thanks to her brother MELAMPUS, Bias (her first cousin) was able to satisfy this condition and marry the girl. See also BIAS.

Perse, Perseis (*Πέρση, Περσηίς*) A daughter of Oceanus and Tethys and the wife of Helios by whom she had Aeetes, Perses, Circe, Pasiphae and Calypso (1).

Persephone (*Περσεφόνη*) The goddess of the Underworld and wife of Hades. She was the daughter of Zeus and Demeter (Table 8), although another tradition makes her the daughter of Zeus and Styx. Hades fell in love with Persephone (his niece) and abducted her while she was picking flowers on the plain around Etna in Sicily. This abduction occurred with the complicity of Zeus and in the absence of Demeter. Eventually Zeus ordered Hades to restore Persephone to her mother. But this was no longer possible, for the young girl had eaten a pomegranate seed, which was enough to tie her to the Underworld for ever (see ASCALAPHUS (1) and DEMETER). As a compromise Zeus decided that she should divide her time between the Underworld and the world above. As Hades' wife Persephone plays a part in the legends of Heracles, Orpheus, Theseus and Pirithous. She was also said to have fallen in love with Adonis. She appears, with Demeter, in the Eleusinian Mysteries. At Rome she was identified with PROSERPINA.

Persepolis (*Περσέπολις*) In certain traditions a son of Odysseus and Nausicaa. In other versions he is the son of Telemachus by Polycaste (1).

Perses (*Πέρσης*) A son of the Titan Crius and of Eurybia. His brothers were Pallas (3) and Astraeus. He himself married Asteria (1). He had several children by her including Hecate. Another tradition makes Perses a son of Helios and Perse. He was said to have been king of Tauris before depriving his brother Aeetes of the kingdom of Colchis, but he was killed by Medus (1) on the instigation of Medea because he wanted to return the kingdom to Aeetes. Another version makes Perses the father of Hecate by a concubine. Hecate supposedly married her uncle Aeetes and became the mother of Circe and Medea.

Perseus (*Περσεύς*) Son of Zeus and Danae (Table 7). For the circumstances of Perseus' birth see ACRISIUS.

Danae contrived to bear Perseus secretly and to keep him in secret for several months. One day, however, the child gave a cry which was heard by Acrisius. Unwilling to believe that his daughter had been seduced by Zeus, Acrisius killed Danae's nurse as an accomplice and had his daughter and grandson thrown into the sea in a wooden chest. The chest was cast up on the island of Seriphos, where mother and child were taken in by a fisherman named Dictys, brother of the tyrant Polydectes. Dictys welcomed them and raised the young Perseus, who became a handsome and courageous young man. Polydectes conceived a passion for Danae, but Perseus guarded his mother well and the king did not dare resort to violence. One day Polydectes invited his friends, including Perseus, to dinner and asked what gift each was willing to offer him. All the other guests said that a horse was a fitting gift, but Perseus declared that he would bring him the head of the Gorgon Medusa. The next day all the princes brought Polydectes a horse, except for Perseus, who brought nothing. Polydectes then ordered him to fetch Medusa's head, saying that otherwise he would take Danae by force. (In another version, Polydectes intended to give all these presents to Hippodamia (1), whom he intended to marry.) In this difficult situation Perseus was helped by Hermes and Athena. On their advice he went first in search of the GRAEAE, who eventually showed him the way to the Nymphs, who possessed winged sandals, a shoulder bag called a *kibisis* and the helmet of Hades which made its wearer invisible. The Nymphs gave these objects to Perseus, while Hermes armed him with the *harpe*, a sickle made of adamant. Perseus then set off to look for the Gorgons, Stheno, Euryale and Medusa. Of the three, only Medusa was mortal, which was why Perseus had some hope of decapitating her. While Medusa was asleep Perseus rose into the air on his winged sandals, and while Athena held a shield of polished bronze over Medusa so that it acted as a mirror he struck off her head. From Medusa's mutilated neck sprang a winged horse, PEGASUS, and a giant, CHRYSAOR. Perseus put the head of Medusa in his shoulder bag and set off home. The victim's two sisters pursued him, but to no avail, for Hades' helmet prevented them from seeing him.

On the way back Perseus travelled through Ethiopia where he came across Andromeda. She was being offered as a sacrifice in expiation of the imprudent words spoken by her mother, Cassiopia, and had been tied to a rock. Perseus fell in love with Andromeda and promised her father, Cepheus (2), that he would release her if he could have her hand in marriage. The bargain was struck and Perseus slew the monster. See ANDROMEDA.

After his marriage Perseus returned to Seriphos accompanied by Andromeda. During his absence Polydectes had tried to rape Danae, who had to seek refuge at the altars of the gods. Perseus took his revenge on Polydectes by turning him to stone. He then handed over the government of Seriphos to Dictys. He gave the sandals, bag and Hades' helmet to Hermes, who returned them to the Nymphs. Athena set the head of Medusa in the middle of her shield. Perseus then left Seriphos with Andromeda and set off for his native land, Argos, to see his grandfather, Acrisius. However Perseus accidentally killed him at Larissa in Thessaly (see ACRISIUS). Not daring to return to Argos in order to claim the kingdom of the man he had killed, he exchanged places with his cousin Megapenthes (2) (Table 7), who thus became king of Argos, while Perseus became king of Tiryns.

Perseus is said to have successfully opposed the introduction of the cult of Dionysus into Argos and even to have fought the god and drowned him in the lake at Lerna (see also HALIAE). He is also said to have killed Ariadne in the same battle (another version gives just Ariadne as Perseus' victim). Mythographers of the Roman period recorded that after Danae and Perseus had been thrown into the sea by Acrisius they landed not at Seriphos but on the coast of Latium. There King Pilumnus (2) married Danae and with her, founded the city of Ardea. Turnus was supposed to be a descendant of this marriage.

Peucetius (*Πευκέτιος*) One of the sons of LYCAON (2). With his brother Oenotrus he went from Arcadia to southern Italy, where he became the ancestor of the Peucetians.

Phaea (*Φαῖα*) The sow killed by Theseus at Crommyon. It was named after the old woman who reared it, and was descended from Echidna and Typhon.

Phaeacians (*Φαίακες*) A mythical nation of sailors. They were descendants of Phaeax (1) who led them out of the land of Hyperia, from which they were driven by the Cyclopes. Phaeax took them to the island of Scheria (but see also NAUSITHOUS (1)). Under King Alcinous the Phaeacians devoted themselves to navigation and trading. For Odysseus' visit to their island and its consequences, see ALCINOUS. The Argonauts also landed on the island of the Phaeacians, and the marriage of Jason and Medea took place there.

Phaeax (*Φαίαξ*)
1. The eponymous hero of the Phaeacians. He was the son of Poseidon and a Nymph called Cercyra. He was king of the island of Scheria (see PHAEACIANS).
2. The man who piloted Theseus' ship when he sailed from Attica to Crete. He was a native of Salamis (see also NAUSITHOUS (2)).

Phaedra (*Φαίδρα*) The daughter of Minos and Pasiphae and the sister of Ariadne. Her brother Deucalion (2) gave her in marriage to Theseus, despite the fact that he was already married to the Amazon Antiope (2) (or Melanippe (3), or Hippolyta (1)). This marriage was the occasion of an attack by the Amazons (see THESEUS, v). Phaedra had two children by Theseus, Acamas (3) and Demophon (2). She fell in love with Hippolytus (1), Theseus' son by his Amazon wife, but Hippolytus refused to give in to his stepmother. For the ensuing events and the death of Phaedra, see HIPPOLYTUS (1).

Phaestus (*Φαίστος*) A son of Heracles. He succeeded Ianiscus to the throne of Sicyon and then, in response to an oracle, went to Crete, where he founded the city that bore his name. He had a son named Rhopalus.

Phaethon (*Φαέθων*) There are two distinct traditions concerning his genealogy. One makes him the son of Eos and Cephalus; the other of Helios and Clymene (1). In the second version Phaethon was brought up by his mother, who kept his father's identity a secret until the boy reached adolescence. Phaethon then requested some acknowledgement of his parentage and asked his father to let him drive his chariot across the sky. Helios gave him permission to do so, and Phaethon started to follow his father's route across the vaults of heaven. But he soon felt afraid at finding himself so high up. The sight of the animals which constitute the signs of the Zodiac frightened him and he left his ordained path. He dropped too low and risked setting fire to the Earth; then he rose too high and the stars complained to Zeus. To prevent a universal conflagration Zeus struck the boy down with his thunderbolt and hurled him into the River Eridanus. His sisters, the Heliades (1), paid him funeral honours.

Phalanthus (*Φάλανθος*) The hero who founded Tarentum (but see also TARAS). During the Messenian war those Lacedaemonians who had not taken part in the expedition were sold into slavery and their children were deprived of their political rights. However, these people (known as Parthenians) plotted an uprising to take place during the Spartiate festival of the Hyacinthids. Phalanthus was chosen as leader and was supposed to give the signal for the revolt by putting on his cap. The Spartiates got wind of the matter, however, and the herald forbade Phalanthus to put on his cap. The Parthenians fled, under the leadership of Phalanthus, and went to Tarentum, where on the instructions of the Delphic oracle they founded a colony. The oracle had also told

Phalanthus that he would be successful in his escape 'when it rained out of a clear sky'. This oracle was fulfilled when Phalanthus' wife Aethra (whose name means 'clear sky') wept on learning of the initial failure of the plot.

Phalces (*Φάλκης*) One of the Heraclids. Phalces seized power in Sicyon one night but agreed to share the government of the city with Lacestades, the previous king, who was also a Heraclid. With his brothers he murdered his father Temenus (3) (see DEIPHONTES).

Phalerus (*Φάληρος*) A hero who gave his name to the Attic port of Phaleron in the Piraeus. He was an Argonaut and fought the Centaurs at the side of Theseus and Pirithous. In his childhood he had been attacked by a snake, but his father Alcon (2) shot the creature with an arrow.

Phanoteus (*Φανοτεύς*) See PANOPEUS.

Phaon (*Φάων*) A hero of the island of Lesbos. He was a ferryman, old, poor and not good-looking, until he ferried Aphrodite, disguised as an old woman, and did not ask her for payment. As a reward the goddess gave him a phial of oil with which he rubbed himself every day. He became very handsome and was beloved by all the women on the island, especially Sappho. He scorned Sappho's love, and at this rejection she threw herself into the waves from the Leucadian rock.

Pharos (*Φάρος*) In one tradition Helen fled from Troy before the capture of the city and bribed Pharos, a ship's captain, to carry her and Menelaus back to Sparta; but a storm cast them up on the coast of Egypt, where a snake bit Pharos and killed him. The island in the estuary of the Nile thenceforth bore his name.

Phasis (*Φᾶσις*) The god of the river of that name in Colchis. He was the son of Helios and of Ocyrrhoe (1). When he caught his mother committing adultery he killed her, was pursued by the Furies and threw himself into the River Arcturus, which then took the name Phasis.

Phegeus (*Φηγεύς*) A king of Phegeia (Psophis) in Arcadia, of which he was the founder. He was a brother of Phoroneus in the genealogy that makes him the son of Inachus. It was to his court that Alcmaeon (1) fled after killing his mother. Phegeus had a daughter, Arsinoe (also called Alphesiboea (2)), and two sons, Pronous and Agenor, or, according to Pausanias, Temenus (2) and Axion.

Pheidippus (*Φείδιππος*) A son of Thessalus (2) who appears in the Catalogue of Ships at the head of a fleet of thirty vessels sailing against Troy. He was one of Helen's suitors. During the first expedition to Troy Pheidippus was sent as an ambassador to Telephus, who was his uncle. He took part in the attack on the city in the Wooden Horse, and after the fall of Troy he settled on the island of Andros.

Phemonoe (*Φημονόη*) A daughter of Apollo and the first Pythia of the

Delphic oracle. She invented hexameter verse as the form in which to express her prophecies. She is also credited with the famous Delphic maxim: 'Known thyself'.

Phereboea (*Φερέβοια*) See PERIBOEA (5).

Phereclus (*Φέρεκλος*) Son of Harmonides, a Trojan who built the boat in which Paris sailed to abduct Helen.

Pheres (*Φέρης*)

1. One of the sons of Cretheus and Tyro (see Tables 1 and 6) who was the founder of the Thessalian city of Pherae. His children include Admetus, Idomene, who married Amythaon, Lycurgus (3) and Periopis who, according to another tradition, was the mother of Patroclus. (For Pheres' refusal to die instead of his son Admetus see ADMETUS.)
2. A son of Medea and Jason (Table 6) who was killed by his mother at the same time as his brother Mermerus.

Philammon (*Φιλάμμων*) A poet and seer, the son of Apollo and Philonis or Chione (3). Chione (or Philonis) mated with both Hermes and Apollo on the same day. The result was twin boys, Autolycus being the son of Hermes and Philammon that of Apollo. Philammon was loved by the Nymph Argiope, but when she became pregnant he refused to have anything to do with her. Argiope fled to Chalcidice and there gave birth to a son, Thamyris.

To Philammon is attributed the invention of girls' choirs and the institution of the Mysteries of Demeter at Lerna. When the Delphians were attacked by the Phlegyans, Philammon came to their rescue at the head of an Argive army. He died during the battle.

Philandrus (*Φίλανδρος*) The inhabitants of the city of Elyros on Crete deposited in Delphi an *ex-voto* offering depicting a nanny-goat suckling two human babies. These children were thought to be Philandrus and Phylacides, two sons of Acacallis by Apollo.

Philoctetes (*Φιλοκτήτης*) Son of Poeas and Demonassa (or Methane) and the keeper of the bow and arrow of Heracles. Philoctetes obtained them either from his father, to whom Heracles had given them, or from Heracles himself as a reward for setting fire to his funeral pyre on Mount Oeta. Heracles had asked Philoctetes to keep the place of his death a secret, and he had promised to do so. Later however, when pressed on the subject, Philoctetes went to Oeta and stamped on the spot where Heracles' pyre had stood. He thus broke his oath without actually speaking. He was punished for this act by a terrible wound which opened up on his foot.

Philoctetes, a native of Thessaly, was listed among Helen's suitors. He joined the Trojan expedition, but did not reach Troy as he was bitten on the foot by a snake during a sacrifice at Tenedos. An intolerable stench of rotting flesh emanated from the wound. Odysseus persuaded the other Greek captains to abandon Philoctetes on the island of Lemnos, where he lived for ten years.

In his tragedy *Philoctetes* Sophocles records that the episode took place not on Tenedos but on the little islet of Chryse. Philoctetes was bitten by a snake while he was tending the altar of Chryse, the goddess who had given her name to the island. A different version claims that Philoctetes was hurt by one of Heracles' poisoned arrows which had been steeped in the blood of the Hydra of Lerna. The arrow struck him in the foot when it accidentally fell out of its quiver and thus caused an incurable wound. (This accident was Heracles' revenge for Philoctetes' betrayal of his oath when he revealed where Heracles' pyre had been located.) One legend recounts that Philoctetes was abandoned because he was unable to suppress his cries of pain which fractured the ritual silence of sacrifices.

At the end of ten years the Greeks had still not taken Troy. Paris was dead and Helenus, who had been refused the hand of Helen, had fled to the mountains where he had been captured by the Greeks. He revealed that one of the preconditions for the capture of Troy was that its enemies should be armed with the arrows of Heracles. These arrows had already conquered the city once (see HERACLES, III); they alone could repeat the exploit. So Odysseus left for Lemnos, either alone or accompanied by Neoptolemus or Diomedes (2), to persuade Philoctetes to come to Troy. There are various accounts of the arguments which Odysseus used. In Euripides, Odysseus and Diomedes seized Philoctetes' weapons by a trick and thus forced the unarmed hero to go with them. In another version they deployed the language of patriotism. Alternatively, they promised that he would be healed by the sons of Asclepius, who were doctors to the Greek forces. Indeed, once Philoctetes arrived at Troy he was tended by either Podalirius or Machaon. Apollo plunged Philoctetes into a deep sleep while Machaon examined the wound, cut out the dead flesh, bathed the wound with vinegar, and applied to it a herb whose secret Asclepius had obtained from the Centaur Chiron.

The death of Paris is frequently attributed to Philoctetes, but this is contradicted by the story of the prophecy of Helenus, since Helenus was not captured until after Paris' death. Thus it was said that the prophecy ordering that Philoctetes should be brought to Troy was made by Calchas (1) and that Philoctetes arrived before the death of Paris.

Once Troy had fallen Philoctetes went home. In the *Odyssey* he reached home safely, but in later legends he founded several cities in southern Italy, including Petelia and Macalla, where he dedicated the arrows of Heracles to Apollo. He died on the battlefield, having come to the aid of the Rhodians, who had arrived in the region under the leadership of Tlepolemus and had been attacked by the native inhabitants.

Philoetius (*Φιλοίτιος*) Odysseus' cattle drover. Like EUMAEUS and unlike MELANTHIUS he remained faithful to Odysseus and hoped that he would return. He disapproved of the regime introduced in Odysseus' absence. He gave hospitality to the returned Odysseus whom he did not recognize in his beggar's disguise, and later helped him to overthrow the suitors. He killed Pisandrus and Ctesippus, and with Eumaeus was given the task of punishing Melanthius by Odysseus.

Philolaus (*Φιλόλαος*) One of the four sons of Minos by the Nymph Paria. When Heracles stopped at Paros on his expedition against the Amazons Philolaus attacked his companions.

Philomela (*Φιλομήλα*) One of the two daughters of Pandion (1), the king of Athens. She had a sister called Procne. When war broke out between Pandion and Labdacus, the king of Thebes, over the question of boundaries, Pandion asked Tereus, a Thracian, for his help; thanks to Tereus, Pandion was victorious. He then gave his ally the hand of Procne in marriage. Procne soon gave birth to a son called Itys. Tereus however fell in love with Philomela. He raped her and then cut out her tongue so that she could not betray him, but she revealed his crime to her sister by embroidering the story on a piece of material. Procne then decided to punish Tereus. She killed Itys, boiled his corpse and served it as a stew to Tereus. Then she fled with Philomela. When he became aware of the crime, Tereus set out in pursuit of the sisters. The two women implored the gods to save them; the gods took pity on them and changed Procne into a nightingale and Philomela into a swallow. Tereus was changed into a hoopoe. In other versions of this legend the roles of Procne and her sister are reversed, Philomela being the wife of Tereus. This version is most widely used by the Roman poets.

Philomelides (*Φιλομηλείδης*) A king of Lesbos who forced travellers to wrestle with him and killed those he defeated. Eventually he himself was killed by Odysseus (or by Odysseus and Diomedes (2)) when the Greek fleet stopped at Lesbos on its way to Troy.

Philotes (*Φιλότης*) The personification of Affection. Hesiod describes her as one of the daughters of Nyx, and sister to Apate (Deceit), Geras (Old Age) and Eris.

Philotis (*Φιλωτίς*) Following the sack of Rome by the Gauls, the Latins under Livius Postumius, attacked Rome. The Latins sent ambassadors asking the Romans to hand over their wives and daughters in order to strengthen the ancestral links between the two races. A slave girl called Philotis (or Tutula) suggested that she, and several other pretty slave girls should be sent to the Latins' camp, dressed as freeborn Roman women. During the night she put a lamp in a fig tree, whereupon the Romans rushed out and slaughtered the Latins. In memory of this event the Nonae Caprotinae, or Nones of the Fig-tree were celebrated. Other Roman antiquaries explained the festival as reflecting the death of Romulus, which happened on the Nones of July when people gathered in the Campus Martius in the place called the *palus Caprae*, or Goat Marsh.

Philyra (*Φιλύρα*) The mother of

the Centaur CHIRON, who was loved by Cronus. In one tradition, Cronus, fearing the jealousy of his wife Rhea, metamorphosed into a horse and mated with Philyra, which explains why Chiron was half horse, half man. In another version Philyra rejected the god's advances and turned herself into a mare to escape from him, but he turned into a stallion and raped her. Chiron was born on Mount Pelion, in Thessaly, where he lived in a cave with his mother.

Phineus (*Φινεύς*)

1. One of the sons of LYCAON. He was struck down by a thunderbolt together with his brothers.
2. The brother of Cepheus (2) and the uncle of ANDROMEDA. Phineus wanted to marry his niece and tried to foment a conspiracy against Perseus when the latter won her instead. In the ensuing battle, Phineus was turned to stone by the sight of Medusa's head. That he suffered this fate makes it impossible to identify him with Phineus (3), but in order to make such an identification possible, certain late mythographers claimed that Phineus was merely blinded by Perseus, not killed by him.
3. A king of Thrace. Having powers of divination, Phineus chose to have a long life at the price of going blind. In indignation the Sun sent the HARPIES to plague him. In other versions Phineus abused his gifts as a seer and revealed the plans of the gods to mortals. Another account claims he had incurred divine wrath by aiding PHRIXUS. Everything that was put before Phineus was snatched away by the Harpies, especially his food; and what they could not carry off they soiled. When the Argonauts asked him to predict the outcome of the expedition Phineus did so, on condition that they rid him of the Harpies. The Boreades, Zetes and Calais, chased the Harpies away. It was said that the Harpies could die only if they were caught by the Boreades; conversely, the latter would die if they failed to catch the Harpies. In the chase the first Harpy fell into a river in the Peloponnese, which was thereafter known as the Harpys; the other reached the Echinades Islands, which were known thereafter as the Strophades, or Islands of Return. At that point Iris appeared and forbade the Boreades to kill the Harpies. In exchange for their lives the Harpies promised to leave Phineus alone, and from then on hid in a cave on Crete.

In another legend Phineus' first wife was Cleopatra (1), the daughter of Boreas. They had two sons, Plexippus and Pandion (3). Phineus then married Idaea (2) (Table 4). Idaea was jealous of her two stepsons and falsely accused them of trying to rape her. Phineus, believing her, had them both blinded. When the Argonauts came to Phineus' court, the Boreades, who were Cleopatra's brothers, took their revenge on Phineus by blinding him in his turn. Asclepius restored the eyesight of Plexippus and Pandion but was punished for doing this by Zeus, who struck him with his thunderbolt.

These variant legends were combined by mythographers, who recounted that Phineus had been punished by Zeus for accusing his children of the crime and blinding them without proof. He was then plagued by the Harpies and the

Argonauts later freed him from them.

Phix (*Φίξ*) According to Hesiod this was the name of the Sphinx.

Phlegethon (*Φλεγέθων*) One of the rivers of the Underworld which joined the Cocytus to form the Acheron. There was a huge waterfall where the two rivers met. The name of the river suggests that it was a river of fire.

Phlegyas (*Φλεγύας*) A king of the LAPITHS and the eponym of the Phlegyans. He was the son of Ares and Dotis or Chryse. He had several children including IXION and CORONIS (1). According to regional traditions, Phlegyas succeeded Eteocles on the throne of Orchomenus, founded a new city, Phlegya, and died without children. His heir was his nephew Chryses (3). Phlegyas went to the Peloponnese to reconnoitre the land for a marauding expedition. During this trip Coronis was seduced by Apollo, which is why ASCLEPIUS was born at Epidauros.

In one account Phlegyas attempted to set fire to the Temple of Apollo at Delphi. Virgil depicts him in Hades suffering torments for his impiety. Apollodorus recounts that Phlegyas was killed by Lycus (3) and Nycteus. His murderers went into exile at Thebes.

Phlias (*Φλίας*) A son of Dionysus and Araethyrea, daughter of Minyas. According to Pausanias he was the husband of Chthonophyle, by whom he had a son called Androdamas. Sometimes Chthonophyle is said to have been the mother of Phlias rather than his wife. Phlias was one of the Argonauts and was the eponym of the city of Phlius in the Peloponnese.

Phlogius (*Φλόγιος*) A son of the Thessalian Deimachus. With his brothers Deileon and Autolycus, he accompanied Heracles on his expedition against the Amazons, but became separated from the hero at Sinope. The three of them spent some time there until the Argonauts passed by and agreed to take them with them.

Phobos (*Φόβος*) The personification of Fear, who accompanied Ares on the battlefield. He was said to be the son of Ares and the brother of Deimos.

Phocus (*Φῶκος*)

1. A native of Glisas in Boeotia who had a daughter called Callirhoe (7). Thirty men wished to marry her. Eventually he announced that, according to the Delphic oracle, the matter would have to be settled by the use of arms. The suitors killed him; Callirhoe fled, and some peasants hid her in a corn-mill. On the festival of the Boeotian federation Callirhoe came as a suppliant to the altar of Athena Itonia and accused the suitors of murdering her father. They fled to Hippotae. The Boeotians forced them to give themselves up and then stoned them to death. The previous evening the murderers had heard a voice coming from the mountains, calling, 'I am here.' It was the voice of Phocus, telling them of their punishment.
2. The eponymous hero of Phocis, a Corinthian and a descendant of

Sisyphus, who was said to be of the blood of Poseidon. He settled in the area around Parnassus, which then became known as Phocis. Phocus is said to have been the husband of ANTIOPE (1). Dionysus had made Antiope mad, but as she was wandering through Greece, Phocus encountered her. He cured her and they then married.

3. The other tradition about Phocus, the eponym of Phocis, makes him the son of Aeacus and Psamathe (1). His half-brothers were Peleus and Telamon, the sons of Aeacus by Endeis. Phocus was so called because to escape from Aeacus' advances Psamathe, who possessed the gift of metamorphosis, changed herself into a seal (Greek φώκη = 'seal'). This did not prevent Aeacus from coupling with her, however. When he reached maturity, Phocus left Salamis, his father's land, for central Greece. He conquered a district which he then called Phocis. He married Asteria (2), the daughter of Deion and Diomede, who bore him twin sons, Crisus and Panopeus.

Later Phocus returned to Aegina; there he was murdered by his half-brothers, who were jealous of him and were perhaps incited to murder by Endeis. Psamathe avenged his death by sending a wolf to destroy Peleus' flocks. However, at Thetis' entreaty, she agreed to change the wolf to stone.

Phoebe (*Φοίβη*)
1. 'The Shining One', one of the Titanides, a daughter of Uranus and Gaia. She married Coeus and bore him Leto and Asteria (1). She is sometimes said to have founded the oracle at Delphi in her capacity as a handmaiden of Themis and to have given it to her nephew Apollo as a present.
2. One of the LEUCIPPIDAE and the wife of Pollux. In literature Phoebe is assumed to be the wife of Castor.
3. One of the HELIADES (1).
4. The daughter of Tyndareus and Leda in the tragic writers.

Phoebus (*Φοῖβος*) An epithet of Apollo.

Phoenix (*Φοῖνιξ*)
1. A mythical bird. It was generally thought to come from Ethiopia. It lived there for 500, 1,461 or 12,954 years, according to different sources. It looked rather like an eagle, but was of considerable size. Its plumage was adorned with brilliant colouring, scarlet, blue, purple and gold, which made it more beautiful than the most splendid peacocks.

The Phoenix did not reproduce normally. When it felt its death impending it collected aromatic plants, incense and *amomum* (a balsam plant) and made a nest. In one tradition it set fire to the nest and a new Phoenix rose from the ashes; in the other it settled upon its nest and impregnated it as it died. The new Phoenix was then born, wrapped up its progenitor's body in a hollow log, and took it to Heliopolis in Egypt where it laid the body on the altar of the Sun. It was then burned by the priests. This was the only time when the Phoenix came to Egypt. It came with an escort of birds, and when it reached the altar of the Sun the priests would compare its appearance with a drawing in the sacred books. When the cremation was over, the young Phoenix would return to Ethiopia where it lived on incense. The birth of the Phoenix was supposed to mark the beginning of the 'Great Year', or one complete cycle of the stars. During the reign of Claudius a Phoenix was said to have been caught in Egypt. It was put on exhibition at Rome, but nobody accepted its authenticity.

2. One of the sons of Agenor (Table 3). He was sent by his father in search of Europa (5), who had been abducted by Zeus. Failing to find her, he settled on the site of the future city of Sidon in Phoenicia. The area owed its name to him. Sometimes, however, he is considered to have been the son of OGYGUS (1), or said to be Europa's father, rather than her brother.

3. The son of Amyntor, king of Eleon in Boeotia, and Hippodamia (4), Cleoboula or Alcimede. Amyntor had a concubine called Phthia, and at the request of his mother, who was jealous, Phoenix seduced his concubine. On learning of this crime, Amyntor had his son blinded. In another version Phthia tried to seduce Phoenix; when she failed she falsely denounced him to Amyntor. Amyntor blinded Phoenix. Phoenix took refuge with Peleus, who took him to the Centaur Chiron who restored his sight. Peleus then entrusted his son Achilles to Phoenix and made him king of the Dolopians. Phoenix left for Troy with Achilles, as his counsellor. Phoenix tried unsuccessfully to persuade his friend to be reconciled to Agamemnon. He was present when Achilles learnt of the death of Patroclus and he also played a part in the funeral games in honour of Patroclus. After Achilles' death, Phoenix went with Odysseus to fetch Neoptolemus. When the Greeks returned from Troy, he travelled with Neoptolemus but died on the journey.

4. The father of Adonis, according to Hesiod's *Catalogue of Women*.

Pholus (*Φόλος*) See CENTAURS.

Phorbas (*Φόρβας*)

1. A descendant of the Lapiths. In some accounts he is the son of Lapithes by Orsinome, in others the son of Triopas, son of Lapithes. He lived in Thessaly, but migrated to Cnidus, or to Rhodes, with his brother Periergus. There is also a Peloponnesian version of the story of Phorbas. He migrated from Thessaly to Olenos in Elis; there Alector, who was afraid of Pelops (1), allied himself with Phorbas and shared his kingdom with him. The alliance of Phorbas and Alector was sealed by a double marriage: Alector married Phorbas' daughter Diogenia, and Phorbas married Alector's sister, Hyrmine. Phorbas had two sons, Augias and Actor (1). On his death they divided Elis between them.

2. The son of Argos (1). He was the father of Triopas. His wife was called Euboea, and MESSENE is sometimes listed among his other children.

3. A Phlegyan who lived at Panope in Phocis. He would attack travellers on the road to Delphi, force them to box with him, and kill them. One day Apollo appeared in the form of a child, challenged Phorbas and vanquished him.

4. The hero who taught Theseus how to drive a chariot. He is sometimes credited with the invention of wrestling.

5. A Trojan sheep-owner, the father of Ilioneus (2).

Phorcys (*Φόρκυς*) One of the sea-gods, the son of Gaia and Pontus. He was the brother of Nereus, Thaumas, Eurybia and Ceto. He married Ceto and had children by her, notably the GRAEAE. He is also said to have been the father of SCYLLA (1). In addition, various sources make Phorcys the father of Echidna and the Hesperides, and sometimes it is claimed that he was the grandfather of the Eumenides.

Phormion (*Φορμίων*) A Spartan who owned the house where Tyndareus had once lived. The Dioscuri came to him disguised as travellers, telling him that they had come from Cyrene. They asked him for hospitality and begged him to give them a specific room, one where they had stayed during their childhood. Phormion placed his whole house at their disposal except the room which they wanted because it was his daughter's room. During the night the young girl, her servants and the Dioscuri all disappeared, and in the girl's room there was a picture of the Dioscuri and some *silphion*, the aromatic plant which was the main product of Cyrene.

Phoroneus (*Φορωνεύς*) According to Peloponnesian legend, Phoróneus was the first mortal. He was the son of the river-god Inachus and Melia (2), and he had two brothers, Aegialeus and Phegeus. Phoroneus was chosen to judge the quarrel between Hera and Poseidon for possession of the Peloponnese: he decided in Hera's favour. Phoroneus first taught people to group themselves together in cities and showed them how to use fire. He brought the cult of the Argive Hera to the Peloponnese. His wife is sometimes called Cerdo, sometimes Teledice, sometimes Europa (3), and sometimes Peitho (3). His children are usually given as Car, the first king of Megara, and NIOBE (1); to these are sometimes added Iasus, Lyrcus (1), Pelasgus and Agenor.

Phosphorus (*Φωσφόρος*) The Morning Star which is also called Heosphorus or Eosphorus. In Latin the name becomes Lucifer.

Phrasius (*Φράσιος*) A seer who visited Egypt during a famine and predicted to BUSIRIS that the famine would end if a stranger were sacrificed every year. Busiris began by sacrificing Phrasius.

Phrixus (*Φρίξος*) One of the offspring of ATHAMAS and Nephele (1), and the brother of Helle. On the advice of his second wife, Ino, Athamas decided to sacrifice Phrixus and Helle to Zeus, but Zeus (or Nephele) sent a ram with a golden fleece which saved them. They flew off East on the ram, but Helle fell into the sea and drowned in the straits thereafter known as the Hellespont (another version says that she was saved by Poseidon, who fell in love with her). Phrixus arrived safely at the court of Aeetes, king of Colchis, who gave him the hand of his daughter Chalciope (2) in marriage. Phrixus sacrificed the ram to Zeus and presented the fleece to AEETES (see also ARGONAUTS and JASON). Phrixus and Chalciope had numerous children, including Argos (3), Melas (2), Phrontis and Cytissorus. Phrixus later died in Colchis.

In a tradition mentioned by Hyginus, Aeetes killed Phrixus because an oracle had predicted that the king would die at the hands of a descendant of Aeolus (1). This text tells how Phrixus and Helle, having been saved from the sacrifice, were driven mad by Dionysus for trying to take revenge on Ino.

Phronime (*Φρονίμη*) Mother of Battus (2), and the daughter of King Etearchus of Axos on Crete. Etearchus remarried. His second wife denounced Phronime, falsely accusing her of a debauched lifestyle. Etearchus believed her and coerced a merchant called Themison into promising to take Phronime away and push her overboard into the open sea. Themison, however, merely dipped her into the sea. He then took her ashore at Thera and arranged for her to marry a local nobleman, Polymnestus, who was Battus' father.

Phrygius (*Φρύγιος*) A king of Miletus, who succeeded when King Phobius gave up his throne after the death of Cleoboea (see ANTHEUS). When Pieria, a daughter of Phytes of Myonte, came to Miletus for the festival of Artemis, he fell in love with her and, by marrying her, put an end to a war between the inhabitants of Myonte and the Milesians.

Phthius (*Φθῖος*) The founder of Phthiotis in Thessaly. Sometimes he is said to be one of the sons of Lycaon (2), sometimes a son of Poseidon by the Nymph Larissa and hence the brother of Achaeus and Pelasgus (3). In another version he is the son of Achaeus and the husband of Chrysippe, daughter of Irus.

Phthonus (*Φθόνος*) The personification of Envy.

Phylacus (*Φύλακος*)

1. A Thessalian hero, the son of Deion, or Deioneus and Diomede (Table 5). He was the father of IPHICLUS (1) and Alcimede, the mother of Jason. Phylacus married Clymene (3). He supposedly founded the city of Phylacae on the River Othrys. He was the owner of a magnificent herd (see MELAMPUS).
2. A Delphian, who appeared in the shape of an armed giant just as the Persians were attacking the sanctuary, and put them to flight, amid lightning and supernatural manifestations. At his side he had another giant, Autonous (cf. HYPERBOREANS).
3. A Trojan warrior killed by Leitus.

Phylas (*Φύλας*)

1. The king of the Thesprotians. Heracles made war on him with the citizens of Calydon, captured his city and then killed him. Phylas' daughter Astyoche was captured by Heracles and bore him a son, Tlepolemus.
2. The father of POLYMELA (1).
3. The king of the Dryopes, who attacked the sanctuary at Delphi. Heracles then made war upon Phylas, killed him and expelled the Dryopes from their territory, which he gave to the Malians. Heracles had a son called Antiochus by Phylas' daughter.
4. The father of Hippotes (1) and

grandfather of Aletes (1), the companion of the HERACLIDS. This Phylas, son of Antiochus, married Leipephile, daughter of Iolaus, who bore him a daughter called Thero.

Phyleus (*Φυλεύς*) One of the sons of Augias. He sided with Heracles against his father over the issue of the payment for cleaning the stables (see HERACLES, II and III). For this he was banished by his father and settled at Dulichium. There he married TIMANDRA or Ctimene (2) who bore him a son named MEGES and a daughter, Eurydamia. After Heracles had conquered Augias, he placed Phyleus on the throne of Elis. Phyleus later gave the throne to his brothers and returned to Dulichium. He took part in the Calydonian boar hunt.

Phylius (*Φύλιος*) An Aetolian hero who played a part in the story of CYCNUS (5).

Phyllis (*Φυλλίς*) On his way back from Troy Demophon (or ACAMAS (3)) was washed up on the coast of Thrace. The king of the region gave him hospitality. The king's daughter, Phyllis, fell in love with him. In one version he married her; in others he promised to marry her, but told her he had to return to Athens to settle his affairs before he could do so. Phyllis agreed to the separation but gave him a casket containing objects sacred to the Great Mother, Rhea. She advised him to open it only when he had abandoned all hope of returning to her. Demophon left her and settled in Cyprus. The day set for his return arrived, but he did not appear. She went down to the harbour nine times to see whether his boat was approaching; in memory of this the place was called the 'Nine Roads'. Phyllis then invoked a curse on Demophon and hanged herself. On the same day in Crete, Demophon opened the casket. The sight of its contents frightened his horse, which bolted. Demophon was thrown, fell on his sword and died. In another version Phyllis was metamorphosed into a leafless almond tree. Her lover embraced the tree which then grew leaves. From that moment the Greek word for leaves, originally 'petala', became 'phylla'.

Phytalus (*Φύταλος*) An Attic hero who lived on the banks of the Ilissus. Demeter visited Attica when she was looking for her daughter, and Phytalus gave the goddess hospitality. In return she gave him some young fig trees. His descendants held the sole right to the cultivation of figs for a long time. They entertained THESEUS when he was on his way back from Corinth and purified him of the murders of Sinis and other brigands.

Picus A very early king of Latium who ruled the Aborigines. He was the father of Faunus and the grandfather of Latinus. His father was sometimes said to be Sterces, or Sterculus, whose name suggests the word 'dung-heap'; he was identifed with Saturn by the mythographers. Picus was an excellent seer, who possessed a green woodpecker, the preeminent prophetic bird. The mythographers claimed that the woodpecker was in fact Picus himself and that he had been changed into that shape by Circe, since he had repulsed Circe's advances because of his love either for his wife, Pomona, or for the Nymph Canens.

Pierides (*Πιερίδες*) Nine maidens who wanted to outshine the Muses. They were the daughters of Pierus (1). They possessed especially beautiful singing voices and challenged the Muses to a singing contest. They were unsuccessful, and to punish them the Muses changed them into magpies, according to Ovid, or into various birds, according to Nicander. According to Pausanias, the Pierides had the same names as the Muses, and the children attributed to the Muses, such as Orpheus, were the children of the Pierides, since the Muses remained eternally virgin.

Pierus (*Πίερος*)
1. The eponym of Pieria, often thought to be the father of the Pierides. Pierus introduced the cult of the Muses into his region. He is sometimes said to have been the father of Linus (2) or of Oeager, and therefore the grandfather of Orpheus.
2. The son of Magnes in some traditions. Pierus was loved by the Muse Clio; Aphrodite had inspired her with the passion as a punishment for deriding the goddess's own love for Adonis. Their son was in some versions said to be HYACINTHUS, in others HYMENAEUS.

Pietas The personification of feelings of duty towards the gods, the state and one's family. Her temple at the foot of the Capitoline dates from the beginning of the second century BC.

Pilumnus
1. A Roman deity who protected new-born babies against the evil tricks and wiles of the malevolent spirit Silvanus. Pilumnus shared his functions with Intercidona and Deverra. Intercidona took her name from the symbolic axe-blows given to the door post at the birth of a child; Deverra derived hers from the broom which was used to sweep the threshold; and Pilumnus was named after the *pilum* (pestle) with which the door was struck. Axe, pestle and broom were symbols of civilization (the axe cut down trees, the pestle pounded corn and the broom swept the threshing floor). These symbols frightened Silvanus, the spirit of the uncivilized wilderness. Pilumnus is also mentioned alongside Picumnus, a deity whose name is reminiscent of PICUS.
2. Virgil mentions a Pilumnus who is grandfather of Turnus and father of Daunus.

Pindus (*Πίνδος*) A son of Macedon (3). When Pindus was out hunting one day he met a monstrous serpent. The creature did not attack him, and to show his gratitude Pindus used to bring the serpent part of the fruits of his hunting expeditions. When Pindus was killed by his three brothers, who were jealous of him, the serpent killed them and guarded Pindus' corpse until his relatives paid him funeral honours.

Piren (*Πειρήν*)
1. The son of Glaucus (3) and the brother of BELLEROPHON who accidentally killed him. See also IO.
2. The son of Argos (1) and Evadne (3). Sometimes his name is given as Piras. In some accounts he is said to be Io's father, but she is more

commonly said to be the descendant of his brother Ecbasus.

Pirene (*Πειρήνη*) The figure who gave her name to the Pirenean spring at Corinth. In one tradition she is one of the twelve daughters of Asopus. When Artemis accidentally killed Cenchrias, her child by Poseidon, Pirene shed so many tears that she changed into a spring. In another tradition Pirene was the daughter of Oebalus (1). A different legend surrounding the Pirenean spring claimed that it was given to Sisyphus by Asopus as a reward for revealing the name of the man who had raped Asopus' daughter AEGINA. In some accounts, Bellerophon met Pegasus by the Pirenean spring.

Pirithous (*Πειρίθοος*) A Thessalian hero. In the *Iliad* he is cited as the son of Zeus and Dia, but he is more usually considered to be the son of Dia and Ixion. The principal events of his legend are his part in the Calydonian boar hunt; his wedding to Hippodamia (2), which was the occasion of the battle with the Centaurs; his meeting with Theseus; his participation in the abduction of Helen; and his visit to Hades.

In the Calydonian boar hunt Pirithous was simply one of the huntsmen and took no special part in the action. In the *Iliad* Pirithous is portrayed as the vanquisher of the CENTAURS, an episode which later became assimilated into his marriage to Hippodamia. She, though sometimes said to be the daughter of Adrastus and Amphithea (Table 1), is more generally described as the daughter of Butes. In one tradition Hippodamia was related to the Centaurs, but as a son of Ixion, Pirithous was himself a 'half-brother' to these monsters. Under the influence of wine the Centaurs tried to rape Hippodamia and carry off the other women present. A battle broke out between the Centaurs and Pirithous' compatriots, the Lapiths, during which many Centaurs were killed. Pirithous and Hippodamia had a son named POLYPOETES (2).

For the friendship between Theseus and Pirithous and their exploits in the Underworld, see THESEUS, VI. For the abduction of Helen, see HELEN.

Pisaeus (*Πισαῖος*) An Etruscan hero named after the city of Pisa in Tuscany. He supposedly invented the trumpet, and battle-rams for warships.

Pisidice (*Πεισιδίκη*)

1. The daughter of the king of Methymna, on Lesbos. When Achilles was besieging the city, Pisidice fell in love with him. She offered to deliver the city to Achilles if he would promise to marry her. Achilles accepted the offer but, once victorious, he had her stoned to death.
2. A girl from Monenia in the Troad. While Achilles was besieging and was about to attack, Pisidice threw a note to him, stating that the citizens were about to surrender because of lack of water. Achilles was consequently able to capture the city without striking a single blow.
3. One of the daughters of Aeolus (1) and Aenarete (Table 5).
4. One of the daughters of Nestor and Anaxibia.
5. A daughter of Pelias.

Pisistratus (*Πεισίστρατος*) The youngest son of NESTOR. He was the same age as TELEMACHUS and went with him on his journey from Pylos to Sparta.

Pistor During the siege of the Capitol by the Gauls, the corn began to run out. Jupiter appeared in a dream to the defenders and advised them to throw their most precious possession at the enemy. The Romans made all of their flour into loaves and hurled them at the enemy. The Gauls despaired of ever starving out an enemy who seemed so well provisioned, and raised the siege. In gratitude the Romans built an altar to Jupiter Pistor (Jupiter the Baker).

Pisus (*Πῖσος*)
1. A son of Perieres (1). He gave his name to the city of Pisa in Elis.
2. The Italian city of Pisa laid claim, in certain traditions, to an eponymous Pisus, who was a king of the Celts and a son of Hyperborean Apollo.
3. A son of Aphareus.

Pitane (*Πιτάνη*)
1. A daughter of the river-god Eurotas who bore Poseidon a child named Evadne (1). This child was exposed at birth by her mother and taken in by AEPYTUS (3). In other versions Pitane herself secretly took the child to Aepytus. The Spartan city of Pitane was named after her.
2. An Amazon who founded the city of Pitane in Mysia, as well as the cities of Cyme and Priene.

Pittheus (*Πιτθεύς*) Son of Pelops (1) and Hippodamia (1) (Table 2) and the brother of Thyestes and Atreus. He succeeded TROEZEN as king of that city, where he founded the oldest Greek temple, that of Apollo Thearius. Pittheus had a reputation for wisdom and eloquence. He was also an excellent seer (see AEGEUS). He was the grandfather of Theseus and he brought him up. Pittheus was also in charge of the education of Hippolytus (1).

Pityreus (*Πιτυρεύς*) A king of Epidaurus, in the Peloponnese, at the time when the Heraclids returned. He gave up his kingdom to the Heraclid Deiphontes without a fight and withdrew with his subjects to Athens.

Pitys (*Πίτυς*) A Nymph whom Pan loved. One day as the girl fled from his advances she was changed into a pine tree (Greek *πίτυς* = 'pine'). In another version Pitys was loved by both Pan and Boreas and yielded to the former. In a fit of jealousy Boreas hurled her off the top of a rock. The Earth, taking pity on her, changed her body into a pine tree. The soul of Pitys is said to weep as Boreas blows through the branches of pine trees.

Pleiades (*Πλειάδες*) The seven sisters who became the seven stars of the constellation of the same name. They were the daughters of Atlas (1) and Pleione. Their names were Taygete, Electra (2), Alcyone (2), Asterope, Celaeno (1), Maia (1) and Merope (1). According to a fragment of Callimachus, the Pleiades were daughters of a queen of the Amazons and were responsible for introducing choral dances and nocturnal festivals. In this poem they are called Coccymo, Glaucia, Protis, Parthenia, Maia, Stonychia, and Lampado. Calypso (1) and Dione are sometimes included among the Pleiades. All the Pleiades married gods except Merope, who married Sisyphus; that is why her star is the least bright in the constellation.

The Pleiades were in Boeotia with Pleione when they met Orion, who fell in love with them. He pursued them for five years and eventually they were turned into doves. Zeus then turned them into stars. In other traditions their transformation was as a result of their grief when their father, Atlas, was condemned to hold up the sky. In another version the Pleiades and their sisters the HYADES were changed into stars after the death of their brother Hyas. When Troy fell, Electra (2) from whom the Trojan royal house was descended (Table 4), left her sisters in despair, and was changed into a comet.

Pleione (*Πληιόνη*) The mother of the PLEIADES and a daughter of Oceanus and Tethys. Her children also included the HYADES and HYAS. Orion fell in love with Pleione as well as her daughters; she too was changed into a star.

Pleisthenes (*Πλεισθένης*) Pleisthenes appears in the genealogy of the family of Atreus and of Pelops (1) but his parentage varies from tradition to tradition. He is most frequently said to be a son of Pelops (1) and Hippodamia (1), and therefore a brother of Thyestes and Atreus (Table 2). In some versions AEROPE (1) is said to be his mother, but other versions make her his wife. Although Agamemnon and Menelaus are usually considered to be the sons of Atreus, Hesiod and Aeschylus claim that Pleisthenes was their father. To make the two traditions correspond it was assumed that Pleisthenes was the father of the two heroes, and was himself the son of Atreus, but he died young, entrusting his two sons and his daughter Anaxibia to their grandfather to bring up. This is why Agamemnon and Menelaus are generally designated under the title Atridae. A tradition mentioned by Hyginus makes Pleisthenes a son of Thyestes.

Plemnaeus (*Πλημναῖος*) A king of Sicyon in the tradition recorded by Pausanias. He is the son of Peratus and father of ORTHOPOLIS. He is said to have introduced the cult of Demeter into Sicyon.

Pleuron (*Πλευρών*) The brother of Calydon and a son of Aetolus and Pronoe. He gave his name to the Aetolian city of Pleuron and married Xanthippe, daughter of Dorus, thus establishing ties between the Aetolians and the Dorians. They had several children: Agenor, Sterope (2), Stratonice and Laophonte. There was a sanctuary dedicated to Pleuron at Sparta.

Plexippus (*Πλήξιππος*)

1. One of the uncles of MELEAGER and the brother of Althaea. He was killed by his nephew during the Calydonian boar hunt.
2. One of the sons of PHINEUS (3) and Cleopatra (1).
3. One of the sons of CHORICUS.

Pluto See PLUTON.

Pluton (*Πλούτων*) The 'Rich Man', a ritual title of HADES. He was assimilated to the Latin deity Dis Pater who, like him, was originally the god of the fields, because the ground was the source of all wealth (see PLUTUS and DEMETER).

Plutus (*Πλοῦτος*) 'Wealth', the son of Demeter and Iasion according to Hesiod's *Theogony*. He was born in Crete. Plutus appears as a young man, or as a child bearing a horn of plenty. Later, as the concept of wealth became associated with material goods, Plutus became the personification of wealth in general; he appears in this form in Aristophanes' comedy. Plutus is represented as being blind, since hs visits the good and the wicked without making any distinction. According to Aristophanes Zeus blinded Plutus to prevent him from rewarding only the virtuous and to oblige him to favour the wicked too.

Podalirius (*Ποδαλείριος*) The brother of Machaon and, like him, a son of Asclepius. His mother's name is sometimes given as Epione, sometimes as Lampetia (2). Podalirius and Machaon were both Helen's suitors and participated in the Trojan War. Both were skilled in healing: Machaon was said to have been principally a surgeon and Podalirius a general practitioner. Podalirius dressed the wounds of Acamas (3) and Epeius, who were badly hurt in the boxing contest at the funeral games in honour of Achilles, and also cured PHILOCTETES. Podalirius outlived his brother, whose death he avenged. After the fall of Troy he returned to Greece and reached Colophon by land. After the death of Calchas (1) at Colophon Podalirius asked the Delphic oracle where he should settle. The oracle instructed him to choose an area where, if the sky fell around him, he would have nothing to fear. The region corresponding to this description was the Chersonese at Caria which is ringed by mountains, and Podalirius settled there. According to another version he was thrown up on the coast of Caria by a storm and rescued by a goatherd who took him to the king of the region, whose name was Damaethus. The king's daughter, Syrna, had just fallen from a roof and Podalirius offered medical assistance. He cured the girl, married her, and was presented with the Carian peninsula, where he founded the city of Syrnos.

There was a sanctuary dedicated to Podalirius in Italy at the foot of Mount Drion. Another sanctuary on the top of the mountain was dedicated to Calchas. Podalirius was said to have founded it, and it was believed that if one sacrificed a black ram to either Podalirius or Calchas and then slept in the animal's skin one had prophetic dreams.

Podarces (*Ποδάρκης*)

1. The name given to Priam when he was young (see HERACLES, III, PRIAM and Table 4).
2. A son of Iphiclus (1) who accompanied his brother Protesilaus to Troy; after the latter's death he succeeded him as commander of the contingent from Phylace. He killed the Amazon Clonia and was himself killed by Penthesilea. The Greeks

paid him special funeral honours and gave him a separate tomb.

Podarge (*Ποδάργη*) One of the HARPIES. She gave birth to Xanthus (7) and Balius (1), the steeds of Achilles, fathered by Zephyrus. She is also said to have been the mother of Phlogaeus and Harpagus, the horses belonging either to Diomedes (1) (but see also HERACLES, II) or to the Dioscuri.

Podes (*Ποδῆς*) A Trojan, and a friend of Hector, who was killed by Menelaus in the fighting over the body of Patroclus.

Poeas (*Ποίας*) The son of Thaumacus. He was married to Methone and was the father of Philoctetes. He appears among the Argonauts. One tradition makes him the conqueror of TALOS (1), although this role is more generally attributed to Medea. Poeas was with Heracles in his dying moments. Some mythographers say that it was he who lit Heracles' funeral pyre when everybody else refused, and in recompense Heracles bequeathed to Poeas his bow and arrows. PHILOCTETES, however, is more frequently credited with this role.

Poemandrus (*Ποίμανδρος*) A Boeotian hero, the son of Chaeresilaus and Stratonice. He married Tanagra, the daugher of Aeolus (1) or Asopus. Poemandrus founded Poemandria (later called Tanagra). Achilles attacked the town when the inhabitants refused to take part in the Trojan War. He carried off Stratonice, but Poemandrus escaped and began fortifying the city. During the course of this work a builder insulted Poemandrus, who hurled a large stone at him. He missed and killed his own son Leucippus (7). As a result of this crime Poemandrus had to leave Boeotia, but as the region was still under siege he asked the enemy to let him leave safely. Achilles granted this request and sent Poemandrus to Elephenor at Chalcis. Elephenor purified Poemandrus, who then built a sanctuary to Achilles.

Poine (*Ποινή*) The personification of Vengeance or Punishment; she is sometimes identified with the Erinyes or Furies whom she accompanied. In later Roman mythology Poena is the mother of the Furies and appears among the demons of the Underworld. Poine was also portrayed as a monster sent by Apollo to avenge the death of Psamathe (2) (cf. COROEBUS (1)).

Polhymnia (*Πολύμνια*) One of the nine Muses, a daughter of Zeus and Mnemosyne. Various traditions attribute to her several inventions, including the lyre and agriculture. In some accounts she is said to be the Muse of Dancing, in others the Muse of Geometry or even of History. An isolated tradition claims that she was Orpheus' mother by Oeager, although Orpheus' mother is more usually said to be Calliope. Plato refers to a legend in which she is the mother of Eros.

Poliporthes (*Πολιπόρθης*) Poliporthes or Ptoliporthes was a son of ODYSSEUS and Penelope, born while his father was ruling the Thesprotians.

Polites (*Πολίτης*)
1. One of the sons of Priam and Hecuba. In the *Iliad* he came to the help of Troilus when he was attacked by Achilles, and he took part in the fighting around the ships, when he saved his brother Deiphobus, who had been wounded. Polites was the last surviving son of Priam. He was killed by Neoptolemus at the palace altar, in his father's presence. Virgil names a son of Polites, called Priamus, among the competitors at the funeral games given for Anchises.
2. A companion of Odysseus who was changed into a pig by Circe. See EUTHYMUS.

Pollux (*Πολυδεύκης*) One of the DIOSCURI, the twin brother of Castor.

Poltys (*Πόλτυς*) A son of Poseidon and king of Aenos in Thrace. He entertained Heracles when he came to Thrace on his way back from the land of the Amazons. He had a brother SARPEDON who was slain by Heracles. During the Trojan War the Trojans sent an embassy to Poltys, asking for his help, but he demanded that Paris should hand Helen over to him in exchange for two other beautiful women. The demand was rejected.

Polybotes (*Πολυβώτης*) One of the giants who fought the gods. See GIANTS.

Polybus (*Πόλυβος*)
1. The king of Thebes, in Egypt, who gave hospitality to MENELAUS and HELEN.
2. A king of Sicyon, son of Hermes and Chthonophyle. Polybus had a daughter called Lysianassa, or Lysimache, whom he gave in marriage to Talaus, king of Argos. She had several children by him, including Adrastus and Pronax (Table 1). ADRASTUS fled to the court of Polybus, and when Polybus died without male children he left his kingdom to Adrastus.
3. A king of Corinth who brought up OEDIPUS.

Polycaon (*Πολυκάων*)
1. The husband of Messene and the younger son of Lelex (1) and Peridea. As he had no hope of inheriting any part of his father's kingdom, he decided to obtain a kingdom of his own. Accompanied by people from Argos and Sparta, he founded the city of Andania and colonized the area of the Peloponnese which he named Messenia (see also MESSENE).
2. The hero who married Evaechme, the daughter of Hyllus and Iole.

Polycaste (*Πολυκάστη*)
1. One of the daughters of Nestor who, in the *Odyssey*, prepared a bath for Telemachus when he came to Pylos to ask after the fate of his father. In later legend Polycaste was said to have married Telemachus and borne him a son called Persepolis.
2. The wife of ICARIUS (2), and Penelope's mother, but in some versions Periboea (1) is given as the wife of Icarius.

Polycrite (*Πολυκρίτη*) A heroine of Naxos. During a war between the Naxians and the Milesians and Erythraeans, Polycrite was taken prisoner. Diognetus, the leader of the Erythraeans, fell in love with his captive. Polycrite was the sister of the leader of the Naxians, Polycles. By means of a note concealed in a cake she warned her brother that she had persuaded her lover to hand over the camp to the Naxians during the night. The Naxians entered the camp and massacred their enemy. However, Polycrite, on returning to Naxos, received so many gifts and wreaths that she suffocated as she was entering the town. She was buried at the spot on which she died. At Polycrite's request, Diognetus' life had been spared during the attack on the camp, although in another version he was killed during the fighting and was buried beside Polycrite.

Polyctor (*Πολύκτωρ*) One of the children of PTERELAUS and Amphimede. With his brothers Ithacus and Neritus he came from Cephalonia to colonize Ithaca and caused the stream from which the inhabitants of Ithaca obtained their water to flow.

Polydamas (*Πολυδάμας*) A Trojan hero, the son of PANTHOUS and Phrontis or Pronome, or else of Antenor and Theano. He was born the same night as Hector, and Hector's prowess in battle was equalled by Polydamas' soundness in council. Polydamas proposed the attack on the Achaean camp; suggested to Hector that he should summon the Trojan chiefs; advised the Trojans to take refuge in Ilion after their defeat and, after Hector's death, to hand over Helen. He had a son, Leocritus.

Polydamna (*Πολύδαμνα*) According to one tradition the wife of the Egyptian king, Thon. In order to protect HELEN from the amorous advances of the king, she took her to the island of Pharos in the Nile delta, and gave her herbs as a protection against the bite of the countless serpents which inhabited the island.

Polydectes (*Πολυδέκτης*) According to some writers, a son of Magnes (Table 5), and one of the Naiads; according to others, he was the son of Peristhenus, a grandson of Nauplius (1) and Androthea, daughter of Pericastor. He had a brother, DICTYS, with whom he settled on the island of Seriphos. It was with Dictys – or, in other traditions, with Polydectes himself – that DANAE sought refuge when she and her son PERSEUS were cast up on the island. Polydectes fell in love with Danae, and in order to remove Perseus he sent him off to look for the head of Medusa.

A version related by Hyginus states that it was at the funeral games organized by Perseus in honour of Polydectes that he accidentally killed his grandfather Acrisius (see also ACRISIUS).

Polydeuces (*Πολυδεύκης*) The Greek form of Pollux, one of the DIOSCURI.

Polydora (*Πολυδώρα*) The daughter of PELEUS and Antigone (3). Polydora had, by the river-god Spercheius, a son named Menesthius. She subsequently married Borus, who sometimes passed for the human father of Menesthius. Some accounts give as her mother Polymela (3). There was also a tradition in which Polydora was not the daughter but the wife of Peleus.

Polydorus (*Πολύδωρος*)
1. Son of Cadmus and Harmonia (1). He married Nycteis, by whom he had Labdacus (Table 3). In some traditions Cadmus left the throne of Thebes to Polydorus when he went to Illyria; in others he gave it to Pentheus, son of his daughter Agave, while Polydorus followed him to Illyria; in others Pentheus dispossessed Polydorus after Cadmus' departure.
2. In the Homeric tradition, the son of Priam and Laothoe. Priam sent him away from the battlefield, but, trusting to his speed as a runner, Polydorus attacked Achilles, who killed him. Achilles removed the silver cuirass from his body; after Achilles' death Thetis gave this trophy to Agamemnon. In later traditions Polydorus was the son of Priam and Hecuba. Priam entrusted the young Polydorus, along with some rich treasures, to his son-in-law Polymestor. Polydorus was murdered by Polymestor, but was later avenged by Hecuba (see HECUBA for details).

In the tradition followed by Virgil, Polymestor buried Polydorus on the coast of Thrace. Aeneas landed there, and was cutting branches from the trees which grew near the tomb when drops of blood oozed from the branches. A voice revealed that he was on the site of Polydorus' tomb and that the trees had sprung from the javelins which had pierced him. The voice recounted the details of Polydorus' death and advised Aeneas to abandon his plans to found a city on the spot. Aeneas gave funeral honours to Polydorus, and departed. Another tradition says that Polymestor handed Polydorus over to Ajax (2) who wanted to use the child as a hostage, and exchange him for Helen. The Trojans refused. Polydorus was then stoned to death before Troy's walls, and his body returned to Hecuba.

Polygonus (*Πολύγονος*) He and Telegonus, the two sons of Proteus and Torone, were bandits who used to challenge travellers to a fight, and then kill them. They were themselves killed by Heracles.

Polyhymnia (*Πολύμνια*) See POLHYMNIA.

Polyidus (*Πολύειδος*)
1. A Corinthian soothsayer, descended from Melampus. His father was Coeranus (1). Polyidus married Eurydamia. They had two sons, Euchenor and Clitus, who took part in the expedition of the Epigoni and later accompanied Agamemnon against Troy. See EUCHENOR.

A tradition which grew up at Megara related that Polyidus came to this city, where he purified ALCATHOUS of the murder of his son Callipolis and built a temple to Dionysus. In this tradition, Polyidus is acknowledged as a son of Coeranus, but his grandfather is given as Abas (3) (Table 1) rather than Clitus (1).

Polyidus advised Bellerophon to go to the spring of Pirene and catch Pegasus. He also advised Iphitus to go to Tiryns to be with Heracles. He saved Teuthras (1) from his madness. But the most famous story of his intervention is that of the resurrection of GLAUCUS (5).
2. A Trojan, the son of the soothsayer Eurydamas, who along with

his brother Abas (4) was slain by Diomedes (2).

Polymede (*Πολυμήδη*) A daughter of Autolycus who married Aeson and became the mother of Jason (Table 6). When her husband was condemned to death by Pelias, she cursed the latter and hanged herself. She left a child called Promachus, but Pelias killed him. Aeson's wife was also known as Alcimede.

Polymela (*Πολυμήλα*)

1. The daughter of Phylas (2) who became by Hermes the mother of EUDORUS. She later married Echecles, a descendant of Actor.
2. The daughter of Aeolus, the god of winds. She was Odysseus' mistress while he was staying at her father's court (see AEOLUS (1) and (2)). Aeolus wanted to punish her, but Diores, his son, was in love with his sister and obtained Aeolus' permission to marry her.
3. A daughter of Actor who, according to certain traditions, married Peleus before his marriage to Thetis (see POLYDORA). Sometimes she is the daughter of Peleus.
4. The daughter of Autolycus, better known as POLYMEDE.

Polymestor (*Πολυμήστωρ*) The king of Thrace, husband of Ilione, the daughter of Priam. For the different versions of this legend, see DEIPYLUS, HECUBA and POLYDORUS (2).

Polymnus (*Πόλυμνος*) When DIONYSUS descended into the Underworld he sought the way from a peasant called Polymnus (or Prosymnus) who gave him the information, but in return asked the god for certain sexual favours. Dionysus promised to bestow these on him on his return. However, when he returned, Polymnus was dead. In order to fulfil his promise, the god carved a fig branch in the shape of a phallus and on Polymnus' tomb performed an act designed to satisfy his shade.

Polynices (*Πολυνείκης*) One of the two sons of OEDIPUS. His brother was Eteocles. Sometimes he is the son of Eurygania (1), but in the tradition followed by the tragic writers, he is the son of Jocasta. Eteocles is sometimes given as his elder, and sometimes as his younger brother. Their rivalry led to the war of the Seven against Thebes and the expedition of ADRASTUS against the city. When Oedipus blinded himself on the discovery of his incest and parricide, his sons insulted him instead of pitying him. Polynices put before him, despite being expressly forbidden to do so, Cadmus' silver table along with his gold cup. This was a way of making fun of him and reminding him of his origins as well as of his crime. Oedipus cursed them both, predicting that they would be incapable of living in peace either during their lifetime or after death. Later, during a sacrifice, the two brothers sent their father the thigh bones of the victim instead of a choice piece. Oedipus hurled the bones to the ground and pronounced a second curse against them, predicting that they would kill each other. Finally, a third curse was pronounced when the brothers had locked Oedipus away in a remote dungeon so that he might be forgotten, and were refusing him the honours to which he was entitled. He predicted that they would divide up their heritage by the sword. More simply, it was said that Oedipus cursed his sons because they had not tried to save him when Creon (2) had banished him from Thebes.

Left as the sole rulers of Thebes, Eteocles and Polynices decided to share the power by reigning alternately, each for a year. Eteocles was the first to reign (or the second, depending on whether he was considered the elder or the younger, in which case he then took over from Polynices after the first year). However, at the end of a year, he refused to hand over power to his brother. Thus, evicted from his homeland, Polynices went to Argos, bearing with him the dress and necklace of Harmonia (1). At that time Adrastus reigned in Argos. Polynices presented himself at his palace one stormy night at the same time as Tydeus (see ADRASTUS). Adrastus gave them his two daughters in marriage (Table 1). Thus Polynices married Argia, and Adrastus promised to help him recover his kingdom. This was the origin of the expedition of the Seven against Thebes. Amphiaraus, the soothsayer, foreseeing the fate of the expedition, tried to dissuade Adrastus. However, Polynices went to IPHIS (1) and asked him how he could force Amphiaraus to join the expedition. Iphis revealed that Amphiaraus was bound by an oath to accept all the decisions of his wife, ERIPHYLE. Polynices then offered her Harmonia's necklace, asking her in return to persuade her husband. Thus the expedition was organized. On their way to Thebes, at Nemea, Polynices won the wrestling at the funeral games organized in honour of Archemorus (see AMPHIARAUS). During the fighting outside Thebes, Polynices was killed by his brother, but as he was dying, Polynices killed Eteocles. Thus Oedipus' curse was fulfilled. For the circumstances surrounding the burial of Polynices, see ANTIGONE.

Polyphemus (*Πολύφημος*)

1. One of the Lapiths, the son of Elatus (2) and Hippe. Poseidon was his divine father and Caeneus his brother. He married Laonome (1). Polyphemus took part in the fight of the Centaurs and Lapiths. He also participated in the Argonauts' expedition, but remained in Mysia, where he founded the city of Cios. He died in the war against the Chalybes.

2. One of the CYCLOPES. He was a son of Poseidon and the Nymph Thoosa. The *Odyssey* depicts him as a horrible giant, the most savage of all the Cyclopes. He was a cave-dwelling shepherd who lived off the produce of his flock of sheep. He knew how to use fire, but ate raw flesh. He knew what wine was but appeared unaware of its affects.

Odysseus and a dozen of his companions were captured by him and imprisoned in his cave. He began to devour them in pairs. Odysseus gave him some of MARON's wine, and the Cyclops found it so good that he got drunk and became more amiable. He asked Odysseus what his name was, to which he replied, 'Nobody'. Out of gratitude for the wine, Polyphemus promised to eat him last. Drowsy with the wine, Polyphemus fell asleep and Odysseus and his companions sharpened an immense stake in the fire and drove it into the giant's only eye. At daybreak Odysseus slipped out of the cave under the belly of a ram, since the Cyclops was guarding the entrance to the cave and feeling everything with his hands. Polyphemus appealed to his fellow Cyclopes for help, but when asked who was attacking him, he had to reply, 'Nobody'. The other Cyclopes thought he was mad and went away. Once Odysseus had set sail he cried out to Polyphemus that he was Odysseus, and taunted him. The Cyclops was enraged, for an oracle had predicted to him that he would be blinded by Odysseus. He threw enormous rocks at the boat, but in vain. It is from this moment that we can trace the hatred of Poseidon, Polyphemus' father, for Odysseus.

After the Homeric poems, Polyphemus became the hero of a love story involving the Nereid Galatea (1): in Theocritus' *Idyll* 11 the Cyclops is in love with a coquette who finds him too brutish. The theme was taken up by Ovid (see ACIS). In a variant tradition Galatea loved the Cyclops and had children by him.

Polyphides (*Πολυφείδης*)
1. A soothsayer, the son of Mantius, and descended from Melampus (Table 1). He received the gift of prophecy from Apollo. As a result of a quarrel with his father, he settled at Hyperasia in Achaea. He had a son, THEOCLYMENUS (1), and a daughter, Harmonide.
2. The twenty-fourth king of Sicyon. He was reigning at the time of the Trojan War according to Eusebius' *Chronicle*, and Menelaus and Agamemnon, while still children, were brought to his court by their nurse to protect them from Thyestes. Polyphides entrusted them to King Oeneus of Aetolia.

Polyphonte (*Πολυφόντη*) According to Antoninus Liberalis, a granddaughter of Ares and companion of Artemis. She scorned Aphrodite, who inspired her with a passion for a bear, by which she bore man-eating twins, Agrius (Wild Man) and Orius (Mountain Man). Zeus wanted to punish them by cutting off their feet and hands, but, following the intervention of Ares, they and their mother were changed into birds.

Polyphontes (*Πολυφόντης*)
1. A son of Autophonus, who commanded the Thebans who ambushed Tydeus during the expedition of the Seven against Thebes. Tydeus massacred them all.
2. A Heraclid who killed Cresphontes in order to seize his kingdom and his wife MEROPE (2). He was in turn killed by the son of the victim (see AEPYTUS (2)).
3. A herald (see OEDIPUS and POLYPOETES (4)).

Polypoetes (*Πολυποίτης*)
1. A son of Apollo and Phthia. He was killed by AETOLUS with his two brothers, Dorus (2) and Laodocus.
2. One of the Greeks who participated in the Trojan War. He was a son of Pirithous and Hippodamia (2) and was born on the day when his father chased the Centaurs from Mount Pelion. His mother died shortly after his birth, and his father went to the court of Theseus at

Athens. When Polypoetes reached manhood, he succeeded Pirithous on the throne. He and his friend Leonteus figure amongst the suitors of Helen. The death of several hundred Trojan warriors is attributed to him, including Damasus and Dresaeus. He participated in the funeral games in honour of Patroclus, and figures amongst the heroes of the Wooden Horse. After the fall of Troy he and Leonteus accompanied CALCHAS (1) to Colophon.

3. The son of ODYSSEUS and Callidice, the queen of the Thesprotians. He succeeded her after her death, while Odysseus returned to Ithaca.

4. A herald (see OEDIPUS and POLYPHONTES (3)).

Polyxena (*Πολυξένη*) The daughter of Priam and Hecuba. She is not mentioned in the *Iliad* and appears only in later epics. It is sometimes stated that Polyxena was at a fountain where Troilus was watering his horse when Achilles appeared, pursued Troilus and killed him. Polyxena escaped, but not before having aroused Achilles' passion. Polyxena is sometimes said to have come with Andromache and Priam to reclaim Hector's body from Achilles. Whereas the hero remained unmoved by the entreaties of Hector's father and widow, Polyxena managed to sway him by offering to be his slave. The story of Achilles' betrayal is also associated with this tradition: in order to win the hand of Polyxena, he suggested to Priam that he would abandon the Greeks, or even fight in the Trojan ranks. The negotiations were to be concluded in the temple of the Thymbrian Apollo, but Paris, hidden behind the statue of the god, killed ACHILLES with an arrow.

In an independent tradition followed by the *Cypria*, Polyxena died from wounds inflicted by Diomedes (2) and Odysseus. She was buried by Neoptolemus. Later, however, it was accepted that Polyxena was sacrificed on the tomb of Achilles either by Neoptolemus or by the Greek leaders at the instigation of Odysseus. This is the version followed by the tragic poets, notably Euripides. The aim of this sacrifice was either to ensure a safe crossing for the Achaean ships or else to appease the ghost of Achilles, which had appeared to his son demanding this offering.

Polyxenus (*Πολύξενος*)

1. Son of Agasthenes and grandson of Augias. He figures among Helen's suitors and commanded a force of Epeians against Troy. After his return from Troy he had a son whom he called Amphimachus after his companion, the son of Cteatus, who had fallen at Troy. After the murder of the suitors Odysseus went to stay with Polyxenus, who gave him a vase on which the story of Trophonius, AGAMEDES and Augias was depicted.

2. One of the sons of Jason and Medea (Table 6).

3. The king of Elis with whom the Taphians hid the oxen which they stole from Electryon. AMPHITRYON recovered them for him.

Polyxo (*Πολυξώ*)

1. The wife of Nycteus and the mother of Antiope (1).

2. Wife of TLEPOLEMUS. He died at Troy, and to honour his memory

Polyxo organized funeral games in which young children took part. Polyxo took vengeance on HELEN to avenge her husband. When Menelaus, returning from Egypt with Helen, arrived within sight of Rhodes, Polyxo gathered all the inhabitants of the island on the shore, armed with torches and stones. Wind drove Menelaus to the shore. He concealed Helen in the ship, dressed up his most beautiful servant-girl in Helen's clothing and allowed the Rhodians to murder the false Helen. Polyxo subsequently allowed Menelaus and the real Helen to leave in peace. In a different version, after the death of Menelaus, Helen's stepsons Nicostratus and Megapenthes (1) evicted her from Sparta. She fled to Polyxo, who pretended to give her a friendly welcome, but secretly planned her revenge. While Helen was bathing she dressed her servants up as the Erinyes and set them on her. Helen was so terrified that she hanged herself. Underneath this 'Tree of Helen' grew a magical plant, Helenium, a remedy for snake bites. On Rhodes Helen was known by the name Dendritis (from δένδρον = tree).

3. The nurse of HYPSIPYLE of Lemnos. She advised her to meet the Argonauts.

Pomona The Roman Nymph of fruit. She had a sacred wood, the Pomonal, on the road from Rome to Ostia. A special priest was in charge of her cult. She was the wife of PICUS. It was for love of her that Picus was said to have rejectd Circe's advances. Ovid makes her the wife of Vertumnus, who was, like her, a divinity linked with fertility and the cycle of the seasons.

Pompo (*Πόμπων*) A daughter of Numa Pompilius and the ancestor of the *gens Pomponia*. According to one tradition Numa's father was Pompilius Pompo.

Pontus (*Πόντος*) The personification of the Sea. He was the son of Gaia and Aether, but by Gaia he fathered Nereus, Thaumas, Phorcys, Ceto and Eurybia. He is occasionally made the father of Briareus and of four Telchines, namely Actaeus, Megalesius, Hormenus and Lycus (5).

Porphyrion (*Πορφυρίων*) One of the giants who fought against the gods. He fell under the arrows of Apollo. There exists another legend in which Porphyrion tried to assault Hera but was killed by Zeus and Heracles (see GIANTS).

Porthaon (*Πορθάων*) A son of Agenor and Epicaste, and consequently the grandson of Pleuron. He ruled over Pleuron and Calydon, and married Euryte, by whom he had Oeneus, Agrius, Alcathous (2), Melas (3), Leucopeus, and Sterope (2). He was the ancestor of Meleager. His name is sometimes written Parthaon or Portheus.

Portheus (*Πορθεύς*)

1. A form of the name PORTHAON.
2. The father of Echion (3), the first of the Greek heroes to emerge from the Wooden Horse, but who fell while jumping out and was killed.

Portunus A Roman divinity who seems, initially, to have been a god of doors, but who in the historic age was a god of the sea watching over harbours. He had a priest, and a special festival, the *Portunalia*. His temple was situated in the Forum Boarium. Portunus was identified with PALAEMON (3) and thus was regarded as the son of MATER MATUTA.

Porus (*Πόρος*) The personification of Expediency and the son of Metis. Married to Penia (Poverty), he was the father of Eros.

Poseidon (*Ποσειδῶν*) The god of the sea and one of the Olympians, the son of Cronus and Rhea. He is sometimes considered older and sometimes younger than his brother ZEUS. The tradition in which Zeus forces his father Cronus to restore to life the children he had swallowed, implies that Zeus is the youngest of the line. Gradually, with the development of birthright, Zeus, who was considered the sovereign ruler, assumed the role of eldest son. Thus, in legends of the Classical period Poseidon was more often considered to be younger than his brother. Poseidon was regarded as having been brought up by the TELCHINES and by Cephira, the daughter of Oceanus. When he reached manhood he fell in love with HALIA (1), the sister of the Telchines, and had by her six sons and a daughter called RHODUS.

Poseidon presided over the Sea. He could command the waves, provoke storms, create landslides on the coast with a flourish of his trident, and cause springs to flow. His power also extended over springs and lakes. Rivers, on the other hand, had their own divinities. His relationship with Zeus was not always friendly. He joined in the gods' conspiracy to put Zeus in chains, but withdrew before the threats of Briareus (see AEGAEON). For a year Poseidon, with Apollo and the mortal Aeacus, participated in the construction of the walls of Troy. However, LAOMEDON refused to give Poseidon the agreed salary, and in order to take vengeance he summoned a sea-monster which caused havoc among the Trojans. That was the origin of Poseidon's resentment against the Trojans, and that is why we see him intervene during the Trojan War on the side of the Achaeans. However, when at the beginning of the *Iliad* the Achaeans decided to fortify their camp by surrounding the ships with a wall, Poseidon protested in the assembly of the gods against this decision because he believed it was likely to diminish the glory he had earned in building the walls of Troy. Zeus managed to calm him down, although Poseidon promised to destroy the wall built by the Achaeans. For a while, he remained uninvolved in the struggle, but when the Trojans got the upper hand he came to the assistance of the Achaeans, taking on the appearance of Calchas (1) to encourage the two Ajaxes and urge on Teucer (2) and Idomeneus until, on instructions from Zeus, he abandoned the battle. Nevertheless it was Poseidon who saved Aeneas when Achilles was about to kill him (see AENEAS). Along with all the gods, Poseidon sought the descruction of the descendants of Priam and, like them also, spared and protected the descendants of Anchises.

When the mortals were organized into cities, the gods each decided to choose one or several towns where they would each be particularly honoured. Sometimes two or three divinities chose the same city, which provoked conflicts amongst them which they submitted to arbitration. In these judgements, Poseidon was in general unlucky. He entered into a dispute with Helios about the city of Corinth. The giant Briareus, as judge, decided in favour of Helios. Similarly, Poseidon wanted to rule over Aegina, but lost out to Zeus. Dionysus prevailed over him at Naxos, Apollo at Delphi, and Athena at Troezen. But the two most famous 'quarrels' were over Athens and Argos. For the dispute over Athens see ATHENA. Phoroneus was appoined to arbitrate in the quarrel between Poseidon and Hera for Argos. Here again, the decision went against Poseidon. In his fury, he blighted the Argolid with a curse and dried up all the rivers of the country. Shortly after, Danaus and his fifty daughters arrived in the Argolid and found no water to drink. Thanks to AMYMONE, with whom Poseidon was in love, the curse was lifted, and the rivers began to flow again. Another version maintained that Poseidon, irritated with Phoroneus and Inachus, had flooded the Argolid with salt water, but Hera forced him to bring the sea back within its bounds. Poseidon did, however, enjoy full possession of ATLANTIS.

Poseidon had numerous love affairs, all fruitful, but his children, like those of Ares, were generally evil and violent. For example, by Thoosa he produced the Cyclops Polyphemus (2); by Medusa, the giant CHRYSAOR and PEGASUS; by Amymone, NAUPLIUS (2); by Iphimedia, the ALOADAE. CERCYON (1), SCIRON, Lamus (1), the king of the LAESTRYGONIANS, and ORION. The sons whom he had by HALIA (1) committed all sorts of excesses and he had to bury them underground in order to save them from punishment.

Poseidon was the progenitor of a great many mythical geneaologies (see, for example, Tables 3 and 6). Particularly noteworthy is the love affair between Poseidon and Demeter, which produced a daughter, whose name it was forbidden to utter, and the horse AREION. Poseidon had a legitimate wife, the goddess AMPHITRITE, a Nereid, by whom he had no children.

He was represented armed with a trident, the weapon used by tuna fishermen, and riding a chariot drawn by monstrous animals, half horse and half serpent. This chariot was surrounded by fish, dolphins and all sorts of sea creatures, as well as by the Nereids and various minor divinities, such as Proteus.

Pothos (*Πόθος*) The personification of Love and Desire. He appears in Aphrodite's retinue beside Eros and Himerus. He was said to be a son of Aphrodite. In Syrian mythology he was supposed to be the son of Cronus and Astarte (Aphrodite).

Prax (*Πράξ*) A descendant of Pergamus, the son of Neoptolemus. Prax came back from Illyria to the Peloponnese and gave his name to the region called Prakiae. He consecrated a sanctuary to Achilles on the road leading from Sparta to Arcadia.

Praxithea (*Πραξιθέα*)

1. The wife of Erechtheus. She was regarded by some as the daughter of the river-god Cephissus, and by others as the daughter of Phrasinus and Diogenia, herself a daughter of Cephissus. Praxithea was a model of patriotism: she sacrificed her daughters after an oracle declared their death necessary to ensure an Athenian victory (see ERECHTHEUS).
2. The Nymph married to Erichthonius and, by him, mother of Pandion (1).
3. Metanira, the wife of Celeus and mother of Demophon (1) and Triptolemus, was sometimes called Praxithea. She was also said to be the nurse of Demophon.

Presbon (*Πρέσβων*) A son of Phrixus and of Iophassa (see PHRIXUS for other traditions relating to his marriage). Presbon had a son, Clymenus (2). After the death of Phrixus, Presbon returned to Orchomenus to reclaim the kingdom of his grandfather, Athamas. The latter had on his deathbed entrusted it to his great-nephews, Haliartus and Coronus, because he believed that his own male line was extinct. On learning of Presbon's return, Haliartus and Coronus welcomed him and restored his kingdom to him. Presbon was the grandfather of ERGINUS (1).

Preugenes (*Πρευγένης*) An Achaean from the valley of the Eurotas. He was the son of Agenor and had two children, Patreus and Atherion. After the arrival of the Dorians, he withdrew with his sons to Achaea, where he founded the city of Patras. Heroic honours were later bestowed on him and Patreus.

Priam (*Πρίαμος*) The youngest of the sons of Laomedon (Table 4). The Trojan War occurred during his reign, when he was quite elderly. The *Iliad* does not mention his mother; later tradition usually made her the daughter of the river-god Scamander and gave her the name Strymo, but other versions called her Placia or Leucippe (1).

Before the siege of Troy Priam fought the Amazons along with Otreus, on the banks of the Sangarius. At the time of the taking of Troy by Heracles Priam, who was still a child, was taken prisoner by the hero along with his sister Hesione. Heracles gave Hesione in marriage to his friend Telamon, and offered her whatever she wished as a wedding present. She asked for her brother, who was then called Podarces. Heracles agreed, and sold him to her in a symbolic fashion. Podarces then took the name of Priam, which means 'the ransomed'. Heracles gave him, as the last surviving son of Laomedon, the entire land of Troy. Priam gradually extended his power over all the region and the islands of the Asiatic coast.

Priam married first Arisbe, the daughter of Merops, who bore him a son named AESACUS, but then abandoned her in order to take Hecuba as his second wife. It was by the latter that he had the majority of his children. The first born was Hector, the second Paris. Then followed Creusa (4), Laodice (4), Polyxena, Cassandra, Deiphobus, Helenus, Pammon,

Polites (1), Antiphus, Hipponous, Polydorus (2) and Troilus, who was also said to be the son of Apollo. Priam had more children by concubines, including Lycaon (1) and Evander (2). Tradition attributes fifty sons to Priam, a number which is not given exactly by any author.

In the *Iliad* Priam is too old to take part in the fighting, but he presides over councils, although even there his opinion does not always prevail. He does not appear to be opposed to Paris' plans, nor to the abduction of Helen; he is well disposed towards the latter and accepts what is fated. His essential characteristic is piety, which brings him Zeus' favours. He sees his children perish one by one, and Hector, one of the last, becomes the most valiant defender of his kingdom. When Hector is killed and borne away by Achilles, Priam humbles himself and seeks out the victor, offering him an enormous ransom for the body of his son. Epics prior to the *Iliad* related the details of Priam's death. When the old king heard the enemy in his palace, he wanted to take up arms, but Hecuba led him into the depths of the palace to an altar so that they might be placed under the protection of the gods. There Priam saw Neoptolemus kill Polites (1) who was also trying to reach the safety of the altar. Neoptolemus then seized the old man by the hair, dragged him from the altar and slit his throat. The body remained unburied. A variant source relates that Neoptolemus dragged Priam to the tomb of Achilles and killed him there.

Priapus (*Πρίαπος*) A fertility deity from the Asiatic town of Lampsacus, usually said to be the son of Dionysus and Aphrodite. He was represented as an ithyphallic figure, the protector of vineyards, gardens and orchards. His essential attribute was the ability to ward off the 'evil eye' and to render harmless the evil spells of people attempting to damage the harvest.

Priapus was included in Dionysus' retinue. Like Silenus, Priapus was often depicted in the company of an ass. During a Dionysiac festival, Priapus met the nymph Lotis. At night he attempted to seduce her, but at the moment he was about to achieve his goal, Silenus' ass began to bray, waking Lotis and all the Bacchic women. Priapus had to abandon his plan. In memory of this incident he was represented in the company of an ass. There is a Roman variant of this legend in which the goddess Vesta is substituted for Lotis. Asses were sacrificed to Priapus, but on the feast of Vesta they were crowned with flowers.

According to other traditions Zeus fell in love with Aphrodite and seduced her. Aphrodite was about to give birth when Hera, fearing that this child would become a threat to the Olympian gods if he possessed the beauty of his mother and the power of his father, and being jealous of her husband's love affairs, touched Aphrodite's womb, with the result that the child was born deformed. The infant Priapus was endowed with enormous genitals. On seeing him, Aphrodite abandoned him in the mountains. There the child was discovered by shepherds who brought him up and established a cult to his virility.

Another tradition made Priapus

the son of Aphrodite and Adonis, attributing likewise his deformity to the malevolence of Hera.

According to Diodorus, Priapus was connected with the myth of Osiris. He was said to be the deification by Isis of Osiris' virility. Diodorus also classes Priapus and Hermaphroditus together.

Prochyte (*Προχύτη*) A Trojan woman related to Aeneas, who was buried on the island of Prochyte to which she gave her name.

Procles (*Προκλῆς*) The son of Aristodemus and Argia, and the twin brother of Eurysthenes. Procles married Lathria, the daughter of the king of Cleonae and had a son called Sous who was the ancestor of Lycurgus, the Spartan legislator.

Procne (*Πρόκνη*) The daughter of Pandion (1), the king of Athens, and the sister of PHILOMELA.

Procris (*Πρόκρις*) One of the daughters of Erechtheus. She was married to Cephalus, but deceived him with Pteleon, who had bought her favours by presenting her with a golden crown. When Cephalus became aware of this deception, Procris fled to Minos. The latter fell in love with her and tried to seduce her. Minos had been cursed by his wife, Pasiphae: on giving himself to another woman, he would bring forth serpents and scorpions which would kill his mistress. In order to free him from this spell, Procris gave him a herb which she had got from Circe. Then, as the price for her favours, she demanded two presents: a dog which never let the game he was pursuing escape, and a javelin which never missed its target. AMPHITRYON later borrowed the dog to chase the fox of Teumessa. Later, Procis returned to Athens where she was reconciled with Cephalus. However, Cephalus, being suspicious, decided to put her to the test by disguising himself and offering her presents (see CEPHALUS for the outcome).

Procrustes (*Προκρούστης*) A robber, also called Damastes or Polypemon, who lived on the road from Megara to Athens. He used to force all travellers to lie down in one of two beds which he possessed: the tall in the little bed (which required cutting off their feet) and the short in the large bed (they were stretched violently to make them fit). Procrustes was killed by Theseus (see THESEUS (2)).

Proculus An Alban noble to whom Romulus appeared after his apotheosis, indicating his wish to be honoured under the name of Quirinus.

Proetides (*Προιτίδες*) The daughters of PROETUS and Stheneboea (Table 7). According to some traditions, there were two of them, Lysippe (1) and Iphianassa (1); other traditions add a third, Iphinoe. The girls were stricken with madness by Hera, sometimes because they claimed to be more beautiful than the goddess; sometimes they were said to have mocked her temple, claiming that their father's palace contained greater riches; sometimes because they had stolen gold from the goddess' dress for their own use. The girls believed that they had been metamorphosed into heifers and escaped into the countryside, wandering here and there and refusing to return home. Another tradition says that Dionysus afflicted them with madness for having refused to adopt his cult. The soothsayer Melampus offered to cure them if Proetus would give him one third of the kingdom of Argos. Proetus refused, finding Melampus' price exorbitant. The Proetides were then seized with a new frenzy and began to run wild over the Argolid and Peloponnese. Proetus again appealed to Melampus, who demanded this time a third of the kingdom for himself, and another for his brother Bias. Proetus agreed to pay the price asked for, fearing that Melampus' demands would become even more exorbitant if he refused. Melampus, taking with him the most robust young men of Argos, then pursued the young girls into the mountains amid great shouting and wild dancing. During the pursuit Iphinoe died of exhaustion. The two others were purified by herbs which Melampus mixed with the water of a spring where they came to drink. Melampus and Bias then married a daughter each. A different tradition relates that it was later, during the reign of the Proetides' nephew ANAXAGORAS, that Melampus cured the collective madness of the women of Argos.

Proetus (*Προῖτος*) A king of Tiryns, the son of Abas (2) and Aglaea, and the twin brother of ACRISIUS (Table 7). Proetus and Acrisius hated one another. They even fought in the womb. On reaching maturity they divided the kingdom: Abas ruled the Argolid, Acrisius over Argos, and Proetus over Tiryns. It is also said that Proetus had seduced his niece DANAE, daughter of Acrisius, and had fathered Perseus, thus offending Acrisius. Proetus fortified Tiryns with massive walls. He was helped by the CYCLOPES. In a different tradition, Acrisius expelled Proetus, who took refuge with Iobates, the king of Lycia, or with Amphianax, whose daughter STHENEBOEA he married. Iobates gave him an army with which he recaptured his kingdom.

When Proetus was married and established at Tiryns, Bellerophon sought sanctuary with him and was falsely implicated in an intrigue with Stheneboea. See BELLEROPHON.

Proetus and Stheneboea had, initially, two or three daughters, the PROETIDES. During the madness of their daughters they had another child, Megapenthes (2) (='Great Sorrow', because of the sorrow caused by their daughters' affliction). Megapenthes succeeded Proetus, but later exchanged the kingdom of Tiryns with Perseus for that of Argos (see PERSEUS).

In his *Metamorphoses*, Ovid has preserved a tradition according to which Proetus attacked Acrisius and was besieging him in Argos when Perseus came to the aid of his grandfather and turned Proetus to stone with the Gorgon's head.

Promachus (*Πρόμαχος*)

1. The son of Aeson and Alcimede (or Perimede) (Table 6), who was killed by Pelias while still very young.
2. The son of Parthenopaeus and one of the EPIGONI.
3. A son of Heracles and PSOPHIS (4).

Prometheus (*Προμηθεύς*) A cousin of Zeus; the son of a Titan, Iapetus (Table 8). Traditions vary as to the name of his mother. She is called Asia, daughter of Oceanus, or Clymene (1) (Table 8; see also EURYMEDON (1)). Prometheus had several brothers: EPIMETHEUS, Atlas (1) and Menoetius (2).

Prometheus was said to have created the first men, fashioning them from potter's clay. But this legend does not appear in Hesiod's *Theogony*, where Prometheus is simply the benefactor of mankind. Once at Mecone, during a sacrifice, he cut up a bull and divided it into two parts: one contained the flesh and the intestines wrapped up in the skin, on top of which he placed the animal's stomach; the other consisted of the bones wrapped in the rich-looking fat. Zeus was then asked to choose his share. He chose the fat and, discovering that it contained nothing but bones, became embittered against Prometheus and mankind. As a punishment, he decided to withhold fire from mortals. However, Prometheus stole some sparks of fire from the sun's 'wheels' and brought them to earth concealed in a hollow tube. Another tradition maintains that he stole the fire from Hephaestus' forge. Zeus punished mankind by sending them a specially fashioned woman, PANDORA. Zeus also had Prometheus bound by steel chains to a rock in the Caucasus and sent an eagle, the offspring of Echidna and Typhon, to consume his liver which would continually renew itself. He swore by the Styx that Prometheus would never be released. Heracles, however, subsequently shot the eagle with an arrow and released Prometheus. Zeus was pleased that this exploit added to his son's fame, but to show that his word was not to be taken too lightly, he forced Prometheus to wear a ring made from the steel chains and to carry a piece of the rock to which he had been attached: a steel bond thus continued to unite the Titan and his rock. At this time the Centaur Chiron had been wounded by one of Heracles' arrows and wanted to die. As he was immortal, he had to find someone who would accept his immortality. Prometheus performed this service for him. Zeus accepted the Titan's freedom and immortality because Prometheus revealed an ancient oracle according to which the son of Zeus and Thetis would be more powerful than Zeus and would dethrone him.

Prometheus, whose name means 'foresight', possessed powers of prophecy. He told Heracles that only Atlas (1) could pick the golden apples from the garden of the Hesperides (see HERACLES, II). Prometheus also showed his son Deucalion (1) how to escape from the great flood which Zeus was planning in order to wipe out the human race, and which he was able to foresee.

Promethus (*Πρόμηθος*) A son of Codrus, who ruled in Colophon with his brother Damasichthon. He accidentally killed the latter, and fled to Naxos, where he died. His ashes were brought back to Colophon by the sons of Damasichthon.

Promne (*Πρόμνη*) The wife of BOUPHAGUS.

Pronax (*Πρῶναξ*) One of the sons

of Talaus (Table 1), and the brother of Adrastus and Eriphyle. He had a daughter, Amphithea, who married ADRASTUS, and had a son, LYCURGUS (3). According to one tradition, Pronax was killed by his cousin AMPHIARAUS at Argos. It was also said that the Nemean games were originally funeral games in his honour.

Propodas (*Προπόδας*) A king of Corinth. Under the reign of his two sons, Doridas and Hyanthidas, the Dorians led by Aletes (1) came into the country.

Propoetides (*Προποιτίδες*) Young girls originally from Amathonta, who denied Aphrodite's divinity. The goddess inflicted them with desires which could not be satisfied. They became the first prostitutes. They ended up being transformed into stone.

Proserpina At Rome, the goddess of the Underworld. Originally a rustic goddess presiding over germination, she was assimilated to the Greek PERSEPHONE. Her cult was officially introduced, along with that of Dis Pater, in 294 BC. The Tarentine Games were celebrated in their honour. The following myth was told about Tarentum: when the children of Valerius became ill, the gods informed him that he and his children should go down the Tiber as far as Tarentum, where they should drink water from the altar of Dis and Proserpina. Valerius set off for Tarentum in the south of Italy, and on the first evening camped at a bend in the Tiber. The local people then told him that this place was called 'Tarentum'. Valerius therefore took some water from the Tiber. His children drank it and were cured. When Valerius began work on an altar to Dis and Proserpina, he discovered a stone bearing an inscription in their honour. This was the altar that the oracle had spoken of.

Prosymna (*Πρόσυμνα*) Prosymna and her sisters Acraea and Euboea were the nurses of Hera. She gave her name to the city of Prosymna.

Protesilaus (*Πρωτεσίλαος*) A Thessalian hero, the son of Iphiclus (1), or Actor, and Astyoche. He was the brother of Podarces (2). His home was the Thessalian city of Phylace. Protesilaus figures among the suitors of Helen and so took part in the Trojan War. He was the first Greek to be killed by the Trojans; as he was leaping from his ship to set foot in Asia, he was struck down by Hector.

Protesilaus had played an important role in the first expedition, which had resulted in the Mysian landing. He snatched away TELEPHUS' shield, thus allowing ACHILLES to wound him. When he set out for Troy, Protesilaus had just married Laodamia (2), but the ritual sacrifices had not been carried out. It was as a punishment for this sacrilege that Laodamia became a widow. See LAODAMIA (2).

Proteus (*Πρωτεύς*) In the *Odyssey*, a god of the sea, charged with tending the flocks of sea-creatures belonging to Poseidon. He usually lived on the island of Pharos near the mouth of the Nile. He had the ability to change himself into whatever form he desired. He used this power particularly when he wanted to elude those asking him questions: he possessed the gift of prophecy, but refused to provide information to those mortals who sought it from him. On the advice of the sea-goddess Idothea (1), Proteus' own daughter, MENELAUS went to question him. Although Proteus metamorphosed himself successively into a lion, a serpent, a panther, an enormous boar, water and a tree, Menelaus did not let him escape. The old man, finally defeated, spoke to him.

The same version is given by Virgil in the episode of ARISTAEUS in the fourth book of the *Georgics*, although the scene is changed from Pharos to Pallene. From Herodotus onwards, Proteus also appears as a king of Egypt rather than as a demon of the sea. Proteus was reigning at Memphis at the time when Helen and Paris were driven by a storm on to the coast of the country. See HELEN. This legend was taken up and modified by Euripides in his *Helen*, where Proteus is king of the island of Pharos. His wife is called PSAMATHE (1). Their two children are Theoclymenus (2) and Idothea (1). While Paris was taking a phantom of Helen, created by Hera, to Troy, the real Helen was entrusted by Hermes to Proteus. It was also said that it was Proteus who created the phantom Helen and gave her to Paris.

A legend related by Conon maintains that Proteus, an Egyptian, had left his country because of the tyranny of BUSIRIS. He followed the sons of Phoenix (2) in their search for Europa (5), and settled at Pallene, where he married Chrysonoe, the daughter of Clitus (2). With Clitus' help he seized the land of the Bisaltes and reigned there. His two sons were called Polygonus and Telegonus (2).

Prothous (*Πρόθοος*)

1. One of the sons of Agrius.
2. The leader of a contingent of Magnesians at Troy. He came from Thessaly. When the Greeks returned from Troy, he perished in the shipwreck off Cape Caphareus.

Protogenia (*Πρωτογένεια*)

1. A daughter of Deucalion (1) and Pyrrha (1) whose name means 'first-born' (Table 5). She and Zeus had two sons, Aethlius and Opus.
2. One of the HYACINTHIDS.
3. The daughter of Calydon (1) and Aeolia (1), and, by Ares, the mother of Oxylus (1).
4. A daughter of Erechtheus (see CHTHONIA (2)).

Psamathe (*Ψαμάθη*)

1. A Nereid who had a son, by Aeacus, named Phocus (3). She had taken on diverse shapes to escape the advances of Aeacus, but nothing prevented him from achieving his aim. When Phocus was killed by his half-brothers Telamon and PELEUS, Psamathe sent a monstrous wolf against the latter's flocks. Later, Psamathe abandoned Aeacus and married PROTEUS.
2. An Argive woman, the daughter of CROTOPUS. By Apollo she had a son, Linus (1) (see also COROEBUS).

Psophis (*Ψῶφις*)

1. A son of Lycaon (2).
2. A seventh-generation descendant of Nyctimus.
3. The daughter of Xanthus (1), himself the son of Erymanthus (2).

4. The daughter of Eryx. While passing through Sicily Heracles married her, but then entrusted her to Lycortas. She later gave birth to two sons of Heracles, Echephron and Promachus (3), who founded the city of Psophis in honour of their mother.

Psyche (*Ψυχή*) The heroine of a tale told by Apuleius in his *Metamorphoses*. Psyche was stunningly beautiful and much admired, but whereas her sisters had found husbands, no one wanted to marry her because her beauty was so daunting. Her father consulted an oracle, which replied that Psyche must be dressed as if for marriage and exposed on a rock, where a horrible monster would come and take possession of her. Her parents were distraught, but obeyed the oracle. The abandoned Psyche was lamenting her fate when she was borne away by the wind to a deep valley and deposited on a lawn, where she fell asleep. On waking she found herself in the garden of a gold and marble palace. Inside the palace rooms voices greeted her and revealed that they were slaves at her service. In the evening Psyche became aware of a presence beside her: this was the husband of whom the oracle had spoken. He did not tell her who he was and warned her that if she ever saw him she would lose him for ever. Psyche was very happy, but, missing her family, who thought she was dead, she persuaded her husband to let her return to them for a while. He warned that this would pose dangers, but still granted the request. The wind bore her to the mountain top where she had been abandoned, from where she returned home. She was greeted with much rejoicing, but when her married sisters saw how happy she was they became jealous. They conspired to sow doubt in her mind. They forced her to admit that she had never seen her husband, then persuaded her to hide a lamp, and, while her husband was sleeping, to discover what he looked like.

Psyche returned to the palace and did as she had been advised. She discovered a beautiful youth sleeping beside her, but she spilled a drop of hot lamp-oil on him. Love (Eros or Cupid, the 'cruel monster' the oracle had spoken of) woke up and fled. Psyche, no longer protected by Love, began to wander the world, pursued by Aphrodite, who was indignant at her beauty. Aphrodite caught her and imprisoned her in her palace, tormenting her and giving her tasks such as sorting grain, gathering wool from wild sheep, and going down to the Underworld. There she had to ask Persephone for a flask of the water of youth, but was forbidden to open it. She did open it, however, and fell into a deep sleep. Love could not forget Psyche however. When he saw her asleep he awoke her with a prick from one of his arrows. He then sought Zeus' permission to marry her. Zeus agreed and Psyche was reconciled with Aphrodite.

In art Psyche is usually depicted as a young girl with butterfly' wings (Greek *Psyche* = 'soul', which was often thought of as a butterfly which escaped from the body after death), playing with Cupids.

Psyllus (*Ψύλλος*) The king of the Psylli, who were renowned in antiquity as snake-charmers. According to Nonnus, when in command of a Libyan fleet, he had wanted to wreak vengeance on the South Wind, whose breath had destroyed his harvests. But as he was approaching the island of Aeolus (2), a storm destroyed his ships.

Pterelaus (*Πτερέλαος*) According to the genealogy most commonly given to him, he was the grandson of Hippothoe and Poseidon, and the son of Taphius (Table 7). In another tradition he was the son of Hippothoe and Poseidon and had two sons, TAPHIUS and TELEBOAS. In a third tradition Teleboas was the father of Pterelaus.

Pterelaus was famous for the war which he waged against Amphitryon and his betrayal by his daughter Comaetho (1). This took place when Electryon was ruling Mycenae, and the sons of Pterelaus came to claim this kingdom, which had belonged to their great-grandfather Mestor, a brother of Electryon (Table 7). Electryon rejected their demands, so in revenge they stole the king's flocks. Electryon's sons challenged them to a fight, from which there was only one survivor from each family: Licymius, a son of Electryon, and Everes, a son of Pterelaus. Electryon planned to go and fight Pterelaus, but died himself before being able to set out. It was Amphitryon who organized the expedition, out of his love for Alcmene. He was victorious, thanks to the aid of Comaetho (see AMPHITRYON).

Ptoliporthes (*Πτολιπόρθης*) See POLIPORTHES.

Pygmalion (*Πυγμαλίων*)
1. A king of Tyre, the son of Mutto and brother of Elissa (see DIDO).
2. A king of Cyprus, who fell in love with an ivory statue of a woman. He was sometimes said to have sculpted it himself. He asked Aphrodite to grant him a woman resembling the statue. On returning home, he discovered that the statue had come alive. He married her, and they had a daughter called Paphos who became the mother of CINYRAS.

Pygmies (*Πυγμαῖοι*) A race of dwarfs, mentioned in the *Iliad*, inhabitants of southern Egypt, or India. Accounts of the Pygmies refer most frequently to their struggles against storks or cranes. A beautiful young girl, Oenoe, was born amongst the Pygmies, but she despised the gods, especially Artemis and Hera. She married a Pygmy named Nicodamas, by whom she had a son, Mopsus (3). However, because Oenoe did not worship Hera as she ought, she transformed her into a stork. The metamorphosed Oenoe tried to repossess her son, who had remained with the Pygmies, but they drove her off. Hence the fear which storks aroused in Pygmies (see also GERANA) and the hatred which the storks bore them. For their clash with Heracles see HERACLES, IV.

Pygmies frequently appear in mosaics and paintings in the midst of the fauna of the Nile, fighting with birds and various animals, attacking crocodiles, and indulging themselves in human activities which they parody by their ugliness and clumsiness.

They are usually depicted with enormous sexual organs.

Pylades (*Πυλάδης*) The great friend of Orestes. He was his first cousin, being the son of Strophius (1) and Anaxibia (Table 2). The two cousins were brought up together at Strophius' court, where Orestes had been put while Clytemnestra was living with Aegisthus during Agamemnon's absence. Pylades advised his friend in his vengeance, and it was said that he fought against the sons of Nauplius (2) when they came to Aegisthus' aid. At the time of Orestes' voyage to Tauris Pylades was of great help to him. He married Electra (3), the elder sister of Orestes, and had two children by her, Medon (3) and Strophius (2).

Pylaemenes (*Πυλαιμένης*) A Paphlagonian, and an ally of the Trojans. Pylaemenes was killed either by Menelaus or by Achilles. Although his death is recounted in Book v of the *Iliad*, he makes an appearance in Book xiii, in the funeral cortège of his son Harpalion.

Pylaeus (*Πυλαῖος*) The son of Lethus. With his brother Hippothous he commanded at Troy a contingent of Pelasgians from Larissa.

Pylas (*Πύλας*) A king of Megara. He was the son of Cleson and the grandson of LELEX (2). He gave his daughter Pylia in marriage to Pandion (2). Later Pylas killed Bias, his father's brother, and had to go into exile. He left his kingdom to Pandion, while he himself, at the head of a band of Leleges, entered the Peloponnese and founded Pylos in Messenia. He was driven out of there by Neleus (1), but then founded Pylos in Elis.

Pylenor (*Πυλήνωρ*) A Centaur, who was wounded by Heracles during the fight at Pholus' home (see CENTAURS). His wound was infected by the blood of the Lernaean Hydra, in which Heracles' arrows had been dipped. He washed his wound in the River Anigrus, which from then on possessed evil properties and an unhealthy smell.

Pylia (*Πυλία*) The wife of Pandion (2) and daughter of PYLAS, the king of Megara.

Pyraechmes (*Πυραίχμης*)

1. In the *Iliad*, one of the two leaders of the Paeonian contingent which had come to help Priam. Pyraechmes killed Eurodorus, the adviser of Patroclus. He was himself killed either by Patroclus or by Diomedes (2), and was buried at Troy.
2. A slinger who ensured the victory of OXYLUS (2) over the Eleans.
3. A king of Euboea, who attacked Boeotia but was defeated by Heracles and torn apart by his horses. This fight took place beside a stream called Heracleius. Horses neighed each time they drank from this water.

Pyramus (*Πύραμος*) According to one tradition Pyramus and Thisbe loved each other so much that they slept together before they were married. Thisbe became pregnant. In despair, she committed suicide. On learning of this, her lover did likewise. The gods metamorphosed them: Pyramus became the Cilician river which bore his name, and Thisbe a spring whose water flowed into that river.

In Ovid's *Metamorphoses* Pyramus and Thisbe were two young Babylonians who loved each other but could not marry because of parental opposition. They saw each other secretly through a crack in the wall which separated their two houses. One night they arranged a rendezvous at the tomb of Ninus. A mulberry tree grew there. Thisbe was the first to arrive but saw a lioness. She fled, but lost her scarf, which the lioness seized in her bloody mouth and tore into pieces. When Pyramus arrived and saw the scarf, he assumed that Thisbe had been eaten by a wild animal, and ran himself through with his sword. When Thisbe returned, she found him dead, and killed herself with the same sword. The fruit of the mulberry, which had until then been white, turned red with all this spilt blood.

Pyrene (*Πυρήνη*)
1. A young girl whose father was King Bebryx. When Heracles crossed his territory on his way to capture Geryon's oxen, he became drunk and raped Pyrene, who gave birth to a serpent. Pyrene fled to the mountains, where she was torn apart by wild animals. Heracles later found her body, paid her funeral honours, and gave the name Pyrenees to the nearby mountains.
2. According to Apollodorus, the mother of CYCNUS (3) and of DIOMEDES (1).

Pyreneus (*Πυρηνεύς*) A king of Daulis who invited the Muses to enter his palace to shelter from a storm, but then assaulted them. The goddesses flew away and Pyreneus, trying to follow them, fell on to some rocks and was killed.

Pyrgo (*Πυργώ*)
1. The wife of ALCATHOUS. She was abandoned by him so that he could marry Evaechme, the daughter of Megareus. Her tomb could be seen at Megara.
2. The nurse of Priam's children. She accompanied Aeneas from Troy and it was she who, at the instigation of Iris, advised the Trojan woman to set fire to the ships.

Pyrias (*Πυρίας*) A boatman from Ithaca who took pity on an old man captured by pirates. The old man was carrying vessels full, apparently, of pitch. These jars later came into the possession of Pyrias, who realized that under the pitch they contained jewels and treasures. In his gratitude Pyrias sacrificed an ox to his unknown benefactor. From this came the proverb: 'Pyrias is the only man to have sacrificed an ox to his benefactor.'

Pyrrha (*Πύρρα*)
1. Daughter of Epimetheus and Pandora. She married DEUCALION (1) and became through him mother of the human race after the flood (Table 5). They created human beings by throwing stones over their shoulders. Deucalion created men, Pyrrha women.
2. The name which ACHILLES bore when he hid among the women of Scyros. His son Neoptolemus was nicknamed Pyrrhus, 'the Redhead'.

Pyrrhicus (*Πύρριχος*) The inventor of the 'pyrrhic', a war-dance performed with the lance, shield and flares. Sometimes he is one of the Curetes, sometimes a Laconian. The name of this dance is also sometimes associated with that of PYRRHUS.

Pyrrhus (*Πύρρος*) The Redhead, the surname of NEOPTOLEMUS, Achilles' son, either because his hair was red, or because he blushed easily or because his father bore the name Pyrrha when he hid among the daughters of Lycomedes on Scyros. Pyrrhus was the eponym of the town of Pyrrhicus in Laconia, and was reputed to have been the inventor of the 'Pyrrhic' war-dance (but see PYRRHICUS).

Pythaeus (*Πυθαεύς*) A son of Apollo, who came from Delphi to Argos and founded a temple there in honour of the 'Pythian' Apollo.

Pythia (*Πυθία*) The prophetic priestess of Pythian Apollo at Delphi.

Python (*Πύθων*) When Apollo decided to found a sanctuary at Delphi, he found near a spring a dragon called Python. Hera had given TYPHON to this monster to bring up. Apollo killed Python with his arrows, since, being a son of Gaia, the dragon could pronounce oracles and was thus a rival to him.

Hyginus told a story in which an oracle had declared that Python would perish at the hands of a son of Leto. When she heard that Leto was pregnant, Hera proclaimed that she could not give birth in any sunlit place. Apollo was born despite this decree, however (see LETO), and three days after his birth killed Python; he founded the Pythian Games in his honour. Python was also said to be buried under the Omphalos of the Temple of Delphi (see also DELPHYNE (2)).

Q

Quirinus A very early Roman god, one of three archaic divinities whose worship made up the Indo-European background of Roman religion. In hierarchical order, he was the last of the three, behind Jupiter and Mars. Ancient sources are nearly unanimous in making him a god of war of Sabine origin, deriving his name either from the Sabine town of Cures, or connecting it with the Sabine name for lance, *curis*. He was apparently the god of the Quirinal hill where, according to tradition, there was a Sabine community.

The modern scholar G. Dumézil has put forward the hypothesis that Quirinus, far from being originally a god of war, was essentially the protector of farmers. This is an attractive hypothesis for which there is some evidence in the writings of Servius, according to whom Quirinus was a 'peaceful Mars' belonging within the city. Further, according to Dumézil the Quirites, whose name is obviously connected with that of the god, were essentially citizens of the city, and it was known that this name, when applied to soldiers, was a deadly insult. It should finally be noted that certain functions assumed by the priest of Quirinus were directed towards the worship of rural divinities (notably Consus). Myths about Quirinus are rare. One was connected with the foundation of the city of Cures by MODIUS FABIDIUS, a son of the god. The main point concerns the assimilation of Romulus and Quirinus. After an appearance of Romulus to Julius PROCULUS, the Romans built a temple to ROMULUS dedicated to Quirinus. At the same time, HERSILIA, Romulus' wife, took the name Hora Quirini.

R

Ramnes An augur of the Rutulian army, under Turnus' command. He was killed by Nisus (2) while he was asleep. Ramnes was the name of one of the three primitive tribes of Rome.

Rarus (*Ῥᾶρος*) In one tradition the son of Cranaus and the father of Triptolemus. In another tradition Rarus was the grandfather of Triptolemus and had a son Celeus (usually considered to be the son of Eleusis). Rarus welcomed Demeter when she was looking for Persephone, and as a reward Demeter taught Triptolemus the art of cultivating wheat. Rarus gave his name to the Plain of Rarus near Eleusis, where wheat was cultivated for the first time.

Ratumena Before his expulsion, Tarquinius Superbus had ordered from craftsmen at Veii a clay chariot to adorn the Temple of Jupiter Capitolinus. When the clay chariot expanded in such an extraordinary way that the oven in which it was being fired had to be dismantled in order to remove it, soothsayers said that this promised power and prosperity to whoever owned the chariot. Consequently the Veians decided not to hand over the chariot, on the pretext that Tarquinius had in the meantime been deposed as king. However, at the games being celebrated at Veii, Ratumena won the chariot race. His horses bolted and raced to Rome, entering through the gate later named Porta Ratumena, where he was thrown from his chariot and killed. The horses continued onwards to the statue of Jupiter Tonans, to whom they appeared to pay homage. In terror the Veians handed over the clay chariot, the guarantee of the greatness of Rome.

Rea Silvia See RHEA SILVIA.

Recaranus Also called Caranus or Garanus, a hero who replaced Hercules in the episode with CACUS. In a related version of the legend, Cacus was a slave, a thief and a subject of King Evander (3). Recaranus would have abandoned his search for the herd which Cacus had stolen had Evander not forced his slave to return them. Recaranus then set up an altar to Jupiter the Finder at the foot of the Aventine: this would be the Ara Maxima, generally attributed to Hercules. In honour of Jupiter he then sacrificed one tenth of his animals on this altar. This was reputedly the origin of the tithe that was offered to Hercules from all the victims sacrificed at the Ara Maxima.

Remus The twin brother of Romulus. According to one isolated explanation, the name Remus was given to the child because he was 'slow' in everything – which would explain why he was supplanted by Romulus. In the legend Remus appears as the unfortunate double of his brother. For their early years see ROMULUS and RHEA SILVIA (1).

Following the incident of the capture of Remus by Amulius and his rescue by Romulus (see ROMULUS, AMULIUS and NUMITOR), the twins set off to found a city. They agreed to found the town on the spot where they had been saved (the future site of Rome), but were unsure exactly where this was. They consulted the omens. Romulus settled himself on the Palatine Hill, Remus on the Aventine. Remus saw six vultures; Romulus saw twelve. The gods having decided in favour of the Palatine (and hence Romulus), the latter set about marking the boundary of the city by digging a ditch with a plough drawn by two oxen. The disappointed Remus ridiculed this boundary which could be crossed so easily, and jumped over the ditch. Annoyed at this sacrilege Romulus killed Remus. In the earliest form of the legend the murder was seemingly the result solely of Remus' sacrilegious action; Romulus was distraught and committed suicide. He buried Remus on the Aventine, which, until the time of Claudius in AD 49, remained outside the *pomerium*, the religious boundary of Rome.

For various genealogies of Remus, see ROMULUS.

Rhacius (*Ῥάκιος*) A Cretan, the son of Lebes, who married MANTO (1), and whose son was the soothsayer MOPSUS (2). He migrated to Colophon, where he met Manto who, on Apollo's orders, had left Thebes after the capture of the city by the Epigoni. He had another child, Pamphylia, the eponym of the country of that name.

Rhadamanthys (*Ῥαδάμανθυς*) A Cretan hero, one of the three sons of Zeus and Europa (5), and brother of Minos and Sarpedon (2) (Table 3). He was adopted by the Cretan king, Asterion, to whom Zeus had given Europa. Rhadamanthys was renowned for his wisdom and justice. He was said to have organized the Cretan code, which had served as a model for the Greek cities, with such skill that after his death he became one of the judges of the dead in the Underworld, alongside Minos and Aeacus.

One tradition maintained that Rhadamanthys fled from Crete to Boeotia and married ALCMENE. In the *Odyssey* Rhadamanthys made a voyage on board the Phaeacian ships to Euboea to look for the giant Tityus. Two children are attributed to Rhadamanthys: Gortys, the eponymous hero of the Cretan town of Gortyn, and Erythrus, the founder of Erythrae in Boeotia.

Rhea (*Ῥεία*) One of the Titanides, daughters of Gaia and Uranus. She married Cronus, with whom she ruled over the world. According to Hesiod's *Theogony*, they produced six children: Hestia, Demeter, Hera, Hades, Poseidon and Zeus, the youngest. Cronus, following an oracle from Uranus and Gaia which warned that one of his children would dethrone him, devoured each as soon as it was born. However, Rhea hid the infant Zeus and gave Cronus a stone wrapped in swaddling clothes to eat instead. There exists an analogous tradition about

Poseidon, saved by his mother by a similar trick. During the Roman period, Rhea was assimilated to CYBELE.

Rhea Silvia

1. Rhea or Rea Silvia, the mother of Romulus and Remus, and sometimes also called ILIA. According to one tradition she was the daughter of Aeneas, and according to the other she was daughter of NUMITOR, the king of Alba. She was secretly loved by Mars, although certain authors attribute the paternity of the twins either to a chance encounter with a lover or to Rhea's uncle, Amulius, who had dethroned Numitor. When it became evident that she was going to give birth, Amulius had her put in prison. She was either killed immediately after giving birth, or died as a result of the harsh treatment which was meted out to her, or else was rescued by Romulus and Remus, when the twins had dealt with Amulius. In the version in which she was killed by Amulius, the latter threw her into the Tiber. The river-god was then seen rising out of the water to greet her and make her his wife. It was also said that it was the god of the River Anio who married her.
2. A priestess with whom Hercules fell in love when he was passing through Rome after his Labour with Geryon's oxen. She had a son, Aventinus, after whom the Aventine hill was named.

Rhesus (*Ῥῆσος*) In Homer, the son of Eioneus; in later authors, the son of Strymon by one of the Muses. Rhesus was famous for his horses, which were snow-white and swift as the wind. He came to the aid of the Trojans in the tenth year, wrought havoc among the Greeks for one day, but was killed at night by Odysseus and Diomedes (2), who took away his horses. An oracle had told Rhesus that if he and his horses drank from the River Scamander, he would be invincible. To prevent this, Hera and Athena told Odysseus and Diomedes to kill Rhesus before he and his horses drank from the river. A tradition related by Conon makes Rhesus the brother of Brangas and Olynthus.

Rhode (*Ῥόδη*) Either a daughter of Poseidon and Amphitrite, and the sister of Triton (Table 8), or one of the daughters of Asopus. All traditions agree that she married Helios (but see RHODUS).

Rhodope (*Ῥοδόπη*) Daughter of the river-god Strymon and wife of HAEMUS (1). See also CICONES.

Rhodopis (*Ῥοδῶπις*) A beautiful Egyptian girl. One day, an eagle flew off with one of her sandals and dropped it at the feet of the king, Psammetichus. Amazed at the finely worked sandal, he had the whole of Egypt searched for the girl to whom it belonged. On her discovery, they were married. It was sometimes stated that Rhodopis was Greek, and had come from Thrace to Egypt, following Charaxus, the brother of the poetess Sappho.

Rhodus (*Ῥόδος*) The wife of Helios, who gave her name to the island of Rhodes, and often confused with RHODE by mythographers. She was sometimes described as the daughter of Aphrodite, sometimes as the daughter of Poseidon and HALIA (1). By Helios she had seven sons, the HELIADES (2).

Rhoecus (*Ῥοῖκος*)
1. There was an oak tree that was so old that it was on the point of falling. Rhoecus had his servants erect a support for it, and thus saved the life of the Hamadryads whose existence was linked to that of the oak. In gratitude, the divinities offered him whatever he wanted. He asked for their favours, which they granted him, but warned him against any unfaithfulness to them. They added that a bee would be their messenger. One day, the bee came to find Rhoecus. However Rhoecus greeted the bee brusquely, with the result that it stung him in the eyes and blinded him.
2. One of the Centaurs killed by ATALANTA.

Rhoeo (*Ῥοίω*) The daughter of STAPHYLUS (3) and sister of Hemithea (1). When LYRCUS (1) was staying with them, she fell in love with him. Zeus later fell in love with her, and she became pregnant by him. Staphylus, not believing that a god was responsible for this, locked his daughter in a chest and put it in the sea. The chest was washed up on the coast of Euboea (or Delos). Rhoeo gave birth to a son called ANIUS (1) and then married Zarex, the son of Carystus. An isolated tradition makes Rhoeo the mother of Jason.

Rhoetus (*Ῥοῖτος*)
1. One of the Giants who took part in the struggle against the gods. He was killed by Dionysus.
2. A Centaur who took part in the fight between the Lapiths and the Centaurs, at the time of Pirithous' wedding. Virgil relates that he was killed by Dionysus. Apollodorus also calls one of the Centaurs Rhoetus.
3. One of the companions of PHINEUS (2) at the time of the marriage of Perseus and Andromeda. He was killed by the hero.
4. The father of ANCHEMOLUS.

Rhopalus (*Ῥόπαλος*) A king of Sicyon. The son of Phaestus. He ruled after Zeuxippus who succeeded PHAESTUS when the latter was exiled to Crete. His son and successor was Hippolytus (3), who surrendered Sicyon to a Mycenaean army which attacked it on Agamemnon's orders. In another tradition Rhopalus was a son of Heracles and the father of Phaestus.

Rhytia (*Ῥυτία*) In the tradition followed by Pherecydes, the mother of the nine Corybantes of Samothrace, whose father was Apollo.

Robigo Robigo and Robigus were two divinities, the first feminine, the second masculine, which watched over the growing wheat and averted blight (*robigo* in Latin). A festival was celebrated in their honour each year in Rome on 25 April.

Roma Roma or Rhome (after the Greek work meaning 'strength'), was a heroine who gave her name to Rome. The oldest tradition makes her a Trojan prisoner who was accompanying Odysseus and Aeneas when the two heroes reached the banks of the Tiber, having been driven by a storm. The captives were tired of wandering and Roma persuaded them to set fire to the ships, which put an end to the voyage. The immigrants settled on the Palatine, where their town prospered; in gratitude they honoured the name of the heroine. Another tradition makes Rhome the daughter of Ascanius. When the Trojans had taken possession of the site of the future Rome, Rhome set up a temple of Faith on the Palatine. The town which grew up on this hill bore the name Rome, in memory of the young girl. A variant tradition claimed that Rhome was the wife of Ascanius. She is also mentioned as the wife of Aeneas, being the daughter of TELEPHUS. She was also said to be the daughter of Telemachus and sister of Latinus. A further tradition mentions a Roma who was the daughter of Evander (3) or Italus (2) and Leucaria. Finally, certain writers maintained that Roma was a soothsayer who advised Evander to choose this spot to found the town of Pallantea, the original nucleus of Rome.

Romis (*Ῥῶμις*) According to Plutarch, an early king of Latium who drove out the Etruscan immigrants and founded the city of Rome.

Romulus The eponymous founder of Rome. He was usually said to be a descendant of Aeneas via the kings of Alba. He and his twin brother Remus were sons of RHEA SILVIA (1) (or ILIA) and grandsons of NUMITOR. There are many variants, however. The series of Alban kings was sometimes omitted and Rhea was made the daughter of Aeneas. Some authors made Romulus and Remus the sons of Aeneas and Dexithea. In this version the twins were brought to Italy when very young. Other traditions make Romulus the son of ROMA and of Latinus. His mother was sometimes called Aemilia and was thus the daughter of Aeneas and Lavinia (for another legend see TARCHETIUS).

Mars was the father of Romulus and Remus. He seduced Rhea Silvia in the sacred wood where she had gone to look for water. It was also said that she was assaulted by the god while she was asleep. Amulius, Rhea's uncle, noticed that she was pregnant and put her in prison. When the children were born, the king exposed them on the banks of the Tiber, at the foot of the Palatine. It was also said that a servant of Amulius put the children in a basket which he then floated on the river, but the river had burst its banks, and a counter-current took it upstream on to the north-west summit of the Palatine. The basket deposited the two children under a fig tree, the Ficus Ruminalis, which was later held to be sacred. There, Romulus and Remus were found by a she-wolf, which had just given birth. She took pity on them and suckled them. The she-wolf was an animal sacred to Mars, and it was believed that this wolf was sent by the god to look after his children. Moreover, a woodpecker (Mars' bird) helped the wolf to feed them. One of the king's shepherds, FAUSTULUS, then saw the children and brought them home to his own wife, ACCA LARENTIA (2), who brought them up.

Faustulus sent the two youths to study at Gabii. Romulus and Remus later came back to the Palatine, where they became involved in robbery. One day Remus attacked Amulius' shepherds who were guarding the king's flocks on the Aventine. The shepherds captured Remus and took him before the Alban king. Meanwhile Faustulus revealed to Romulus the secret of his birth, and asked him to save his brother. Romulus hurried to Alba, overran Amulius' palace, revealed his identity to the king whom he then killed, and freed Remus. He handed sovereignty over to his grandfather Numitor. The twins then decided to found a city (see REMUS for the choice of the site and the early stages of its foundation). Romulus eventually killed Remus. The city was founded on 21 April, the festival of the Parilia (the festival of Pales). The year was either 754, 752 or even 772 BC.

It is usually agreed that Romulus' city included only the Palatine *pomerium*, that is the hill itself. But several episodes of the legend of Romulus imply that the city also included the Capitol, notably the *asylum* in the hollow which marked the summit of the hill. Plutarch even situates the ritual events of the foundation of the city and the consecration of the *mundus* (the centre of augury in the new city) on the Comitium.

When the city was founded, Romulus was concerned to populate it. As local resources were insufficient he created a place of refuge on the Capitol, between the two sacred woods, that of the Arx (the Citadel) and the Capitol itself (the southern summit of the hill). There all the Italian outlaws could take refuge: exiles, murderers, runaway slaves etc. This was the nucleus of the first population of Rome. However there were no women. Romulus therefore thought of abducting women from his Sabine neighbours. He organized horse races on the Festival of Consus on 21 August. People from the surrounding area attended, along with their wives and children. At a given signal Romulus' men abducted all the young women, of whom there were either 30 or 527, or even 683. Only one of them, HERSILIA, was a married woman. An army was soon formed under the Sabine king, Titus Tatius, which marched against Rome. Tatius managed to get inside the Capitoline citadel by surprise, thanks to the treachery of TARPEIA. One section of the Sabine army then tried to take from the rear the Roman toops of Romulus who were holding a position at the foot of the Capitol facing north. They would have succeeded if the gods JANUS and JUPITER had not intervened and turned the battle in the Romans' favour.

The Romans and Sabines subsequently signed a treaty of friendship uniting the two people. It was said that the Sabine women abducted by the Romans had thrown themselves between the combatants and had begged their fathers, brothers and new husbands to cease this sacrilegious fight. This episode took place in the Forum. This was how Titus Tatius came to be associated with the rule of Romulus, and the union of the two peoples came about. But Tatius died soon after and Romulus became sole ruler of the two peoples.

The reign of Romulus lasted for 33 years, and was marked by the development of the young Rome, with the result that the people gave the king the title of Father of the Nation. Romulus ended his earthly life at the age of 54. On the Nones (7th) of July he was reviewing his army on the Campus Martius in a part known as the *palus Caprae* (the Goat's marsh) when a storm broke, accompanied by an eclipse of the sun. Everything disappeared under a deluge. When the storm was over, the king was found to be missing. He had disappeared off the face of the earth. A Roman, Julius Proculus, claimed that Romulus had appeared to him in a dream and had revealed that he had been abducted by the gods and had become the god QUIRINUS. In addition he had asked that a sanctuary be raised to him on the Quirinal Hill. This was done. For the feast of the *Nonae Caprotinae* commemorating the disappearance of Romulus, see PHILOTIS.

Romus In certain traditions, the eponymous founder of Rome. He was said to have been the son of Imathion who had been sent from Troy by Diomedes (2), or else the son of AENEAS. According to other traditions he was the son of Ascanius (compare ROMA). He was sometimes considered to be one of the children of Odysseus and Circe. He had two brothers, Antias and Ardeas, the eponyms of the cities Ardea and Antium. A later legend made Romus the son of Roma. His brothers were thus Romulus and Telegonus (1). See also LEUCARIA.

Ruturi A tribe from central Italy whose capital was Ardea in Latium. They opposed the arrival of AENEAS, and took up arms against him at the instigation of TURNUS, their king.

S

Sabazius (*Σαβάζιος*) A Phrygian god, who was considered to be an earlier Dionysus. The idea of domesticating oxen and yoking them to the plough was attributed to him. He was depicted with horns on his forehead. It was said that Sabazius was conceived when Zeus took the form of a serpent to sleep with Persephone. The serpent was the most sacred animal of the god, and played a role in his mysteries. There is a story that Sabazius, in the form of a serpent, slept with one of his priestesses in Asia Minor, and that children were born of this union.

Sabbe (*Σάββη*) The Babylonian Sibyl. She was of Hebraic origin, a daughter of Berosus and Erymanthe.

Sabus According to one tradition, the son of the Roman god SANCUS and the eponym of the Sabines. According to others, Sabus was a Lacedaemonian who established himself in the region of Reate (modern Rieti).

Sagaritis (*Σαγαρîτις*) A Hamadryad in Ovid's version of the myth of ATTIS.

Salacia A Roman divinity of the sea. She was the personification of salt water, and akin to Venilia, the divinity of coastal water, but distinct from her.

Salamis (*Σαλαμίς*) One of the daughters of ASOPUS. She was abducted by Poseidon, by whom she had a son, CYCHREUS, to the island which subsequently took the name of Salamis (off the coast of Attica).

Salius (*Σάλιος*) A companion of Aeneas. He came from Samothrace, Mantinea in Arcadia, or from Tegea. The war-dance of the Roman college of priests, the *Salii*, was attributed to him (see also CATHETUS).

Salmoneus (*Σαλμωνεύς*) One of the sons of Aeolus (1) and Aenarete (Table 5). He was born in Thessaly but emigrated to Elis, where he founded the city of Salmonia. He married Aleus' daughter Alcidice, by whom he had a daughter, Tyro. After Alcidice's death he married Sidero, who turned out to be a cruel stepmother. Salmoneus tried to imitate Zeus' thunder by constructing a bronze road and riding a chariot with copper and iron wheels on it, dragging chains behind it. He threw burning torches to imitate Zeus' lightning. Zeus struck him down with a real thunderbolt, destroying Salmonia and its inhabitants.

Salus In Rome the personification of health and preservation in general. She had a temple on the Quirinal. She was gradually associated with HYGIEIA.

Samon (*Σάμων*) According to certain traditions, the eponymous hero of Samothrace. He was the son of

Hermes and a Nymph called Rhene. He emigrated from Arcadia to Samothrace with DARDANUS.

Sanape (*Σανάπη*) An Amazon who gave her name to the town of Sinope, on the Black Sea. She had an excessive liking for wine, which earned her the name of Sanape, meaning 'drunkard' in the local dialect. This name was corrupted into Sinope, and became that of the city.

Sancus His full name was Semo Sancus, a divinity of the earliest Roman religion. He was also identified with Dius Fidius. His worship was said to have been introduced by the Sabines. He was sometimes considered to be the father of SABUS.

Sangarius (*Σαγγάριος*) The god of the river of that name in Asia Minor. He was a son of Oceanus and Tethys. He was sometimes made out to be the father of Hecuba, whom he sired on either Metope (1), Eunoe or Evagora. He was also the father of ALPHAEUS. Sangarius plays a role in the myth of his daughter NANA and the birth of ATTIS (see also AGDISTIS).

Saon (*Σάων*) A Boeotian who consulted the oracle at Delphi during a drought. The oracle ordered him to go to Lebadea to question the oracle of Trophonius. At Lebadea, he discovered that no one there knew of an oracle, but he saw some bees and, following them, went into a cave where the hero Trophonius gave him all the instructions necessary for the foundation of a cult as well as an oracle in his honour.

Sardus (*Σάρδος*) A son of Maceris, the name the Libyans and Egyptians gave to Heracles. He led a force of Libyans to an island known as Iehnooussa, which subsequently took the name of Sardinia.

Saron (*Σάρων*) A legendary king of Troezen. He erected a magnificent temple to Artemis on the shore of the Gulf of Troezen. He was a great hunter; one day a hind which he was chasing leapt into the sea. He swam in pursuit of it until he drowned. His body was washed up by the waves not far from the temple he had founded. The gulf was then called the Saronic Gulf.

Sarpedon (*Σαρπηδών*)

1. A giant, the son of Poseidon, who was killed by Heracles (see POLTYS).
2. One of the sons of Europa (5) and Zeus (Table 3). He was brought up by Asterius, who married Europa, with his two brothers, Minos and Rhadamanthys. He later quarrelled with Minos, either over who should obtain the Cretan throne, or because they were both in love with the same boy, Miletus. Sarpedon left Crete and went to Asia Minor. He settled in the region of Miletus in Lycia. He became king there, and was sometimes credited with the foundation of Miletus.
3. The *Iliad* spoke of a Sarpedon, leader of a Lycian contingent, who fought alongside the Trojans. He was said to be the son of Zeus and Laodamia (1), the daughter of Bellerophon. Sarpedon played a major role in the attack on the Achaean camp and the assault on the walls. He was killed by Patroclus, and a great battle was fought around his body.

To distinguish Sarpedon (2) from Sarpedon (3) Diodorus constructed the following genealogy: Sarpedon (2), the son of Europa (5), went to Lycia. He had a son called Evander (1) who married Deidamia (or Laodamia (1)) the daughter of Bellerophon. The fruit of this marriage was Sarpedon (3), grandson of the first, who took part in the Trojan War.

Saturn A very old Italian god identified with CRONUS. He was said to have come from Greece to Italy in very early times, when JUPITER (Zeus) dethroned him and hurled him from Olympus. He established himself on the Capitol, on the site of the future Rome, and founded a village there which bore the name of Saturnia. He was welcomed there by the god JANUS. The reign of Saturn over Latium (thus called because the god had hidden himself there; from the verb *latere*) was extremely prosperous. This was the GOLDEN AGE. Saturn taught people how to cultivate the ground. At this time the Italian population was composed of ABORIGINES, who owed their first laws to Saturn. He was depicted armed with a scythe and his name was associated with the invention of viticulture. He was however sometimes considered as a god of the Underworld.

The days sacred to Saturn were the *Saturnalia*, the end of December and of the year. They were marked by festivals during which the social order was inverted: slaves gave orders to their masters and the latter waited at the table.

Satyria (*Σατυρία*) A daughter of Minos. She was loved by Poseidon, and gave him a son Taras. She gave her name to Cape Satyrion. It was sometimes claimed that she was the mother of ITALUS (1).

Satyrs (*Σάτυροι*) Demons of nature who appeared in Dionysus' train. They were represented sometimes with the lower part of the body resembling that of a horse and the upper part that of a man, and sometimes with their animal half in the form of a goat. They had a long, thick tail, like that of a horse, and a perpetually erect penis of enormous proportions. They were depicted as dancing, drinking with Dionysus and pursuing the Maenads and the Nymphs. They were gradually represented with less obviously bestial characteristics: their lower limbs became human, they had feet and not hooves. Only the tail remained, as evidence of their old form. MARSYAS was a Satyr (see also SILENUS).

Saurus (*Σαῦρος*) A bandit from Elis who robbed travellers until he was killed by Heracles.

Scamander (*Σκάμανδρος*) The river flowing through the plain of Troy. It also bore the name of Xanthus (11) (Tawny), either because of the colour of its water, or else because it was said that its water stained red the fleece of the sheep which bathed in it. Aphrodite dipped her hair in its water to give it golden highlights before submitting herself to the Judgement of Paris.

Heracles, finding himself in the Troad, was thirsty, and begged Zeus, his father, to show him a spring. Zeus made a little stream well up out of the ground but Heracles found this insufficient. He then dug the ground (in Greek σκάπτω) and found a large reservoir of water which became the source of the Scamander.

In the *Iliad*, the Scamander appears as a god, the son of Zeus. Indignant at receiving vast quantities of bodies and blood in its water, Scamander determined to put an obstacle in Achilles' way; so he overflowed his banks and threatened to drown Achilles until Hephaestus forced the river to return within his banks and remain neutral. Scamander had by the Nymph Idaea a son Teucer (1) (Table 4). The river-god was thus one of the founders of the royal family of Troy.

Scamandrius (*Σκαμάνδριος*)
1. The name given by Hector to his son ASTYANAX.
2. A Trojan who was killed by Menelaus.

Schedius (*Σχέδιος*) One of Helen's suitors. He took part in the war against Troy, commanding a force of Phocians together with his brother Epistrophius. They were both sons of Iphitus (2). He was killed by Hector.

Schoeneus (*Σχοινεύς*)
1. The father of Atalanta and Clymenus (3). He was of Boeotian origin, but migrated to Arcadia. He gave his name to towns in both countries.
2. A son of Autonous who was changed into a bird (see ACANTHIS).
3. A son of Athamas and Themisto.

Sciapodes (*Σκιάποδες*) An Indian or Ethiopian people whose name in Greek means 'shady feet': they had such enormous feet that in summer they lay down on the ground and sheltered from the sun, using their feet as parasols.

Sciron (*Σκίρων*) A Corinthian, the son of Pelops (1) or Poseidon, who settled in Megara at a place called the Scironian Rocks, near the coastal road. He would force travellers to wash his feet and would push them into the sea, where an enormous tortoise tore their bodies to pieces. Theseus, on his way from Troezen to Athens, killed him. Historians of Megara however claimed that Sciron was a kindly hero who was married to Chariclo (2). There was one daughter from this marriage, Endeis, the wife of Aeacus and mother of Telamon and Peleus. According to this version Theseus killed Sciron after he had become king of Athens, while on his way to take Eleusis. According to another tradition, Sciron was the son of Canethus and Henioche, the sister of Theseus' mother Aethra. Theseus and Sciron were thus first cousins. It was said that he had founded the Isthmian Games in honour of Sciron to atone for this murder (see also SINIS).

Sciron was also said to be a son of Pylas, the king of Megara. He married one of the daughters of Pandion (2) of Athens. He clashed with Nisus (1), one of his brothers-in-law, after Pandion's death, because Nisus had obtained the throne of Megara. Both agreed to abide by Aeacus' decision: he decreed that they share the power between them, giving the kingship to Nisus and control of the army to Sciron.

Scirus (*Σκῖρος*)

1. A soothsayer from Dodona who arrived at Eleusis during the war between this town and Athens at the time of Erechtheus. He was killed in the fighting and buried on the Sacred Way at Eleusis, at the place which was called Sciron.
2. A Salaminian who gave Theseus some experienced sailors, notably his helmsman Nausithous (2), when Theseus set off to kill the Minotaur. This Scirus is often confused with the SCIRON of Megara.

Scylla (*Σκύλλη*)

1. A sea-monster who lived in the straits of Messina, on the Italian coast. She had the form of a woman with six dogs' heads around the lower part of her body; these creatures devoured all that passed within their reach.

When Odysseus' ship passed by Scylla's cave the dogs leapt out and consumed six of the hero's companions. In the *Odyssey* Scylla is the daughter of a goddess, Crataeis. Elsewhere her father is called Trienus or Phorcys. Other genealogies made her the daughter of Hecate, or Typhon and Echidna, or else of Lamia (2).

Ovid related how Glaucus (4) loved Scylla and scorned the love of Circe on this account. To have her revenge on her rival Circe mixed magic herbs with the water of the fountain where Scylla bathed. Scylla was immediately transformed: six terrifying dogs grew from her groin. It was also claimed that Poseidon fell in love with Scylla and that Aphrodite persuaded Circe to metamorphose her. Another version maintained that Scylla, in love with Glaucus, had refused Poseidon's advances and he had therefore punished her in this way. The death of Scylla was sometimes attributed to Heracles: she devoured a number of the oxen of Geryon which he was bringing back with him. Heracles killed her but Phorcys returned her to life by magical operations performed by torchlight.

2. The daughter of Nisus (1). When Minos came to lay siege to Megara as punishment for the murder of Androgeos, Scylla fell in love with him. Nisus was invincible as long as he had a purple lock of hair (some sources speak of a lock of golden hair) on his head. Scylla cut off this lock of hair, having made Minos promise that he would marry her if she betrayed her homeland. Minos thus gained possession of Megara but was so horrified at Scylla's crime that he attached her to the prow of his boat so that she drowned. The gods transformed her into an egret.

Scythes (*Σκύθης*) The eponymous hero of the Scythians. He was sometimes considered to be a son of Heracles and a female monster identified with ECHIDNA. His brothers were Agathyrsus and Gelonus. Echidna asked him what she ought to do with their children once they were grown up. Heracles gave her one of the two bows he was carrying and his baldric. He added that whichever of the children could draw the bow and use the baldric as he could should rule over the country. The others would have to be exiled. Scythes was the only one of the three able to fulfil the conditions. A tradition reported by Diodorus made Zeus Scythes' father.

Selene (*Σελήνη*) The personification of the Moon. She was sometimes said to be the daughter of Hyperion and Theia, sometimes of the Titan Pallas (3) or else of Helios. She was depicted as a beautiful young girl who rode across the heavens in a silver chariot drawn by two horses. She had a daughter, Pandia, by Zeus, and in Arcadia her lover was the god Pan. She was usually described as the lover of ENDYMION.

Selinus (*Σέλινος*) A son of Poseidon who ruled Aegialia (the ancient name for Achaea). When ION wanted to wage war against him, Selinus gave him in marriage his only daughter, Helice (1). Ion succeeded him on the throne.

Semele (*Σεμέλη*) The daughter of Cadmus and Harmonia (1). She was loved by Zeus and by him conceived Dionysus (Table 3). The jealous Hera suggested to her that she ask her lover to appear before her in all his glory. Zeus, who had rashly promised to grant Semele everything she asked for, had to appear before her with his thunderbolts. Semele was immediately burnt to death. Her sisters spread the rumour that she had had a mortal lover but had boasted of having enjoyed Zeus' favours, whereupon the god had struck her down with his lightning as a punishment. For this calumny a curse was laid on the sisters' descendants (see ACTAEON, LEUCOTHEA (1), PENTHEUS). Later, DIONYSUS went down to the Underworld to look for his mother. Semele was taken up to the heavens where she was given the name of Thyone.

A Laconian version states that Dionysus was born to Semele quite normally at Thebes but that Cadmus abandoned mother and son in a chest at sea. The waves threw the chest up on the coast of Laconia, where Semele, who had died, was buried.

Semiramis (*Σεμίραμις*) A Bablyonian queen. Diodorus tells us that a goddess called Derceto was worshipped at Ascalon in Syria. She lived in a lake near the town and had a woman's face with the body of a fish. Aphrodite made Derceto fall in love with CAYSTRUS, a Syrian, by whom she had a daughter. However, Derceto exposed the child, killed Caystrus and hid at the bottom of the lake. The child was brought up by doves, who stole milk and cheese from nearby shepherds. The shepherds finally discovered the girl and brought her to their chief. He named her Semiramis, 'the one who comes from the doves'.

Semiramis was still a girl when one of the king's advisers, Onnes, was ordered to inspect the flocks. He saw Semiramis and fell in love with her. He took her back with him to Nineveh and married her. They had two children, Hyapate and Hydaspe. Semiramis was very clever and gave her husband such good advice that he succeeded in all his endeavours. At about this time King Ninus, who ruled in Babylon, organized an expedition against Bactria. He overwhelmed the country by the sheer number of his troops and only the capital, Bactra, held out against him. Onnes, who was with the army and was missing Semiramis, asked her to join him. She noticed that the attack was being directed from the plain, while both attackers and defenders were ignoring the citadel. She took charge of a group of soldiers, scaled the cliffs and turned the flank of the enemy defences. The besieged soldiers surrendered. Ninus was full of admiration for Semiramis and very soon her beauty made him want to have her as his wife. He offered to give Onnes his own daughter Sosana in exchange but Onnes refused. Ninus threatened to tear his eyes out, whereupon in despair Onnes hanged himself. Ninus then married Semiramis and they had a son, Ninyas. Semiramis succeeded Ninus on the throne.

She began her reign by building a mausoleum to Ninus at Nineveh. She then decided to have a city built for herself on the Babylonian plain. The new city was marked out on horseback on the river bank. Its perimeter was 66 kilometres long, and six harnessed chariots could ride abreast along the walls. The city was defended by 250 towers. The Euphrates was crossed by a bridge 900 metres long and was lined with great quays for 30 kilometres. At each end of the bridge was built a fortified castle, the queen's residence, linked by a subterranean passage under the river. In the citadel of the western castle the queen had her famous Hanging Gardens built. However, according to Diodorus it was not Semiramis who built the Hanging Gardens, but a Syrian king. One of his concubines asked him for a representation of the 'paradises', the vast pleasure gardens of her homeland. These were created by superimposing square terraces one on top of the other, like the steps in an amphitheatre. Each of these terraces rested on vaulted galleries, covered with a thick layer of lead, on top of which was put rich soil. Inside these galleries the royal apartments were laid out. A system of hydraulic machines brought the water from the river to the gardens.

Semiramis set out at the head of a large army to go to Media. On the way she built a vast park opposite Mount Bagistan, and continued on her route, leaving behind her a trail of works of art of all sorts, notably at Ecbatana, which she filled with fountains. She travelled all over Asia and then went to Egypt to consult the oracle of Ammon. She asked the oracle when she would die. It replied that she would meet her end when her son Ninyas conspired against her. She then conquered Ethiopia and returned home to Bactra. She planned to conquer India, and succeeded in crossing the Indus, but her troops were soon put to flight, and she herself was injured. Shortly afterwards Ninyas along with the eunuchs of the palace plotted against her. Recalling the prophecy of the oracle, Semiramis handed the empire over to Ninyas and disappeared. It was said that she was changed into a dove and borne up to heaven, where she was deified.

Serestus One of Aeneas' companions. He was separated from Aeneas during a storm but rejoined him at Carthage. He secretly took the fleet away when Aeneas wanted to leave Dido. He guarded the camp at the mouth of the Tiber in Aeneas' absence and later fought alongside him when the camp was besieged by Turnus.

Sergestus A companion of Aeneas. He was separated from Aeneas during a storm and rejoined him at Carthage. During the regattas organized in honour of Anchises, he commanded the *Centaur*. He took part in the final assault against Turnus.

Servius Tullius The sixth king of Rome. It was said that he was the son of a slave of Tarquin the Elder, who conceived him by uniting with a phallus of ash (see LARES). Another version maintained that he was the posthumous son of Tullius who reigned at Corniculum when the town was taken by the Romans. His mother was at Rome as a prisoner of Tarquin when she gave birth to her son. One day, while the little Servius was sleeping, his head was surrounded by flames. Tarquin's wife, Tanaquil, prevented the child from being woken up or the flames from being extinguished, and when the child woke up the flames went out. From that point onwards Tanaquil and Tarquin brought up their captive's son with the greatest of care. When he reached manhood, Tarquin gave him his own daughter in marriage and designated him as his successor. When Tarquin was assassinated, Tanaquil took steps to assure that Servius could assume power without difficulty. Later Servius had his elevation ratified by democratic election.

Sevechorus (*Σευήχορος*) A legendary king of Babylon. An oracle had told him that he would be deprived of his kingdom by a son of his daughter. He consequently locked her up in a tower, but this did not prevent her from conceiving a son. The guardians of the tower, fearing for their lives, hurled the child from the top of the tower as soon as he was born. However, an eagle rescued the child before he hit the ground and carried him off to a garden whose keeper brought him up and gave him the name of Gilgamus. This Gilgamus, the hero Gilgamesh, later ruled over Babylon.

Seven against Thebes Adrastus, Amphiaraus, Capaneus, Hippomedon, Parthenopaeus, Polynices and Tydeus. See ADRASTUS.

Sibyl (*Σιβύλλη*) A priestess who made known the oracles of Apollo. According to certain traditions, the first Sibyl was a young girl of this name, the daughter of Dardanus and Neso. Possessing the gift of prophecy she had a great reputation as a soothsayer and the name of Sibyl was given generally to all prophetesses. Another tradition maintains that the earliest Sibyl was a daughter of Zeus and Lamia (1) who was called Sibyl by the Libyans and who uttered prophecies. The second Sibyl was Herophile, a native of Marpessus in the Troad. She was born before the Trojan War and predicted that Troy would be destroyed through the fault of a woman born in Sparta (Helen). There was a hymn sung at Delos which she had composed in honour of Apollo. This Sibyl spent most of her life on Samos but also visited Claros, Delos and Delphi. She carried with her a stone which she mounted before prohesying. She died in the Troad, but her stone could be seen at Delphi in the time of Pausanias.

The most famous of all the Greek Sibyls was the one from Erythrae, in Lydia. Her father was Theodorus, a shepherd of Mount Ida, and her mother was a Nymph. Immediately after her birth she grew suddenly and began to prophesy in verse. While still young she was dedicated by her parents to Apollo. She predicted that she would be killed by an arrow of her god. She lived for the lifetime of nine men, each of 110 years. One tradition maintained that this Sibyl of Erythrae was the same as the Sibyl of Cumae in Campania. This Italian Sibyl was sometimes referred to as Amalthea, sometimes as Demophile or even as Herophile. She pronounced oracles in a cave. Apollo had given her as many years to live as the number of grains of sand she could hold in her hand, but on the condition that she never returned to Erythrae. She settled in Cumae. In one version the Erythraeans inadvertently sent her a letter with a seal made from the earth of their country and on seeing this fragment of her homeland she died. It was also related that in asking Apollo for a long life, she had omitted to ask him for youth. The god offered it to her in exchange for her virginity but she refused. So as she aged she became smaller and wizened, with the result that she ended up looking like a cicada, and she was hung up in a cage like a bird, in the temple of Apollo at Cumae. Children would ask her: 'Sibyl, what do you want?' and she would reply: 'I want to die.' The Cumaean Sibyl was said to have come to Rome during the reign of Tarquinius Superbus, bringing with her nine collections of prophecies. She offered to sell them to the king but Tarquinius found them too expensive. At each refusal the Sibyl burnt three of them. In the end Tarquinius bought the last three and deposited them in the temple of Capitoline Jupiter. Until the time of Augustus, these 'Sibylline books' were consulted in times of trouble or of any extraordinary event. Religious instructions were found inside them: the introduction of a new cult, an expiatory sacrifice, etc., all designed to cope with an unforeseen situation. In the *Aeneid*, the Cumaean Sibyl was Aeneas' guide for his descent into the Underworld. There was another Sibyl of lesser reputation at Samos called Phyto. For the Hebrew Sibyl, see SABBE.

Sicelus (*Σικελός*) The eponymous king of the Siceli, who migrated from southern Italy to Sicily. According to Dionysius of Halicarnassus, Sicelus originally lived at Rome but was evicted from there. He took refuge with King Morges, who gave Sicelus part of his kingdom, whose inhabitants then took the name of Siceli. Sicelus was sometimes considered to be a son of Italus or even of Poseidon.

Sicinnus (*Σίκιννος*) The inventor of the dance peculiar to the Satyrs, the Sicinnis. This was sometimes attributed to a Phrygian Nymph, Sicinnis, an attendant of Cybele.

Sicyon (*Σικυών*) The second founder and eponym of Sicyon in the Peloponnese. The town had been founded by Aegialeus. There were several traditions about Sicyon's genealogy. He was sometimes made a son of Marathon and a brother of Corinthus, but he was usually considered to be the son of Metion and grandson of Erechtheus, king of Athens. He was thus the brother of Daedalus. King Lamedon summoned him as an ally, and gave his daughter Zeuxippe (2) to him in marriage.

Side (*Σίδη*)
1. One of the daughters of Danaus and eponym of the town of Side in the Peloponnese.
2. According to a legend recorded by Apollodorus, ORION married a woman called Side, who was hurled into the Underworld by Hera for daring to rival the goddess' beauty.

Sidero (*Σιδηρώ*) The second wife of Salmoneus and stepmother of Tyro. She maltreated Tyro very badly. She was later killed by Pelias, one of Tyro's sons, in the sanctuary of Hera.

Silenus (*Σιληνός*) A general term applied to an old Satyr, but also the name of a character who brought up Dionysus. He was said to be a son of Pan, or of Hermes and a Nymph, or alternatively to have been born from drops of Uranus' blood when he was mutilated by Cronus. Silenus was exceptionally wise, but had to be forced to reveal this wisdom to men. He was once captured by Midas, to whom he passed on many wise words. Virgil imagines in the sixth *Eclogue* that shepherds could force Silenus to sing. Silenus was said to be the father of the Centaur Pholus by a Nymph of the ash trees. Silenus was very ugly, with a snub nose, thick lips and the gaze of a bull. He was very fat and was usually described as riding an ass, on which he could barely stay upright as he was so drunk.

Sillus (*Σίλλος*) A grandson of Nestor through his father, Thrasymedes. He had a son named Alcmaeon (2). At the time of the invasion of the Peloponnese by the Heraclid, he fled to Attica, where his son became the progenitor of the noble Athenian family of the Alcmaeonidae.

Silvanus A Roman divinity of the woods (*silvae*). He was not clearly distinguished from Faunus, and became identified with Pan. He was an old man, but possessed all the strength of youth. His worship was linked to that of Heracles and also to the Lares. Silvanus lived ordinarily in sacred woods, near villages or in the open country. At the time of the expulsion of the Tarquins, the Etruscan and Roman armies had fought each other, but the result of the day's fighting was unclear. At night a divine voice could be heard proclaiming that the Romans had won as they had lost one man less than their opponents. The Etruscans lost courage and fled. Once the dead had been counted, it was realized that the mysterious voice – Silvanus' – had spoken the truth (see AIUS LOCUTIUS for an analogous legend).

Silvius A son of Aeneas and LAVINIA, and half-brother of Ascanius. Ascanius had first of all made way for him in Lavinium and, so as not to offend him, had gone off to found Alba. When he died Ascanius left the throne of Alba to Silvius; the latter ruled for 29 years and left his kingdom on his death to his son, Aeneas Silvius.

Other traditions make Silvius the son of Ascanius, who was himself the son of Aeneas and Lavinia. Finally he was sometimes considered to be the son of Aeneas and Silvia, the wife of Latinus, whom Aeneas married after the latter's death.

Simois (*Σιμόεις*) A river in the Trojan plain. It is described, in Hesiod, as a son of Oceanus and Tethys. It played a role in the *Iliad*, where SCAMANDER called for his help in driving back ACHILLES and stopping the massacre of the Trojans. Simois had two daughters: Astyoche and Hieromneme. The first was the wife of Erichthonius and mother of Tros; the second was the wife of Assaracus and mother of Capys (Table 4).

Sinis (*Σίνις*) One of the robbers killed by Theseus (see THESEUS, II). He was a son of Poseidon, and a giant endowed with prodigious strength. He was nicknamed 'the bender of pine-trees', because he used to bend trees to the ground and tie a man between them. He would then let the trees spring up again, which would tear the man apart. According to another tradition, he would force any traveller to help him bend a pine-tree, but would then let the tree go so that the man would be catapulted into the distance and killed.

It was supposedly in honour of Sinis that Theseus founded the Isthmian games, considered as funeral games for Sinis (for an analogous tradition, see SCIRON). Sinis had a daughter, Perigoune. While Theseus was killing her father, she hid herself in an asparagus patch. She and Theseus then had a child, MELANIPPUS (4). Their descendants were particularly fond of asparagus as their ancestor owed her life to this plant.

Sinon (*Σίνων*) Son of Aesimus and the first cousin of Odysseus. When the Greeks had constructed the Wooden Horse, they had to persuade the Trojans to take it into the town. So they weighed anchor and slipped away to wait secretly behind the island of Tenedos. Sinon had been left behind, however, and got himself captured by the Trojan shepherds. He was taken before Priam and interrogated. He said that he had been persecuted by Odysseus and had fled so as not to be offered as a sacrifice to the gods. He claimed to be a relation of Odysseus' enemy PALAMEDES and that Calchas (I), in league with Odysseus, had decreed that Sinon should be sacrificed to the gods. Sinon said that he had escaped and hidden in a marsh before he was captured. The Trojans asked why the Greeks had left the Wooden Horse on the shore. Sinon said it was an offering to Pallas Athena, as expiation for Odysseus' sacrilege in stealing the PALLADIUM; various extraordinary happenings had frightened the Greeks and Calchas had told them that the goddess demanded an offering in the form of a horse to replace the stolen statue. Sinon added that Calchas interpreted the gods' wishes as promising the Trojans supremacy over the Greeks if they worshipped the horse in their city. The Trojans believed Sinon's story, and the omen of LAOCOON's death confirmed their decision. Sinon was freed, a hole made in the walls, and the horse brought into the city. At nightfall Sinon opened the side of the horse to allow the concealed soldiers to emerge and massacre the sleeping Trojans. At the same time he signalled to the Greek ships with a lighted flare from the top of the city.

Sinope (Σινώπη) The eponymous heroine of the town of Sinope, on the Asiatic coast of the Euxine Sea. She was a daughter of Asopus. Apollo abducted her and took her to Asia Minor, where she gave birth to a son, Syrus, who gave his name to the Syrians. Another tradition made her a daughter of Ares and Aegina. Zeus fell in love with her and swore to grant her whatever she wanted. The girl asked him to preserve her virginity. Zeus respected her wishes and gave her the land of Sinope as a dwelling. She later extracted the same promises from Apollo and Halys, the river-god, nor did she allow any mortal to take what the gods had not been able to obtain.

Sirens (Σειρῆνες) Sea demons, half woman and half bird. They were said to be the daughters of Achelous and either Melpomene, Sterope (3) or Terpsichore. Phorcys is sometimes named as their father, while Libanius relates that they were born of the blood of Achelous when he was wounded by Heracles.

There were two Sirens in the *Odyssey*, but later traditions name four or more often three. They were remarkable musicians; according to Apollodorus, one played the lyre, another sang, and the third played the flute. The Sirens lived on an island in the Mediterranean and attracted passing sailors with their music: the ships would approach too close to the rocky coast and thereby come to grief. The Sirens would then devour the sailors. The Argonauts sailed close to the Sirens, but Orpheus sang whilst they were within earshot of them, so none of the sailors were lured towards them except BUTES (3) (see also ERYX). In their vicinity Odysseus, advised and warned by Circe, ordered his sailors to block up their ears with wax, he had himself tied to the mast and forbade his men to untie him, no matter how strongly he pleaded. As soon as he heard the Sirens' song Odysseus felt an overwhelming desire to go to them, but his companions prevented him. In frustration at having failed, the Sirens threw themselves into the sea and drowned.

Ovid relates that the Sirens were once ordinary girls, companions of Persephone. When she was abducted by Pluto, they asked the gods for wings to help them in their search for their companion. Other authors attribute this transformation to the anger of Demeter since they failed to prevent the abduction of her daughter. It was also said that Aphrodite deprived them of their beauty because they scorned the pleasures of love. It was also said that after their transformation they tried to rival the Muses, who removed all their feathers. Traditionally the Sirens' island was off the coast of southern Italy, near the Sorrento peninsula. The tomb of the Siren Parthenope was said to be in Naples, where her body had been cast up on the shore.

According to another tradition Parthenope was a beautiful Phrygian girl who fell in love with Metiochus but did not want to break the vow of chastity she had made. She cut off her hair and went into exile in Campania, where she dedicated herself to Dionysus. In anger Aphrodite turned her into a Siren. The Sirens were sometimes said to sing for the blessed in the Islands of the Blessed. They could play the celestial harmonies, and because of this they were often depicted on Sarcophagi.

Siris (*Σῖρις*) The eponym of a town on the gulf of Tarentum. She was sometimes said to be the daughter of the Italian king MORGES, and sometimes the first wife of King METAPONTUS. Metapontus evicted her in order to marry Arne, the daughter of Aeolus (1). Arne had her killed by her sons Boeotus and Aeolus (2).

Sisyphus (*Σίσυφος*) The most cunning of mortals. He was the son of Aeolus (1) (Table 5). He founded Corinth, then called Ephyra. He was considered to have been CORINTHUS' successor and avenger, or else MEDEA's successor.

Autolycus had stolen flocks from Sisyphus, but he was able to reclaim them by pointing to his name, which he had engraved under the hoof of each of his animals. That particular day was the eve of the marriage of Anticleia, the daughter of Autolycus, and Laertes. During the night Sisyphus found his way into the girl's bed. She conceived Odysseus. According to certain mythographers, Autolycus gave his daughter spontaneously to Sisyphus, as he wanted to have a grandson as wily as he.

When Zeus abducted Aegina he passed through Corinth and was sighted by Sisyphus. When Aegina's father, Asopus, came in search of her, Sisyphus promised to reveal the kidnapper's name on condition that Asopus made a spring gush on the citadel of the town. Asopus agreed, and Sisyphus told him that Zeus was the guilty one. One version maintained that Zeus struck him with a thunderbolt and hurled him into the Underworld, where he was condemned to roll an enormous rock eternally up a hill. But this punishment, related in the *Odyssey*, was said to have another explanation in which Zeus sent the spirit of Death (Thanatos) to Sisyphus in order to bring about his end. Sisyphus, however, took Thanatos by surprise and chained him up, so that for a while no mortal died. Zeus had to force Sisyphus to free Thanatos so that he could continue his task. The first victim was Sisyphus. However, Sisyphus secretly enjoined his wife not to pay him any funeral honours. On arriving in the Underworld Sisyphus complained strongly of his wife's impiety, and obtained Hades' permission to return to earth to punish her. Once on earth again, Sisyphus lived to a ripe old age. But when he finally died, the gods of the Underworld were anxious to avoid any possible escape, and so set him a task which left him no free time and no possibility of leaving.

There was another episode in the legend of Sisyphus which has reached us only in a damaged fragment of Hyginus. Sisyphus hated his brother Salmoneus and asked the oracle of Apollo how he could kill 'his enemy'. Apollo told him that he would find men to take revenge if he slept with his own niece, Tyro, who was Salmoneus' daughter. Tyro had twins by Sisyphus but, learning of the oracle, killed her two children while they were young. The text breaks off here, but when it resumes we find Sisyphus in the Underworld, rolling his stone.

The foundation of the Isthmian Games is sometimes attributed to Sisyphus, in honour of his nephew MELICERTES. Sisyphus was married to MEROPE (1). His descendants included Glaucus (3) and Bellerophon.

Sithon (*Σίθων*) A king of Thrace and eponym of the Sithonian peninsula, the middle one of the three peninsulas of the Chersonese in Thrace. He was a son of Ares, or of Poseidon and the Nymph Ossa. He married Anchinoe (or Anchiroe), the daughter of Nilus, and had two daughters by her, Rhoeteia and Pallene (1). Nonnus related that Dionysus fell in love with Pallene and killed Sithon with a stroke of his thyrsus's before marrying the girl. An allusion in Ovid suggests that Sithon became a woman.

Smaragus (*Σμάραγος*) One of the evil demons who enjoyed shattering vases in potters' kilns. Artisans would pray to them before firing any pottery.

Smerdius (*Σμέρδιος*) The son of Leucippus (4) and the king of Naxos. During his reign Theseus, returning from Crete, abandoned Ariadne.

Smicrus (*Σμῖκρος*) Abandoned by his father in Asia, Smicrus was befriended by a son of Eritharses who was keeping watch over a herd of goats in the country. Eritharses offered him a home and treated him as his own son. One day Smicrus and his adopted brother found a swan, and fought with the local children to see to whom the bird would belong. The goddess Leucothea (1) appeared before them, and ordered them to ask the Milesians to set up a gymnastic competiton in her honour. Smicrus later married the daughter of a noble Milesian, by whom he had BRANCHUS. Another variant states that the apparition urged Eritharses to pay the greatest possible attention to Smicrus. Eritharses gave Smicrus his daughter in marriage and it was she who was the mother of Branchus.

Smintheus (*Σμινθεύς*)

1. One of the companions of Echelas, the son of PENTHILUS. An oracle had foretold that his daughter would be drowned at sea. The young girl's lover, Enalus, hurled himself into the sea with her. Touched by such devotion, the gods saved them both.
2. A cult title of Apollo.

Smyrna (*Σμύρνα*)

1. An Amazon who founded several cities in Asia Minor, notably Ephesus and Smyrna.
2. The mother of ADONIS, who was also called Myrrha. She was sometimes said to be the daughter of Theias, or the daughter of King Cinyras.

Sol The Sun, whose worship was reputedly introduced in Rome at the same time as that of the Moon by the first Sabine king, Titus Tatius. For the Hellenic legends about the sun, see HELIOS.

Solois (*Σολόεις*) A young Athenian who accompanied Theseus in his expedition against the Amazons. On his return, Theseus brought back Antiope (2), and while on board Solois fell in love with her. Antiope refused to give in to Solois who, in desperation, threw himself overboard and was drowned. Theseus then remembered an oracle of the Pythian priestess by which he had been ordered to found a city on the day when he was afflicted by a great sadness during a voyage in a foreign land. Obeying this command, Theseus founded the city of Pythopolis, in Bithynia, in honour of the Pythian Apollo. He called the nearby river Solois, in memory of the young Athenian, whose brothers, along with another Athenian, Hermus, he settled in the city.

Sopatrus (*Σώπατρος*) When mortals lived only on fruit and vegetables and did not yet offer blood sacrifices to the gods, a foreigner named Sopatrus lived in Athens. During a sacrifice, just as Sopatrus had placed his offering on the altar, a bull appeared which consumed the plants and grain of the sacrifice. Sopatrus seized an axe and killed the animal. Then, regretting his action, he went into voluntary exile in Crete. After his departure the country was struck by famine. The gods decreed that only Sopatrus could provide the remedy. The slaughtered animal had to be brought back to life, and the murderer punished. Envoys were therefore sent in search of Sopatrus and he was discovered conscience-stricken in Crete. Sopatrus accompanied them home and devised the following plan. During a general meeting of all Athenians, he had a bull brought in, and girls offered him water with which he purified a knife which had been sharpened by other Athenians. He killed the animal, which was cut up and skinned by others, so that everyone took part in the murder. Afterwards the flesh of the bull was shared out, the skin was stuffed with hay, and this artificial bull was then harnessed to a plough. Finally, a tribunal was set up to judge the murderer, in which it was proven that the guilty agent was the knife, which was condemned to be hurled into the sea. This was done. The bull having been 'resurrected' in the form of the stuffed animal and the guilty party executed, the famine ceased. This rite of sacrifice was thus established in Athens, where it was celebrated by Sopatrus' descendants, the Sopatrides.

Sophax (*Σόφαξ*) When Heracles had murdered Antaeus, he slept with his wife TINGE. She gave birth to Sophax, who reigned in Mauretania. Sophax had a son Diodorus, who extended his father's empire and founded the dynasty of the Mauretanian kings.

Soranus The god worshipped at the summit of Mount Soracte. Soranus, sometimes identified with Dis Pater, was more generally considered to be Apollo, and it is as such that he was invoked by Virgil in the *Aeneid*.

Sparta (*Σπάρτα*) The eponym of

the city of Sparta, daughter of the river-god Eurotas and Cleta, and wife of LACEDAEMON. She was the mother of Amyclas and EURYDICE (2). She was sometimes also said to be the mother of Himerus and Asine.

Spartoi (*Σπαρτοί*) The 'sown men' who sprang up from the teeth of the dragon killed by CADMUS.

Spercheius (*Σπερχειός*) The god of the river of the same name, a son of Oceanus and Tethys. Peleus dedicated Achilles' hair to him to ensure that his son should return safely from Troy. Spercheius was Achilles' brother-in-law, because he had married Peleus' daughter, POLYDORA. He was the father of DRYOPS and perhaps of the Nymphs of the Othrys.

Sphaerus (*Σφαῖρος*) The name given posthumously to CILLAS, the charioteer of Pelops (1). He gave his name to the island of Sphaeria, near Troezen, and while making a sacrifice to him AETHRA was surprised by Poseidon (see also AEGEUS and THESEUS, I).

Sphinx (*Σφίγξ*) A monster with the face of a woman, the chest and feet of a lion and wings like a bird of prey. The Sphinx was particularly associated with the myth of OEDIPUS and the Theban cycle, and was mentioned as early as Hesiod's *Theogony*. It was sometimes said to be the offspring of Echidna and Orthrus, but usually its father was TYPHON. Another tradition makes it a daughter of Laius, king of Thebes, or of the Boeotian Ucalegon (2). The Sphinx was sent by Hera to Thebes to punish LAIUS for loving CHRYSIPPUS. The Sphinx lived in a mountain west of Thebes, where it ravaged the countryside, devouring mortals who passed by. It would ask riddles of passers-by and eat those who could not answer them. In particular it asked, 'What creature has only one voice, walks sometimes on two legs, sometimes on three, sometimes on four, and which, contrary to the general law of nature, is at its weakest when it uses the most legs?' There was also another riddle: 'There are two sisters; one gives birth to the other, and she in turn gives birth to the first.' The answer to the first riddle is 'Man' (as a baby he crawls on all fours, then walks on two legs, and ends up supporting himself on a stick). The answer to the second is 'Day and Night' (day and night are feminine nouns in Greek and therefore 'sisters'). Oedipus eventually solved the riddles, and in despair the monster threw itself from the top of a rock and was killed. In other traditions Oedipus killed it with his spear. In another version the Thebans assembled every day to try to solve the riddle together, but unsuccessfully. At the end of each day the Sphinx would eat one of them. It was said to have eaten Haemon (1), the son of Creon (2).

Staphylus (*Σταφυλός*)

1. A shepherd of the Aetolian king Oeneus. He noticed that one of the goats returned later than the others and seemed more frolicsome. He followed it and saw that it was eating fruit which he did not recognize. He told the king what had happened, and the latter had the idea of pressing

the grapes and making wine. The new liquid was given the name of the king (*οἶνος* in Greek means 'wine'). The fruit itself was then called 'staphylus'.

2. A son of Silenus. He was reputedly the first to introduce the custom of mixing water and wine.

3. A child of Dionysus and Ariadne, although one tradition made him the son of Theseus. He was the brother of Thoas (1), Oenopion and Peparethus, to whom were sometimes added Latramys, Evanthes and Tauropolis. Staphylus married Chrysothemis (2) by whom he had Molpadia (2), Rhoeo and Parthenus (2) (and, according to certain authors, Hemithea (1)). Through RHOEO he was the grandfather of ANIUS (1). For the other sisters, see PARTHENUS (1) and LYRCUS (1). Staphylus was said to be one of the Argonauts.

4. A character in the *Dionysiaca* of Nonnus.

Stentor (*Στέντωρ*) In the *Iliad* a Stentor could shout as loudly as 50 men. His name became proverbial. He was a Thracian who had engaged in a shouting match against Hermes (the gods' herald), and when he had lost he was put to death.

Sterope (*Στερόπη*)

1. One of the Pleiades. She married Ares, by whom she had a son, Oenomaus. One tradition maintained that she married Oenomaus himself. Another tradition said that she was married to Hyperochus, who fathered OENOMAUS.

2. One of the daughters of Pleuron.

3. The mother of the SIRENS and the daughter of Porthaon and Euryte. She married Achelous.

4. The daughter of CEPHEUS (1).

5. A daughter of Acastus, the king of Iolcus (Table 6). When PELEUS took refuge at Acastus' court, Astydamia, Acastus' wife, who was in love with the hero, claimed in a letter which she sent to Antigone (3), Peleus' wife, that Peleus wanted to marry Sterope. This caused Antigone's suicide.

Steropes (*Στερόπης*) One of the CYCLOPES.

Stheneboea (*Σθενέβοια*) The wife of King Proetus. She was usually said to be the daughter of Iobates and to have married PROETUS when the latter, evicted by ACRISIUS, migrated to Asia Minor. She was also said to be the daughter of Amphianax, king of Lycia, or of the Arcadian king Aphidas. In the *Iliad*, the same heroine was called Anteia rather than Stheneboea. The latter was the name most commonly used by the tragic writers. Stheneboea provided Proetus with several daughters, the PROETIDES, and a son, Megapenthes (2). Her happiness was disrupted by the arrival in Tiryns of Bellerophon, whose beauty fascinated her. She made advances to him but was rejected. In anger she denounced him to Proetus for having tried to seduce her. For the consequences of this, see BELLEROPHON.

The end of the story, after Bellerophon's victories, was dramatized by Euripides in his lost tragedy *Stheneboea*: the hero returned from Lycia determined to avenge himself, but Proetus stalled for time and allowed Stheneboea to escape on Pegasus,

Bellerophon's winged horse. However, Stheneboea was unseated by Pegasus, fell into the sea and was killed. Another tradition maintained that Stheneboea committed suicide on learning of Bellerophon's return.

Sthenelas (*Σθενέλας*) A son of Crotopus, of the family of Phorbas. He succeeded his father on the throne of Argos.

Sthenelus (*Σθένελος*)

1. The son of Actor, and companion of Heracles, whom he followed in his expedition against the Amazons. He was wounded, died on the way back in Paphlagonia and was buried near the coast. Later, when the Argonauts were passing nearby, Persephone granted Sthenelus permission to return briefly to earth to see them. The Argonauts made a sacrifice to him, as to a hero.
2. A son of Androgeos and consequently a grandson of Minos, and a brother of Alceus. See EURYMEDON (2).
3. Son of Capaneus, one of the EPIGONI. His mother was Evadne (2). He had inherited one third of the kingdom of Argos from IPHIS (1). He figures amongst Helen's suitors and thus took part in the Trojan War. But from the fall of Thebes onwards (prior to the Trojan War), he became the great friend of Diomedes (2). At Troy he distinguished himself in battle, especially in the service of Diomedes, whose squire he seems to have been. He had earlier been wounded in the foot, and could fight only from a chariot. After returning from Troy, he accompanied DIOMEDES (2) to Aetolia to restore the throne to Oeneus. It was probably the same Sthenelus who was the father of the COMETES (1).
4. One of the sons of Perseus and Andromeda (Table 7). He married Nicippe, the daughter of Pelops (1) and had several children, including EURYSTHEUS and Iphis (2). He ruled over Mycenae, which had been founded by Perseus.

Stilbe (*Στίλβη*)

1. The daughter of the Thessalian river-god Peneius and of the Nymph Creusa (1). By Apollo she became the mother of Centaurus and Lapithes. She was also said to have had another son, Aeneus, the father of Cyzicus.
2. The daughter of Eosphorus, sometimes said to be the mother of Autolycus.

Stirus or **Styrus** An Albanian prince who, in Valerius Flaccus' *Argonautica*, claimed the hand of Medea. As the Scythian king, Anausis, also wanted to marry the girl, they fought and were both wounded. After Medea's abduction by Jason, Stirus followed her, but was drowned in the storm raised by Hera.

Striges Winged female demons, with talons like those of birds of prey, who fed off the blood and entrails of children (see CARNA).

Strophius (*Στρόφιος*)

1. The son of CRISUS. His mother was Antiphatia, the daughter of Naubolus. Through his wife, Anaxibia, he was Agamemnon's brother-in-law (Table 2). PYLADES was his son. See also ORESTES.

2. The grandson of Strophius (1), the son of Pylades and Electra (3).

Strymo (*Στρυμώ*) The daughter of the river-god Scamander. She married Laomedon (Table 4) and was the mother of Priam. Sometimes, Priam's mother was said to be Placia or Leucippe (1) instead of Strymo.

Strymon (*Στρυμών*) The god of the river of the same name in Thrace. He was the father of RHESUS by one of the Muses. He was also described as the father of Brangas and OLYNTHUS and of Tereine and Evadne (3). One legend relates that Strymon was a king of Thrace and a son of Ares. When Rhesus was killed at Troy, Strymon threw himself in despair into a river, which subsequently took his name.

Stymphalus (*Στύμφαλος*) One of the five sons of Elatus (1) and Laodice (1). He was the eponynous hero of the town of Stymphalus in the Peloponnese, by the lake of the same name (see HERACLES, II). He had several sons: Agamedes, Gortys, Agelaus, and a daughter, Parthenope. Stymphalus successfully defended Arcadia against Pelops (1) until the latter pretended to effect a reconciliation with Stymphalus but killed him during a feast. He then dismembered him and dispersed the pieces.

Styx (*Στύξ*) A river of the Underworld. In Hesiod's *Theogony*, Styx was the oldest of the children of Oceanus and Tethys. But Hyginus mentioned her as one of the children of Nyx and Erebus. She featured amongst Persephone's companions in the Homeric *Hymn to Demeter*, but there was also a tradition, related by Apollodorus, according to which she was Persephone's mother. Styx is usually said to be married to Pallas (3), by whom she became the mother of Zelus, Nike, Cratos and Bia. During the fight between Zeus and the Giants, she and her children supported Zeus. In recognition of this Zeus gave her the honour of being the surety of oaths sworn by the gods. According to a fragment of Epimenides, Styx conceived a child by a certain Peiras (*Πείρας*), and give birth to ECHIDNA. Finally, one of the children attributed to Styx was ASCALAPHUS (1).

Styx was the name of a spring in Arcadia which emerged from a rock above ground, then disappeared underground again. Its water was poisonous for humans and cattle and could break iron, metal and pottery, though a horse's hoof was unharmed by it. Alexander the Great was supposedly poisoned by water from this spring. The water of the Styx was usually said to possess magical properties. It was in this river that Thetis dipped ACHILLES in order to make him invulnerable. Above all, the water of the Styx was used by the gods for pronouncing oaths: Zeus would send Iris to draw an ewer of water from the Styx, and bring it back to Olympus, so that it 'witnessed' the oath. If the god subsequently perjured himself, he became unable to breathe for an entire year and could not drink either ambrosia or nectar. At the end of a year, another test was forced on him. For nine years he took no part in the deliberations or the feasts of the gods. He resumed his privileges only in the tenth year. The Styx was a branch of Oceanus. In Virgil's description of the Styx, it meanders around the kingdom of Hades nine times, completely surrounding it (see ACHERON).

Summanus A Roman god associated with Jupiter: he was the god of the nocturnal heaven. A statue of Summanus existed on the temple of Jupiter on the Capitol, but its head was severed by a flash of lightning in 278 BC and hurled into the Tiber. This omen was interpreted as a sign that the god wanted to have a separate temple, and one was consecrated to him on 20 July in the Circus Maximus. Summanus was said to have been introduced to Rome by Titus Tatius.

Sybaris (*Σύβαρις*)

1. A female monster from Phocis, also called LAMIA (2) (see ALCYONEUS (2)). A spring welled up out of the rock at the spot where the monster was killed, and became known as the Sybaris. Locrian settlers gave this name to the town which they founded in southern Italy.
2. A Trojan companion of Aeneas, who was killed by Turnus.
3. The father of a young girl, Alia, who slept with a monster in a wood sacred to Artemis. The race of the Ophiogenians, or the 'sons of the serpent', was the fruit of this union. They lived in the Hellespont region. This tribe cured serpents' bites by their incantations. It was also said that the ancestor of the Ophiogenians was a serpent who had been changed into a man.

Syceus (*Συκεύς*) According to one tradition, one of the Titans who saved his mother, Ge, as she was being pursued by Zeus. He made a fig tree grow, which she sheltered under to protect herself from Zeus' thunderbolts.

Sychaeus (*Συγχαῖος* or *Συχαῖος*) DIDO's husband. He is also known as Sicharbas, but in the *Aeneid* he is called Sychaeus. He was murdered by Dido's brother Pygmalion (1) (see DIDO), who left the body unburied. Dido did not know what had happened until Sychaeus appeared to her in a dream, explained the events, advised her to flee and revealed the spot where he had buried his treasure. Dido built a sanctuary to Sychaeus in her palace and faithfully preserved his memory until the arrival of Aeneas. Full of remorse for her infidelity to Sychaeus' memory, she committed suicide after Aeneas' departure. She was united with Sychaeus in the Underworld. A tradition independent of the *Aeneid* makes Sychaeus the husband of Dido's sister Anna.

Syleus (*Συλεύς*) A wine-grower who would stop passers-by and force them to work in his vineyard before putting them to death. During his servitude to Omphale, Heracles began working for him but instead of tilling the vines he tore them up. He then killed Syleus with a hoe. Syleus had a brother called Dicaeus ('the just one'). They were both sons of Poseidon. After killing Syleus, Heracles was welcomed by Dicaeus. Heracles then fell in love with Syleus' daughter and married her. He went away for some time, during which the young girl died, not being able to bear the absence of her lover.

The region in which Syleus lived was sometimes given as Lydia, and sometimes as Aulis, Thermopylae or Pelion in Thessaly. A tradition existed according to which HERACLES was sold as a slave to Syleus and not to Omphale as a punishment for spilling the blood of Iphitus (1).

Syme (*Σύμη*) A daughter of IALYSUS and Dotis, she was abducted by Glaucus (4). Having taken possession of the island of Syme between Rhodes and Cnidos, he gave it his wife's name. Syme had a son by Poseidon called Chthonius.

Syrinx (*Σύριγξ*) An Arcadian Hamadryad who was loved by Pan. The god pursued her, but just as he was about to catch her, she changed herself into a reed on the banks of the River Ladon. As the wind's breath was making the reeds sigh, Pan had the idea of joining reeds of different lengths together with wax. He thus made a musical instrument which he called the Syrinx. It was also related that there was a grotto near Ephesus where Pan had brought the first Syrinx. Young girls who claimed they were virgins were shut up in it and, if they really were pure, the sounds of a Syrinx would soon be heard, and the girl would appear, crowned with pine. If a girl was not pure, funeral cries could be heard from within and when the grotto was opened, she would have disappeared.

Syrna (*Σύρνα*) The eponym of the city of Syrnos and daughter of Damaethus, the king of Caria. See PODALIRIUS.

Syrus (*Σύρος*) The eponym of the Syrians. According to some he was the son of SINOPE, but according to others Syrus was one of the sons of Agenor and Telephassa, and thus a brother of Cadmus, Phoenix (2) and Cilix. The invention of arithmetic and the introduction of the doctrine of metempsychosis were attributed to him.

T

Tages An Etruscan labourer was ploughing when he saw a clod of earth rise up and become a child which he named Tages. Tages was said to be the son of the Genius Iovialis. He was gifted with great wisdom and possessed powers of prophecy. He predicted the future for the villagers who had come running to the field where he was born, instructed them in the rules of haruspication, then died. His words were written down and formed the basis of Etruscan books devoted to prophecy.

Talassio A ritual cry, made during marriages at the moment when the bride was carried over the threshold. Talassus was one of Romulus' companions. At the time of the rape of the Sabine women, the royal shepherds had abducted a young girl and, on bringing her back, cried out, so that no one should take her from them: 'She is for Talassus' (in Latin: *Talassio*). As Talassus' marriage was a happy one, this cry of good omen was preserved in the marriage ritual. Another explanation was also given, connecting the word with the Greek *Ταλασία* (wool-spinning). After the rape of the Sabine women, it was agreed that the women would not be made to perform any menial tasks, but would content themselves with spinning wool. The cry of *Talassio* was said to recall this agreement.

Talaus (*Ταλαός*) The son of BIAS or CRETHEUS and the father of ADRASTUS. He ruled over a part of the kingdom of Argos which had been allocated to his father by PROETUS. His mother was Pero. Talaus' wife is sometimes called Lysimache, and is said to be the daughter of Abas (3) (see Table 1); she is also called Lysianassa, the daughter of POLYBUS (2). Talaus figures among the Argonauts.

Talos (*Τάλως*)

1. A figure of Cretan legend, a bronze robot. Talos was considered to be either the work of Hephaestus, who made a present of him to Minos, or of Daedalus, the official artist to the king, or else the last representation on earth of the Bronze Age.

Talos was indefatigably vigilant, and had been chosen by Minos, or Zeus, for the task of protecting the island of Crete. Each day he walked fully armed three times around the island, preventing strangers from entering it and the inhabitants from leaving without Minos' permission. Talos' favourite weapons were enormous stones which he hurled great distances. However, if anyone got through his first barrage, Talos would leap into a fire, make himself red-hot, embrace his victims and burn them. He was invulnerable except in the lower part of his leg, where there was a vein closed at the top by a nail. When the ARGONAUTS arrived, Medea succeeded through her magic in opening up the vein and Talos died. Another version relates that Philoctetes' father, Poeas, one of the Argonauts, pierced this vein with an arrow. Talos had a son, Leucus (see IDOMENEUS).

2. An Athenian, a nephew of DAEDALUS, who was killed by the latter because he was jealous of his skill.

Talthybius (*Ταλθύβιος*) One of Agamemnon's heralds who took part with him in the Trojan War. His colleague was the herald Eurybates. In the *Iliad*, Talthybius was given the responsibility of taking Briseis away from Achilles, and was sent as ambassador to Machaon. It was also said that he had accompanied Iphigenia to Aulis for the sacrifice, and that he had been part of the embassy to CINYRAS. At Sparta there was a sanctuary to him.

Tanais (*Τάναις*) The god of the river we know as the Don and the son of Oceanus and Tethys.

Tantalus (*Τάνταλος*)

1. A son of Zeus and Pluto, the daughter of Cronus or of Atlas (1). He reigned on Mount Sipylus. He was extremely rich and was loved by the gods, who welcomed him to their feasts. He had married the Pleiad Dione. But Euryanassa, daughter of the river-god Pactolus, is also mentioned as his wife. His children were Pelops (1) and Niobe (2); Broteas, Dascylus and several others are sometimes added (see Table 2).

Tantalus perjured himself in order to hand over to Hermes Zeus' dog, which had been entrusted to him by PANDAREOS. Zeus shut Tantalus up under Mount Sipylus before he was condemned to the Underworld. In another adventure Ilus (2) reputedly evicted him from Asia Minor after the misfortunes of his daughter Niobe. A final episode makes him the abductor of GANYMEDE. What made Tantalus famous was the punishment he underwent in the Underworld, a description of which is given in Book XI of the *Odyssey*. Tantalus was accused of pride: he had been invited by the gods to dine with them, but revealed their divine secrets to humans. Alternatively he is accused of having stolen nectar and ambrosia during these banquets and having given some to his mortal friends. For another accusation, see PELOPS (1). Like Lycaon (1), Tantalus immolated his son to serve him as a dish to the gods. His punishment was described in various ways. Sometimes in the Underworld he was placed under an enormous stone, which was always on the point of falling, but remained continuously balanced. According to other versions, he felt an eternal hunger and thirst: he was plunged into water up to his neck, but the water withdrew whenever he tried to dip his mouth into it. Similarly, a branch laden with fruit hung just above his head, but if he raised his arm the branch sprang out of reach.

2. A son of Thyestes or of Broteas, both sons of Tantalus (1). In one version he had been killed by Atreus because of his hatred for Thyestes and served to the latter in a stew; in another, he was the first husband of CLYTEMNESTRA and was killed by Agamemnon, his nephew (Table 2).

3. One of the sons of Amphion and Niobe (2).

Taphius (*Τάφιος*) A son of Poseidon and Hippothoe (Table 7). His son was PTERELAUS. Taphius was the eponymous hero of the island of Taphos.

Taras (*Τάρας*) The eponym of Tarentum in southern Italy. He was a son of Poseidon and a local Nymph, Satyra or Satyria, who was often said to be the daughter of Minos (hence the tradition of the Cretan origin of Tarentum). For another founder of Tarentum, see PHALANTHUS.

Taraxippus (*Ταράξιππος*)
1. 'Horse-troubling', a demon which haunted the racecourse at Olympia and frightened the horses near a bend where there was an altar. It was said that it was the soul of the hero ISCHENUS, or that of Olenius, a famous Olympian chariot-driver, or else of Dameon, daughter of Phlious, who took part in Heracles' expedition against Augias and who was killed by Cteatus at the same time as her horse. It was also said that Taraxippus was Alcathous (2), son of Porthaon, who had been put to death by Oenomaus when he tried to obtain the hand of Hippodamia (1). Taraxippus had a dual link with the legend of Oenomaus. It was said that Pelops (1) had buried at this spot a 'charm' which he used to frighten Oenomaus' horses and thus win the race. The second legend was that Pelops was buried in the Olympia racecourse and continued to disrupt the races there. It was, however, also suggested that there was a laurel growing near the altar and that the shadows caused by the leaves blowing in the wind were sufficient to startle horses racing on the track.
2. Another Taraxippus existed on the Corinth racetrack. It was the soul of the hero GLAUCUS (3), who had been devoured by his horses.

Tarchetius (*Ταρχέτιος*) According to Plutarch's *Life of Romulus*, Tarchetius was a king of Alba, in whose house a phallus appeared one day. The goddess Tethys told him that a young girl should be united with the phallus and that the first child of this union would have a glorious life. Tarchetius ordered one of his daughters to follow Tethys' instructions, but she sent a servant-girl in her place. As punishment Tarchetius bound the two girls to a spinning stool and promised to release them only when they had finished a specified piece of work. When they were asleep Tarchetius sent other servants who undid their work. The servant-girl who had given herself to the phallus eventually gave birth to twins. Tarchetius wanted to put them to death, but she gave them to a man called Teratius who exposed them. They were suckled by a she-wolf, and later dethroned and killed Tarchetius.

Tarchon (*Τάρχων*) An Etruscan hero, founder of the cities of Tarquinia, Mantua and Cortona. He was sometimes considered to be the brother of Tyrrhenus and son of Telephus. He led the Etruscan immigrants from Lydia to Italy. He was born with white hair, a sign of great destiny. In the *Aeneid*, Virgil makes Tarchon an ally of Evander (3) and, consequently, of Aeneas.

Tarpeia A Roman heroine, eponym of the Capitol (*Tarpeius Mons*) or, more particularly, of the Tarpeian rock, from which certain criminals were thrown. She was the daughter of Sp. Tarpeius, who had been put in charge of the Capitol by Romulus after the rape of the Sabine women; while the Sabine king, Tatius, was encamped with his army at the foot of the Capitol Tarpeia fell in love with him. She promised to turn the citadel over to him either on the condition that he agreed to marry her, or that he and his soldiers give her 'what they were wearing on their left arms', meaning their gold bracelets. Tatius accepted and Tarpeia betrayed the Capitol. But instead of marrying the young girl Tatius had her crushed to death beneath his men's shields, which they wore on their left arms.

There was a local cult devoted to Tarpeia on the Capitol. There was also a story that she was Tatius' daughter and had been abducted by Romulus. Therefore her treason was revenge against her abductor. In one version the Sabines put her to death because of her refusal to reveal to Tatius what Romulus' battle plans were. It was also said that Tarpeia had planned to deliver the Sabines into the hands of the Romans. She pretended to betray Romulus, asking in return for what the Sabines were wearing on their left arms. She meant their shields and hoped that once the Sabines had entered the citadel, deprived of their main protection, they would be easily killed by the Romans. She was betrayed, however, and when Tarpeia asked Tatius for his and his soldiers' shields, he had her crushed to death beneath them.

Tartarus (*Τάρταρος*) In the Homeric poems and in Hesiod's *Theogony*, Tartarus is the deepest region of the world, placed beneath the Underworld itself. There was the same distance between Hades (the Underworld) and Tartarus as between Heaven and Earth. It was in Tartarus that successive generations of the gods locked away their enemies (see CYCLOPES, CRONUS, ZEUS, GYGES (1)). Tartarus remained a place feared by the Olympians. When any one of them defied Zeus he would threaten to lock the rebel away there. When APOLLO killed the Cyclopes with his arrows, he only just escaped this punishment because of Leto's pleading: instead of being hurled into Tartarus, her son was only condemned to enter into the service of a mortal. The ALOADAE and SALMONEUS were thrown into Tartarus, which became increasingly identified with the Underworld where serious criminals were tortured. Tartarus was the antitype of the Elysian Fields, where the Blessed lived. In Hesiod's *Theogony*, Tartarus is personified and represents one of the primordial elements of the world, along with Eros, Chaos and Gaia. By Gaia Tartarus produced several monsters: Typhon, Echidna and, according to some sources, Zeus' eagle and Thanatos.

Tatius Titus Tatius was traditionally second king of Rome. He was of Sabine origin from the town of Cures. He was commander-in-chief of the Sabine confederacy, which wanted to avenge the abduction of their women (see TARPEIA). After the two peoples were reconciled through the initiative of HERSILIA and the Sabine women, it was decided that Tatius and Romulus would share the power in the city which was thus formed. This city would keep the name of Rome from its founder, but its citizens would be called Quirites in memory of Tatius' homeland. Tatius would dwell on the Capitol and Romulus on the Palatine. This joint reign lasted for five years, but in the fifth year some of Tatius' relations and compatriots quarrelled with some Laurentine ambassadors who were on their way to Rome and killed them. Romulus wanted to punish this attack on the rights of his people but Tatius successfully saved his relations. However friends of the victims killed Tatius during a sacrifice which the two kings were offering at Lavinium. Romulus brought Tatius' body back to Rome and gave him great funeral honours. He was buried on the Aventine, near the *Armilustrium*.

Taurus (*Ταῦρος*) It was related that the Minotaur was not an animal but a certain Taurus, whose name means 'the Bull', leader of Minos' armies and a cruel man. The young people sent from Athens as tribute were not, it was said, put to death by Minos, but proposed as prizes at the funeral games given in honour of Androgeos. The first winner of these games was Taurus, who seriously mistreated those whom he won. Theseus undertook the expedition to Crete to take vengeance on him. Minos was happy to be rid of a general who had become a nuisance and who also had fallen in love with the queen, Pasiphae. That was why Minos assisted Theseus' enterprise and even gave him his daughter Ariadne in marriage.

Taygete (*Ταυγέτη*) One of the Pleiades. She yielded to Zeus' advances only when unconscious, but was so ashamed when she recovered that she hid herself under Mount Taygetus, in Laconia. In due course she gave birth to Lacedaemon. It was also said that in order to protect her from Zeus, Artemis disguised the girl as a doe. When she was restored to her original form, Taygete in gratitude dedicated the Ceryneian Hind to the goddess (see HERACLES, II).

Tecmessa (*Τέκμησσα*) The daughter of the Phrygian king Teleutas, who was abducted by Ajax (2). She journeyed to Troy with the hero and gave him a son, Eurysaces. Tecmessa plays an important role in Sophocles' tragedy *Ajax*.

Tectamus (*Τέκταμος*) The son of Dorus (1) (Table 5). He invaded Crete at the head of the Pelasgians and Aeolians. There he married the daughter of Cretheus and had by her a son, ASTERION. He consolidated his authority over the entire island. Tectamus represents the Dorian component of the Cretan population.

Tectaphus (*Τέκταφος*) An Indian prince. Taken prisoner by Deriades, he had been locked away and left to die in hunger. But Tectaphus' daughter, Aeria, who had just given birth, obtained the guards' permission to go into the prison, simply, she claimed, to bring her father a supreme consolation. She was searched but no food was found on her. She was thus allowed to enter, where she gave her father milk from her breast. Deriades learned of this act of piety and freed his enemy.

Tegeates (*Τεγεάτης*) A son of Lycaon (2) and the founder of the city of Tegea. He married Atlas' daughter MAERA (1). They had several sons, including Scephrus and LEIMON. Another tradition made Tegeates the father of CYDON, Archedius, Gortys and CATREUS. See also RHADAMANTHYS.

Tegyrius (*Τεγύριος*) A king of Thrace, who welcomed EUMOLPUS (1) and Ismarus when they were banished from Ethiopia.

Telamon (*Τελαμών*) Father of Ajax (2). In one tradition his parents were Actaeus and Glauce (3), the daughter of CYCHREUS; in the other, Telamon is the son of Aeacus and Endeis (Cychreus' granddaughter), and thus the brother of Peleus and Alcimache, who married OILEUS, thus establishing a link between the two Ajaxes. For Telamon's early childhood see PELEUS. After the murder of his half-brother Phocus, he was exiled along with Peleus and settled in Salamis, from where he unsuccessfully tried to reinstate himself in his father's favour. In this tradition Telamon married Glauce (3) at Salamis, and when her father Cychreus died without sons he inherited the kingdom. When Glauce died Telamon married PERIBOEA (5) or Eriboea (Table 2). They had one son, Ajax (2).

Telamon took part in the Calydonian boar hunt and in the voyage of the ARGONAUTS, where he rowed alongside Heracles. He reproached the Argonauts for abandoning Heracles in Mysia after the HYLAS episode. Telamon also played a part in the sack of Troy by Heracles (see HERACLES, III). Heracles gave him HESIONE (3), the daughter of LAOMEDON. By Hesione he had a son, Teucer (2). Telamon was still alive at the end of the Trojan War in which his sons Ajax and Teucer took part. When Teucer returned without Ajax, Telamon threw him out. We have only very vague information concerning Telamon's death.

Telchines (*Τελχῖνες*) Actaeus, Megalesius, Hormenus and Lycus (5), demons from Rhodes, sons of Pontus and Gaia. Along with Caphira they helped bring up Poseidon, who subsequently had children by their sister HALIA (1). The Telchines conceived the idea of sculpting statues of the gods; they could cause rain, hail or snow to fall; they could assume any form they chose and were very reluctant to reveal their talents. They had a premonition about the Flood and scattered around the world; Lycus (5) went to Lycia, where he built the temple of Lycian Apollo on the banks of the Xanthus. The Telchines were depicted with the lower part of their body as a fish or serpent, or else as web-footed. Their gaze was terrifying and they could cast evil spells: Ovid says that for this reason Jupiter drowned them in the sea.

Telchis (*Τελχίς*) In the tradition related by Pausanias, one of the kings of Sicyon, the son of Europs and father of Apis. In the tradition related by Apollodorus, Telchis and Thelxion were heroes who rid the country of the tyranny of Apis.

Teleboas (*Τηλεβόας*) The eponymous hero of the Teleboeans who from the neighbouring island of Taphos took possession of the island of Leucas. Teleboas was either the son or the father of PTERELAUS.

Teledamus (*Τηλέδαμος*) One of the twins born of the love of Cassandra and Agamemnon (Table 2). He was killed while very young, along with his brother, and buried at Mycenae.

Telegonus (*Τηλέγονος*)

1. The son of Odysseus and Circe (according to one version, of Odysseus and Calypso (1)). Telegonus does not appear in the *Odyssey*, but he inspired an epic poem, the *Telegonia*, by Eugammon of Cyrene.

Telegonus was brought up on the island of Circe, after Odysseus' departure. On reaching manhood, he learnt who his father was, and went to Ithaca to make himself known. He began to raid cattle belonging to the king. Odysseus defended his property and in the fight was wounded by his son, whose lance was tipped with the bones of a ray (a fish thought to be deadly). The wound was fatal and Odysseus died. Telegonus then recognized his victim and bitterly lamented his crime. He brought back the body, which Penelope insisted on accompanying, to Circe's island. There he married Penelope, and Circe sent both of them to the Isles of the Blessed. It was sometimes claimed that ITALUS (2) was born of this marriage. The founding of Tusculum and Praeneste was sometimes attributed to Telegonus.

2. See POLYGONUS.

Telemachus (*Τηλέμαχος*) The only son of Odysseus and Penelope, according to the *Odyssey*. He was born shortly before the Trojan War and had never known his father. His legend is developed particularly in the first four books of the *Odyssey*, which form what is sometimes known as the *Telemachia*, but mythographers acknowledged a whole series of Telemachus' adventures both earlier and later than the Homeric story. For events in Telemachus' infancy see ODYSSEUS, II and PALAMEDES. When he was a child, Telemachus, had fallen into the sea: he was saved by dolphins, and that was why Odysseus' shield bore the emblem of a dolphin.

According to the *Odyssey*, Telemachus grew up at the court of Ithaca under the care of Mentor, Odysseus' old friend. But when he was about 17 the importunities of Penelope's suitors began. Telemachus determined to evict them. He undertook a voyage to seek news of his father from Nestor, who had come back to Pylos, and from Menelaus, who was at Sparta. In the course of his visit to Nestor, he was greeted by POLYCASTE (1). From Menelaus, he learnt that Odysseus was a prisoner of Calypso (1). Back in Ithaca, Telemachus soon saw his father return, disguised as a stranger. Their first meeting was arranged by the herdsman Eumaeus. Then the plot against the suitors was hatched, followed by the massacre (see ODYSSEUS, IV).

Mythographers added various other episodes. The *Telegonia* related that after Odysseus was killed by TELEGONUS (1), the latter married Penelope, and Telemachus married Circe. LATINUS was born of this marriage. There was another legend, according to which Odysseus had been warned by an oracle to mistrust his son. He therefore had Telemachus exiled. In fact, the oracle alluded to Telegonus (1) and nothing could prevent destiny from being fulfilled nor Odysseus from being accidentally killed by the son he and Circe produced. Telemachus then reigned over Ithaca.

Telemachus was much used by mythographers who studied and commented on the legend of Odysseus. Developing the Homeric episode of Telemachus and Polycaste (1), they affirmed the existence of two children born of this union: Persepolis and Homer himself. Similarly, they conceived of a marriage between Telemachus and Nausicaa, from which Persepolis was born. The Attic orator Andocides claimed amongst his distant ancestors Telemachus and Nausicaa.

Telemus (*Τήλεμος*) A soothsayer from the land of the Cyclopes who predicted to Polyphemus (2) that Odysseus would blind him.

Telephassa (*Τηλέφασσα*) The wife of Agenor and the mother of Cadmus, Cilix, Phoenix (2), Thasos and Europa (5) (Table 3). She set off in search of Europa after the latter had been abducted by Zeus. She died in Thrace where Cadmus buried her.

Telephus (*Τήλεφος*) The son of Heracles and Auge. For the circumstances of his birth and exposure, see AUGE. He was found by some shepherds of King Corythus (2) being suckled by a hind. Corythus brought him up and gave him the name Telephus, which recalls the Greek word *ἔλαφος*, meaning 'deer' or 'hind'. On reaching manhood, Telephus interrogated the oracle at Delphi in order to locate his mother. He was told to go to Mysia, where he found her at the court of King Teuthras (1). It was said that earlier, while at Tegea, he had accidentally killed his mother's two brothers, Hippothous and Pereus, thus fulfilling an ancient oracle. This murder was the subject of Sophocles' lost tragedy the *Aleadae*. Hounded from Arcadia, Telephus consulted the Delphic oracle, which ordered him to go to Mysia without uttering a single word during the journey and until Teuthras had purified him.

At the same time as Telephus arrived at Teuthras' court, the Argonaut Idas tried to rob Teuthras of his kingdom. Teuthras asked Telephus, who had come into Mysia accompanied by PARTHENOPAEUS, for his help. He promised him the hand of Auge, whom he had considered his adopted daughter ever since she had landed in Mysia. Telephus won the victory, and the promised marriage was arranged. However Auge, faithful to the memory of Heracles, did not want to marry a mortal, and entered the nuptial chamber carrying a sword. An enormous serpent, sent by the gods, rose up between her and her son, and Auge and Telephus recognized each other. Incest and crime were avoided, and mother and son returned to Arcadia.

It was more commonly accepted that Telephus, having been recognized by Auge, remained in Mysia, where Teuthras made him his heir. He gave him his daughter Argiope in marriage. At this point Telephus fought against the Greeks who were going to Troy and was wounded by Achilles. The Greeks, being unaware of the correct route to Troy disembarked in Mysia, believing themselves to be in Phrygia. Some authors claim that they did it deliberately, wanting to diminish the power of the Mysians before attacking Troy so as to prevent Priam from seeking help from them. Telephus went to meet the invaders and killed many of them, but when Achilles appeared before him, Telephus fled. In the chase, he caught his foot in a vine and tripped. Achilles wounded him in the thigh with his lance. It was claimed that Dionysus himself caused him to fall over because Telephus had not paid him the honours to which he was entitled. The Greeks then re-embarked.

The Greeks spent eight years gathering another army, which assembled once again at Aulis, but they did not know how to reach the Troad. Telephus, whose wound was not healing, came from Mysia to Aulis and offered to show the Greeks the way if Achilles agreed to heal him, as Apollo had predicted to Telephus that he who had wounded him would heal him. Achilles agreed; he applied some of the rust from his lance to Telephus' wound, which then healed. Telephus then guided the fleet to Troy. In his tragedy *Telephus*, Euripides relates how, on Clytemnestra's advice, Telephus seized the infant Orestes and threatened to kill him if the Greeks did not agree to having Achilles cure him.

Telephus played no part in the Trojan War, although his son EURYPYLUS (4) did. But by this time Telephus was already dead.

Telephus was linked with Italian myths through his two sons Tarchon and Tyrsenus (or Tyrrhenus). Tarchon and Tyrsenus emigrated to Etruria after the capture of Troy. Likewise ROMA, one of the heroines to whom the foundation of Rome was attributed, was sometimes considered a daughter of Telephus and wife of Aeneas.

Tellus The personification of the productive power of the earth in Rome. She was sometimes honoured under the name of *Terra Mater*, the Earth Mother, and identified with the Greek goddess GAIA. In the Ancient period she was paired with a masculine *numen*, Tellumo.

Telphousa (*Τέλφουσα*) The Nymph of a spring in Boeotia. On his return from the Hyperboreans, Apollo was enchanted by the coolness of the spot and wanted to set up his sanctuary there. Telphousa was afraid that the number of her conquests would diminish if a great god established himself near her, so she advised him to go to Delphi. Apollo did this, but after his victory over Python, realizing that he had been tricked, he returned to reproach Telphousa and, as a punishment, concealed the spring under the cliffs. He then dedicated an altar to himself in the place.

Temenus (*Τήμενος*)

1. A native of Stymphalus in the Peloponnese. He was the son of Pelasgus and it was he who brought up the goddess Hera. He dedicated three sanctuaries in her honour: to

Hera the Child, Hera the Married Woman, and Hera the Widow.

2. One of the two sons of Phegeus. He and his brother Axion killed Alcmaeon. Phegeus' sons were more usually called Pronous and Agenor.

3. A Heraclid, the son of Aristomachus and great-grandson of Hyllus in one tradition, the son of Cleodaeus and grandson of Hyllus in another. Along with his brother CRESPHONTES he was given the task of conquering the Peloponnese (see HERACLIDS). After the victory Temenus was given Argos: he asked Erigaeus, a descendant of Diomedes (2), to remove the Palladium, which had been brought by Diomedes to Argos, and he thus deprived the city of its protection (see LEAGRUS). Temenus gave his daughter Hyrnetho in marriage to the Heraclid Deiphontes, thus arousing the hatred of his own sons, who assassinated him (see DEIPHONTES).

Temon (*Τέμων*) The Aenians, evicted from Pelasgiotis by the Lapiths, wanted to settle on the banks of the Inachus. An oracle had warned the Inachians that they would lose their country if they surrendered the smallest part of it, and had promised the Aenians that if the inhabitants gave up as much as a tiny part of their land, then the Aenians could become rulers of the whole country. Thus an Aenian called Temon disguised himself as a beggar and went to the king of the Inachians. The king made fun of him and gave him a lump of earth instead of bread. The old men of the country recalled the ancient oracle, and asked him to prevent Temon from leaving with a piece of their land. Temon fled, promising Apollo a hecatomb if he extricated him from this difficulty. Apollo protected him and he escaped. Later, Phemius, the king of the Aenians, engaged King Hyperochus of the Inachians in single combat. Phemius killed him with a stone when Hyperochus turned round to chase away the dog which had accompanied him. The Aenians then took possession of the country. In memory of these events, they devoted a special cult to stones and, during the sacrifices, they would offer the descendants of Temon a cut of meat called 'the beggar's meat'.

Tenerus (*Τήνερος*) The king of Thebes, son of the Nymph MELIA and Apollo. He was a priest of the temple of Apollo Ptoius and a famous soothsayer.

Tenes (*Τένης*) The eponymous hero of the island of Tenedos, off the Trojan coast. He was generally considered to be the son of CYCNUS (3) and, more rarely, of Apollo. His mother was Procleia, a daughter of Laomedon, and he had one sister, Hemithea (2). When Procleia died, Cycnus remarried, to a woman called Philonome, who slandered Tenes to Cycnus, claiming that he had tried to rape her, whereas in fact he had remained unmoved by her advances. Cycnus believed her, and put both his children in a chest which he then abandoned at sea. The chest was protected by the gods, particularly by Poseidon (the grandfather of Tenes), and was washed up on the coast of the island of Leucophrys, which was subsequently called Tenedos. The inhabitants of the island took Tenes as their king. Later, when Cycnus realized his error, he had Philonome buried alive and tried to bring about a reconciliation with his son, but Tenes refused, and when Cycnus visited Tenedos, he cut the moorings of his father's boat to signify that all was over between them. When the Greeks, sailing to Troy, appeared off Tenedos, Tenes tried to prevent them from disembarking by bombarding them with stones, but Achilles wounded him in the chest and he died.

There was another tradition, according to which Tenes was killed while trying to protect Hemithea from the amorous advances of Achilles. He was burned on the same spot where his temple was later to stand. No flute player had permission to enter the temple, as a flautist called Eumolpus (or Molpus (3)), bribed by Tenes' stepmother, had slandered him. In the myth of Achilles in its post-Homeric form, the death of Tenes linked the hero to his destiny. Thetis warned that if Achilles killed a 'son of Apollo' he could not himself escape a violent death at Troy.

Terambus (*Τέραμβος*) Son of Eusirus, himself the son of Poseidon, and the Nymph Idothea. He lived on Mount Othrys, where he kept large flocks. He had a melodious voice and was skilled at playing the shepherds' pipes; he was reputedly the first mortal to sing to his own accompaniment on the lyre. The Nymphs came to listen to him and Pan was well-disposed to him. Towards the end of summer, Pan advised him to take his flocks back down to the plain, as winter would be early and harsh. Terambus scorned this advice and began slandering the Nymphs, claiming that they were not the daughters of Zeus. He also said that Poseidon, who was in love with one of them, Diopatra, had transformed the other Nymphs into poplar trees while he satisfied his passion for her. The Nymphs said nothing, but with the onset of winter Terambus' flocks disappeared and he alone was left on the mountain. Then the Nymphs took their revenge by transforming him into a wood-eating stag-beetle, a creature which had enormous horns in the shape of a lyre (see CERAMBUS).

Tereus (*Τηρεύς*) The king of Thrace and son of Ares. See PHILOMELA.

Termerus (*Τέρμερος*) The eponymous hero of the city of Termera in Caria. He was a pirate, probably to be identified with the pirate of whom Plutarch writes that he would kill travellers by head-butting them. This monster was killed by Heracles.

Terminus An old Roman divinity whose shrine stood on the Capitol, inside the temple of Jupiter. His introduction into the Roman religion was attributed to the Sabine Titus Tatius. He was the god identified with the boundaries of fields, and was by his very nature immovable. During the construction of the temple of Jupiter Optimus Maximus, the various divinities occupying the chosen site agreed to withdraw. Terminus alone refused to move and his shrine had to be incorporated within the temple. Since Terminus could exist only under the open sky, an opening was made in the roof for his exclusive use. The *Terminalia* were celebrated in his honour on 23 February each year.

Terpsichore (*Τερψιχόρη*) One of the nine MUSES, a daughter of Zeus and Mnemosyne. She was sometimes said to be the mother of the SIRENS by the river-god Achelous, and also of LINUS (2) and of Rhesus.

Tethys (*Τηθύς*) The personification of the feminine fecundity of the sea, the daughter of Uranus and Gaia, and the youngest of the Titanides. She married Oceanus, one of her brothers, by whom she had more than 3,000 children, who were all the rivers of the world. Tethys brought up HERA who had been entrusted to her by Rhea during Zeus' struggle against Cronus. As a sign of her gratitude, Hera managed to reconcile Tethys and Oceanus who had fallen out. Tethys' dwelling was usually situated in the far West, beyond the country of the Hesperides.

Teucer (*Τεῦκρος*)

1. The son of the Phrygian river-god Scamander and Idaea (1), a Nymph from Mount Ida (Table 4), although other traditions make Teucer a foreigner who migrated to the Troad from Crete, or, more precisely, from Cretan Ida, along with his father, Scamander. An oracle had commanded them to settle on the spot where they would be attacked by the 'sons of the earth'. One night while they were camping in the Troad, their weapons, shields and the strings of their bows were gnawed by mice. Realizing that the prophecy had been fulfilled, they founded a temple to Apollo Smintheus (Apollo of the Mice) at this spot, and settled there. Attic mythographers claimed that Teucer came originally from Attica and that he migrated to the Troad from there.

Teucer was the ancestor of the Trojan royal family. He welcomed DARDANUS and gave him his daughter Batieia (or Arisbe) (see Table 4).

2. A son of Telamon and Hesione (3) (Table 4). He was the half-brother of Ajax (2) but, through his mother, belonged to the Trojan royal family. In the *Iliad* he was younger than Ajax and the best archer in the whole Greek army. He took part in the expedition to Troy, even though Priam was his uncle. His exploits were considerable: he killed numerous Trojan heroes, wounded Glaucus (2) and was himself wounded by Hector but saved by Ajax. In the course of other fights he just failed to kill Hector. Finally, he participated in the funeral games, where he took part in the archery contest.

In later poems, some of his other adventures are described. At the time of Ajax's death he was absent in Mysia, but he returned in time to protect his brother's body against the insults of the Atrides. Teucer was one of the soldiers inside the Wooden Horse. His return to Greece was not a happy one. He got as far as Salamis, where Telamon reigned, but was separated from his nephew EURYSACES. Telamon gave him an unfriendly reception; he reproached him for not protecting Ajax, and also for not avenging his death. Teucer was then forced into exile.

Before leaving, he made a speech from his boat in the Attic bay of Phreattys to justify himself. The custom of exiles trying for a last time to justify themselves at this spot before leaving the country was traced back to this episode.

He went to Syria, where he was welcomed by King Belus, who settled him on Cyprus, which he had recently conquered. Teucer founded the new Salamis and married Eune, the daughter of King Cyprus, eponym of the island. They had one daughter, Asteria (3). According to another tradition, Teucer settled peacefully on the island, where he married Eune, the daughter of CINYRAS. From some writers we learn that Teucer lived on Cyprus until he died, or alternatively that he tried to return to Salamis in Attica. Telamon was being evicted from his kingdom and had found refuge in Aegina. Teucer was reconciled with his father and re-established him on the throne. It was also said that he undertook the voyage to Attica after hearing the news of the death of Telamon, but he was driven off by Eurysaces.

Teutamus (*Τεύταμος*) The king of Assyria, also called Tautanes. His reign coincided with the period of the Trojan War. Priam asked him for help. Teutamus gave him 10,000 Ethiopians, 10,000 men of Susa and 200 war chariots. This army was placed under the command of MEMNON.

Teuthras (*Τεύθρας*)

1. A king of Mysia. He killed a boar which begged for mercy in a human voice after having taken refuge in the sanctuary of Artemis Orthosia. As a punishment the goddess afflicted him with madness. His mother, with the help of the soothsayer Polyidus (1), appeased Artemis' anger and Teuthras recovered. The mountain on which Teuthras had this adventure was called Teuthrania in memory of it.

Teuthras welcomed Auge when she was sold by Nauplius (2). It was sometimes said that he married her and later adopted TELEPHUS. Occasionally it was also claimed that he treated Auge as though she was his daughter. Teuthras died without any male issue and Telephus succeeded him.

2. A Greek killed by Hector at Troy.

Thalia (*Θαλία*)

1. A Muse. Although she had originally no particular function, she ended up presiding particularly over comedy and light verse. She was said to have borne Apollo sons, the Corybantes. One version of the legend of DAPHNIS made her one of the hero's lovers (in this story she is also called Pimplea).

2. One of the Charites (Graces), the daughter of Zeus and Eurynome (1). Like her sisters, she presided over vegetation.

3. A Nereid, daughter of Nereus and Doris.

Thalassio See TALASSIO.

Thalpius (*Θάλπιος*) Thalpius and his brother Antimachus were two of the leaders who commanded the Epeians from Elis. They were the sons of the MOLIONIDAE. Thalpius' mother was Theraephone, daughter of Dexamenus, and his father was Eurytus (4). Thalpius figures amongst the suitors of Helen and the heroes inside the Wooden Horse. His tomb could be seen at Elis, along with that of his brother.

Thamyris (*Θάμυρις*) Thamyris (or Thamyras) was one of the mythical musicians to whom various poems and musical innovations were attributed. He composed a Theogony, a Cosmogony and a Titanomachy. He was also said to have invented the Dorian mode.

He was the son of the musician PHILAMMON and the Nymph Argiope, but other traditions made him the son of Aethlius and grandson of Endymion. Similarly, his mother was sometimes one of the Muses, Erato or Melpomene. He was of great beauty and excelled both in singing and playing the lyre, which Linus (2) taught him. He was sometimes said to be Homer's teacher. Homer related how he tried to rival the musical talents of the Muses, but was defeated. The angry goddesses blinded him and deprived him of his musical skills. He had asked, had he won, to be granted successively the favours of all the Muses. Thamyris then threw his useless lyre into the River Balyra (whose name contains the words meaning 'to throw' and 'lyre') in the Peloponnese.

Thanatos (*Θάνατος*) The personification of Death. In the *Iliad* he appears as the brother of Sleep (Hypnos). Hesiod makes these two spirits the sons of Nyx. In the theatre Thanatos was sometimes introduced as a character. This innovation went back to the tragedian Phrynichus in his *Alcestis*, now lost. Euripides made Thanatos fight with Heracles in his *Alcestis*. See also SISYPHUS for another of Thanatos' misadventures.

Thasus (*Θάσος*) The eponymous hero of the island of Thasos. He was a Phoenician, sometimes said to be a son of Agenor and brother of Cadmus (Table 3) and sometimes connected with the family of Europa (5) (notably as either a son of Cilix, or of Phoenix (2)). He took part in the quest for Europa. He stopped at Thasos, to which he gave his name.

Thaumas (*Θαύμας*) One of the sons of Pontus and Gaia. He was the brother of Nereus, Phorcys, Ceto and Eurybia, and thus belonged to the group of primordial sea divinities. By Electra (1) he had as daughters the Harpies and Iris.

Theano (*Θεανώ*) The daughter of the king of Thrace, who married the Trojan ANTENOR. They had several children: Iphidamas, Archelochus, Acamas (1), Glaucus (1), Eurymachus (2), Helicaon and POLYDAMAS. She also brought up Pedaeus, whom Antenor had fathered on another woman. At Troy she undertook the functions of a priestess of Athena. At the time of Odysseus' and Menelaus' embassy before the opening of hostilities, she welcomed them as her husband's guests. So, with Antenor and their children, she was spared during the fighting after the capture of the city and was able to leave Asia and travel to Illyria. A later tradition related that she and Antenor betrayed the city and handed the Palladium over to the Greeks.

2. Wife of King Metapontus of Icaria. See AEOLUS (2).

Thebe (*Θήβη*)
1. Thebes in Boeotia was linked sometimes to a Thebe who was the daughter of Prometheus and a Nymph.
2. The daughter of Zeus and Iodama, a descendant of Deucalion (1) (Table 5).
3. The youngest daughter of Asopus and Metope (1).
4. Thebes in Cilicia had a heroine Thebe, the daughter of Adramys the Pelasgian, who had promised her hand to whoever could defeat him at running. Heracles managed to do so, and married Thebe. In her memory, he founded a city in Cilicia, and gave it his wife's name. Another genealogy linked her with the lineage of Cadmus, by making her the daughter of Cilix. The eponym of the Egyptian Thebes belonged to the same genealogy: she was a granddaughter of Nilus (Table 3).

Theia (*Θεία*) One of the Titanides, a daughter of Uranus and Gaia. By Hyperion she had three children: Helios, Eos and Selene.

Theias (*Θείας*) In one form of the legend of ADONIS, he was father of the latter and son of the Babylonian king, Belus. He married the Nymph Orithyia and had a daughter, Smyrna (2).

Theiodamas (*Θειοδάμας*) A hero whose legend was sometimes associated with the land of the Dryopians and sometimes with Cyprus. In the case of the former he was said to be the father of HYLAS (see also HERACLES, III).

Thelxion (*Θελξίων*) The fifth king of Sicyon. Another hero of this name, possibly the same person, was one of the two murderers of APIS.

Themis (*Θέμις*) The goddess of Law who belongs to the lineage of the Titans. She was the daughter of Uranus and Gaia. She featured amongst the divine wives of Zeus, as the second, after METIS. By Zeus, she gave birth to the Horae; to the Moirae; to Astraea, the personification of Justice; and to the Nymphs of the River Eridanus. Sometimes the Hesperides were said to have been born of this union.

Aeschylus made Themis the mother of Prometheus, and the same name was sometimes given to the Arcadian Nymph called CARMENTA in the Roman tradition. As the personification of Justice or Eternal Law, Themis was Zeus' adviser. She ordered him to clothe himself in the Aegis, and to use it as a breastplate during the fight against the Giants. Sometimes she was also credited with having suggested the Trojan War, to remedy the overpopulation of the earth. Themis was one of the few first-generation divinities to be associated with the Olympians and to share their life on Olympus. She owed these honours to her relationship with Zeus and to the services which she had rendered to the gods. She taught Apollo prophecy and she possessed the Pythian sanctuary at Delphi before it came to belong to him. A certain number of her oracles are quoted, such as the one warning Atlas (1) that a son of Zeus would steal the golden apples from the Hesperides and the oracle concerning the progeny of Thetis.

Themisto (Θεμιστώ) The daughter of Hypseus and Creusa (1). She married ATHAMAS. They had four children: Leucon, Erythrius, Schoeneus (3) and Ptous (see LEUCOTHEA (1)).

Theoclymenus (Θεοκλύμενος)

1. A soothsayer, a son of POLYPHIDES (1). He was a native of Argos, but had to go into exile after an assassination. He took refuge in Pylos, where he met Telemachus, whom he accompanied to Ithaca. He predicted, in Penelope's presence, that Odysseus was not far away. He also announced the fate that awaited the suitors.

2. A son of Proteus and Psamathe (1). In Euripides' *Helen*, after the death of Proteus, a king of lower Egypt, he succeeded him on the throne. He was a cruel man who sacrificed all those on whom he laid hands. He tried to seduce Helen, who had taken refuge at his court, and, when she tricked him, he tried to kill his own sister, THEONOE (1), whom he accused of complicity with Helen.

Theonoe (Θεονόη)

1. The daughter of Proteus and sister of THEOCLYMENUS (2). In Euripides' *Helen*, she is the sympathetic adviser, who possessed powers of prophecy. She helped Helen escape from Egypt and, in doing so, incurred her brother's wrath. She was saved only by the intervention of the Dioscuri. One tradition maintained that she fell in love with Menelaus' pilot, CANOPUS.

2. The daughter of Thestor. She had a brother, Calchas (1), and sister, Leucippe (3). One day she was abducted by pirates and sold to Icarus, the king of Caria. Thestor set out to look for her, but he was shipwrecked and was washed up on the coast of Caria. He was arrested, taken to the king, and enslaved. Leucippe set off to look for her father and sister, following an order from the oracle of Delphi. She shaved her hair and disguised herself as a priest. When she reached Caria, Theonoe saw her but did not recognize her and, assuming her to be a man, fell in love with her. Hindered by her disguise, Leucippe declined her advances, whereupon Theonoe had her arrested and thrown into prison. She then commanded one of her slaves to kill her. This slave happened to be Thestor. The latter began to lament the fate which forced him, having lost his two daughters, Theonoe and Leucippe, to commit a crime. Leucippe then realized with whom she was dealing, revealed who she was, and determined to kill Theonoe. She was about to succeed when Theonoe called on her father, Thestor, which led to a recognition scene. King Icarus showered them all with presents and sent them back to their own country.

Theophane (Θεοφάνη) The daughter of King Bisaltes. Many noble suitors wished to marry her but Poseidon fell in love with her and transported her to the island of Crumissa. Her suitors set off to look for her. To deceive them, Poseidon transformed the young girl into a ewe, himself into a ram and the inhabitants of the island into sheep. When the suitors reached the island they found only sheep and set about eating them. Seeing this, Poseidon turned them into wolves. He and Theophane, in this guise of sheep, produced the ram with the golden fleece which was to bear away Phrixus and Helle.

Theras (*Θήρας*) Son of Autesion of Sparta. Theras' sister Argia's two sons, Procles and Eurysthenes, were tutored by Theras when their father, Aristodemus, died. Theras was regent in their name until they came of age. He then left with a number of Minyan exiles and settled on the island of Calliste, which was subsequently called Thera after him.

Thero (*Θηρώ*) A third-generation descendant of Iphicles. By Apollo, she had a son Chaeron, the eponym of Chaeronea in Boeotia (Table 7).

Thersandrus (*Θέρσανδρος*)
1. The son of Sisyphus and Merope (1). He had two sons, Haliartus and Coronus, eponyms of the Boeotian cities of Haliartus and Coronea.
2. A son of Polynices and Argia (Table 1). He took part in the expedition of the Epigoni against Thebes, and it was he who gave the peplos of Harmonia (1) to ERIPHYLE. After the capture of the city, Thersandrus came to power. He married Demonassa, the daughter of Amphiaraus, and had by her a son, Tisamenus (2). He took part in the expedition against Troy which resulted in the disembarkation at Mysia. He was killed by Telephus, and his funeral rites were celebrated by Diomedes (2). Virgil refers to another tradition, according to which Thersandrus participated in the Trojan War and figured amongst the soldiers inside the Wooden Horse.

Thersites (*Θερσίτης*) Son of Agrius. With his brothers Onchestus, Prothous (1), Celeutor, Lycopeus and Melanippus (3) he drove his uncle OENEUS from the throne of Calydon (see DIOMEDES (2)).

According to the *Iliad*, Thersites was the ugliest and most cowardly of the Greeks at Troy. He limped and was bandy-legged, with round shoulders and only the odd hair on his head. When Agamemnon put his men to the test by urging them to lift the siege, Thersites was one of the first to accept this solution. Odysseus beat him with his staff and Thersites collapsed, to the accompaniment of the soldiers' jeers. It was also said that he took part in the hunting of the boar of Calydon, but fled in terror on seeing the animal. The cyclical epics tell us that when Penthesilea, the Amazon, was killed by Achilles, the latter fell in love with her as he saw her die. Thersites taunted the hero about this love and, with the point of his lance, gouged out the young woman's eyes. Achilles beat Thersites to death with his fists.

Theseus (*Θησεύς*) The pre-eminent Attic hero. Our main sources for his legend are the *Life* written by Plutarch, and the references made by Apollodorus and Diodorus. Theseus was said to have lived a generation before the Trojan War, in which his two sons DEMOPHON (2) and ACAMAS (3) took part. He was younger than

Heracles by at least a generation, though certain traditions link the two heroes together in the quest for the Golden Fleece (see the ARGONAUTS) and the war against the Amazons.

I. ORIGINS AND CHILDHOOD

There are two traditions about the origins of Theseus. The first makes him a son of Aegeus and Aethra, thus uniting the families of Erechtheus and, through the latter's father, Erichthonius, of Hephaestus with those of Pelops (1) and Tantalus (Table 2) (see AEGEUS).

It was also said that Theseus was the son of Poseidon. The same night in which Aethra slept with Aegeus she went to offer a sacrifice on an island, following a dream sent to her by Athena, and was raped by Poseidon. The son whom she conceived as a result was believed by Aegeus to be his own.

Theseus spent his early years at Troezen in the care of his grandfather Pittheus, for Aegeus had not wished to bring the child to Athens, fearing his nephews, the PALLANTIDAE. Just before he had left Troezen, Aegeus had hidden a sword and a pair of sandals underneath a rock, and had confided this secret to Aethra, advising her to reveal it to her son only when he was strong enough to move the rock and take the objects hidden there. Then, wearing the sandals and armed with the sword, he was to set off in search of his father, secretly, so that the Pallantidae would have no chance to plot his downfall. Theseus' tutor was Connidas. A story was also told in Troezen which demonstrated the child's courage: one day, Heracles was Pittheus' guest, and removed his lion's skin. The children of the palace, thinking that a real lion had got into the room, fled, shrieking. Theseus however, then aged seven, took a weapon and attacked the monster. When he reached adolescence, Theseus went to Delphi where, following the custom, he offered some of his hair to the god. Instead of entirely shaving his head, however, he shaved only the forepart, in the manner of the Abantes, thus instituting a fashion which was still carried on in the historical period.

II. RETURN TO ATHENS

When he was 16, Theseus was so strong that Aethra decided that the moment had come to tell him the secret of his birth. She led him to the rock where Aegeus had hidden the sword and the sandals. The young man moved the rock, took the objects concealed there, and set off for Athens to make himself known. Aethra urged him to take the sea route from Troezen to Athens, and Pittheus added his entreaties to hers. At that time Heracles was in the service of Omphale in Lydia, and all the monsters which had recently hidden for fear of the hero were once again setting about their devastation. Thus the Isthmus of Corinth was infested with bandits. But Theseus, envying Heracles' fame, decided to imitate him. He killed, one after another: PERIPHETES (1), at Epidaurus; the bandit SINIS at Cenchreae; and the sow of Crommyon, a ferocious animal which had already killed many men. It was said to be the offspring of Typhon and Echidna, and was called Phaea, after the old woman who fed it. Theseus killed the animal with a blow of his sword. When he reached the Scironian Rocks, he killed SCIRON. Next, he fought and killed CERCYON (1) at Eleusis. Further on, he gave Damastes the punishment he deserved (see PROCRUSTES).

Theseus then reached the banks of the river Cephissus, where he was met by members of the Phytalides, who agreed to purify him of the murders he had committed. Thus purified, Theseus entered Athens on the eighth day of the month of Hecatombaeum. Aegeus was then under the spell of MEDEA, who had promised to deliver him from his sterility through her magic. Theseus arrived, preceded by a great reputation as a destroyer of monsters, and Medea immediately guessed his real identity. Aegeus, however, unaware that this stranger was his son, was afraid. Medea persuaded Aegeus to invite the young man to dinner on the pretext of honouring him, but in fact in order to poison him. Theseus accepted the invitation, but did not want to declare his identity immediately. In the course of the meal, however, he drew the sword which his father had left him to cut his meat. On seeing this, Aegeus knocked over the cup of poison which was prepared for Theseus, and officially recognized his son before all the assembled citizens. Medea was exiled by Aegeus.

It was also said that before she tried to poison him, Medea attempted to kill Theseus by sending him to fight a montrous bull which was wreaking havoc on the plain of Marathon, and which was sometimes described as being the Cretan Bull brought back by Heracles to the Peloponnese, from where it had escaped (see HERACLES, II). This bull breathed fire from its nostrils. but Theseus captured and chained it up, offering it as a sacrifice to Apollo Delphinius. This sacrifice took place in the presence of Aegeus, and when Theseus (who had not yet declared himself) drew his sword to cut off some hair from the animal's head Aegeus recognized the weapon which he had left under the rock at Troezen. During the pursuit of the bull at Marathon the episode of Hecale, related by Callimachus in a famous poem, took place (see HECALE).

Once he had been officially recognized by his father, Theseus had to fight against his cousins, the 50 sons of Pallas (7) (see PALLANTIDAE). It was often said that Theseus was exiled from Athens and had to spend a year at Troezen to expiate his murder of the Pallantidae. This was the version followed by Euripides in his *Hippolytus*; but he added that Theseus was then accompanied by Phaedra, and that it was there that she conceived her passion for her stepson. This involves some modification of the more usual chronology of events, making the expedition against the Amazons take place before the massacre of the Pallantidae.

III. THE CRETAN CYCLE

Following the death of his son ANDROGEOS, Minos had demanded from the Athenians a tribute, payable every nine years, of seven young men and seven young women. When the time came to provide this tribute for the third time, the Athenians began to murmur against Aegeus. Theseus then offered himself as one of the victims to be sent to Crete. It was also said that Minos himself chose the victims, and that he asked for Theseus, insisting that the young people come unarmed, though he agreed that, if they succeeded in killing the MINOTAUR to whom they were to be thrown, they would have the right to return. Theseus set off on an Athenian boat on the sixth day of the month of Mounichion. The pilot was NAUSITHOUS (2), a man from Salamis, whom the king of that city, Scirus, had given to Theseus since his grandson Menesthes was amongst the young people being sent to Minos. Amongst the young girls were Eriboea, or Periboea (5), the daughter of Alcathus, the king of Megara. Theseus prevented Minos from having sexual relations with the girl during the crossing (see PERIBOEA (5)). Later Theseus was said to have married her.

On his departure, Theseus received two sets of sails for the boat from his father, one black, one white. The black sails were for the outward journey and symbolized its funereal nature, but in the hope that the return journey would be a joyful one, Aegeus provided Theseus with white sails with which to indicate that his mission had been successful. On arriving in Crete, Theseus and his companions were confined in the Minotaur's palace, the Labyrinth. Theseus, however, was glimpsed by ARIADNE, one of Minos' daughters; she fell in love with him, and gave him a ball of thread so that he would not lose his way in the Labyrinth.

According to another version, Ariadne did not give him a ball of thread, but a luminous crown which she had received as a wedding gift from Dionysus. It was by the light of this crown that Theseus was able to find his way in the dark Labyrinth. This divine crown was sometimes said to be a gift not of Ariadne but of Amphitrite, given to him when he had gone to Poseidon's palace to look for the ring of Minos. As a condition of helping Theseus, Ariadne asked that he should marry her and take her home with him. Theseus agreed and kept his promise. After he had killed the Minotaur he sabotaged the Cretan ships so that no attempt could be made to follow him, and set sail at night, accompanied by Ariadne and the young Athenians who had been saved by his exploit.

According to the most famous version of the legend, Theseus reached Naxos and put into port there. Ariadne fell asleep, and when she awoke, she was alone. On the horizon she saw Theseus' ship. Some mythographers maintain that Theseus loved another woman, Aegle, the daughter of Panopeus of Phocis, while others claim that Dionysus ordered him to abandon Ariadne, as he himself had fallen in love with her. Others say that the god kidnapped her during the night, or even that Athena or Hermes urged Theseus to abandon her. Dionysus then married her. Another version of this episode claims that the ship carrying Ariadne and Theseus was swept by a storm to Cyprus. Ariadne, who was pregnant, disembarked. Theseus boarded the ship again to keep watch over it, but a gust of wind dragged it out to sea. The women of the island cared for Ariadne, and brought her letters which they had written themselves and which they said had come from Theseus. Ariadne died in childbirth. Theseus later returned and established a ritual and a sacrifice in honour of Ariadne.

On his return trip Theseus stopped at Delos, where he consecrated in the temple a statue of Aphrodite which Ariadne had given him. There, along with the other young people who were saved, he performed a complicated dance which represented the windings of the Labyrinth. Once he arrived in sight of the coast of Attica, Theseus forgot to lower the black sails of his boat and to hoist the white sails of victory. Aegeus, waiting on the cliffs for his return, saw the black sails and, believing that his son had died, hurled himself into the sea, which was thereafter called the Aegean. It was also said that the old king was looking out over the sea from the top of the Acropolis. When he saw the black sail, he fell from the top of the cliff and was killed.

IV. POLITICAL ACTIVITY IN ATHENS

Once Theseus had disposed of the PALLANTIDAE after Aegeus' death, he assumed power in Attica. His first act was to unite in a single city the inhabitants who had previously been spread around the countryside. Athens became the capital of the state which he then set up. Theseus endowed it with essential political institutions, such as the Boule, instituted the festival of the Panathenaea, a symbol of the political unity of Attica, minted money, and divided society into three classes: the Nobles, the Artisans and the Farmers. He conquered Megara and incorporated it into the state he had created. At the frontier between the Peloponnese and Attica, he erected a column to mark the border between the two countries: the Dorian lands on one side, the Ionian on the other. Theseus founded, or rather reorganized, the Isthmian Games at Corinth in honour of Poseidon.

During the reign of Theseus the expedition of the Seven against Thebes took place (see ADRASTUS). Theseus granted protection to OEDIPUS when the latter sought refuge at Colonus; similarly, he guaranteed the burial of heroes who had fallen outside the city. His son Demophon (2) was to carry on the same practice when the HERACLIDS returned.

V. THE WAR AGAINST THE AMAZONS

Accounts differ as to the origins of this war. It was often said that Theseus had taken part in the expedition of HERACLES (II) and that he had been given Antiope (2), one of the captured Amazons, as a reward for his exploits, but most mythographers relate that he had gone alone to abduct Antiope. After landing in the kingdom of the Amazons, he was warmly welcomed and they had sent him presents. Antiope brought these gifts to him, and Theseus invited her to come on board ship, but as soon as she joined him, he treacherously set sail. The Amazons then sailed in force against Athens, took Attica and established their camp in the city itself. The decisive battle took place beside the Pnyx, at the front of the Acropolis. The Amazons won an initial success, but when one of their wings was penetrated by the Athenians, they were forced to sign a peace treaty.

According to some writers, however, the Amazons attacked Attica because Theseus rejected Antiope and decided to marry Phaedra, given to him by Deucalion (2), the son of Minos. Antiope, who had borne a son by Theseus named Hippolytus, wanted vengeance, and organized an expedition against Attica. The attack took place on the day of the marriage of Theseus and Phaedra, but the guests managed to close the doors of the banqueting hall and kill Antiope. In the version which describes the expedition as an attempt by the Amazons to rescue Antiope, Theseus remained faithful to her, and Antiope, who supported Theseus against her sisters, was killed in the battle. In this version, it was only after her death that Theseus married Phaedra.

VI. FRIENDSHIP WITH PIRITHOUS

The friendship between Theseus and the Lapith hero PIRITHOUS originated when Pirithous, having heard of Theseus' exploits, decided to put him to the test. He set himself the task of stealing some of Theseus' flocks in the Marathon area, but when the two men met they were amazed at each other's beauty. Pirithous refused to fight and spontaneously offered to make reparation to Theseus for the stock which he had stolen, and declared himself Theseus' slave. Theseus refused this offer and offered Pirithous his friendship. Theseus took part in the fight between the Lapiths and Centaurs alongside Pirithous. One day the two friends decided to marry only daughters of Zeus, since they were themselves sons of two of the greatest gods: Theseus of Poseidon, Pirithous of Zeus. So Theseus decided to seek Helen's hand, and Pirithous Persephone's. They began by abducting Helen (see HELEN and also ACADEMUS, AETHRA and DEMOPHON (2)) and then set out to find Persephone. Helen was subsequently recovered by her brothers, the Dioscuri, who invaded Attica, took Aethra prisoner and installed Menestheus on the Athenian throne. Menestheus gathered around him many nobles who were discontented with Theseus' political reforms.

In the Underworld, hunting for Persephone, Theseus and Pirithous were victims of their rashness. They were well received by Hades, who invited them to sit down with him to join in a feast. But they found themselves fixed to their seats, unable to rise, and were kept as prisoners. When Heracles went down to the Underworld, he tried to free them, but of the two only Theseus received permission from the gods to return to earth. Pirithous remained permanently seated on the chair of oblivion.

VII. THE DEATH OF THESEUS

After being rescued by Heracles, Theseus returned to Athens to find political affairs problematic. In despair at ever being able to restore himself to the throne, he sent his children secretly to Euboea to be with Elephenor, the son of Chalcodon (1), and went into exile, cursing Athens. It was sometimes said that he tried to take refuge in Crete with Deucalion (2), his brother-in-law, but that a storm washed him up on the coast of Scyros; it was also said that he went to Scyros of his own accord to find Lycomedes, to whom he was related. Moreover, he had family estates on the island. Lycomedes greeted him with apparent favour but, taking him up to a mountain to show him a view of the island, pushed Theseus off a cliff, killing him. Other authors maintain that Theseus was killed accidentally, while walking in the mountains. Menestheus continued to reign in Athens, as the Dioscuri had intended, and Theseus' two sons ACAMAS (3) and DEMOPHON (2) took part in the Trojan War. On Menestheus' death, they returned, and refounded the kingdom of Athens.

During the battle of Marathon the Athenian soldiers saw a hero of enormous size fighting at their head and realized that it was Theseus. After the Persian wars, the Delphic oracle ordered the Athenians to gather up the bones of Theseus and give them an honourable burial in the city. Cimon carried out the oracle's instructions. He conquered Scyros and there saw an eagle perched on a mound, scratching the earth with its claws. Cimon realized the significance of this sign. He dug up the mound and found a coffin containing a hero of enormous stature, and alongside him a bronze lance and a sword. Cimon brought these relics back and the Athenians gave their hero's bones a magnificent burial in the city, near the site of a refuge for fugitive slaves and poor people who were being persecuted by the rich, for Theseus had been the champion of democracy in his lifetime.

Thespius (*Θέσπιος*) The eponymous hero of the Boeotian town of Thespiae, and a son of Erechtheus, king of Attica. He left Attica and founded a kingdom in Boeotia. It was with him that Heracles, at the age of 18, began his exploits by killing the lion of Cithaeron. Thespius had 50 daughters, either by Megamede daughter of Arneus, or by various concubines. While the lion hunt was going on, Heracles stayed with Thespius and slept with one of his daughters every night. Thespius wanted to have grandsons fathered by Heracles, and the latter was so exhausted after each day's outing that he was not aware that each night he was sleeping with a different daughter. Other traditions maintained that he slept with all the daughters in seven nights, or even in a single night. Each one conceived a son by Heracles, and the eldest and the youngest had twins. Most of the children, known as the Thespiades, were, on Heracles' instructions, taken by Iolaus to Sardinia where they settled. Two came back to Thebes, and seven remained in Thespiae. Thespius also purified Heracles after the murder of the children he had had by Megara. For Thespius, father of Hypermestra (2), see THESTIUS.

Thesprotus (*Θεσπρωτός*) One of the sons of Lycaon (2). He left Arcadia and settled in Epirus, in the area which took the name of the country of the Thesprotians. In one version of the legend Thyestes took refuge with him.

Thessalus (*Θεσσαλός*)

1. A king who came from the country of the Thesprotians, who conquered Thessaly and founded his kingdom there. Thessalus was a son of Graicus, to whom the foundation

of the city of Thessalonica was sometimes attributed.

2. A son of Heracles and Chalciope (1), or of Astyoche (in which case he was the brother of Tlepolemus). He was king of Cos and sent his two sons, Phidippus and Antiphus, to take part in the Trojan War. After the sack of Troy, the sons settled in the country, which was called Thessaly in memory of their father.

3. The son of Medea and Jason; at the time of the death of Adrastus he fled from Corinth to Iolcus, where he assumed power. He too was said to have given his name to Thessaly.

4. Son of HAEMON (2).

Thestius (Θέστιος) A king of Pleuron and an Aetolian hero. His mother was Demonice and his father Ares. His wife was sometimes said to be Eurythemis, sometimes Deidamia, daughter of Perieres, sometimes Leucippe (2), or again Laophonte (daughter of Pleuron and therefore his great-aunt). He had numerous children, among whom were Althaea, mother of Meleager, Leda, Hypermestra (2), Iphiclus (2), Evippus, Plexippus (1), Eurypylus (6) and Meleager's uncles, sometimes called the Thestiades, who were killed during the hunt of Calydon. Hypermestra (2) is perhaps identical with Hypermestra (3) the daughter of Thespius, for the names Thestius and Thespius are often interchanged in the manuscripts. For the legend of Thestius and Calydon, see CALYDON (2).

Thestor (Θέστωρ) Son of Apollo and Laothoe, and father of Calchas (1), Leucippe (3) and THEONOE (2).

Thetis (Θέτις) One of the daughters of Nereus and Doris. She was a divinity of the sea, and the most famous of all the Nereids. Thetis was brought up by Hera, and several episodes involving her are explicable in terms of the bonds of affection linking the two: Thetis took in HEPHAESTUS after he was hurled from Olympus by Zeus for having tried to intervene on behalf of Hera; Thetis, at Hera's command, took the helm of the *Argo* during the passage of the Symplegades; Thetis rejected the love of Zeus so as not to distress Hera. Other traditions, however, claimed that both Zeus and Poseidon had wanted to possess her until it was revealed by an oracle of Themis that the son born to Thetis would be more powerful than his father. The two gods then made hasty attempts to give her to a mortal. Other versions attribute this prophecy to Prometheus, who stated explicitly that the son born of an affair between Zeus and Thetis would become ruler of Heaven. Chiron the Centaur learnt of this, and advised his protégé Peleus to take advantage of this opportunity to marry a divinity. Thetis made his task extremely difficult. She had the ability to change shape at will, and she used this gift to elude Peleus, though he eventually succeeded in overpowering and marrying her.

Thetis' attempts to obtain immortality for her son ACHILLES brought about the breakdown of the marriage between herself and Peleus. When Achilles was nine years old and Calchas (1) announced that Troy could not be taken without the help of Achilles, Thetis, knowing that her son would die at Troy, took him to Lycomedes, on Scyros, and concealed him amongst his daughters. Achilles could not escape his destiny however and he set off for the war. Thetis provided Achilles with a companion whose task was to prevent him from making fatal errors, though he did not stop the killing of TENES. She forbade Achilles to be the first ashore at Troy because the first hero to disembark would also be the first to fall in battle. She gave him arms and, after the death of Patroclus, had others made for him by Hephaestus. She tried to dissuade Achilles from killing Hector, as he would himself die soon after. After Achilles' death, Thetis took a strong interest in her grandson NEOPTOLEMUS. She advised him not to return with the other Achaeans, and to wait several days on Tenedos, thus saving his life (see also MOLOSSUS).

Thoas (*Θόας*)

1. One of the sons of Dionysus and Ariadne, although he was sometimes said to be the son of Theseus, as were his brothers Oenopion and Staphylus (3). He was born on the island of Lemnos, and he reigned over the city of Myrina, whose eponym was his wife. By her he had a daughter HYPSIPYLE. When the women of Lemnos decided to massacre all the men on the island as a result of the curse of Aphrodite, Hypsipyle spared Thoas, who was the only man on Lemnos to survive the massacre. In one tradition Hypsipyle hid him in a chest; in another she gave him the sword with which she was supposed to kill him, and brought him in disguise to the temple of Dionysus, where she hid him. The next morning she took him to the coast, dressed as Dionysus, on the god's ritual chariot, on the pretext of purifying the god of the night's murders. Thoas put to sea in an old boat, and landed at Tauris. Another tradition claims that he landed on Sicinos (one of the Cyclades), which then bore the name of Oenoe. There was a story that he reached the island of Chios, where his brother Oenopion was ruler.

2. A grandson of Thoas (1) and the son of Jason and HYPSIPYLE. He was twin brother of EUNEUS (Table 6).

3. The king of Tauris at the time when IPHIGENIA became a priestess of Artemis there. This character was sometimes identified with THOAS (1) who found refuge in Tauris after his escape from Lemnos. When Orestes and Pylades came to the country, the king wanted Iphigenia to sacrifice them, following the local custom, but they fled with her and the goddess's statue to CHRYSES (2). Thoas pursued them there, but was killed.

4. The son of Andraemon, leader of an Aetolian contingent in the *Iliad*. His mother was Gorge (1). He was one of Helen's suitors and, at the end of the Trojan War, one of the warriors inside the Wooden Horse. ODYSSEUS took refuge with him when evicted from Ithaca by Neoptolemus; he married his daughter, by whom he had a son called Leontophonus. Thoas did Odysseus the service of mutilating him to make him unrecognizable for one of his espionage operations.

5. The grandson of Sisyphus, through his father Ornytion. He succeeded his father as ruler of Corinth. He was in turn succeeded by his own son Damophon, who maintained his kingship until the coming of the Heraclids. This, at least, was the Corinthian tradition.

6. Son of Icarius (2) and brother of Penelope (2).

7. A giant, the brother of Agrius. He was killed by the Moirae (see GIANTS).

Thon (*Θών*) or **Thonis** (*Θῶνις*) A king of Egypt who welcomed Menelaus and Helen on their return to Greece. Overcome by Helen's beauty he tried to rape her. Menelaus killed him. For a different tradition see POLYDAMNA.

Thoosa (*Θόωσα*) The daughter of Phorcys and beloved of Poseidon, by whom she had a son, Polyphemus (2), the Cyclops.

Thrace (*Θράκη*) The eponymous heroine of Thrace.

Thrasymedes (*Θρασυμήδης*) One of the sons of Nestor. He accompanied his father and brother ANTILOCHUS to the Trojan War. He played a part in the fight around his brother's body against Memnon, and he was among the warriors inside the Wooden Horse. He returned successfully to Pylos at the end of the war and welcomed Telemachus there. He had a son called Sillus and a grandson, Alcmaeon (2).

Thriae (*Θριαί*) The Prophetesses, three sisters, daughters of Zeus, and Nymphs of Parnassus. They brought up Apollo. The invention of divination by means of pebbles was attributed to them. They were very fond of honey, which was offered to them when their advice was sought.

Thyestes (*Θυέστης*) The twin brother of Atreus and the son of Pelops (1) and Hippodamia (1) (Table 2). His legend is concerned primarily with his hatred for Atreus, and the vengeance which the two brothers alternately wreaked upon one another. This tragic subject was used by poets and was complicated by the addition of episodes each more atrocious than the last. For the broad outline of this legend, see ATREUS.

After Thyestes had been tricked by Atreus into eating his own children, he fled to THESPROTUS, who lived in Epirus, and from there went to Sicyon, where his daughter Pelopia (1) was living. An oracle had told him that only a son born incestuously from his daughter could take vengeance on his brother. This son, AEGISTHUS, managed to kill Atreus and gave back to Thyestes the kingdom from which he had been ejected.

Thyia (*Θυία*) A Nymph, daughter of the river-god Cephissus, or of the hero Castalius, one of the earliest inhabitants of Delphi. Thyia was loved by Apollo, by whom she had a son, DELPHUS. Thyia was the first person to celebrate the cult of Dionysus on the slopes of Parnassus, and it was in memory of this that the Maenads sometimes bore the name Thyades. It was also said that Poseidon had been in love with her. Another tradition claimed that Thyia was a daughter of Deucalion (1), and had two sons by Zeus, Magnes and Macedon (1).

Thymoetes (*Θυμοίτης*)

1. In a tradition related by Diodorus, a son of Laomedon and thus one of Priam's brothers. But Thymoetes

was more usually described as the husband of CILLA and consequently Priam's brother-in-law. Thymoetes never forgave Priam for putting Cilla to death, and to take vengeance he was one of the first to bring the Wooden Horse into Troy.

2. A king of Attica (see MELANTHUS).

Thyone (*Θυώνη*) In some traditions the name of Dionysus' mother, more usually called SEMELE. This difference in name was explained in two ways: either it was not the same Dionysus, or Semele was the 'mortal' name of the mother of the god and Thyone the 'divine' name.

Tiberinus

1. In Roman legend he has a dual character: on the one hand he was the god of the Tiber, a poetic abstraction along Greek lines; on the other hand, he was a king of Alba, a tenth-generation descendant of Aeneas. He died while fighting by the River Albula, which thereafter became known as the Tiber.

2. The eponym of the River Tiber, but of divine origin. He was the son of the god Janus and of Camasene, a Nymph from Latium. He drowned in the river to which he gave his name.

Tiburnus Tiburnus, or Tibartus, the eponymous hero and founder of the Latin city of Tibur (Tivoli). He was sometimes considered to be one of the three sons of Amphiaraus who came to Italy to found colonies (see also CATILLUS).

Timalcus (*Τίμαλκος*) The eldest son of Megareus, the king of Megara. When the Dioscuri were looking for Helen, who had been abducted by Theseus, they passed by Megara. Timalcus joined forces with them, and took part in the capture of Aphidna, but was killed by Theseus.

Timandra (*Τιμάνδρα*) One of the daughters of Tyndareus and Leda (Table 2). She married ECHEMUS and had a son, EVANDER (3). She irritated Aphrodite by neglecting to offer ritual sacrifices to her, however, was struck with madness by the goddess, and allowed herself to be abducted by PHYLEUS.

Tinge (*Τίγγη*) The wife of the giant Antaeus. She bore a son SOPHAX who founded the city of Tingis (modern Tangiers) in her honour.

Tiphys (*Τῖφυς*) The first pilot of the ship *Argo*. He was the son of Hagnias, and was originally from Siphae in Boeotia. He possessed a detailed knowledge of the winds and the course of the stars which he had learnt from Athena herself, but was never described as participating in fighting on land. Tiphys died from an illness while staying with King Lycus (7) in the land of the Mariandyni.

Tiresias (*Τειρεσίας*) A soothsayer. Through his father, Everes, who was descended from Oudaeus, he belonged to the race of the Spartoi (see CADMUS). His mother was the Nymph CHARICLO (3). One tradition stated that Tiresias was blinded by Pallas Athena because he had seen the goddess naked, but at Chariclo's request Pallas gave him the gift of prophecy in compensation. In the most famous version, however, whilst walking on Mount Cyllene (or Cithaeron), the young Tiresias saw two serpents mating. Tiresias either separated the serpents, or wounded them, or killed the female. Whichever was the case, the result of his intervention was that he became a woman. Some years later, walking by the same spot, he again saw the serpents mating. He intervened in the same way and regained his former sex. This incident made him famous, and one day when Hera and Zeus were quarrelling over whether the man or the woman experienced the greater pleasure in love-making, they decided to consult Tiresias, the only individual to have experienced both. Tiresias said that if the enjoyment of love was constituted out of ten parts, the woman possessed nine and the man one. Hera was so furious that she struck Tiresias blind. Zeus, in compensation, gave him the gift of prophecy and the privilege of living for seven human generations.

Tiresias revealed to Amphitryon the real identity of his rival for ALCMENE; he disclosed the crimes of which OEDIPUS was unwittingly guilty and advised Creon (2) to drive Oedipus from Thebes; at the time of the expedition of the Seven against Thebes, he prophesied that the city would be spared if MENOECEUS (2) was sacrificed to appease the anger of Ares; he advised the Thebans, during the expedition against the Epigoni, to conclude an armistice with them and to leave the town secretly at night in order to avoid a general massacre; he advised Pentheus not to oppose the introduction of the cult of Dionysus in Boeotia, and also revealed the fate of the Nymph Echo after her metamorphosis. He also predicted the death of Narcissus. In the *Odyssey*, on Circe's advice, Odysseus undertook the journey to Hades in order to consult Tiresias. Zeus had given Tiresias the privilege of retaining his gift of prophecy even after his death. Tiresias had a daughter, the soothsayer Manto (1), who was the mother of the soothsayer MOPSUS (2). After the capture of Thebes by the Epigoni, Tiresias followed the Thebans in their exodus and stopped with them near a spring called Telphousa. He drank this water, which was extremely cold, and then died. According to another version, Tiresias remained in the city with his daughter. They were taken prisoner and were sent to Delphi to be consecrated to Apollo. On the way Tiresias, who was very old, died of exhaustion.

Tisamenus (*Τισαμενός*)

1. Son of Orestes and Hermione. He succeeded Orestes on the throne of Sparta, but was killed fighting the Heraclids in one tradition, or driven out but allowed to withdraw in safety in another. He sought refuge with the Ionian settlers on the north coast of the Peloponnese, but they attacked him. Tisamenus was killed but his soldiers were victorious. They besieged the Ionians in the city of Helice, but later allowed them to go to Attica, where they were received by the Athenians. Tisamenus' companions gave him a magnificent funeral and took control of the region taken from Ionians, which was called Achaea. Tisamenus' eldest son, Cometes (2), succeeded him.

His other sons were Diamenes, Sparton, Tellis and Leontomenes.

2. A son of Thersandrus (2) and Demonassa. At the time of the second Trojan expedition his father had already died at the house of Telephus during the landing in Mysia (see THERSANDRUS (2)), but Tisamenus was too young to command the Theban contingent. PENELEOS rather than Tisamenus avenged the king's death by killing Telephus' son Eurypylus (4). When he reached manhood, Tisamenus ruled over Thebes. He had one son, Autesion, but he had to be exiled, and joined forces with the Heraclids. Tisamenus was succeeded by Damasichthon, grandson of Peneleos.

Tisiphone (*Τεισιφόνη*)

1. The Avenger of Murder, one of the three Erinyes. One tradition portrays her as in love with CITHAERON, whom she killed by having him bitten by a snake which she plucked from her hair.

2. A lost tragedy of Euripides calls one of Alcmaeon's daughters Tisiphone. She was given by her father to Creon (1), and sold into slavery.

Titanides (*Τιτανίδες*) Six of the daughters of Uranus and Gaia: Theia (or Thia), Rhea, Themis, Mnemosyne, Phoebe (1) and Tethys. After they slept with their brothers, the Titans, they gave birth to divinities of different kinds (Table 8).

Titans (*Τιτᾶνες*) The generic name borne by six of the male children of Uranus and Gaia. The youngest amongst them was CRONUS from whom the Olympians were descended. They had six sisters, the Titanides, on whom they fathered a whole cycle of divinities (Table 8).

After the castration of Uranus by Cronus, the Titans seized power. Oceanus refused to help Cronus, however, and remained independent. He later helped Zeus to dethrone Cronus. This struggle, which brought the Olympians to power, was known as the Titanomachia and is related in Hesiod's *Theogony*. Zeus' allies in this struggle were not only the Olympians, such as Athena, Apollo, Hera, Poseidon, and Pluto, but also the HECATONCHEIRES, who had suffered under the Titans, and even Prometheus, although he was the son of the Titan Iapetus.

Tithonus (*Τιθωνός*) Although one tradition often makes him the son of Eos and Cephalus, Tithonus was more usually regarded as one of the sons of Laomedon (Table 4) and Strymo. He was therefore the elder brother of Priam. Tithonus was extremely handsome, and was noticed by Eos, who fell in love with him and abducted him to Ethiopia. They had two sons, Emathion and MEMNON. Motivated by her love for Tithonus, Eos asked Zeus that he might be granted immortality, but she forgot to obtain eternal youth for him. So, while Eos remained unchanged, Tithonus grew older, and shrank to the point where he had to be put in a wicker basket like a child. In the end Eos changed him into a cicada.

Tityus (*Τιτυός*) A giant, the son of Zeus and Elara. Fearing Hera's jealousy, Zeus concealed his lover when she was pregnant in the depths of the earth, from where Tityus emerged at his birth. When Leto gave birth to Zeus' children Artemis and Apollo, Hera unleashed Tityus against her, but he was struck by one of Zeus' thunderbolts and fell into the Underworld, where two snakes or two eagles devoured his liver, which grew again in accordance with the phases of the moon. According to other authors, it was Leto's two children who killed the monster with their arrows. Tityus returned permanently into the ground, where his body covered over two acres.

Tlepolemus (*Τληπόλεμος*) A son of Heracles and Astyoche. After Heracles' death, the HERACLIDS tried to return to the Peloponnese, but when they were forced after each attempt to withdraw into Attica, Tlepolemus and his great-uncle Licymnius, along with Licymnius' children, were granted permission by the Argives to settle in Argos. During a quarrel between Tlepolemus and his great-uncle, the latter was killed by a blow from a stick. According to some authors this was accidental; Tlepolemus had meant either to strike an ox, or to punish a slave, and the stick had unfortunately missed its mark. Licymnius' relations forced Tlepolemus to exile himself from Argos. He left, along with his wife Polyxo (2), and settled in Rhodes. There he founded three cities, Lindos, Ialysus and Camirus.

Tlepolemus was one of the suitors for the hand of Helen. He set out for the Trojan War, leaving POLYXO (2) at Rhodes as regent. He was killed by Sarpedon (2).

Tmolus (*Τμῶλος*) Omphale's widowed husband.

Toxeus (*Τοξεύς*)

1. The Archer, one of the sons of Eurytus (2). He was killed by Heracles at the same time as his brothers.
2. One of the sons of Oeneus, the king of Calydon, and of Althaea. Oeneus killed him because he jumped over a ditch (cf. the death of REMUS).

Triopas (*Τριόπας*) Or Triops. He was sometimes said to be the son of Canace (1) and Poseidon, sometimes of Lapithes and Orsinome, or (in the Argive tradition) of Phorbas (2) and Euboea, of the family of Niobe (1) and Argos (1). The name of Triopas was also borne by one of the HELIADES (2). The foundation of the city of Cnidus was sometimes attributed to Triopas.

Triptolemus (*Τριπτόλεμος*) The archetype of the Eleusinian hero linked to the myth of DEMETER. In the earliest version of the legend, he was a king of Eleusis. Later he was said to be the son of King Celeus and Metanira and brother of Demophon (1). Other traditions made him the son of Dysaules and Baubo, or of the hero Eleusis, or of Gaia and Oceanus. In return for the hospitality which Demeter had received at Eleusis from Triptolemus' relations, she gave him a chariot drawn by winged dragons and ordered him to travel throughout the world sowing grains of wheat everywhere. In some countries Triptolemus encountered strong resistance: the king of the Getae, Carnabon, killed one of his dragons, but Demeter immediately replaced it; at Patras Antheias tried to harness the dragons to the goddess's divine chariot while Triptolemus was asleep and to sow the wheat himself, but he fell from the chariot and was killed.

Triptolemus later became 'judge of the Dead' in the Underworld and he figured alongside Aeacus, Minos and Rhadamanthys. The introduction of the festival of the Thesmophoria at Athens was attributed to Triptolemus. For Demeter's attempt to give immortality to one of the sons of Celeus, see DEMOPHON (1). Often it was Triptolemus who was said to have been the victim of the goddess's spells. For the children attributed to Triptolemus in local traditions, see CROCON.

Triton (*Τρίτων*) A sea-god, usually said to be the son of Poseidon and Amphitrite (Table 8). Although his abode was generally the entire sea, he was often considered to be the god of Lake Tritonis in Libya. A daughter, Pallas (2), was attributed to him, and also a priestess of Athena called Triteia, who was loved by Ares, by whom she had a son, Melanippus (1).

Triton was involved in the expedition of the Argonauts. Disguised as Eurypylus (5), he gave a clod of earth to EUPHEMUS as a present for his hospitality and indicated to the sailors the route to take in order to regain the Mediterranean. Triton also appeared in a Boeotian legend, at Tanagra, where, during a festival of Dionysus, Triton attacked the local women while they were bathing in the lake. But Dionysus came to their aid and drove off Triton. It is also said that Triton plundered the shores of the lake, carrying off herds, until the day when a jug of wine appeared on the shore. Triton drank it. He fell asleep and was killed with an axe. This was the 'rational' interpretation of the victory of Dionysus. The name of Triton was often applied to a whole range of beings who made up Poseidon's retinue. The upper half of their bodies took the form of men's bodies, but the lower half were like those of fishes. They were usually depicted as blowing into shells which they used as horns (see MISENUS (2)).

Trochilus (*Τροχίλος*) An Argive, the son of Io and a priest of Demeter. The invention of the chariot was attributed to him, and in particular the sacred chariot used in the Argive cult of Hera. Hounded by Agenor, he fled and took refuge in Attica, where he married an Eleusinian woman and had two sons, Eubouleus (1) and Triptolemus. Later he was said to have been placed amongst the stars, where he formed the constellation of the Charioteer.

Troezen (*Τροιζήν*)The eponym of the city of Troezen on the Saronic Gulf. According to the local tradition, he was the son of Pelops (1) and Hippodamia (1) and brother of PITTHEUS (Table 2). During the reign of King Aetius, Pittheus and Troezen migrated to the city which was to take the latter's name, and the three of them reigned together. Troezen had two sons, Anaphlystus and Sphettus, who migrated to Attica.

Troilus (*Τρωίλος*) The youngest son of Priam and Hecuba, although it was often claimed that Apollo was his father. There was a prophecy which stated that Troy would never be taken if Troilus reached the age of

20, but he was killed by Achilles shortly after the arrival of the Greeks. He was either killed by Achilles near the Scaean Gates (see also POLYXENA), or was taken prisoner and sacrificed to the hero. Another variant claimed that Achilles fell in love with him. Troilus fled and took refuge in the temple of the Thymbrian Apollo. Achilles tried to entice him out but finally lost his temper and killed him inside the sanctuary.

Trophonius (*Τροφώνιος*) The hero of Lebadeia in Boeotia, where there was a famous oracle. Sometimes he is described as the son of Apollo and Epicaste and thus stepson of AGAMEDES; he was also said to be one of the children of Erginus (1). He was suckled by Demeter. He was known for his skill as an architect. The construction of several famous buildings was attributed to Agamedes and him: Amphitryon's house at Thebes; one of the temples of Apollo at Delphi; the treasure-houses of Augias at Elis and of Hyrieus at Hyria; and the temple of Poseidon at Mantinea. When he put his talent to improper use it caused his downfall (see AGAMEDES). There existed several versions of his death. It was often said that this was the price given by Apollo for the construction of his temple, as death was the finest reward which the gods could give to man.

Tros (*Τρώς*) The eponym of the Trojans and of Troy. He was the son of Erichthonius, himself the son of Dardanus, and of Astyoche, daughter of the river-god Simois (Table 4). He married Callirhoe (4), and by her had a daughter, Cleopatra (4), and three sons, Ilus (2), Assaracus and Ganymede.

Turnus An Italic hero, the king of the Rutuli at the time of the arrival of Aeneas. He was the son of King Daunus, and grandson of Pilumnus (2). His mother was the Nymph Venilia. According to the form of the legend which probably goes back to Cato's *Origines*, Turnus became an ally of Latinus after the marriage between the latter's daughter and Aeneas. Latinus had asked for his help in defending himself against Trojan banditry. In an early battle Latinus was killed. Turnus fled to MEZENTIUS at Caere. He then returned to attack Aeneas, but in the course of a second battle he was killed. According to another version, Aeneas and Latinus were allies and were both attacked by Turnus and the Rutuli. During a battle, both Latinus and Turnus were killed.

Virgil made Turnus the brother of Juturna and engaged to Lavinia, one of Latinus' granddaughters, who had been promised to him by Latinus' wife, Amata. Turnus was a violent young man who would not allow foreigners to settle in central Italy and stirred up all the neighbouring peoples against the Trojans. He was eventually killed by Aeneas in single combat.

Tutula See PHILOTIS.

Tyche (*Τύχη*) The personification of Chance or Fortune. She assumed great importance which continually increased into the Hellenistic period and similarly at Rome (see FORTUNA).

She eventually became assimilated with certain goddesses, such as Isis and Nemesis. Every city had its Tyche, depicted as being crowned with towers to symbolize her role as a guardian of cities. She was sometimes represented as being blind.

Tychius (*Τυχίος*) A cobbler from Boeotia who made the leather shield for Ajax.

Tydeus (*Τυδεύς*) An Aetolian hero, son of the second marriage of King Oeneus and Periboea (6). According to one tradition Oeneus seduced Periboea before he married her, and abandoned her to the swineherds, amongst whom Tydeus grew up. It was also often claimed that Oeneus, on Zeus' orders, seduced his own daughter Gorge, and that Tydeus was the product of this intrigue.

When he reached manhood, Tydeus murdered either Oeneus' brother, Alcathous (2); or the eight sons of Melas (3); or his own brother Olenias. Tydeus had to leave his homeland and he arrived to stay with ADRASTUS at the same time as Polynices. Adrastus purified Tydeus of his murder, gave him one of his daughters, Deipyle, and promised to restore Polynices and Tydeus to their homelands. As a result of this Tydeus came to take part in the expedition of the Seven against Thebes.

In the episode of Archemorus, Tydeus took HYPSIPYLE's side and fought against LYCURGUS (2). Amphiaraus and Adrastus settled the quarrel. Tydeus won the boxing at the games celebrated in honour of Archemorus (these became the Nemean Games). Tydeus was sent as an ambassador to Thebes, but Eteocles refused to listen to him. So Tydeus challenged the Thebans individually to single combat, and defeated them one after the other. As he was leaving, the Thebans set an ambush of 50 men for him, but Tydeus killed them all except MAEON (1). During the siege Ismene, Eteocles' sister, who was in love with a young Theban called Theoclymenus, had arranged to meet him outside the city. Warned by Athena, Tydeus waited for the young couple and took them by surprise. Theoclymenus escaped; Ismene, taken prisoner, tried to arouse Tydeus' pity. He remained unmoved, and killed her.

In the decisive battle outside Thebes, Tydeus' adversary was Melanippus (2). Although Melanippus wounded him mortally, Tydeus nevertheless defeated him. Athena was with Zeus' approval getting ready to make Tydeus immortal. But Amphiaraus learned of the goddess's intentions, cut off Melanippus' head, and then presented it to Tydeus. The latter split the skull of his enemy in two, and devoured the brains. Disgusted by this, Athena decided to deprive Tydeus of immortality. Tydeus' burial was carried out by Maeon, in gratitude for having spared him. Another tradition maintains that the body was carried off by Theseus' Athenians and buried at Eleusis. Tydeus was the father of DIOMEDES (2).

Tyndareus (*Τυνδάρεως*) The father of the Dioscuri, of Helen and of Clytemnestra, as well as of Timandra and Phylonoe. According to some traditions, he was the son of Oebalus (1) and the Naiad Batieia. Sometimes his father was said to be Perieres (1), or even Cynortas, who was usually said to be the father of Perieres. In the latter two traditions, Tyndareus' mother was Gorgophone. His brothers or half-brothers, depending on the tradition, were Icarius, Aphareus and Leucippus (1); sometimes a sister Arena was added to this list.

On the death of Oebalus, HIPPOCOON drove his brothers out and kept the kingdom of Sparta for himself. Tyndareus fled to the court of Thestius in Calydon, where he married the king's daughter, Leda. Later, Heracles restored the kingdom of Sparta to Tyndareus. According to another tradition, Hippocoon and Icarius remained in Sparta and agreed to evict Tyndareus, who took refuge at Pellene in Achaea, or with his half-brother Aphareus in Messenia.

After the death of Atreus, the children Menelaus and Agamemnon were entrusted to Oeneus at Calydon. When Tyndareus returned from Calydon to Sparta, he took the two children with him, and brought them up in his own house. There the brothers met Helen and Clytemnestra. After the deification of his two sons, Castor and Pollux, Tyndareus bequeathed the kingdom of Sparta to Menelaus. During the Trojan War Tyndareus gave his granddaughter HERMIONE in marriage to Orestes. It was sometimes maintained that he outlived Agamemnon and was ORESTES' prosecutor before the Areopagus, or at Argos before the people's tribunal. Tyndareus is included among those brought back to life by Asclepius. He was honoured as as a hero at Sparta.

Typhon (*Τυφών*) Typhon, or Typheus, was a monster who was the youngest son of Gaia and Tartarus. In a different tradition, Gaia, displeased about the defeat of the Giants, slandered Zeus in the presence of Hera, who went to Cronus to ask for a means of taking revenge. Cronus gave her two eggs coated with his own semen: once buried, these eggs would give birth to a demon capable of dethroning Zeus. This monster was Typhon. According to another tradition Typhon was a son of Hera whom she had produced herself without any male assistance (cf. HEPHAESTUS). She gave her monstrous son to the serpent PYTHON who lived at Delphi, for him to bring up.

Typhon was half man and half animal. He was higher than the mountains, and his head often touched the stars. When he stretched out his arms, one of his hands reached the East and the other the West. Instead of fingers, he had 100 dragons' heads. From his waist down he was encircled by snakes. His body had wings and his eyes shot forth flames. When the gods saw him attacking Olympus, they fled to Egypt and took on animal forms. Only Athena and Zeus resisted him. Zeus hurled thunderbolts at him and in closer conflict struck him with his steel sickle. This struggle took place on Mount Casius, on the borders of Egypt and Arabia Petraea. Typhon succeeded in wresting the sickle from Zeus' hands. He cut the tendons in Zeus' arms and legs, and carried him off to Cilicia where he shut him up in the Corycian Cave. He concealed Zeus' tendons and muscles in a bearskin and gave them to the dragon Delphyne (I) for safe keeping. Hermes and Pan, or, in some accounts, Cadmus, stole the tendons and restored them to Zeus' body. He recovered his strength and began striking Typhon with thunderbolts. Typhon fled and, in the hope of increasing his strength, tried to taste the magic fruits which grew on Mount Nysa after being promised by the Moirae, who wanted to lure him there, that these would cure him. Zeus caught up with him there and the pursuit continued. In Thrace, he threw mountains at Zeus, who forced them back on to the monster with his thunderbolts. While Typhon was crossing the sea to Sicily, Zeus hurled Mount Etna at him, which crushed him. The flames which erupt from Etna are either those poured forth by the monster or the remains of the thunderbolts with which Zeus struck him down. Typhon was said to be the father of Orthrus, the Hydra of Lerna, and the Chimaera, whom he had by Echidna.

Tyro (*Τυρώ*) The daughter of Salmoneus and Alcidice. She was brought up by Salmoneus' brother, Cretheus. She fell in love with the river-god Enipeus, and would often go to his banks to lament her passion. One day the god Poseidon emerged from the water and in the form of Enipeus seduced her. She secretly gave birth to twins, PELIAS and NELEUS (I) (Table 6). Her stepmother Sidero, the second wife of Salmoneus, maltreated her. When her children were grown up, they came and killed Sidero. Tyro then married Cretheus, by whom she had Aeson, Pheres (I) and Amythaon (Table 6). For a different legend concerning Tyro whose fragmented story has been partly preserved for us by Hyginus, see SISYPHUS.

Tyrrhenus (*Τυρρηνός*) The eponymous hero of the Tyrrhenians (the Etruscans). He was sometimes said to be the brother of Lydus and son of Atys and Callithea, sometimes a son of Manes (I) and Callirhoe (I), sometimes a son of Heracles and the inventor of the trumpet. In this case, his mother was Omphale. He was also said to be a son of Telephus; which makes Tarchon his brother. The Tyrrhenus of Lydian origin was exiled after the fall of Troy – or else during the famine – and settled in central Italy where he became the progenitor of the Etruscan race.

Tyrrhus The head shepherd of Latinus. He took command of the Latin peasants to avenge the death of the sacred doe killed by ASCANIUS. After the death of Aeneas, LAVINIA, frightened of her stepson, took refuge with Tyrrhus to give birth to SILVIUS.

Tyrus (*Τύρος*) A Phoenician Nymph, loved by Heracles. Her dog ate a purple shellfish (a murex) and came back with his nose coloured purple. Tyrus told Heracles that she would no longer love him unless he gave her a garment of the same colour. Heracles went off to look, and found purple dye, the glory of Tyre.

U

Ucalegon (*Οὐκαλέγων*)
1. A Trojan and a friend of Priam. He appears in the Council of Elders of the city. His house, which was adjacent to Aeneas', was destroyed when Troy fell.
2. The father of the Sphinx in one tradition.

Ulixes See ODYSSEUS.

Ulysses See ODYSSEUS.

Uranus (*Οὔρανος*) The personification of the Sky as a fertile element. In Hesiod's *Theogony* he is the son of Gaia. Other poems make him the son of AETHER in a tradition which goes back to the *Titanomachia*. In the Orphic *Theogony* Uranus and Gaia are two of the children of Nyx.

The best-known legends of Uranus are those in which he appears as the husband of Gaia. By her he had a large number of children (see e.g. Table 8), namely six male Titans, the six female Titanides, the three Cyclopes and the three Hecatoncheires. Gaia tired of endless childbirth and asked her sons to protect her against her husband. They all refused except CRONUS, who ambushed his father and, with the help of a sickle which his mother had lent him, cut off Uranus' testicles and threw them into the sea. This act of mutilation is usually said to have taken place at Cape Drepanum, which is supposed to have taken its name from Cronus' sickle (Greek *δρέπανον* = 'sickle'); sometimes it is situated off Corcyra, the land of the Phaeacians. The island is said to be the sickle itself, which was thrown into the sea by Cronus, and the Phaeacians were born of the god's blood. Alternatively, the scene is set in Sicily, which was fertilized by the god's blood, which is why that island is so fertile.

In a tradition recorded by Diodorus Siculus, Uranus was the first king of the Atlantes. He was the first to teach them civilization and to initiate them into culture. He was himself a skilled astronomer: he devised the first calendar from the movement of the stars and predicted the principal events which would occur in the world. On his death divine honours were paid to him. Gradually he became identified with the sky itself. In this tradition Uranus had 45 children, 18 by Titae (who later took the name Gaia): from their mother they took the name Titans. His daughters were Basileia and, later, Cybele and Rhea (who was also called Pandora). Basileia inherited the throne of Uranus and married Hyperion, one of her brothers, by whom she had two children, Helios and Selene. Among the other children of Uranus, Diodorus mentions Atlas (1) and Cronus; according to Plato, Oceanus and Tethys are also children of Uranus. Hesiod preserves the memory of two prophecies attributed jointly to Uranus and Gaia: first, the prophecy which warned Cronus that his reign would end when he had been conquered by one of his sons: second, the prophecy that put ZEUS on his guard against the child he would have by METIS. It was in response to this prophecy that Zeus swallowed Metis when she was pregnant with Athena.

V

Vacuna An ancient Sabine goddess who had a sanctuary near Horace's villa. She has been identified with Diana, Minerva, and even with Victory.

Valeria During an epidemic which ravaged the city of Falerii, an oracle commanded that a virgin should be sacrificed every year to Juno. One year the chosen victim was a girl called Valeria Luperca. Just as she was about to kill herself with a sword at the altar, an eagle appeared, plucked the sword from her, and dropped a small stick by the ritual hammer which was lying on the altar. The eagle flew off and dropped the sword on a heifer. Valeria grasped the meaning of the signs given by the bird. She sacrificed the heifer and, taking the hammer with her, touched those who had been stricken by the epidemic with it. They were cured immediately.

Veiovis A Roman god, identified with Apollo, who had an ancient shrine on the Capitol and another on the Insula Tiberina. He was associated with the Underworld, and seems to have presided originally over swamps and volcanic movements. He was a god of the *gens Julia*.

Venus A very ancient Latin divinity who had a shrine near Ardea which was established before the foundation of Rome. In the second century BC she was assimilated into the legend of the Greek APHRODITE. The *gens Julia*, which claimed to be descended from AENEAS, assumed that Venus was one of their ancestors.

Vertumnus A god who had a statue in Rome in the Etruscan district at the entrance to the Forum. Vertumnus personified the idea of change. To him was attributed the ability to take on as many shapes as he wished. Ovid describes a love affair of his with POMONA.

Vesta A Roman goddess who presided over the fire in the domestic hearth. Like the Greek HESTIA, she belonged to the group of the 12 great gods. Her cult was controlled directly by the chief high priest assisted by the Vestal Virgins. The cult of Vesta was introduced to Rome, according to most authors, by Romulus, even though her temple (round in shape, like the earliest huts of Latium) stood not inside the Palatine city but on the edge of it, in the Roman forum, and consequently outside the boundaries of the city attributed to Romulus. On the day of the *Vestalia* in mid-June, young asses were garlanded with flowers and did not work. A legend of Hellenistic origin describes how the goddess, chaste above all others, was protected by a donkey from the amorous designs of PRIAPUS.

Virbius A demon whose worship was linked with that of Diana, in the sacred woods surrounding Nemi (Aricia). The fact that horses were not allowed to enter this wood gave rise to the belief that Virbius was HIPPOLYTUS, who had been killed by his horses, revived by Asclepius, and transported by Artemis to Italy. This interpretation was suppported by a pun, breaking Virbius up into *vir* (man) and *bis* (twice): thus, he who had been a man twice, and this was seen as an allusion to the resurrection of the hero.

Volturnus An old Roman divinity who had a festival, the *Volturnalia*, on 27 August. One legend maintained that this Volturnus was the father of the Nymph JUTURNA.

Vulcan A Roman deity, possessing a festival called the *Vulcanalia*, which took place on 23 August. He was said to have been introduced to Rome by Titus Tatius, but there was a tradition which attributes the construction of his first shrine to Romulus. During the festival of Vulcan, little fish and often other animals were sometimes thrown into the fire. These offerings represented human lives and they were offered to Vulcan in order to preserve lives. He has been identified with HEPHAESTUS. Vulcan was sometimes said to be the father of CACUS, or of CAECULUS, or even of SERVIUS TULLIUS (more usually considered to be the son of the household god or Lar).

Xanthippe (*Ξανθίππη*) Daughter of Dorus (1) and wife of PLEURON.

Xanthus (*Ξάνθος*)

1. Son of Erymanthus (2) and father of Psophis.
2. A king of Thebes who was killed in single combat by MELANTHUS.
3. In the *Iliad*, a Trojan, the son of Phaenops, who was killed by Diomedes (2).
4. A son of Niobe (2), according to Pherecydes.
5. Son of Aegyptus.
6. Son of Triopas.
7. One of Achilles' horses.
8. One of the mares of Diomedes (1).
9. In the *Iliad*, one of the horses of Hector.
10. One of Castor's horses, according to Stesichorus.
11. A river of the Troad. According to Homer it was called SCAMANDER by mortals and Xanthus by the gods.

Xuthus (*Ξοῦθος*) Son of Hellen and Othreis or Orseis, and the brother of Dorus and Aeolus (1). In some traditions he is the father of Ion by Creusa (2), although in Euripides' *Ion* Apollo is Ion's father and Xuthus his stepfather (see ION). In this version Xuthus is descended from Zeus through Aeolus (2). Pausanias says that Xuthus was driven out of Attica by the sons of Erechtheus. He went to Aegialus in the northern Peloponnese, where he died.

Z

Zacynthus (*Ζάκυνθος*) The eponymous hero of the island of Zacynthus (modern Zante). He was said to be either the son of Dardanus (Table 4) or an Arcadian from the city of Psophis.

Zagreus (*Ζαγρεύς*) The son of Zeus and Persephone, and considered the 'first Dionysus'. Zeus was said to have taken on the form of a serpent in order to beget him. He intended to make Zagreus his successor and bestow on him sovereignty over the world, but the Fates decided otherwise. Anticipating Hera's jealousy, Zeus entrusted the infant Zagreus to Apollo and the Curetes, who brought him up in the forest of Parnassus, but Hera discovered where he was and gave the Titans the task of abducting him. Zagreus tried to escape from them by changing shape, metamorphosing himself, notably into a bull; however the Titans cut him into pieces and ate him, partly cooked and partly raw. Athena could save only the heart, which was still beating. Several scattered pieces of him were gathered up by Apollo, who buried them near the tripod at Delphi. Zeus wanted him restored to life, and this occurred either through Demeter, who reconstituted what remained of him, or because Zeus forced Semele to consume Zagreus' heart and then give birth to a 'second Dionysus'. It was also said that Zeus consumed the child's heart before fathering Zagreus/Dionysus on Semele. Zagreus was an Orphic god, and the preceding legend belongs to Orphic theology. Aeschylus, on the other hand, called Zagreus an underworld Zeus and likened him to Hades.

Zelus (*Ζῆλος*) Zeal or Emulation, a son of Styx and Oceanus. He was the brother of Nike, Cratos and Bia.

Zephyrus (*Ζέφυρος*) The god of the west wind, the son of Eos and Astraeus and the brother of Boreas. See FLORA, HARPIES and HYACINTHUS.

Zetes (*Ζήτης*) One of the BOREADES.

Zethus (*Ζῆθος*) See AMPHION.

Zeus (*Ζεύς*) Generally regarded as the greatest god of the Greek pantheon. He was essentially the god of Light, of clear skies as well as of thunder.

His personality, that of the king of men and of gods, enthroned in the luminous heights of the sky, was created in the Homeric poems. Usually he presided on Mount Olympus, but he also travelled. He could be found, for example, living with the Ethiopians, a pious race above all others, whose sacrifices found particular favour with him. Gradually the word *Olympus* came to mean merely the ethereal region where the gods lived. Zeus not only presided over celestial manifestations – causing rain, thunder and lightning

– but above all he maintained order and justice in the world. He was responsible for purifying murderers of the stain of blood, and he ensured that oaths were kept, and that the appropriate duties were carried out to one's hosts. He was the guarantor of royal powers and, more generally, of the social hierarchy. He exercised prerogatives not only towards mortals, but also towards the gods. He himself was subject to Fate, which he interpreted and defended against the whims of the other gods. For example, he considered the destinies of Achilles and Hector, and when the scale bearing the latter went down to Hades, Zeus forbade Apollo to intervene, and abandoned the hero to his enemy. He was the distributor of good and evil. Homer relates in the *Iliad* that at the gate of his palace there were two jars, one containing good, the other evil. Zeus' custom with each mortal was to take a portion from both jars. But sometimes he used only one of them, and the resulting destiny was either entirely good or, more usually, entirely evil.

For the Stoics (notably Chrysippus, who dedicated a poem to him), Zeus was the symbol of a single god, the incarnation of the Cosmos. The laws of the world were nothing but the thought of Zeus, but that was the extreme point of the god's evolution, beyond the limits of mythology towards theology and philosophy.

I. BIRTH OF ZEUS

Zeus was the son of the Titan CRONUS and of RHEA, and the last-born (Table 8). Cronus was warned by an oracle that one of his children would dethrone him and tried to prevent this by devouring his sons and daughters as Rhea gave birth to them. On the birth of the sixth, Rhea used a trick to save Zeus. She gave birth to him secretly at night and, in the morning, gave Cronus a stone wrapped up in a blanket. Cronus ate this stone which he thought was a child, and Zeus was saved. There were two distinct traditions about the place of Zeus' birth. The most frequently mentioned place was in Crete, on Mount Aegeon, Mount Ida or Mount Dicte. The other tradition, defended by Callimachus in his *Hymn to Zeus*, situates it in Arcadia (see NEDA). However, Callimachus says that Zeus' earliest years were spent in a Cretan hiding place, where his mother had entrusted him to the CURETES and the Nymphs. His nurse was the Nymph (or goat) Amalthea, who suckled him. When this goat died, Zeus used its skin for his shield: this was the *aegis* whose power was first put to the test at the time of the fight against the Titans. The divine child was nourished on honey: the bees of Mount Ida produced honey especially for him (for the euhemeristic interpretations of this, see MELISSA and MELISSEUS (1)). The Cretans did not merely show the spot where, according to them, Zeus was born; they would also point out a so-called Tomb of Zeus.

II. THE CONQUEST OF POWER

When Zeus reached adulthood, he wanted to seize power from Cronus. He asked METIS for advice, and she gave him a drug which made Cronus vomit up the children whom he had swallowed. With the aid of his brothers and sisters now restored to life, Zeus attacked Cronus and the

Titans. The struggle lasted ten years until Zeus and the Olympians were victorious, and the Titans were expelled from Heaven. To win this victory Zeus, on Gaia's advice, had had to liberate the Cyclopes and the Hecatoncheires from Tartarus, where Cronus had locked them up. To do this, he killed their guardian, Campe. The Cyclopes then gave Zeus thunder and lightning which they had made; they gave Hades a magic helmet which made the wearer of it invisible; Poseidon received a trident, which could shake the sea and the land at a blow. Having won their victory, the gods shared power out among themselves by drawing lots. Zeus obtained Heaven; Poseidon the Sea; Hades the Underworld. In addition Zeus was to preside over the Universe. The victory of Zeus and the Olympians was soon contested. They had to fight against the GIANTS, aroused against them by Gaia, who was annoyed at having her sons, the Titans, locked away in Tartarus. Finally, Zeus had to overcome TYPHON.

III. MARRIAGE AND THE AFFAIRS OF ZEUS

The earliest of his wives was Metis, the daughter of Oceanus. Metis took on several forms in order to try and escape from the god, but finally submitted, and conceived a daughter. Gaia predicted to Zeus that if Metis gave birth to a daughter, she would then produce a son who would dethrone his father. So Zeus swallowed Metis and, when the time came for the delivery of the child, Prometheus or Hephaestus split Zeus' skull with an axe, and the goddess Athena emerged fully armed. Zeus then married Themis, one of the Titanides, and had daughters by her who were called the Horae, named Eirene (Peace), Eunomia (Good Order) and Dike (Justice). Then he fathered the Moirae who were the agents of Destiny.

Zeus fathered APHRODITE on Dione, one of the Titanides, in one tradition. By Eurynome (1) he fathered the CHARITES. By Mnemosyne he had the MUSES. Finally, by Leto, he fathered Apollo and Artemis.

It was only at this moment that, according to Hesiod, the 'sacred marriage' with Hera, his own sister, took place, but it was generally considered to have happened much earlier. Hebe, Eilithyia and Ares were born of this marriage. By another of his sisters, Demeter, Zeus had a daughter, Persephone. Zeus' intrigues with mortals were countless. There was hardly a region in the Greek world which did not boast an eponymous hero who was a son born of one of Zeus' love affairs. Similarly, most of the great families of legend were connected with Zeus. The Heraclids, for example, were descended not only from the union of the god and Alcmene but also, earlier, from the union of Zeus and Danae (Table 7). Achilles and Ajax (2) were descended from Zeus through the Nymph Aegina, and the ancestor of Agamemnon and Menelaus, Tantalus, was said to be the son of Zeus and Pluto (Table 2). The race of Cadmus was connected with Zeus through Io and her son Epaphus (Table 3). The Trojans, through their ancestor Dardanus, were born of the affairs between Zeus and Electra (2) (Table 4). The Cretans claimed connections with Europa (5) and the three sons she had by Zeus: Minos, Sarpedon (2) and Rhadamanthys. The Arcadians had an ancestor called Arcas, son of Zeus and Callisto (1), and the Argives took their name from Argos (1), the son (like his brother Pelasgus (1), eponym of the Pelasgians) of Zeus. Finally, the Lacedaemonians claimed descent from the god and the Nymph Taygete. There were sometimes particular reasons which led the god to father children on mortals. The birth of Helen was explained as a desire to diminish the excessive population of Greece and Asia by provoking a bloody conflict. Similarly, the birth of Heracles was intended to provide a hero capable of ridding the world of destructive monsters. Many of these unions took place with Zeus disguised as an animal or in some other form: with Europa (5) he took the form of a bull; with Leda a swan; with Danae a shower of gold. These adventures often exposed Zeus to Hera's anger. One explanation given by ancient writers for the god's metamorphoses was the desire to be concealed from his wife. Zeus' lovers often took animal forms. Thus Io was metamorphosed into a cow, and Callisto became a she-bear.

IV. VARIOUS LEGENDS

The *Iliad* related a plot against Zeus by Hera, Athena and Poseidon, which was an attempt to chain him up. He was saved by Aegaeon. On another occasion he hurled Hephaestus into space, making the god lame thereafter, as a punishment for having sided with Hera. He re-established order in the world after PROMETHEUS' theft by chaining the latter to the Caucasian mountains, but, confronted by the wickedness of mankind, he caused the great flood, from which the human race was saved only thanks to DEUCALION (1). Thus it was to Zeus the Liberator that Deucalion made his first sacrifice once this flood was over.

Zeus intervened in the quarrel between Apollo and Heracles concerning the tripod of Delphi; between Apollo and Idas about MARPESSA; between Pallas (2) and Athena, thus bringing about, quite unintentionally, the former's death; between Athena and Poseidon who were fighting over possession of Attica; between Aphrodite and Persephone who were arguing over ADONIS. He also punished a number of criminals, Salmoneus, Ixion (thus avenging a particular insult) and Lycaon (2). We see him intervening also in the Labours of Heracles, giving him weapons against his enemies, or removing him from their hands when he is injured. Zeus was said to have abducted GANYMEDE in the Troad, and made him his own cup-bearer as a replacement for Hebe. At Rome Zeus was identified with JUPITER, like him god of heaven, and protector of the city in his temple on the Capitol.

Zeuxippe (*Ζευξίππη*)

1. The wife of Pandion (1) and mother of Erechtheus, Butes (2), Procne and Philomela.
2. The daughter of Lamedon, king of Sicyon. She married Sicyon, by whom she had a daughter Chthonophyle.
3. The daughter of Hippocoon. She married Antiphates, the son of Melampus, and by him had two sons: Oecles and Amphalces (Table 1).

GENEALOGICAL TABLES

TABLE 1

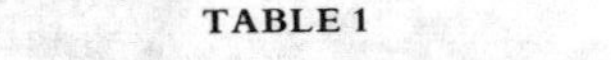

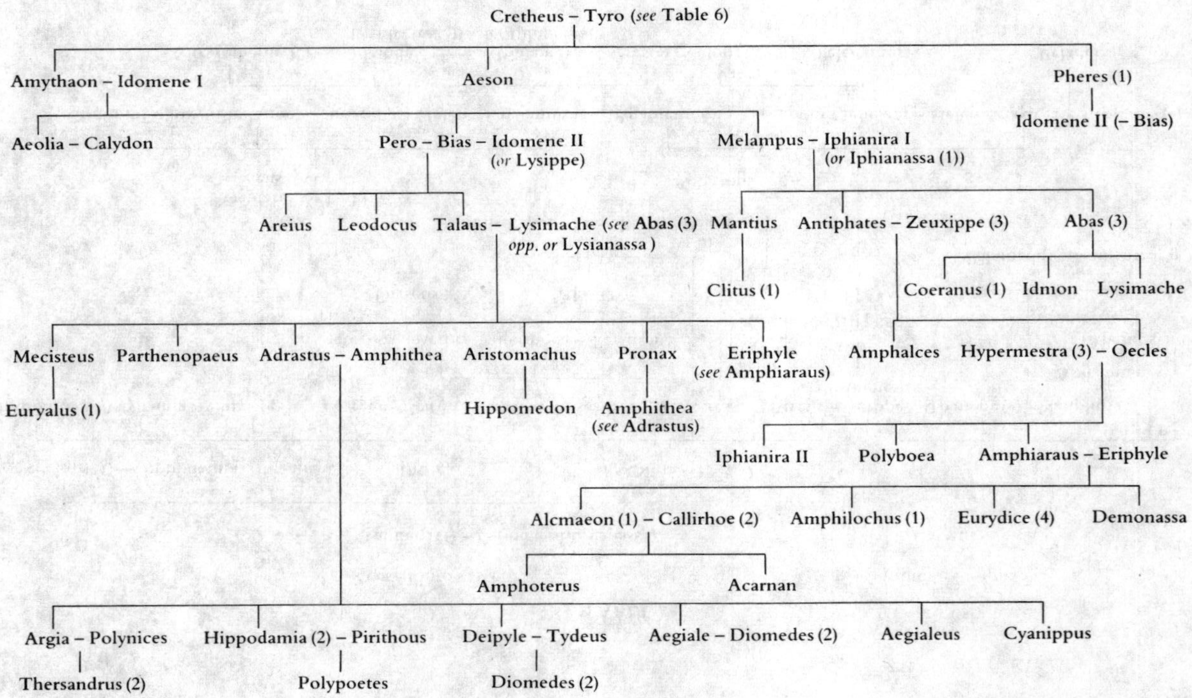

Cretheus – Tyro (*see* Table 6)

Amythaon – Idomene I
Aeson
Pheres (1)

Children of Pheres (1):
Idomene II (– Bias)

Children of Amythaon – Idomene I:
Aeolia – Calydon
Pero – Bias – Idomene II (*or* Lysippe)
Melampus – Iphianira I (*or* Iphianassa (1))

Children of Pero – Bias:
Areius
Leodocus
Talaus – Lysimache (*see* Abas (3) *opp. or* Lysianassa)

Children of Melampus – Iphianira I:
Mantius
Antiphates – Zeuxippe (3)
Abas (3)

Children of Mantius:
Clitus (1)

Children of Abas (3):
Coeranus (1)
Idmon
Lysimache

Children of Talaus – Lysimache:
Mecisteus
Parthenopaeus
Adrastus – Amphithea
Aristomachus
Pronax
Eriphyle (*see* Amphiaraus)

Children of Antiphates – Zeuxippe (3):
Amphalces
Hypermestra (3) – Oecles

Children of Mecisteus:
Euryalus (1)

Children of Aristomachus:
Hippomedon

Children of Pronax:
Amphithea (*see* Adrastus)

Children of Hypermestra (3) – Oecles:
Iphianira II
Polyboea
Amphiaraus – Eriphyle

Children of Amphiaraus – Eriphyle:
Alcmaeon (1) – Callirhoe (2)
Amphilochus (1)
Eurydice (4)
Demonassa

Children of Alcmaeon (1) – Callirhoe (2):
Amphoterus
Acarnan

Children of Adrastus – Amphithea:
Argia – Polynices
Hippodamia (2) – Pirithous
Deipyle – Tydeus
Aegiale – Diomedes (2)
Aegialeus
Cyanippus

Children of Argia – Polynices:
Thersandrus (2)

Children of Hippodamia (2) – Pirithous:
Polypoetes

Children of Deipyle – Tydeus:
Diomedes (2)

TABLE 2

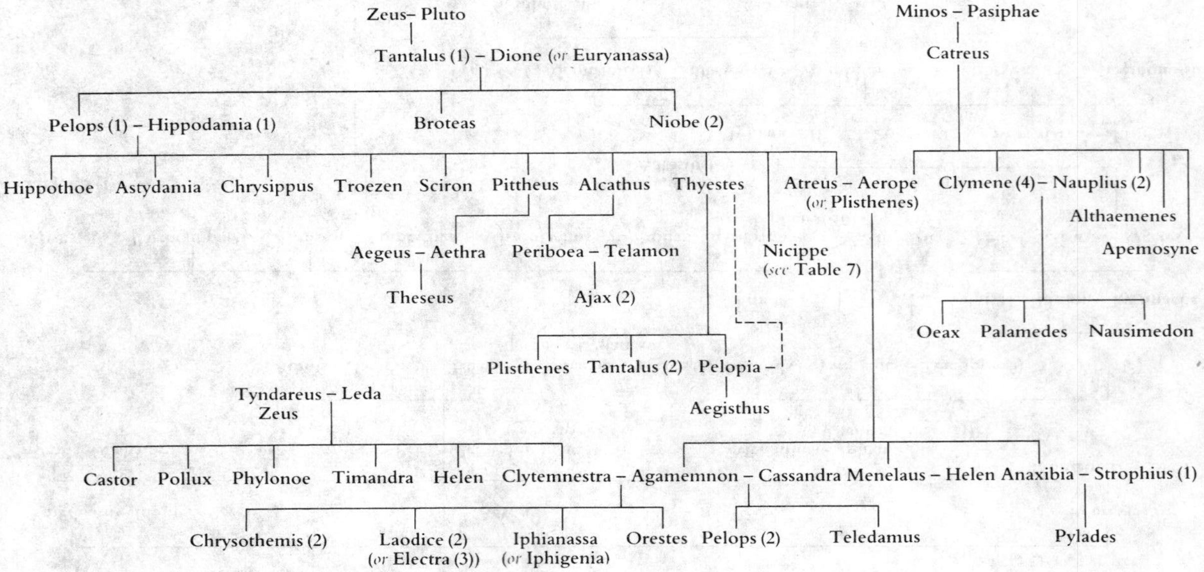

Zeus – Pluto

Tantalus (1) – Dione (*or* Euryanassa)

Pelops (1) – Hippodamia (1) Broteas Niobe (2)

Hippothoe Astydamia Chrysippus Troezen Sciron Pittheus Alcathus Thyestes Nicippe (*see* Table 7) Atreus – Aerope (*or* Plisthenes)

Aegeus – Aethra Periboea – Telamon

Theseus Ajax (2)

Plisthenes Tantalus (2) Pelopia –

Aegisthus

Minos – Pasiphae

Catreus

Aerope Clymene (4) – Nauplius (2) Althaemenes Apemosyne

Oeax Palamedes Nausimedon

Tyndareus – Leda
Zeus

Castor Pollux Phylonoe Timandra Helen Clytemnestra – Agamemnon – Cassandra Menelaus – Helen Anaxibia – Strophius (1)

Chrysothemis (2) Laodice (2) (*or* Electra (3)) Iphianassa (*or* Iphigenia) Orestes Pelops (2) Teledamus Pylades

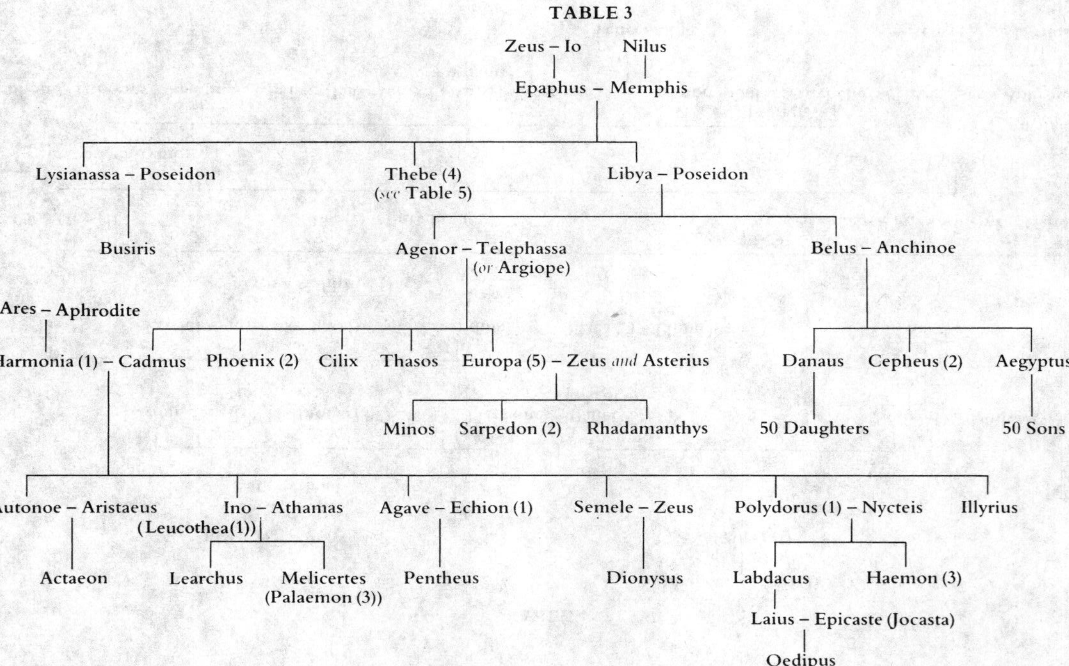
TABLE 3
Zeus – Io
Nilus
Epaphus – Memphis
Lysianassa – Poseidon
Thebe (4)
(see Table 5)
Libya – Poseidon
Busiris
Agenor – Telephassa
(or Argiope)
Belus – Anchinoe
Ares – Aphrodite
Harmonia (1) – Cadmus
Phoenix (2)
Cilix
Thasos
Europa (5) – Zeus and Asterius
Danaus
Cepheus (2)
Aegyptus
Minos
Sarpedon (2)
Rhadamanthys
50 Daughters
50 Sons
Autonoe – Aristaeus
Ino – Athamas
(Leucothea(1))
Agave – Echion (1)
Semele – Zeus
Polydorus (1) – Nycteis
Illyrius
Actaeon
Learchus
Melicertes
(Palaemon (3))
Pentheus
Dionysus
Labdacus
Haemon (3)
Laius – Epicaste (Jocasta)
Oedipus

TABLE 4

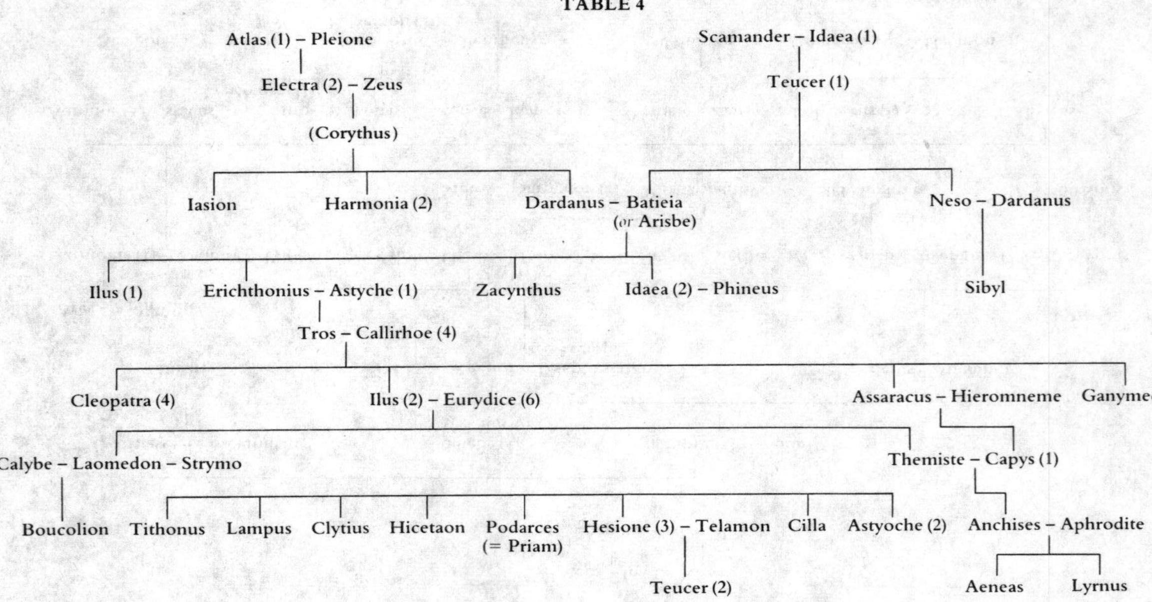
Atlas (1) – Pleione
Electra (2) – Zeus
(Corythus)
Scamander – Idaea (1)
Teucer (1)
Iasion
Harmonia (2)
Dardanus – Batieia
(or Arisbe)
Neso – Dardanus
Ilus (1)
Erichthonius – Astyche (1)
Zacynthus
Idaea (2) – Phineus
Sibyl
Tros – Callirhoe (4)
Cleopatra (4)
Ilus (2) – Eurydice (6)
Assaracus – Hieromneme
Ganymede
Calybe – Laomedon – Strymo
Themiste – Capys (1)
Boucolion
Tithonus
Lampus
Clytius
Hicetaon
Podarces
(= Priam)
Hesione (3) – Telamon
Cilla
Astyoche (2)
Anchises – Aphrodite
Teucer (2)
Aeneas
Lyrnus

TABLE 5

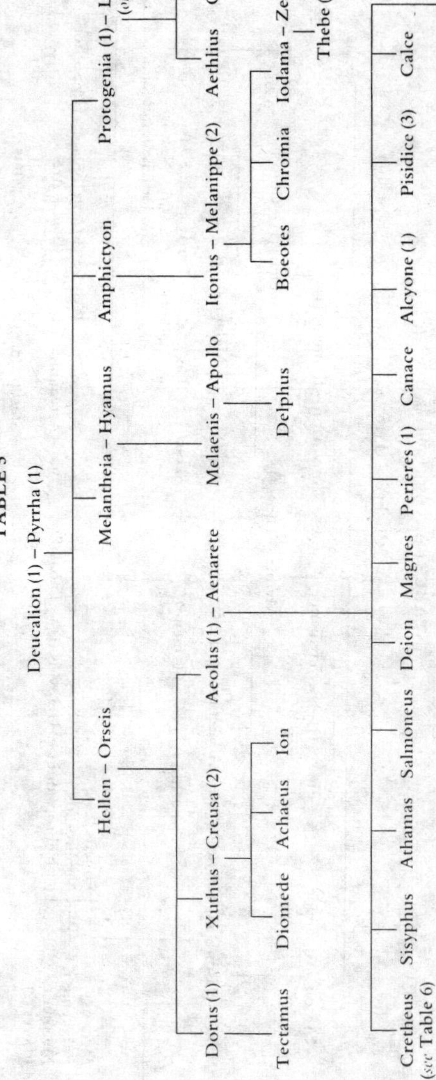

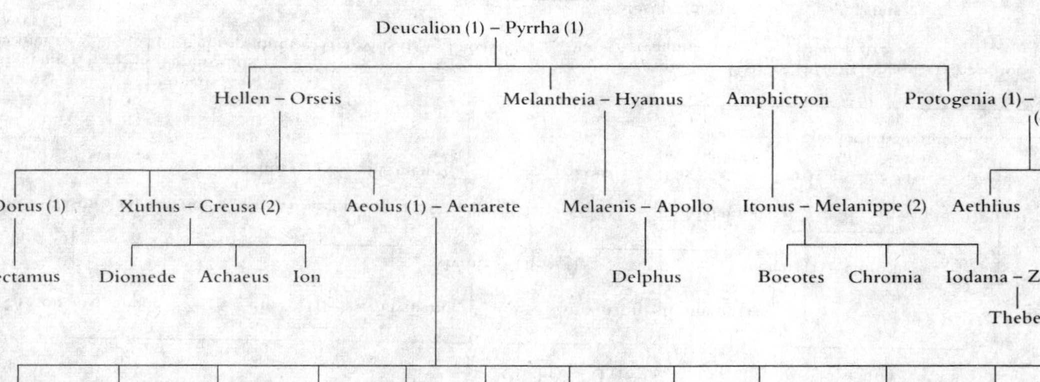
Deucalion (1) – Pyrrha (1)
Hellen – Orseis
Melantheia – Hyamus
Amphictyon
Protogenia (1) – Locrus (*or* Zeus)
Dorus (1)
Xuthus – Creusa (2)
Aeolus (1) – Aenarete
Melaenis – Apollo
Itonus – Melanippe (2)
Aethlius
Opus
Tectamus
Diomede
Achaeus
Ion
Delphus
Boeotes
Chromia
Iodama – Zeus
Thebe (2)
Cretheus (*see* Table 6)
Sisyphus
Athamas
Salmoneus
Deion
Magnes
Perieres (1)
Canace
Alcyone (1)
Pisidice (3)
Calce
Perimede

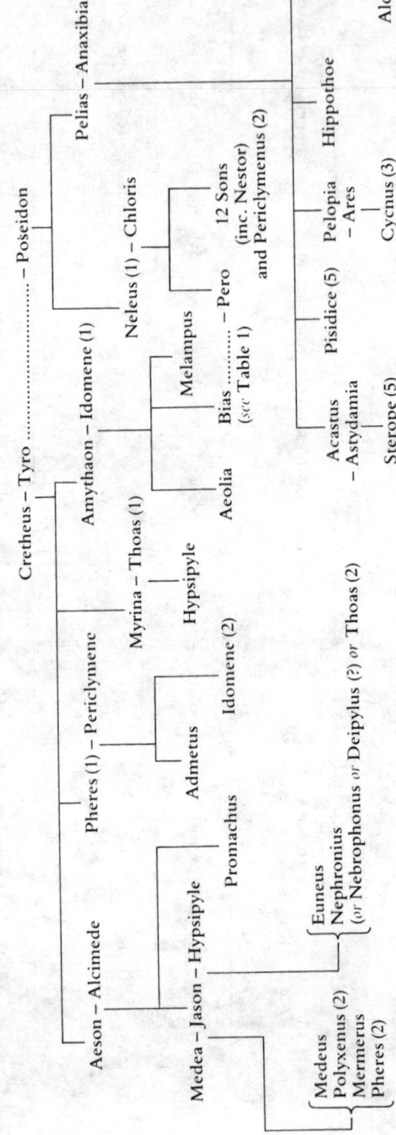
TABLE 6 (*see* also Table 1)
Cretheus – Tyro .... – Poseidon
Aeson – Alcimede
Pheres (1) – Periclymene
Amythaon – Idomene (1)
Neleus (1) – Chloris
Pelias – Anaxibia
Medea – Jason – Hypsipyle
Promachus
Admetus
Idomene (2)
Myrina – Thoas (1)
Hypsipyle
Aeolia
Melampus
Bias .... – Pero
(*see* Table 1)
12 Sons
(inc. Nestor)
and Periclymenus (2)
Acastus
– Astydamia
Sterope (5)
Pisidice (5)
Pelopia
– Ares
Cycnus (3)
Hippothoe
Alcestis
Medeus
Polyxenus (2)
Mermerus
Pheres (2)
Euneus
Nephronius
(*or* Nebrophonus *or* Deipylus (?) *or* Thoas (2)

TABLE 7

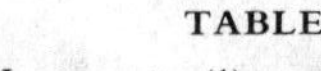

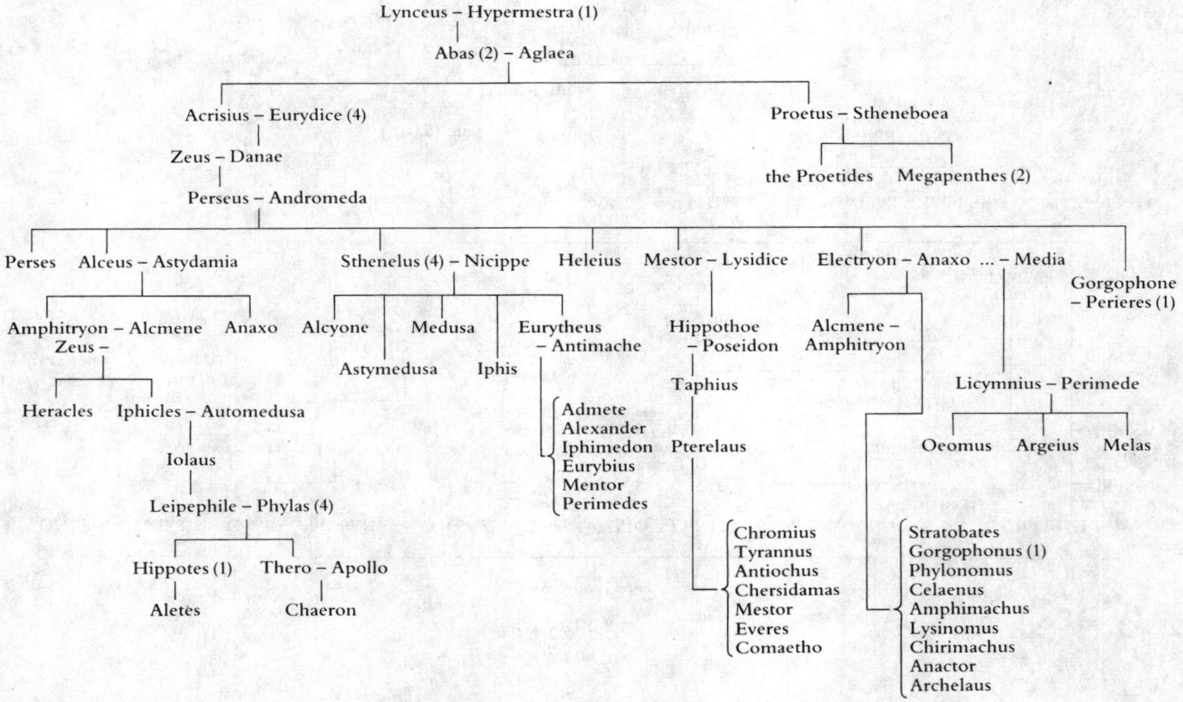

- Lynceus – Hypermestra (1)
  - Abas (2) – Aglaea
    - Acrisius – Eurydice (4)
      - Zeus – Danae
        - Perseus – Andromeda
          - Perses
          - Alceus – Astydamia
            - Amphitryon – Alcmene – Zeus –
              - Heracles
              - Iphicles – Automedusa
                - Iolaus
                  - Leipephile – Phylas (4)
                    - Hippotes (1)
                      - Aletes
                    - Thero – Apollo
                      - Chaeron
            - Anaxo
          - Sthenelus (4) – Nicippe
            - Alcyone
            - Astymedusa
            - Medusa
            - Iphis
            - Eurytheus – Antimache
              - Admete, Alexander, Iphimedon, Eurybius, Mentor, Perimedes
          - Heleius
          - Mestor – Lysidice
            - Hippothoe – Poseidon
              - Taphius
                - Pterelaus
                  - Chromius, Tyrannus, Antiochus, Chersidamas, Mestor, Everes, Comaetho
          - Electryon – Anaxo
            - Alcmene – Amphitryon
            - Stratobates, Gorgophonus (1), Phylonomus, Celaenus, Amphimachus, Lysinomus, Chirimachus, Anactor, Archelaus
          - Electryon ... – Media
            - Licymnius – Perimede
              - Oeomus
              - Argeius
              - Melas
          - Gorgophone – Perieres (1)
    - Proetus – Stheneboea
      - the Proetides
      - Megapenthes (2)

TABLE 8

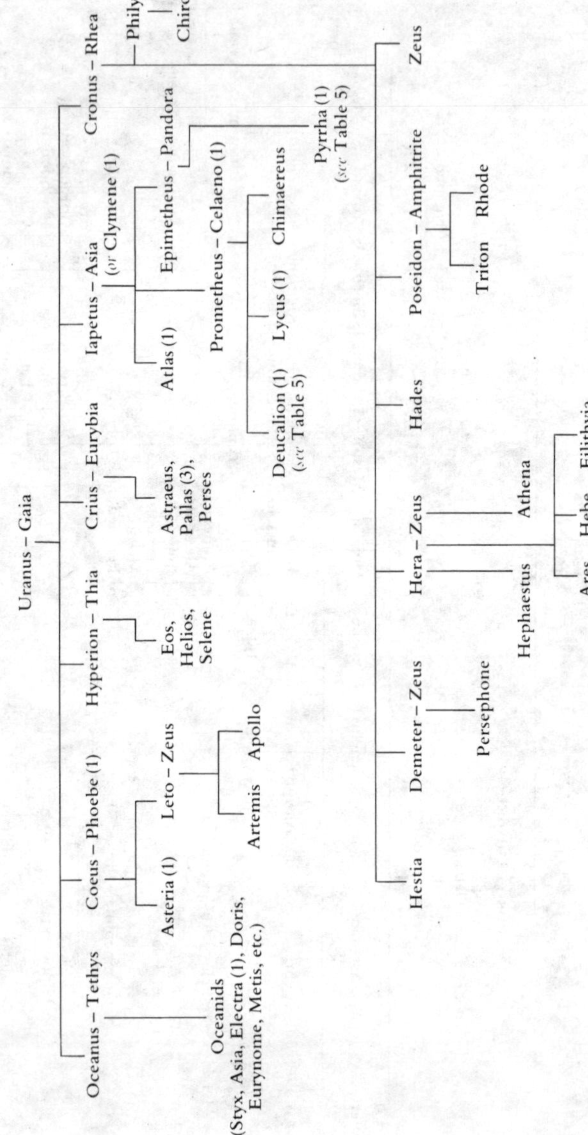
Uranus – Gaia
Oceanus – Tethys
Coeus – Phoebe (1)
Hyperion – Thia
Crius – Eurybia
Iapetus – Asia
(or Clymene (1))
Cronus – Rhea
Philyra
Chiron
Oceanids
(Styx, Asia, Electra (1), Doris,
Eurynome, Metis, etc.)
Asteria (1)
Leto – Zeus
Artemis
Apollo
Eos,
Helios,
Selene
Astraeus,
Pallas (3),
Perses
Atlas (1)
Epimetheus – Pandora
Prometheus – Celaeno (1)
Deucalion (1)
(see Table 5)
Lycus (1)
Chimaereus
Pyrrha (1)
(see Table 5)
Hestia
Demeter – Zeus
Persephone
Hera – Zeus
Hephaestus
Athena
Ares
Hebe
Eilithyia
Hades
Poseidon – Amphitrite
Triton
Rhode
Zeus

READ MORE IN PENGUIN

In every corner of the world, on every subject under the sun, Penguin represents quality and variety – the very best in publishing today.

For complete information about books available from Penguin – including Puffins, Penguin Classics and Arkana – and how to order them, write to us at the appropriate address below. Please note that for copyright reasons the selection of books varies from country to country.

In the United Kingdom: Please write to *Dept. EP, Penguin Books Ltd, Bath Road, Harmondsworth, West Drayton, Middlesex UB7 ODA*

In the United States: Please write to *Consumer Sales, Penguin Putnam Inc., P.O. Box 12289 Dept. B, Newark, New Jersey 07101-5289.* VISA and MasterCard holders call 1-800-788-6262 to order Penguin titles

In Canada: Please write to *Penguin Books Canada Ltd, 10 Alcorn Avenue, Suite 300, Toronto, Ontario M4V 3B2*

In Australia: Please write to *Penguin Books Australia Ltd, P.O. Box 257, Ringwood, Victoria 3134*

In New Zealand: Please write to *Penguin Books (NZ) Ltd, Private Bag 102902, North Shore Mail Centre, Auckland 10*

In India: Please write to *Penguin Books India Pvt Ltd, 11 Community Centre, Panchsheel Park, New Delhi 110017*

In the Netherlands: Please write to *Penguin Books Netherlands bv, Postbus 3507, NL-1001 AH Amsterdam*

In Germany: Please write to *Penguin Books Deutschland GmbH, Metzlerstrasse 26, 60594 Frankfurt am Main*

In Spain: Please write to *Penguin Books S. A., Bravo Murillo 19, 1° B, 28015 Madrid*

In Italy: Please write to *Penguin Italia s.r.l., Via Benedetto Croce 2, 20094 Corsico, Milano*

In France: Please write to *Penguin France, Le Carré Wilson, 62 rue Benjamin Baillaud, 31500 Toulouse*

In Japan: Please write to *Penguin Books Japan Ltd, Kaneko Building, 2-3-25 Koraku, Bunkyo-Ku, Tokyo 112*

In South Africa: Please write to *Penguin Books South Africa (Pty) Ltd, Private Bag X14, Parkview, 2122 Johannesburg*

READ MORE IN PENGUIN

DICTIONARIES

Abbreviations
Ancient History
Archaeology
Architecture
Art and Artists
Astronomy
Biographical Dictionary of Women
Biology
Botany
Building
Business
Challenging Words
Chemistry
Civil Engineering
Classical Mythology
Computers
Contemporary American History
Curious and Interesting Geometry
Curious and Interesting Numbers
Curious and Interesting Words
Design and Designers
Economics
Eighteenth-Century History
Electronics
English and European History
English Idioms
Foreign Terms and Phrases
French
Geography
Geology
German
Historical Slang
Human Geography
Information Technology
International Finance
International Relations
Literary Terms and Literary Theory
Mathematics
Modern History 1789–1945
Modern Quotations
Music
Musical Performers
Nineteenth-Century World History
Philosophy
Physical Geography
Physics
Politics
Proverbs
Psychology
Quotations
Quotations from Shakespeare
Religions
Rhyming Dictionary
Russian
Saints
Science
Sociology
Spanish
Surnames
Symbols
Synonyms and Antonyms
Telecommunications
Theatre
The Third Reich
Third World Terms
Troublesome Words
Twentieth-Century History
Twentieth-Century Quotations